한국의 토익 수험자 여러분께,

토익 시험은 세계적인 직무 영어능력 평가 시험으로, 지난 40여 년간 비즈니스 현장에서 필요한 영어능력 평가의 기준을 제시해 왔습니다. 토익 시험 및 토익스피킹, 토익라이팅 시험은 세계에서 가장 널리 통용되는 영어능력 검증 시험으로, 160여 개국 14,000여 기관이 토익 성적을 의사결정에 활용하고 있습니다.

YBM은 한국의 토익 시험을 주관하는 ETS 독점 계약사입니다.

ETS는 한국 수험자들의 효과적인 토익 학습을 돕고자 YBM을 통하여 'ETS 토익 공식 교재'를 독점 출간하고 있습니다. 또한 'ETS 토익 공식 교재' 시리즈에 기출문항을 제공해 한국의 다른 교재들에 수록된 기출을 복제하거나 변형한 문항으로 인하여 발생할 수 있는 수험자들의 혼동을 방지하고 있습니다.

복제 및 변형 문항들은 토익 시험의 출제의도를 벗어날 수 있기 때문에 기출문항을 수록한 'ETS 토익 공식 교재'만큼 시험에 잘 대비할 수 없습니다.

'ETS 토익 공식 교재'를 통하여 수험자 여러분의 영어 소통을 위한 노력에 큰 성취가 있기를 바랍니다.

감사합니다.

Dear TOEIC Test Takers in Korea,

The TOEIC program is the global leader in English-language assessment for the workplace. It has set the standard for assessing English-language skills needed in the workplace for more than 40 years. The TOEIC tests are the most widely used English language assessments around the world, with 14,000+ organizations across more than 160 countries trusting TOEIC scores to make decisions.

YBM is the ETS Country Master Distributor for the TOEIC program in Korea and so is the exclusive distributor for TOEIC Korea.

To support effective learning for TOEIC test-takers in Korea, ETS has authorized YBM to publish the only Official TOEIC prep books in Korea. These books contain actual TOEIC items to help prevent confusion among Korean test-takers that might be caused by other prep book publishers' use of reproduced or paraphrased items.

Reproduced or paraphrased items may fail to reflect the intent of actual TOEIC items and so will not prepare test-takers as well as the actual items contained in the ETS TOEIC Official prep books published by YBM.

We hope that these ETS TOEIC Official prep books enable you, as test-takers, to achieve great success in your efforts to communicate effectively in English.

Thank you.

입문부터 실전까지 수준별 학습을 통해 최단기 목표점수 달성!

ETS TOEIC® 공식수험서
스마트 학습 지원

**구글플레이, 앱스토어에서
ETS 토익기출 수험서 다운로드**

구글플레이   앱스토어

ETS 토익 모바일 학습 플랫폼!

ETS® 토익기출 수험서 어플

교재 학습 지원
1. 교재 해설 강의
2. LC 음원 MP3
3. 교재/부록 모의고사 채점 및 분석
4. 단어 암기장

부가 서비스
1. 데일리 학습(토익 기출문제 풀이)
2. 토익 최신 경향 무료 특강
3. 토익 타이머

모의고사 결과 분석
1. 파트별/문항별 정답률
2. 파트별/유형별 취약점 리포트
3. 전체 응시자 점수 분포도

ETS TOEIC 공식카페 ▼

etstoeicbook.co.kr

ETS 토익 학습 전용 온라인 커뮤니티!

ETS TOEIC® Book 공식카페

강사진의 학습 지원   토익 대표강사들의 학습 지원과 멘토링

교재 학습관 운영   교재별 학습게시판을 통해 무료 동영상
강의 등 학습 지원

학습 콘텐츠 제공   토익 학습 콘텐츠와 정기시험
예비특강 업데이트

ETS® TOEIC®

토익® 정기시험
기출문제집 1

1000
READING

YBM

토익 정기시험
기출문제집 1
1000
READING

발행인	허문호
발행처	YBM

편집	노경미, 허유정
디자인	김혜경, 이현숙
마케팅	정연철, 박천산, 고영노, 박찬경, 김동진, 김윤하

초판발행	2018년 12월 17일
37쇄발행	2024년 7월 1일

신고일자	1964년 3월 28일
신고번호	제 300-1964-3호
주소	서울시 종로구 종로 104
전화	(02) 2000-0515 [구입문의] / (02) 2000-0429 [내용문의]
팩스	(02) 2285-1523
홈페이지	www.ybmbooks.com

ISBN	978-89-17-23056-7

토익® 정기시험
기출문제집 1
1000
READING

Preface

Dear test taker,

English-language proficiency has become a vital tool for success. It can help you excel in business, travel the world, and communicate effectively with friends and colleagues. The TOEIC® test measures your ability to function effectively in English in these types of situations. Because TOEIC scores are recognized around the world as evidence of your English-language proficiency, you will be able to confidently demonstrate your English skills to employers and begin your journey to success.

The test developers at ETS are excited to help you achieve your personal and professional goals through the use of the ETS® TOEIC® 정기시험 기출문제집 1000 Vol.1. This book contains test questions taken from actual, official TOEIC tests. It also contains three tests that were developed by ETS to help prepare you for actual TOEIC tests. All these materials will help you become familiar with the TOEIC test's format and content. This book also contains detailed explanations of the question types and language points contained in the TOEIC test. These test questions and explanations have all been prepared by the same test specialists who develop the actual TOEIC test, so you can be confident that you will receive an authentic test-preparation experience.

Features of the ETS® TOEIC® 정기시험 기출문제집 1000 Vol.1 include the following.

- Seven full-length actual tests plus three full-length tests of equal quality created by ETS for test preparation use, all accompanied by answer keys and official scripts
- Specific and easy to understand explanations for learners
- The very same ETS voice actors that you will hear in an official TOEIC test administration

By using the ETS® TOEIC® 정기시험 기출문제집 1000 Vol.1 to prepare for the TOEIC test, you can be assured that you have a professionally prepared resource that will provide you with accurate guidance so that you are more familiar with the tasks, content, and format of the test and that will help you maximize your TOEIC test score. With your official TOEIC score certificate, you will be ready to show the world what you know!

We are delighted to assist you on your TOEIC journey with the ETS® TOEIC® 정기시험 기출문제집 1000 Vol.1 and wish you the best of success.

최신 기출문제 전격 공개!

'출제기관이 독점 제공한' 기출문제가 담긴 유일한 교재!

이 책에는 정기시험 기출문제 7세트와 ETS가 제공한 출제 예상문제 3세트가 수록되어 있다. 기출문제로
실전 감각을 키우고, 최신 경향을 반영한 예상문제로 시험에 확실하게 대비하자!

기출 포인트를 꿰뚫는 명쾌한 해설!

최신 출제 경향을 가장 정확하게 알 수 있는 기출문제를 풀고 출제포인트가 보이는 명쾌한 해설로
토익을 정복해 보자!

'ETS가 제공하는' 표준 점수 환산표!

출제기관 ETS가 독점 제공하는 표준 점수 환산표를 수록했다. 채점 후 환산표를 통해
자신의 실력이 어느 정도인지 가늠해 보자!

What is the TOEIC?

TOEIC은 어떤 시험인가요?

Test of English for International Communication(국제적 의사소통을 위한 영어 시험)의 약자로서, 영어가 모국어가 아닌 사람들이 일상생활 또는 비즈니스 현장에서 꼭 필요한 실용적 영어 구사 능력을 갖추었는가를 평가하는 시험이다.

시험 구성

구성	Part	내용		문항수	시간	배점
듣기(L/C)	1	사진 묘사		6	45분	495점
	2	질의 & 응답		25		
	3	짧은 대화		39		
	4	짧은 담화		30		
읽기(R/C)	5	단문 빈칸 채우기(문법/어휘)		30	75분	495점
	6	장문 빈칸 채우기		16		
	7	독해	단일 지문	29		
			이중 지문	10		
			삼중 지문	15		
Total	**7 Parts**			**200문항**	**120분**	**990점**

TOEIC 접수는 어떻게 하나요?

TOEIC 접수는 한국 토익 위원회 사이트(www.toeic.co.kr)에서 온라인 상으로만 접수가 가능하다. 사이트에서 매월 자세한 접수 일정과 시험 일정 등의 구체적 정보 확인이 가능하니, 미리 일정을 확인하여 접수하도록 한다.

시험장에 반드시 가져가야 할 준비물은요?

신분증 규정 신분증만 가능

(주민등록증, 운전면허증, 기간 만료 전의 여권, 공무원증 등)

필기구 연필, 지우개 (볼펜이나 사인펜은 사용 금지)

시험은 어떻게 진행되나요?

09:20	입실 (09:50 이후는 입실 불가)
09:30 – 09:45	답안지 작성에 관한 오리엔테이션
09:45 – 09:50	휴식
09:50 – 10:05	신분증 확인
10:05 – 10:10	문제지 배부 및 파본 확인
10:10 – 10:55	듣기 평가 (Listening Test)
10:55 – 12:10	독해 평가 (Reading Test)

TOEIC 성적 확인은 어떻게 하죠?

시험일로부터 약 12일 후, 오후 3시부터 인터넷과 ARS(060-800-0515)로 성적을 확인할 수 있다. TOEIC 성적표는 우편이나 온라인으로 발급 받을 수 있다(시험 접수시, 양자 택일). 우편으로 발급 받을 경우는 성적 발표 후 대략 일주일이 소요되며, 온라인 발급을 선택하면 유효기간 내에 홈페이지에서 본인이 직접 1회에 한해 무료 출력할 수 있다. TOEIC 성적은 시험일로부터 2년간 유효하다.

TOEIC은 몇 점 만점인가요?

TOEIC 점수는 듣기 영역(LC) 점수, 읽기 영역(RC) 점수, 그리고 이 두 영역을 합계한 전체 점수 세 부분으로 구성된다. 각 부분의 점수는 5점 단위이며, 5점에서 495점에 걸쳐 주어지고, 전체 점수는 10점에서 990점까지이며, 만점은 990점이다. TOEIC 성적은 각 문제 유형의 난이도에 따른 점수 환산표에 의해 결정된다.

토익 경향 분석

1인 등장 사진
주어는 He/She, A man/woman, One of the men/women 등이며 주로 앞부분에 나온다.

2인 이상 등장 사진
주어는 They, Some men/women/people 등이며 주로 중간 부분에 나온다.

사물/배경 사진
주어는 A car, Some chairs 등이며 주로 뒷부분에 나온다.

사람 또는 사물 중심 사진
주어가 일부는 사람, 일부는 사물이며 주로 뒷부분에 나온다.

사람 또는 사물 중심 사진 **33**%   1인 등장 사진 **33**%

PART 1 최신 출제 경향

사물/배경 사진 **17**%   2인 이상 등장 사진 **17**%

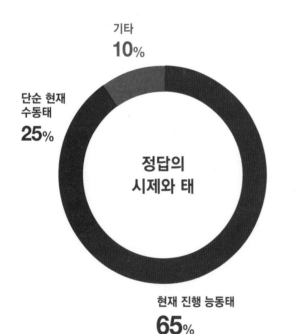

기타 **10**%

단순 현재 수동태 **25**%

정답의 시제와 태

현재 진행 능동태 **65**%

현재 진행 능동태
〈is/are + 현재분사〉 형태이며 주로 사람이 주어이다.

단순 현재 수동태
〈is/are + 과거분사〉 형태이며 주로 사물이 주어이다.

기타
〈is/are + being + 과거분사〉 형태의 현재 진행 수동태, 〈has/have + been + 과거 분사〉 형태의 현재 완료 수동태, '타동사 + 목적어' 형태의 단순 현재 능동태, There is/are와 같은 단순 현재도 나온다.

평서문
질문이 아니라 객관적인 사실이나 화자의 의견 등을 나타내는 문장이다.

명령문
동사원형이나 Please 등으로 시작한다.

의문사 의문문
각 의문사마다 1~2개씩 나온다. 의문사가 단독으로 나오기도 하지만 What time ~?, How long ~?, Which room ~? 등에서처럼 다른 명사나 형용사와 같이 나오기도 한다.

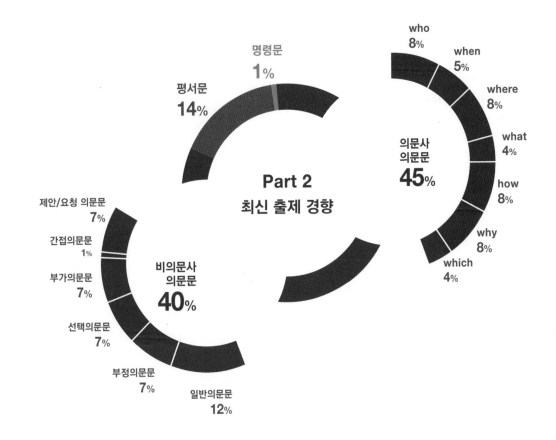

Part 2
최신 출제 경향

명령문 1%
평서문 14%
제안/요청 의문문 7%
간접의문문 1%
부가의문문 7%
선택의문문 7%
부정의문문 7%
일반의문문 12%
비의문사 의문문 40%

who 8%
when 5%
where 8%
what 4%
how 8%
why 8%
which 4%
의문사 의문문 45%

비의문사 의문문
일반(Yes/No) 의문문 적게 나올 때는 한두 개, 많이 나올 때는 서너 개씩 나오는 편이다.
부정의문문 Don't you ~?, Isn't he ~? 등으로 시작하는 문장이며 일반 긍정 의문문보다는 약간 더 적게 나온다.
선택의문문 A or B 형태로 나오며 A와 B의 형태가 단어, 구, 절일 수 있다. 구나 절일 경우 문장이 길어져서 어려워진다.
부가의문문 ~ don't you?, ~ isn't he? 등으로 끝나는 문장이며, 일반 부정 의문문과 비슷하다고 볼 수 있다.
간접의문문 의문사가 문장 처음 부분이 아니라 문장 중간에 들어 있다.
제안/요청 의문문 정보를 얻기보다는 상대방의 도움이나 동의 등을 얻기 위한 목적이 일반적이다.

PART 3 　짧은 대화 Short Conversations　　　총 13대화문 39문제 (지문당 3문제)

- 3인 대화의 경우 남자 화자 두 명과 여자 한 명 또는 남자 화자 한 명과 여자 두 명이 나온다. 따라서 문제에서는 2인 대화에서와 달리 the man이나 the woman이 아니라 the men이나 the women 또는 특정한 이름이 언급될 수 있다.
- 대화 & 시각 정보는 항상 파트의 뒷부분에 나온다.
- 시각 정보의 유형으로 chart, map, floor plan, schedule, table, weather forecast, directory, list, invoice, receipt, sign, packing slip 등 다양한 자료가 골고루 나온다.

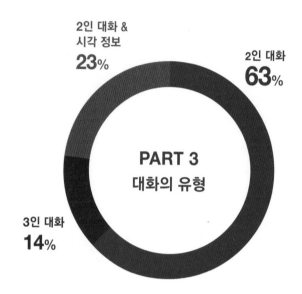

- 주제, 목적, 이유, 대화의 장소, 화자의 직업/직장 등과 관련된 문제는 주로 대화의 첫 번째 문제로 나오며 다음 행동/일어날 일 등과 관련된 문제는 주로 대화의 세 번째 문제로 나온다.
- 화자의 의도 파악 문제는 주로 2인 대화에 나오지만, 가끔 3인 대화에 나오기도 한다. 시각 정보 연계 대화에는 나오지 않고 있다.
- Part 3 안에서 화자의 의도 파악 문제는 2개가 나오고 시각 정보 연계 문제는 3개가 나온다.

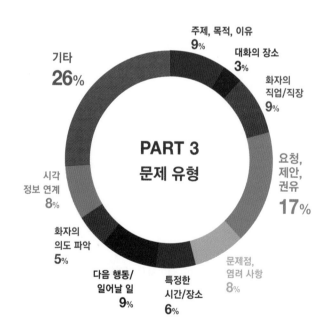

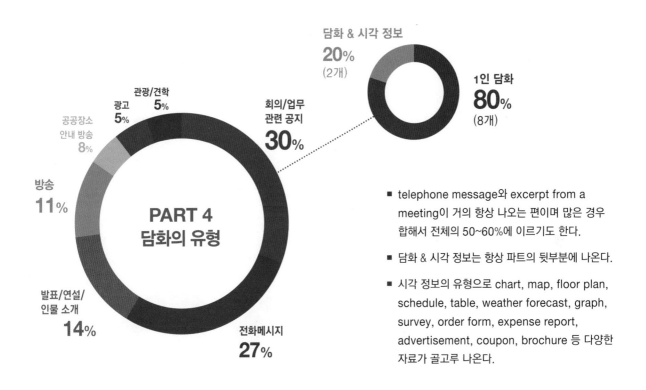

- telephone message와 excerpt from a meeting이 거의 항상 나오는 편이며 많은 경우 합해서 전체의 50~60%에 이르기도 한다.

- 담화 & 시각 정보는 항상 파트의 뒷부분에 나온다.

- 시각 정보의 유형으로 chart, map, floor plan, schedule, table, weather forecast, graph, survey, order form, expense report, advertisement, coupon, brochure 등 다양한 자료가 골고루 나온다.

- 문제 유형은 기본적으로 Part 3과 거의 비슷하다.

- 주제, 목적, 이유, 담화의 장소, 화자의 직업/직장 등과 관련된 문제는 주로 담화의 첫 번째 문제로 나오며 다음 행동/일어날 일 등과 관련된 문제는 주로 담화의 세 번째 문제로 나온다.

- Part 4 안에서 화자의 의도 파악 문제는 3개가 나오고 시각 정보 연계 문제는 2개가 나온다.

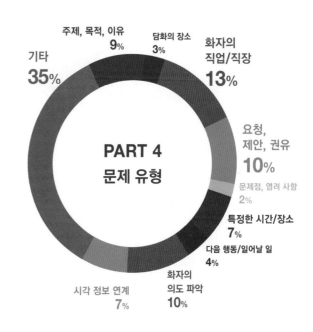

토익 경향 분석

문법 문제

시제와 대명사와 관련된 문법 문제가 2개씩, 한
정사와 분사와 관련된 문법 문제가 1개씩 나온
다. 시제 문제의 경우 능동태/수동태나 수의 일
치와 연계되기도 한다. 그 밖에 한정사, 능동태/
수동태, 부정사, 동명사 등과 관련된 문법 문제
가 나온다.

어휘 문제

동사, 명사, 형용사, 부사와 관련된 어휘
문제가 각각 2~3개씩 골고루 나온다. 전
치사 어휘 문제는 3개씩 꾸준히 나오지
만, 접속사나 어구와 관련된 어휘 문제는
나오지 않을 때도 있고 3개가 나올 때도
있다.

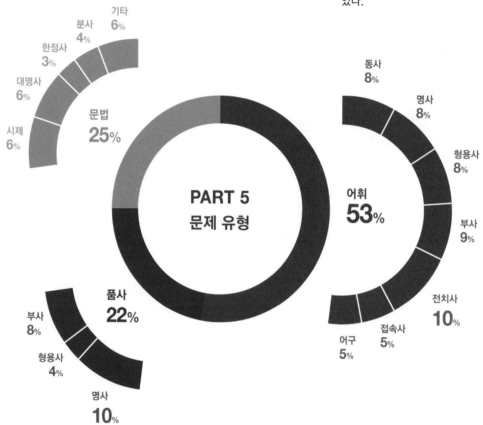

품사 문제

명사와 부사와 관련된 품사 문제가 2~3개
씩 나오며, 형용사와 관련된 품사 문제가
상대적으로 적은 편이다.

한 지문에 4문제가 나오며 평균적으로 어휘 문제가 2개, 품사나 문법 문제가 1개, 문맥에 맞는 문장 고르기 문제가 1개 들어간다. 문맥에 맞는 문장 고르기 문제를 제외하면 문제 유형은 기본적으로 파트 5와 거의 비슷하다.

어휘 문제

동사, 명사, 부사, 어구와 관련된 어휘 문제는 매번 1~2개씩 나온다. 부사 어휘 문제의 경우 therefore(그러므로)나 however(하지만)처럼 문맥의 흐름을 자연스럽게 연결해 주는 부사가 자주 나온다.

문맥에 맞는 문장 고르기

문맥에 맞는 문장 고르기 문제는 지문당 한 문제씩 나오는데, 나오는 위치의 확률은 4문제 중 두 번째 문제, 세 번째 문제, 네 번째 문제, 첫 번째 문제 순으로 높다.

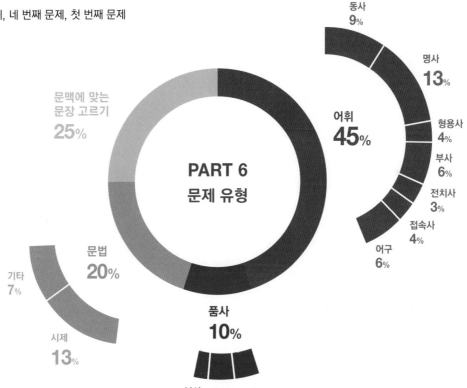

문맥에 맞는 문장 고르기 **25%**

PART 6 문제 유형

어휘 **45%**

동사 **9%**
명사 **13%**
형용사 **4%**
부사 **6%**
전치사 **3%**
접속사 **4%**
어구 **6%**

문법 **20%**

기타 **7%**

시제 **13%**

품사 **10%**

부사 **2%**   형용사 **4%**   명사 **4%**

문법 문제

문맥의 흐름과 밀접하게 관련이 있는 시제 문제가 2개 정도 나오며, 능동태/수동태나 수의 일치와 연계되기도 한다. 그 밖에 대명사, 능동태/수동태, 부정사, 접속사/전치사 등과 관련된 문법 문제가 나온다.

품사 문제

명사나 형용사 문제가 부사 문제보다 좀 더 자주 나온다.

PART 7 독해 Reading Comprehension

지문 유형	지문당 문제 수	지문 개수	비중 %
단일 지문	2문항	4개	약 15%
	3문항	3개	약 16%
	4문항	3개	약 22%
이중 지문	5문항	2개	약 19%
삼중 지문	5문항	3개	약 28%

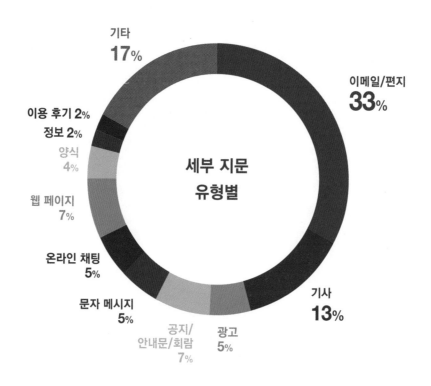

- 이메일/편지, 기사 유형 지문은 거의 항상 나오는 편이며 많은 경우 합해서 전체의 50~60%에 이르기도 한다.

- 기타 지문 유형으로 agenda, brochure, comment card, coupon, flyer, instructions, invitation, invoice, list, menu, page from a catalog, policy statement, report, schedule, survey, voucher 등 다양한 자료가 골고루 나온다.

(이중 지문과 삼중 지문 속의 지문들을 모두 낱개로 계산함 – 총 23지문)

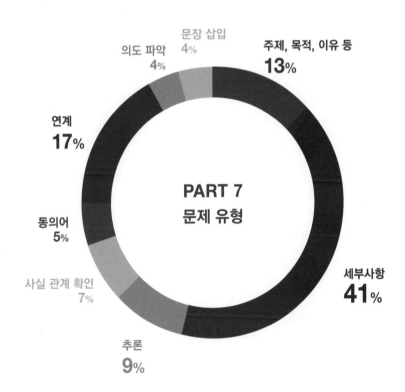

의도 파악
4%

문장 삽입
4%

주제, 목적, 이유 등
13%

연계
17%

동의어
5%

사실 관계 확인
7%

추론
9%

세부사항
41%

PART 7
문제 유형

■ 동의어 문제는 주로 이중 지문이나 삼중 지문에 나온다.
■ 연계 문제는 일반적으로 이중 지문에서 한 문제, 삼중 지문에서 두 문제가 나온다.
■ 의도 파악 문제는 문자 메시지(text-message chain)나 온라인 채팅(online chat discussion) 지문에서 출제되며 두 문제가
  나온다.
■ 문장 삽입 문제는 주로 기사, 이메일, 편지, 회람 지문에서 출제되며 두 문제가 나온다.

점수 환산표 및 산출법

점수 환산표 이 책에 수록된 각 Test를 풀고 난 후, 맞은 개수를 세어 점수를 환산해 보세요.

LISTENING Raw Score (맞은 개수)	LISTENING Scaled Score (환산 점수)	READING Raw Score (맞은 개수)	READING Scaled Score (환산 점수)
96–100	475–495	96–100	460–495
91–95	435–495	91–95	425–490
86–90	405–475	86–90	395–465
81–85	370–450	81–85	370–440
76–80	345–420	76–80	335–415
71–75	320–390	71–75	310–390
66–70	290–360	66–70	280–365
61–65	265–335	61–65	250–335
56–60	235–310	56–60	220–305
51–55	210–280	51–55	195–270
46–50	180–255	46–50	165–240
41–45	155–230	41–45	140–215
36–40	125–205	36–40	115–180
31–35	105–175	31–35	95–145
26–30	85–145	26–30	75–120
21–25	60–115	21–25	60–95
16–20	30–90	16–20	45–75
11–15	5–70	11–15	30–55
6–10	5–60	6–10	10–40
1–5	5–50	1–5	5–30
0	5–35	0	5–15

점수 산출 방법

아래의 방식으로 점수를 산출할 수 있다.

자신의 답안을 수록된 정답과 대조하여 채점한다. 각 Section의 맞은 개수가 본인의 Section별 '실제 점수 (통계 처리하기 전의 점수, raw score)'이다. Listening Test와 Reading Test의 정답 수를 세어, 자신의 실제 점수를 아래의 해당란에 기록한다.

	맞은 개수	환산 점수대
LISTENING		
READING		
총점		

Section별 실제 점수가 그대로 Section별 TOEIC 점수가 되는 것은 아니다. TOEIC은 시행할 때마다 별도로 특정한 통계 처리 방법을 사용하며 이러한 실제 점수를 환산 점수(converted[scaled] score)로 전환하게 된다. 이렇게 전환함으로써, 매번 시행될 때마다 문제는 달라지지만 그 점수가 갖는 의미는 같아지게 된다. 예를 들어 어느 한 시험에서 총점 550점의 성적으로 받는 실력이라면 다른 시험에서도 거의 550점대의 성적을 받게 되는 것이다.

실제 점수를 위 표에 기록한 후 왼쪽 페이지의 점수 환산표를 보도록 한다. TOEIC이 시행될 때마다 대개 이와 비슷한 형태의 표가 작성되는데, 여기 제시된 환산표는 본 교재에 수록된 Test용으로 개발된 것이다. 이 표를 사용하여 자신의 실제 점수를 환산 점수로 전환하도록 한다. 즉, 예를 들어 Listening Test의 실제 정답 수가 61~65개이면 환산 점수는 265점에서 335점 사이가 된다. 여기서 실제 정답 수가 61개이면 환산 점수가 265점이고, 65개이면 환산 점수가 335점 임을 의미하는 것은 아니다. 본 책의 Test를 위해 작성된 이 점수 환산표가 자신의 영어 실력이 어느 정도인지 대략적으로 파악하는 데 도움이 되긴 하지만, 이 표가 실제 TOEIC 성적 산출에 그대로 사용된 적은 없다는 사실을 밝혀 둔다.

토익 정기시험
기출문제집

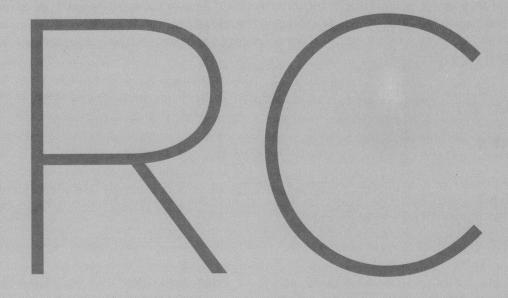

RC

기출 TEST

01

READING TEST

In the Reading test, you will read a variety of texts and answer several different types of reading comprehension questions. The entire Reading test will last 75 minutes. There are three parts, and directions are given for each part. You are encouraged to answer as many questions as possible within the time allowed.

You must mark your answers on the separate answer sheet. Do not write your answers in your test book.

PART 5

Directions: A word or phrase is missing in each of the sentences below. Four answer choices are given below each sentence. Select the best answer to complete the sentence. Then mark the letter (A), (B), (C), or (D) on your answer sheet.

101. Ms. Durkin asked for volunteers to help ------- with the employee fitness program.
    (A) she
    (B) her
    (C) hers
    (D) herself

102. Lasner Electronics' staff have extensive ------- of current hardware systems.
    (A) know
    (B) known
    (C) knowledge
    (D) knowledgeable

103. ------- a year, Tarrin Industrial Supply audits the accounts of all of its factories.
    (A) Once
    (B) Immediately
    (C) Directly
    (D) Yet

104. Ms. Pham requested a refund ------- the coffeemaker she received was damaged.
    (A) despite
    (B) why
    (C) concerning
    (D) because

105. Information ------- the artwork in the lobby is available at the reception desk.
    (A) across
    (B) about
    (C) upon
    (D) except

106. With the Gema XTI binoculars, users can ------- see objects that are more than 100 meters away.
    (A) ease
    (B) easy
    (C) easily
    (D) easier

107. The Physical Therapy Association is committed to keeping costs ------- for its certification programs.
    (A) affordable
    (B) permitted
    (C) cutting
    (D) necessary

108. Mr. Brennel ------- positions in various areas of the company before he became president.
    (A) occupation
    (B) occupational
    (C) occupying
    (D) occupied

109. To remain on schedule, editors must submit all ------- to the book to the authors by Friday.
    (A) ideas
    (B) essays
    (C) revisions
    (D) suggestions

110. ------- industry professionals are allowed to purchase tickets to the Kuo Photography Fair.
    (A) Only
    (B) Until
    (C) Unless
    (D) Quite

111. At Pharmbeck's banquet, Mr. Jones ------- a trophy for his performance in this year's quality-improvement initiative.
    (A) accepted
    (B) congratulated
    (C) nominated
    (D) hoped

112. Ms. Suto claims that important market trends become ------- with the use of data analysis.
    (A) predict
    (B) prediction
    (C) predictable
    (D) predictably

113. One of Grommer Consulting's goals is to enhance the relationship ------- salespeople and their customers.
    (A) inside
    (B) within
    (C) around
    (D) between

114. Depending on your answers to the survey, we ------- you to collect additional information.
    (A) may call
    (B) are calling
    (C) have been called
    (D) must be calling

115. ------- Jemburger opened its newest franchise, the first 100 customers were given free hamburgers.
    (A) Now
    (B) When
    (C) As if
    (D) After all

116. Please include the serial number of your product in any ------- with the customer service department.
    (A) corresponds
    (B) correspondence
    (C) correspondingly
    (D) correspondent

117. The award-winning film *Underwater Secrets* promotes awareness ------- ocean pollution and its effects on our planet.
    (A) of
    (B) to
    (C) from
    (D) with

118. BYF Company specializes in ------- promotional items to help companies advertise their brand.
    (A) personally
    (B) personalized
    (C) personality
    (D) personalizes

119. ------- the rent increase is less than 2 percent, Selwin Electrical Supply will continue to lease the space.
    (A) As long as
    (B) Along with
    (C) Not only
    (D) Otherwise

120. Belden Hospital's chief of staff meets regularly with the staff to ensure that procedures ------- correctly.
    (A) to be performed
    (B) would have performed
    (C) had been performed
    (D) are being performed

GO ON TO THE NEXT PAGE

121. Any requests for time off should be addressed to the ------- department supervisor.
   - (A) urgent
   - (B) appropriate
   - (C) subsequent
   - (D) deliverable

122. World Fish Supply delivers the freshest fish possible thanks to innovative ------- and shipping methods.
   - (A) preserves
   - (B) preserved
   - (C) preserve
   - (D) preservation

123. Company executives are currently reviewing the annual budget ------- submitted to them by the Financial Planning department.
   - (A) requirements
   - (B) deliveries
   - (C) developers
   - (D) qualities

124. Even the CEO had to admit that Prasma Designs' win was ------- the result of fortunate timing.
   - (A) parts
   - (B) parted
   - (C) partly
   - (D) parting

125. Mr. Singh took notes on ------- the focus group discussed during the morning session.
   - (A) each
   - (B) several
   - (C) another
   - (D) everything

126. Last year, Tadaka Computer Solutions ranked third ------- in regional earnings.
   - (A) together
   - (B) overall
   - (C) consecutively
   - (D) generally

127. ------- the popularity of the BPT39 wireless speaker, production will be increased fivefold starting next month.
   - (A) On behalf of
   - (B) Whether
   - (C) Moreover
   - (D) As a result of

128. Zypo Properties has just signed a lease agreement with the law firm ------- offices are on the third floor.
   - (A) how
   - (B) what
   - (C) whose
   - (D) wherever

129. ------- events this year caused profits in the second and third quarters to differ significantly from original projections.
   - (A) Total
   - (B) Marginal
   - (C) Representative
   - (D) Unforeseen

130. The timeline for the pathway lighting project was extended to ------- input from the environmental commission.
   - (A) use up
   - (B) believe in
   - (C) make into
   - (D) allow for

PART 6

Directions: Read the texts that follow. A word, phrase, or sentence is missing in parts of each text. Four answer choices for each question are given below the text. Select the best answer to complete the text. Then mark the letter (A), (B), (C), or (D) on your answer sheet.

Questions 131-134 refer to the following advertisement.

With Global Strength Gym's 30-day trial period, you get the opportunity to try out our classes,

equipment, and facilities. ------- . It's completely risk-free! To sign up, we require your contact
          131.

information and payment details, but you will only be charged if you are a member for

------- 30 days. If you decide within this time that you no longer want to be a member of
132.

Global Strength, ------- visit our Web site at www.gsgym.com. On the Membership page, elect to
                133.

------- your membership and enter the necessary information. It's that easy!
134.

131. (A) Throughout the trial, you pay nothing
        and sign no contract.
     (B) Weight-lifting classes are not currently
        available.
     (C) A cash deposit is required when you
        sign up for membership.
     (D) All questions should be e-mailed to
        customerservice@gsgym.com.

132. (A) not even
     (B) almost
     (C) over
     (D) less than

133. (A) justly
     (B) regularly
     (C) evenly
     (D) simply

134. (A) extend
     (B) renew
     (C) cancel
     (D) initiate

GO ON TO THE NEXT PAGE

Questions 135-138 refer to the following instructions.

As a Hanson-Roves employee, you are entitled to sick absences, during which you will be paid for time off work for health ------- . To avoid deductions to your pay, you ------- to provide a

135.   136.
physician-signed note as documentation of your illness. ------- should include the date you were

137.
seen by the doctor, a statement certifying that you are unable to perform the duties of your position, and your expected date of return. Your supervisor will then forward the documentation to Human Resources. ------- . Employee health records can be accessed only by those with a valid

138.
business reason for reviewing them.

135. (A) reasons
 (B) origins
 (C) senses
 (D) contributions

136. (A) were required
 (B) require
 (C) are required
 (D) are requiring

137. (A) Those
 (B) They
 (C) I
 (D) It

138. (A) Hanson-Roves ensures the privacy of your health information.
 (B) Absences may be caused by a number of factors.
 (C) You should then explain why a physician's note is not available.
 (D) Take note of the duties you were originally assigned.

Questions 139-142 refer to the following e-mail.

To: fcontini@attmail.com
From: btakemoto@arolischems.co.uk
Date: 15 July
Subject: Your first day at Arolis

Dear Mr. Contini,

Welcome to Arolis Chemicals! Thank you for ------- the full-time, permanent position of laboratory
            139.
assistant. We look forward to your arrival on 1 August in the Harris Building. Please report to the

front desk and ask for Jack McNolan. He ------- you to the Human Resources office. There, you
                                  140.
will obtain your employee badge ------- all documents necessary to start work. Note that because
                          141.
of its large size, the Leicester campus of Arolis can be difficult to navigate. Studying a campus

map will help orient you to the location of the different buildings. ------- .
                                              142.

Should you have any questions, please do not hesitate to contact me.

Sincerely,

Brandon Takemoto
HR Administrative Officer

---

139. (A) offering
   (B) accepting
   (C) discussing
   (D) advertising

140. (A) accompany
   (B) did accompany
   (C) accompanies
   (D) will accompany

141. (A) too
   (B) also
   (C) as well as
   (D) additionally

142. (A) Please sign all the documents.
   (B) I will provide you with a replacement.
   (C) Construction will be completed next
      year.
   (D) You can download one from our Web
      site.

GO ON TO THE NEXT PAGE

(18 April)—MKZ Foods, Inc., the region's largest exporter of pecans, expects its outgoing shipments to increase significantly over the next few months. This ------- is based on the fact that **143.**
the region's pecan farmers expanded their land area by 20 percent last year. According to spokesperson Katharina Seiler, MKZ's exports could reach a colossal 50,000 metric tons this year. ------- .
144.

MKZ buys most of the yield from the region's pecan farms and processes it ------- export **145.**
throughout the world. "The availability of new land for ------- in the region is creating opportunities **146.**
for growth," said Ms. Seiler. "I believe MKZ is going to have a truly outstanding year."

143. (A) cost
(B) delay
(C) decision
(D) forecast

144. (A) Such a figure is unprecedented in the company's history.
(B) Moreover, Ms. Seiler holds an advanced degree in economics.
(C) Pecans are high in vitamins and minerals.
(D) Still, MKZ shares have been profitable in recent years.

145. (A) on
(B) for
(C) in
(D) by

146. (A) farming
(B) farmer
(C) farmed
(D) farm

PART 7

Directions: In this part you will read a selection of texts, such as magazine and newspaper articles, e-mails, and instant messages. Each text or set of texts is followed by several questions. Select the best answer for each question and mark the letter (A), (B), (C), or (D) on your answer sheet.

Questions 147-148 refer to the following text message.

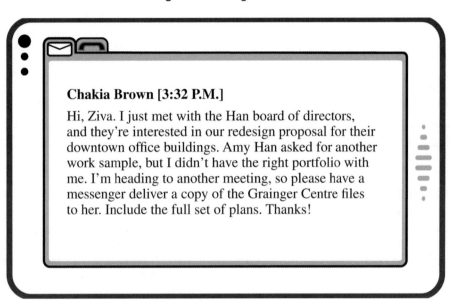

Chakia Brown [3:32 P.M.]

Hi, Ziva. I just met with the Han board of directors, and they're interested in our redesign proposal for their downtown office buildings. Amy Han asked for another work sample, but I didn't have the right portfolio with me. I'm heading to another meeting, so please have a messenger deliver a copy of the Grainger Centre files to her. Include the full set of plans. Thanks!

147. Where does Ms. Brown most likely work?

(A) At an accounting firm
(B) At an architectural firm
(C) At a Web design company
(D) At a market research company

148. What is Ziva asked to do?

(A) Reply to a text message
(B) Create a portfolio
(C) Set up a meeting
(D) Send a work sample

GO ON TO THE NEXT PAGE

Questions 149-150 refer to the following e-mail.

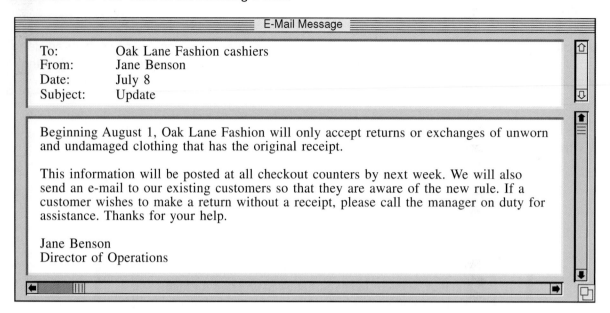

E-Mail Message

To: Oak Lane Fashion cashiers
From: Jane Benson
Date: July 8
Subject: Update

Beginning August 1, Oak Lane Fashion will only accept returns or exchanges of unworn and undamaged clothing that has the original receipt.

This information will be posted at all checkout counters by next week. We will also send an e-mail to our existing customers so that they are aware of the new rule. If a customer wishes to make a return without a receipt, please call the manager on duty for assistance. Thanks for your help.

Jane Benson
Director of Operations

149. What is the purpose of the e-mail?

(A) To request a sales report
(B) To announce a new policy
(C) To discuss a fashion trend
(D) To describe an upcoming sale

150. According to the e-mail, what will managers do?

(A) Decide how to display new merchandise
(B) Train staff to use the cash register
(C) Help customers with special requests
(D) Decide what items get price discounts

Questions 151-152 refer to the following Web page.

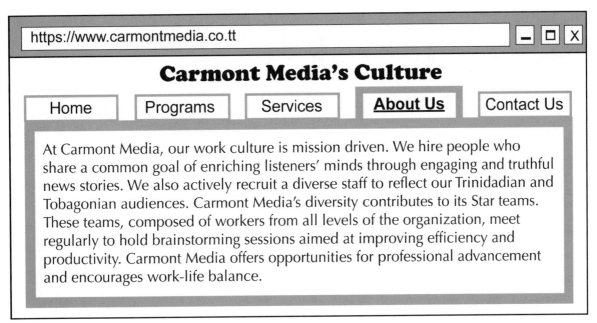

151. What is mentioned about Carmont Media's employees?

(A) They get experience in various departments.
(B) They enjoy working for the organization.
(C) They come from a variety of backgrounds.
(D) They are recruited through a staffing agency.

152. What is a purpose of Carmont Media's Star teams?

(A) Seeking new employees
(B) Raising funds for projects
(C) Promoting work-life balance
(D) Finding creative solutions

GO ON TO THE NEXT PAGE

Louisa Santos   **9:30 A.M.**
Kenji, where are you? The job candidates are here.

Kenji Muro   **9:31 A.M.**
Sorry! The bridge is closed. My bus had to take a detour. I should be there in 30 minutes. Please start without me.

Louisa Santos   **9:34 A.M.**
OK. I'm going to interview Elena Crenshaw first.

Kenji Muro   **9:34 A.M.**
Good. She's the one with experience at another T-shirt company.

Louisa Santos   **9:35 A.M.**
Yes. Can you believe our small company has grown so much that we need to hire someone just to process orders?

Kenji Muro   **9:36 A.M.**
I know! OK. I'll see you soon.

153. What does Mr. Muro want Ms. Santos to do?

(A) Process some orders
(B) Make a hiring decision
(C) Reschedule a meeting
(D) Talk to a job candidate

154. At 9:36 A.M., what does Mr. Muro mean when he writes, "I know"?

(A) He is also surprised by the company's growth.
(B) He thinks salaries should be higher.
(C) He has met Ms. Crenshaw before.
(D) He is certain his bus will arrive in 30 minutes.

Questions 155-157 refer to the following article from a company newsletter.

TEST 1

Mark Chandler is Back!

The Administrative Services Division welcomes back to headquarters Associate Director Mark Chandler. —[1]—. Mark spent the last month in Ottawa attending an advanced training session about corporate information security. Corporate-security training allows a company to safeguard its sensitive, confidential, and proprietary information.

Mark is among a growing number of corporate executives who have successfully graduated from this rigorous course. —[2]—. A member of the National Organization of Corporate Security Officers (NOCSO), Mark was formally recognized by the organization for his part in developing software that keeps electronic documents safe. —[3]—. Well done, Mark! —[4]—.

155. What is the purpose of the article?

(A) To recognize an employee's accomplishments
(B) To introduce a new staff member
(C) To clarify what information is considered confidential
(D) To describe the challenges of corporate security

156. How did Mr. Chandler improve corporate security?

(A) He trained his company's security officers.
(B) He helped design a system for securely storing documents.
(C) He assisted in developing new safety guidelines.
(D) He recruited employees who specialize in corporate security.

157. In which of the positions marked [1], [2], [3], and [4] does the following sentence best belong?

"The training included 60 hours of instruction and a comprehensive written exam."

(A) [1]
(B) [2]
(C) [3]
(D) [4]

Congratulations on purchasing Megagroome, the world's finest rechargeable shaver! To keep your shaver in top condition, clean your shaver weekly by running it under hot water. Once a month, disassemble the shaver and clean the internal portion thoroughly as shown in the owner's manual. The shaving heads should be replaced every year with the replacement parts listed in the manual.

The Megagroome shaver has a lithium ion battery that should last for several years. Please charge the shaver as often as needed. It is not necessary to fully discharge the battery before recharging it. Use only the included charger, because use of any other charger may void the warranty. Complete instructions and details can be found in the owner's manual.

Megagroome

158. Where would the card most likely be found?

(A) Inside a box with a product
(B) On a bulletin board
(C) In a product display at a store
(D) In the pages of a magazine

159. How often should the shaver be taken apart?

(A) Daily
(B) Weekly
(C) Monthly
(D) Annually

160. What is indicated about the shaver's battery?

(A) It must run out before charging.
(B) It may be charged whenever necessary.
(C) It is able to hold a charge for a week.
(D) It will work with different chargers.

Questions 161-163 refer to the following Web page.

http://www.diversifymuseum.org

DIVERSIFY MUSEUM

A Museum of Cross-Cultural History and Artifacts

We are proud to announce our newest exhibit: *South American Art.*

The exhibit will open on 7 June as part of the museum's ongoing Arts Around the World programme. All museum patrons who have paid the museum entrance fee may view the exhibit. It will feature historical and contemporary artwork displays from renowned South American artists.

The curator of the six-week exhibition, Julio Carrera, will bring his vast expertise to the museum. Before joining the museum's management in March of this year, Mr. Carrera was the curator for the Brazilian Institute of the Arts for six years and spent three years studying ancient artifacts for the Centro de la Historia del Arte, an art preservation centre in Venezuela.

The *South American Art* exhibit will include paintings, sculptures, crafting tools, clothing, jewellery, murals, and clay pottery from six South American countries. Visiting artists from these countries will provide art workshops on select dates in July. The cost for each workshop is £10 in addition to the regular admission fee and includes basic art supplies.

161. What is indicated about the *South American Art* exhibit?

(A) It is the first exhibit in the Arts Around the World program.
(B) It will be on display only through the end of June.
(C) It includes both old and new art.
(D) It focuses on wall hangings and murals.

162. Who is Mr. Carrera?

(A) A visiting artist
(B) An art journalist
(C) A volunteer tour guide
(D) A museum employee

163. According to the Web page, what can museum patrons do for an extra fee?

(A) Watch a video on South America
(B) Attend an art class
(C) Explore a new exhibit
(D) Sponsor an upcoming exhibit

GO ON TO THE NEXT PAGE

Questions 164-167 refer to the following online chat discussion.

Oliver Koh (10:15 A.M.)
Hi, Aaron and Denise. Do you know if a package has arrived for me? I was supposed to get a delivery of some documents today, but maybe they were sent to someone else by mistake. It's from Schrantz Farm Organics and should be labeled urgent.

Aaron Koskinen (10:17 A.M.)
There's nothing for you here at the front desk. You might want to check with the print shop on the ground floor.

Denise Matova (10:18 A.M.)
There's a package from Schrantz Farm Organics here in the mail room, but there's no name on it.

Oliver Koh (10:18 A.M.)
That must be the one for me. Could you please look at the delivery slip again?

Denise Matova (10:19 A.M.)
Sorry, it does have your name on it. It was so small I didn't notice it.

Oliver Koh (10:20 A.M.)
Great! Could you have the package sent up to my office please?

Denise Matova (10:20 A.M.)
No problem. I'm going upstairs in a minute anyway.

Oliver Koh (10:21 A.M.)
OK, thanks for your help.

164. Why did Mr. Koh start the online chat discussion?

(A) He received a damaged package.
(B) He has a meeting with a client soon.
(C) He is expecting some important documents.
(D) He delivered a shipment to the wrong person.

165. What does Mr. Koskinen recommend doing?

(A) Calling Schrantz Farm Organics
(B) Changing a meeting place
(C) Going to the front desk
(D) Checking a different location

166. At 10:19 A.M., what does Ms. Matova most likely mean when she writes, "Sorry"?

(A) She misplaced a delivery slip.
(B) She arrived late to work today.
(C) She would like Mr. Koh to repeat his instructions.
(D) She made a mistake reading a label.

167. What will Ms. Matova probably do with the package?

(A) Take it to Mr. Koh
(B) Send it out by express mail
(C) Leave it at the front desk
(D) Remove the items from it

From:	Won Ho Kim
To:	Management Team
Date:	12 August
Subject:	Improving employee satisfaction

Management Team:

— [1] —. Over the next few months, the Human Resources department will be engaging with the Management Team in a variety of conversations about increasing productivity and employee satisfaction. — [2] —.

Telecommuting, in which employees are permitted to work from home all or part of the time, is an approach that many companies are using because it allows employees to work on tasks that may be difficult to complete in an office full of disruptions. With the building reconfiguration project coming up in January, we would like to take the opportunity to consider whether telecommuting would be a good solution for our company. Our final decision on this matter will influence the way in which the work space is reorganized.

I am writing to ask for your feedback. — [3] —. At this point, Human Resources is simply gathering information. Please complete the telecommuting survey, which is found on the Human Resources Web site. — [4] —. Just look for the link on the left side of the home page.

Thank you in advance, and please let me know if you have any questions.

Won Ho Kim
Human Resources Manager
GHTY Engineering, Inc.

168. Why was the e-mail sent?

(A) To remind employees about a policy
(B) To request participation in a survey
(C) To discuss upcoming meetings
(D) To encourage employees to attend an event

169. What is mentioned as a benefit of telecommuting?

(A) It helps employees work without interruptions.
(B) It frees up space in the building for new workers.
(C) It is good for the environment.
(D) It saves the company money.

170. What is the company planning to do in the new year?

(A) Hire a new human resources manager
(B) Reorganize the management team
(C) Change the layout of its building
(D) Introduce a new Web site

171. In which of the positions marked [1], [2], [3], and [4] does the following sentence best belong?

"It should be noted that no decisions about telecommuting have been made."

(A) [1]
(B) [2]
(C) [3]
(D) [4]

GO ON TO THE NEXT PAGE

The Uppsala International Book Fair   **22–24 September • Berglund Conference Hall • Uppsala, Sweden**
Schedule for Friday, 22 September

Outthinking Public Opinion   **12:00 noon–1:00 P.M., Salon A**
Touring to promote his latest book, *Outthinking Public Opinion*, author Damian Schnauz makes a stop at the Uppsala International Book Fair to discuss his latest subject, take questions, and sign his books.

Introductory Course in Graphic Design   **1:30–2:30 P.M., Visual Media Centre**
Professional digital designers Allen Doubek and Ivanette Lacasse will present useful techniques and provide attendees with hands-on practice opportunities.

Seminar on Online Publishing   **3:00–4:30 P.M., Lindqvist Auditorium**
Releasing and promoting e-books and audiobooks on the Internet. Speakers: Kenneth Pulaski, editor-in-chief of Vendler Publishing, and Tina Savona, marketing manager at Vendler Publishing. All accompanying materials will be sold at the venue immediately before and after the seminar.

Readership in the Digital Age   **5:00–6:30 P.M., Room 210**
Is literacy promoted or inhibited by digital media? Debate moderated by Greg Gunnarson.

- To attend these or any other sessions, purchase a daily admission ticket for 100 kr.

- Note that reservations are not required for any session, but seating is limited, so please arrive a few minutes before the scheduled time to ensure a seat. Also note that while photos are permitted, no video recordings may be made of any presentation.

- Meals are available for purchase at locations throughout Berglund Conference Hall. Information about accommodations may be obtained on our Web site at uibf.se/hotels.

172. What is suggested about the first day of the Uppsala International Book Fair?

(A) It is being organized by a team of publishers.
(B) No sessions are scheduled for the morning hours.
(C) Attendance is expected to be the highest on that day.
(D) Mr. Schnauz will announce the subject of his next book.

173. Where will book fair attendees be able to participate in interactive activities?

(A) In Salon A
(B) In the Visual Media Centre
(C) In Lindqvist Auditorium
(D) In Room 210

174. What is mentioned about the accompanying materials for the seminar?

(A) They can be purchased on-site.
(B) They can be downloaded online.
(C) They are available in limited numbers.
(D) They should be ordered from the presenters.

175. What are book fair attendees encouraged to do?

(A) Ask questions after sessions
(B) Post photos on social media
(C) Rearrange seats as necessary
(D) Arrive early for sessions

Questions 176-180 refer to the following Web page and e-mail.

http://www.mountainandforest.ca/custserv/shippinginfo

| Clothing | Gear | **Customer Service** | About Us |

Mountain and Forest Company
The Leader in Quality Camping and Hiking Gear

Please note that most regular electronic or phone orders can be processed and made ready for shipping almost immediately. Custom and personalized orders may take up to five days for processing before they are shipped.

Please direct any questions or concerns to our customer service department at service@mountainandforest.ca. We will respond within 24 hours.

Our shipping rates:

Order cost with tax	Overnight shipping (1 day)	Express shipping (3 days)	Standard (6–8 days)
Under $25	$8	$5	$3
$25 to $100	$13	$7	$5
Over $100	$18	$15	FREE

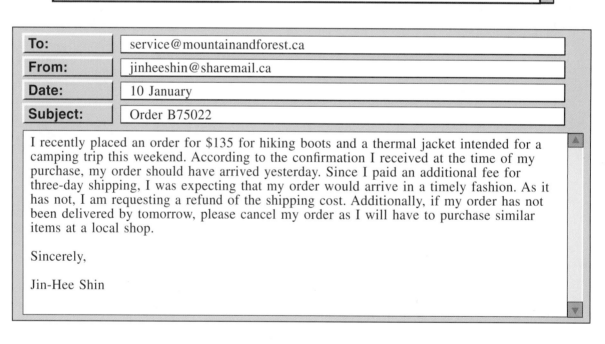

To:	service@mountainandforest.ca
From:	jinheeshin@sharemail.ca
Date:	10 January
Subject:	Order B75022

I recently placed an order for $135 for hiking boots and a thermal jacket intended for a camping trip this weekend. According to the confirmation I received at the time of my purchase, my order should have arrived yesterday. Since I paid an additional fee for three-day shipping, I was expecting that my order would arrive in a timely fashion. As it has not, I am requesting a refund of the shipping cost. Additionally, if my order has not been delivered by tomorrow, please cancel my order as I will have to purchase similar items at a local shop.

Sincerely,

Jin-Hee Shin

176. In the Web page, what is indicated about Mountain and Forest's shipping?

(A) Standard shipping is free for orders under $25.
(B) Some shipped orders may take up to eight days to arrive.
(C) The shipping cost depends on the total weight of an order.
(D) Custom orders are not eligible for standard delivery.

177. In the Web page, the word "direct" in paragraph 2, line 1, is closest in meaning to

(A) address
(B) supervise
(C) prescribe
(D) handle

178. What is the purpose of the e-mail?

(A) To suggest a new service policy
(B) To inquire about an order packing error
(C) To request a personalized item
(D) To report a delivery problem

179. How much did Ms. Shin pay for shipping?

(A) $5
(B) $8
(C) $15
(D) $18

180. According to the e-mail, why might Ms. Shin decide to visit a local shop?

(A) She expects to purchase her items for a lower price.
(B) She wants to support businesses in her town.
(C) She needs to have her items before a certain date.
(D) She hopes to find a greater selection of sportswear.

GO ON TO THE NEXT PAGE

Society for Trade and Industry (STI) **"The Role of Distance Education in Professional Training"** **City University of Abu Dhabi, 11–13 October** DRAFT: Schedule for Wednesday, 11 October	
7:30 A.M.–9:00 A.M.	Conference Registration
9:00 A.M.–9:10 A.M.	Welcome and Opening Remarks: Yasmin Al Gaood, Conference Chair
9:15 A.M.–10:00 A.M.	Opening Keynote Address: Ayumi Murakami, STI President
10:05 A.M.–10:50 A.M.	Title of presentation unknown: representative to be selected, Yaoundé College of Agriculture, Cameroon
10:55 A.M.–11:40 A.M.	Innovative Online Resources: Chia Po Cheng, Taipei Business Management Institute, Taiwan
11:45 A.M.–1:20 P.M.	Lunch (Turquoise Center, central campus)
1:30 P.M.–2:15 P.M.	Distance Education in the Film Industry: representative from Scotland to be selected
2:20 P.M.–3:05 P.M.	Improving Course Content Quality: Andrei Durchenko, Moscow Journalism Academy, Russia
3:10 P.M.–4:00 P.M.	Learner Support Systems: Marcel Peralta, School of Pediatric Dentistry, Asunción, Paraguay

From:	Ayumi Murakami <amurakami@sti.org>
To:	Yasmin Al Gaood <yasmin.algaood@cuad.ac.ae>
Subject:	Re: Draft conference schedule for Wednesday
Date:	25 August

Hello, Yasmin,

As per your request, I have filled the slots that were listed as still available on the tentative conference schedule for Wednesday. Dr. Alban Buchanan in Scotland says that he is eager to talk about distance education as it is practiced within the film academies in his country. Also, my contact in Yaoundé wrote to let me know that Ms. Marie-Thérèse Tchangou will be the school's representative.

Mr. Andrei Durchenko has informed me that he is withdrawing from the conference. His replacement from the same school, Ms. Melina Vakhitova, will submit the title of her presentation shortly.

I also wanted to add that I will be arriving in Abu Dhabi at 6:00 A.M. on Wednesday. That should give me plenty of time to set up for my presentation.

Regards,

Ayumi

181. What is indicated about Ms. Murakami?

(A) She will speak on the first day of the conference.
(B) She was recently elected STI president.
(C) She will be available to answer questions.
(D) She is scheduled to present in the afternoon.

182. When will a specialist in business management be speaking?

(A) At 10:05 A.M.
(B) At 10:55 A.M.
(C) At 2:20 P.M.
(D) At 3:10 P.M.

183. In the e-mail, in paragraph 1, line 1, the word "slots" is closest in meaning to

(A) reservations
(B) machines
(C) openings
(D) buildings

184. What presentation will have to be canceled?

(A) Innovative Online Resources
(B) Distance Education in the Film Industry
(C) Improving Course Content Quality
(D) Learner Support Systems

185. According to the e-mail, what information is Ms. Murakami expecting to receive?

(A) The title of a presentation
(B) The name of a replacement speaker
(C) The conference schedule for Thursday
(D) The contact information for Mr. Buchanan

GO ON TO THE NEXT PAGE

From:	mstoch@hesidionclinic.com
To:	lstawinski@nostilde.com
Date:	March 20
Subject:	Hesidion Clinic's Health Awareness Day

Dear Ms. Stawinski,

In appreciation of your loyalty as a long-time patient of Hesidion Clinic, we are pleased to invite you to our clinic's Health Awareness Day to be held at the clinic on Saturday, April 10. We would be delighted to see you attend, as we will offer a number of activities designed to promote health awareness in our community. If you sign up for this special event by responding to this e-mail by March 31, you will receive a code to present at the clinic for a surprise benefit.

Martin Stoch, Communications Director, Hesidion Clinic

Hesidion Clinic Health Awareness Day, April 10
Tasks and Responsibilities

• Communications: Martin Stoch

• Advertising: Adilene Walker

• Presentations: Jillian Opala (Nutrition),
  Lance Verhoeven (Fitness)

• Kids' Health Game: Susan Hayashi

• Health Checkups/Talks: Anne Spillane,
  Rami Al-Araj, Kurt Yin, Thierry Daumas

Health Day at Hesidion Clinic

by Shai Herzog on April 14

Hesidion Clinic hosted a successful Health Awareness Day this past Saturday. The event was held as a way to thank the community for supporting the clinic over the past 15 years. It was well attended by both Hesidion Clinic patients and members of the general public.

Attendees participated in a variety of presentations and everyone received free water bottles, notepads, and other items from event sponsors. Participants who provided a special code were offered a complimentary physical checkup from the team of clinic physicians.

During the event, a sizable line formed at Dr. Thierry Daumas' table. "I came out today to learn about skin care and advances in eye-care technology. But Dr. Daumas' talk about how to prevent cavities and improve oral health provided me with the most helpful information," said attendee Liana Stawinski.

By far the most popular event was nutritionist Jillian Opala's presentation on healthy eating habits. More than 100 people, many of them retirees, flocked to hear the latest on super foods. The event took nearly twice as long as expected, as Ms. Opala answered a steady stream of participant questions.

Children were delighted to take part in a health contest involving questions about general health and hygiene. The winners received toys and certificates from the game host. The day was such a success that Hesidion Clinic director, Lance Verhoeven, is already considering making it an annual event.

186. What is Ms. Stawinski encouraged to do?

(A) Complete a survey
(B) Go to an event
(C) Organize some activities
(D) Meet with Mr. Stoch

187. How did some attendees get a free health checkup?

(A) By arriving when the clinic opened
(B) By attending Dr. Daumas' talk
(C) By responding to an e-mail from Mr. Stoch
(D) By winning a competition

188. What does Dr. Daumas most likely specialize in?

(A) Skin
(B) Ears
(C) Eyes
(D) Teeth

189. What is indicated about the presentation on food?

(A) It was filmed.
(B) It was postponed.
(C) It attracted a lot of attention.
(D) It was given by a retired clinic employee.

190. Who most likely distributed certificates?

(A) Mr. Stoch
(B) Ms. Hayashi
(C) Ms. Spillane
(D) Mr. Verhoeven

GO ON TO THE NEXT PAGE

STUDY BUSINESS IN SINGAPORE

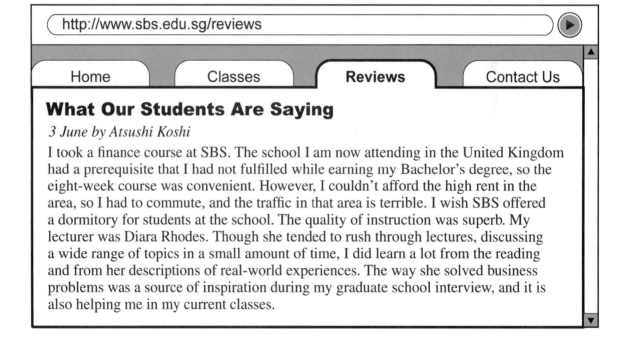

The Singapore Business School (SBS) is located in the heart of Singapore's financial district. We offer a range of high-quality courses aimed at preparing students for graduate school. Between classroom sessions you can explore the city and cultivate business connections. We offer content-based classes, such as finance, economics, and international marketing, as well as classes on preparing graduate school applications, including developing CVs and writing personal statements.

We have helped thousands of students gain entry into graduate programmes around the world. We boast a number of high-profile part-time instructors who are experts in their fields, including Diara Rhodes, chief financial officer of Auto Drive Korea, and Farah Wan, vice president of the Kuala Lumpur Union Lenders. For more information about our impressive faculty and course offerings, or to enroll online, visit our Web site at www.sbs.edu.sg.

---

http://www.sbs.edu.sg/reviews

| Home | Classes | **Reviews** | Contact Us |

What Our Students Are Saying

3 June by Atsushi Koshi

I took a finance course at SBS. The school I am now attending in the United Kingdom had a prerequisite that I had not fulfilled while earning my Bachelor's degree, so the eight-week course was convenient. However, I couldn't afford the high rent in the area, so I had to commute, and the traffic in that area is terrible. I wish SBS offered a dormitory for students at the school. The quality of instruction was superb. My lecturer was Diara Rhodes. Though she tended to rush through lectures, discussing a wide range of topics in a small amount of time, I did learn a lot from the reading and from her descriptions of real-world experiences. The way she solved business problems was a source of inspiration during my graduate school interview, and it is also helping me in my current classes.

```
┌─────────────────────────────────────────────────────────────┐
│                        *E-mail*                              │
├─────────────────────────────────────────────────────────────┤
│  To:          atsushi.koshi@scholarmail.co.uk                │
│  From:        lsommersell@sbs.edu.sg                         │
│  Subject:     Your review                                    │
│  Date:        15 August                                      │
├─────────────────────────────────────────────────────────────┤
│  Dear Mr. Koshi,                                             │
│                                                             │
│  Thank you for your feedback. You're not the first person    │
│  to voice this particular concern. Just so you know, we plan  │
│  on addressing it by following your recommendation.          │
│  Students who take classes with us starting as early as 1    │
│  January will be able to take advantage of this new benefit. │
│  Please be sure to mention this to anyone you know who       │
│  is thinking about taking a class with us.                   │
│                                                             │
│  Kind regards,                                               │
│                                                             │
│  Lauri Sommersell                                            │
│                                                             │
└─────────────────────────────────────────────────────────────┘
```

191. Who is the brochure intended for?

(A) Business professionals
(B) Potential graduate students
(C) Instructors seeking employment
(D) Aspiring writers

192. What is indicated about SBS?

(A) It is located in a busy area.
(B) It offers financial assistance.
(C) It provides internship opportunities.
(D) It has employment-assistance services.

193. What does Mr. Koshi mention about his lecturer?

(A) She required a lot of reading.
(B) She covered topics quickly.
(C) She provided few examples.
(D) She encouraged in-class participation.

194. Where does Mr. Koshi's instructor work when she is not teaching?

(A) At SBS
(B) At a bank in Singapore's financial district
(C) At Auto Drive Korea
(D) At Kuala Lumpur Union Lenders

195. How will SBS be addressing Mr. Koshi's complaint?

(A) By hiring more faculty
(B) By reducing the length of classes
(C) By adding more transportation options
(D) By building student housing on campus

GO ON TO THE NEXT PAGE

SEEKING FULL-TIME LINE COOK

The Delphine Street Grill is a high-profile restaurant serving New Orleans since 1924. We are seeking a line cook to prepare select sautéed items and sauces under the supervision of the executive chef. The ideal candidate will have at least one year of related cooking experience or will have completed a two-year apprenticeship in a well-established restaurant. Demonstrated ability to prepare innovative dishes as well as classic Cajun-style cuisine is required. To apply, go to www.delphinestreetgrill.com/careers.

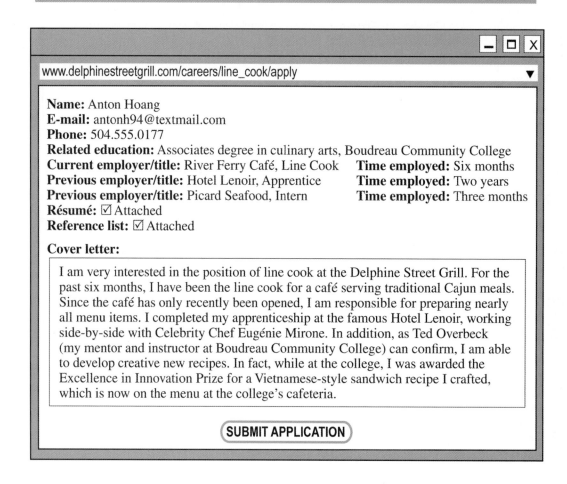

www.delphinestreetgrill.com/careers/line_cook/apply ▼

Name: Anton Hoang
E-mail: antonh94@textmail.com
Phone: 504.555.0177
Related education: Associates degree in culinary arts, Boudreau Community College
Current employer/title: River Ferry Café, Line Cook   **Time employed:** Six months
Previous employer/title: Hotel Lenoir, Apprentice   **Time employed:** Two years
Previous employer/title: Picard Seafood, Intern   **Time employed:** Three months
Résumé: ☑ Attached
Reference list: ☑ Attached

Cover letter:

I am very interested in the position of line cook at the Delphine Street Grill. For the past six months, I have been the line cook for a café serving traditional Cajun meals. Since the café has only recently been opened, I am responsible for preparing nearly all menu items. I completed my apprenticeship at the famous Hotel Lenoir, working side-by-side with Celebrity Chef Eugénie Mirone. In addition, as Ted Overbeck (my mentor and instructor at Boudreau Community College) can confirm, I am able to develop creative new recipes. In fact, while at the college, I was awarded the Excellence in Innovation Prize for a Vietnamese-style sandwich recipe I crafted, which is now on the menu at the college's cafeteria.

(SUBMIT APPLICATION)

BOUDREAU COMMUNITY COLLEGE
School of Culinary Arts

Marie Beaumont
Delphine Street Grill
3248 Delphine Street
New Orleans, LA 70117

Dear Ms. Beaumont:

I am writing in regard to Anton Hoang's application for employment. Since Mr. Overbeck is on leave this semester, he asked me to respond in his place. Mr. Hoang, who graduated in the top five of his class, demonstrated exceptional culinary skill and a strong desire to learn. He received a glowing review from Sabine Riou, the renowned chef who supervised his three-month internship. I am confident Mr. Hoang will be a valuable asset to your establishment.

Sincerely,

Liz Flores

Liz Flores
Associate Director of Culinary Arts

---

196. What is indicated about the line cook position?

(A) It is a two-year contract.
(B) It requires working the late-night shift.
(C) It includes supervising the apprentices.
(D) It involves preparing a limited variety of dishes.

197. What is true about Mr. Hoang?

(A) He is applying to work at several restaurants.
(B) He meets the requirements of the position.
(C) He has appeared on television with Ms. Mirone.
(D) He taught at a culinary school in Vietnam.

198. Who is Mr. Overbeck?

(A) An executive chef
(B) An associate director
(C) A culinary teacher
(D) A restaurant owner

199. What is suggested about Boudreau Community College?

(A) It gives out culinary awards.
(B) It offers free cooking workshops.
(C) It needs a new chef for its cafeteria.
(D) It invites celebrity chefs as guest speakers.

200. Where does Ms. Riou most likely work?

(A) At the River Ferry Café
(B) At Hotel Lenoir
(C) At Picard Seafood
(D) At the Delphine Street Grill

Stop! This is the end of the test. If you finish before time is called, you may go back to Parts 5, 6, and 7 and check your work.

토익® 정기시험
기출문제집

RC

기출 TEST

02

READING TEST

In the Reading test, you will read a variety of texts and answer several different types of reading comprehension questions. The entire Reading test will last 75 minutes. There are three parts, and directions are given for each part. You are encouraged to answer as many questions as possible within the time allowed.

You must mark your answers on the separate answer sheet. Do not write your answers in your test book.

PART 5

Directions: A word or phrase is missing in each of the sentences below. Four answer choices are given below each sentence. Select the best answer to complete the sentence. Then mark the letter (A), (B), (C), or (D) on your answer sheet.

---

101. Ms. Carpenter will be attending the conference with ------- marketing team.

(A) she
(B) her
(C) hers
(D) herself

102. ------- the last ten years, Bay City's population has grown by about 27 percent.

(A) As
(B) Against
(C) During
(D) Below

103. Please congratulate Alan Schmit, ------- of the Leadership Award in Nursing at Knoll Hospital.

(A) won
(B) wins
(C) winning
(D) winner

104. Ireland's largest software producer will ------- be opening a large facility in Cork.

(A) soon
(B) such
(C) ever
(D) like

105. Ashburn Bank's online service has been in high demand -------.

(A) lateness
(B) later
(C) lately
(D) latest

106. The ------- of videos to electronic press releases can help companies showcase their products.

(A) content
(B) addition
(C) pictures
(D) promotion

107. Ms. Hyun is reviewing the training manual to see if updates -------.

(A) have need
(B) needing
(C) are needed
(D) to be needed

108. When leaving the auditorium, please exit ------- the doors on the lower level.

(A) except
(B) inside
(C) without
(D) through

109. The judges for this year's screenplay competition include ------- from Hanovi Studios.

(A) represents
(B) representatives
(C) represented
(D) represent

110. I have attached my résumé detailing my ------- experience in the hotel industry.

(A) extensive
(B) punctual
(C) prospective
(D) accepted

111. Remember to check the spelling of Mr. Kamashi's name when ------- the document.

(A) revising
(B) revises
(C) revised
(D) revise

112. Residents visited City Hall to ask ------- developers will preserve the historic properties.

(A) although
(B) since
(C) whether
(D) both

113. The Ford Group's proposed advertising campaign is by far the most ------- we have seen so far.

(A) innovate
(B) innovative
(C) innovations
(D) innovatively

114. Solei Landscaping announced that the design for the Cherry Hill building complex is ------- complete.

(A) almost
(B) nearby
(C) anytime
(D) yet

115. Daniel Nishida, the chief supply officer, asked that ------- be given full responsibility for approving all invoices.

(A) he
(B) him
(C) his
(D) himself

116. In preparation for Mr. Kumar's retirement at the end of March, the Carolex Corporation will need to ------- a new facilities director.

(A) resume
(B) compete
(C) recruit
(D) conduct

117. The team's contributions to the Ripton Group's marketing plan were very ------- acknowledged.

(A) favor
(B) favorably
(C) favorable
(D) favored

118. ------- receiving the engineering award, Ms. Kwon made a point of thanking longtime mentors.

(A) Onto
(B) Unlike
(C) About
(D) Upon

119. Please read the list of ------- qualifications to ensure that you have the necessary education and experience for the position.

(A) slight
(B) equal
(C) obliged
(D) essential

120. Choosing the best software tool to eliminate computer viruses is rarely simple, ------- it is important to seek expert advice.

(A) why
(B) then
(C) nor
(D) so

GO ON TO THE NEXT PAGE

121. Ms. Delgado would like to meet with all loan officers ------- reviewing any more loan applications.

(A) now that
(B) as though
(C) before
(D) often

122. Cedar Branch Hill has a ------- as a business-friendly environment that provides efficient licensing and other legal processes.

(A) prediction
(B) courtesy
(C) reputation
(D) statement

123. The actors held an additional rehearsal ------- perfect their performance in the final scene.

(A) considerably
(B) in order to
(C) nevertheless
(D) as a result of

124. RZT Technology will double the size of its Toronto laboratory to ------- the organization's rapid growth.

(A) assign
(B) investigate
(C) experience
(D) accommodate

125. Even though Smithton Electronics' second quarter was not -------, the company plans to invest large sums on research.

(A) profitable
(B) profiting
(C) profitability
(D) profitably

126. The Williamsport Hotel is an ideal venue for the conference because of its ------- to the airport.

(A) achievement
(B) proximity
(C) competence
(D) exception

127. The second training session is for employees ------- responsibilities include processing payroll forms.

(A) whose
(B) which
(C) what
(D) who

128. ------- poorly the high-speed printer may be functioning, it is still making copies that are adequate for our purposes.

(A) Rather
(B) Seldom
(C) However
(D) Thoroughly

129. The long-awaited Weka 2XG digital camera will finally be ------- at a product exhibition on August 16.

(A) reduced
(B) unveiled
(C) consulted
(D) resolved

130. Northeast Community Finance ------- an online system in order to shorten service lines at branch locations.

(A) has implemented
(B) to be implementing
(C) to have been implementing
(D) is implemented

PART 6

Directions: Read the texts that follow. A word, phrase, or sentence is missing in parts of each text. Four answer choices for each question are given below the text. Select the best answer to complete the text. Then mark the letter (A), (B), (C), or (D) on your answer sheet.

Questions 131-134 refer to the following advertisement.

Garden Shade Tree Landscaping

Garden Shade creates tree landscapes and hedges to suit every garden, no matter the size. Our

designs have ------- small urban gardens as well as large-scale projects commissioned by
                   131.

architects and property developers. ------- . However, no single nursery can offer trees of all
                                      132.

species and sizes. That is why Garden Shade has developed close relationships with many

specialist growers ------- to provide us with the trees we need. Such resources give us the variety
                    133.

necessary to complete any ------- . In other words, whatever your landscape design dream, we can
                           134.

make it happen.

---

131. (A) transformed
     (B) related
     (C) collected
     (D) planted

132. (A) We are here to answer your
         landscaping questions.
     (B) For most projects, we use trees from
         our own nurseries.
     (C) Some trees have specific growing
         requirements.
     (D) Under normal conditions, nursery stock
         is guaranteed for one year.

133. (A) readiness
     (B) readies
     (C) readiest
     (D) ready

134. (A) study
     (B) form
     (C) order
     (D) survey

GO ON TO THE NEXT PAGE

To: Staff
From: Amy Henwith
Date: 15 January
Subject: Exciting news

Dear Staff,

Thanks for a great year! In case you haven't heard, Henwith Home Supply will be ------- our second
                                                                                          135.
store this spring. This additional retail site will be located in the shopping centre at the corner of

Aberton Parkway and Sutton Avenue in Derbyshire.

We will be accepting applications for cashiers and sales positions ------- 1 April. The personnel
                                                                            136.
director will review applicants' qualifications from 2 April to 6 April, and ------- is scheduled to
                                                                                137.
begin one week later. ------- .
                       138.

Best,

Amy Henwith, CEO
Henwith Home Supply

135. (A) moving
     (B) renovating
     (C) expanding
     (D) opening

136. (A) until
     (B) following
     (C) according to
     (D) for

137. (A) trainer
     (B) training
     (C) train
     (D) trained

138. (A) Feel free to share this news with any
         interested friends.
     (B) Make sure you have received all of the
         material.
     (C) Contact Henwith Home Supply if you are
         still waiting for a response.
     (D) Access to the main entrance will be
         blocked by construction.

Amon Donates to Music School in Grenel City

A spokesperson for Brenda Amon ------- that the pianist made a sizeable donation toward the
                                              139.

expansion of the Grenel City Conservatory of Music. "Without her generous support," said

Marc Diaz, director of facility planning, "we would have been limited in our renovation plans going

forward."

------- . Now, a new wing will be constructed on the south end of the ------- conservatory. Once
140.   **141.**

completed, the building will boast a 700-seat auditorium, state-of-the-art recording studios, and

new faculty and administrative offices. Additionally, private practice rooms will be located

------- the current student lounge.
142.

---

139. (A) confirm
(B) confirmation
(C) has confirmed
(D) will confirm

140. (A) Ms. Amon's performance at the
conservatory was outstanding.
(B) The project had been delayed
because of budget cuts.
(C) Student enrollment has decreased
over the past few years.
(D) The original conservatory is being
converted into student housing.

141. (A) temporary
(B) existing
(C) corrected
(D) proposed

142. (A) adjacent to
(B) even though
(C) instead of
(D) as well as

GO ON TO THE NEXT PAGE

Questions 143-146 refer to the following e-mail.

Date: 11 January
To: Mitchell Parker <mparker@allmail.co.za>
From: Inez Lofaro <ilofaro@daqtex.co.za>
Subject: Product recall

Dear Mr. Parker,

Thank you for your recent ------- of the Daqtex Mini-V camera. We are contacting everyone who
                               143.

has recently bought this product to inform them that certain models are being recalled for repair.

In these models, the electronic chip that enables the digital conversion of light is faulty.

------- . Please ------- whether your camera has this problem by checking the serial number on the
144.   **145.**

bottom of the camera. If it ends with the letters TVX, a repair will be required. Daqtex will pay all

shipping costs for sending your Mini-V back to us. In addition, we will repair ------- free of charge.
                                                                                146.

Thank you,

Inez Lofaro, Customer Service Manager
Daqtex Industries

---

143. (A) purchase
(B) review
(C) gift
(D) demonstration

144. (A) We hope you will enjoy the product for
many years to come.
(B) It is covered in the troubleshooting
section of the manual.
(C) This defect will eventually interfere with
the clarity of your images.
(D) This special feature is unavailable on
some older models.

145. (A) verification
(B) verified
(C) verify
(D) verifies

146. (A) mine
(B) it
(C) theirs
(D) these

PART 7

Directions: In this part you will read a selection of texts, such as magazine and newspaper articles, e-mails, and instant messages. Each text or set of texts is followed by several questions. Select the best answer for each question and mark the letter (A), (B), (C), or (D) on your answer sheet.

Questions 147-148 refer to the following notice.

Fastest Fleet

RATE OUR SERVICES AND WIN FREE TRAVEL!

Visit our Web site at www.fastestfleet.com/feedback and fill out the 5-minute questionnaire. You could win one of 10 FREE round-trip bus trips to any destination within the continental United States!

You must be 18 or older to participate. Only customers who have previously traveled with Fastest Fleet are eligible to enter.

147. Where would the notice likely be seen?

(A) In an airport
(B) In a bus station
(C) In a train station
(D) In a ferry terminal

148. What are customers asked to do?

(A) Provide feedback
(B) Buy a round-trip ticket
(C) Take advantage of a discount
(D) Join a customer loyalty program

GO ON TO THE NEXT PAGE

Questions 149-150 refer to the following online chat discussion.

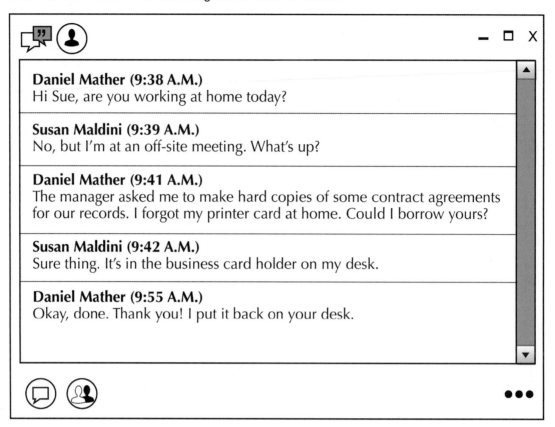

Daniel Mather (9:38 A.M.)
Hi Sue, are you working at home today?

Susan Maldini (9:39 A.M.)
No, but I'm at an off-site meeting. What's up?

Daniel Mather (9:41 A.M.)
The manager asked me to make hard copies of some contract agreements for our records. I forgot my printer card at home. Could I borrow yours?

Susan Maldini (9:42 A.M.)
Sure thing. It's in the business card holder on my desk.

Daniel Mather (9:55 A.M.)
Okay, done. Thank you! I put it back on your desk.

---

149. What task was Mr. Mather given?

(A) To send out contracts
(B) To repair the photocopier
(C) To monitor employee attendance
(D) To make copies of some documents

150. At 9:42 A.M., what does Ms. Maldini most likely mean when she writes "Sure thing"?

(A) She can lend Mr. Mather her card.
(B) She will return to the office.
(C) She will contact the manager.
(D) She can copy the agreements.

MEMO

To: Westhauser Laboratories Staff
From: Area manager
Date: March 22
Re: Break-time beverages

Beginning immediately, staff members are asked to contribute toward the cost of hot beverages available in our kitchenette. For each cup of coffee or tea you pour for yourself, we are requesting that you leave fifty cents. Please note that this amount is still far less than what you would pay at the café next to our building.

Each time you prepare a beverage, just place your payment in the marked can on the counter next to the sink. As in the past, a variety of high-quality tea and coffee supplies will be made available, and products will be restocked monthly. Your understanding is appreciated so that everyone can continue to enjoy conveniently located hot beverages throughout the workday.

151. What is the purpose of the memo?

(A) To explain a new policy
(B) To discourage long breaks
(C) To provide a budget update
(D) To address staff complaints

152. What are staff members asked to do?

(A) Bring their own beverages to work
(B) Leave payments in a container
(C) Submit requests for supplies
(D) Keep the kitchenette tidy

Attention Milwaukee Modern Art Museum Visitors

The Meacham Room is closed temporarily as we prepare the space for the Modern Artist Showcase, which will run from April 1 to June 30.

We encourage you to return to experience this much-anticipated exhibit that will feature paintings, sculpture, and multimedia works by acclaimed international artists such as Sally Acosta, Frank Kember, Kimberly Hong, and Matilda Breeland. Of note is newcomer Theodore Carmody's sculpture collection that was dubbed "most exciting debut of the decade" by Ethan Lerner, renowned and respected critic of the *Ireland Arts Chronicle*. More information about the featured artists and the exhibit can be found at www.milwaukeemodernart.org. Or download our museum app to keep current with all upcoming events.

---

153. What is indicated about the museum?

(A) It is promoting an upcoming exhibit on its Web site.
(B) It is known for its sculpture exhibits.
(C) It will be closed for renovations in April.
(D) Its upcoming exhibit is free for museum members.

154. Who is Ms. Breeland?

(A) A journalist
(B) An artist
(C) A museum curator
(D) An art critic

155. Who was praised by Mr. Lerner?

(A) Ms. Acosta
(B) Mr. Kember
(C) Ms. Hong
(D) Mr. Carmody

Questions 156-157 refer to the following form.

Change of Work Order

General Contractor:
Howard Kleiber, Mercrest Construction
106 Pickens Way, Columbus, OH 43211

Property Owner: Oscar Copeland, 866 Andell Road, Columbus, OH 43215

Project Start Date: July 10

Project End Date: July 15

The contractor is hereby instructed to make the following changes to the contract documents:

Description of Work Added/Deleted:
Client will now be supplying the countertops and faucet in addition to the kitchen cabinets. Therefore, the total project cost will be adjusted to only include the cost of installation.

Original Contract Price: $3,496

Net Reduction from Previous Contract: -$2,412

Total Project Cost with Approved Changes: $1,084

Revised Payment Schedule:
15% of total project cost ($162) is due upfront to secure contractor, $222 is due on project start date, and the remainder ($700) is due upon project completion.

Accepted by:

Contractor: _Howard Kleiber_

Property Owner: _Oscar Copeland_

---

156. Why has the price of a project been adjusted?

(A) The client is providing all the materials.
(B) The client wants to match a competitor's price.
(C) The contractor installed countertops incorrectly.
(D) The contractor overestimated the cost of labor.

157. How much money will Mr. Copeland most likely give Mr. Kleiber on July 15 ?

(A) $162
(B) $222
(C) $700
(D) $1,084

GO ON TO THE NEXT PAGE

To:	Dahlia Pawar <dpawar@bronsonco.ca>
From:	Anna Bondell <abondell@noaaa.com>
Subject:	Information
Date:	August 25

Dear Ms. Pawar:

Thank you for your continued membership in the North American Architects Association. I'm writing to remind you that preregistration for the annual conference closes on September 15. — [1] —. This year's conference features more than 100 sessions, an exhibit hall, and special workshops. — [2] —.

Preregistration will save you $30 off the regular registration fee. — [3] —. At the same time, you'll be able to sign up in advance for a group tour of the city and for the VIP Banquet, which always fills up quickly. Visit our Web site to register online. — [4] —. If you prefer to register by telephone, contact us at 1-249-555-0177. Please have your membership number available.

Looking forward to seeing you in Mexico City!

Sincerely,

Anna Bondell
Membership Coordinator

158. What most likely is Ms. Pawar's occupation?

(A) Architect
(B) Writer
(C) Travel agent
(D) Conference organizer

159. What is NOT a benefit of conference preregistration?

(A) A tour of Mexico City
(B) A hotel room upgrade
(C) Admission to a dinner
(D) Reduced registration fees

160. In which of the positions marked [1], [2], [3], and [4] does the following sentence best belong?

"You will also find the complete conference program there."

(A) [1]
(B) [2]
(C) [3]
(D) [4]

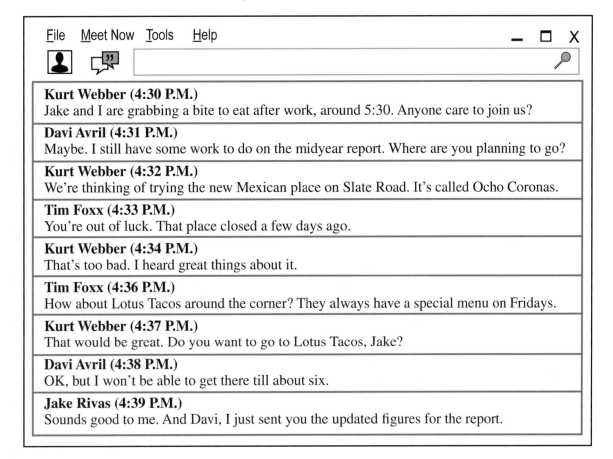

File   Meet Now   Tools   Help   — □ X

Kurt Webber (4:30 P.M.)
Jake and I are grabbing a bite to eat after work, around 5:30. Anyone care to join us?

Davi Avril (4:31 P.M.)
Maybe. I still have some work to do on the midyear report. Where are you planning to go?

Kurt Webber (4:32 P.M.)
We're thinking of trying the new Mexican place on Slate Road. It's called Ocho Coronas.

Tim Foxx (4:33 P.M.)
You're out of luck. That place closed a few days ago.

Kurt Webber (4:34 P.M.)
That's too bad. I heard great things about it.

Tim Foxx (4:36 P.M.)
How about Lotus Tacos around the corner? They always have a special menu on Fridays.

Kurt Webber (4:37 P.M.)
That would be great. Do you want to go to Lotus Tacos, Jake?

Davi Avril (4:38 P.M.)
OK, but I won't be able to get there till about six.

Jake Rivas (4:39 P.M.)
Sounds good to me. And Davi, I just sent you the updated figures for the report.

161. What are the writers discussing?
(A) Where to hold a company banquet
(B) What restaurant serves the best food
(C) What is on the menu at Ocho Coronas
(D) Where to go for dinner

162. What information does Mr. Foxx provide about Ocho Coronas?
(A) People have recommended it to him.
(B) It usually opens early on Fridays.
(C) The food there is not very authentic.
(D) It is no longer in business.

163. At 4:34 P.M., why most likely does Mr. Webber write, "That's too bad"?
(A) He wanted to try a new restaurant.
(B) Mr. Foxx cannot complete a project.
(C) Slate Road is too far away.
(D) He has a scheduling conflict.

164. What does Mr. Avril decide to do?
(A) Research nearby restaurants
(B) Work extra hours tomorrow
(C) Join his coworkers for a meal
(D) Have food delivered to the office

Multinational Voice Magazine
PO Box 17999
Greenlane
Auckland 1546

Tuata Wehi
16 Page Street
Wellington 6023

Dear Mr. Wehi,

On 25 March, your three-month trial subscription to *Multinational Voice Magazine* will expire. To continue to receive this vital news resource, please fill out the postage-paid renewal card included with this letter and mail it in before the end of this month. You may select from a three-month, six-month, one-year, or two-year subscription. Do note that our two-year offer is by far the most economical. Also, the one- and two-year options include the "Notable People of the Year" special edition.

Thank you once again for choosing *Multinational Voice Magazine*. We continually strive to provide the best commentary on global affairs from a New Zealand perspective. To provide your feedback, please visit www.mvmagazine.co.nz and fill out our online comment form.

Sincerely,
Estelle Pearson, Customer Service Representative

---

165. Why was the letter sent to Mr. Wehi?

(A) To report a late payment
(B) To offer him a refund
(C) To promote a new service
(D) To remind him to resubscribe

166. For about how long has Mr. Wehi been receiving *Multinational Voice Magazine*?

(A) For three months
(B) For six months
(C) For one year
(D) For two years

167. What is one thing that Mr. Wehi is encouraged to do?

(A) Call Ms. Pearson directly
(B) Offer his opinion
(C) Attend an event
(D) Confirm his address

```
*E-mail*
```

From:	info@morganairportshuttle.com
To:	tgrant@tivimail.com
Subject:	re: Suitcase on board
Date:	January 19

Dear Mr. Grant,

Thanks for your inquiry. There are a number of suitcases in our storeroom that match the description you provided, but we have not found one bearing a name tag identifying you as the owner. You will need to come over and find yours on-site at 620 Baker St. Please note that you will be asked to indicate what time your bus left the airport terminal or, better yet, to present your ticket if you still have it.

We are open 6 A.M.–10 P.M. every day. Please do not delay. Due to the large number of items found by our drivers, we have no choice but to limit storage time to 7 days only, after which we dispose of the item.

Regards,

Gina Steiner
Morgan Airport Shuttle

168. Where does Ms. Steiner work?

(A) At a transportation service
(B) At an insurance company
(C) At a car rental company
(D) At a travel agency

169. What did Mr. Grant most likely inquire about?

(A) Reservation options
(B) Luggage limitations
(C) Travel expenses
(D) Lost property

170. What information will Mr. Grant be asked to provide?

(A) His address
(B) His phone number
(C) His departure time
(D) His final destination

171. What is Mr. Grant advised to do?

(A) Take advantage of a discount
(B) Compare payment options
(C) Visit the office as soon as possible
(D) Print out an electronic ticket

GO ON TO THE NEXT PAGE

Spectacular Bridge Created with Super Cranes

By Marcia Brunon

March 14

Five years ago, the town of Stonewell, situated at the foot of the Marshall Mountains, decided to finance the building of a bridge across the Stonewell River. It was planned as a much-needed northern route for the town. — [1] —. The efficiency of the project was directly attributable to two RWC451 cranes, manufactured by Ronsonworks, a company based in England.

The two identical tower cranes were owned by the construction firm Redding Builders. One crane was assembled at the south bank of the river, while the other one was placed on a concrete pylon in the center of the Stonewell River. — [2] —. The assembly of the second crane was particularly challenging, as it required the use of another crane on a floating barge.

"Any large project is going to require unforeseen adjustments that may disrupt an official construction schedule," said Roger Lee, chief engineer of Redding Builders. — [3] —. In this case, the metal anchors that connected the bridge to the pylons were determined to be too small. The new anchors weighed 22 tons, which is within the safe lifting capacity of an RWC451 crane. — [4] —. Engineers reinforced the existing cranes for extra security, and the cranes performed well.

Today, this postcard-worthy bridge is the pride of Stonewell, featuring viewing platforms for pedestrians, hikers, and visitors at the base of each pier overlooking the mountainous valley. Construction materials and colors harmonize beautifully with the local environment. All design elements, including the piers, viewing platforms, and railings, complement the natural landscape, making the bridge a hit with everyone from hikers to the truck drivers who now include it in their regular route.

172. What is mentioned about the cranes?

(A) They are owned by Ronsonworks.
(B) They were designed specifically for the Stonewell Bridge project.
(C) They were assembled on the Stonewell Bridge construction site.
(D) They weigh more than 22 tons.

173. What is indicated by Mr. Lee?

(A) His professional specialty is bridge construction.
(B) He believes that projects like the Stonewell Bridge always present problems.
(C) He delayed the Stonewell Bridge project for budgetary reasons.
(D) His first project as a chief engineer was the Stonewell Bridge.

174. What is NOT suggested about the Stonewell Bridge?

(A) It provides a northward exit out of town.
(B) It was designed for both pedestrians and vehicles.
(C) It was designed to blend with the natural setting.
(D) It required more workers than first estimated.

175. In which of the positions marked [1], [2], [3], and [4] does the following sentence best belong?

"The project, which was expected to take four years, was completed in less than three."

(A) [1]
(B) [2]
(C) [3]
(D) [4]

GO ON TO THE NEXT PAGE

To: Absalom and Twigg Law Firm employees
From: Shawna Montgomery, Office Manager
Subject: March plans
Sent: February 12
Attachment: Schedule

As most of you are aware, our schedule will be a bit challenging during the first week in March. Various rooms and offices will need to be vacated for certain periods to allow work crews to repaint, recarpet, and replace old furniture. Affected employees will need to box up *all* their office items by 3 P.M. on the day before their room is scheduled for work (please see the attached schedule). Two teams of workers will be on-site, so more than one room at a time will need to be vacated. Note that any rooms due for work on Monday must be packed up and vacated by Friday afternoon, February 27.

Boxes will be provided. Leave your boxes in the rooms for the work crews to remove. Please label them with your name and office number so that the crews can return them to the correct offices once the work is complete.

Please make arrangements to continue working on your assignments while the work crews are in your rooms. The conference room (Room 409) will remain available to be used as a workspace during the entire week. Another possible option is to request permission from your supervisor to telecommute for one or two days.

Please have patience with these temporary inconveniences and do not hesitate to contact me with any questions or concerns.

WORK SCHEDULE—March 2 to March 6		
MONDAY, March 2	Room 401 (Meeting room)	Room 403 (Allie Stevens & Matt Beale)
TUESDAY, March 3		
WEDNESDAY, March 4	Room 402 (Marlene Asbury & Luke Roe)	Room 408 (Meeting room)
THURSDAY, March 5		
FRIDAY, March 6	Room 407 (Jung Li)	Room 404 (Elliot Hagburg & Ana Keller)

176. Why was the memo sent to employees?

(A) To alert them to upcoming renovations
(B) To announce that the firm will be relocating
(C) To request feedback about new workplace facilities
(D) To address their complaints about building maintenance

177. What are employees instructed to do?

(A) Report for work early
(B) Schedule a meeting with a manager
(C) Indicate which office supplies are theirs
(D) Update their contact information online

178. What is stated about Room 409 ?

(A) It will be available for videoconferencing.
(B) Employees may gather there for work.
(C) A scheduling meeting will be held there.
(D) Its furniture will be removed temporarily.

179. When should Ms. Asbury be ready to vacate her office?

(A) On February 12
(B) On February 27
(C) On March 3
(D) On March 4

180. What is suggested about Mr. Hagburg?

(A) He shares an office with a colleague.
(B) He will work off-site on March 5.
(C) He is the head of a department.
(D) He requested the use of a conference room.

GO ON TO THE NEXT PAGE

Livrou Farm

Fresh Organic Produce—From Our Farm to Your Home

Livrou Farm in Bromont, Quebec, invites you to participate in its community-supported agriculture program. Members enjoy fresh farm produce during our growing season from June to November.

Sign up for a farm share and receive these benefits:
• More than 30 varieties of in-season vegetables, fruits, and herbs, harvested by our farm staff and prepared for you to pick up at our barn
• A selection of pick-your-own strawberries, apples, and other fruits
• Access to our member Web site with recipes, farm updates, and a farm newsletter
• Discounts on events at the farm, such as the annual summer music festival. Events typically cost $15, but members pay $10.

Members pick up their shares once a week at the farm. A full-size share is $700 per season, and a half-size share is $350. Half-size shareholders receive half the amount of produce each week. All other benefits remain the same.

Our farm produce is grown without the use of pesticides or herbicides, and we use only naturally occurring fertilizers. For more information or to register for a membership, please see our Web site at www.livroufarm.ca.

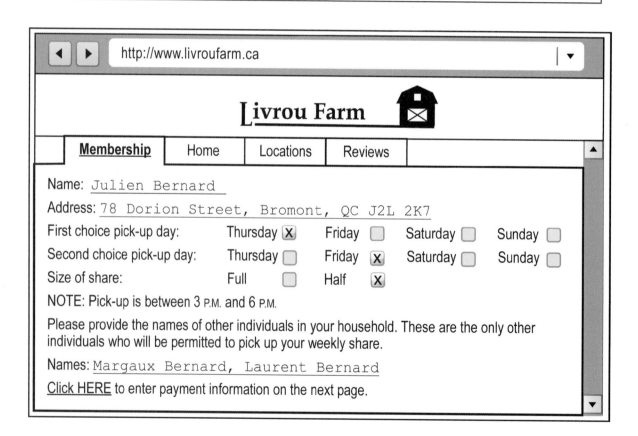

http://www.livroufarm.ca

Livrou Farm

| **Membership** | Home | Locations | Reviews |

Name: Julien Bernard
Address: 78 Dorion Street, Bromont, QC J2L 2K7

First choice pick-up day:	Thursday [X]	Friday ☐	Saturday ☐	Sunday ☐
Second choice pick-up day:	Thursday ☐	Friday [X]	Saturday ☐	Sunday ☐
Size of share:	Full ☐	Half [X]		

NOTE: Pick-up is between 3 P.M. and 6 P.M.

Please provide the names of other individuals in your household. These are the only other individuals who will be permitted to pick up your weekly share.

Names: Margaux Bernard, Laurent Bernard

Click HERE to enter payment information on the next page.

181. What is the purpose of the flyer?

(A) To invite people to a farm festival
(B) To promote community service opportunities
(C) To share recipes for healthy eating
(D) To advertise a farm program

182. What is suggested about the workers at Livrou Farm?

(A) They collect farm produce from June to November.
(B) They update the farm's Web site once a week.
(C) They create meals using the farm's products.
(D) They sell farm products at several local markets.

183. What is NOT indicated about Livrou Farm?

(A) It publishes a newsletter.
(B) It uses natural fertilizers.
(C) It hosts musical performances.
(D) It offers cooking classes.

184. What is true about Mr. Bernard's membership?

(A) He must pick up his produce on Sundays.
(B) He is the only person allowed to pick up his farm share.
(C) He will be allowed to pick some of his own fruit.
(D) He will be able to plant and grow his own vegetables.

185. How much should Mr. Bernard pay for the membership?

(A) $10
(B) $15
(C) $350
(D) $700

GO ON TO THE NEXT PAGE

http://www.communitylinkforum.org/burlingtonvermont ▼

▲

Professional Seeking Apartment in Burlington
Jorge Janssen <jjanssen@blitzer.com>

Topic: Real Estate and Housing
Date: June 23

I accepted a new position in Burlington and need to relocate near the downtown area before my start date on August 15. I'm seeking a simple, clean, one-bedroom rental or larger, depending on price. A relaxing location with outdoor seating for entertaining friends or family would be a plus. I do have a car, but I'd appreciate having good access to public transportation. I have a budget of around $1,400 monthly to cover all housing costs, including utilities.

▼

http://www.communitylinkforum.org/burlingtonvermont ▼

▲

Apartment for Rent in Burlington
Eloise McMahon <mcmahonrental@hmail.com>

Topic: Real Estate and Housing
Date: June 23

Be the first to rent this two-bedroom apartment upon completion of extensive renovations. This property is anticipated to be move-in ready on August 1. It will feature a clean modern look, new floors throughout, and all-new appliances. The apartment is situated downtown, and students are welcome as it's less than ten minutes by bus to Denton University. On-street parking is available with a decal from the City Transportation Office. Cats or small dogs are potentially permitted, but with conditions, so please inquire. $1,400 rent also pays for water, sewer, garbage pickups, and general upkeep of the property. Electricity and natural gas will be the responsibility of the tenant. A one-time security deposit equal to one month's rent should be paid upon signing the rental agreement.

▼

To:	Eloise McMahon <mcmahonrental@hmail.com>
From:	Jorge Janssen <jjanssen@blitzer.com>
Re:	Apartment
Date:	June 24

Dear Ms. McMahon,

I noticed your rental listing on communitylinkforum.org. From the description it sounds as if it may be just what I've been looking for. I'm eager to look over the apartment, and I just happen to be in Burlington all this week. My last day in town will be Sunday, June 30. If the place suits me, I'd want to move in the same day that it's expected to be available. The timing would be perfect! I hope to hear from you soon.

Thank you.

Jorge Janssen
(802) 555-0122

186. Why is Mr. Janssen relocating?

(A) To begin a new job
(B) To return to his hometown
(C) To study part-time
(D) To start his retirement

187. What aspect of the property does NOT match Mr. Janssen's preferences?

(A) The location
(B) The monthly costs
(C) The parking availability
(D) The size

188. For what situation does Ms. McMahon mention that she will need additional information?

(A) When changes to the decor are preferred
(B) When a tenant is ready to pay a security deposit
(C) When repairs to the apartment are needed
(D) When someone wants to keep an indoor pet

189. Why does Mr. Janssen send the e-mail?

(A) To agree to the terms of a rental contract
(B) To change the details of a residential advertisement
(C) To ask about a feature of an apartment
(D) To make arrangements to view a property

190. When does Mr. Janssen wish to start living in the residence?

(A) On June 24
(B) On June 30
(C) On August 1
(D) On August 15

GO ON TO THE NEXT PAGE

Kitchenware Utopia Food Processor—Model C3

You will never need to buy another food processor! Our best-selling model, the C3, is made of high-quality plastic and easy-to-clean stainless steel.

FEATURES The unique blade design and powerful motor make this a professional-grade appliance, ideal for busy restaurants of any size.

WARRANTY We include a seven-year warranty on all parts and labor—a reassurance to you that our food processor will last a long time.

Special purchase price: $319.00/KU Club Members: $299.00

---

www.kitchenwareutopia.com/C3/reviews/454

Rating: ★ ★ ★ ★

Review: This product is amazing! I work as a caterer, and I've used a lot of different food processors. Kitchenware Utopia's C3 is by far the best I've found. Its motor is very powerful, and the many different blades and settings make it extremely versatile. The settings are also straightforward. It's expensive but well worth the investment, and since I'm a loyalty club member, the price was reasonable. My only complaint would be that it's very heavy and therefore not as portable as I'd hoped. Overall, though, I'm exceptionally satisfied with this product.

Posted by Eli Perles on March 27

We are very glad to hear you are happy with our C3 food processor. Customer satisfaction is our number one priority. We would like to respond to your complaint and provide a suggestion regarding your concerns. Our C2 processor might be better suited to your professional needs. The C2 offers the same motor size as the C3, but it is much smaller than the C3 in general. However, this model does cost slightly more than the C3. You can view the product description by visiting www.kitchenwareutopia.com/C2.

Posted by Kitchenware Utopia Customer Service on March 28

191. What is NOT mentioned in the product description as a feature of the C3 food processor?

(A) It is very durable.
(B) It is suitable for commercial kitchens.
(C) It is larger than competitors' food processors.
(D) It is a popular model.

192. What is indicated in the customer review?

(A) The C3 comes with detailed instructions.
(B) Mr. Perles is pleased with his purchase.
(C) Kitchenware Utopia's customer service is very good.
(D) Users find the C3 difficult to clean.

193. What is suggested about Mr. Perles?

(A) He paid $299 for the food processor.
(B) He purchased some optional parts for the processor.
(C) He catered a large-scale event on March 27.
(D) He has never used a food processor before.

194. Why would the C2 processor likely be recommended as more suitable for Mr. Perles?

(A) It is inexpensive.
(B) It is dishwasher safe.
(C) It is easy to assemble.
(D) It is lightweight.

195. In the online response, the word "regarding" in paragraph 1, line 3, is closest in meaning to

(A) looking after
(B) about
(C) in comparison
(D) admiring

GO ON TO THE NEXT PAGE

Ment Hall to Host Piasek Cup Final

Ment Hall, which is currently undergoing extensive renovation, will be ready to host the final game of the Piasek Cup Volleyball Championship to be held in Warsaw this June. Although the project has been in the works for some time, it was the opportunity to host this championship that provided the economic incentive to push the project to its completion. City officials have confirmed that the construction is progressing according to schedule and will be complete well before the finals of the championship.

Since Ment Hall is the only major arena in the country that has never hosted a Piasek Cup event, the hall's owners were proud to have been chosen to host this year's finale. The final game will inaugurate the refurbished hall. The event is expected to draw thousands of volleyball fans, and the organizers are confident that Ment Hall will live up to the occasion. Seating 19,000 spectators, Ment Hall will be double its previous size.

Piasek Cup Volleyball Championship

Quarterfinal Games

Venezuela-Australia 10 June, 3:00 P.M. Loave Arena, Bydgoszcz	Poland-France 10 June, 6:00 P.M. Timpani Hall, Katowice	Brazil-USA 11 June, 3:00 P.M. Polana Center, Cracow	Cuba-Egypt 11 June, 6:00 P.M. Mistrz Arena, Wroclaw

Semifinal Games

Winners of 10 June games 13 June, 3:00 P.M. Timpani Hall, Katowice	Winners of 11 June games 13 June, 3:00 P.M. Polana Center, Cracow

Final Game

16 June, 6:00 P.M.
Ment Hall, Warsaw

NOTE: Tickets for the final game are selling fast, so don't wait until after the semifinal games to order. Reserved seating only, no general admission. No refunds.

News Update
HALLAX RADIO 108.3 FM

Sports—Volleyball, 10 June

At 3:00 P.M., Venezuela will take on Australia for qualification to the semifinals. Our guest announcer will be Vin Cote, retired coach of last year's winning team from Canada.

At 6:00 P.M., host team Poland will face off against France. The game will be covered live by Jeremy Bosko.

196. In the article, the word "draw" in paragraph 2, line 7, is closest in meaning to

(A) promote
(B) attract
(C) sketch
(D) remove

197. What will be changed about Ment Hall?

(A) Its ownership
(B) Its ticket prices
(C) Its seating capacity
(D) Its location

198. When will the first game be held at a new host venue?

(A) On June 10
(B) On June 13
(C) On June 14
(D) On June 16

199. In the schedule, what are people advised to do?

(A) Request a refund for tickets that they do not plan to use
(B) Order tickets immediately after the semifinal games
(C) Buy tickets for the final game as soon as possible
(D) Arrive at the final game early

200. Where will Mr. Cote be reporting from?

(A) Bydgoszcz
(B) Katowice
(C) Cracow
(D) Wroclaw

Stop! This is the end of the test. If you finish before time is called, you may go back to Parts 5, 6, and 7 and check your work.

토익® 정기시험
기출문제집

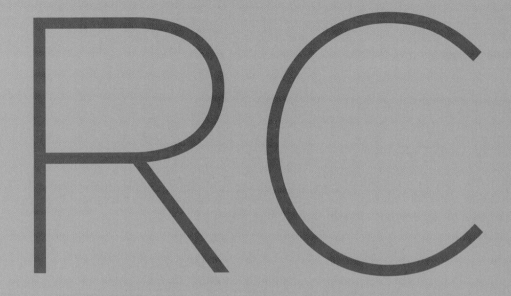

RC

기출 TEST

03

READING TEST

In the Reading test, you will read a variety of texts and answer several different types of reading comprehension questions. The entire Reading test will last 75 minutes. There are three parts, and directions are given for each part. You are encouraged to answer as many questions as possible within the time allowed.

You must mark your answers on the separate answer sheet. Do not write your answers in your test book.

PART 5

Directions: A word or phrase is missing in each of the sentences below. Four answer choices are given below each sentence. Select the best answer to complete the sentence. Then mark the letter (A), (B), (C), or (D) on your answer sheet.

101. York Development Corporation marked the ------- of the Ford Road office complex with a ribbon-cutting ceremony.

(A) opens
(B) opening
(C) opened
(D) openly

102. Staff at the Bismarck Hotel were ------- helpful to us during our stay.

(A) quite
(B) enough
(C) far
(D) early

103. Ms. Luo will explain some possible consequences of the ------- merger with the Wilson-Peek Corporation.

(A) proposed
(B) proposal
(C) proposition
(D) proposing

104. The Springdale supermarket survey ------- will be released a week after they are evaluated.

(A) events
(B) stores
(C) results
(D) coupons

105. The new printer operates more ------- than the previous model did.

(A) quickest
(B) quickness
(C) quick
(D) quickly

106. Here at Vanguard Buying Club, ------- help members find quality merchandise at the lowest possible prices.

(A) us
(B) our
(C) we
(D) ourselves

107. Management announced that all salespeople would be receiving a bonus this year, ------- in time for summer vacations.

(A) just
(B) as
(C) only
(D) by

108. According to *Florida Digital Designer Magazine*, many graphic designers do not consider ------- to be traditional artists.

(A) it
(B) their
(C) themselves
(D) itself

109. A wooden bridge crossing the wading pond ------- to the hotel's nine-hole golf course.

(A) prepares
(B) leads
(C) presents
(D) takes

110. A special sale on stationery ------- on the Write Things Web site yesterday.

(A) was announced
(B) announced
(C) was announcing
(D) to announce

111. All produce transported by Gocargo Trucking is refrigerated ------- upon pickup to prevent spoilage.

(A) lately
(B) promptly
(C) potentially
(D) clearly

112. The Ferrera Museum plans to exhibit a collection of Lucia Almeida's most ------- sculptures.

(A) innovative
(B) innovation
(C) innovatively
(D) innovate

113. The bank's cashier windows are open daily from 8:00 A.M. to 4:00 P.M. ------- on Sundays.

(A) except
(B) until
(C) nor
(D) yet

114. Inventory control and warehousing strategies ------- within the responsibilities of the supply chain manager.

(A) have
(B) cover
(C) mark
(D) fall

115. Of all the truck models available today, it can be difficult to figure out ------- would best suit your company's needs.

(A) when
(B) why
(C) which
(D) where

116. CEO Yoshiro Kasai has expressed complete faith in Fairway Maritime's ------- to deliver the product on time.

(A) belief
(B) measure
(C) problem
(D) ability

117. At Derwin Securities, trainees alternate ------- attending information sessions and working closely with assigned mentors.

(A) along
(B) against
(C) between
(D) near

118. Company Vice President Astrid Barretto had no ------- to being considered for the position of CEO.

(A) objected
(B) objecting
(C) objects
(D) objection

119. Belinda McKay fans who are ------- to the author's formal writing style will be surprised by her latest biography.

(A) fortunate
(B) readable
(C) comparable
(D) accustomed

120. The Southeast Asia Business Convention will feature ------- known and respected leaders from countries across the region.

(A) widen
(B) wider
(C) widely
(D) wide

GO ON TO THE NEXT PAGE

121. ------- the high cost of fuel, customers are buying smaller, more efficient cars.

(A) Together with
(B) Instead of
(C) As well as
(D) Because of

122. Over the past ten years, Bellworth Medical Clinic ------- Atlan Protection officers for all security needs.

(A) is hiring
(B) were hiring
(C) has hired
(D) was hired

123. The driver will make three ------- to deliver the package before it is returned to our warehouse.

(A) attempts
(B) pursuits
(C) aims
(D) experiences

124. We congratulate all Riverside employees, whose ------- effort has resulted in a 20 percent reduction in waste disposal costs.

(A) collect
(B) collective
(C) collects
(D) collector

125. Andrzej Ptak's photography Web site will be available online ------- we have finished organizing and cataloging his work.

(A) how
(B) once
(C) so too
(D) not only

126. The initial feedback from early buyers of the Sunbell XC2 mobile phone indicates that they found it ------- to use.

(A) conveniences
(B) conveniently
(C) convenience
(D) convenient

127. ------- space in the bathroom was limited, the contractor managed to fit in two sinks and a shower.

(A) Both
(B) So that
(C) Whether
(D) Even though

128. The staff must ------- as much market-research data as possible before planning the advertising campaign.

(A) equip
(B) compile
(C) endorse
(D) compose

129. ------- a national holiday falls on a Thursday, the Barstow Company allows employees to take off Friday as well.

(A) Even
(B) For
(C) Nearly
(D) Whenever

130. ------- materials for the advanced Farsi course include an audio CD and a DVD.

(A) Supplementary
(B) Consequential
(C) Persistent
(D) Cooperative

PART 6

Directions: Read the texts that follow. A word, phrase, or sentence is missing in parts of each text. Four answer choices for each question are given below the text. Select the best answer to complete the text. Then mark the letter (A), (B), (C), or (D) on your answer sheet.

Questions 131-134 refer to the following article.

(3 September)—Five years ago, Brian Trang signed a five-year lease to open his restaurant, Trang's Bistro, at 30 Luray Place. Mr. Trang admits that the first two years of operation were quite ------- . "We offer spicy food from Vietnam's central region," he explains. "We didn't do well at first
131.

------- the cuisine is based on unfamiliar herbs and hot flavors. It took a while to catch on with
132.

customers." But Mr. Trang was confident the food would gain in popularity, and he was correct.

------- . Mr. Trang has just signed another five-year lease, and he is planning ------- the space
133.   **134.**

next year.

131. (A) competitive
 (B) potential
 (C) challenging
 (D) rewarding

132. (A) because
 (B) unless
 (C) despite
 (D) besides

133. (A) Originally from Hue, Mr. Trang moved to London at age five with his family.
 (B) Reservations at Trang's Bistro must now be made a week in advance.
 (C) This situation was not expected to last so long.
 (D) The restaurant will relocate in March.

134. (A) renovate
 (B) being renovated
 (C) renovates
 (D) to renovate

This manual provides guidelines for inventory control at Malanta facilities. Our advanced manufacturing procedures depend on ------- inventory control. Only by maintaining a precise flow
135.

of inventory ------- minimize costs and ensure prompt shipments. To achieve this goal, we must
136.

avoid shortages. When stock is in the correct location at the time it is ordered, shipments are made at regular shipping costs and within estimated time frames. ------- . Therefore, the
137.

procedures in this manual must always be faithfully ------- .
138.

135. (A) accurate
(B) seasonal
(C) expensive
(D) industrialized

136. (A) is able to
(B) to be able
(C) our ability to
(D) are we able to

137. (A) We have calculated the costs for you.
(B) Please allow at least two weeks for delivery.
(C) Unfortunately, some items are currently not in stock.
(D) However, this is not possible when unexpected shortages occur.

138. (A) implemented
(B) reproduced
(C) corrected
(D) recorded

To: Alan Porto <aporto@silverwing.ky>

From: Tuchman's Billing <billing@tuchmans.ky>

Subject: Autopay

Date: 19 February

Dear Mr. Porto:

Congratulations on your recent ------- in Tuchman's Autopay system. Thank you for signing up for
                                  139.

this convenient billing system. Your automatic payments will begin with the next billing cycle on

1 March. ------- . Your statements will come to you electronically and your payment will be
          140.

deducted from your designated bank account. You may ------- the account from which the funds
                                                        141.

are withdrawn. Simply log in to the My Account section on our Web site https://www.tuchmans.ky,

select Autopay, and follow the instructions to enter the alternate account information. Please

contact customer service if you have ------- using Tuchman's Autopay.
                                      142.

Tuchman's Billing Department

---

139. (A) enroll
(B) enrolled
(C) enrolls
(D) enrollment

140. (A) Our billing clerks are happy to serve you.
(B) You will no longer receive a bill by post.
(C) We appreciate our loyal customers.
(D) Take advantage of our special offers.

141. (A) own
(B) settle
(C) open
(D) change

142. (A) any difficulties
(B) more difficult
(C) the difficulty
(D) too difficult

GO ON TO THE NEXT PAGE

12 December
Lenny Howe
222 Easton Boulevard
Port Douglas QLD 4877

Dear Mr. Howe,

The Irwin Neighbourhood Association is proud to ------- a summer event called Park Fest, to be
                                                    143.
held at Fern Park on 10 January, from 1 P.M. to 8 P.M. Park Fest will feature numerous

family-friendly activities and a delicious picnic dinner to be served at 6 P.M. A per person fee of

ten dollars will be collected. The proceeds will ------- go towards a park enhancement project.
                                                  144.
The plan is to hire a contractor to landscape the park grounds, while a smaller portion will be

spent on an advertising campaign. This event ------- to be great fun. ------- .
                                             145.   **146.**

Regards,

Faye Mason-Jones
Director, Irwin Neighbourhood Association

143. (A) announce
     (B) admit
     (C) recall
     (D) state

144. (A) entirely
     (B) often
     (C) primarily
     (D) together

145. (A) promise
     (B) promises
     (C) promising
     (D) promised

146. (A) You can help by disposing of all
         rubbish.
     (B) The park was established 75 years
         ago.
     (C) We hope you will be able to attend.
     (D) Fern Park attracts over 20,000 visitors
         a year.

PART 7

Directions: In this part you will read a selection of texts, such as magazine and newspaper articles, e-mails, and instant messages. Each text or set of texts is followed by several questions. Select the best answer for each question and mark the letter (A), (B), (C), or (D) on your answer sheet.

Questions 147-148 refer to the following form.

Lastico Employee Badge
Application Form

To receive a new Lastico employee badge, please fill out the following form. Write in pen only. Please PRINT clearly.

Name _LAURA CONSTANTINI_   Division _CUSTOMER SUPPORT_

Employee No. _2378_   Employed at Lastico since _FEB 10_

My previous badge ☑ expired   ☐ was lost ☐ was damaged
(Leave blank if you are applying for the first time)

Submitted _AUG 2_   Signed _Constantini_

---

147. Why did Ms. Constantini fill out the form?

(A) To authorize a charge to her credit card
(B) To be assigned to a new company division
(C) To request a document renewal
(D) To report lost equipment

148. What instructions are included?

(A) Where to send the form
(B) How to complete the form
(C) When to submit the application
(D) What documentation to attach

★ ★ ★ ★ ★ ★ ★ ★

VACANCY

The Golden Lagoon has been serving Montego Bay for 18 years. We are an award-winning restaurant with a reputation that spans the Caribbean. Currently we have vacancies for the position of waitstaff. Duties include taking customers' orders, serving food and beverages, preparing itemized bills, and accepting payments. Experience is preferred but not required. We offer an excellent hourly rate and flexible work schedule. Apply in person, supplying a résumé and three employment references.

The Golden Lagoon
Shahine Kincaid, Manager
135 Concertina Dr.
Montego Bay, Jamaica
Business hours: Monday–Friday, 11:00 A.M.–11:00 P.M.
Saturday and Sunday, noon–10:00 P.M.

★ ★ ★ ★ ★ ★ ★ ★

149. What is stated about The Golden Lagoon?

(A) It is closed on Sundays.
(B) It regularly has positions available.
(C) It has been in business for over a decade.
(D) It was bought by Ms. Kincaid eighteen years ago.

150. What is mentioned about job applicants?

(A) They will be working on a fixed schedule.
(B) They must go to the restaurant to file their job request.
(C) They must have worked in a restaurant before.
(D) They will learn how to cook Jamaican dishes.

TEST 3

```
========================== *E-mail* ==========================

    To:          Staff

    From:        Asta Lindstrom

    Subject:     Reminder

    Date:        11 April
```

To All Staff:

This is a reminder that the water in the Tolliver building will be temporarily shut off tomorrow at 8 a.m. while repairs are completed. I understand that most employees who work in the building will be off-site at a software training session and will not be affected.

For those of you who will be working in Tolliver tomorrow, the Hillcrest Water Department has assured me that the water will be off for no more than four hours. We will provide complimentary bottled water in the lobby for all staff during this time. The cafeteria will remain closed until the water has been turned on again. At that point meal service and food sales will resume. I apologize for the inconvenience.

Sincerely,

Asta Lindstrom
Facilities Manager

151. What will happen tomorrow?

(A) New computers will arrive.
(B) Maintenance work will be done.
(C) A new employment policy will take effect.
(D) The location of a training session will be announced.

152. What will employees NOT be able to do in the Tolliver building in the morning?

(A) Use new software
(B) Drink bottled water
(C) Purchase food items
(D) Walk through the lobby

GO ON TO THE NEXT PAGE

Questions 153-154 refer to the following text-message chain.

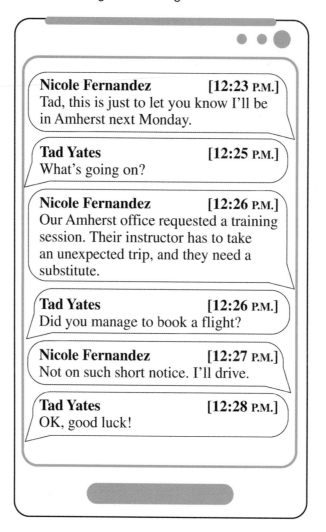

Nicole Fernandez [12:23 P.M.]
Tad, this is just to let you know I'll be in Amherst next Monday.

Tad Yates [12:25 P.M.]
What's going on?

Nicole Fernandez [12:26 P.M.]
Our Amherst office requested a training session. Their instructor has to take an unexpected trip, and they need a substitute.

Tad Yates [12:26 P.M.]
Did you manage to book a flight?

Nicole Fernandez [12:27 P.M.]
Not on such short notice. I'll drive.

Tad Yates [12:28 P.M.]
OK, good luck!

153. What will Ms. Fernandez do next Monday?

(A) Teach a training course
(B) Meet an instructor
(C) Go on a vacation
(D) Apply for a job

154. At 12:27 P.M., what does Ms. Fernandez mean when she writes, "Not on such short notice"?

(A) She will not arrive on time.
(B) She will not travel by plane.
(C) She cannot accept an invitation.
(D) She cannot make a payment.

refer to the following e-mail.

To:	Jake Taera <jtaera@tritmail.com>
From:	Natalie Satter <nsatter@coldings.com>
Subject:	Information
Date:	30 September
Attachment:	📎 Coldings1

Dear Mr. Taera:

Welcome to the Coldings Home Store family! You have been hired as a sales associate. Your training session begins on 8 October at 8:30 A.M. at the Auckland store, 42 Crossbill Road. Please report to Human Resources to begin your orientation as a Coldings Home Store team member. During your first two weeks with our company, you will learn about our team approach and the many benefits of working at Coldings Home Store. You will be working from 8:30 A.M. to 5:00 P.M. After training, you might be assigned to a different work shift and you will be eligible for benefits including flexible days off, sick days, and our employee discount.

Please sign and return the attached document indicating your willingness to accept the position as sales associate. Please let me know if you have any questions or need directions. I look forward to seeing you at the Auckland store on 8 October.

Sincerely,

Natalie Satter
Human Resources Coordinator

155. What is the purpose of the e-mail?

(A) To thank an employee
(B) To provide job information
(C) To explain a new policy
(D) To announce a special sales event

156. According to Ms. Satter, what might happen after two weeks?

(A) Mr. Taera's work schedule might change.
(B) Mr. Taera's might be transferred to another location.
(C) The company might train Mr. Taera for a new responsibility.
(D) The company might mail Mr. Taera new benefits information.

157. What did Ms. Satter send with the e-mail?

(A) A store map
(B) An events calendar
(C) A list of benefits
(D) An employment agreement

GO ON TO THE NEXT PAGE

For immediate release

Contact: Desmond Hawkes, Office of Public Relations
Telephone: (02) 5555 6506
E-mail: dhawkes@carlisle.org.au

New Exhibition at Sydney's
Carlisle Art Museum

SYDNEY (3 June)—The Carlisle Art Museum's latest exhibition, *Deep Waters*, will open on 15 June. The exhibition will feature 38 realist and abstract paintings portraying the beauty and vastness of the world's oceans. All the works were created by Australian artists based in Sydney, and among them will be six by the critically acclaimed oil painter Harold Bernstein.

The exhibition will run until 15 July. Tickets are $10. Museum visitors may view the exhibition between 9 A.M. and 4 P.M. on Tuesdays, Wednesdays, and Thursdays, and between 2 P.M. and 9 P.M. on Fridays and Saturdays. On each day of the exhibition, at least one of the artists will be present and available to answer visitors' questions about the creative process. Mr. Bernstein will be available on 30 June only.

On 23 July, the exhibition will open at the Muriel Art Gallery in Melbourne, where ocean-themed paintings from Melbourne artists will be added to the collection.

158. What is one purpose of the press release?

(A) To advertise an upcoming art show
(B) To publicize paintings available for purchase
(C) To profile an art gallery owner
(D) To announce the opening of a new museum

159. Who is Mr. Bernstein?

(A) An art critic
(B) A museum director
(C) A public relations specialist
(D) An artist

160. What is implied about the exhibition in Melbourne?

(A) It will be open to the public in the evenings only.
(B) It will include more paintings than the exhibition in Sydney will.
(C) It will feature demonstrations of painting techniques by artists.
(D) It will include paintings of landscapes in addition to paintings of oceans.

```
┌─────────────────────────────────────────────────────────────────────────┐
│                              *E-mail*                                     │
├─────────────────────────────────────────────────────────────────────────┤
│  From:        evaluation@crawfordds.com                                   │
│  To:          trosinsky@mailssen.com                                      │
│  Subject:     Crawford Design Contest                                     │
│  Date:        April 2                                                     │
├─────────────────────────────────────────────────────────────────────────┤
│  Dear Ms. Rosinsky,                                                       │
│                                                                           │
│  Thank you for entering the Crawford Design Studio Awards Contest. Today  │
│  we received your project titled "Old Rexto Factory Restoration,"         │
│  including a total of nine photographs and an 18-page description file.   │
│  — [1] —. Your submission has been forwarded for further processing and   │
│  has been assigned the entry number P1298. — [2] —.                       │
│                                                                           │
│  Your project will now be reviewed by a panel of judges, which consists   │
│  of our in-house experts as well as outside designers. — [3] —. You will  │
│  be able to check on the status of your entry via the "Submissions Being  │
│  Processed" link in our Web site's Main Menu.                             │
│                                                                           │
│  Should you have any questions, please do not hesitate to call us. — [4] —.│
│                                                                           │
│  Kind regards,                                                            │
│                                                                           │
│  Crawford Design Studio                                                   │
└─────────────────────────────────────────────────────────────────────────┘
```

161. What is the purpose of the e-mail?

(A) To report missing documents
(B) To inquire about building costs
(C) To confirm receipt of materials
(D) To request additional photographs

162. What is Ms. Rosinsky advised to do online?

(A) Read the contest rules
(B) Obtain a map and directions
(C) Update her contact information
(D) Track the progress of her submission

163. In which of the positions marked [1], [2], [3], and [4] does the following sentence best belong?

"Please use it when you contact us regarding your entry."

(A) [1]
(B) [2]
(C) [3]
(D) [4]

GO ON TO THE NEXT PAGE

Questions 164-167 refer to the following article.

May 5—Boston law firm Warner and Arnes announced this morning that it is merging with the Philadelphia law firm Hamilton Jones to create Warner, Hamilton, and Associates. With more than 655 attorneys, the merger will make this the largest law firm in the northeastern United States.

"This is a welcome merger of two well-managed firms who share similar corporate cultures and philosophies," said Andrea Warner, codirector of the former Warner and Arnes, who will serve as managing partner of Warner, Hamilton, and Associates. "Our combined expertise makes Warner, Hamilton, and Associates uniquely placed to provide clients with even higher levels of counsel and service. We look forward to continuing our practices in Boston and Philadelphia and expect to open yet another office in Hartford within the next twelve months."

According to a press release, Ms. Warner has garnered attention through her representation of clients across the country in prominent cases involving workers' rights, equal pay, and social justice.

The firm expects to keep all of its current lawyers and staff and will "combine management teams made up of partners from each firm to ensure a seamless transition," the release said.

164. Why was the article written?

(A) To profile the career of a prominent lawyer
(B) To promote legal services
(C) To discuss the joining of two firms
(D) To announce a firm's relocation

165. What does Warner, Hamilton, and Associates plan to do?

(A) Hire additional lawyers
(B) Expand to a third city
(C) Change its leadership
(D) Close its Philadelphia office

166. What is suggested about Ms. Warner?

(A) She is based in Hartford.
(B) She plans to retire soon.
(C) She sometimes offers free legal counsel.
(D) She is well-known nationally.

167. The word "seamless" in paragraph 4, line 4, is closest in meaning to

(A) in a single piece
(B) without problems
(C) in close range
(D) without hurry

Questions 168-171 refer to the following e-mail.

To:	maria_bellandini@pweb.net
From:	thomas.mclaren@delicatessenmag.com
Date:	Tuesday, October 2
Subject:	Food Photography Article

Dear Ms. Bellandini:

I have some news regarding your article that is scheduled to be published in the next issue of *Delicatessen Magazine.* — [1] —. Yesterday, we learned that a major advertiser canceled their contract with us, and as a result, we will have to reduce the number of pages in our upcoming issue. This is extremely unfortunate, but we just do not have enough money without these ads to publish the magazine in its current format. — [2] —.

We know that readers have enjoyed reading about your experiences in Italy. — [3] —. While your eight-page story about working as a food photographer is excellent, in order to fit in the slimmer issue, it will need to be cut by about thirty percent. Although I sincerely hope you agree to having your article published in our upcoming issue, I will understand if you would rather have the article published in full at a later time. However, I have to let you know that the magazine industry is not always the most stable business, and for this reason, I do not know if there will be space for your story in the future. — [4] —.

Please let me know as soon as possible what you would like to do. Should you agree to edit the story, I will need the new version by Monday.

Best regards,

Thomas McLaren, Editor-in-Chief

168. What is implied about *Delicatessen Magazine*?

(A) It plans to merge with another magazine.
(B) It gives discounted subscriptions to staff.
(C) It relies on advertisements for funding.
(D) It offers long-term contracts to writers.

169. How would Ms. Bellandini most likely revise her article?

(A) By making it shorter
(B) By changing the topic
(C) By adding more information
(D) By including more images of food

170. What does Mr. McLaren NOT suggest to Ms. Bellandini?

(A) Her previous articles were well liked.
(B) She should submit her article to another magazine.
(C) Her article might not be published in full at a later date.
(D) She should notify him of her decision.

171. In which of the positions marked [1], [2], [3], and [4] does the following sentence best belong?

"Of course, this is your choice, and I will respect whatever decision you make."

(A) [1]
(B) [2]
(C) [3]
(D) [4]

GO ON TO THE NEXT PAGE

Delroy Gerew (1:29 P.M.):
Hi, Ms. Chichester, we'd like to order another 10 shirts, featuring the company's name, Magnalook, and its logo. We need four small, two medium, and four large sizes. Could you fill the order by Friday?

Nina Chichester (1:32 P.M.):
That's two days from today, so a $75 rush-order fee will be added.

Delroy Gerew (1:34 P.M.):
How can we avoid the fee?

Nina Chichester (1:36 P.M.):
By choosing the standard 5-day production option. Your order would be ready Monday of next week.

Delroy Gerew (1:38 P.M.):
I guess it can't be helped. Since we have employees starting this Friday and you open at 8:00 A.M., can I pick up the shirts at that time?

Nina Chichester (1:39 P.M.):
Pick-up time is normally after 1:00 P.M., but I'll see to it they're ready by 8:00 A.M.

Delroy Gerew (1:41 P.M.):
Thank you. Actually, my assistant will be picking them up.

Nina Chichester (1:42 P.M.):
That's fine. Could you please e-mail me your logo again? The computer on which I had it stored crashed the other day and is awaiting repair.

Delroy Gerew (1:44 P.M.):
Will do. Thanks, and please charge the credit card you have on file for us.

172. What is suggested about the company Ms. Chichester works for?

(A) It currently has no large-sized shirts in stock.
(B) It has filled an order for Mr. Gerew before.
(C) It offers discounts on large orders.
(D) It is open every evening.

173. Why is Mr. Gerew ordering new shirts?

(A) Additional staff members have been hired.
(B) More were sold than had been anticipated.
(C) The company's logo has been changed.
(D) The style currently in use has become outdated.

174. At 1:38 P.M., what does Mr. Gerew mean when he writes, "I guess it can't be helped"?

(A) He will pay a $75 rush-order fee.
(B) He will ask his assistant to help him.
(C) He will meet Ms. Chichester at 1:00 P.M.
(D) He will select the standard production option.

175. What will Mr. Gerew likely do next?

(A) Provide payment information to Ms. Chichester
(B) Schedule a meeting with Ms. Chichester
(C) Send an e-mail to Ms. Chichester
(D) Fix Ms. Chichester's computer

GO ON TO THE NEXT PAGE

E-Mail Message

To: staffmailinglist@coltonmedical.org
From: Melvin Myers <mmyers@coltonmedical.org>
Date: June 10
Subject: Parking area reassignment

Dear Colleagues:

I just want to remind everyone that crews will begin construction on the new Colton Medical Nutrition Center on June 18.

Effective June 15, parking areas F and G will be closed until August 20, when construction is expected to be completed. Staff currently assigned to park in areas F and G will be given temporary "guest" parking stickers and must park in the guest-parking garage. The Property Maintenance Office will place stickers in staff mailboxes by 4 P.M. today. The sticker should be displayed on the driver's side window of the vehicle.

A construction access road will be created by closing the entrance and exit roads to parking areas F and G. This will also block access to the security building and the pond. However, a temporary alternative entranceway to those locations will be created. To help eliminate excessive traffic, please visit those places only when absolutely necessary. Take note that the Information Center at the main entrance will remain open during construction.

Please e-mail me directly with any questions regarding parking stickers.

Sincerely,

Melvin Myers
Property Maintenance

**WELCOME TO COLTON MEDICAL CAMPUS INFORMATION CENTER
PLEASE CHECK IN BEFORE PROCEEDING**

ATTENTION STAFF:
PARKING AREAS F & G CLOSED UNTIL SEPTEMBER 10

Staff members who normally use these areas and who have not yet received a temporary parking sticker should request one at the security station. A valid access card and staff I.D. are required.

Cars will be immediately towed away if parked next to pedestrian areas, including all walkways, temporary rest areas, and construction tents. Owners of cars parked in the garage without a sticker displayed on the window will be fined $25 per day.

Security officers are available to assist you.

176. Why are parking areas being closed?

(A) They are being resurfaced.
(B) They are being reserved for guests.
(C) An outdoor event will be held on them.
(D) A construction project is scheduled to begin.

177. According to the e-mail, who will receive a temporary parking sticker?

(A) Anyone who is visiting the medical campus
(B) Anyone who usually parks in areas F and G
(C) Anyone who usually parks in the parking garage
(D) Anyone who requests one from the maintenance office

178. Why should staff members limit their visits to the security building?

(A) So that visitors can enjoy the pond
(B) So that fewer cars will be in the area
(C) So that security staff can monitor traffic
(D) So that visitors can get to the Information Center

179. What changed after the e-mail was sent on June 10 ?

(A) Which parking areas are being closed
(B) Where staff should park their vehicles
(C) Where parking stickers should be displayed
(D) How long some parking areas will be closed

180. According to the notice, why might a staff member's car be towed?

(A) If it is parked near a walkway
(B) If it is parked in the visitors' area
(C) If it does not display a parking sticker
(D) If it is parked in the garage after August 20

TEST 3

GO ON TO THE NEXT PAGE

SURVEY

Please take a few minutes to complete this survey about your shopping experience at Woodruff's. Indicate your answer using the 5-point scale to the right of each statement. (1 = Strongly Disagree, 2 = Disagree, 3 = No Opinion, 4 = Agree, 5 = Strongly Agree)

Statement	1	2	3	4	5
The store was clean and organized in appearance.	☐	☐	☐	■	☐
There was a wide selection of items in my size.	☐	☐	☐	☐	■
There were dressing rooms available for me to use.	☐	☐	☐	☐	■
The salespeople were courteous and attentive to me.	☐	■	☐	☐	☐
The items were priced well compared to other stores.	☐	☐	☐	☐	■
I am satisfied overall with my experience at Woodruff's.	☐	☐	☐	■	☐

Amount you spent on this purchase: $60

Age (optional): ☐16-25 ☐26-35 ■36-45 ☐46-55 ☐56-65 ☐66+

Name (optional): Consuela Torres **E-mail (optional):** catorres81@aumail.co.au

---

E-Mail Message

From: Customer Service <custserv@woodruff.co.au>
To: Consuela Torres <catorres81@aumail.co.au>
Date: Friday, 27 April 2:40 P.M.
Subject: Survey
Attachment: ▯ Voucher

Dear Ms. Torres:

Thank you for taking the time to complete a survey about your recent experience at Woodruff's. We appreciate that so many people took the time to provide us with feedback since it helps us to improve the quality of our service.

We were happy to learn that your overall experience shopping at Woodruff's was a positive one. However, we were sorry to see that you shared one area of dissatisfaction with a significant proportion of the customers who responded to the survey. I want you to know that we are taking the survey results seriously. We plan to improve this area with training soon.

As an apology for our failure to meet high standards in all areas, I have attached a voucher for 15% off a future purchase (good for one year) at any of our three Clarksville locations. We look forward to serving you in the future.

Sincerely,

Marietta Passante

181. What type of business is Woodruff's?

(A) A computer software company
(B) A clothing store
(C) A mobile-phone service provider
(D) A consulting firm

182. With what statement about Woodruff's would Ms. Torres most likely agree?

(A) It is located close to her home.
(B) It has a large staff.
(C) It is relatively inexpensive.
(D) It is open later than other businesses.

183. In the e-mail, the word "appreciate" in paragraph 1, line 2, is closest in meaning to

(A) increase
(B) order
(C) understand
(D) value

184. What most likely is Woodruff's planning to do?

(A) Teach its employees to be more friendly and helpful to customers
(B) Make the workplace cleaner and more organized
(C) Open an additional location in Clarksville
(D) Offer a discount voucher to all customers who complete a survey

185. What is suggested about the survey?

(A) It has been taken by many customers.
(B) It was created by Ms. Passante.
(C) It is accessible on the company Web site.
(D) It has been in use for one year.

GO ON TO THE NEXT PAGE

McGivern Wholesale

1486 Beden Trail, Brampton ON L6R 2K7
905-555-0158 • www.mcgivernwholesale.ca

Ordered By: Deshauna's Creations
Order Date: October 12

Item	Item Name	Quantity	Price Each	Amount
14L	3 m table linens, cream	4	$26.00	$104.00
17P	25 cm dinner plates, pale blue	40	$4.40	$176.00
18S	50 cm serving dishes, white	20	$7.95	$159.00
21G	350 ml water goblets, amber	40	$3.25	$130.00
			Subtotal	$569.00
			Tax (HST)	$73.97
			Shipping	$30.00
			Total	$672.97

Payment is due upon receipt.

E-mail

To:	Pete McGivern <pete.mcgivern@mcgivernwholesale.ca>
From:	Deshauna Jacques <deshaunajacques@deshaunascreations.ca>
Subject:	October order
Date:	October 17

Dear Mr. McGivern,

I received my October order, but there were some errors. I received 20 dinner plates instead of 40, and seven water goblets arrived with cracks in the glass. Have you switched shipping carriers recently?

I have been a loyal customer since you opened five years ago, and never before have I experienced problems with an order. Incidentally, you might like to know that I spoke this morning with Ed Salek, owner of nearby Salek's Café. He mentioned that his last delivery from you had some mistakes too.

How soon can you fix my order? I have three parties coming up next week, so I need these items quickly.

Sincerely,

Deshauna Jacques

To:	Deshauna Jacques <deshaunajacques@deshaunascreations.ca>
From:	Pete McGivern <pete.mcgivern@mcgivernwholesale.ca>
Subject:	Re: October order
Date:	October 17

Dear Ms. Jacques,

I was very sorry to learn about your order, and about Mr. Salek's as well; I will extend my apology to him today. You are a valued customer, and I am embarrassed that you received such a poor shipment. We are in the middle of moving to a new warehouse, and it has not gone as smoothly as I had hoped. Regardless, I want to make amends as soon as possible. I have put in an order to correct the mistakes, and I hope you will accept a 15 percent discount on your next shipment. Just use code 15D when placing your order.

Please let me know if there is anything else I can do to correct this.

Yours sincerely,

Pete McGivern

TEST 3

186. Why was the first e-mail sent?

(A) To ask for customer feedback
(B) To seek a solution to a problem
(C) To request a refund on an item
(D) To cancel an order for tableware

187. What item was received damaged?

(A) 14L
(B) 17P
(C) 18S
(D) 21G

188. In the second e-mail, the word "extend" in paragraph 1, line 1, is closest in meaning to

(A) offer
(B) delay
(C) continue
(D) increase

189. What is NOT indicated about McGivern Wholesale?

(A) It does business with restaurants.
(B) It is changing the location of a facility.
(C) It has been operating for five years.
(D) It is revising its price list.

190. What will McGivern Wholesale give to Ms. Jacques?

(A) A rebate on shipping charges
(B) An extra package of table linens
(C) A reduced price on her next order
(D) An updated invoice

GO ON TO THE NEXT PAGE

Questions 191-195 refer to the following form, notice, and e-mail.

Reddford Construction ➐			Date: March 15	
450 Matilda Drive			**Cost Estimate No.:** 50190	
Lexington, Kentucky 40502				
Prepared for: Jenny Choi, 518 Buffalo Springs Road				
Prepared by: Gabriel Nunez				

Description	Amount	Cost
Unglazed ceramic floor tiles (@ $2.49/tile)	400	$996.00
Premium bright white grout (@ $32.99/gallon)	5	$164.95
Labor for preparation, installation, and cleanup (@ $35/hour)	16	$560.00
ESTIMATE TOTAL $1,720.95		
All estimates are valid for one month unless otherwise specified.		

<u>New Lexington City Ordinance</u>

As of March 30, all construction companies must have a building permit ($100 for residential buildings; $300 for commercial buildings) before beginning a renovation project for each client. To complete an application for your construction project, contact City Hall at 859-555-0103.

To:	Gabriel Nunez <gnunez@reddfordcon.com>
From:	Jenny Choi <jchoi86@citymail.com>
Date:	Friday, April 2 10:12 A.M.
Subject:	Permits

Dear Mr. Nunez:

I'm writing concerning the job in my dining room that I'd like to contract you for. I'd like work to begin on April 10, but after looking at the estimate you sent me, I have a question about your calculation of the total cost. Specifically, does your estimate take into account any permits that would be needed for the job? A colleague told me that there is an ordinance that went into effect last month requiring building permits for any renovation project. I really liked the job you did installing carpeting and painting in my living room last year, and I would prefer to work with a company that I know. However, I am on a tight budget, so I need to consider the charge for the building permit in the overall cost of the project. Could you please get back to me at your earliest convenience?

Sincerely,

Jenny Choi

191. On April 10, what work does Ms. Choi want Mr. Nunez to do for her?

(A) Deliver furniture
(B) Install tiles
(C) Clean the living room carpets
(D) Paint the dining room walls

192. What will happen after April 15 ?

(A) Ms. Choi's application will be reviewed.
(B) Ms. Choi will receive a final bill.
(C) The new city ordinance will go into effect.
(D) The cost estimate will become invalid.

193. How much will likely be added to Ms. Choi's estimate?

(A) $32.99
(B) $35.00
(C) $100.00
(D) $300.00

194. In the e-mail, the word "contract" in paragraph 1, line 1, is closest in meaning to

(A) reduce
(B) retain
(C) collect
(D) purchase

195. What does Ms. Choi indicate about Reddford Construction?

(A) She has hired them for a job before.
(B) She needs to reschedule an appointment with them.
(C) She thinks that their prices are too high.
(D) She believes that they bought too many tiles.

GO ON TO THE NEXT PAGE

Cardiff Daily Times

In Brief—20 March

As reported earlier this year, Gold Kettle Grocery is opening an additional regional distribution centre in Cardiff. Construction was postponed for a time because of an unanticipated problem related to the ground conditions on the site. However, the problem has been resolved, and the 40,000-square-metre centre should be fully operational in June. The grand opening is planned for the fourth of June. The warehouse has a special area with state-of-the-art equipment to store foods that need to be kept frozen or cool. The site will also include loading bays and offices.

The distribution centre is expected to create more than 400 new jobs, according to Myles Simler, vice president of operations. Because of the size and scope of the project, a variety of jobs will be needed, from warehouse loaders and drivers to clerical positions.

E-mail

To:	Myles Simler <msimler@goldkettle.co.uk>
From:	Raadhika Baral <rbaral@goldkettle.co.uk>
Subject:	Information
Date:	26 June
Attachment:	📎 Notification comparison

Dear Myles:

Thanks for giving me a lift to the grand opening earlier this month. I do not believe I have ever seen such a well-planned event. We should send Ping Chen something to show him our appreciation for organising it.

Now that the centre in Cardiff has been open for a few weeks, I think we should consider hiring a company that forwards automatic notifications to employees' mobile phones. Such a service would allow us to get messages to them quickly and also prevent mistakes with shipments. I have a contact who has worked in customer service at Calls For You. I think it's a good company, but Raven Notifications also looks good, and their rates are lower. I have attached information about both companies to help you decide which one we might use. Let me know what you think.

Sincerely,

Raadhika Baral

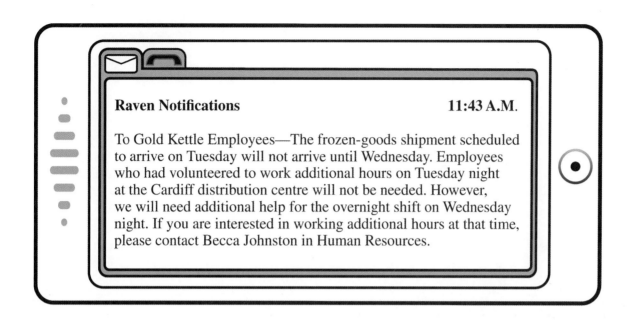

Raven Notifications   **11:43 A.M.**

To Gold Kettle Employees—The frozen-goods shipment scheduled to arrive on Tuesday will not arrive until Wednesday. Employees who had volunteered to work additional hours on Tuesday night at the Cardiff distribution centre will not be needed. However, we will need additional help for the overnight shift on Wednesday night. If you are interested in working additional hours at that time, please contact Becca Johnston in Human Resources.

196. What is the purpose of the article?

(A) To provide an update on a local project
(B) To discuss state-of-the-art warehouse equipment
(C) To report on local businesses that plan to hire more workers
(D) To explain difficulties encountered on a construction project

197. In the article, the word "scope" in paragraph 2, line 4, is closest in meaning to

(A) instrument used for viewing
(B) evaluation
(C) time of completion
(D) extent

198. What is most likely true about the Cardiff distribution center?

(A) It had a problem with food storage.
(B) Its grand opening was successful.
(C) Mr. Simler was recently hired there.
(D) Ms. Baral was unhappy with its service.

199. What company was chosen by Mr. Simler?

(A) The company that Ms. Baral's contact works for
(B) The company with the most reliable customer-service representatives
(C) The company that has lower rates than a competitor
(D) The company with an overnight call center

200. What does the text message ask employees who want additional work to do?

(A) Arrive on Tuesday night
(B) Contact the personnel office
(C) Reply to the message with the hours they can work
(D) Go to a different distribution center

Stop! This is the end of the test. If you finish before time is called, you may go back to Parts 5, 6, and 7 and check your work.

토익® 정기시험
기출문제집

RC

기출 TEST

04

READING TEST

In the Reading test, you will read a variety of texts and answer several different types of reading comprehension questions. The entire Reading test will last 75 minutes. There are three parts, and directions are given for each part. You are encouraged to answer as many questions as possible within the time allowed.

You must mark your answers on the separate answer sheet. Do not write your answers in your test book.

PART 5

Directions: A word or phrase is missing in each of the sentences below. Four answer choices are given below each sentence. Select the best answer to complete the sentence. Then mark the letter (A), (B), (C), or (D) on your answer sheet.

101. The regional manager will arrive tomorrow, so please ensure that all ------- documents are ready.
    (A) she
    (B) her
    (C) hers
    (D) herself

102. The historic Waldridge Building was constructed nearly 200 years -------.
    (A) away
    (B) enough
    (C) ago
    (D) still

103. Consumers ------- enthusiastically to the new colors developed by Sanwell Paint.
    (A) responding
    (B) response
    (C) responsively
    (D) responded

104. The ------- files contain your employment contract and information about our company.
    (A) directed
    (B) attached
    (C) interested
    (D) connected

105. Please submit each reimbursement request ------- according to its category, as outlined in last month's memo.
    (A) separately
    (B) separateness
    (C) separates
    (D) separate

106. Customers can wait in the reception area ------- our mechanics complete the car repairs.
    (A) whether
    (B) except
    (C) while
    (D) during

107. No one without a pass will be granted ------- to the conference.
    (A) admission
    (B) is admitting
    (C) admitted
    (D) to admit

108. To receive an electronic reminder when payment is due, set up an online account ------- Albright Bank.
    (A) of
    (B) about
    (C) over
    (D) with

109. The registration fee is ------- refundable up to two weeks prior to the conference date.

(A) fullest
(B) fuller
(C) fully
(D) full

110. All identifying information has been ------- from this letter of complaint so that it can be used for training purposes.

(A) produced
(B) extended
(C) removed
(D) resolved

111. ------- this time next year, Larkview Technology will have acquired two new subsidiaries.

(A) To
(B) By
(C) Quite
(D) Begin

112. Table reservations for ------- greater than ten must be made at least one day in advance.

(A) plates
(B) meals
(C) sizes
(D) parties

113. Because of ------- weather conditions, tonight's concert in Harbin Park has been canceled.

(A) worsening
(B) worsens
(C) worsen
(D) worst

114. Ms. Al-Omani will rely ------- team leaders to develop employee incentive programs.

(A) onto
(B) into
(C) within
(D) upon

115. Survey ------- analyze the layout of a land area above and below ground level.

(A) technicians
(B) technically
(C) technical
(D) technicality

116. ------- assemble your Gessen product, first read all instructions and gather all required tools.

(A) For the purpose of
(B) To be sure
(C) In order to
(D) For example

117. Online shoppers who experience long waits for their orders tend ------- the business low ratings.

(A) have given
(B) gave
(C) to give
(D) giving

118. ------- of the new Delran train station will begin in late September.

(A) Association
(B) Construction
(C) Violation
(D) Comprehension

119. The computing power of the new laptop is ------- to any desktop computer in the same price range.

(A) compare
(B) comparing
(C) comparison
(D) comparable

120. Dr. Yuina Hashimoto recently added another doctor to her practice, ------- allowing more patients to be seen.

(A) that
(B) thus
(C) which
(D) so that

GO ON TO THE NEXT PAGE

121. Graden Hotel ------- its superior reputation thanks to the leadership of its president, Marcia Clemente.

(A) practiced
(B) treated
(C) heard
(D) earned

122. Aki Katsuro's latest novel is his most exciting ------- and is sure to make Radin Books' best-seller list.

(A) just
(B) later
(C) yet
(D) very

123. Thanks ------- to pastry chef Ana Villagra, Lauducci's Restaurant has become a favorite with local patrons.

(A) largely
(B) larger
(C) large
(D) largest

124. At Crintack Manufacturing, we acknowledge our ------- to provide a safe workplace for our employees.

(A) assumption
(B) valuation
(C) perception
(D) obligation

125. ------- Mr. Donovan had expected the charity event to be a success, the response from the community still overwhelmed him.

(A) Whenever
(B) Although
(C) Even so
(D) In spite of

126. This free mobile app provides ------- calendar updates, so salespeople will never miss an appointment.

(A) casual
(B) equal
(C) continual
(D) eventual

127. Most senior managers approved the architect's proposal for the office layout, although ------- expressed concerns about the cost.

(A) one
(B) one another
(C) each other
(D) other

128. Greenville Library has hired an office assistant not only to perform general office duties ------- to support an ongoing special project.

(A) but also
(B) only if
(C) other than
(D) as for

129. The lease with The Pawlicki Group ------- if modifications to the existing offices are made.

(A) had continued
(B) will be continued
(C) was continuing
(D) has been continuing

130. Wrazen Associates ------- a summary with a list of recommendations as a routine part of any audit.

(A) realizes
(B) induces
(C) causes
(D) issues

PART 6

Directions: Read the texts that follow. A word, phrase, or sentence is missing in parts of each text. Four answer choices for each question are given below the text. Select the best answer to complete the text. Then mark the letter (A), (B), (C), or (D) on your answer sheet.

Questions 131-134 refer to the following e-mail.

From: Facilities Department
To: All Staff
Subject: AC issues
Date: 4 February

Please be advised that an equipment contractor, Torrono Sheet Metal, is scheduled to start work on the chiller enclosure at the rear of the building tomorrow morning. The contractor will be installing a steel cover to ------- protect the inner workings of our heating and cooling equipment.
131.

Expect to see technicians entering and leaving the building repeatedly, carting large machine parts and tools. There will be some noise associated with this project, and we ask for your patience. ------- , you should probably look for on-street parking. The contractor's vans ------- much of the
132.   **133.**
driveway. ------- .
134.

Jorge Carreras, Facilities Director

131. (A) better
     (B) quicker
     (C) sooner
     (D) harder

132. (A) As a result
     (B) Also
     (C) Nevertheless
     (D) However

133. (A) are blocking
     (B) will block
     (C) had blocked
     (D) block

134. (A) Send us your suggestions for a new facility.
     (B) I am writing to let you know about a maintenance issue.
     (C) Rather, they were not my first choice for this contract.
     (D) The work is expected to be completed by 2:00 P.M.

GO ON TO THE NEXT PAGE

To: Melina Ramos Sandoval

From: welcome@sourcework.ca

Date: 25 October

Subject: Registration complete

Dear Ms. Sandoval,

Welcome to the Source Work jobs network, the leading online career matching service. Your e-mail address, work experience, and preferences ------- in our database. This information will be
135.
used to identify employers who are seeking job candidates just like ------- . In the future, you will
136.
receive periodic notifications about open positions in your area.

------- . Therefore, we will not share your name or address with anyone. At any point, you can
137.
select the link at the bottom of any e-mail you receive from us to unsubscribe or change your e-mail preferences.

Thank you for ------- . If you have any questions or comments, feel free to contact us.
138.

Sincerely,

The Source Work team

---

135. (A) they record
(B) are recording
(C) that the record
(D) have been recorded

136. (A) us
(B) me
(C) you
(D) ours

137. (A) Privacy is important to us.
(B) Finding the perfect job can be difficult.
(C) Our jobs database is updated weekly.
(D) Your résumé has recently been reviewed.

138. (A) investing
(B) attending
(C) competing
(D) registering

Questions 139-142 refer to the following memo.

From: Noora Simola, Vice President of Operations
To: All Employees
Date: February 8
Re: Payroll changes

Beginning on March 15, we will be using a new payroll service that will affect a number of our current payroll processes. First, weekly payroll checks will be mailed on Thursday instead of Friday. Direct-deposit payroll payments will also be processed a day ------- . Second, pay stubs for
       139.
direct-deposit payments will no longer be e-mailed. Instead, employees will be able to

------- this information by accessing their payroll accounts online.
140.

Other processes will remain the same. All time cards will continue to be due to the payroll department by Monday at 6:00 P.M. ------- . A complete, updated list of instructions for payroll
       141.
procedures ------- to all employees on or before March 1. If you have any questions before then,
    142.
please contact Leonti Belousov at ext. 5810.

139. (A) twice
(B) following
(C) earlier
(D) previously

140. (A) view
(B) correct
(C) reject
(D) enter

141. (A) Please note the change of day and time.
(B) Most employees begin work at 8:00 A.M.
(C) The payroll department is not operational.
(D) Old time card forms will also still be valid.

142. (A) will distribute
(B) will be distributed
(C) was distributed
(D) distributing

GO ON TO THE NEXT PAGE

Tasty Treat in Kentron

Kentron's own Groovato Gelato was founded in 2010 when Luciano Algieri, an Italian immigrant to the United States, bought a ------- on Coverby Avenue. The building had previously housed the
143.
Hopscotch Ice Cream Company, and Algieri was able to hire many former Hopscotch employees.

Teaching ------- ice-cream crafters to make gelato proved to be an easy task.
144

------- his product, Algieri started with an old family recipe. He then enhanced the flavor with
145.
secret ingredients plus unusual combinations of fruits and nuts. ------- .
146.

There are now three store locations in the Kentron area. Residents are lucky to have this gem!

---

143. (A) dessert
(B) vehicle
(C) machine
(D) factory

144. (A) experiences
(B) experience
(C) experiencing
(D) experienced

145. (A) To create
(B) Creates
(C) Had created
(D) Creation

146. (A) Banana walnut is slightly more expensive.
(B) Some people still prefer Hopscotch ice cream.
(C) The result is a rich and satisfying mixture of flavors.
(D) Please try a sample and give us your feedback.

PART 7

Directions: In this part you will read a selection of texts, such as magazine and newspaper articles, e-mails, and instant messages. Each text or set of texts is followed by several questions. Select the best answer for each question and mark the letter (A), (B), (C), or (D) on your answer sheet.

Questions 147-148 refer to the following notice.

TASTE! SHARE! WIN!

Here at Sawadee World Bistro, our talented chefs bring the world to you by serving flavorful specialties from around the globe. Now with the click of a button, you can share your dining experience with the world!

Just take a picture of your meal and post it on our Web site. You will automatically be entered for a chance to win a $100 gift card.

What are you waiting for?

www.sawadeeworldbistro.com/tastesharewin

147. Where would the notice most likely be posted?

(A) On the wall of a restaurant
(B) On the back page of a cookbook
(C) On the cover of a photography magazine
(D) On the door of a kitchen supply store

148. How can readers enter a contest?

(A) By writing a review
(B) By creating a recipe
(C) By making a donation
(D) By submitting a photograph

GO ON TO THE NEXT PAGE ➡

·ıı||ıı· ● ● ●

Susan Rollins (10:12 A.M.)
I just looked through your preliminary design plans for the Miller house on Greenwood Lane. Everything looks great, especially the kitchen and main living area. My only concern is the practicality of the glass sunroom. Glass rooms often run over budget.

Myles Hart (10:15 A.M.)
The clients insisted I include the sunroom. They're going to try to find a way to finance it.

Susan Rollins (10:17 A.M.)
We'll need to make sure that's arranged before we finalize these plans. In the meantime, can you come up with a new design that leaves off this addition?

Myles Hart (10:18 A.M.)
Shouldn't be a problem. I'll work on it now. I'd planned to talk to the Millers later today, so I can discuss the budget with them then.

149. Where do the writers most likely work?

(A) At a bank
(B) At a glass factory
(C) At an architectural firm
(D) At a home-furnishings store

150. At 10:18 A.M., what does Mr. Hart mean when he writes, "Shouldn't be a problem"?

(A) The project is well within the budget.
(B) He is willing to draft an alternate plan.
(C) He can meet with the Millers later today.
(D) The Millers have agreed with a suggestion.

Verita Model JX41Ci–Instructions for Use

• Ensure that the electrical cord is untangled and then plug it into a nearby wall outlet.

• Choose the appropriate setting (floor, low carpet, high carpet) by using the dial on top of the machine.

• Turn the machine on by pushing the power button at the base of the handle. Run slowly and steadily over an area two or three times to pick up dirt and debris.

• If there is still debris in corners or other hard-to-reach areas, connect the appropriate attachment and use it on the specified area.

TEST 4

151. What is the purpose of the machine referred to in the instructions?

(A) Preparing food
(B) Heating
(C) Packaging
(D) Cleaning

152. What are users instructed to do each time before using the machine?

(A) Connect all of the machine's attachments
(B) Adjust the machine's controls
(C) Clean every part of the machine
(D) Allow the machine to warm up

GO ON TO THE NEXT PAGE

Questions 153-154 refer to the following text message.

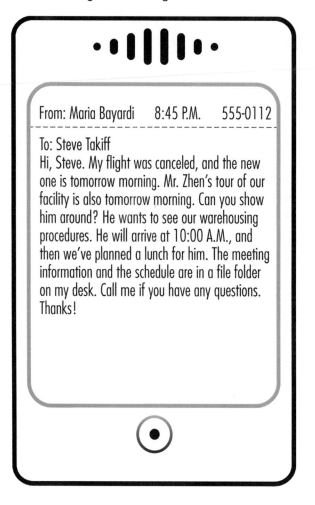

From: Maria Bayardi   8:45 P.M.   555-0112

To: Steve Takiff
Hi, Steve. My flight was canceled, and the new one is tomorrow morning. Mr. Zhen's tour of our facility is also tomorrow morning. Can you show him around? He wants to see our warehousing procedures. He will arrive at 10:00 A.M., and then we've planned a lunch for him. The meeting information and the schedule are in a file folder on my desk. Call me if you have any questions. Thanks!

---

153. Why did Ms. Bayardi send the text to Mr. Takiff?

(A) To find out when his flight arrives
(B) To ask for directions to the warehouse
(C) To give him an update
(D) To cancel an appointment

154. What does Ms. Bayardi ask Mr. Takiff to do?

(A) Plan a lunch
(B) Give a tour
(C) Reschedule an event
(D) Call Mr. Zhen

Questions 155-157 refer to the following e-mail.

E-mail

To:	Bo Xiao
From:	David Morisseau
Date:	May 16
Re:	Order # 3A556

Dear Mr. Xiao,

Thank you very much for your recent purchase from Yippee.com! — [1] —. We are grateful for your business. We are proud to sell only high-quality products that we believe in and use ourselves. We also take pride in providing you with the best customer service possible. — [2] —.

To say thank you for your purchase, we would like to offer you 15% off your next order as well as free shipping. Visit our Web site at www.yippee.com to place your order. — [3] —. This offer expires 60 days from the date of this e-mail.

As part of our ongoing efforts to provide the best service available, Yippee.com routinely asks our customers for their feedback. Therefore, we invite you to visit www.yippee.com/survey to complete our customer-satisfaction survey. — [4] —.

Thank you again,

David Morisseau
Vice President of Customer Service
Yippee.com

---

155. What is the main purpose of the e-mail?

(A) To offer a refund
(B) To clarify some information
(C) To express appreciation
(D) To advertise a new product

156. What is Mr. Xiao asked to do?

(A) Attend a celebratory event
(B) Evaluate a company's service
(C) Send an e-mail within 60 days
(D) Visit a new store that is opening soon

157. In which of the positions marked [1], [2], [3], and [4] does the following sentence best belong?

"Please use code XB84RD when completing your order to receive the discount."

(A) [1]
(B) [2]
(C) [3]
(D) [4]

GO ON TO THE NEXT PAGE

Questions 158-160 refer to the following advertisement.

JON CHEUNG'S HOME REPAIR
No job is too small • Licensed and insured • Free estimates

➤ Laying and removal of carpet, tile, and wood flooring

➤ Installation of doors and replacement windows

➤ Construction and repair of decks and porches

➤ Installation of kitchen countertops and cabinets

➤ Minor plumbing and electrical work

For high-quality work at affordable prices, call 910-555-0148. If there is no answer, please leave a message, and someone will contact you by the following day. References available upon request.

---

158. What is indicated about Mr. Cheung?

(A) He recently started a business.
(B) His company is hiring.
(C) His rates are reasonable.
(D) He works part-time.

159. What is NOT mentioned as a task Mr. Cheung can do?

(A) Fixing porches
(B) Painting houses
(C) Replacing floor coverings
(D) Putting in new windows

160. According to the advertisement, what may a customer ask for?

(A) Tile and carpet samples
(B) Recommendations from other clients
(C) Bigger work crews for rush jobs
(D) Discounts for large-scale work

Washington State to Introduce Its Very Own Apple

By Julia Richards for *The Agri Monthly*

Scientists at Scales University reported last month that they have completed the development of the "Shiner Crisp," the first apple that Washington state farmers will have trademarked all to themselves. — [1] —. The first Shiner Crisp is expected to become available to consumers as early as next year. — [2] —.

Apple breeders design new apples especially to better compete with such traditional apple varieties as Reds and Juiceys. The development process involves a considerable investment of time and money in repeated taste tests for their new fruits. — [3] —. Whereas Reds and Juiceys average $1.29 per pound, new types of apples (such as the hugely popular Branburs and Honey-Sweets) are raking in at least three times as much.

These additions have major long-term impacts on the market, too. Two decades ago, Reds and Juiceys comprised over 50 percent of all apple sales; now their sales are less than 25 percent of the market. It is no wonder that apple breeders are racing to come up with the next popular apple! — [4] —.

161. What is the purpose of the article?

(A) To give an opinion on Shiner Crisp prices
(B) To recruit students for Scales University
(C) To provide a detailed explanation of price differences in the apple industry
(D) To announce the design of a new apple

162. According to the article, what is true about Reds and Juiceys?

(A) They are uniquely trademarked to Washington state.
(B) They are less expensive than Honey-Sweets.
(C) They have increased their sales recently.
(D) They were bred by university scientists.

163. In which of the positions marked [1], [2], [3], and [4] does the following sentence best belong?

"In other words, these new types of apples are designed for big flavor and big profits."

(A) [1]
(B) [2]
(C) [3]
(D) [4]

GO ON TO THE NEXT PAGE

Questions 164-167 refer to the following e-mail.

To:	Theresa Pearle <tpearle@praguequarterly.cz>
From:	Marek Koubek <mkoubek@bistrokoubek.cz>
Re:	Press release
Date:	15 March

Dear Ms. Pearle,

Per our phone call earlier today, please find the press release for my new restaurant, Bistro Koubek, below. Thank you again for offering to print it in your magazine. It was interesting to hear your views on the growing English-speaking community in Prague that your publication caters to. We hope the restaurant will appeal to Czech citizens as well as Americans and other foreigners residing in or visiting Prague.

Best regards,

Marek Koubek

FOR IMMEDIATE RELEASE: CZECH-AMERICAN BISTRO OPENING ITS DOORS

PRAGUE (15 March)—Bistro Koubek, located at V Celnici 437/4, 110 00 Prague 1, will celebrate its grand opening with a party on Friday, 21 May, beginning at 6:00 P.M.

According to owner and head chef Marek Koubek, the restaurant will feature Cajun-Czech fusion cooking, combining popular menu items from New Orleans, Louisiana, such as gumbo and jambalaya, with traditional Czech cuisine.

Complimentary samples and beverages will be available during the grand opening event, but full meals will not be served. Normal hours of operation are 5:00 P.M. until midnight, seven days a week, beginning on 22 May. The menu can be viewed at www.bistrokoubek.cz.

Chef Koubek lived in Prague until age sixteen, when he moved with his family to New Orleans, where his father opened a restaurant. There, he worked in the kitchen while studying at the Louisiana Academy of Culinary Arts. After graduating, he was hired as head chef at Crescent City Eatery, where he earned four major awards for his unique menus and flair for meal presentation. He is thrilled to return to his childhood home and share the culinary heritage of two cultures with the city's diners.

164. Why did Mr. Koubek e-mail Ms. Pearle?

(A) To invite her to a party
(B) To provide content for an article
(C) To announce the launch of a new Web site
(D) To request her assistance in editing some text

165. The phrase "appeal to" in paragraph 1, line 4, is closest in meaning to

(A) attract
(B) join together
(C) benefit
(D) call upon

166. What is indicated about the event on May 21 ?

(A) It will begin at 5:00 P.M.
(B) Only a few people have been invited.
(C) All items will be served free of charge.
(D) Patrons must have a ticket to enter.

167. What is NOT stated about Mr. Koubek?

(A) He grew up in Prague.
(B) He has traveled extensively in Europe.
(C) He worked in his father's restaurant.
(D) He has won several cooking prizes.

Peter Harrer [9:30 A.M.]	Hi, everyone. I'll make this brief as I know you're all busy reading the manuscripts for the editorial meeting on Friday.
Cora Grant [9:31 A.M.]	Did we change the time for that?
Peter Harrer [9:32 A.M.]	It's still at 2:00, right?
Meili Shu [9:32 A.M.]	Yes. At first we talked about having it in the morning, but I have an appointment at 10:00.
Peter Harrer [9:33 A.M.]	OK. I'm glad we got that sorted out. I'd like to share Kwang's idea. Kwang, do you want to explain it?
Kwang Chun [9:35 A.M.]	Sure. What if we encourage our customers to sign up to receive a newsletter each month by e-mail? We would include information about our special promotions or book giveaway contests. We could even have some of our authors write occasional articles.
Cora Grant [9:36 A.M.]	Yes, they could give insights into their work or maybe discuss a favorite book.
Meili Shu [9:37 A.M.]	It's a great idea! This kind of thing is getting more popular in business these days. And people always like a chance to win free books.
Peter Harrer [9:38 A.M.]	Well, keep in mind we are a small press with a small budget. Would one of you like to get this idea off the ground?
Kwang Chun [9:39 A.M.]	I suppose I should, since I'm proposing it. Maybe Meili would help?
Meili Shu [9:40 A.M.]	Of course.
Peter Harrer [9:41 A.M.]	OK, thanks everyone. See you all on Friday.

168. Who most likely are the participants in the online chat discussion?

(A) Staff at a marketing firm
(B) Reporters at a local newspaper
(C) Presenters at a conference
(D) Colleagues at a publishing company

169. At 9:33 A.M., what does Mr. Harrer mean when he writes, "we got that sorted out"?

(A) The manuscripts have all been assigned.
(B) A meeting time has been agreed upon.
(C) An appointment has been canceled.
(D) New work policies have been followed.

170. What project is Mr. Chun taking on?

(A) Developing a newsletter
(B) Revising a budget
(C) Reviewing a book
(D) Writing an advice column

171. What does Ms. Shu agree to do?

(A) Assist a colleague
(B) Change her schedule
(C) Interview an author
(D) Take a business trip

GO ON TO THE NEXT PAGE

Haswell Tire Company Maintenance Warranty

At Haswell Tire Company, we know you depend on your tires to take you where you want to go. That's why we offer a lifetime warranty on tire maintenance for every tire you purchase from us. It covers tire inspection, rotation, and repairs free of charge.

Inspection: Our service crew will check the pressure, inflate the tires if necessary, and let you know when the tread is getting low.

Rotation: It's important to rotate your vehicle's tires periodically. Our team can perform this service for you in less than half an hour.

Repair: If you have a flat tire, our team will make every effort to repair the damage. If the tire can't be repaired, we'll offer you 20 percent off the regular price when you purchase a new tire.

Bring in your vehicle during regular business hours and our friendly service staff will help you get back on the road quickly. No appointment is necessary. Just show the receipt from your tire purchase. This warranty covers service for the life of the tires under the original purchaser and is not transferrable to other vehicles or owners.

Your satisfaction is our top priority. Unlike our competitors, we do not just sell tires. During our three decades as a local family-owned business, we have developed lasting relationships with our customers by providing outstanding service. Thank you for your business.

---

172. The word "perform" in paragraph 3, line 2, is closest in meaning to

(A) entertain
(B) operate
(C) portray
(D) complete

173. According to the document, when will Haswell Tire Company provide a discount?

(A) When a customer buys a replacement tire
(B) When service takes longer than half an hour
(C) When the company holds a special sale day
(D) When a customer purchases tires for more than one vehicle

174. What must a customer have in order to receive a service covered by the warranty?

(A) Proof of tire purchase
(B) Documentation of a previous inspection
(C) A copy of the warranty
(D) A scheduled appointment

175. What is suggested about Haswell Tire Company?

(A) It offers lower prices than other tire stores.
(B) It emphasizes good customer relations.
(C) It manufactures the tires that it sells.
(D) It is an international corporation.

GO ON TO THE NEXT PAGE

Questions 176-180 refer to the following e-mail and article.

To:	Michael Kaelo <mkaelo@hawthorneclinic.bw>
From:	Sophie Thabado <sthabado@Gaboronestar.bw>
Date:	20 February
Subject:	RE: Event
Attachment:	📎 Dinner and lunch menu options

Dear Mr. Kaelo,

Thank you for considering the Gaborone Star Hotel for your event. Regarding your inquiry, we have four ballrooms that accommodate large groups: Jupiter, Saturn, Neptune, and Venus. They seat 400, 300, 200, and 100 guests respectively.

I've attached some lunch and dinner menu options, but we are happy to work with you regarding specific requests. We can arrange a sit-down meal or buffet-style service. We also provide audiovisual equipment for business presentations or celebrations.

Please let me know if you need any additional information.

Sincerely,

Sophie Thabado, Director of Events

Gaborone Times
20 May

Local Happenings

On 15 May, family members, friends, and colleagues of Dr. Patrick Matambo gathered at the Gaborone Star Hotel to celebrate his retirement, which will take effect on 1 June. For twenty years, Dr. Matambo has been the director of the Hawthorne Clinic, located near Hawthorne City University. Among the nearly 180 well-wishers in attendance were also some former patients who attested to the honoree's kindness and professionalism.

Dr. Matambo has also been a familiar face at local charity events, and in particular, he has helped to raise money for many area schools. His immediate plans are to take a month-long vacation on a cruise ship with his wife, Alicia Matambo.

Although Dr. Matambo is retiring, he will remain involved with the clinic as a consultant. A new director has been approved by the Hawthorne Clinic's board of trustees and is expected to be announced later this week.

176. Why did Ms. Thabado send the e-mail?

(A) To promote a new hotel
(B) To offer special hotel discounts
(C) To confirm her attendance at an event
(D) To respond to a request for information

177. What was sent with the e-mail?

(A) Photographs of event ballrooms
(B) Information about meal choices
(C) A list of hotel services
(D) A form for ordering audio equipment

178. In what ballroom was the celebration most likely held?

(A) Jupiter
(B) Saturn
(C) Neptune
(D) Venus

179. What is NOT mentioned about Dr. Matambo?

(A) He is planning leisure travel.
(B) He moved to Hawthorne City twenty years ago.
(C) He was in charge of a medical facility.
(D) He has helped many local schools.

180. According to the article, what does Dr. Matambo plan to do?

(A) Remain professionally active
(B) Spend more time on hobbies
(C) Teach some classes
(D) Interview his replacement

TEST 4

GO ON TO THE NEXT PAGE

Questions 181-185 refer to the following e-mail and schedule.

To:	Vincent Reister <vreister@hexagonmail.com>
From:	Florence Zhang <fzhang@zhtours.com.hk>
Re:	Hong Kong Tour
Date:	3 May
Attachment:	📎 Tour Schedule

Dear Mr. Reister:

Thank you for your inquiry about tours with Zhang Hong Kong Tours, Inc. Thank you also for the compliment—I am very happy to hear that your business partner, Mr. Brown, was satisfied with our Creative HK tour last month and that he recommended our services to you.

We have a number of tours scheduled during your short visit to our city during the week of 24 May. I gather from your e-mail that you are most interested in viewing historical landmarks. We have a couple of options that I believe you would especially enjoy. As you can see from the attached schedule, one of those tours is already fully booked. I suggest that you book soon if you would like to secure a place on the other tour. I will be more than happy to reserve a seat for you as soon as you confirm. I look forward to your reply.

Sincerely,

Florence Zhang, Zhang Hong Kong Tours, Inc.

Zhang Hong Kong Tours, Inc.–May Tour Schedule
For more information about these and other tours, visit www.zhtours.com.hk

Date	Tour	Primary Stops	Hours/Duration	Price (US$)	Availability
25 May	HK for Shoppers	✓ Mall of Hong Kong ✓ Hong Kong Markets	9 A.M.–3 P.M. (6 hours)	$45.00	*4 spaces left*
26 May	Creative HK	✓ Film Archive ✓ Gallery of Modern Art	12 noon–5 P.M. (5 hours)	$45.00	*3 spaces left*
27 May	HK History (Central District)	✓ Lo Pan Temple ✓ Bishop's House ✓ Queen's Pier	10 A.M.–2 P.M. (4 hours)	$45.00	*Sold out*
28 May	HK Outdoors	✓ Kowloon Park ✓ Cheung Sha Beach	1 P.M.–6 P.M. (5 hours)	$35.00	*3 spaces left*
30 May	HK History (Islands District)	✓ Tin Hau Temple ✓ Yeung Hau Temple ✓ Yuk Hui Temple	10 A.M.–2 P.M. (4 hours)	$50.00	*2 spaces left*

181. What is the purpose of the e-mail?

(A) To provide a referral
(B) To answer a question about a company's service
(C) To update an itinerary for a new customer
(D) To confirm a booking

182. How did Mr. Reister hear about Zhang Hong Kong Tours?

(A) From a colleague
(B) From a travel agent
(C) From an advertisement
(D) From an Internet search

183. What did Mr. Brown most likely see on his tour?

(A) Markets
(B) Temples
(C) Paintings
(D) Parks and beaches

184. What is suggested about Mr. Reister?

(A) He is on a limited budget.
(B) He will soon start a business.
(C) He is interested in Chinese cuisine.
(D) He will be in Hong Kong temporarily.

185. According to Ms. Zhang, what tour is most suitable for Mr. Reister?

(A) HK Outdoors
(B) HK for Shoppers
(C) HK History (Islands District)
(D) HK History (Central District)

GO ON TO THE NEXT PAGE

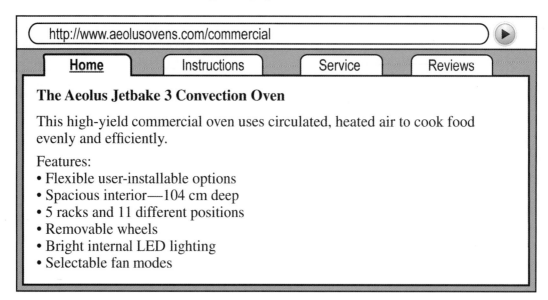

http://www.aeolusovens.com/commercial

Home	Instructions	Service	Reviews

The Aeolus Jetbake 3 Convection Oven

This high-yield commercial oven uses circulated, heated air to cook food evenly and efficiently.

Features:
- Flexible user-installable options
- Spacious interior—104 cm deep
- 5 racks and 11 different positions
- Removable wheels
- Bright internal LED lighting
- Selectable fan modes

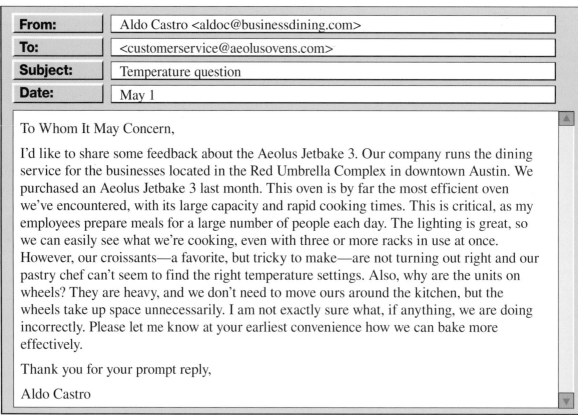

From:	Aldo Castro <aldoc@businessdining.com>
To:	<customerservice@aeolusovens.com>
Subject:	Temperature question
Date:	May 1

To Whom It May Concern,

I'd like to share some feedback about the Aeolus Jetbake 3. Our company runs the dining service for the businesses located in the Red Umbrella Complex in downtown Austin. We purchased an Aeolus Jetbake 3 last month. This oven is by far the most efficient oven we've encountered, with its large capacity and rapid cooking times. This is critical, as my employees prepare meals for a large number of people each day. The lighting is great, so we can easily see what we're cooking, even with three or more racks in use at once. However, our croissants—a favorite, but tricky to make—are not turning out right and our pastry chef can't seem to find the right temperature settings. Also, why are the units on wheels? They are heavy, and we don't need to move ours around the kitchen, but the wheels take up space unnecessarily. I am not exactly sure what, if anything, we are doing incorrectly. Please let me know at your earliest convenience how we can bake more effectively.

Thank you for your prompt reply,

Aldo Castro

From:	Iris Martz <imartz@aeolusovens.com>
To:	Aldo Castro <aldoc@businessdining.com>
Subject:	Your question
Date:	May 5

Dear Mr. Castro,

Thank you for your recent e-mail about the Aeolus Jetbake 3. My guess is that the trouble you are having is related to the 1.0 control panel that is standard on most of our models. This is interchangeable with panel 2.0, which allows for finer adjustments and includes a feature to set the heat-circulating fan to three different modes. I will ship one to you without charge. Please reply with your shipping address and the serial number of your oven. It is located on the back, just under the factory inspection certificate.

Thank you for your purchase!

Yours sincerely,

Iris Martz
Customer Care

186. In the first e-mail, the word "critical" in paragraph 1, line 4, is closest in meaning to

(A) judgmental
(B) important
(C) dangerous
(D) unexpected

187. What feature of the oven listed on the Web page is NOT referred to in Mr. Castro's e-mail?

(A) Ability to select fan modes
(B) Spacious interior
(C) Use of multiple racks
(D) Bright internal LED lighting

188. What does Mr. Castro's company do?

(A) Prepare meals for business employees
(B) Design food service equipment
(C) Supply baked goods to local restaurants
(D) Publish an online food magazine

189. Why does Ms. Martz write to Mr. Castro?

(A) To provide information on how to remove the oven's wheels
(B) To give him guidance in addressing an installation issue
(C) To request his assistance with a cooking seminar
(D) To offer a solution to a baking problem

190. What does Ms. Martz ask Mr. Castro to do?

(A) Ship a part to her
(B) Send her some product information
(C) Consult an online resource
(D) Write a follow-up review

GO ON TO THE NEXT PAGE

To:	jacknajarian@sellomail.com
From:	guestservices@pamakanihotel.com
Subject:	Surfing lessons
Date:	May 10

Dear Mr. Najarian,

Thank you for writing to us at the Pamakani Hotel to ask if we could recommend a surfing school nearby. You will be happy to know that Lauloa Surf School (www.lauloasurfschool.com) is located on the beach just a few steps from our hotel. The prices are fair, and their lessons are quite good. Having taken a 4-hour lesson with the legendary Alana Kapaku myself, I can personally recommend them.

We look forward to greeting you and your daughter when you arrive on June 4. Please let us know if you have any further questions or needs before or during your stay. We are at your service.

Sincerely,

Regina Manibog
Representative, Guest Services, Pamakani Hotel

---

http://www.lauloasurfschool.com/lessons

Lauloa Surf School • 2495 Kekau Road, Honolulu, HI 96815 • 808-555-0142

Group Lesson
For beginning and lower-intermediate surfers. Group lessons consist of 3 instructors and a maximum of 12 students. We'll form a group for you if you don't already have one.
• 2-hour lesson / $75 per person
• Must be at least 13 years old.

Private Lesson
For all levels, beginning through advanced. You'll have our instructor all to yourself, and you'll learn whatever you want to learn about how to surf.
• 2-hour lesson / $125 per person
• For safety reasons, children under 13 years old require a private lesson.

Family and Friends Lesson
For beginning to upper-intermediate surfers. No more than 4 people. This lesson is for those who want one instructor just for themselves. You will surf more waves than in our regular Group Lesson.
• 2-hour lesson / $100 per person
• Must be at least 13 years old.

Professional Lesson
For advanced surfers. Learn advanced techniques from former professional surfer Alana Kapaku. Alana competed professionally for over 10 years. Her students have included famous movie stars!
• One-on-one 4-hour lesson/$200 per person
• Must be at least 13 years old.

All surf lessons include: protective swim shirt, reef shoes, board leash, and surfboard rental.

```
╔══════════════════════ *E-mail* ══════════════════════╗
║                                                       ║
║  To:        information@lauloasurfschool.com          ║
║                                                       ║
║  From:      jacknajarian@sellomail.com                ║
║                                                       ║
║  Subject:   Surfing lessons                           ║
║                                                       ║
║  Date:      June 17                                   ║
║                                                       ║
╠═══════════════════════════════════════════════════════╣
```

Greetings,

I'm writing to thank you on behalf of my 12-year-old daughter for the wonderful surfing lesson she had during the week when she and I visited Hawaii. I've already told her that when we visit again, I'll purchase another lesson and even sign up with her this time, so we can both learn more about how to surf.

Thank you again. We can't wait to get back and enjoy the beach and waves together at Lauloa Surf School.

Sincerely,

Jack Najarian

---

191. Why did Ms. Manibog write the first e-mail?

(A) To confirm a reservation
(B) To reply to an inquiry
(C) To obtain a recommendation
(D) To introduce an instructor

192. In the first e-mail, the word "fair" in paragraph 1, line 4, is closest in meaning to

(A) generous
(B) objective
(C) reasonable
(D) light

193. What is most likely true about Ms. Manibog?

(A) She is an advanced-level surfer.
(B) She is the manager of Guest Services at Pamakani Hotel.
(C) She previously worked for Lauloa Surf School.
(D) She is a close friend of Mr. Najarian's family.

194. How much did Mr. Najarian pay for his daughter's lesson?

(A) $75
(B) $100
(C) $125
(D) $200

195. What is indicated about Mr. Najarian and his daughter?

(A) They met Ms. Kapaku on the beach.
(B) They travel on vacation to Hawaii every year.
(C) They plan to stay at the Pamakani Hotel again.
(D) They expect to take a surfing lesson together.

GO ON TO THE NEXT PAGE

Pop Superstar Coming Home

LAFONT (May 23)—Sonia Benitez is coming back to where it all started, and she's giving back. The international pop superstar announced that she has added a free concert in Lafont to her Long Road tour, which begins on June 2. Benitez will perform in Lafont on July 17.

Born in nearby Ollender, Benitez moved to Lafont with her family when she was five years old. She graduated from Jasper High School, where she first caught the attention of peers and teachers by winning the school-wide talent show at the age of fourteen, the first time she ever set foot on a stage. Since then, she has embarked on a professional career that has taken her to five continents and has won her millions of fans all over the world.

Benitez made the decision to add a concert in Lafont when her manager, Jeremy Hampton, brought to her attention a three-day break after a show in Chicago. "It was obvious to both of us," Benitez said in a phone call from her recording studio in Los Angeles. "To be so close to Lafont with an extra three days and not do a show would be unthinkable. It was a very easy decision to make."

The only challenge was finding a venue that would accommodate all of Benitez' hometown fans. The town's largest theater seats only 1,200. Lafont Mayor Ellis Swanson came up with a creative solution. "He suggested an outdoor concert," said Benitez. "Not at a stadium, but at a local farm outside of town. That way there won't be a limit on how many people can attend. We'll just set up a stage in the middle of a huge field."

Local radio DJ Taylor Wendel estimates that as many as 8,000 fans might turn out for the concert.

"Considering how popular Sonia is around here, and considering the concert is free, I think that's a conservative estimate," says Wendel. "It's going to be a memorable event."

Benitez Plays to Big Crowd

LAFONT (July 18)—Sonia Benitez' homecoming concert last night in a field at Gingham Hills Farm was nothing short of phenomenal. The crowd of 10,000-plus was delighted to welcome the hometown hero, who was making her first trip back to Lafont in more than 12 years. Benitez put on quite a show, extending her usual two-hour set of songs by another hour with an additional eight songs.

The evening's most memorable moment (of which there were many) came when Benitez was joined onstage by pianist Genevieve Parker, another native of Lafont and friend of Sonia's since the age of six. While perhaps not as well known as Benitez, Parker is an equally accomplished musician, having studied classical piano in Vienna and having toured internationally with the Vienna Touring Orchestra.

Sonia Benitez in Lafont
Special Notes

Gingham Hills Farm is proud to host Sonia Benitez' homecoming concert. Among the songs that Sonia will perform tonight are those listed below, which have special significance for Sonia and the Lafont community.

"The Butterfly Song"	Sonia's first composition, cowritten with her sister when she was eleven years old
"Dinner by the Riverbank"	A song about the Walton River, which runs through Lafont, with backing vocals by the Jasper High School Choir
"A Single Morning"	Sung by Sonia at her first-ever performance during high school
"Everybody Smiles"	Sonia will be accompanied by a childhood friend on the piano

---

196. What is suggested about Lafont?

(A) It has a new mayor.
(B) It is Ms. Benitez' birthplace.
(C) It is located near Chicago.
(D) It will be the first stop on a concert tour.

197. According to the first article, what problem with the concert had to be addressed?

(A) Finding extra musicians
(B) Locating a large enough space
(C) Determining a possible date
(D) Setting an affordable ticket price

198. What is indicated about the song "A Single Morning"?

(A) It is about life in Lafont.
(B) It is usually performed with a choir.
(C) It was Ms. Benitez' first song played on the radio.
(D) It was sung by Ms. Benitez at a talent show.

199. How did the concert in Lafont differ from Ms. Benitez' usual concerts?

(A) It was an hour longer.
(B) It was held in the daytime.
(C) Attendees were seated in a stadium.
(D) The Vienna Touring Orchestra opened the show.

200. What song did Ms. Parker perform in?

(A) "The Butterfly Song"
(B) "Dinner by the Riverbank"
(C) "A Single Morning"
(D) "Everybody Smiles"

Stop! This is the end of the test. If you finish before time is called, you may go back to Parts 5, 6, and 7 and check your work.

토익® 정기시험
기출문제집

RC

기출 TEST

05

READING TEST

In the Reading test, you will read a variety of texts and answer several different types of reading comprehension questions. The entire Reading test will last 75 minutes. There are three parts, and directions are given for each part. You are encouraged to answer as many questions as possible within the time allowed.

You must mark your answers on the separate answer sheet. Do not write your answers in your test book.

PART 5

Directions: A word or phrase is missing in each of the sentences below. Four answer choices are given below each sentence. Select the best answer to complete the sentence. Then mark the letter (A), (B), (C), or (D) on your answer sheet.

---

101. Ms. Tillinghast has received several awards ------- her innovative ideas.

(A) away
(B) for
(C) often
(D) across

102. Using proper techniques to ------- items drastically reduces the risk of back injury.

(A) select
(B) lift
(C) damage
(D) attract

103. Restaurants in Rondale must follow all ------- health guidelines.

(A) local
(B) locals
(C) locally
(D) localize

104. Sinee's Catering is always ------- to deliver outstanding food to your special events.

(A) ready
(B) skillful
(C) complete
(D) delicious

105. A ------- way to support economic growth in Ludlow City is to shop at area businesses.

(A) practice
(B) practicing
(C) practical
(D) practically

106. A record number of appliance ------- came into the Port of Reece last month.

(A) shipments
(B) shipping
(C) shipment
(D) shipped

107. At Sloat Publishing, interns are assigned to a ------- of positions with increasing responsibility.

(A) frequency
(B) length
(C) shortage
(D) series

108. The conference fee ------- admittance to more than twenty workshops and seminars.

(A) include
(B) includes
(C) is included
(D) including

109. Cabinetmaker Finley Orcheta uses the finest woodworking machines imported ------- Denmark.

(A) from
(B) against
(C) about
(D) before

110. Senior hotel manager salaries differ ------- by company, location, and experience.

(A) great
(B) greater
(C) greatly
(D) greatest

111. Pantep, Inc., works ------- with customers to establish long-term partnerships.

(A) nearly
(B) closely
(C) recently
(D) newly

112. Adalet Farm's unique method of irrigating vegetables has proved to be ------- effective.

(A) far
(B) correctly
(C) highly
(D) much

113. Customers who submit payments ------- March 10 will be charged a late fee.

(A) after
(B) behind
(C) quite
(D) almost

114. The poll shows how often company executives make financial decisions that are ------- by employee opinions.

(A) acted
(B) trained
(C) reminded
(D) influenced

115. Prices at Taylor City Books are ------- lower than at other online bookstores.

(A) more significant
(B) significant
(C) significance
(D) significantly

116. The ------- of this workshop is to equip business leaders with the tools to make prudent financial decisions.

(A) guide
(B) experience
(C) aim
(D) solution

117. A marketing campaign was designed to target ------- of the three demographics we identified.

(A) which
(B) other
(C) either
(D) each

118. ------- food critics recommend ZJ's Bistro as the best restaurant in the area, most local residents prefer Dree's Café.

(A) Whenever
(B) Although
(C) So that
(D) Among

119. Green Grocer customers should request assistance from staff instead of removing products from the top shelves -------.

(A) themselves
(B) their own
(C) them
(D) their

120. Skovent Products' sales revenue showed a ------- improvement at the end of last quarter.

(A) respective
(B) crowded
(C) marked
(D) diverse

GO ON TO THE NEXT PAGE

121. Before work can begin at the construction site, the ------- permit applications must be processed.

(A) relevant
(B) relevantly
(C) relevance
(D) relevancies

122. During negotiations, Mr. DuPont insisted that price ------- be implemented without delay.

(A) expectations
(B) institutions
(C) sensations
(D) reductions

123. After the team meeting next week, Ms. Li ------- whether the project deadline needs to be changed.

(A) to decide
(B) deciding
(C) will decide
(D) has decided

124. ------- the proposal for the Southside Library garden was incomplete and had an unclear timetable, it was rejected.

(A) Until
(B) Because
(C) While
(D) Unless

125. As the rental agreement with the Smith Group is set ------- soon, the available office space can be advertised.

(A) expired
(B) to expire
(C) will have expired
(D) expiring

126. Any furniture purchased at Marty's Superstore throughout February will be delivered ------- five business days.

(A) since
(B) between
(C) within
(D) above

127. The manager presented data on employee performance with ------- on measurable achievements.

(A) emphatic
(B) emphasis
(C) emphasize
(D) emphasized

128. Even employees who ------- were not familiar with the new software program have found it easy to use.

(A) initially
(B) annually
(C) successfully
(D) inadvertently

129. Supervisors will not ------- approve time off for employees during peak operational months.

(A) generalization
(B) generalize
(C) generally
(D) general

130. Toronto is one of three cities being ------- as the host for the next convention of the Global Society of Accountants.

(A) found
(B) categorized
(C) known
(D) considered

PART 6

Directions: Read the texts that follow. A word, phrase, or sentence is missing in parts of each text. Four answer choices for each question are given below the text. Select the best answer to complete the text. Then mark the letter (A), (B), (C), or (D) on your answer sheet.

Questions 131-134 refer to the following announcement.

We are pleased to announce that the installation of the new manufacturing equipment in our main plant has been completed. The new machines ------- work flow by allowing for flexibility in
        131.
production. With six mixing tanks of ------- sizes, we expect to be able to fill a wider range of
                                132.
orders, from small to very large. This ------- is an important way to ensure that Balm
                          133.
Manufacturing continues to be a leader in the fragrance industry.

------- . Jim Martel, who is organizing this effort, will contact each of you soon with details.
134.

131. (A) have been improved
     (B) were improving
     (C) will improve
     (D) improved

132. (A) varying
     (B) varies
     (C) vary
     (D) variation

133. (A) proposal
     (B) contract
     (C) impression
     (D) upgrade

134. (A) Supervisors completed a tour of the plant yesterday.
     (B) Unfortunately, the installation cost more than we had anticipated.
     (C) As you are aware, our industry is increasingly competitive.
     (D) All personnel must be trained on the new equipment by the end of the month.

GO ON TO THE NEXT PAGE

Questions 135-138 refer to the following Web page.

---

www.kateweicommunications.com

Marketing your business can be confusing. Newspapers and magazines are ------- useful venues
135.

for advertising. ------- , social media platforms have become even more critical marketing outlets.
136.

Kate Wei Communications utilizes both traditional outlets and the latest communication

platforms. ------- . In addition to exceptional print services, Kate Wei Communications has the
137.

expertise to help you ------- your online presence. Why wait? Choose our award-winning firm to
138.

strengthen your company's image today!

---

135. (A) still
    (B) nowhere
    (C) soon
    (D) evenly

136. (A) As a result
    (B) To demonstrate
    (C) Otherwise
    (D) However

137. (A) Marketing professionals give conflicting
       advice.
    (B) Traditional methods have the best
       impact.
    (C) We will develop a diverse plan for your
       business.
    (D) We have recently changed our terms of
       service.

138. (A) optimal
    (B) optimize
    (C) optimization
    (D) optimum

To: Emily Swanton <eswanton@swantonfarmfeed.com>
From: Arnold Hansen <AHansen@poltonfairgrounds.org>
Subject: Polton Farm Fair
Date: June 2

This e-mail serves as a receipt for your registration ------- confirms your participation in the
                                                        139.
Seventeenth Annual Polton County Farm Fair from July 14 to July 16. As a returning exhibitor,

Swanton Farm Feed will be offered ------- space at a discounted rate.
                                   140.

Please be aware of a new requirement when preparing your space. This year, all booths must be

completely ready by 8 P.M. on July 13. ------- . Tables will be provided by the organizer, as in past
                                       141.
years.

Thank you once again for your participation in our ------- .
                                                   142.

Arnold Hansen, Assistant Coordinator
Polton County Farm Fair

---

139. (A) whereas
    (B) rather than
    (C) in case
    (D) and also

140. (A) rent
    (B) rental
    (C) rents
    (D) renting

141. (A) This includes the removal of trash and packing materials.
    (B) The number of food vendors has increased in recent years.
    (C) The exact schedule will be announced later.
    (D) The Livestock Pavilion will be located next to the south exit.

142. (A) discovery
    (B) survey
    (C) event
    (D) vote

Sparkle Pro Enterprises Opens American Factory

Worldwide News

MANCHESTER (10 April)—Sparkle Pro Enterprises, a leading Belgium-based ------- of cleaning
                                                                        143.
products, is expanding its territory. The company has just opened its first plant in the United
States, in Indianapolis. For more than forty years, Sparkle Pro has been making and distributing
household and industrial cleaners to a wide range of vendors, including retail outlets and hotel
chains, throughout Europe. ------- .
                           144.

The Indianapolis facility will require the company to hire 300 additional employees ------- the end
                                                                                    145.
of this year in order for it to achieve full capacity. According to Egon Bretz, the new director of
North American operations, Sparkle Pro is confident that it will be able to train a large number of
personnel quickly. Mr. Bretz expects no significant ------- in meeting these needs.
                                                     146.

143. (A) produced
     (B) producing
     (C) producer
     (D) produce

144. (A) Water-based cleaners have become
         more expensive.
     (B) The company's Web site lists all of its
         major vendors.
     (C) The hotels are conveniently located in
         most cities.
     (D) Other factory facilities were gradually
         sold.

145. (A) by
     (B) despite
     (C) as
     (D) except

146. (A) decrease
     (B) challenges
     (C) project
     (D) candidates

PART 7

Directions: In this part you will read a selection of texts, such as magazine and newspaper articles, e-mails, and instant messages. Each text or set of texts is followed by several questions. Select the best answer for each question and mark the letter (A), (B), (C), or (D) on your answer sheet.

Questions 147-148 refer to the following notice.

Notice

The sidewalk along Crestview Boulevard is scheduled to be repaired next week. Due to safety concerns, the front door of the Queenstown Financial Services (QFS) building will be inaccessible from Monday, 15 January, to Wednesday, 17 January. QFS employees and customers are advised to use the north entrance on Sycamore Avenue. To get to the receptionist on the second floor, take either the staircase or the elevator, both of which can be found near the north entrance.

147. What is the purpose of the notice?

(A) To introduce changes to certain safety regulations
(B) To announce the temporary closure of an entryway
(C) To report the installation of a new elevator
(D) To disclose the new location of a company

148. What is suggested about the QFS building?

(A) Many employees work there.
(B) It will reopen on Thursday.
(C) The main entrance is on Crestview Boulevard.
(D) The renovation project will take more than a week.

GO ON TO THE NEXT PAGE

Questions 149-150 refer to the following e-mail.

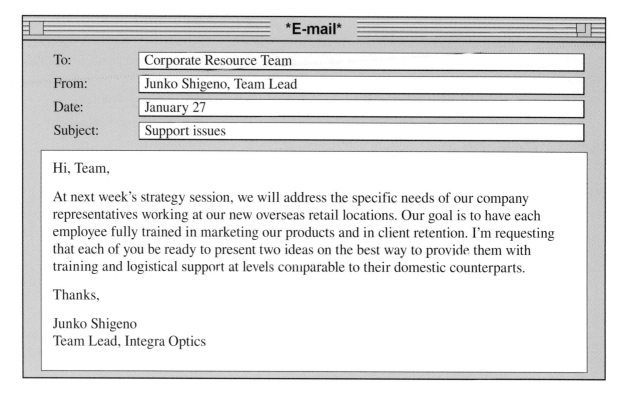

Hi, Team,

At next week's strategy session, we will address the specific needs of our company representatives working at our new overseas retail locations. Our goal is to have each employee fully trained in marketing our products and in client retention. I'm requesting that each of you be ready to present two ideas on the best way to provide them with training and logistical support at levels comparable to their domestic counterparts.

Thanks,

Junko Shigeno
Team Lead, Integra Optics

149. According to the e-mail, what is true about Integra Optics?

(A) It markets corrective eyewear.
(B) It has an international presence.
(C) It plans to open several more stores.
(D) It just produced a new line of products.

150. What does Ms. Shigeno ask employees to do?

(A) Evaluate a proposal
(B) Contact clients
(C) Attend training sessions
(D) Prepare for a meeting

Important Information

At the Froehling Company, we take great pride in our high-quality, easy-to-assemble furniture, and we want you to be completely satisfied with your purchase.

Before beginning to assemble the product, check the parts list to make sure that all parts have been included in the box.

If your item is missing parts or assembly hardware, or if it has been damaged during shipping, do not return the product to the store from which you purchased it; stores do not stock replacement parts. Rather, contact us directly and we will send you the item(s) required free of charge. You can reach us by
• visiting us at www.froehlingco.com to order replacement parts online;
• sending us an e-mail at parts@froehlingco.com; or
• calling us anytime at 555-0128.

---

151. What is the purpose of the information?

(A) To inform customers where to obtain product assembly instructions
(B) To notify customers how to resolve a problem involving their purchase
(C) To offer a gift to loyal customers of a company
(D) To help customers find nearby retail stores

152. What is suggested about the Froehling Company?

(A) It has customer service representatives available at all times.
(B) It recommends returning damaged goods to the retailer.
(C) It has a new system for keeping track of inventory.
(D) It supplies a product catalog with each order.

GO ON TO THE NEXT PAGE

Marina Tincheva   9:01 A.M.
Hi Luis. I'm at the restaurant. I need to start setting up the dessert tables for the wedding banquet this afternoon, but the door's locked and I left my key at home.

Luis Machado   9:03 A.M.
Ms. Howell isn't there? She usually shows up hours ahead of an event to get things ready.

Marina Tincheva   9:04 A.M.
I know. It doesn't make sense. You'll be in late today, right?

Luis Machado   9:06 A.M.
Yes. Actually, I'm on my way to a conference for managers, but I can be there in 10 minutes to let you in.

Marina Tincheva   9:07 A.M.
Thank you so much! I'll wait at the café next door.

153. Who most likely is Mr. Machado?

(A) A café waiter
(B) A dessert chef
(C) A wedding florist
(D) A restaurant manager

154. At 9:04 A.M., what does Ms. Tincheva most likely mean when she writes, "It doesn't make sense"?

(A) The bride should be there already.
(B) Her coworker usually arrives early.
(C) She received the wrong paperwork.
(D) She does not know where her key is.

Visiting Carlin County? Don't miss these points of interest!

Avevo Botanical Garden
Open daily, 9 A.M.–6 P.M.; $8 admission
With stunning views of Gull Bay, the Avevo Botanical Garden is a beautiful place
to examine and learn about the region's abundant and diverse plant life.

Rever Concert Hall
Open to the public Monday to Friday, 10 A.M.–4 P.M.
Designed by renowned architect Ang Zhao, the Rever Concert Hall has striking
architecture and is well worth a visit. Guided tours are available for $2 per person.

Carlin County Museum of Art
Open daily, 10 A.M.–7 P.M.; $5 admission
This lovely art museum focuses on works by local artists. Special exhibits rotate
monthly.

The Maritime Museum
Open Wednesday to Sunday, 9 A.M.–4 P.M.; no fee, but donations are welcome
An impressive collection of historical artifacts makes the Maritime Museum a
wonderful place to learn about the region's seafaring history. This museum is
located on a retired ship on East Beach.

TEST 5

155. What is the purpose of the information?

(A) To provide a schedule of events
(B) To give directions to notable landmarks
(C) To highlight the accomplishments of
local artists
(D) To describe tourist destinations

156. What is indicated about Carlin County
Museum of Art?

(A) It is closed on Mondays.
(B) It was designed by a famous architect.
(C) It features collections from around the
world.
(D) It changes some exhibits periodically.

157. According to the information, what do the
Avevo Botanical Garden and the Maritime
Museum have in common?

(A) Both charge a small admission fee.
(B) Both are located near water.
(C) Both display historical artifacts.
(D) Both offer guided tours.

GO ON TO THE NEXT PAGE

Bingham Man Receives Award

by Timur Kardos

9 October—A Bingham native received this year's Contributors Award from the Association for the Construction of Steel Bridges (ACSB), a trade organisation. Scott Moore, 66, was presented the award during yesterday's annual ACSB meeting in Norwalk.

According to an ACSB press release, the award is given every year to "an individual who has contributed significantly to the betterment of the steel industry." ACSB spokesperson Cora Schroeder said, "Mr. Moore devotes his spare time to ensuring quality in our industry. For the past decade, he has dedicated himself to helping the ACSB monitor and refine steel-production standards and practices. This year, he chaired a committee that created an improved set of standards for structural steel used in the construction of bridges."

Mr. Moore was born and raised in Bingham and received his engineering degree from Bingham University. After graduating, he worked as a construction manager during the building of Bingham's new city hall. He joined Marshall Steel 39 years ago as a building supervisor, ultimately rising to his current position of senior project engineer.

158. What is suggested about Mr. Moore?
   (A) He led efforts to raise standards for steel use.
   (B) He designed a new type of bridge.
   (C) He serves on a committee with Ms. Schroeder.
   (D) He has received several awards from the ACSB.

159. According to the article, what happened ten years ago?
   (A) Mr. Moore moved to Norwalk.
   (B) Mr. Moore began to help the ACSB.
   (C) The ACSB revised its membership requirements.
   (D) The ACSB first presented its award.

160. What was Mr. Moore's first job at Marshall Steel?
   (A) Senior project engineer
   (B) Company spokesperson
   (C) Construction manager
   (D) Building supervisor

http://www.goldendayimages.com

Golden Day Stock Photographs

Using stock images in your materials can significantly improve your company's ability to communicate—not only with external clients but with employees as well. A well-chosen image can serve many functions, from increasing employee engagement with internal communications, to catching the attention of potential clients, to helping readers of documents better understand complex ideas.

Golden Day's images come from a unique international network of contributors, so our selection is not only large but also truly diverse. No matter the size of your organization, and no matter where you are located and with whom you do business, you will find the perfect photo to enhance your message.

Our monthly subscription plans range from $49 to $495 based on the quantity and resolution of the images you download. Once you download an image, there are no limits on its usage.

Don't miss our special introductory offer: first-time subscribers qualify for consultations with our branding experts for six months at no extra cost! Our experts will help you ensure that all your client-facing materials are cohesive and make your company stand out.

161. What reason to use stock images is NOT mentioned in the advertisement?

(A) To encourage employees to read company newsletters
(B) To keep current customers interested in a company's brand
(C) To attract new customers
(D) To help clarify written information

162. According to the advertisement, why are Golden Day's images special?

(A) They are a larger size than is typically offered.
(B) They are created by famous photographers.
(C) They are used by multinational companies.
(D) They are sourced from all over the world.

163. The word "resolution" in paragraph 3, line 1, is closest in meaning to

(A) level of detail
(B) statement of agreement
(C) subject matter
(D) firmness of purpose

164. What is Golden Day offering to new customers?

(A) Free marketing advice
(B) Discounts on subscription plans
(C) Limited-time access to additional photo collections
(D) Introductions to potential new clients

GO ON TO THE NEXT PAGE

We're Doing Something Right

by Ariel Garman

SUSTERN (November 8)—According to a recent study conducted by the Mid-Atlantic Hotel Association, tourism at our beaches improved significantly this past summer, and the hotel industry showed greater profits this year than last. Hotel occupancy averaged 94 percent during the peak summer months. — [1] —.

Sustern saw the opening of the area's largest hotel, The Glaston, last spring. The new hotel was at full capacity nearly every weekend during the summer. Weekday occupancy also exceeded expectations.

The hotel's manager, Anika Bastien, said, "Tourists were thrilled with the array of amenities offered, including 24-hour dining options, a free shuttle to nearby beaches, and free Wi-Fi. In fact, many have already reserved rooms for next summer. — [2] —."

Sustern has become the most popular tourist destination in the region, with about 20 percent more beachgoers than the Delmire shore, its biggest competitor. — [3] —. Experts attribute this to the growing number of outlet stores in Sustern, overall lower prices, and an abundance of new restaurants, hotels, and community events. Tourists continue to visit the area after the prime beach months, keeping hotel rooms occupied longer. — [4] —.

165. What is the purpose of the article?

(A) To announce the opening of a new hotel
(B) To provide information about the local tourism industry
(C) To discuss job opportunities in the hotel industry
(D) To compare the quality of beaches in two locations

166. What is NOT indicated about Sustern?

(A) Its beach is more popular than Delmire's.
(B) Its new hotel employs Ms. Bastien.
(C) It hosts a wide variety of events.
(D) It recently held a beach cleanup weekend.

167. In which of the positions marked [1], [2], [3], and [4] does the following sentence best belong?

"This was a big increase from last summer's average of just 77 percent."

(A) [1]
(B) [2]
(C) [3]
(D) [4]

GO ON TO THE NEXT PAGE

E-mail

To:	All staff
From:	Jessica Perry
Subject:	Conference
Date:	19 July
Attachment:	🔗 Workshop application

Hello everyone,

The fourth annual Australian National Sales and Marketing Conference (ANSMC) will take place from 18 to 22 November here in Perth. Conference organizers have asked local marketing specialists to help out by giving a keynote speech, leading a workshop, or working in the exhibition hall. — [1] —.

Our chief executive officer, Martin Hughes, wants us to take advantage of this excellent opportunity for Hughes Australia Marketing to achieve visibility on a national stage. It is sure to help us to expand our client base. Mr. Hughes has already agreed to give a keynote speech about using survey results to create successful marketing campaigns. — [2] —. I am designing our company's booth for the exhibition hall. If you would like to help, please come to Room C556 at 2:00 P.M. next Tuesday, 23 July, for a planning meeting. — [3] —.

If you would like to lead a workshop, please complete the attached proposal form and return it to me by 26 July. — [4] —. You may present alone or with a partner. Workshop ideas will be discussed and approved at a managers' meeting on 29 July.

Thanks,

Jessica

168. What is the purpose of the e-mail?

(A) To remind staff to register for a conference
(B) To apologize for missing a deadline
(C) To invite staff to submit an application
(D) To request responses to a marketing survey

169. What is suggested about Hughes Australia Marketing?

(A) It is hosting the ANSMC.
(B) It is located in Perth.
(C) It has been in business for four years.
(D) It serves clients throughout Australia.

170. According to the e-mail, why does Mr. Hughes want employees to participate in the ANSMC?

(A) So they can learn new marketing strategies
(B) So they can share the results of a survey
(C) So they can attract new clients
(D) So they can listen to his keynote speech

171. In which of the positions marked [1], [2], [3], and [4] does the following sentence best belong?

"This will help me ensure that none of our workshop topics overlap."

(A) [1]
(B) [2]
(C) [3]
(D) [4]

GO ON TO THE NEXT PAGE

Questions 172-175 refer to the following online chat discussion.

Alberto Ovando [11:15 A.M.]
When we met last week, production was nearly finished on the boxes and other packaging for Redmond's. Rani, where are we now?

Rani Verma [11:16 A.M.]
The refrigerator and dishwasher boxes were supposed to arrive at Redmond's warehouse on Wednesday, but the snowstorm really backed up our delivery schedule.

Alberto Ovando [11:17 A.M.]
Have you told them this?

Stacy Pfeiffer [11:18 A.M.]
I will, but I was waiting to hear from the drivers. George, can you help?

George Kellerman [11:19 A.M.]
I spoke with them ten minutes ago. They're back on the road now, so they only lost a day. They should have everything before the end of the week.

Stacy Pfeiffer [11:21 A.M.]
OK. I'll tell them to expect delivery by Friday at the very latest.

Rani Verma [11:22 A.M.]
At least the packaging materials for the smaller appliances shipped before the storm; only the larger boxes are affected.

Alberto Ovando [11:23 A.M.]
The contract is for us to provide packaging materials for all of Redmond's products, not just the smaller ones. Let's make sure we stay on the revised schedule.

172. For what type of business do the people most likely work?

(A) A restaurant supply company
(B) An appliance repair shop
(C) A packaging manufacturer
(D) A furniture delivery service

173. What problem are the people discussing?

(A) A shipment was delayed.
(B) A warehouse was closed.
(C) An order was incorrect.
(D) A driver did not report for work.

174. What will Ms. Pfeiffer most likely do next?

(A) Cancel a shipment
(B) Sign the contract
(C) Call a driver
(D) Contact the client

175. At 11:18 A.M., what does Ms. Pfeiffer most likely mean when she writes, "can you help"?

(A) She thinks Mr. Kellerman should load some boxes.
(B) She needs Mr. Kellerman to drive to the warehouse.
(C) She wants Mr. Kellerman to provide delivery information.
(D) She expects Mr. Kellerman to pay the drivers.

GO ON TO THE NEXT PAGE

PAGA's Seventeenth Annual Botanical and Horticultural Expo, July 10–13
Starkey Convention Center, Pittsburgh, Pennsylvania

The Pittsburgh Area Garden Association (PAGA) invites companies to support its garden exhibition, which last year was attended by nearly 40,000 visitors. This is a cost-effective means of reaching home gardeners and outdoor enthusiasts and enhances your firm's commercial performance.

PAGA is pleased to offer the following levels of corporate sponsorship with corresponding benefits. (For inquiries, contact Ms. Carita Aragon, PAGA's Event Coordinator, at 925-555-0142. To register, e-mail sponsors@paga.org.)

Workshop Patron—$1,250
A representative of your company will have the honor of introducing the presenter(s) of a workshop, to be conducted on the second day of the event.

Charging Station Patron—$2,000
There will be eight mobile-device charging stations in the exhibition hall, each with a sponsor sign next to it.

Bag Patron—$3,500
Your company's emblem will be on all fabric tote bags, to be distributed to every visitor.

General Program Patron—$5,000
Two executives of your company will attend the PAGA Gala Banquet on the opening night of the expo.

From:	caragon@paga.org
To:	mkee@wimosol.com
Date:	May 15
Subject:	Thank you

Dear Mr. Kee:

Thank you for registering Wireless Monitoring Solutions as a sponsor of the Pittsburgh Area Garden Association (PAGA) Expo. Your sponsorship not only helps to make this year's event possible, but also to generate interest in gardening.

Your contribution of $2,000 has been processed. Additionally, we are offering you sponsorship of our expo bags at no additional cost. This offer is a token of our appreciation for the long-standing support of PAGA and its programs. To finalize the promotional materials, please send us the artwork of your company's logo.

Carita Aragon, PAGA Event Coordinator

176. What is the purpose of the flyer?

(A) To promote the benefits of participating in an event

(B) To present a breakdown of the costs of hosting an activity

(C) To report on the financial success of a fund-raising campaign

(D) To encourage community members to join a nature preservation project

177. According to the flyer, when should a call be placed to PAGA's office?

(A) When a contribution cannot be processed

(B) When a payment has not been received

(C) When additional information is required

(D) When a change in sponsorship level must be made

178. What will happen on July 10 ?

(A) Attendance figures from last year's expo will be released.

(B) Mobile-device charging stations will be installed.

(C) A workshop will be presented.

(D) A formal dinner will be held.

179. What is suggested about PAGA's event?

(A) It is partially funded by the Pittsburgh city government.

(B) It is held at a different venue every year.

(C) It is intended to promote enthusiasm for gardening.

(D) It attracts more than 40,000 visitors annually.

180. What is NOT indicated about Wireless Monitoring Solutions?

(A) Its name will be featured in various locations at the convention center.

(B) It will install wireless monitoring devices in the exhibition hall.

(C) It has sponsored PAGA's exhibition on various occasions.

(D) Its logo will be displayed on souvenir bags.

GO ON TO THE NEXT PAGE

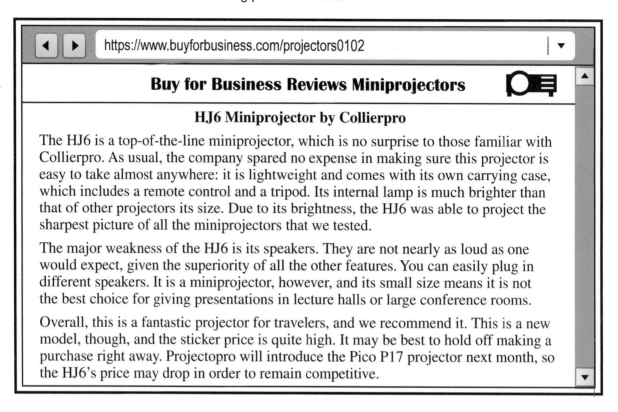

https://www.buyforbusiness.com/projectors0102

Buy for Business Reviews Miniprojectors

HJ6 Miniprojector by Collierpro

The HJ6 is a top-of-the-line miniprojector, which is no surprise to those familiar with Collierpro. As usual, the company spared no expense in making sure this projector is easy to take almost anywhere: it is lightweight and comes with its own carrying case, which includes a remote control and a tripod. Its internal lamp is much brighter than that of other projectors its size. Due to its brightness, the HJ6 was able to project the sharpest picture of all the miniprojectors that we tested.

The major weakness of the HJ6 is its speakers. They are not nearly as loud as one would expect, given the superiority of all the other features. You can easily plug in different speakers. It is a miniprojector, however, and its small size means it is not the best choice for giving presentations in lecture halls or large conference rooms.

Overall, this is a fantastic projector for travelers, and we recommend it. This is a new model, though, and the sticker price is quite high. It may be best to hold off making a purchase right away. Projectopro will introduce the Pico P17 projector next month, so the HJ6's price may drop in order to remain competitive.

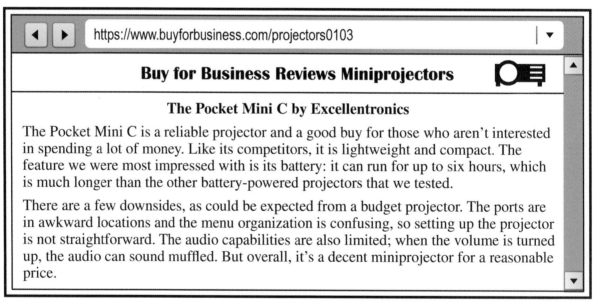

https://www.buyforbusiness.com/projectors0103

Buy for Business Reviews Miniprojectors

The Pocket Mini C by Excellentronics

The Pocket Mini C is a reliable projector and a good buy for those who aren't interested in spending a lot of money. Like its competitors, it is lightweight and compact. The feature we were most impressed with is its battery: it can run for up to six hours, which is much longer than the other battery-powered projectors that we tested.

There are a few downsides, as could be expected from a budget projector. The ports are in awkward locations and the menu organization is confusing, so setting up the projector is not straightforward. The audio capabilities are also limited; when the volume is turned up, the audio can sound muffled. But overall, it's a decent miniprojector for a reasonable price.

181. What is suggested about Collierpro?

(A) It is owned by *Buy for Business*.
(B) It makes high-quality electronics.
(C) It is a new company.
(D) It offers discounts for business travelers.

182. What is mentioned as a feature of the HJ6 Miniprojector?

(A) It is less expensive than the Pico P17.
(B) It is sold with a spare power cord.
(C) It has a rechargeable battery.
(D) It produces a very clear image.

183. Why should customers wait before purchasing the HJ6 Miniprojector?

(A) The model's features will be updated soon.
(B) The projector might become less expensive soon.
(C) Minor problems with the machine will be fixed soon.
(D) Another company will buy the projector's manufacturer soon.

184. What criticism do both of the reviewed projectors receive?

(A) They are too heavy.
(B) They are not easy to set up.
(C) Their sound systems do not work well.
(D) Their projections are not large enough.

185. According to the second review, what is the best feature of the Pocket Mini C?

(A) Its design is attractive.
(B) It is easier to carry than other projectors.
(C) It has more ports than other projectors.
(D) Its battery lasts for a long time.

GO ON TO THE NEXT PAGE

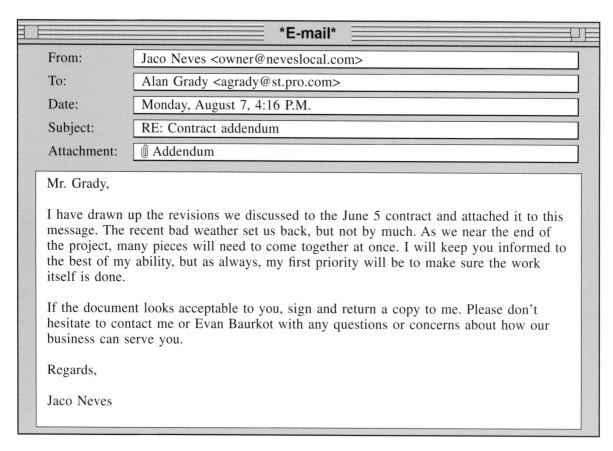

From:	Alan Grady <agrady@st.pro.com>
To:	Jaco Neves <owner@neveslocal.com>
Date:	Monday, August 7, 9:31 A.M.
Subject:	Contract addendum

Mr. Neves,

Thanks for calling to discuss your progress on the house construction. To summarize our conversation, even with the delay until September 22, the house should be ready for me to move into before my apartment lease expires on October 10. I've thought more about the status reports we discussed, and twice a week would be best. My understanding is that you will now document these changes to the contract so that I can sign off on them this week.

Thanks, as always, for your careful attention to this project.

Alan Grady

E-mail

From:	Jaco Neves <owner@neveslocal.com>
To:	Alan Grady <agrady@st.pro.com>
Date:	Monday, August 7, 4:16 P.M.
Subject:	RE: Contract addendum
Attachment:	🖇 Addendum

Mr. Grady,

I have drawn up the revisions we discussed to the June 5 contract and attached it to this message. The recent bad weather set us back, but not by much. As we near the end of the project, many pieces will need to come together at once. I will keep you informed to the best of my ability, but as always, my first priority will be to make sure the work itself is done.

If the document looks acceptable to you, sign and return a copy to me. Please don't hesitate to contact me or Evan Baurkot with any questions or concerns about how our business can serve you.

Regards,

Jaco Neves

CONTRACT ADDENDUM

1. Because of work that could not be performed due to unavoidable circumstances from July 24 to July 28, the completion date for all construction will be moved from September 17 to September 22. The Client will not be charged any additional labor costs as a result of this change. Any charges resulting from an extension of building permits will be paid by the Contractor.

2. Effective immediately, the Contractor will submit a report of all work completed (including any delays incurred or anticipated) once every week, beginning on Monday, August 12.

186. Who is Mr. Grady?

(A) A business partner of Mr. Neves'
(B) A client of Mr. Neves'
(C) An assistant to Mr. Baurkot
(D) A legal advisor of Mr. Baurkot's

187. What is planned for October?

(A) A lease will be extended.
(B) A contract will be changed.
(C) A project schedule will be revised.
(D) A house will be occupied.

188. In the second e-mail, the phrase "drawn up" in paragraph 1, line 1, is closest in meaning to

(A) raised
(B) sketched
(C) prepared
(D) straightened

189. When was the work most likely affected by bad weather?

(A) On June 5
(B) On July 24
(C) On August 12
(D) On September 22

190. What information in the contract is different from what Mr. Grady requested?

(A) The frequency of the reports
(B) The charge for additional labor
(C) The date of completion
(D) The number of permits required

GO ON TO THE NEXT PAGE

More Improvements Ahead

At its meeting on Tuesday, the Eldonbury Town Council voted to explore options for additional work to be done on town facilities. According to Charles Gruber, town clerk, the renovation of the Eldonbury Community Centre came in well under budget. The council, therefore, decided to compile a list of smaller improvement projects that could be done with the leftover funds.

Some suggested projects include adding a covered entryway to the Eldonbury Public Library, improving lighting in Westfall Park, and replacing floors in the Town Hall. According to Mr. Gruber, the council will solicit ideas from members of the public. Interested parties may voice their opinions at the council's meeting on Tuesday, 20 March, at 4:00 P.M. or send an e-mail to the council office before 31 March. After the period of public comment, the planning committee will put forth a final list for the council to discuss, with a decision expected by 15 April.

E-mail

From:	mccaffrey32@citymail.co.uk
To:	towncouncil@eldonbury.org.uk
Date:	25 March
Subject:	Additional Project

Dear Town Council Members,

I read that you are accepting suggestions for the use of the leftover money from the Community Centre renovation. Because of a previously scheduled appointment, I was not able to attend the council meeting, but I would like to express my support for the idea of expanding the lighting in the park. While the cost of that project is likely to be reasonable compared to that of the other possibilities, the improved lighting would increase the usability of Westfall Park and would benefit many people, especially in the dark winter months. A well-lit, nicely maintained park is an obvious source of civic pride, and something we could all appreciate. I hope the council will seriously consider this project.

Sincerely,

Heather McCaffrey

From:	sunil.pai@hgnetworks.co.uk
To:	towncouncil@eldonbury.org.uk
Date:	27 March
Subject:	Town projects

Dear Mr. Gruber,

I was glad to hear that the latest renovation project was completed with money to spare. Although the Community Centre does sponsor activities for citizens of all ages, it is, for the most part, visited by adolescents and parents with children. Therefore, I would like to suggest that the next project focus on a place more often used by Eldonbury's older people.

The public library is a natural gathering place for older adults, and a new entryway would provide a dry, protected place for people to chat or wait for transportation. It would be a noticeable improvement, likely to be applauded by citizens who did not feel that they gained much from the improvements to the Community Centre. In April, when the votes are cast, please consider this suggestion to balance the interests of all members of the Eldonbury public.

Thank you,

Sunil Pai

TEST 5

191. Why does the town of Eldonbury have funds available?

(A) The town council has canceled a project.
(B) The town has raised the tax rate.
(C) A group of citizens has donated money.
(D) An earlier project cost less than expected.

192. In the article, the phrase "put forth" in paragraph 2, line 12, is closest in meaning to

(A) grow
(B) exert
(C) propose
(D) request

193. When did Ms. McCaffrey have an appointment?

(A) On March 20
(B) On March 25
(C) On March 31
(D) On April 15

194. What does Mr. Pai mention in his e-mail about the Eldonbury Community Centre?

(A) It is located near public transportation.
(B) It is used mainly by younger residents.
(C) Its building previously served another purpose.
(D) Its programs will run year-round.

195. On what point would Ms. McCaffrey and Mr. Pai most likely agree?

(A) The chosen project should be beneficial to the entire community.
(B) The town should spend as little money as possible on its next project.
(C) The town council should extend the deadline for public comment.
(D) The patrons of the library and the park should work together to raise money.

GO ON TO THE NEXT PAGE

TAHARA AIR

Delayed Luggage Form

Dear Tahara Air Customer,

We regret that the arrival of your luggage has been delayed. Please provide the following details to help us track down and return your luggage more quickly. A Tahara Air representative will contact you by phone as soon as your luggage is located. Should your luggage remain missing for more than three days, please visit www.tahara-air.com/baggage for further instructions.

Date: _12 October_
Name: _Marzena Majewska_
Local Address: _Hotel Dantes, Rua Jau, 1300 Lisbon, Portugal_
Telephone: _+44 1632 812110_
Flight Number: _J77FG2_

Delayed Luggage Information

	Quantity	Description
☑ Suitcase	1	small black suitcase with wheels; "Marzena Majewska" on the name tag
☐ Backpack		
☐ Purse		
☑ Box	1	small cardboard box with "Marzena Majewska, Saltoni Foods" written on it
☐ Other		

From:	hgilbert@saltonifoods.co.uk
To:	mmajewska@saltonifoods.co.uk
Subject:	Re: Sauce samples
Date:	12 October, 2:03 P.M.

Dear Marzena,

I'm sorry to hear about your luggage. At least the airline has located your suitcase.

Since it's impossible to determine when the rest of your luggage will be found and returned, I've sent you more samples by overnight shipping. That way, you will not have to go empty-handed to tomorrow's meeting with the clients. There are five packets of each flavour as well as two small sauce jars with labels. I sent the items by BDW Shipping to your hotel. The package will be delivered by 8:30 a.m. so that you are sure to have the sauce samples and packaging to show when you speak at the meeting at 11.

Take care,

Harry Gilbert

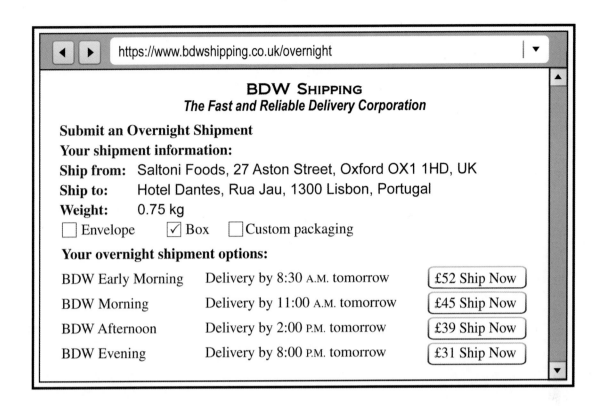

BDW SHIPPING
The Fast and Reliable Delivery Corporation

Submit an Overnight Shipment
Your shipment information:
Ship from: Saltoni Foods, 27 Aston Street, Oxford OX1 1HD, UK
Ship to: Hotel Dantes, Rua Jau, 1300 Lisbon, Portugal
Weight: 0.75 kg
☐ Envelope   ☑ Box   ☐ Custom packaging

Your overnight shipment options:

BDW Early Morning	Delivery by 8:30 A.M. tomorrow	£52 Ship Now
BDW Morning	Delivery by 11:00 A.M. tomorrow	£45 Ship Now
BDW Afternoon	Delivery by 2:00 P.M. tomorrow	£39 Ship Now
BDW Evening	Delivery by 8:00 P.M. tomorrow	£31 Ship Now

196. What is indicated about Tahara Air?

(A) It requires customers to include name tags on all pieces of luggage.
(B) It guarantees that missing luggage will be returned in three days.
(C) It will notify Ms. Majewska when her luggage is found.
(D) It will reimburse Ms. Majewska for her lost luggage.

197. Where did Ms. Majewska most likely pack her samples?

(A) In a box
(B) In a purse
(C) In a suitcase
(D) In a backpack

198. What is implied about Mr. Gilbert?

(A) He is meeting with clients in Portugal.
(B) He travels frequently for Saltoni Foods.
(C) He is a Tahara Air customer service agent.
(D) He wants the clients to review some products.

199. According to the e-mail, what will Ms. Majewska do tomorrow at 11 A.M.?

(A) Accept a delivery
(B) Make a presentation
(C) Check out of the hotel
(D) Confirm her return flight

200. How much was Mr. Gilbert charged for shipping?

(A) £31.00
(B) £39.00
(C) £45.00
(D) £52.00

Stop! This is the end of the test. If you finish before time is called, you may go back to Parts 5, 6, and 7 and check your work.

토익 정기시험
기출문제집

RC

기출 TEST

06

READING TEST

In the Reading test, you will read a variety of texts and answer several different types of reading comprehension questions. The entire Reading test will last 75 minutes. There are three parts, and directions are given for each part. You are encouraged to answer as many questions as possible within the time allowed.

You must mark your answers on the separate answer sheet. Do not write your answers in your test book.

PART 5

Directions: A word or phrase is missing in each of the sentences below. Four answer choices are given below each sentence. Select the best answer to complete the sentence. Then mark the letter (A), (B), (C), or (D) on your answer sheet.

---

101. Jesper Associates currently has ------- with 26 different food suppliers.

(A) contracting
(B) contracts
(C) contractor
(D) contract

102. Passengers must be at the gate ------- 25 minutes prior to boarding their flight.

(A) at least
(B) as much
(C) in case
(D) by then

103. Deltran analytics software can help ------- identify issues, predict trends, and improve business.

(A) you
(B) your
(C) yours
(D) yourself

104. The technology department ------- to purchase three new servers next year.

(A) announces
(B) thinks
(C) predicts
(D) plans

105. Jennson Motors hired an ------- new efficiency expert last month.

(A) approximate
(B) angular
(C) exceptional
(D) eventual

106. Mr. Winkel's ------- responsibilities include auditing and financial review of large clients.

(A) accounts
(B) accounted
(C) accounting
(D) accountable

107. The prime minister greeted foreign diplomats ------- a luncheon today in London.

(A) at
(B) had
(C) such
(D) where

108. The management team at Ofto Corporation offers incentives ------- employee productivity.

(A) stimulate
(B) to stimulate
(C) will stimulate
(D) are stimulating

109. In response to customer -------, Lopez Naturals will release a line of organic soaps.
(A) demand
(B) permit
(C) arrival
(D) account

110. Before the computers leave the factory, they are ------- thoroughly to ensure they have no defects.
(A) selected
(B) inspected
(C) attached
(D) managed

111. WRUZ Radio will broadcast a new show ------- to business news and economic analysis.
(A) allowed
(B) prepared
(C) dedicated
(D) introduced

112. Mr. Okada met ------- with the building manager to discuss the demolition project.
(A) frequent
(B) frequenting
(C) frequently
(D) frequented

113. Mr. Montri politely ------- the job offer from Barranca Shipping Company.
(A) declined
(B) decreased
(C) prevented
(D) converted

114. Written permission must ------- before using Thavor Corporation's logo.
(A) to obtain
(B) obtained
(C) be obtained
(D) obtaining

115. ------- it is relatively small, the fitness center at Ginder Apartments is very popular with residents.
(A) Reasoning
(B) Essentially
(C) Although
(D) Throughout

116. All communications must be approved by the public relations director before they can be shared -------.
(A) certainly
(B) externally
(C) deeply
(D) utterly

117. Providing precision welding to a ------- array of industries, Mistone Metalworks recently celebrated a century of service in Quebec.
(A) widely
(B) widen
(C) width
(D) wide

118. Mr. Kim considers punctuality a crucial ------- for all his assistants to have.
(A) device
(B) type
(C) action
(D) trait

119. The chief financial officer has ------- the importance of attracting new customers next quarter.
(A) applied
(B) demanded
(C) administered
(D) emphasized

120. Seowerd Furnishings is closing some of its showrooms because customers are ------- ordering furniture online.
(A) increasing
(B) increase
(C) increasingly
(D) increased

GO ON TO THE NEXT PAGE

121. ------- construction in progress at the old town hall building, tourist groups will not be allowed to enter the site.
(A) Now that
(B) While
(C) Even if
(D) Due to

122. Several drilling-technology experts will present the results of their ------- on June 23.
(A) comprehension
(B) resolution
(C) investigation
(D) specification

123. The store had a ------- display to promote the newest book from the best-selling mystery author.
(A) default
(B) grateful
(C) talented
(D) massive

124. Most of the people ------- attended yesterday's workshop have already submitted their feedback.
(A) who
(B) those
(C) whose
(D) some

125. Both tasty and healthy, the tomato salad at Alfredi's Bistro is also large ------- to be served as a main dish.
(A) enough
(B) fully
(C) nearly
(D) well

126. The Klassin Group's booth at the Liberty Architecture Expo has garnered much -------.
(A) interest
(B) interests
(C) interested
(D) interesting

127. Save 25 percent on any printer ------- you buy a laptop computer at Diego's Electronics.
(A) whereas
(B) whenever
(C) such as
(D) seeing that

128. The recently adopted policy restructures the company's debt according to a ------- five-step plan.
(A) managing
(B) manageably
(C) manages
(D) manageable

129. The quality assurance department needs to hire additional staff ------- production has increased by 50 percent.
(A) even though
(B) since
(C) because of
(D) therefore

130. Your order cannot ------- until we have received full payment.
(A) to process
(B) be processed
(C) being processed
(D) has processed

PART 6

Directions: Read the texts that follow. A word, phrase, or sentence is missing in parts of each text. Four answer choices for each question are given below the text. Select the best answer to complete the text. Then mark the letter (A), (B), (C), or (D) on your answer sheet.

Questions 131-134 refer to the following Web page.

Commercial relocation may at first appear ------- , but Mester Movers will work with you to make
131.

the process as simple as possible. Whether you are relocating an office, factory, or laboratory

across town or across the country, we have the people, technology, and resources to ------- your
132.

move with efficiency.

We take special care when packing small and delicate objects. ------- , we make sure that large
133.

items such as desks, filing cabinets, and chairs are also ready for the move by providing you with

special tags. ------- .
134.

131. (A) complication
(B) complicated
(C) complicates
(D) complicate

132. (A) handling
(B) handled
(C) handle
(D) handles

133. (A) Rather
(B) In brief
(C) In other words
(D) At the same time

134. (A) Our Moving Guide will explain how to
properly affix them.
(B) Your employer will tell you when the
move will occur.
(C) We travel on back roads to get them
moved quickly.
(D) We have a dozen moving trucks on
our fleet.

GO ON TO THE NEXT PAGE

Purchase Order Guidelines

Mapleshades Medical Center authorizes certain employees to purchase goods and services for company-related business. To purchase a ------- item or service, fill out the online request form.
135.

Use the form to ------- a description of the item needed. Also, briefly explain why the purchase is
136.

necessary. Note that your ------- may affect subsequent decisions. If the request entails replacing
137.

a device that is out of order, bring the matter to the attention of Mr. Rowen, head of the

Maintenance Division, before submitting the request. ------- . Please direct any questions you may
138.

have related to the purchase of office supplies and equipment to the Purchasing Department.

135. (A) specify
(B) specific
(C) specifics
(D) specifically

136. (A) view
(B) change
(C) provide
(D) find

137. (A) retirement
(B) score
(C) experience
(D) justification

138. (A) He has studied all possible options in detail.
(B) He will determine whether such action is warranted.
(C) It has a staff of six who service our two office buildings.
(D) It is usually maintained on a monthly basis.

From: Hong Kong Princess Center Administration
To: All Princess Center residents
Date: 17 October
Subject: Higwam workers to maintain C-level elevators

------- the past week you may have experienced increased wait times for our C-level elevators,
   139.
which service floors 25 through 36. We have contacted Higwam, our elevator maintenance

contractor, who ------- repairs in the elevator shafts.
                140.

This is to alert all residents that beginning tomorrow and through the end of the week, you are

likely to see Higwam technicians working in the lobby. They are planning to work on one unit at a

time in order to keep the others operational while repairs are in progress, so for the next few

------- , there may continue to be prolonged wait times. ------- .
141.   **142.**

For any questions, please contact our office. We apologize for the inconvenience and appreciate

your patience.

139. (A) Between
(B) After
(C) Over
(D) Inside

140. (A) was conducting
(B) will be conducting
(C) would conduct
(D) is now conducting

141. (A) hours
(B) days
(C) weeks
(D) months

142. (A) Alternatively, you may use the service
elevator in the rear of the building.
(B) Complimentary refreshments will be
available to the workers in the lobby.
(C) Elevator repairs can be costly, which is
why we request your collaboration.
(D) Our B-level elevators suffered a
service disruption last month as well.

Questions 143-146 refer to the following article.

DAKAR (August 4)—Nentique Laboratories, Inc., announced today the development of a new variety of organic wheat that _____ heat. Dozens of plants were cross-pollinated over many years
143.
to produce this variety, known as GR-712. It joins a growing list of _____ that can withstand high
144.
temperatures during extended dry periods. "Some farmers in regions close to the equator focus
_____ on rice production because rice grows well in hot climates. But in the Sahara, it is too dry
145.
for much of the year," explains company spokesman Ahmad Niang. "But for a small investment in
GR-712 seeds, farmers will now be able to grow wheat in our region." _____ . This added income
146.
can, in turn, be reinvested in better machinery, which will encourage more environmentally
friendly farming practices.

143. (A) tolerates
(B) tolerable
(C) tolerate
(D) tolerating

144. (A) fuels
(B) materials
(C) vehicles
(D) crops

145. (A) exclude
(B) exclusion
(C) exclusive
(D) exclusively

146. (A) There is more rainfall in the region in August and September.
(B) Nentique believes diversification of this kind will lead to greater profits.
(C) A common name for the new species is yet to be determined.
(D) This merger will also help streamline Nentique's production process.

Directions: In this part you will read a selection of texts, such as magazine and newspaper articles, e-mails, and instant messages. Each text or set of texts is followed by several questions. Select the best answer for each question and mark the letter (A), (B), (C), or (D) on your answer sheet.

Questions 147-148 refer to the following text-message chain.

Jane Equi [10:41 A.M.]
Hi Mateo. Brian Jaffers just called to cancel tomorrow's walk-through at 721 Union Street.

Mateo Rodriguez [10:42 A.M.]
That's too bad. That apartment is just right for him. Did you reschedule?

Jane Equi [10:44 A.M.]
Yes, for Thursday, just before you show the Rockledge Place property to the Kim family. The two sites are very close to each other.

Mateo Rodriguez [10:45 A.M.]
Great. Could you please confirm the time with Ms. Kim today?

Jane Equi [10:47 A.M.]
Sure.

147. Who most likely is Mr. Rodriguez?

(A) A landscape designer
(B) An administrative assistant
(C) A human resources director
(D) A real estate agent

148. At 10:45 A.M., what does Mr. Rodriguez most likely mean when he writes, "Great"?

(A) He is excited about the results of his work.
(B) He is glad about his company's new location.
(C) He is pleased with Ms. Equi's work.
(D) He is interested in contacting Mr. Jaffers.

GO ON TO THE NEXT PAGE

Wallaby Decking
Serving Queensland and Beyond

Congratulations on your new timber deck! Follow these tips to keep it in top shape for years to come.

- ✓ Apply a coat of UV sealant annually to shield the deck from the effects of moisture and heat.

- ✓ Keep the gaps between boards free of dirt and debris. Air must flow around and between the boards to prevent moisture buildup.

- ✓ Wash the deck periodically. Use a soft-bristled brush, a hose, and a chemical-free detergent to clean away dirt without removing the finish.

- ✓ Avoid water stains and mildew. Do not allow potted plants or other large, heavy objects to rest directly on the surface of the deck.

---

149. What is indicated about the boards?

(A) They should be installed in shady areas.
(B) They are waterproof.
(C) They have space between them.
(D) They are sold only in Queensland.

150. What is NOT mentioned as a tip for deck maintenance?

(A) Applying a weather-resistant coating
(B) Cleaning the surface regularly
(C) Removing stains with a chemical cleaner
(D) Keeping plants off the surface

Hapkell Industries Pairs Up with E&T Recycling Center

June 19—The computer technology company Hapkell Industries just announced it will begin working with E&T Recycling Centers. This partnership will enable consumers to responsibly recycle computer equipment, at no personal cost, simply by taking it to a collection center.

"Used computers make up a rapidly growing waste source," said CEO Indira Kapoor. "As a major producer of computer products, we believe it is our obligation to reuse what we can and keep heavy metals out of the landfills. This is what prompted us to go forward with this initiative."

Hapkell Industries originally sponsored two pilot E&T collection sites and, given their success, aims to add ten more sites by year's end. To learn more about the initiative and for a map of current and proposed collection sites, visit ETrecyclingcenter.com.

TEST 6

151. According to Ms. Kapoor, why did her company partner with a recycling firm?

(A) To manufacture more affordable computer products

(B) To follow a government environmental policy

(C) To meet a responsibility as an industry leader

(D) To pursue a rewarding financial opportunity

152. What is stated about collection sites?

(A) They are not getting as much use as expected.

(B) They are no longer accepting volunteers.

(C) Their sanitary requirements are very strict.

(D) Their locations can be found on an online map.

GO ON TO THE NEXT PAGE

```
╔══════════════════════════════════════════════════════════════════╗
║                            *E-mail*                                ║
╠══════════════════════════════════════════════════════════════════╣
```

To:	Stan Anyati
From:	Stella Gerraldi
Date:	May 1
Subject:	Café Marti

Dear Stan,

I called your shop yesterday and spoke with Andre about my vintage espresso maker. I was surprised that he was able to find replacement parts for such an old machine. He also re-created some parts that are no longer made. Apparently, there is a brass holder for the manufacturer's nameplate that has not yet arrived from Italy. Once that arrives, the restoration can be completed.

As we discussed earlier, I need the machine delivered by May 7. On May 8 we will celebrate the tenth anniversary of the café's opening. The espresso machine has always been our centerpiece. We use it on all our advertising. Even without the nameplate, I need to have this vintage machine working for our celebrations.

Regards,

Stella

153. What is indicated about the espresso machine?

(A) It is a symbol of the Café Marti.
(B) It has never worked very well.
(C) It was designed by Stan Anyati.
(D) It is ten years old.

154. What is suggested about the brass holder?

(A) It has been redesigned.
(B) It will need to be re-created.
(C) The machine can function without it.
(D) The manufacturer in Italy sent it to the wrong address.

To:	Department Managers
From:	Margaret Langley
Date:	December 27
Subject:	Extended-absence greeting
Attachment:	📎 Sample message #5

Dear Managers,

In preparation for the upcoming holiday when offices will be closed, I'd like to remind you that company policy requires each of our departments to replace the traditional greeting on their voice messaging systems with an extended-absence greeting that will play next week when callers are diverted to voice mail. This will involve making a new recording, saving it to the system, and programming the system to activate the recording at the close of our business day on Friday. Once you activate the extended-absence greeting, it will override the traditional greeting through the holiday.

The attached document contains the text of the greeting you should record. This is the same text we have used in the past, but as usual, the dates have been changed to reflect the current closure. Please use this document to record your holiday greeting. Make sure you activate it before you leave for the day on Friday.

155. What is the subject of the e-mail?

(A) A newly established company policy
(B) An improved way to access voice mail
(C) A procedure related to a holiday closing
(D) A change to the traditional shift schedule

156. What is included as an attachment?

(A) A script to be read aloud
(B) A flyer announcing a company event
(C) Instructions for installing a new phone
(D) Transcripts of recorded customer calls

157. What is indicated in the e-mail about the attached document?

(A) It is ready for publication.
(B) It is distributed annually.
(C) It is handed out to customers.
(D) It is intended only for new employees.

GO ON TO THE NEXT PAGE

Kimfor
Marketing
Solutions

Thank you for your purchase of Kimfor Marketing Solutions e-mail software. We are confident that this product will help you to develop your business.

As an added bonus, we are pleased to announce that free training is offered for all of our products. These short but effective online seminars are a great opportunity for businesses that are new to our products to ensure that they are utilizing the software to its full potential.

Our instructors are professionals who have used our tools to grow their own businesses. For more information and to make a reservation for a seminar, please visit our Web site at kimformarketingsolutions.com/seminarsignup.

---

158. What is one purpose of the notice?

(A) To inform customers about a service
(B) To discuss a new product line
(C) To introduce a marketing instructor
(D) To remind customers of an upcoming deadline

159. According to the notice, what qualification do instructors share?

(A) They have worked for the company for many years.
(B) They are experienced users of the e-mail software.
(C) They participated in designing the software.
(D) They work in the marketing department.

160. The word "grow" in paragraph 3, line 1, is closest in meaning to

(A) become
(B) expand
(C) produce
(D) move

Chef and lifestyle coach Lana Watson has announced her first foray into cosmetics with the launch of a new skin care business. Her Summer Garden skin care line consists solely of products made from organic ingredients and features extracts from plants, fruits, and vegetables. — [1] —.

"I've always served the healthiest possible food in my restaurant," said Ms. Watson. "Natural ingredients nourish our health and beauty from the inside out.

— [2] —. My skin care line utilizes only the vitamins and proteins in foods, such as spinach and cucumber, and combines them to create powerful moisturizers and cleansers that are free from artificial chemicals. — [3] —."

Summer Garden products are suitable for those with dry, sensitive, or combination skin and will be available online and at select retail stores beginning this September. — [4] —.

161. What is the article mainly about?

(A) Local organic farms
(B) Online shopping trends
(C) A new business venture
(D) A company merger

162. What is indicated about Summer Garden products?

(A) They are suitable for all ages.
(B) They are available for purchase now.
(C) They are relatively inexpensive.
(D) They contain no artificial ingredients.

163. In which of the positions marked [1], [2], [3], and [4] does the following sentence best belong?

"It seemed logical to then create products to nurture our skin from the outside in."

(A) [1]
(B) [2]
(C) [3]
(D) [4]

GO ON TO THE NEXT PAGE

Maria Zuccarini 5:30 P.M. Hi. This is my first time using the Dubonville community chat room. Do any neighbors have experience laying a ceramic tile floor?

Yuqiu Wang 5:35 P.M. Hi, Maria. Are you looking to do it yourself? I put in a tile floor in my kitchen last year and did all the work myself. I regret my decision, though.

Maria Zuccarini 5:37 P.M. I want to save money, so I'd rather not hire a professional. But I've never done a project like this on my own before.

Dennis Gurka 5:41 P.M. People who are comfortable with home repairs can lay tile flooring if they watch videos or attend a class. But it does take effort, time, and precision.

Yuqiu Wang 5:44 P.M. In my case, I had helped a friend with a tiling project prior to working on my own kitchen. I also watched several videos on myhomefix.com before getting started. In the future, I'd get professional help, though.

Yuqiu Wang 5:45 P.M. Dennis, do you have experience in this area? Do you think Maria could tackle this project without a professional?

Maria Zuccarini 5:51 P.M. Interesting. Thanks for sharing your experience.

Dennis Gurka 5:58 P.M. I have my own flooring business. Whether she can depends on several factors. Maria, will you need to cut the tile, install a drain, or flatten an uneven floor?

Maria Zuccarini 6:06 P.M. I just need to replace a few broken tiles, but I suspect this is not a job for an amateur. Dennis, is the business in Dubonville? Could you send me your contact information?

Dennis Gurka 6:07 P.M. It's just outside the city limits. It's called Floors Forever. The phone is 642-555-0143.

164. For whom is the chat room intended?

(A) People who live in the same town
(B) People who attend the same online class
(C) People who work together for a large company
(D) People who are planning a trip together

165. At 5:35 P.M., what does Ms. Wang most likely mean when she writes, "I regret my decision, though"?

(A) She did not end up saving money.
(B) She should have hired a professional.
(C) She would have preferred different tiles.
(D) She did not need to remodel her kitchen.

166. What is probably true about Mr. Gurka?

(A) He is Ms. Zuccarini's coworker.
(B) He has broken tiles in his home.
(C) He has a lot of experience laying tiles.
(D) He is taking a class at myhomefix.com.

167. What will Ms. Zuccarini most likely do next?

(A) Go shopping for ceramic tiles
(B) Search for a video on laying tiles
(C) Return a box of broken tiles
(D) Contact a business near Dubonville

TEST 6

GO ON TO THE NEXT PAGE

To:	nora.simmons@heltlx.edu
From:	e.agbayani@periodicalquest.com
Date:	February 28
Subject:	Periodical Quest

Dear Ms. Simmons,

This is a courtesy message to inform you that your monthly Periodical Quest membership fee for March could not be processed due to an expired credit card. To avoid any service disruptions, please visit periodicalquest.com/useraccount and update your billing information. If you have any difficulties, I will be happy to take you through the process.

Incidentally, while reviewing your account I noticed that you are not using our full range of services. As a member, you have unlimited online access to our library of over 3,000 journals, newspapers, and magazines. Additionally, as a professor you can also benefit from our resources for teaching and research purposes. It would seem that you did not complete your member profile when you signed up for our service four months ago. Please take a moment to review your member preferences. We want to make sure that you are taking advantage of all that Periodical Quest has to offer.

Feel free to contact me if you have any questions regarding your account. If you wish to cancel your membership, no further action is required.

Sincerely,

Elena Agbayani
Periodical Quest

168. Why was Ms. Simmons contacted?

(A) A new service is now available.
(B) A payment was not processed.
(C) An order will be delivered soon.
(D) An article needs to be revised.

169. What is indicated about Periodical Quest?

(A) It charges a monthly fee.
(B) It has just doubled its journal collection.
(C) Its Web site is easy to navigate.
(D) Its customer support team is available 24 hours a day.

170. What is indicated about Ms. Simmons?

(A) She works in the field of education.
(B) She recently e-mailed customer service.
(C) She has been a Periodical Quest member for many years.
(D) She intends to cancel her Periodical Quest membership.

171. Who most likely is Ms. Agbayani?

(A) A magazine editor
(B) A bank representative
(C) A computer programmer
(D) An accounts manager

GO ON TO THE NEXT PAGE

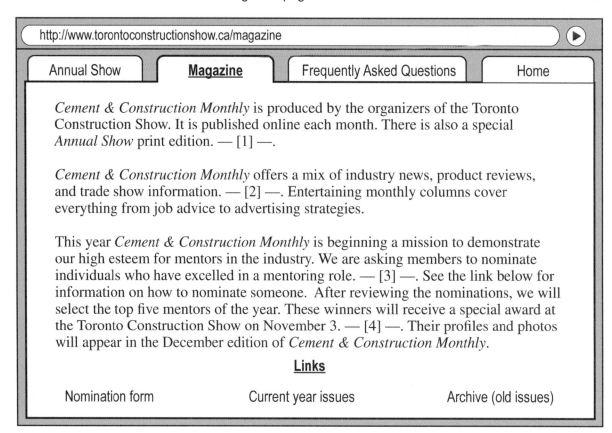

http://www.torontoconstructionshow.ca/magazine

| Annual Show | **Magazine** | Frequently Asked Questions | Home |

Cement & Construction Monthly is produced by the organizers of the Toronto Construction Show. It is published online each month. There is also a special *Annual Show* print edition. — [1] —.

Cement & Construction Monthly offers a mix of industry news, product reviews, and trade show information. — [2] —. Entertaining monthly columns cover everything from job advice to advertising strategies.

This year *Cement & Construction Monthly* is beginning a mission to demonstrate our high esteem for mentors in the industry. We are asking members to nominate individuals who have excelled in a mentoring role. — [3] —. See the link below for information on how to nominate someone. After reviewing the nominations, we will select the top five mentors of the year. These winners will receive a special award at the Toronto Construction Show on November 3. — [4] —. Their profiles and photos will appear in the December edition of *Cement & Construction Monthly*.

Links

Nomination form   Current year issues   Archive (old issues)

172. What is a purpose of the Web page?

(A) To explain a registration process
(B) To update a convention schedule
(C) To review a product
(D) To promote a trade publication

173. What new feature is being announced?

(A) A plan to honor mentors
(B) An online discussion forum
(C) On-site job interviews
(D) Monthly advice columns

174. What will happen on November 3 ?

(A) A special news report will be shown.
(B) Awards will be given out.
(C) Election results will be published.
(D) A photo collection will be displayed.

175. In which of the positions marked [1], [2], [3], and [4] does the following sentence best belong?

"This is distributed to all registered visitors to the show."

(A) [1]
(B) [2]
(C) [3]
(D) [4]

GO ON TO THE NEXT PAGE

62nd Annual Samsville Home and Garden Show
March 31 to April 2, Samsville Conference Pavilion

Exhibitor Application

Company name: Castillo Landscape Design
Contact name: Valia Castillo
Phone: 302-555-0198
E-mail: vcastillo@castillold.com
Web site: www.castillold.com

Items/services to be exhibited:
I will display photographs, plans, and models of available outdoor design services that my company offers.

Additional information or requests:
I would like to request a second parking pass since one of my employees will also be attending and helping to transport materials.

NOTE: This application is not a contract and does not guarantee a booth at the show. Space is available on a first-come basis. Once your completed application is received, a coordinator will contact you within five business days to finalize your reservation and payment. Discounts for members of Samsville Home and Garden will be automatically applied at the time of payment. Any questions can be directed to our exhibition organizer, Ms. Faye Li, at fli@samsvillehg.org. All applications are due by January 31.

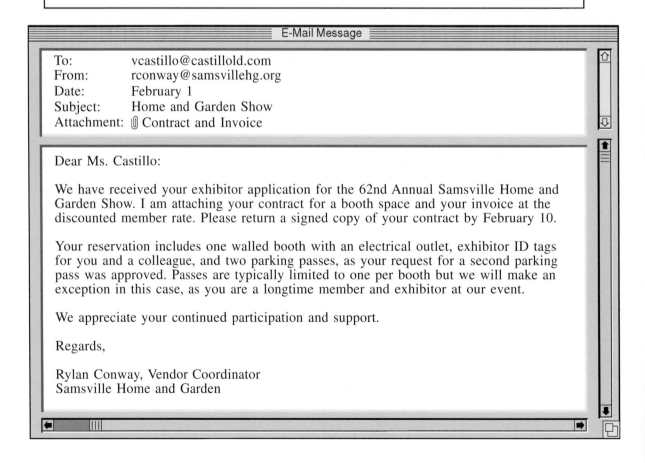

E-Mail Message

To: vcastillo@castillold.com
From: rconway@samsvillehg.org
Date: February 1
Subject: Home and Garden Show
Attachment: 📎 Contract and Invoice

Dear Ms. Castillo:

We have received your exhibitor application for the 62nd Annual Samsville Home and Garden Show. I am attaching your contract for a booth space and your invoice at the discounted member rate. Please return a signed copy of your contract by February 10.

Your reservation includes one walled booth with an electrical outlet, exhibitor ID tags for you and a colleague, and two parking passes, as your request for a second parking pass was approved. Passes are typically limited to one per booth but we will make an exception in this case, as you are a longtime member and exhibitor at our event.

We appreciate your continued participation and support.

Regards,

Rylan Conway, Vendor Coordinator
Samsville Home and Garden

176. What is Ms. Castillo planning to bring to the show?

(A) Pictures of gardens
(B) Sample trees and plants
(C) Sample project estimates
(D) Gardening tools

177. What is typically included in a booth reservation?

(A) An exhibitor sign
(B) A parking permit
(C) An annual membership
(D) A directory of local vendors

178. When did Ms. Castillo most likely submit her application?

(A) In January
(B) In February
(C) In March
(D) In April

179. What is suggested about Ms. Castillo?

(A) She works at Samsville Home and Garden.
(B) She has lived in Samsville for ten years.
(C) She requested an additional electrical outlet.
(D) She will pay a reduced price for her booth space.

180. Why does Mr. Conway make an exception for Ms. Castillo?

(A) She is a past organizer for the event.
(B) She often participates in the show.
(C) She agreed to pay an extra fee.
(D) She submitted a very strong application.

TEST 6

GO ON TO THE NEXT PAGE

http://www.projectelements.com

| Team Plans | About Us | Resources | FAQ |

All of your project management needs—All in one place—All online.

Project Elements LLC develops project management software for use in companies both small and large. Our proprietary software will serve you from start to finish, helping your teams to communicate, schedule, and manage information.

Team Basic

Get your team of five started with our Basic solution. Task management, file sharing, and mobile accessibility will be at your fingertips. Add 100 GB of online data storage space in the cloud for a small additional fee.

Team Creative

This option is the best solution for small teams of up to 35 creative professionals. In addition to all the Team Basic features, get video editing tools, graphic design software, and 300 GB of cloud storage for all of your design needs.

Team Player

Teams of up to 50 excel with this enhanced service. Get all the features of Team Basic, plus timelines, advanced integration with second-party platforms, and up to 400 GB of cloud space for your team.

Team Leader

This option is best for teams of up to 100. Get all of the features of Team Player, plus enhanced options for personalization, resource tracking, time tracking, 500 GB of cloud space, and fast video uploads for a seamless team experience.

Need more convincing? We were recognized for our software quality with the Gold Star Start-Up Awards by *Work Winner Magazine* two years in a row. To hear more about Project Elements success stories, check out our client testimonials in the About Us tab.

To:	ebennis@projectelements.com
From:	jasbury@clarelcommunications.com
Subject:	Project Elements Upgrade
Date:	December 5

Dear Mr. Bennis,

I am the new director of digital advertising for Clarel Communications. Robert Roust, the former director, told me how valuable the Project Elements platform has been, and I want to explore with you a potential change in Clarel's current plan. We are presently a team of 45 but anticipate growing to 55 members over the next year. The team likes the storage feature, but they would be interested in a plan with more than 400 GB and better personalization options. Is there a plan that will fit our needs?

Looking forward to hearing from you,

Julia Asbury
Director of Digital Advertising
Clarel Communications

181. How would Project Elements software most likely be used?

(A) For ordering products online
(B) For working together as a team
(C) For training new managers
(D) For monitoring social media posts

182. What is true about Project Elements LLC?

(A) It has received an industry award.
(B) It has been in business for over ten years.
(C) It purchased Clarel Communications.
(D) It publishes a technology magazine.

183. Why was the e-mail sent?

(A) To register a product
(B) To request technical help with a product
(C) To explain a product registration issue
(D) To seek advice in choosing a product

184. Which product will Mr. Bennis probably recommend?

(A) Team Basic
(B) Team Creative
(C) Team Player
(D) Team Leader

185. In the e-mail, the word "fit" in paragraph 1, line 6, is closest in meaning to

(A) match
(B) agree to
(C) rely on
(D) adjust

GO ON TO THE NEXT PAGE

Ride-Away Vehicles Summer Special

Save 15 percent off our rates* during the month of July for travel within Ireland.

Compact Car €21
Standard Car €32
Full-Size Sedan €46
Van €52

Call 020 917 1212 or book online at www.ride-awayvehicles.co.ie.

*Price advertised is the daily rate for eligible drivers, inclusive of value-added tax (VAT) and the basic protection plan. Additional fees may apply. Please contact a Ride-Away Vehicles representative for more information.

To:	yayoiadachi@jrengineering.co.jp
From:	info@rideawayvehicles.co.ie
Date:	14 July
Subject:	Reservation confirmation - #122055

Dear Ms. Adachi,

Your car rental reservation is confirmed. Here are the details per the terms of your rental:

Pickup: 21 July, 9:00 A.M. at Ride-Away Vehicles, Shannon Airport, Shannon, Ireland

Drop-Off: 29 July, 5:00 P.M. at Ride-Away Vehicles, Cork City Centre, Cork City, Ireland

Rate: €21/day X 8 days = €168 (includes unlimited mileage and navigational system/GPS)

Model: Colaba Seasider or similar

Important Information: The driver must present a valid driving licence at pickup. Additional charges may apply for any changes to the reservation, including changes to the pickup or drop-off date, time, or location. A €25 service fee will be assessed for vehicles returned without a full tank of petrol in addition to the cost of fuel.

Thank you for choosing Ride-Away Vehicles. Please call 020 917 1212 with any questions.

Ride-Away Vehicles Return Form

Completed By: _Henry Riordan, Assistant Manager, Cork City Centre location_

Driver Name: _Yayoi Adachi_   Date/Time of Return: _29 July, 4:40 P.M._

Model/Number Plate: Condition of Vehicle: _No damage_
Colaba Seasider, 161-C-45329
          Odometer Reading:
Gas Tank: _Half full_   _33,763 kilometers_

Yayoi Adachi
Driver's Signature

---

186. What is Ride-Away Vehicles advertising?

(A) A free day of rental
(B) A reduced daily rate
(C) A free upgrade to a larger vehicle
(D) A waiver of additional fees

187. What will happen on July 21 ?

(A) A promotion period will end.
(B) A confirmation will be sent.
(C) Ms. Adachi will be at Shannon Airport.
(D) Ms. Adachi will add a driver to her contract.

188. What does the e-mail indicate about Ride-Away Vehicles?

(A) They operate from multiple locations.
(B) They charge a fee for the use of a GPS.
(C) They apply a discount on rentals one week or longer.
(D) They receive payment before confirming a reservation.

189. What type of vehicle did Ms. Adachi rent?

(A) A compact car
(B) A standard car
(C) A full-size sedan
(D) A van

190. What is suggested about Ms. Adachi?

(A) She did not receive a GPS.
(B) She returned her car late.
(C) She did not get the car she requested.
(D) She will be charged a €25 service fee.

GO ON TO THE NEXT PAGE

http://www.styleno.com/printers/RD525

| Home | Computers | **Printers** | Ink & Toner | Accessories | Support |

Product: Stylero RD525 Three-in-One Printer

Price: Regularly $120.00 Now $99.99 (Offer valid March 1–March 15)

Includes one complimentary Stylero-01 (black) ink cartridge with purchase! Stylero color ink cartridges sold separately.

The RD525 is one of our most popular models: a wireless color printer, scanner, and photocopier in one. It's perfect for everyday printing needs in homes, classrooms, and small offices. Though compatible with many brands of ink cartridges, we recommend our own Stylero-brand ink, which lasts up to twice as long as other products. A three-year warranty is available for $7.95.

---

http://www.loveitornot.com/productreviews/stylero/RD525

(April 3) I bought the Stylero RD525 last month for my home office. I give digital photography lessons out of my home several nights per week and need easy access to color prints for my students' work in my classes. I haven't had any trouble with the photocopier or scanner, and the quality of the prints is excellent in both color and in black and white. However, I've been experiencing delays with the printer feature at times. There is a five-minute lag between sending my prints from the computer and when the printing actually begins. I can't use this device for instant prints in class, or I lose valuable class time. I wish I'd bought a different printer, or at least bought the warranty to get it repaired!

Alicia Boisvert

(April 5) I bought this printer for my classroom and noticed the same issue that Ms. Boisvert described. There is a relatively simple fix though. Most printers go into "sleep mode" to conserve energy between prints. If the length of time before entering sleep mode is set for too short a time, there will be a delay between sending the photos from the computer and the actual printing because the printer will need to warm up each time. Make sure you adjust the sleep mode feature to wait at least an hour before going to sleep. The instructions are in the manual. I always turn the printer on a few minutes before class and it doesn't pose an issue. It's an easy adjustment and I think the RD525 is a good product for the price.

Antonio Thompson

191. What is indicated about the Stylero RD525 ?

(A) It requires Stylero brand ink.
(B) It can function as a photocopier.
(C) It was sold at a discount for a month.
(D) It will be discontinued after March 15.

192. What did Ms. Boisvert most likely spend additional money on?

(A) A monitor
(B) A three-year warranty
(C) A scanner
(D) Color ink cartridges

193. What does Ms. Boisvert say about the Stylero RD525 ?

(A) It is durable.
(B) It produces good prints.
(C) It is expensive.
(D) It requires regular maintenance.

194. What is suggested about both Ms. Boisvert and Mr. Thompson?

(A) They are teachers.
(B) They returned the Stylero RD525.
(C) They enjoy photography.
(D) They have printers at home.

195. What advice does Mr. Thompson give regarding the Stylero RD525 ?

(A) Unplug it between uses.
(B) Replace its power button.
(C) Adjust one of its features.
(D) Turn it on an hour in advance.

TEST 6

GO ON TO THE NEXT PAGE

Baardsen Laundry Machine Series

Model	Load Capacity	Loading Door Position	Automatic Detergent Dispenser	Pre-wash Cycle
Lute	9 kg	Front	Yes	No
Xenon	10 kg	Front	No	No
Indium	12 kg	Front	Yes	Yes
Mercury	14 kg	Front	Yes	Yes

Note: Baardsen washers with a load size greater than 10 kg are outfitted with Fluxstat water-saving technology.

Issue with Baardsen
Posted by: Patricia Canton

I bought my Baardsen washing machine five months ago for use at my bed and breakfast inn. Overall, I have been satisfied with the appliance features. The extra rinse cycle is helpful for guests who are sensitive to chemicals or perfumes in laundry detergent. I needed a washer with the largest capacity so it could handle my typical volume of bed linens and towels. The main issue with my machine has been an annoying banging sound. It happens sometimes when the guests use the machine. It is a problem because the laundry room is situated just off the patio where guests often dine. I sent a message to the company asking for help and they informed me that the load needs to be evenly distributed in the wash tub. But that didn't prove to be the source of the problem. How can I get rid of this noise?

Patty's Bed and Breakfast Guest Services:

Kitchen:

Enjoy the lovely spring weather by taking your breakfast, served between 8:00 and 9:30 A.M., on the patio. We offer self-service for coffee and tea around the clock. The household coffeemaker and tea kettle are next to the stove, and supplies are stored in the cupboard nearby.

Laundry Room:

Fresh towels are provided daily and bed linens are changed weekly. If you would like to use the washing machine, please choose the eco-saving setting. Select your preferred temperature and power setting. When adding detergent, make sure the detergent drawer is closed tightly before you start the machine. If not properly secured, it may open during the rinse cycle and cause a bothersome noise. Also, the extra-rinse option is recommended if you have any sensitivity to laundry soap.

Patricia Canton, Proprietor

---

196. According to the chart, what is true about all Baardsen laundry-machine models?

(A) They use the same water-saving feature.
(B) They are energy efficient.
(C) They release laundry detergent automatically.
(D) They are loaded through a door on the front of the appliance.

197. What washing machine model did Ms. Canton most likely purchase?

(A) Lute
(B) Xenon
(C) Indium
(D) Mercury

198. According to Ms. Canton's query, when is a noise particularly annoying?

(A) When she uses the machine
(B) When guests of the inn are sleeping
(C) When guests of the inn are eating
(D) When the laundry dryer is also running

199. According to the notice, what is available to guests at any time?

(A) Fresh towels
(B) Hot beverages
(C) Box lunches
(D) Refrigerators in guest rooms

200. What advice did Ms. Canton most likely receive as a reply to her query?

(A) Avoid overloading the washing machine.
(B) Always use the water-saving setting.
(C) Always select the extra-rinse feature.
(D) Ensure that the soap drawer is firmly closed.

Stop! This is the end of the test. If you finish before time is called, you may go back to Parts 5, 6, and 7 and check your work.

토익® 정기시험
기출문제집

RC

기출 TEST

07

READING TEST

In the Reading test, you will read a variety of texts and answer several different types of reading comprehension questions. The entire Reading test will last 75 minutes. There are three parts, and directions are given for each part. You are encouraged to answer as many questions as possible within the time allowed.

You must mark your answers on the separate answer sheet. Do not write your answers in your test book.

PART 5

Directions: A word or phrase is missing in each of the sentences below. Four answer choices are given below each sentence. Select the best answer to complete the sentence. Then mark the letter (A), (B), (C), or (D) on your answer sheet.

101. If ------- are not satisfied with an item, return it for a full refund within 30 days of purchase.
    (A) you
    (B) your
    (C) yours
    (D) yourself

102. The location of next month's online gaming forum is yet to be -------.
    (A) concluded
    (B) prevented
    (C) invited
    (D) decided

103. Guests were ------- with the table decorations for the company banquet.
    (A) impressive
    (B) impressed
    (C) impressing
    (D) impressively

104. The Shubert Company is ------- effective at helping power plants reduce their carbon dioxide emissions.
    (A) once
    (B) far
    (C) early
    (D) very

105. Mr. Hodges ------- that volunteers sign up to assist with the Hannock River cleanup by Friday.
    (A) requesting
    (B) to be requested
    (C) requests
    (D) to request

106. Last year, the *Daejeon English News* ------- the number of readers by adding a digital subscription option.
    (A) needed
    (B) increased
    (C) joined
    (D) asked

107. Before the updated design can go into -------, it must be approved by management.
    (A) product
    (B) producer
    (C) productive
    (D) production

108. The economic development summit will be held ------- the Xi'an Trade Tower on September 22.
    (A) to
    (B) at
    (C) down
    (D) of

109. Inclement weather was ------- responsible for the low turnout at Saturday's Exton Music Festival.
(A) largely
(B) large
(C) largest
(D) larger

110. Our most recent survey was sent to clients just last week, ------- it is too soon to send another one.
(A) when
(B) since
(C) so
(D) finally

111. ------- necklace that is shipped from Gillis Designers is given a thorough quality check.
(A) Whenever
(B) Also
(C) All
(D) Each

112. Ms. Valdez' sales numbers are good ------- for her to be considered for the employee-of-the-month award.
(A) forward
(B) even
(C) ahead
(D) enough

113. Aaron Park's new book features photographs of homes designed and built by the homeowners -------.
(A) itself
(B) himself
(C) themselves
(D) ourselves

114. It is ------- for the audience to hold its applause until the speaker has finished.
(A) enthusiastic
(B) casual
(C) exclusive
(D) customary

115. Despite ------- that Legend Air would perform poorly with the entry of cheaper competition, it posted strong second-quarter earnings.
(A) predicted
(B) predictable
(C) predicts
(D) predictions

116. Mr. Nigam was ------- retirement when his boss asked him to be the head of security at the new facility.
(A) under
(B) ahead of
(C) nearby
(D) close to

117. Main Street Restaurant offers a menu of ------- prepared lunch and dinner meals.
(A) thought
(B) thoughtfulness
(C) thoughts
(D) thoughtfully

118. ------- our public relations manager, Ms. Ghazarian has just been appointed vice president of media relations.
(A) Sincerely
(B) Immediately
(C) Solely
(D) Formerly

119. Videos of Korean pop music have become very popular ------- adolescents worldwide.
(A) including
(B) whereas
(C) among
(D) within

120. Milante Shoes ------- altered the firm's marketing strategy after a recent economic shift.
(A) quick
(B) quickest
(C) quickly
(D) quicken

GO ON TO THE NEXT PAGE

121. The annual report has been posted online, ------- the director's office has not yet received a printed copy.
(A) but
(B) why
(C) with
(D) once

122. Hasin Fariz turned a study on the ------- effects of sleep into a best-selling book.
(A) favorable
(B) favor
(C) favors
(D) favorably

123. Wynston Containers is ------- a yearly shutdown of its factory so that it can be evaluated for safety and efficiency.
(A) involving
(B) participating
(C) implementing
(D) producing

124. The Girard Botanical Archive has almost 300,000 plant -------, all neatly pressed onto archival paper.
(A) authorities
(B) specimens
(C) founders
(D) specifics

125. Hotels and universities are ------- to recycle their used mattresses through the city's recycling program.
(A) systematic
(B) eligible
(C) familiar
(D) successful

126. The ------- to review plans to replace the Tronton Bridge will be scheduled soon.
(A) heard
(B) hears
(C) hearing
(D) hear

127. Kovox Ltd. aims to optimize quality ------- reducing the impact on the environment.
(A) which
(B) while
(C) because
(D) unless

128. The grocery store ------- vegetables from out of town until local prices went down last month.
(A) is buying
(B) will be buying
(C) has been buying
(D) had been buying

129. All Hershel Industries employees must have a valid ID card ------- enter the building.
(A) in order to
(B) as long as
(C) regarding
(D) always

130. ------- and cost factored equally in choosing Cantavox as our main supplier.
(A) Reliability
(B) Allowance
(C) Dependence
(D) Estimation

PART 6

Directions: Read the texts that follow. A word, phrase, or sentence is missing in parts of each text. Four answer choices for each question are given below the text. Select the best answer to complete the text. Then mark the letter (A), (B), (C), or (D) on your answer sheet.

Questions 131-134 refer to the following letter.

Dear PGD Account Holder,

PGD Bank strives ------- the highest levels of client security and service. This applies not only to
     131.
online- and telephone-based services, but also to our brick-and-mortar locations. Our three

branch offices have proudly been a part of the community ------- a combined total of 40 years.
     132.

To assist you even better in the future, our Smithville branch will be temporarily closed for

renovations July 8–22. ------- . In the meantime, our other two regional branches in Pine Grove and
     133.
Bradford will maintain normal business ------- . We value your feedback and will respond to any
     134.
concerns that you may have as soon as possible.

Sincerely,

Edwin Chen, Operations Manager
PGD Bank

131. (A) to provide
    (B) provided
    (C) providing
    (D) to be provided

132. (A) except
    (B) amid
    (C) near
    (D) for

133. (A) Unfortunately, services will be limited.
    (B) We thank you for trusting in PGD Bank
       over these years.
    (C) We apologize for any inconvenience
       this may cause.
    (D) Traffic on the boulevard has increased
       lately.

134. (A) investments
    (B) hiring
    (C) hours
    (D) interests

GO ON TO THE NEXT PAGE

To: Samuel Archerson <sarcherson@vona.co.uk>

From: James Darrers <jdarrers@sky.co.uk>

Date: 10 January

Subject: Cost Accountant position

Dear Mr. Archerson,

Thank you for taking the time to meet with me today. I ------- our conversation, and I remain very
                                                       135.

interested in the position of cost accountant. I would welcome the opportunity to return for the

third and final round of ------- .
                          136.

I am confident my years of accounting experience would benefit your firm. As discussed, over the

last ten years, I have helped many companies save a ------- amount of money. I am especially
                                                     137.

adept at analysing the day-to-day operations of a business and helping to determine more

cost-effective methods.

I checked regarding your question about a potential start date. ------- . I hope to hear from you in
                                                                138.

the near future.

Sincerely,

James Darrers

135. (A) enjoy
     (B) enjoyed
     (C) enjoying
     (D) will enjoy

136. (A) revisions
     (B) promotions
     (C) interviews
     (D) receptions

137. (A) substance
     (B) substantiate
     (C) substantially
     (D) substantial

138. (A) I have four additional questions to ask
         you.
     (B) I would be able to begin during the first
         week of February.
     (C) I am confident I have the potential for this
         position.
     (D) Thank you for the offer of employment.

To: Mason Wu <mwu@wustudios.co.nz>
From: Trent Tuiloma <ttuiloma@canterburyairport.co.nz>
Subject: Canterbury Airport project
Date: Monday, 2 July

Dear Mr. Wu,

Thank you for agreeing to consult on the Canterbury Airport redesign project. ------- **139.** . As a result, I am particularly eager to hear your ideas about upgrading our main terminal.

Can we meet this week? There are a number of ------- **140.** restaurants near my office. If you are available this Friday, we could meet at Celia's Café on Cumberland Street. I would also like a few of my colleagues to ------- **141.** us. They would appreciate ------- **142.** ways to enhance the airport user's experience.

I look forward to hearing from you soon.

Sincerely,

Trent Tuiloma
Chairman, Canterbury Airport Redesign Team

TEST 7

139. (A) I can meet you when you arrive.
(B) Scheduling flights can be quite tricky.
(C) I have long admired your work on regional airports.
(D) There are several dining options at the airport.

140. (A) excel
(B) excellent
(C) excellently
(D) excelled

141. (A) join
(B) pay
(C) remind
(D) defend

142. (A) to discuss
(B) discussing
(C) discuss
(D) discussed

GO ON TO THE NEXT PAGE

Questions 143-146 refer to the following article.

SHIRESBERRY (February 15)—The second annual Shiresberry Film Festival begins on April 18

and ------- for five weeks. This year's offerings will not be limited to entries from North America and
    143.

Europe. We will also be presenting ------- from Asia and South America. And everyone's favorite
        144.

feature from last year's festival will be back: directors and screenwriters will hold

question-and-answer sessions after their films' initial screening. Make sure you do not miss this

------- event. Tickets always sell out quickly. ------- . Shiresberry Film Club members can now
145.   **146.**

purchase priority tickets. Visit the Shiresberry Theater box office or www.shiresberrytheater.com.

---

143. (A) run
(B) has run
(C) will run
(D) ran

144. (A) movies
(B) clothing
(C) food
(D) books

145. (A) political
(B) popular
(C) practical
(D) preliminary

146. (A) The awards will be presented by
Hunter Johns.
(B) Renovations to the space are nearly
complete.
(C) The later offerings were an even
bigger success.
(D) Sales are open to the general public
on March 3.

Directions: In this part you will read a selection of texts, such as magazine and newspaper articles, e-mails, and instant messages. Each text or set of texts is followed by several questions. Select the best answer for each question and mark the letter (A), (B), (C), or (D) on your answer sheet.

Questions 147-148 refer to the following advertisement.

Sedwick Electronics Hiring Event
March 2, 10 A.M.–5 P.M.
22 Myer Street, Hanover, PA 17331

Sedwick Electronics is opening a new manufacturing facility in Hanover, Pennsylvania, and we need to fill many positions. We offer a wonderful work environment and great benefits to our employees.

Come to the event and hear from employees from our Lancaster facility about their experience, learn about the open positions, and speak with our recruiters. No RSVP is necessary. Bring copies of your résumé.

147. For whom is the advertisement intended?

(A) Recruiters
(B) Job seekers
(C) Local business owners
(D) Current Sedwick Electronics employees

148. What is stated about Sedwick Electronics?

(A) It is moving its headquarters.
(B) It offers a training program for new employees.
(C) It requires employees to wear uniforms.
(D) It will have more than one location.

TEST 7

GO ON TO THE NEXT PAGE

Aguni Plumbing Supply Returns

Beginning March 1 at all Aguni Plumbing Supply locations, customers will be able to come to our stores to return purchases made online. For a complete refund, the return must be made within 30 days of purchase and must be accompanied by a receipt. In addition, the merchandise must be returned in the original packaging, and all components must be included. After 30 days, refunds will be limited to in-store credit only. Defective items may be exchanged for the same item only.

149. What will happen on March 1 ?

(A) A shipment will be returned.
(B) A new policy will go into effect.
(C) A promotional sale will take place.
(D) A customer survey will be published.

150. What is NOT a requirement for a complete refund?

(A) The return must be made at the original purchase location.
(B) The return must be made within a certain time frame.
(C) The item must be returned with all its components.
(D) The item must be returned in the original packaging.

Springfield Community School
Computer Courses

Internet Safety
This course teaches students everything they need to navigate the Web safely.

Course ID	Class Time	Instructor	Room
249800: 01	Tuesday 5:30–7:30 P.M.	Patrick McCann	211
249800: 02	Saturday 1:00–3:00 P.M.	Nora Farid	166

Spreadsheet Basics
This course teaches the basics of online spreadsheets. Students will learn how to create effective charts for calculating and analyzing data clearly and easily.

Course ID	Class Time	Instructor	Room
225810: 01	Thursday 5:30–8:30 P.M.	Remi Sanders	118
225810: 02	Sunday 1:00–4:00 P.M.	Nora Farid	315

TEST 7

151. Why would people enroll in the course taught by Ms. Sanders?

(A) To practice designing Web sites
(B) To improve their Internet searches
(C) To get tips on creating spreadsheets
(D) To learn how to advertise on the Internet

152. What is indicated about Ms. Farid?

(A) She also teaches children.
(B) She is Ms. Sanders' supervisor.
(C) She teaches twice a week.
(D) She used to work as a data analyst.

GO ON TO THE NEXT PAGE

Questions 153-154 refer to the following text-message chain.

Sally Witham (4:47 P.M.)
Hi Wakiko. I just finished up here at the Kyoto store. I'll be on the train that arrives in Tokyo at 11:35 tomorrow morning. How should I get to your location?

Wakiko Ohara (4:48 P.M.)
I'll have an associate pick you up at the station. How do things look in Kyoto?

Sally Witham (4:49 P.M.)
The Kyoto store is doing a great job. It has everything that we at the home office are looking for. Athletic shoes and sandals are displayed according to specifications, and sales associates are friendly and knowledgeable.

Wakiko Ohara (4:51 P.M.)
You should like things here, too. Do you want to begin your visit after lunch, say at 2:00?

Sally Witham (4:52 P.M.)
Sounds good. See you tomorrow.

153. Why did Ms. Witham contact Ms. Ohara?

(A) To review sales figures
(B) To arrange a store visit
(C) To discuss employee performance reviews
(D) To determine the most convenient train to take

154. At 4:51 P.M., what does Ms. Ohara most likely mean when she writes, "You should like things here, too"?

(A) The Tokyo store is being run according to corporate policy.
(B) Ms. Witham will find the athletic shoes she needs.
(C) Ms. Ohara's associate is always punctual.
(D) The Tokyo store is located next to a popular restaurant.

GO ON TO THE NEXT PAGE

Structure: Blaine River Drawbridge	Location: Ridgeline Highway, KM 147
Main span material: Steel girder	Owner: State Highway Agency
Age of structure: 30 years	Report completed by: Vivian Tulio
	Date: October 17

Notes:
The bridge is overall structurally sound. Inform Department of Transportation about small cracks in asphalt.

Bridge component	Rating	Key to ratings
Support elements	4	**1** Failed; immediate closure required
Towers	4	**2** Deteriorated; may fail soon
Road surface	3	**3** Shows deterioration but still functions within acceptable parameters
Drainage features	4	**4** Shows minor wear
Safety barriers	5	**5** New condition
Sidewalk or walkway	6	**6** Not applicable

155. What did Ms. Tulio most likely do?

(A) Make repairs
(B) Hire a contractor
(C) Perform an inspection
(D) Authorize a construction plan

156. What part of the structure is in most need of maintenance?

(A) The support elements
(B) The road surface
(C) The drainage features
(D) The safety barriers

157. What is probably true about the Blaine River Drawbridge?

(A) It was not designed for pedestrian use.
(B) It will be closed for the month of October.
(C) It does not have the required signage.
(D) It is the oldest bridge on the Ridgeline Highway.

Subway Sound to be Upgraded

BOSTON (April 1)—The public address systems at selected subway stations are scheduled to be refurbished, the Transit Authority announced this week. The systems are used to make announcements to commuters both on the platforms and in the stations.

Local commuters welcomed the news, although for some it was long overdue.

"It can be pretty difficult to understand the announcements at some of the stations I use most frequently," said Ian Miller, who has taken the subway to work nearly every week for the past eighteen years. "I had heard the reports about it on TV, and all I can say is that it is about time!"

Some of the systems currently in use are more than 30 years old. Worn-out speakers, wiring, microphones, and amplifiers will be replaced with new, more reliable devices. The work should be completed in October and cost more than $11 million.

Boston's subway system came together in stages over the course of several years. The foundational component of the system's Green Line first opened on Tremont Street in the late 1890s. It was the first of its kind in the United States.

---

158. What is the purpose of the article?

(A) To clarify where subway riders can locate information

(B) To describe improvements at some subway stations

(C) To announce the creation of a new subway line

(D) To explain why subway schedules will be revised

159. How does Mr. Miller feel about the plans?

(A) He expects the project to fail.

(B) He is concerned about the cost.

(C) He believes the work is unnecessary.

(D) He has been waiting for the changes.

160. The word "stages" in paragraph 5, line 2, is closest in meaning to

(A) steps

(B) scenes

(C) train cars

(D) platforms

GO ON TO THE NEXT PAGE

To:	All Staff
From:	Selene Hong
Date:	March 25
Subject:	Reminder

Dear Staff,

I would like to draw your attention to several new procedures regarding business trip expense reports. — [1] —. Beginning next month, business-related dining receipts must be accompanied by a listing of each dinner attendee. Also, please make sure that you do not include receipts for any non-work-related items or activities with your report. — [2] —. Finally, note that our accounting software will now automatically calculate for you the total to be reimbursed. You need only to upload images of your receipts for the software to do this.

I will be happy to respond to your questions. — [3] —. However, I will be flying to Tokyo this Friday to meet clients, so I will not be checking e-mail that day. — [4] —.

Sincerely,

Selene Hong
Assistant Director, Human Resources Department
Datoric Systems

161. What is indicated about Datoric Systems?

(A) It has increased the spending amount allowed for business dinners.
(B) It will adopt new procedures for filing travel expense reports.
(C) It has office locations in several countries.
(D) It plans to hold a company celebration.

162. Why is the accounting software mentioned?

(A) To highlight a special capability it has
(B) To encourage staff to install it
(C) To help employees log on to it
(D) To point out that it will be replaced

163. In which of the positions marked [1], [2], [3], and [4] does the following sentence best belong?

"Following these steps will enable us to quickly issue your reimbursement payment."

(A) [1]
(B) [2]
(C) [3]
(D) [4]

E-Commerce Opening Doors for African Fashion Industry

ADDIS ABABA (6 May)—Africa's role as a consumer of fashion has been on the rise in recent years. This trend is largely due to the emergence of e-commerce, which provides Africans with the opportunity to buy clothing from retailers with no physical presence on the continent.

Perhaps more importantly, though, the growth of e-commerce is enabling small-scale African designers to also become *producers* of fashion, as they showcase their collections to consumers worldwide. African shopping Web sites like Jumjum and Longa are making the work of African designers available for purchase not just throughout the continent, but also as far away as London and New York. — [1] —.

"African designers are finally gaining visibility," says Mazaa Absher, founder of Abbi Sportscore, Africa's fastest-growing athletic footwear company. "We have always had terrific design and production capacity here on the continent, but it was hard getting it out into the world. Now we are generating more sales online than we are in our stores." — [2] —.

Even as Ms. Absher has transformed her company into an international powerhouse, she continues to highlight the advantages of manufacturing its products in her home city of Nazret. — [3] —. Africa's strong textile sector and innovative designs combine tradition and wearability, and this formula is allowing companies like hers to set their sights beyond the continent.

"As more cities in Ethiopia—and all over Africa—improve their manufacturing capacity, it will become easier to reach the rest of the world," says Ms. Absher. — [4] —.

164. What is the main topic of the article?

(A) New trends in marketing athletic footwear
(B) Increased competition in the African clothing market
(C) Recent growth in the African fashion industry
(D) The largest clothing companies in Africa

165. What is indicated about Abbi Sportscore?

(A) It sells its products only online.
(B) It manufactures its shoes in Nazret.
(C) It will be moving its main offices soon.
(D) It was the first shoe company in Ethiopia.

166. What is suggested about the Jumjum and Longa Web sites?

(A) They sell only handcrafted goods.
(B) They receive orders from around the world.
(C) They offer free shipping to London and New York.
(D) They are planning to open retail stores.

167. In which of the positions marked [1], [2], [3], and [4] does the following sentence best belong?

"The city boasts four garment factories, with a fifth scheduled to be built this year in nearby Wonji."

(A) [1]
(B) [2]
(C) [3]
(D) [4]

TEST 7

Questions 168-171 refer to the following text-message chain.

Gary Park (10:23 A.M.)
I e-mailed you the cover design for our September issue a few minutes ago. Did you receive it?

Jill Riley (10:26 A.M.)
Yes, but is this the latest version? I thought we agreed that the background color should be lighter so the article titles are more visible.

Gary Park (10:28 A.M.)
I forgot—sorry about that! I'm just now sending the file with the most recent version.

Jill Riley (10:30 A.M.)
Opening it now… That's more like it. I'll forward it to Graphics and request a sample printout.

Jill Riley (10:35 A.M.)
Good morning, Mr. Ojeda. Our new cover design is ready. When do you think you'll have a chance to work on it?

Frank Ojeda (10:38 A.M.)
Send it to me now. I'll have a print copy ready for your approval after lunch.

168. Where do the people most likely work?

(A) At a bookstore
(B) At a public library
(C) At a television studio
(D) At a magazine publisher

169. Why does Mr. Park apologize?

(A) He sent the wrong file.
(B) He used an old e-mail address.
(C) He missed a project deadline.
(D) He lost an important document.

170. At 10:30 A.M., what does Ms. Riley most likely mean when she writes, "That's more like it"?

(A) The budget is more reasonable.
(B) The color looks better.
(C) The story is more interesting.
(D) The schedule is more realistic.

171. What will Mr. Ojeda do by the afternoon?

(A) Approve a marketing plan
(B) Produce a sample
(C) Repair a printer
(D) Make copies of an agreement

8 February

Ms. Mala Chelvi
60 Jalan Tun Razak
54200 Kuala Lumpur

Dear Ms. Chelvi,

We are delighted to inform you that you have been nominated as a finalist for the Small Business Challenge competition this year. Now in its fifth year, this competition is designed to highlight innovative products and services launched by young entrepreneurs. The Web application that you developed, which provides a means of matching charitable organizations with volunteers, earned one of the top scores from our panel of judges.

In the next round of the challenge, you will participate in a live presentation about your product before a panel of expert judges. The three people with the best presentations will receive one-time grants of MYR 10,000 each to invest in their businesses.

Please go to sbc.org/competition and submit an outline of your presentation, a brief video that clearly illustrates the use of your application, and a passport-sized photograph of yourself. You will also need to sign a consent form allowing us to use your name and photo, if needed, in promotional materials on our Web site. The deadline for submission of these materials is 10 March.

Best regards,

Felix Pang

Felix Pang
Chairperson, Small Business Challenge Committee

TEST 7

172. What is the purpose of the letter?

(A) To seek volunteers for an event
(B) To notify a contest finalist
(C) To sell business consultation services
(D) To offer a small-business loan

173. What does Ms. Chelvi most likely specialize in?

(A) Law
(B) Technology
(C) Finance
(D) Marketing

174. The word "illustrates" in paragraph 3, line 2, is closest in meaning to

(A) represents
(B) translates
(C) lightens
(D) decorates

175. What is Ms. Chelvi asked to do by March 10 ?

(A) Update a Web page design
(B) Give a presentation
(C) Sign a consent form
(D) Pay a fee

GO ON TO THE NEXT PAGE

To:	riedewald@parasur.net.sr
From:	client_services@mhf.ca
Date:	April 2, 12:21 P.M.
Subject:	Your feedback

Dear Mr. Riedewald,

Thank you for filling out the McMann Home Furnishings (MHF) survey. To show our appreciation, we have added reward points to your account. They can be applied to the purchase of products offered online as well as those offered in our retail stores. Clearance items and those priced $15.00 and above may not be purchased using credits.

To use your reward points for an online purchase, select the items you would like to purchase and then check out. At the bottom of the page, select "Apply credits." The value of the applied credits will appear on your order receipt as a special discount.

If you would prefer to use reward points at one of our retail locations, you can do so by logging in to your account on our Web site. Go to the My Rewards page, and then select "Print as a coupon." The coupon will have a bar code that can be scanned at the store's checkout counter.

Sincerely,

Client Services, McMann Home Furnishings

Online Order #1157
McMann Home Furnishings Store
March 19, 11:31 A.M.

Hand-Painted Picture Frame
Quantity: 1
Price: 10.00
Special Discount: -10.00

Sailboat Ceramic Mug
Quantity: 4
Price: 40.00
Clearance Discount: -20.00

Floral Blanket
Quantity: 1
Price: 25.00

Photo Album
Quantity: 1
Price: 34.00
Seasonal Item Discount: -17.00

Item total: 62.00
Shipping: Free
Total: 62.00

176. According to the e-mail, how did Mr. Riedewald receive reward points?

(A) He won an online contest.
(B) He participated in a customer survey.
(C) He spent a certain amount of money.
(D) He returned an item.

177. In the e-mail, the phrase "filling out" in paragraph 1, line 1, is closest in meaning to

(A) emptying
(B) supplying
(C) completing
(D) expanding

178. How can customers apply their reward points in an MHF retail store?

(A) By entering their account number
(B) By entering their phone number
(C) By scanning a coupon's bar code
(D) By going to the Client Services Department

179. According to the receipt, what is true about Mr. Riedewald?

(A) He paid for delivery of the items.
(B) He purchased the items in the evening.
(C) He paid over $70 for all items combined.
(D) He purchased only one item at regular price.

180. What item did Mr. Riedewald most likely purchase using reward credits?

(A) The picture frame
(B) The ceramic mug
(C) The floral blanket
(D) The photo album

GO ON TO THE NEXT PAGE

Two Swan Press
72 Holywell Road, Edinburgh EH8 8PJ

4 December

Mr. Albert Morello
17 Peyton Avenue
Kingston 5
Jamaica, W.I.

Dear Mr. Morello:

Enclosed please find your royalty payment for *Understanding Our Oceans*. You should have recently received an e-mail that listed the sales figures and the royalties due to you for the print and electronic versions of your book.

We are proud to announce that Two Swan Press was given the Publisher of the Year Award by the UK Book Industry in October. We thank the authors who have worked with us since our founding five years ago.

All Two Swan Press authors are entitled to an author discount of 40 percent off any title on our Web site. Simply use the code AUX1417 for your discount.

If you have any questions at all, please do not hesitate to contact me.

Kind regards,

Sarah Wicklin
Sarah Wicklin

Encl.

---

https://www.twoswanpress.co.uk/orderconfirmation

THANK YOU FOR YOUR ORDER!

Special December Offer—free shipping on all orders over £35

Name:	Duncan Booth
E-mail:	mbooth@silvertech.co.uk
Date of purchase:	12 December
Ship to:	Duncan Booth 321 Maslin St. Coatbridge ML5 1LZ, Scotland, UK

1 *Business in Our Lives* by Elaine Schuyler	£75.00
Discount Applied (AUX1417)	−30.00
Balance Due	£45.00
Paid by Credit Card ****5732	

Items from multiple orders may be combined in the same package. We will notify you when your order has shipped.

181. What is a purpose of the letter?

    (A) To ask Mr. Morello to write a book
    (B) To explain an enclosed contract
    (C) To notify Mr. Morello of a payment
    (D) To describe an updated personnel policy

182. What was sent in a previous message to Mr. Morello?

    (A) Incorrect contact information
    (B) Detailed sales numbers
    (C) A list of suggested changes
    (D) A link to an electronic book

183. What does Ms. Wicklin mention about Two Swan Press?

    (A) It moved to a new location in October.
    (B) It has launched a new program for its fifth anniversary.
    (C) It has won an industry award.
    (D) It has decided to focus on scientific publications.

184. What is suggested about Mr. Booth?

    (A) He is a Two Swan Press author.
    (B) He wrote *Business in Our Lives*.
    (C) He is an acquaintance of Mr. Morello.
    (D) He has purchased items from Two Swan Press before.

185. What is indicated about the order?

    (A) It has been delayed.
    (B) It has not yet been paid.
    (C) It contains multiple books.
    (D) It includes free shipping.

GO ON TO THE NEXT PAGE

To:	All Staff
From:	Personnel Department
Date:	June 20
Subject:	Mentoring Program
Attachment:	📎 Application

Employees who have been with Broadside Electronics for less than eighteen months are invited to apply to participate in a new mentoring program that will match a maximum of ten junior employees with long-term company veterans. The goal is that junior employees will sharpen corporate skills, better understand company culture, and develop a more focused career path. Mentees will be assigned to a mentor based strictly on their work assignment and professional interests. The pairs will meet at mutually convenient times throughout the year, from three to five hours per month.

To be considered for participation in this initiative, complete the attached application and return to Mentoring Program Director Tim Wrigley at t.wrigley@broadsideelec.com by July 1. Mr. Wrigley will send notification of his selections by July 15.

MENTORING PROGRAM APPLICATION

Name: <u>Cara Drummond</u>   Extension: <u>144</u>

Division: <u>Sales</u>

Professional areas of interest:
<u>I am most interested in learning about our markets abroad and developing my sales-presentation abilities for these international markets. I am also interested in general career guidance.</u>

Best workdays and times for meeting:
<u>Any weekday morning except Monday.</u>

The Broadside Company Newsletter

Mentoring Program Sees Results

Long-time employee and Vice President of Sales Alena Russo was intrigued when a Personnel Department director approached her about mentoring a less experienced employee under a program that began last year. She is glad to have accepted the assignment. "After working with Ms. Drummond, I am more satisfied with my own duties, because I know I have helped a professional who is just getting started. I only wish that I had had someone looking out for me in my early years," remarked Ms. Russo.

Ms. Drummond explains that she "needed pointers on how to make better sales pitches." She reports that her sales are up by 20 percent now. She better understands the opportunities Broadside Electronics has to offer and what is required to become a manager. "Thanks to Ms. Russo, I have been able to define my career goals, and I am a happier person when I arrive to work every day."

New mentorship pairs are now being formed. Interested parties should contact Tim Wrigley in the Personnel Department.

---

186. What does the e-mail indicate about the mentoring program?

(A) It is popular industry-wide.
(B) The number of participants is limited.
(C) It is designed for staff in the sales division.
(D) Participants must attend an orientation meeting.

187. How will the junior employees most likely be selected?

(A) They will be chosen from a management-training group.
(B) They will undergo competitive interviews.
(C) They will be evaluated by Mr. Wrigley.
(D) They will be recommended by a local business school.

188. What is suggested about Ms. Drummond?

(A) She has worked at Broadside Electronics for less than eighteen months.
(B) She has just transferred from another department.
(C) She has received a positive annual review.
(D) She has made many successful presentations abroad.

189. What is most likely true about Ms. Russo?

(A) She is planning to retire soon.
(B) She has international sales experience.
(C) She has mentored many junior employees.
(D) She recently joined the hiring team.

190. What benefit from the mentoring program have both Ms. Drummond and Ms. Russo enjoyed?

(A) Increased job satisfaction
(B) Quick promotions
(C) Paycheck bonuses
(D) Clearer career goals

GO ON TO THE NEXT PAGE

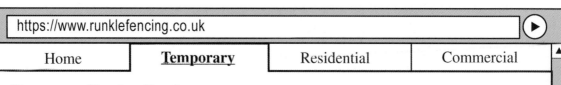

https://www.runklefencing.co.uk ▶

| Home | **Temporary** | Residential | Commercial | ▲ |

Temporary Fencing Service

Need a temporary fence installed at your residence, workplace, or special event? Our expert team will deliver and install chain-link fencing on the booked date and time. When the fence is no longer needed, we will take it down and haul it away. Like our residential and commercial fencing, our temporary fences are obtained from the best manufacturers using the finest materials. Our fences have a tidy, sturdy, professional appearance that local residents and businesses appreciate. We also see to all legally required inspections and certifications.

Ready for a price quote? Contact us today via our Online Quote service. Be sure to provide the following information so we can provide an accurate estimate:

1. The preferred height of your fence (Be aware that local regulations commonly allow a maximum height of three metres.)
2. The perimeter of the area you need to enclose
3. The number of gated entrances needed
4. The number of days the fence needs to be up

| **Name:** | Marguerite Carhart | **Phone:** (0117) 555-9102 |

Installation Address: 438 Stretford Way, Bristol BS5 7TB
E-mail: mcarhart@stockporteventcentre.co.uk
Today's date: 8 August

Fence Details:

I need a temporary three-metre-tall fence installed around the Stockport Event Centre within the next two weeks. This is to prevent the public from entering while we make renovations from 18 to 30 August. Two gates are needed so that workers and vehicles may enter and leave the location.

To:	mcarhart@stockporteventcentre.co.uk
From:	hmontalbo@runklefencing.co.uk
Date:	9 August
Subject:	Quote Number 080817
Attachment:	📎 fencequote_mcarhart

Dear Ms. Carhart,

Thank you for your enquiry. Please see the attached estimate for the work you requested. Note that the price of delivery is included at no further charge unless a rush order—one providing less than three weeks' notice—is required. This is a rough estimate based on the information you provided. If you ring us at (0117) 555-2938 and provide us with a missing detail, I can give you a more accurate quote.

You might also consider including a plastic curtain with your order. This would be wrapped around and fastened to the fence, hiding the construction site from the view of pedestrians. If this interests you, we can include it in the revised quote.

Best Regards,

Howard Montalbo

191. What does the Web site indicate about fences taller than three meters?

(A) They are made of plastic.
(B) They are usually prohibited by law.
(C) They require special transportation.
(D) They must be ordered directly from the manufacturer.

192. According to the form, why does Ms. Carhart need a temporary fence installed?

(A) To mark a property line
(B) To draw attention to an exhibit
(C) To control a crowd at a special event
(D) To limit public access to a work site

193. What information does Ms. Carhart fail to give about the fence she needs?

(A) The height of the fence to be erected
(B) The dates when the fence is needed
(C) The perimeter of the area to be enclosed
(D) The number of entrances needed

194. What is implied about Ms. Carhart's fence project?

(A) There will be a charge for delivery.
(B) The project involves work at several job sites.
(C) Extra workers must be hired to install the fence.
(D) Inspectors must first approve the project.

195. Why does Mr. Montalbo recommend adding a curtain?

(A) It would act as a noise barrier.
(B) It would help keep in dust.
(C) It would serve as a visual screen.
(D) It would improve safety conditions.

GO ON TO THE NEXT PAGE

To:	Daniel Rodrigues Pereira
From:	Livia Romero
Subject:	Company outing
Date:	August 5

Hello Daniel,

I hope you are settling in well. I'm sure you have had a busy few weeks. Around this time of year, the office manager typically begins arranging our annual company outing. I think we mentioned this during your interview in June. Previously, we have done things like going to a concert and taking a local river cruise. The outing is always great for morale, and everyone looks forward to it.

This year, I think it would be a good idea to get tickets to a sporting event. I know that many staff members are fans of the San Jose Starlings baseball team. It should be an evening game when the team is playing at home. We have a budget of $600.00 this year. Looking at the ticket prices, it seems that will be just enough to get a ticket for every staff member.

I'm sure Elise can assist you with this; she has often helped organize the outings. Let me know if you have any questions.

Best,

Livia Romero
Director of Administration, Loftgren Consulting

Plan your next event with the San Jose Starlings!

Discounted tickets are available for groups of ten or more. The more tickets you buy, the more you save —perfect for family gatherings, company outings, or charity fund-raisers! Get perks such as free tickets for the organizer, discounts on food, and your group's name displayed on the scoreboard.

Group Ticket Pricing

10 tickets	$130.00
30 tickets	$360.00
50 tickets	$550.00
70 tickets	$700.00

Contact **grouptickets@sanjosestarlings.com** or call **408-555-0101** for more information.

Date	Day	Time	Opposing Team	Home or Away
San Jose Starlings				
August Schedule				
August 13	Sunday	1:05 P.M.	Aspen Monarchs	Home
August 15	Tuesday	7:05 P.M.	Aspen Monarchs	Home
August 19	Saturday	1:05 P.M.	Philipsburg Pinstripes	Away
August 22	Tuesday	7:05 P.M.	Philipsburg Pinstripes	Away

Purchase tickets online at **www.sanjosestarlings.com/tickets**.

196. Why did Ms. Romero send the e-mail to Mr. Rodrigues Pereira?

(A) To tell him about an upcoming budget cut
(B) To invite him to a concert
(C) To introduce him to his new assistant
(D) To ask him to arrange an event

197. What does the e-mail imply about Mr. Rodrigues Pereira?

(A) He recently attended a San Jose Starlings game.
(B) He will be leaving in a few weeks to go on vacation.
(C) He is a professional party planner.
(D) He recently began working for Loftgren Consulting.

198. According to the flyer, what is a benefit of buying tickets as a group?

(A) Reduced ticket prices
(B) Free food
(C) Front-row seating
(D) T-shirts with the team's logo

199. How many employees does Loftgren Consulting most likely have?

(A) 10
(B) 30
(C) 50
(D) 70

200. On what date could Loftgren Consulting employees attend a game?

(A) August 13
(B) August 15
(C) August 19
(D) August 22

Stop! This is the end of the test. If you finish before time is called, you may go back to Parts 5, 6, and 7 and check your work.

토익 정기시험
기출문제집

RC

ETS TEST

08

READING TEST

In the Reading test, you will read a variety of texts and answer several different types of reading comprehension questions. The entire Reading test will last 75 minutes. There are three parts, and directions are given for each part. You are encouraged to answer as many questions as possible within the time allowed.

You must mark your answers on the separate answer sheet. Do not write your answers in your test book.

PART 5

Directions: A word or phrase is missing in each of the sentences below. Four answer choices are given below each sentence. Select the best answer to complete the sentence. Then mark the letter (A), (B), (C), or (D) on your answer sheet.

---

101. Ms. Villanueva has extensive experience in corporate ------- and budgeting.

(A) financially
(B) financed
(C) financial
(D) finance

102. Because Mr. Lewis works so -------, he was given a pay raise.

(A) bright
(B) hard
(C) tight
(D) sharp

103. Full of old-fashioned charm, the Bronstad Inn ------- offers modern conveniences.

(A) plus
(B) else
(C) also
(D) less

104. Franklin Bookstore will be moving next month ------- a larger location on Queen Street.

(A) to
(B) at
(C) out
(D) over

105. Marina Hou ------- considered becoming an actor before deciding to write plays instead.

(A) briefly
(B) briefs
(C) briefing
(D) briefed

106. On Fixit Time's Web site, homeowners will find economical solutions for ------- repairs.

(A) dark
(B) broken
(C) cleaning
(D) common

107. Walter Keegan was ------- hired as a salesperson, but he soon became head of the marketing department.

(A) originality
(B) original
(C) originals
(D) originally

108. Durr Island has become popular with tourists ------- its rich culture of art and music.

(A) provided that
(B) because of
(C) even
(D) how

109. While he is not enthusiastic about the suggestions, Mr. Shang ------- them.

(A) considering
(B) to consider
(C) will consider
(D) consider

110. The design ------- of Tavalyo Toys has been relocated to the company's headquarters.

(A) division
(B) specification
(C) allowance
(D) construction

111. The Merrick Travel Agency organizes tours of national monuments and other ------- sites in the St. Petersburg area.

(A) historian
(B) historic
(C) historically
(D) histories

112. The MHS wireless speaker not only works with smartphones ------- is waterproof as well.

(A) but
(B) and
(C) however
(D) besides

113. Assistant managers are largely responsible for the day-to-day operations in ------- departments.

(A) theirs
(B) them
(C) their
(D) they

114. Customers must ------- review the terms of the fitness center's membership agreement before they sign it.

(A) smoothly
(B) probably
(C) legibly
(D) thoroughly

115. We made a ------- estimate of how many tourists to expect in the coming month.

(A) conservative
(B) conservation
(C) conservatism
(D) conservatively

116. Once they have completed three years of employment, the workers at Loruja ------- additional vacation time.

(A) reserve
(B) earn
(C) continue
(D) find

117. ------- has time at the end of the day should make sure that all of the file cabinets are locked.

(A) Whom
(B) Who
(C) Whoever
(D) Whose

118. North River Linens promises next-day shipping ------- Asia.

(A) without
(B) between
(C) throughout
(D) along

119. ------- last year, the unpublished novel by Martin Sim has attracted intense interest from several publishing companies.

(A) Discover
(B) Discovery
(C) Discovered
(D) Discovering

120. Hoonton Realty clients can search property listings in ------- neighborhood by using a special online database.

(A) other
(B) several
(C) all
(D) any

GO ON TO THE NEXT PAGE

121. Exceptional service is what sets our hotels apart from those of our -------.
    - (A) compete
    - (B) competing
    - (C) competitive
    - (D) competition

122. The Internet connection will be closely monitored ------- the source of the slowdown can be confirmed.
    - (A) why
    - (B) until
    - (C) due to
    - (D) just as

123. Thank you for being one of Danton Transportation's most ------- customers over the past ten years.
    - (A) valuation
    - (B) valued
    - (C) value
    - (D) values

124. Mr. Tang is a successful recruiter because he can quickly ------- talented sales agents from the rest.
    - (A) distinguish
    - (B) persuade
    - (C) alter
    - (D) assist

125. Ms. Penner assured us that ------- work stopped during the power failure, production targets would be met.
    - (A) although
    - (B) at
    - (C) her
    - (D) never

126. Please provide the exact dimensions of the custom fence you would like built, and your quote will be adjusted -------.
    - (A) namely
    - (B) accordingly
    - (C) frequently
    - (D) supposedly

127. The vice president of Chestonville Bank believes that ------- employees is vital to the company's success.
    - (A) empowered
    - (B) empower
    - (C) empowering
    - (D) empowers

128. The ------- for the city council's Monday meeting is posted on the municipal Web site by 3:00 P.M. on the preceding Friday.
    - (A) catalog
    - (B) inventory
    - (C) agenda
    - (D) record

129. The building inspector declared the new facility ------- sound and ready to open.
    - (A) structured
    - (B) structuring
    - (C) structural
    - (D) structurally

130. Dr. Huertas received the ------- Brighton Award for her groundbreaking work in plant biology.
    - (A) overwhelmed
    - (B) intentional
    - (C) prestigious
    - (D) deserving

PART 6

Directions: Read the texts that follow. A word, phrase, or sentence is missing in parts of each text. Four answer choices for each question are given below the text. Select the best answer to complete the text. Then mark the letter (A), (B), (C), or (D) on your answer sheet.

Questions 131-134 refer to the following e-mail.

To: All Staff
From: George Ruiz
Date: Wednesday, 18 July
Subject: Important guests

Food critics from two ------- newspapers, the *Toronto Day* and *Toronto Rising*, are expected to dine
        131.
here this week. Let's make a special effort to do our work flawlessly.

Photographs of the critics will be placed at our welcome station. Using these ------- , hosts will be
                                                                              132.
responsible for identifying the critics and telling the wait staff, who should alert the kitchen.

Servers must strive to be prompt. They should also recommend our daily specials.

------- .
133.

I am confident that everyone ------- these critics with our great food and service.
                              134.

Thank you,

George Ruiz
General Manager

131. (A) local
     (B) locals
     (C) locally
     (D) more locally

132. (A) reviews
     (B) issues
     (C) menus
     (D) images

133. (A) These are the most creative dishes we
         offer.
     (B) We have already placed an
         advertisement.
     (C) Work schedules are posted by the rear
         entrance.
     (D) One of them was unhappy with the
         timing.

134. (A) impressed
     (B) will impress
     (C) is impressing
     (D) has impressed

GO ON TO THE NEXT PAGE

Cherville Simplifies Local Tourism

10 May—The city of Cherville boasts charming architecture and a breathtaking countryside that has long been appreciated by residents. Thanks to the recent introduction of a train service, tourists are now able to ------- the city as well. As a result of Cherville's rise in popularity, existing
135.
tourism-related businesses are booming. ------- .
136.

To help tourists and businesses, the Cherville Commerce Bureau has debuted the Citycard. When swiped, the card automatically applies ------- at local businesses and attractions. The Bureau
137.
believes that the Citycard will please tourists, who will benefit from lower prices. ------- , the card
138.
should encourage retail traffic, leading to increased profits for businesses.

135. (A) revisit
(B) enjoy
(C) depart
(D) bypass

136. (A) Furthermore, the architect will be building a tower.
(B) The mayor will be giving a welcome speech.
(C) The train allows locals to travel more easily.
(D) In fact, restaurants and hotels keep opening.

137. (A) discounts
(B) discounted
(C) to discount
(D) discounting

138. (A) Instead
(B) Until then
(C) At the same time
(D) Despite that

To: All Macaw Store Managers
From: Mary Van Vliet, Chief Technology Officer
Date: 22 May
Re: Payment system upgrade

Next week new payment processing terminals will be installed at each sales register in Macaw stores located in St. Thomas. Payment System 4.0 ------ in our stores in Puerto Rico for several months.
139.
So far, no issues with the system have been reported by ------ customers or managers there.
140.

------ . It is faster and handles more transaction types than the current payment system. It also
141
eliminates the need for ------ verification of transactions under $25.00.
142.

Please feel free to contact me with any questions about the installation.

---

139. (A) to operate
(B) will operate
(C) is operating
(D) has operated

140. (A) like
(B) extra
(C) either
(D) total

141. (A) Payment System 4.0 offers a variety of benefits.
(B) New payroll software will be released soon.
(C) We are having a special sale in June.
(D) I will e-mail each of you the exact installation date.

142. (A) available
(B) additional
(C) reserved
(D) economical

GO ON TO THE NEXT PAGE

Questions 143-146 refer to the following review.

App Review: Forward Path

In the world of ------- apps, those developed by Arvedlon, Inc., stand out for their innovation and
     143.

ease of use. The newly released Forward Path app ------- tablets and smartphones is no
     144.

exception. Forward Path connects with home exercise equipment such as stationary bicycles

and rowing machines. Users can select video footage of dozens of real-world routes. Then they

can choose from several speed options ------- the video to the pace of their workouts.
     145.

------- . While nothing can replace an outdoor workout, Forward Path comes closer than any
146.

other app currently on the market. Our testers highly recommend it.

---

143. (A) translation
   (B) fitness
   (C) landscaping
   (D) navigation

144. (A) into
   (B) by
   (C) near
   (D) for

145. (A) to time
   (B) time
   (C) are timing
   (D) timed

146. (A) They can even specify the weather
      conditions and season.
   (B) The choices are somewhat limited
      compared to other apps.
   (C) At this price, it should be very popular.
   (D) The minimum is 30 minutes a day.

PART 7

Directions: In this part you will read a selection of texts, such as magazine and newspaper articles, e-mails, and instant messages. Each text or set of texts is followed by several questions. Select the best answer for each question and mark the letter (A), (B), (C), or (D) on your answer sheet.

Questions 147-148 refer to the following notice.

Area Traffic Alert and Transportation Authority Update

The Regional Transportation Authority will begin repairing and replacing signs on Highway 675 in January. The new signs are designed to be more reflective and thus easier to read. They will also be better located.

Most of the activity will entail partial closures of thruway lanes at night when the traffic volume is lowest. Vehicular traffic during the daytime will not be affected. The work is expected to last six to eight weeks; all scheduled activities are weather dependent.

---

147. What is the purpose of the notice?

(A) To warn about increased traffic
(B) To outline work-zone safety tips
(C) To describe an improvement project
(D) To announce plans for a new highway

148. What is a feature of the new signs?

(A) They will last much longer.
(B) They come in many colors.
(C) They are significantly larger.
(D) They offer improved readability.

GO ON TO THE NEXT PAGE

Lorene Industries
Reimbursement Request Form

Name: Timothy Oswell   **Supervisor's name:** Laura Cho
Department: Advertising
ID: 8123976
Position: Project manager
Itemized expenses:

Date	Description	Cost
28/1	Travel to meeting	£3
28/1	Lunch with Yannick Le Mignon, Mazzira Group	£55
28/1	Return travel to office	£3
	Total reimbursement	**£61**

Funds will not be issued to employees without itemized receipts. Credits for claimed reimbursements will be added to the employee's regular biweekly paycheck. Amounts over £100 will not be processed during the current pay period. Instead, they will be reimbursed at the end of the following quarter.

Employee signature: *Timothy Oswell*
Supervisor signature: *Laura Cho*

Form received date: 30/1   **Receipts attached?** Yes

Finance department reimbursement officer approval: Tia Jegerfalk

---

149. What can be reimbursed using the form?

(A) Only amounts less than £100
(B) Only transportation costs
(C) Only charges submitted with a receipt
(D) Only the expenses of senior staff members

150. What is suggested about Mr. Oswell?

(A) He used a company credit card.
(B) He gets paid at the end of every week.
(C) He conducted business with a new client.
(D) He will receive a credit with his next paycheck.

To:	All Staff
From:	Takashi Imura
Sent:	Thursday, October 07, 9:04 A.M.
Subject:	Elevator inspections

The City Code Enforcement Office will perform annual elevator inspections beginning at 11:00 A.M. tomorrow. — [1] —. The purpose is to ensure that our elevators meet all safety requirements. Our elevators are well maintained, so I do not anticipate any problems.

There will be periods when individual elevators will be out of service. — [2] —. However, at least one elevator in the building will be in service at any given time. The testing is officially scheduled to last until 2:00 P.M. I will send an e-mail to let you know when all elevators are in service again. — [3] —. A message will also be posted on the building's Facilities Web site.

We apologize for any inconvenience caused by the inspection process, and we will work to minimize the impact on staff and clients using the building. — [4] —.

Takashi Imura, Building Supervisor

151. How often are the elevators inspected?

(A) Once a month
(B) Every six months
(C) Once a year
(D) Every two years

152. Why might the inspection be inconvenient for staff and clients?

(A) Offices on the top floor will be closed after 11:00 A.M.
(B) An elevator they often use may not be working.
(C) The elevators will be out of service until 2:00 P.M. Monday.
(D) Officials may have to operate some elevators for riders.

153. In which of the positions marked [1], [2], [3], and [4] does the following sentence best belong?

"Thank you for your patience, and let me know if you have any questions."

(A) [1]
(B) [2]
(C) [3]
(D) [4]

TEST 8

Katie Milerre: (10:36 A.M.)
Mr. del Mar, I'm finalizing the catering order for next month's client-appreciation banquet. We haven't received responses from our clients at Hartford and Mason Law Firm. Should I call to confirm with them?

Alberto del Mar: (10:38 A.M.)
No, that's not necessary. I spoke with Mr. Hartford yesterday, and he told me they won't be able to make it. They'll be traveling out of state for an appointment that day.

Katie Milerre: (10:39 A.M.)
I see. Would you like me to have a gift basket sent to their office since they won't be attending?

Alberto del Mar: (10:41 A.M.)
Yes. Please also include a gift card to the restaurant where the banquet is being held and an invitation to attend lunch with me there at a later date.

Katie Milerre: (10:42 A.M.)
Certainly. I will bring the card to your office this afternoon for a signature.

Alberto del Mar: (10:42 A.M.)
Thank you, Katie.

154. What is indicated about Mr. Hartford?

(A) He is unable to attend an upcoming event.
(B) He will contact Ms. Milerre in the afternoon.
(C) He is organizing a conference.
(D) He has not made travel plans yet.

155. At 10:39 A.M., what does Ms. Milerre most likely mean when she says, "I see"?

(A) She is looking at some information about a client.
(B) She understands an explanation provided by Mr. del Mar.
(C) She is currently viewing some photographs of gift baskets.
(D) She knows that Mr. del Mar wants her to purchase a card.

I have spent most of my life in the woods of rural Colorado, where I have always looked to the beauty of nature for inspiration. My plates, bowls, and cutting boards are hand carved from pieces of wood that were foraged from fallen trees that I discovered while on various hikes through the forest.

Each object in my wooden kitchenware collection is one of a kind and has been carved to bring out the natural curves and grain patterns of the wood. These unique pieces can last a lifetime if stored and treated properly. They should never be left to soak in water, as prolonged exposure to water will cause them to warp. It is also a good idea to apply a light coat of mineral oil from time to time to prevent the colors from fading. For more tips on how to best protect your natural wood product from deterioration, visit www.hollyhollingsworth.com. Thank you for purchasing my products!

— Holly Hollingsworth

156. Where would the information most likely be found?

(A) Inside a package with a product
(B) Near a piece of art in a museum
(C) In an article in a nature magazine
(D) In an advertisement in a newspaper

157. According to the information, what can readers do on a Web site?

(A) Browse new items available for sale
(B) Compare the different types of wood
(C) Read detailed product-care instructions
(D) Learn about wood-carving techniques

TEST 8

Pernely Hotel

Thank you for choosing Pernely Hotel for your recent event! Please take a moment to fill out this survey. We hope you will share your positive experience with associates and friends. If we receive a booking based on your referral, we will give you a 5% discount on the cost of your next event.

Customer name and e-mail: _Aika Otani, a.otani@bipmail.com_

Event date: _April 6_

Event location: _Oakwood Dining Room_

Please rate the following aspects of your experience with us. (N/A = not applicable)

	Poor	Fair	Good	Excellent	N/A
Quality of food				X	
Quantity of food			X		
Friendliness of staff				X	
Room setup/atmosphere	X				
Overnight accommodations					X

Comments/Suggestions:

The Pernely event coordinator provided excellent support in putting this annual event together. The food was delicious—the guests raved about the roast chicken! The dining room got quite noisy as it filled up. We will plan to use Pernely again next year, though we will definitely request a different room.

---

158. How can Ms. Otani become eligible for a discount?

(A) By booking an event before April 6
(B) By referring someone who books an event
(C) By reserving a block of hotel rooms
(D) By completing an online survey

159. What problem did Ms. Otani experience?

(A) There was too much noise.
(B) There was not enough food.
(C) The menu was limited.
(D) The room was small.

160. What is NOT indicated on the form?

(A) The guests enjoyed the food.
(B) The event was held in the Oakwood Dining Room.
(C) Many of Ms. Otani's guests stayed overnight.
(D) A Pernely Hotel staff member helped with planning.

Questions 161-163 refer to the following article.

CAPE TOWN (26 October)—Locally based Roebling Vision announced yesterday that it will be merging with Novianto Technology, headquartered in Nairobi, Kenya. This action will allow Roebling Vision to expand its research division to include a team that specializes in cutting-edge vision technology.

"There is no doubt that we will be releasing new eyewear solutions in the upcoming year," said Roebling Vision CEO Obakeng Van Dyk. "With our joint efforts, there will be no limit to what we can do."

Before the two companies join forces, Roebling Vision's laboratories in Johannesburg will be expanded to be able to accommodate a much larger workforce.

Headquartered here in Cape Town, Roebling Vision has centres throughout the country. Its popularity grew about ten years ago, after several South African celebrities began wearing Roebling glasses. The company is best known for manufacturing eyeglasses and contact lenses. Less known is the fact that it also has a small division devoted to research and technology located in Johannesburg.

---

161. What is the purpose of the article?

(A) To critique new types of eyewear
(B) To report on the opening of a vision center
(C) To announce the uniting of two companies
(D) To discuss recent fashion trends

162. What will Roebling Vision do soon?

(A) Increase its laboratory capacity
(B) Move its headquarters to Nairobi
(C) Discontinue a product line
(D) Hire a new CEO

163. The phrase "devoted to" in paragraph 4, line 8, is closest in meaning to

(A) admiring of
(B) focused on
(C) elected to
(D) supported by

GO ON TO THE NEXT PAGE

Questions 164-167 refer to the following online chat discussion.

Marguerite Ogus (9:30 A.M.)
Hi, team. How are we progressing on the free Healthy Lifestyle series for our employees?

Peter Jellis (9:31 A.M.)
As we discussed at our lunch meeting in the cafeteria in February, we're starting with nutrition.

Taewon Yoon (9:31 A.M.)
I talked to Adam Rickert, who writes the column on healthy living for our hospital newsletter.

Peter Jellis (9:32 A.M.)
So are we on target to start the series on March 1, Taewon?

Marguerite Ogus (9:33 A.M.)
Marvelous. I remember seeing his interview on television about the need for quality sleep. Is he comfortable with presenting live in front of people?

Peter Jellis (9:34 A.M.)
Well, last month he delivered a major conference presentation.

Taewon Yoon (9:34 A.M.)
Yes. Adam Rickert committed to doing the first three sessions in the series.

Marguerite Ogus (9:35 A.M.)
Good. What about the room?

Peter Jellis (9:36 A.M.)
The atrium on the north side of the hospital has been reserved through May for the full series.

Taewon Yoon (9:37 A.M.)
And we have already chosen the second topic in the series: physical fitness.

Marguerite Ogus (9:38 A.M.)
Excellent. Let's move on to picking the third speaker of the series, who will discuss the importance of social relationships in our April sessions.

---

164. What is suggested about the speaker series?

(A) It will include lunch.
(B) It will be held in a hospital.
(C) It will be open to the public.
(D) It will be shown on television.

165. At 9:33 A.M., what does Ms. Ogus mean when she writes, "Marvelous"?

(A) She is satisfied with the latest newsletter.
(B) She is pleased that Mr. Jellis has joined the chat.
(C) She is happy with Mr. Yoon's choice of speaker.
(D) She is glad to speak as part of the series.

166. When is Mr. Rickert scheduled to speak?

(A) In February
(B) In March
(C) In April
(D) In May

167. According to the chat, what topic will most likely NOT be discussed in the speaker series?

(A) Physical exercise
(B) Eating well
(C) Sleep habits
(D) Healthy relationships

LONG ISLAND REGIONAL ENERGY AUTHORITY
Residential Audit

Prepared for customer: Darrah Henninger

Property address: 337 Barrel Street, Hempstead, NY 11550

Reason for audit request: The customer reported unusually high energy bills and an inefficient cooling system during the warmest months.

Date of visit: August 26

Inspection summary: The building size is approximately 366 square meters, and there is an exterior air-conditioning unit on the west side of the structure. — [1] —. The unit was installed new and is six years old.

The size of the cooling unit is more than sufficient for the building size. — [2] —. However, the return air flows through a vent that is too small. Expanding the current vent size or creating an additional vent on an adjacent wall will correct this issue.

The building has a vaulted metal roof that is poorly insulated. Reinsulating the roof is recommended. — [3] —. The use of ceiling fans on the upper level should be avoided in the warm months. Because the roof is not insulated well, the fans use an excessive amount of energy to combat the heat transfer through the ceiling during the summer, and therefore the rooms cannot be adequately cooled.

This audit has been performed by a certified energy auditor. — [4] —.

Audit prepared by: Kevin Anders

---

168. Why most likely did Ms. Henninger request the audit service?

(A) She would like to enlarge her living space.
(B) She needs some heating equipment repaired.
(C) She is interested in purchasing a property.
(D) She wants to lower her summer energy costs.

169. What is indicated about the air-conditioning unit?

(A) It is an adequate size.
(B) It has a satisfactory venting system.
(C) It is a discontinued model.
(D) It has been producing warm air.

170. What does Mr. Anders advise about the ceiling fans?

(A) They should be replaced.
(B) They should be reinstalled in other locations.
(C) They should be used instead of the air-conditioning unit.
(D) They should be turned off for part of the year.

171. In which of the positions marked [1], [2], [3], and [4] does the following sentence best belong?

"This should be a top priority."

(A) [1]
(B) [2]
(C) [3]
(D) [4]

Questions 172-175 refer to the following conference schedule.

Conference Schedule for May 25
7:00–8:00 A.M.   **Registration** (main auditorium, ground floor)
8:00–9:15 A.M.   **Software Solutions** Learn about the latest and best software systems for keeping track of fleets and product shipments and for facilitating communication between drivers and dispatchers. Instructor: Nicklas Massen
9:30–10:30 A.M.   **Air Cargo Units** Explore new insights into air cargo operations in the areas of domestic and overseas transport, calculating rates and charges, safeguarding valuable items, and troubleshooting possible complications. Instructor: Ezinne Chioke
10:45–11:45 A.M.   **Effective Driver Training** It's the law! The National Transportation Council holds employers responsible for ensuring that all drivers are familiar with government laws and requirements. The latest rule updates will be addressed as will tips on how to organize an effective training program. Instructor: Ching-Lien Wu
12:00–1:00 P.M.   **Maintaining Vehicle Fleets** Examine recent trends in managing fleets of vehicles (cars, buses, trucks, and delivery equipment), which include anticipating and controlling the costs associated with vehicles, mechanics, drivers, vendors, and fuel consumption. Instructor: Nicklas Massen
All sessions will be held in the Geneva Conference Room on the fourth floor, except the 12 P.M. session, which will be held in the Harkness Conference Room on the second floor. Presenters who need help setting up should see Facilities staff in room G14.

172. Who most likely would attend the conference?

(A) Transportation company owners
(B) Computer software programmers
(C) Truck and bus drivers
(D) Business management professors

173. What is NOT a subject likely to be covered during the 9:30 A.M. session?

(A) Pricing
(B) International shipments
(C) Solving common difficulties
(D) Improving staff communication

174. When will the session on following regulations be held?

(A) At 8:00 A.M.
(B) At 9:30 A.M.
(C) At 10:45 A.M.
(D) At 12:00 P.M.

175. Where will Ms. Chioke lead her session?

(A) In the main auditorium
(B) In the Geneva Conference Room
(C) In the Harkness Conference Room
(D) In room G14

TEST 8

GO ON TO THE NEXT PAGE

Placid Moon Coffee
March Sales Report—Prepared April 4 by Cora Lin, Store Manager
In-Store Sales of All Products

Product	Revenue	Notes
Coffee, whole bean, one-pound bags	$14,000	Overall, sales revenue was higher. Bags of whole-bean Misty Heights Blend were a top seller, bringing in just over $3,000.
Coffee, prepared drinks	$18,200	A number of drinks were not offered while the espresso machine was being serviced. Sales should recover in April.
Tea, prepared drinks	$5,500	Sales are comparable with previous months.
Bottled drinks	$2,200	Sales are comparable with previous months.
Baked goods	$3,400	This is a 7 percent increase from last month.
Retail (nonperishable goods)	$750	Placid Moon Coffee mugs are still out of stock as our vendor has not yet fulfilled our order.
March Promotion		
Customer loyalty program	N/A	Few loyalty discount cards were distributed to customers this month. We should better train staff in promoting this benefit.

E-mail

To:	coralin@placidmooncoffee.com
From:	tyrellharris@placidmooncoffee.com
Date:	April 4, 6:23 P.M.
Subject:	Re: March sales report

Thank you for promptly submitting your March report. I'm pleased with the strong sales of the new whole-bean product we introduced last month. Let's keep a close eye on sales of this coffee blend through April. We may be able to add it to our regular lineup.

I like your suggestion regarding the customer loyalty program. In addition, I propose putting up a poster advertising the cards by the registers and another one in the employee lounge. Please inform me at the end of the month if these efforts have an impact.

Finally, I have good news to share. Yukihiro Asakawa began serving our Bold Macaw variety at his flagship restaurant in December, and he now wants Placid Moon to be the exclusive provider for all his restaurants. This expansion of our business is all thanks to you, since you introduced Mr. Asakawa to our coffee not long ago.

Tyrell Harris
Placid Moon Coffee, Owner

176. What product sold less than expected?

(A) Prepared coffee drinks
(B) Prepared tea drinks
(C) Bottled drinks
(D) Baked goods

177. What problem does Ms. Lin have?

(A) Some desserts did not sell as desired.
(B) Some mugs have not been delivered.
(C) Some coffee beans are out of stock.
(D) Some posters have unclear information.

178. What does Ms. Lin recommend?

(A) A better espresso machine should be purchased.
(B) The customer loyalty program should be discontinued.
(C) Part-time staff should be hired on a permanent basis.
(D) Employees should receive additional training.

179. What is suggested about the Misty Heights Blend?

(A) It was offered for the first time in March.
(B) It will no longer be sold by Placid Moon Coffee.
(C) It is more expensive than other types of coffee.
(D) It has a stronger flavor than other blends.

180. What is most likely true about Ms. Lin?

(A) She agreed to take on an added responsibility.
(B) She requested a new espresso maker from Mr. Harris.
(C) She recommended products to Mr. Asakawa.
(D) She renovated the employee lounge.

GO ON TO THE NEXT PAGE

Audition for a TV Baking Show

DUNMORE, PA—Think you have what it takes to be the next baking star? Get your cake pans and pastry brushes ready because the popular baking competition show, *Toni's Baking Ace*, has just scheduled auditions for its fifth season!

Toni's Baking Ace has become a huge TV hit since it premiered five years ago. The show is named for its celebrated host, pastry chef Adrianna Toni. Long before becoming a TV celebrity, she founded multinational bakery chain TKL Creations and published *Dolce Dancing*, a dessert cookbook that has become a classic.

If you are an amateur baker, that is, if you have never baked as part of a business, you stand a chance of appearing on *Toni's Baking Ace*. The first step is to complete an online application. The show's producers will select about 50 promising candidates and send each an invitation for an in-person interview. Those who make it through this first round will attend an intensive two-day baking audition in front of the TV judges. From this audition, sixteen lucky finalists will be selected as participants to compete for the Baking Ace title!

Have your baked goods always impressed your family and friends? Do not hesitate to submit your application—and get baking!

---

http://www.tonisbakingace.com ▶

| Home | Recipes | Video | **Audition Application** |

Name: Dennis Farah
Phone: 414-555-0112
E-mail: dfarah@chemail.com

• **Current Occupation:**
I have been working as a high school chemistry teacher for the past nine years.

• **When did you begin to bake, and how did you learn?**
I started baking with my father when I was five years old. He loved to bake for family and friends, and I became his kitchen assistant. I can remember researching cooking techniques, watching baking shows, and developing some of my own recipes.

• **Do you have a specialty item?**
Pies, especially because I like to experiment with new pie filling.

• **Why do you want to be on the show?**
I am passionate about baking. I have been watching Toni's Baking Ace since it first aired, and it has greatly increased my own skills, as I have tried out many top recipes that I've seen on the show. Last week a friend heard about this audition, and she persuaded me to submit an application.

• **Have you ever marketed and sold any baked goods?**
My formal baking experience amounts to donating cupcakes to be sold at our school's annual Christmas sale to support the school's sports programs.

Please upload a 60-second video introducing yourself and showing a baked creation of yours. Go to the Video tab to upload your video.

181. What does the article indicate about *Toni's Baking Ace* ?

(A) It accepts teenagers as contestants.
(B) It often selects international participants.
(C) It awards prize money to winners.
(D) It is hosted by a famous author.

182. In the article, the word "hit" in paragraph 2, line 2, is closest in meaning to

(A) success
(B) impact
(C) expense
(D) encouragement

183. What requirement is mentioned in the online application?

(A) Signing a contract
(B) Passing a baking speed competition
(C) Including an introductory video
(D) Participating in a past contest

184. What does Mr. Farah state in his application?

(A) He has a kitchen assistant.
(B) He is an educator.
(C) He has never watched the show.
(D) His father will soon appear on the show.

185. Why most likely does Mr. Farah give details about an annual event?

(A) To show how popular his baking is
(B) To indicate he is familiar with contests
(C) To provide evidence that he is not a professional baker
(D) To prove he can bake with limited equipment

TEST 8

GO ON TO THE NEXT PAGE

https://www.lanarktheater.org/advertise ▼

Advertise with Lanark Theater!

When you place an advertisement in our printed programs, your business will be seen by thousands of our patrons. Our upcoming season has just been announced, and we have an exciting lineup of theater, music, and dance groups that will perform throughout the year. You can feature your business in our programs for a full year or a partial year and also choose the size of your advertisement. The basic advertising options are as follows.

Description	Full Page	Half Page	Quarter Page
Full year (12 months)	$4,165	$2,200	$1,700
Half year (6 months)	$2,550	$1,120	$780
Quarter year (3 months)	$1,330	$760	$440
One-time advertisement	$440	$300	$150

Keep in mind that full-year advertisers receive a special discount card that is good for 15% off tickets for any Lanark Theater event for the duration of the advertising contract!

To get started, submit an advertisement request form. We will contact you to help you select the most suitable advertising package. The request form can be found at www.lanarktheater.org/advertisement-request.

Lanark Theater
Advertisement Request Form

Name: Louise Sanderson

E-mail: l.sanderson@stanmorebistro.com

Phone: 716-555-0145

Company: Stanmore Bistro

Have you advertised with us before? No

How did you learn about this advertising opportunity?
I frequently see performances at Lanark Theater. Not too long ago, I noticed that a friend's business is being advertised in your programs. He is the owner of Braedale Apparel, and he has highly recommended that I advertise my own business in your program as well. I certainly think that Lanark Theater patrons would enjoy dining at my bistro!

What type of advertisement are you interested in?
Full year _____ Half year _X_ Quarter year _____ One-time _____ Not sure _____

What is your maximum budget? $850

To:	Maciej Ritchie <m.ritchie@braedaleapparel.com>
From:	Rosa Chokphel <rosa.chokphel@lanarktheater.org>
Subject:	Advertisement renewal
Date:	December 13

Dear Mr. Ritchie,

Thank you for renewing Braedale Apparel's advertisement package for the upcoming season. You are once again confirmed for a quarter-page advertisement for the full year. We at Lanark Theater could not fulfill our mission of offering the community rich and thought-provoking artistic performances without the help of local businesses like yours!

We also want to thank you for your recent referral. Because of your recommendation, Louise Sanderson will be advertising in our programs. Your support is greatly appreciated!

All the best,

Rosa Chokphel
Marketing Associate, Lanark Theater

186. What is the purpose of the Web page?

(A) To promote upcoming shows
(B) To review recent performances
(C) To announce advertising opportunities
(D) To profile the lineup of performers

187. What is mentioned about Lanark Theater?

(A) It offers a variety of artistic performances.
(B) It advertises in a local newspaper.
(C) It has only recently opened.
(D) It features performances exclusively from local groups.

188. What type of business does Ms. Sanderson own?

(A) An advertising company
(B) A clothing store
(C) A theater
(D) A restaurant

189. What advertisement option will Ms. Sanderson most likely purchase?

(A) A full-page advertisement
(B) A half-page advertisement
(C) A quarter-page advertisement
(D) A one-time advertisement

190. What is suggested about Mr. Ritchie?

(A) He is a co-owner at Stanmore Bistro.
(B) He will receive discounted tickets.
(C) He has upgraded his advertising package.
(D) He prefers music performances to dance performances.

GO ON TO THE NEXT PAGE

http://www.cheverlyartmuseum.com

| Home | About | Exhibits | **Summer Program** | Contact |

After viewing our world-class art exhibits, come and enjoy some free music during Cheverly Art Museum's tenth annual Summer Concert Series. From July 14 through August 4, musical performances will be held either on our Atrium Stage near the main entrance or on our Chillum Stage in the outdoor plaza. Concerts are held from 7–9 P.M. Tickets are $10 in advance or $15 at the door, if still available.

July 14 Atrium Stage
Local trio Killaloe Sounds will start our series off with lively traditional Irish music.

July 21 Atrium Stage
Renowned jazz pianist Lillian Cathey will play soulful songs from her *Keyboard Sway* recording, which has been a best seller for over five years.

July 28 Chillum Stage
The nationally renowned Tulla Stompers play traditional American folk music. The performance will feature Rhianon Lewis on lead vocals, Hector Freeman on banjo, Lynn Truman on mandolin, and Wyatt Davenport on fiddle.

August 4 Chillum Stage
The Hennessy String Quartet will play selections from their recent recording, *Summertime Classics*.

To:	Rhianon Lewis <rhianon.lewis@tgd.com>
From:	James Sabo <j.sabo@cheverlyartmuseum.com>
Subject:	Summer concert performance
Date:	July 17

Dear Ms. Lewis:

I am the program coordinator for the Cheverly Art Museum. We are so excited to have you perform with us this season. Our concerts are always well received and well attended.

Please note that we run a sound check onstage an hour before each performance to make sure that all equipment is working properly, so we recommend that musicians arrive by at least two hours before the scheduled start time. Also, if you or your bandmates need tickets for friends or family members, please let me know, and I will be happy to coordinate it. Tickets are no longer available, but we have a few seats reserved that I can offer you.

I look forward to meeting you!

Sincerely,

James Sabo
Program Coordinator, Cheverly Art Museum

To:	James Sabo <j.sabo@cheverlyartmuseum.com>
From:	Rhianon Lewis <rhianon.lewis@tgd.com>
Subject:	RE: Summer concert performance
Date:	July 17

Hi, James,

Thanks for the information. I will be driving with the group from Arlington, so we are all set for transportation. We plan to arrive at 5:30 p.m.

On a separate matter, I hope it is not too late to request a change in venue. I came to see the July 14 performance, and the group that performed then showed a video on the screen behind them as they played. My group also has images and videos that we would like to display during our performance. I've spoken with the stage manager, and he said that our scheduled space would not allow for such a setup. While these elements are not a necessary part of our show, our audiences have found them to be very powerful; thus, we would love to incorporate them if we can.

Thank you,

Rhianon

---

191. What does the Web page indicate about the concert series?

(A) It is held every year.
(B) It focuses on classical music.
(C) It is open only to museum members.
(D) It is organized by a well-known artist.

192. According to the Web page, what act has recently recorded music?

(A) Killaloe Sounds
(B) Lillian Cathey
(C) The Tulla Stompers
(D) The Hennessy String Quartet

193. What is suggested about the Tulla Stompers concert?

(A) It has already sold out.
(B) It will begin two hours early.
(C) It will feature a local guest musician.
(D) It has been moved to a different date.

194. According to the first e-mail, why should musicians arrive early?

(A) To find parking
(B) To sign a contract
(C) To test sound equipment
(D) To select a stage manager

195. What is indicated about Ms. Lewis?

(A) She recorded a song with Lillian Cathey.
(B) She has requested transportation to Cheverly Art Museum.
(C) She has never used video in her performance before.
(D) She attended a performance by Killaloe Sounds.

TEST 8

Business Outlook Monthly

Articles in the March Issue:

The Right Candidates   **Page 11**
Spot the applicant that will make a difference. Doug Tenor spoke with four
managers about their approach to interviewing.

The Right Questions   **Page 27**
How do the big international corporations look for new employees? Lilly Zimble
visits three of the biggest HR departments in the world to see what goes into job
postings and recruiting.

Being There   **Page 38**
Gina Pimentel looks at the strengths and weaknesses of virtual conferencing.
What is the future for distance meetings, and is this what we want? While useful
for brief meetings, will they ever excel for longer interactions? Surprisingly, some
studies show that virtual conferencing has little effect on employee engagement.

Benefits of the Phrase Book   **Page 44**
Melissa Dyson shares tips on communicating with locals when conducting
business abroad. Clients warm to visitors who make the effort to learn some
of their language.

Extended Stay   **Page 52**
Greg McDaniel went to five hotels in five weeks to experience their extended-stay
options. He details each hotel's pros and cons.

---

http://www.farolgrandehotel.com/updates

The Farol Grande Hotel—Updates

We recently learned that we were reviewed in the March issue of *Business Outlook Monthly*
magazine! The review was performed by an "undercover operation"—the reporter used a
fictional name, posed as a regular guest, and stayed with us for five nights—so we didn't
know he was here until we saw the article! Access the magazine here to read the thorough
analysis of our facilities: http://www.bom.com/currentissues/march.

> *Business Outlook Monthly*
>
> To the Editor:
>
> I read with interest Gina Pimentel's take on the status of videoconferencing and other virtual meeting technologies. Although I sympathize with the author's sentiment that video and conference calls are no real alternative to meetings in person, it seems to be the trend of the future. But even with recent technological advances, in my experience, videoconferences are most effective for short meetings such as status checks. When it comes to negotiations, however, there is nothing like face-to-face interactions.
>
> —Emre Osman

196. How are the first two articles in the magazine similar?

(A) Both discuss employee hiring practices.
(B) Both focus on new uses of technology.
(C) Both discuss how a new position is advertised.
(D) Both critique negative interview behaviors.

197. On what page is there advice for international travelers?

(A) Page 11
(B) Page 27
(C) Page 38
(D) Page 44

198. According to the Web page, what did the reporter do?

(A) He visited the hotel in March.
(B) He hid his real identity.
(C) He canceled a reservation.
(D) He arrived late at night.

199. Who stayed at the Farol Grande Hotel?

(A) Mr. Tenor
(B) Ms. Zimble
(C) Ms. Dyson
(D) Mr. McDaniel

200. On what do Ms. Pimentel and Mr. Osman agree about virtual meetings?

(A) They increase employee engagement.
(B) They should be phased out in the future.
(C) They should replace in-person meetings.
(D) They work well for quick exchanges of information.

Stop! This is the end of the test. If you finish before time is called, you may go back to Parts 5, 6, and 7 and check your work.

토익®정기시험
기출문제집

RC

ETS TEST

09

READING TEST

In the Reading test, you will read a variety of texts and answer several different types of reading comprehension questions. The entire Reading test will last 75 minutes. There are three parts, and directions are given for each part. You are encouraged to answer as many questions as possible within the time allowed.

You must mark your answers on the separate answer sheet. Do not write your answers in your test book.

PART 5

Directions: A word or phrase is missing in each of the sentences below. Four answer choices are given below each sentence. Select the best answer to complete the sentence. Then mark the letter (A), (B), (C), or (D) on your answer sheet.

101. Every batch of sauce at Generita's Bistro is processed meticulously by ------- expert chefs.

(A) they
(B) their
(C) them
(D) themselves

102. Computerization of medical records ------- increases a physician's ability to diagnose and treat patients.

(A) great
(B) greatly
(C) greatness
(D) greatest

103. At Rojelle's Fine Dining, we use the freshest ------- available to make our salads.

(A) applications
(B) subjects
(C) ingredients
(D) factors

104. Professor Benguigui will present his paper ------- the natural history conference tomorrow.

(A) by
(B) at
(C) of
(D) on

105. The chefs are still waiting for a ------- date for the new convection oven that was ordered two weeks ago.

(A) shipper
(B) ships
(C) shipments
(D) shipping

106. Mr. Kang works ------- with our internal team members as well as various regional sales representatives.

(A) mildly
(B) nearly
(C) closely
(D) narrowly

107. Fashion designer Hye-Ja Pak knows ------- to update her line in response to changing tastes.

(A) and
(B) when
(C) need
(D) for

108. The samba class was so well ------- that the Yulara Dance School decided to make the course a permanent offering.

(A) attended
(B) educated
(C) gathered
(D) protected

109. The factory will be situated away ------- the city's residential area to reduce complaints about noise and emissions.

(A) from
(B) about
(C) with
(D) out

110. Ms. Kuramoto selected the most ------- mailing option available.

(A) economical
(B) economy
(C) economize
(D) economized

111. Companies without information technology specialists can ------- on Vyber Software Advisers for assistance with online services.

(A) reliable
(B) reliably
(C) rely
(D) relying

112. Next year, our team will have a new task, ------- is to review design portfolios.

(A) although
(B) which
(C) after
(D) because

113. Cook the meat for 30 minutes to ensure ------- readiness to be eaten.

(A) both
(B) this
(C) its
(D) that

114. Amoxitron's research team will hire ------- interns to assist with laboratory duties.

(A) given
(B) several
(C) whole
(D) natural

115. ------- the new acai juice blend has proved so popular, we should move quickly to increase our production volume.

(A) If
(B) Whether
(C) Since
(D) Unless

116. New emissions standards have forced Rider Auto to modify the process of engine -------.

(A) construction
(B) constructed
(C) constructive
(D) construct

117. Maki Kayano's book offers techniques for ------- business tasks with speed and precision.

(A) executing
(B) equipping
(C) returning
(D) involving

118. To control costs, updated credit card readers will be installed in branch stores -------.

(A) gradual
(B) gradually
(C) more gradual
(D) most gradual

119. In this quarter, the Montel Beverage Company is expecting sales ------- £160,000 and £180,000.

(A) without
(B) among
(C) throughout
(D) between

120. Because Mount Akoyola is so challenging for climbers, ------- have reached its peak.

(A) any
(B) either
(C) other
(D) few

GO ON TO THE NEXT PAGE

121. King Street Bridge will be closed in the month of September ------- repair work.

(A) because of
(B) so that
(C) as if
(D) rather than

122. Ms. Taniguchi's supervisor commended her for negotiating ------- with Furuyama Corporation.

(A) effective
(B) effecting
(C) effected
(D) effectively

123. Staff members may reserve the conference room ------- they need it.

(A) somewhere
(B) whatever
(C) everything
(D) anytime

124. The public relations director must have a high level of ------- in English and Spanish.

(A) proficiency
(B) advancement
(C) routine
(D) strength

125. Patterson Products ------- seeks innovative ways of meeting changing consumer demand.

(A) dually
(B) favorably
(C) continually
(D) generically

126. Mr. Volante is working at home tomorrow so he ------- the technical report without any distractions.

(A) can finish
(B) would finish
(C) finished
(D) has been finishing

127. All of the billing procedures remain the same, ------- new payment codes need to be inserted into the invoice documents.

(A) in order that
(B) during
(C) across from
(D) except that

128. The lightweight design of the new sedan is ------- because it can cause the vehicle to slide on icy roads.

(A) possible
(B) mechanical
(C) questionable
(D) multiple

129. When the bank president retired, the common ------- was that the vice president would take over.

(A) assume
(B) assumption
(C) assuming
(D) assumable

130. West Bengali Airlines ------- fees for oversized items that are still within weight limitations.

(A) invites
(B) cooperates
(C) transports
(D) waives

Directions: Read the texts that follow. A word, phrase, or sentence is missing in parts of each text. Four answer choices for each question are given below the text. Select the best answer to complete the text. Then mark the letter (A), (B), (C), or (D) on your answer sheet.

Questions 131-134 refer to the following e-mail.

To: pmendoza@factmail.co
From: recruiting@analystsassoc.org
Date: May 2
Subject: Joining ASA

Dear Mr. Mendoza,

Thank you for expressing your interest in our organization during the recent ------- . It was a pleasure
131.
meeting you at the ASA booth during the Weber Information Systems Convention. As you may

recall from our conversation, we discussed how ASA membership ------- your career through
132.
networking opportunities as well as the industry insights offered in our monthly newsletter. The

normal fee for members is just $120 a year; however, we are currently offering a new-member

discount. ------- .
133.

If you are still interested in joining, please reply to ------- with your mailing address. I will then
134.
forward you an application packet.

Sincerely,

Ashlee Loren, President
Association of Systems Analysts

131. (A) election
    (B) broadcast
    (C) conference
    (D) performance

132. (A) can benefit
    (B) is benefiting
    (C) has benefited
    (D) will have benefited

133. (A) Discounts on rental cars are included
        in the annual membership.
    (B) Our jobs board is quite comprehensive.
    (C) We are the first organization of our
        kind.
    (D) This month you can join for just half
        the usual rate.

134. (A) it
    (B) me
    (C) them
    (D) anyone

GO ON TO THE NEXT PAGE

To: Sam Heinz
From: Northways Professional Development
Sent: April 20
Subject: Workshop 4/28–4/30

Dear Workshop Participants,

We look forward to seeing you at the digital storytelling workshop. On the first day, when you enter the Albin College campus, attendants will ------- you to lot 43 and the Toteman Building. We will
135.
begin each day in conference room 9. Coffee, tea, snacks, and fruit ------- in the mornings. Lunch
136.
will be sandwiches and salads from Black Horse Restaurant. ------- .
137.

In the afternoons, we will be working in the computer lab. We suggest that you assemble some images that you would like to use for your project. It will be ------- for you to have them saved on a
138.
digital storage device beforehand. If you have any questions, please e-mail us.

Very Best,
Gina Kapuski

135. (A) offer
(B) direct
(C) pass
(D) instruct

136. (A) will be provided
(B) were provided
(C) providers
(D) are providing

137. (A) Some prior experience working with digital files is assumed.
(B) Please do not bring any copyrighted material to the workshop.
(C) Please let us know if you have any dietary restrictions.
(D) There is a one-time parking charge of fifteen dollars.

138. (A) useful
(B) surprised
(C) difficult
(D) amazing

Venley Foods Responsive to Changing Consumers

Who cares where the tomatoes in your salad actually came from? ------- , an increasing number of
139.
people do, according to a study conducted by the Consumer Group. In fact, the study shows that

many consumers would pay an average of 10 percent more when given the exact source of a

fresh food product. ------- . Some grocery stores, such as Venley Foods in Boston, have taken
140.
advantage of the trend and used it to implement ------- branding and marketing. "If we can tell a
141.
story about our product," says Venley Foods CEO Minji Kim, "then we've added ------- in the
142.
minds of consumers."

---

139. (A) Carefully
(B) Apparently
(C) Formerly
(D) Rarely

140. (A) Fresh food can be refrigerated for up
to two days.
(B) Many grocery stores have been
extending their hours.
(C) Most studies are published in
consumer magazines.
(D) The number increases to 20 percent in
large cities.

141. (A) smarts
(B) smartly
(C) smarter
(D) smartness

142. (A) value
(B) time
(C) obstacles
(D) bonus

Nylobe, Inc., Announces Newest Development Project

SEATTLE (May 1)—Researchers at technology firm Nylobe, Inc., are working to develop a sensor capable of detecting corrosion caused by environmental exposure. Corrosion is a major contributor to ------- losses in the aircraft industry each year. "This will be a major ------- for commercial airline
    143.   144.
fleets," says Mel Laveau, Nylobe's CEO. "The sensor will decrease both labor and maintenance costs without being too expensive."

According to Ms. Laveau, the sensor will work by detecting corrosion in its early stages, when the problem can be corrected simply by removing the corroded material. ------- . In the structure of large
                                                145.
aircraft, some critical joints can be particularly susceptible to corrosion. ------- , the sensor can be
                                                            146.
used to inspect these areas and then target the most likely areas of concern.

143. (A) financially
    (B) financed
    (C) financial
    (D) finances

144. (A) balance
    (B) examination
    (C) expectation
    (D) asset

145. (A) This will reduce the need for making expensive structural repairs.
    (B) The parts have all been replaced with higher quality materials.
    (C) The next stage of the project involves scanning the affected areas.
    (D) Its style and sleek design made it popular with the public.

146. (A) Meanwhile
    (B) Similarly
    (C) Otherwise
    (D) Fortunately

Directions: In this part you will read a selection of texts, such as magazine and newspaper articles, e-mails, and instant messages. Each text or set of texts is followed by several questions. Select the best answer for each question and mark the letter (A), (B), (C), or (D) on your answer sheet.

Questions 147-148 refer to the following invoice.

Invoice 3987

Shawqi Office Services, Dubai, UAE
Report requested in English

18 October

Jenkins Press
P.O. Box 2291
Dubai, UAE

Service

On 14 October, replaced bulb and repaired paper tray on copier per call received on 12 October. Replaced copy ink in two machines. Performed routine yearly maintenance on five copiers per existing service contract.

Labor cost	AED 330.00
Paper tray	AED 50.00
Bulb	AED 30.00
Copy ink	AED 220.00
Total	**AED 630.00**

Total amount must be received by 31 October.
Thank you for your business!

147. What is indicated about Jenkins Press?

(A) It has several offices around the world.
(B) Its copiers get checked every year.
(C) Its office equipment is outdated.
(D) It is a new customer of Shawqi Office Services.

148. When is payment due?

(A) October 12
(B) October 14
(C) October 18
(D) October 31

Harbour View Apartment—Porthmadog, Wales

This one-bedroom apartment is perfect for a holiday escape! Located in a quiet area, it boasts a patio with a lovely view of the harbour. Recently renovated, the unit includes an eat-in kitchen with stove, refrigerator, microwave, and coffeepot; bathroom with walk-in shower; and a living room with a large-screen TV. Other amenities of the property include:

• Short distance to restaurants and shops
• Five-minute walk to the beach
• Public gardens and historic sites within a 20-minute drive
• Heat and electricity included
• Towels and bed linens provided on-site
• Daily cleaning service available (extra fee)
• Wireless Internet access (extra fee)

Reserve this lovely gem now! Signing a contract by March 30 will reduce the rental cost by 10 percent. To sign a contract, contact Dylan Barrett at dbarrett@telarentals.co.uk.

---

149. Who would the advertisement most likely interest?

(A) Business travelers
(B) Residents of Porthmadog
(C) Property investors
(D) Short-term vacationers

150. What is indicated about the rental fee?

(A) It includes tours of historic places.
(B) It does not cover all of the apartment's features.
(C) It includes vouchers to use at local restaurants.
(D) It requires a minimum 30 percent deposit in advance.

151. Why should an individual contact Mr. Barrett by March 30 ?

(A) To get a discount on rent
(B) To schedule apartment renovations
(C) To rent the last available property
(D) To sell the property before the end of the season

Jason Salter (1:45 P.M.)
Liz, the meeting is starting in fifteen minutes. Where are you?

Liz Ortiz (1:47 P.M.)
The train has been stopped on the tracks for a while. There seems to be some kind of problem. I still hope to make the meeting.

Jason Salter (1:50 P.M.)
Okay. I'll save you a seat.

Liz Ortiz (1:59 P.M.)
There's just been an announcement. There's a disabled train up ahead. It'll be awhile.

Jason Salter (2:00 P.M.)
Don't worry. If there are any questions for our department, I'll handle them.

Liz Ortiz (2:01 P.M.)
Thanks. I'll call you later.

152. What is suggested about Mr. Salter?

(A) He is leading the meeting.
(B) He commutes to work by train.
(C) He has many questions for Ms. Ortiz.
(D) He works in the same department as Ms. Ortiz.

153. At 1:59 P.M., what does Ms. Ortiz imply when she writes, "It'll be awhile"?

(A) The meeting is running late.
(B) She is still preparing her notes.
(C) She will likely miss the meeting.
(D) She has not boarded the train yet.

TEST 9

GO ON TO THE NEXT PAGE

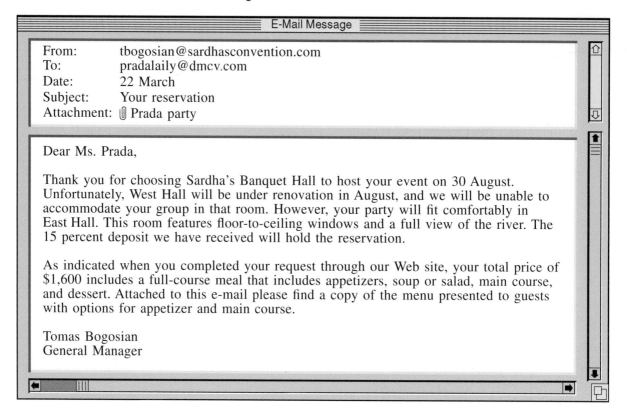

E-Mail Message

From:	tbogosian@sardhasconvention.com
To:	pradalaily@dmcv.com
Date:	22 March
Subject:	Your reservation
Attachment:	📎 Prada party

Dear Ms. Prada,

Thank you for choosing Sardha's Banquet Hall to host your event on 30 August. Unfortunately, West Hall will be under renovation in August, and we will be unable to accommodate your group in that room. However, your party will fit comfortably in East Hall. This room features floor-to-ceiling windows and a full view of the river. The 15 percent deposit we have received will hold the reservation.

As indicated when you completed your request through our Web site, your total price of $1,600 includes a full-course meal that includes appetizers, soup or salad, main course, and dessert. Attached to this e-mail please find a copy of the menu presented to guests with options for appetizer and main course.

Tomas Bogosian
General Manager

154. What is one purpose of the e-mail?

(A) To cancel a reservation
(B) To apologize for an error
(C) To indicate a room change
(D) To request an extra deposit

155. What is suggested about Ms. Prada?

(A) She has paid her bill in full.
(B) She eats at Sardha's regularly.
(C) She works in the food industry.
(D) She made the reservation online.

MEMO

To: All Employees
From: IT Supervisor
Subject: OS Update
Date: 27 May

All company computers in the Melbourne and Victoria offices require an update to the operating system. This update will prepare our computers for the new version of our accounting software, which should arrive in the first week of July. Technicians will install the new operating system beginning on 3 June. We expect the process to be completed around 16 June, providing time to work out any bugs with the operating system before the accounting software is uploaded.

Completing the entire process will require you to log in so that we can verify the system is working as anticipated. Therefore, if you plan to go on holiday during this period, please inform IT Support immediately of the dates you will be out so that we can plan an alternate date to accommodate your schedule.

If you have any questions, please contact IT Support staff at extension 48.

156. When is the installation of the operating system expected to be finished?
(A) In the first week of June
(B) In the middle of June
(C) At the end of June
(D) In the first week of July

157. Who is asked to contact IT Support?
(A) Employees who do not need the accounting software
(B) Accountants already using the new operating system
(C) Staff who work outside the offices
(D) Employees who are taking time off

GO ON TO THE NEXT PAGE

Clarke-Ellis Construction
#20 Murphy Industrial Park
St. Michael BB23028
1-246-555-0126
Full-service commercial contractor serving all of Barbados

4 June

Ida Gutierrez
Darling Cove Inn
Mango Drive
Folkestone BB24017

Dear Ms. Gutierrez,

Thank you for contacting Clarke-Ellis Construction for your roofing project.
— [1] —. After inspecting the property, I have confirmed that the inn's main roof is
in good condition and requires no repairs at this time. However, the roof of the inn's
porch appears to be at least twenty years old and is worn beyond repair. — [2] —.
Clarke-Ellis Construction can remove and dispose of the existing porch roof and
install a new one. The replacement will be comparable to the quality, style, and
colour of the inn's main roof. We will use only commercial-grade leak barriers,
insulation, and shingles manufactured by West Indies Weatherproofing, Inc. The
estimated total cost, inclusive of labour and materials, is $3,260. — [3] —.
Additional fees would apply should you want us to make other improvements, such
as painting the porch or replacing porch screens.

Please call me at the number above to discuss scheduling or any questions you have
about the work. — [4] —. I hope to hear from you soon.

Sincerely,

Grayson Clarke

Grayson Clarke, Co-owner, Clarke-Ellis Construction

---

158. Why did Mr. Clarke write the letter?

(A) To provide a work proposal
(B) To ask for a project extension
(C) To request an inspection report
(D) To submit a revised cost estimate

159. What is indicated about West Indies
Weatherproofing, Inc.?

(A) It is installing a new porch at Darling
Cove Inn.
(B) It provides painting services.
(C) It produces roofing materials.
(D) It is owned by Clarke-Ellis Construction.

160. In which of the positions marked [1], [2], [3],
and [4] does the following sentence best
belong?

"It must be replaced."

(A) [1]
(B) [2]
(C) [3]
(D) [4]

Position: Assistant Editor   **Date Posted: March 15**

Description

Goldhorse Press, an independent book publishing company focusing on North American gardening, has provided gardening advice for home gardeners for over 50 years. We are currently seeking an assistant editor to join our expanding team in Charlotte, North Carolina. We offer an excellent benefits package that includes medical and dental insurance.

Responsibilities

Assist editors in the acquisition of titles with mainstream appeal; develop manuscripts, collaborate with outside support, and work closely with two managing editors.

Requirements/Qualifications

• Bachelor's degree in a related field
• Minimum of one year of experience in the publishing industry
• Ability to pay close attention to detail
• Comfortable working as a team member
• Some experience in gardening preferred
• Immediate availability

E-mail résumé and salary requirements to humanresources@goldhorsepress.com.

---

161. What title would most likely be published by Goldhorse Press?

(A) *Growing Your Baking Business*
(B) *A Tour Guide to North Carolina*
(C) *Planting Perennial Flowers*
(D) *The Efficient Executive*

162. What is indicated about Goldhorse Press?

(A) It is hiring two assistant editors.
(B) It provides insurance to employees.
(C) It publishes trade journals.
(D) It is a newly established company.

163. What is a requirement for the advertised position?

(A) A passion for gardening
(B) An aptitude for noticing details
(C) A master's degree in a related field
(D) An ability to work without supervision

164. What are applicants asked to do?

(A) Submit a job application form
(B) Submit a list of references
(C) Indicate availability
(D) Indicate desired pay

TEST 9

```
┌─────────────────────────────────────────────────────────────────┬─────────┐
│                                                        │ − │ □ │ X │
└─────────────────────────────────────────────────────────────────┴─────────┘
```

Derek Marshall [8:19 A.M.]

Hi, everyone. I wanted to give an update on our merger with Ridgewood, Inc., and see if you have had any meetings.

Mai Chung [8:20 A.M.]

Have we worked out which of our Derek Boutique locations will stay open?

Derek Marshall [8:21 A.M.]

Yes, Derek Boutique will keep 35 stores open with the full line of clothing. The other 12 will move their inventory to the Ridgewood, Inc., locations.

Nikita Tamboli [8:22 A.M.]

When should the moves be scheduled? This month?

Derek Marshall [8:23 A.M.]

No, the 12 locations don't need to be vacated until the end of next month. Could you schedule this for five weeks from now?

Anthony Rossi [8:24 A.M.]

I met over lunch with my managers earlier this week, including the two that I just hired.

Nikita Tamboli [8:25 A.M.]

That would work.

Mai Chung [8:27 A.M.]

I'll be meeting with the managers on my staff, too, to review the transition plan.

Derek Marshall [8:28 A.M.]

This is good work, everyone.

Anthony Rossi [8:29 A.M.]

When will the whole process be complete?

Derek Marshall [8:30 A.M.]

Within about 6 months.

165. Where do the writers most likely work?

(A) At a marketing firm
(B) At a clothing company
(C) At a real estate agency
(D) At a newspaper publisher

166. How many stores will be closing?

(A) 5
(B) 6
(C) 12
(D) 35

167. At 8:25 A.M., what does Ms. Tamboli most likely mean when she writes, "That would work"?

(A) The current inventory will be doubled.
(B) Ridgewood, Inc., will close in two weeks.
(C) Mr. Marshall will meet with the managers.
(D) She can schedule the moves in the proposed time frame.

168. What is suggested about Ms. Chung and Mr. Rossi?

(A) They supervise other employees.
(B) They often shop at Ridgewood, Inc.
(C) They recently went to lunch together.
(D) They have concerns about the merger.

From the Shadows to the Limelight

By Calum Ellwood

Dr. Esther Nujoma, an agricultural biotechnologist with the Namibia Institute of Applied Sciences, is the author of several books on the practical applications of biotechnology. — [1] —. According to book critic Paige Kinnock of the *London Daily Register*, "Dr. Nujoma has increased the public's awareness of the role of biotechnology in daily life through her ability to translate highly complex scientific material into simple language."

Her latest work, *Shining Behind Shadows*, marks a departure from her usual subject matter. — [2] —. Rather, the book highlights the lives and careers of twelve of her peers from Africa and Asia. The idea came to her three years ago at a conference in Chile. As Dr. Nujoma recalls, "Listening to one speaker after another, I realized that many of my colleagues are from regions of the world, such as Africa and Asia, that were underrepresented." — [3] —.

The book is quite compelling. Dr. Nujoma brings to life the stories of how her peers were drawn to the profession and the effort they pour into their work.

The book does, however, fall short in one respect: it provides insights only into the lives and careers of those working in the field of agricultural biotechnology. I would have welcomed the stories of those specializing in animal, marine, or medical biotechnology, too. — [4] —. Even so, Dr. Nujoma has again succeeded in creating a work that speaks to experts and laypeople alike.

169. What is NOT indicated about Dr. Nujoma?

(A) She has visited Chile.
(B) She is a talented writer.
(C) She is based out of Namibia.
(D) She was interviewed by the *London Daily Register*.

170. What does Mr. Ellwood say about *Shining Behind Shadows*?

(A) It focuses on scientists from Africa and Asia.
(B) It was released three years ago.
(C) It details why Dr. Nujoma chose her career.
(D) It describes various branches of biotechnology.

171. In which of the positions marked [1], [2], [3], and [4] does the following sentence best belong?

"Its focus is not on applying biotechnology in real-life situations."

(A) [1]
(B) [2]
(C) [3]
(D) [4]

KINGSTON-GARNET ISLAND PASSENGER FERRY SERVICE

General Information

Beginning on 15 May, the Kingston-Garnet Island Passenger Ferry Service will resume service for eight weeks during the summer season. Ferries run daily every half hour from 7 a.m. to 8 p.m. The last ferry to Garnet Island will depart at 7:30 p.m. The last ferry from Garnet Island will leave at 8 p.m.

Bicycles are permitted on the passenger ferries. Bicyclists should arrive 30 minutes prior to departure and wait in the special bicycle lane to be loaded first. There are five racks that hold 50 bicycles on every passenger ferry.

No motorized vehicles are permitted on Garnet Island. Overnight parking is allowed in the main ferry terminal lot in Kingston. Rates are $5 per hour for up to 4 hours and a flat fee of $25 for four to 24 hours.

Visit our Web site at www.kgferryservice.com for photographs of the ferry boats, a map of Garnet Island, lists of local attractions on the island, and information about peak-hour fare increases and group discounts.

172. What is indicated about the ferry service?

(A) It is available only seasonally.
(B) Its boats were recently upgraded.
(C) It takes an hour to reach the island.
(D) It runs more frequently on weekends.

173. What is true about bicyclists on the ferries?

(A) They are last to board the boat.
(B) They must purchase a special ticket.
(C) They cannot travel on the 7:30 P.M. trip.
(D) They should arrive at the terminal early.

174. What is not allowed on Garnet Island?

(A) Renting bicycles
(B) Driving cars
(C) Camping overnight
(D) Taking photographs

175. What is indicated about the ferry tickets?

(A) They can be purchased at stores in Kingston.
(B) They are less expensive for children.
(C) They vary in price depending on the time of travel.
(D) They are more expensive if purchased on the boat.

TEST 9

GO ON TO THE NEXT PAGE

Thank you for shopping at Green Stripe Press.

Order Number: GSP20896
Customer Information: Shoebox Mountain
Jason Ho <jasonho@shoeboxmountain.com>
Order Date: December 14 (PREPAID: online order)
Expected Delivery: December 18–20

Quantity	Item #	Item	Price
1	CAL201	Complimentary Wild Animals Calendar	$ 0.00
7	ARB132	Accounting Record Book ($19.99 each)	$139.93

Subtotal:	$139.93
Discount:	$ 0.00
Tax @ 6%:	$ 8.40
Shipping & Handling:	$ 0.00
Total:	**$148.33**

There is no charge for shipping and handling for corporate accounts. For questions regarding this order, please contact customerservice@greenstripepress.com.

To:	<customerservice@greenstripepress.com>
From:	Jason Ho <jasonho@shoeboxmountain.com>
Date:	December 18
Subject:	Order #GSP20896

Dear Green Stripe Press,

I am writing regarding my most recent order (#GSP20896), which was delivered today. If you check my original order, you will see that I ordered six accounting record books. You sent us seven copies. I'd like to return the one I didn't order and have our corporate credit card refunded, together with the shipping cost the return will incur. Let me know how you would like me to proceed.

On a different note, congratulations on the calendar you included in my order! The photos are even more stunning than those in the *Ancient Castles* calendar you sent us last year. Some staff members saw mine and want copies of their own. Would you mind sending two more our way?

Best,

Jason Ho, Owner
Shoebox Mountain

176. Why was Mr. Ho not charged a shipping fee?

    (A) He took advantage of a promotion.
    (B) He made the purchase for his company.
    (C) He picked up his order in person.
    (D) He overpaid for shipping on a previous order.

177. What is true about Mr. Ho's order?

    (A) It was damaged in transit.
    (B) It included fragile items.
    (C) It was paid for by check.
    (D) It was delivered on time.

178. According to the e-mail, what was Mr. Ho sent by mistake?

    (A) A castle book he did not order
    (B) A calendar for last year
    (C) An incorrect refund check
    (D) An extra accounting book

179. What is one reason Mr. Ho wrote the e-mail?

    (A) To offer praise for an item
    (B) To complain about a price
    (C) To order some photo albums
    (D) To recommend a graphic designer

180. In the e-mail, the phrase "our way" in paragraph 2, line 4, is closest in meaning to

    (A) in our style
    (B) to our address
    (C) at our expense
    (D) for our benefit

GO ON TO THE NEXT PAGE

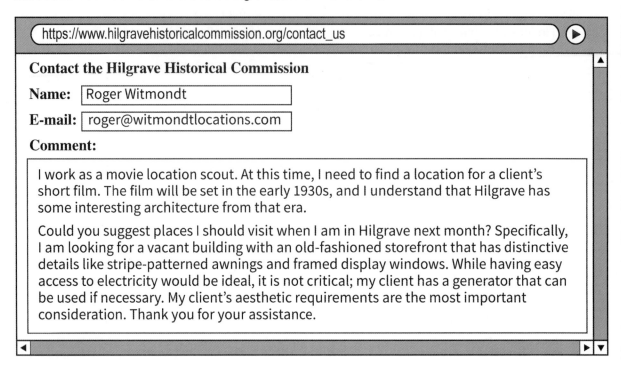

https://www.hilgravehistoricalcommission.org/contact_us

Contact the Hilgrave Historical Commission

Name: Roger Witmondt

E-mail: roger@witmondtlocations.com

Comment:

I work as a movie location scout. At this time, I need to find a location for a client's short film. The film will be set in the early 1930s, and I understand that Hilgrave has some interesting architecture from that era.

Could you suggest places I should visit when I am in Hilgrave next month? Specifically, I am looking for a vacant building with an old-fashioned storefront that has distinctive details like stripe-patterned awnings and framed display windows. While having easy access to electricity would be ideal, it is not critical; my client has a generator that can be used if necessary. My client's aesthetic requirements are the most important consideration. Thank you for your assistance.

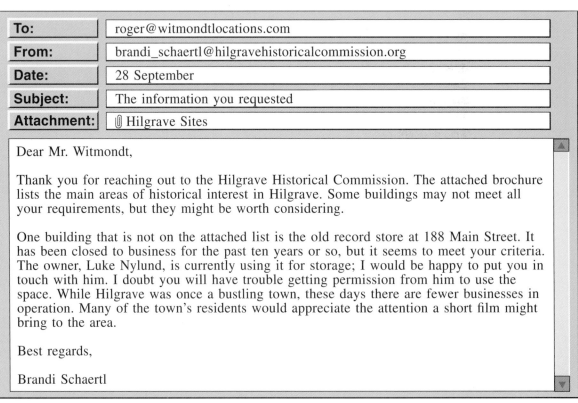

To:	roger@witmondtlocations.com
From:	brandi_schaertl@hilgravehistoricalcommission.org
Date:	28 September
Subject:	The information you requested
Attachment:	📎 Hilgrave Sites

Dear Mr. Witmondt,

Thank you for reaching out to the Hilgrave Historical Commission. The attached brochure lists the main areas of historical interest in Hilgrave. Some buildings may not meet all your requirements, but they might be worth considering.

One building that is not on the attached list is the old record store at 188 Main Street. It has been closed to business for the past ten years or so, but it seems to meet your criteria. The owner, Luke Nylund, is currently using it for storage; I would be happy to put you in touch with him. I doubt you will have trouble getting permission from him to use the space. While Hilgrave was once a bustling town, these days there are fewer businesses in operation. Many of the town's residents would appreciate the attention a short film might bring to the area.

Best regards,

Brandi Schaertl

181. Why is Mr. Witmondt looking for a filming location in Hilgrave?

(A) It is known for its scenic mountain views.
(B) It is a short distance from his office.
(C) Its business district has appeared in other films.
(D) Its buildings represent a particular time period.

182. On the contact form, the word "critical" in paragraph 2, line 4, is closest in meaning to

(A) judgmental
(B) essential
(C) sustainable
(D) available

183. What is implied about 188 Main Street?

(A) It was once used as a residence.
(B) It is frequently visited by tourists.
(C) It has several floors.
(D) It has decorative design features.

184. What does Ms. Schaertl offer to do?

(A) Advertise a forthcoming film
(B) Arrange to have a building cleaned
(C) Connect Mr. Witmondt with a building's owner
(D) Help Mr. Witmondt acquire necessary permits from the town

185. What does Ms. Schaertl suggest that Hilgrave needs?

(A) More publicity
(B) Additional parking
(C) A storage facility
(D) A business directory

GO ON TO THE NEXT PAGE

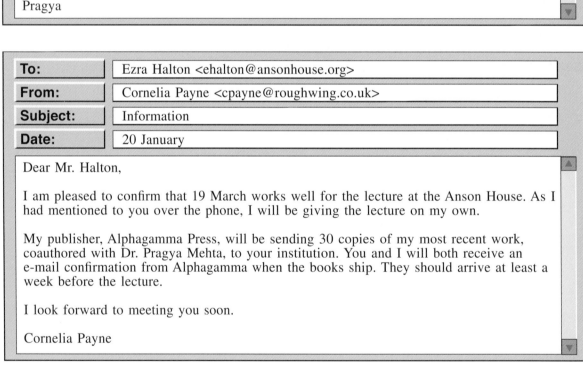

To:	Cornelia Payne <cpayne@roughwing.co.uk>
From:	Pragya Mehta <pmehta@airsky.in>
Subject:	Lecture
Date:	18 January
Attachment:	📎 Notes

Dear Cornelia,

I am sorry for the late notice, but I will not be able to join you for the lecture. My new position at the university in Mumbai requires me to remain on campus.

Although I know you are fully prepared to deliver the lecture on your own, I have attached a copy of the notes I had prepared for the presentation. After you review them, let me know if there is anything else I can add.

I had very much looked forward to traveling to Freeport, The Bahamas, for the first time and to seeing you again. I certainly miss working with you at the City University.

Good luck with the lecture.

Pragya

To:	Ezra Halton <ehalton@ansonhouse.org>
From:	Cornelia Payne <cpayne@roughwing.co.uk>
Subject:	Information
Date:	20 January

Dear Mr. Halton,

I am pleased to confirm that 19 March works well for the lecture at the Anson House. As I had mentioned to you over the phone, I will be giving the lecture on my own.

My publisher, Alphagamma Press, will be sending 30 copies of my most recent work, coauthored with Dr. Pragya Mehta, to your institution. You and I will both receive an e-mail confirmation from Alphagamma when the books ship. They should arrive at least a week before the lecture.

I look forward to meeting you soon.

Cornelia Payne

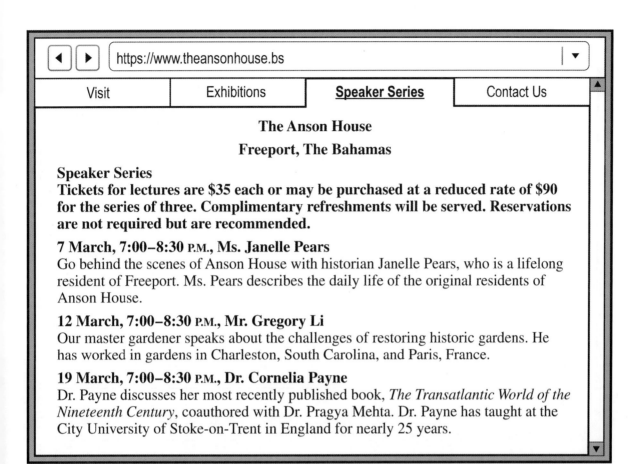

https://www.theansonhouse.bs

| Visit | Exhibitions | **Speaker Series** | Contact Us |

The Anson House
Freeport, The Bahamas

Speaker Series
Tickets for lectures are $35 each or may be purchased at a reduced rate of $90 for the series of three. Complimentary refreshments will be served. Reservations are not required but are recommended.

7 March, 7:00–8:30 P.M., Ms. Janelle Pears
Go behind the scenes of Anson House with historian Janelle Pears, who is a lifelong resident of Freeport. Ms. Pears describes the daily life of the original residents of Anson House.

12 March, 7:00–8:30 P.M., Mr. Gregory Li
Our master gardener speaks about the challenges of restoring historic gardens. He has worked in gardens in Charleston, South Carolina, and Paris, France.

19 March, 7:00–8:30 P.M., Dr. Cornelia Payne
Dr. Payne discusses her most recently published book, *The Transatlantic World of the Nineteenth Century*, coauthored with Dr. Pragya Mehta. Dr. Payne has taught at the City University of Stoke-on-Trent in England for nearly 25 years.

186. Why did Dr. Mehta send the e-mail to Dr. Payne?

(A) To cancel a vacation plan
(B) To request lecture notes
(C) To confirm a meeting
(D) To offer an apology

187. According to the second e-mail, what did Dr. Payne do?

(A) Arrange a delivery
(B) Give Mr. Halton a gift
(C) Revise her presentation
(D) Announce an address change

188. What is indicated about Alphagamma Press?

(A) It has headquarters in The Bahamas.
(B) It regularly ships materials to Anson House.
(C) It published *The Transatlantic World of the Nineteenth Century*.
(D) It is paying Dr. Payne's travel and accommodation expenses.

189. Where were Dr. Mehta and Dr. Payne most likely colleagues?

(A) In Mumbai
(B) In Freeport
(C) In Stoke-on-Trent
(D) In Charleston

190. What is indicated about the Speaker Series in the Web page?

(A) Discounts are unavailable.
(B) Reservations are optional.
(C) Events are held in the morning.
(D) Refreshments are not included.

TEST 9

GO ON TO THE NEXT PAGE

CRYN Group: We find the best employees for your company.

Posted: November 25

Position title and codes:
- Director of Operations, TL0015
- Marketing Director, TL0023
- Quality Control Director, TL0027
- Director of Category Management, TL0045

To apply: Send your résumé to mdoro@cryngroup.ca.com with posting number 2098 in the subject line.

Company:

Our client plans to chart an aggressive growth path in Latin America, where it plans to start operations next year. It is a well-established company widely known for marketing consumer-health products in North America, and more recently in Europe and Asia.

Qualifications:

Candidates must have a formal business degree and a proven management record in at least one international setting. Experience with online sales and marketing preferred.

To:	Sven Arvidson <sarvidson@barkent.de.com>
From:	Maria Doro <mdoro@cryngroup.ca.com>
Re:	Posting number 2098
Date:	December 10

Dear Mr. Arvidson,

Thank you for submitting your résumé. I'd like to schedule a preliminary telephone conversation with you as soon as possible to determine whether you would be a good choice for our client. I would particularly like to discuss whether you would be prepared to work at our client's new facility overseas.

Let me know if you are available for a 30-minute phone call sometime between 10:00 A.M. and 2:00 P.M. EST on Monday or Tuesday of next week. Please respond to me by e-mail at your earliest convenience.

Maria Doro
CRYN Group

Tayerson Ltd. Names New Director

Toronto, April 5—Tayerson Ltd. continues to staff its new international outpost, which opens one month from today. In this case, the lucky candidate is Sven Arvidson. "Category Management is a relatively new area—and one that I'm sure I'll enjoy exploring and developing as director," Mr. Arvidson said. "As a major online marketer of nutritional supplements, Tayerson is poised to lead the way toward better living while becoming a more vibrant, more profitable corporation."

Mr. Arvidson has held several key management positions throughout his career, most recently at Barkent Pharmaceuticals in Germany. He was also a partner at MSZ Consulting Group, where he provided marketing guidance to leading consumer-product companies in Canada and China.

---

191. According to the advertisement, what qualification is not required of applicants?

(A) A degree in business
(B) Previous employment in a managerial position
(C) Experience working overseas
(D) Online sales and marketing experience

192. What most likely is the location of the position for which Mr. Arvidson applied?

(A) Latin America
(B) North America
(C) Europe
(D) Asia

193. What does Ms. Doro ask Mr. Arvidson to provide in his reply?

(A) Information on his leadership skills
(B) His availability for an interview
(C) A current résumé
(D) The names of two references

194. What job code did Mr. Arvidson most likely reference in his application?

(A) TL0015
(B) TL0023
(C) TL0027
(D) TL0045

195. According to the press release, what does Tayerson Ltd. sell?

(A) Medical devices
(B) Accounting software
(C) Nutritional supplements
(D) Exercise equipment

TEST 9

GO ON TO THE NEXT PAGE

FGJ's Business Expert Series
Prospect Data Purchasing
45-Minute Webinar
11 May, 2:30 P.M.

Every department in an organisation needs information to make business decisions. Marketing professionals in particular rely on accurate data about potential customers to be successful. In this Webinar, Briana Carrera, chief financial officer of Pile One Market Data, explains how to avoid the pitfalls of acquiring incomplete data and provides tips on what to ask your prospective data provider to ensure that your next batch of data leads to the results you want.

E-mail

To:	Sandra Lescure
From:	Gino Stelleti
Date:	12 May
Subject:	Subject: FGJ's Webinar

Dear Sandra,

You had asked me to give you a report on the Webinar I attended yesterday about acquiring data. To be honest, even though the facilitator was clearly knowledgeable, she did not tell me anything I didn't already know. I was hoping that she would show us the differences between the many types of databases out there, but she never touched on that topic. I am not so sure all these Webinars are useful; in the end, they always seem to be steering us to purchase from one particular company or another—in this case it was Pile One. Having said that, the new schedule just came out, and there is another Webinar coming up soon that I am hoping will provide the information I want about how to store and sort data. I have already signed up for it; I will keep you posted about what I learn.

Gino

Upcoming 45-Minute Webinars in FGJ's Business Expert Series

Basics of Market Research	1 June, 9:30 A.M.	Ed Quinones	€12.00
Tips for Accelerating Sales	12 June, 9:30 A.M.	Cameron Stone	€16.00
What is Market Automation?	5 July, 11:00 A.M.	Ed Quinones	€12.00
Choosing the Right Database	17 July, 2:00 P.M.	Selina Tucci	€12.00

The Business Expert Series is organised by Tuyet Nguyen. Please address any questions to her at tnguyen@fgj.org. To access Webinar content, attendance is required as Webinars are not recorded for later viewing.

196. According to the brochure, who would benefit most from the Prospect Data Purchasing Webinar?

(A) A financial analyst
(B) A marketing manager
(C) A customer-service representative
(D) An information-technology specialist

197. What was Mr. Stelleti's complaint about the Webinar?

(A) He did not like the format.
(B) He did not learn anything new.
(C) He had difficulty hearing everything.
(D) He found the topic to be too complex.

198. What does Mr. Stelleti suggest about Ms. Carrera?

(A) She recently joined a new company.
(B) She has experience managing databases.
(C) She had asked him to sign up for the Webinar.
(D) She tried to sell her company's services.

199. When will Mr. Stelleti most likely attend another Webinar?

(A) On June 1
(B) On June 12
(C) On July 5
(D) On July 17

200. According to the schedule, what do all of the Webinars have in common?

(A) They cost the same amount.
(B) They are held in the morning.
(C) They last the same amount of time.
(D) They are recorded for future playback.

Stop! This is the end of the test. If you finish before time is called, you may go back to Parts 5, 6, and 7 and check your work.

토익 정기시험
기출문제집

RC

ETS TEST

10

READING TEST

In the Reading test, you will read a variety of texts and answer several different types of reading comprehension questions. The entire Reading test will last 75 minutes. There are three parts, and directions are given for each part. You are encouraged to answer as many questions as possible within the time allowed.

You must mark your answers on the separate answer sheet. Do not write your answers in your test book.

PART 5

Directions: A word or phrase is missing in each of the sentences below. Four answer choices are given below each sentence. Select the best answer to complete the sentence. Then mark the letter (A), (B), (C), or (D) on your answer sheet.

101. Please contact the product distributor, not the retail store, if ------- need replacement parts.
(A) your
(B) you
(C) yourself
(D) yours

102. AGU Group's insurance rates have remained steady ------- the last three years.
(A) at
(B) by
(C) to
(D) for

103. Sage Bistro's menu features a ------- variety of seafood items than Almaner Pavilion's.
(A) wide
(B) widest
(C) wider
(D) widely

104. Frequent training enables our technicians to resolve most computer problems -------.
(A) swiftly
(B) avoidably
(C) doubtfully
(D) rigidly

105. Most of the manufacturing sector has reported higher profits as a result of the trade -------.
(A) agreement
(B) agreeing
(C) agreeably
(D) agrees

106. The cooking instructions call for reducing the heat and letting the sauce simmer ------- it thickens.
(A) whereas
(B) likewise
(C) instead
(D) until

107. The Cullingford Bridge took a ------- short amount of time to be repaired.
(A) surprise
(B) surprisingly
(C) surprising
(D) surprised

108. The company's summer picnic is ------- held outside town, in Warren County Lakeside Park.
(A) apart
(B) always
(C) much
(D) far

109. Ms. Navarro wants to fill the administrative assistant ------- as soon as possible.

(A) worker
(B) employment
(C) position
(D) experience

110. The item that Ms. Bak ordered from our catalog is ------- until 16 October.

(A) unavailable
(B) occupied
(C) uneventful
(D) delivered

111. Kespi Brand cookies, delicious by -------, are even better when paired with a glass of milk.

(A) they
(B) theirs
(C) them
(D) themselves

112. The North India Electricians Association ------- various online courses covering licensure, safety, and technology.

(A) offers
(B) takes
(C) pays
(D) allows

113. The latest survey shows that our downtown store is more ------- for local shoppers than our suburban location.

(A) conveniences
(B) conveniently
(C) convenience
(D) convenient

114. *Weaving Fire* is the most popular television show ------- women ages 18–34.

(A) among
(B) toward
(C) within
(D) along

115. ------- a designer has completed a prototype product, the rest of the team will be invited to critique it.

(A) So that
(B) Whether
(C) From
(D) After

116. Rather than archiving routine e-mails, please delete them -------.

(A) especially
(B) likewise
(C) quite
(D) instead

117. Mr. Khana made a phone call yesterday during which he ------- for the delay in the shipment of the clothing order.

(A) to apologize
(B) apologized
(C) apologize
(D) will be apologizing

118. Following many months of research, the marketing team finally decided on a ------- for the new perfume bottle.

(A) force
(B) style
(C) belief
(D) request

119. For more information about product warranties or ------- your new appliance, please contact customer service.

(A) to register
(B) registered
(C) registers
(D) registration

120. There will be a software upgrade tomorrow, ------- please back up any important files you have stored on the server.

(A) rather
(B) while
(C) so
(D) because

GO ON TO THE NEXT PAGE

121. Ambassador Chaturvedi wrote in his memoir that his parents taught him to do each job well, ------- it was.

(A) whoever
(B) anyone
(C) everything
(D) whatever

122. Yields from your garden will ------- rise as you add Natrium Compost to the soil.

(A) steady
(B) steadying
(C) steadily
(D) steadier

123. The Tokyo division handles product ------- and customer service for the company.

(A) distribute
(B) distributor
(C) distribution
(D) distributed

124. Our newest executive assistant will be responsible for ------- between the marketing and accounting departments.

(A) coordination
(B) attention
(C) appreciation
(D) consideration

125. Hemlin Corporation is looking for a sales representative ------- primary role will be expanding business in the northwest region.

(A) that
(B) whose
(C) who
(D) which

126. To eliminate ------- inventory of winter outerwear, Ashley Fashions has cut prices on all coats, hats, and scarves.

(A) chilly
(B) adequate
(C) excess
(D) revised

127. Search the Labesse Financial Web site for the most current and detailed ------- of investment options.

(A) explain
(B) explanation
(C) to explain
(D) explainable

128. The last paragraph ------- to have been added to the contract as an afterthought.

(A) arranged
(B) permitted
(C) transferred
(D) appeared

129. Unless the shipment of tiles arrives early, work on the lobby floor ------- after the holiday.

(A) has commenced
(B) commencing
(C) will commence
(D) commenced

130. Neeson Pro garments are made of a synthetic blend that is ------- to staining.

(A) exposed
(B) automatic
(C) limited
(D) vulnerable

PART 6

Directions: Read the texts that follow. A word, phrase, or sentence is missing in parts of each text. Four answer choices for each question are given below the text. Select the best answer to complete the text. Then mark the letter (A), (B), (C), or (D) on your answer sheet.

Questions 131-134 refer to the following memo.

To: All Employees
Subject: Server Maintenance Reminder
Date: March 11

Please be advised it is time for the IT department to ------- mandatory server maintenance and
            131.
updates. ------- . There will be no Internet service in the building from 7:00 P.M. Wednesday,
   132.
March 12, until 9:00 A.M. Thursday, March 13. In addition, please note there will be no remote

access available. Therefore, you will not be able to log in to the server from outside the office.

------- this regularly scheduled maintenance, you will not have access to your e-mail, calendar, or
133.
contacts. Employees should plan accordingly. We ------- any inconvenience this may cause.
                                     134.

131. (A) suggest
(B) perform
(C) cancel
(D) revise

132. (A) The updates will be e-mailed to all
employees.
(B) Please reply if you would like to
participate.
(C) The process will begin tomorrow
evening.
(D) A memo will be distributed indicating
the start time.

133. (A) During
(B) Now
(C) When
(D) Finally

134. (A) regret
(B) regretting
(C) regrettable
(D) regrettably

GO ON TO THE NEXT PAGE

TEST 10

Questions 135-138 refer to the following letter.

22 April

Ms. Anna Schoorl
Rodezand 334
3011 AV Rotterdam
Netherlands

Dear Ms. Schoorl,

Congratulations on your remarkable ------- in the Netherlands, Belgium, and Luxembourg. Your
                                    135.
region has improved its on-time delivery performance for each of the past seven quarters.

------- .
136.

I am pleased to offer you a promotion to Director of European Operations. The position

------- in Hamburg, Germany. I realize that relocating may be difficult for you. ------- , I certainly
137.   **138.**
hope that you will take time to consider this opportunity. Please call me at your earliest

convenience so that we can discuss any concerns you may have.

Thank you for being a part of the Unocity Shipping family.

Sincerely,

Xia Hsu, Director of Operations
Unocity Shipping, Inc.

---

135. (A) speeches
(B) shops
(C) visits
(D) efforts

136. (A) Such work deserves recognition.
(B) Please meet with your assistant.
(C) It was shipped about a week ago.
(D) I will be in Belgium next month.

137. (A) was based
(B) is based
(C) basing
(D) bases

138. (A) In addition
(B) For instance
(C) However
(D) Similarly

Questions 139-142 refer to the following e-mail.

To: Wu Investment Services employees
From: Eileen Suen, Office Manager
Re: Jacob Wu
Date: 15 August

To All Staff,

As many of you are aware, Jacob Wu, our long-standing Chief Executive Officer, ------- on 1
                                                                                  139.
October. Twenty years ago, Mr. Wu set out to create a Hong Kong-based services firm with an

international scope. ------- . Wu Investment Services currently serves clients in seventeen
                     140.
countries, 95 percent of whom have chosen to invest with us for the long term.

Mr. Wu will be ------- by Thomas Wu, his son, who has served as Vice President of
                141.
Wu Investment Services for the past four years.

A gathering will be held on 28 September to celebrate Mr. Wu's ------- career. I will send further
                                                                142.
information about the event closer to the date. Thank you.

Eileen

---

139. (A) retired
  (B) will be retiring
  (C) would retire
  (D) was to retire

140. (A) You will soon receive a formal
      invitation.
  (B) The event will take place in the staff
      room.
  (C) He certainly achieved his goal.
  (D) There, he graduated with academic
      distinction.

141. (A) succeeded
  (B) achieved
  (C) accomplished
  (D) resolved

142. (A) promising
  (B) technical
  (C) foremost
  (D) distinguished

TEST 10

GO ON TO THE NEXT PAGE

From: Madeleine DeVries, Director of Operations

To: All Employees

Date: June 1

Re: Travel Policy

To help reduce ------- , the officers have voted to change the company's travel policy. The revised
143.

policy will be ------- on June 15. From that point forward, employees traveling within the country will
144.

be required to submit their travel requests to the accounting office no later than three weeks before

the date of departure. ------- .
145.

------- exceptions to this policy will be decided on a case-by-case basis and must first be approved
146.

by the individual employee's supervisor.

143. (A) spend
(B) spends
(C) spender
(D) spending

144. (A) instituted
(B) examined
(C) purchased
(D) overturned

145. (A) The accounting office will be closed for
renovations next week.
(B) Travel is important for maintaining
relationships with clients.
(C) The officers periodically review and
revise key company policies.
(D) Requests for international travel must
be sent at least one month in
advance.

146. (A) Any
(B) Additional
(C) Previous
(D) These

Directions: In this part you will read a selection of texts, such as magazine and newspaper articles, e-mails, and instant messages. Each text or set of texts is followed by several questions. Select the best answer for each question and mark the letter (A), (B), (C), or (D) on your answer sheet.

Questions 147-148 refer to the following receipt.

Siobhan's Toronto, Ontario

April 14   09:23 a.m.   Dine-in
Order: 55234   Server: Antonio K.

1 Medium Coffee $2.25
No sugar
No milk

1 Large Coffee $2.75
3 sugars
No milk

2 Croissants $4.00

Subtotal $9.00
HST 13% $1.17
Total   **$10.17**

****

Tell us how we did today and get a free medium coffee!
Just fill out our online survey at www.siobhans.ca/survey.
You will be given a code to receive a free medium coffee
when you buy any regular-priced pastry.

---

147. What type of business most likely provided the receipt?

(A) A caterer
(B) A vegetable market
(C) A café
(D) An online retailer

148. How much money can survey participants save?

(A) $2.25
(B) $2.75
(C) $4.00
(D) $9.00

> ### Country Gardening Today
>
> Growing plants can be easy. It just takes knowing the right tips and tricks. That's why our award-winning *Country Gardening Today* is the most widely read gardening magazine in all of New Zealand. Most of our readers say they had never planted a single seed before ordering our magazine, and now they take pride in their beautiful flowers and scrumptious vegetables. Our articles cover every aspect of gardening, and they are written by expert landscape designers, horticulturalists, and botanists. This fun and practical magazine also offers do-it-yourself landscaping ideas, product recommendations (no ads!), and step-by-step guides. Don't miss this spectacular offer! Subscribe before the end of February and save 25% off the retail cover price! Just go to www.countrygardeningtoday.com.

149. For whom is the advertisement most likely intended?

(A) Beginning gardeners
(B) Landscape designers
(C) Plant store owners
(D) Magazine publishers

150. According to the advertisement, what does the magazine feature?

(A) Product advertisements
(B) Gardening tips from readers
(C) Articles by gardening professionals
(D) Botanical artwork

To:	Pedro Alamilla
From:	Emma Golding
Date:	16 April
Subject:	Labels

Dear Pedro,

Per your request, below is the text for the labels for the new "Think Green Paper" line. The labels will be placed on the edge of the packaged reams of paper, so their size should not exceed 3 cm by 8 cm. The design should include the tree graphic we discussed yesterday. The text should read as follows:

- Think Green Paper
- 100% from recycled products
- 90 g/m2 bond
- Bright white

Please create a true-to-size and true-to-color sample version of the label by Wednesday, 21 April, and send it to the attention of my assistant, Dora Kensington. I will be out of the office on Wednesday, but I will review the sample and approve it as soon as I am back in the office on Thursday morning.

Emma

151. Who most likely is Mr. Alamilla?

(A) An administrative assistant
(B) A graphic designer
(C) An accountant
(D) A store manager

152. What is indicated about the sample?

(A) It will include an image.
(B) It will be larger than its final version.
(C) It will be printed with green ink.
(D) It will require Ms. Kensington's approval.

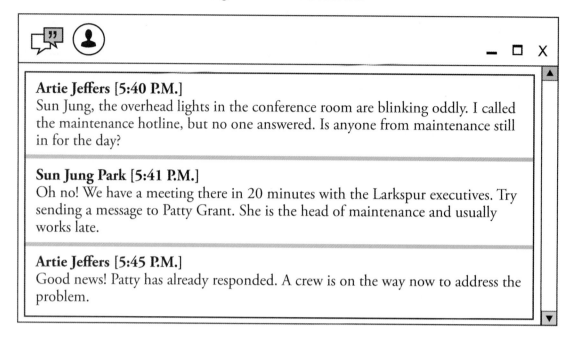

Artie Jeffers [5:40 P.M.]
Sun Jung, the overhead lights in the conference room are blinking oddly. I called the maintenance hotline, but no one answered. Is anyone from maintenance still in for the day?

Sun Jung Park [5:41 P.M.]
Oh no! We have a meeting there in 20 minutes with the Larkspur executives. Try sending a message to Patty Grant. She is the head of maintenance and usually works late.

Artie Jeffers [5:45 P.M.]
Good news! Patty has already responded. A crew is on the way now to address the problem.

153. Why does Mr. Jeffers write to Ms. Park?

(A) To schedule a meeting
(B) To find out whether she can work late
(C) To ask about staff availability
(D) To postpone an upcoming event

154. At 5:41 P.M., what does Ms. Park most likely mean when she writes, "Oh no"?

(A) She did not set up the conference room.
(B) She cannot find Ms. Grant's phone number.
(C) She is unable to attend an executive meeting.
(D) She is concerned about a maintenance issue.

Bill Gallardo's Suits

Item details

Purchaser: Richard Sawyer

Garment: #PC36 (navy/wool)

Price: $89.99   Tax: $5.40

Alteration: no charge (see remarks)

Sold By: Larry Wei

Assigned to: Florian Gartner

Alterations

Jacket	Pants
Collar:	Waist:
Sleeves: shorten	Length:
Shoulders:	Thigh:
Length:	Knee:
Waist:	Hem:

Remarks

clerical error during initial measurement

155. Who most likely is Mr. Wei?

(A) A tailor
(B) A designer
(C) A salesperson
(D) A business owner

156. Where does the item not fit Mr. Sawyer correctly?

(A) On his legs
(B) On his arms
(C) Around his neck
(D) Around his waist

157. Why will the alterations be free?

(A) A coupon was redeemed.
(B) The item was purchased online.
(C) The item was sold with a defect.
(D) A staff member made a mistake.

GO ON TO THE NEXT PAGE

Posted by Padma Pradhan on Friday, September 23, at 12:34 P.M.

I took my mobile phone to the Vivi's Tech Fix location on Rivas Boulevard and 23rd Street for help with a cracked screen. I dropped off the phone on a Tuesday afternoon, and by Wednesday morning I had received a quote by e-mail letting me know the cost to fix it. I called to accept the quote and give my credit card number, and I was able to pick up the mobile the next day on my way home from work—as good as new. If you are looking for responsible professionals, Vivi's Tech Fix is the right place.

While I was in the store picking up my mobile, another customer came in. She was also picking up a damaged mobile; however, the technicians had informed her that the device could not be fixed because of severe water damage, so she owed them nothing. I was impressed that customers can get a free diagnostic from the technicians and don't need to pay anything if a device is beyond repair.

158. What is implied about Vivi's Tech Fix?

(A) It has multiple stores.
(B) It was recently established.
(C) It repairs mobile phones only.
(D) It accepts payment by credit card only.

159. When did Ms. Pradhan pick up her mobile phone?

(A) On Tuesday
(B) On Wednesday
(C) On Thursday
(D) On Friday

160. In paragraph 2, line 5, the word "beyond" is closest in meaning to

(A) superior to
(B) very costly to
(C) in immediate need of
(D) outside the reach of

PLEASE READ IMMEDIATELY

To: All Staff
From: Information Technology Services
Date: July 28

Last night, we experienced an outage of the main webmail server that has affected e-mail and web service throughout the company. — [1] —. Our host server, webmail.raass.net, failed overnight, and this has interrupted our mail service. — [2] —. As a result, it takes much longer to open e-mail. In many cases, accounts may not respond at all.

At this moment, service has still not been fully restored. We are investigating the cause of the problem and working to resolve it. — [3] —. We will keep you posted with further notices via automated voice messages, so please do not ignore your phone. We apologize for the inconvenience. — [4] —.

---

161. What does the memo explain?

(A) How passwords should be changed
(B) How to apply for new e-mail accounts
(C) Why staff have received so many voice messages
(D) Why staff have had difficulty accessing e-mails

162. What are employees asked to do?

(A) Contact the help desk
(B) Post messages on a board
(C) Update their user information
(D) Wait for further announcements

163. In which of the positions marked [1], [2], [3], and [4] does the following sentence best belong?

"Unfortunately, it is unclear when that will happen."

(A) [1]
(B) [2]
(C) [3]
(D) [4]

GO ON TO THE NEXT PAGE

TEST 10

To:	jgonzalez@centralavemarketing.com
From:	pamison@dantonpubliclibrary.org
Subject:	Library update
Date:	May 10
Attachment:	📎 Volunteer opportunities

Dear Ms. Gonzalez,

Thank you for your generosity in donating to the Danton Public Library once again last year. Because of donations from you and others, we were able to purchase twenty new computers for our patrons' use. — [1] —. We also acquired a new collection of nonfiction books for our children's room.

At this time, I would like to tell you about another project we hope to complete with additional funds: converting many of our old, worn-out books into electronic files to help preserve their content for future use. This is a costly endeavor. — [2] —. If you are able to contribute even a small amount toward this new goal, it would be greatly appreciated.

If you are unable to make another monetary donation, please consider helping us complete some small renovation projects that we have scheduled for this year. — [3] —. A list of those projects is attached. We hope you will find one that interests you. — [4] —. We look forward to working alongside enthusiastic and engaged community members like yourself to ensure the library's future success.

Sincerely,

Peter Amison, Community Outreach Coordinator
Danton Public Library

164. Why did Mr. Amison send the e-mail to Ms. Gonzalez?

(A) Because she has a history of helping the library
(B) Because she is overseeing a new project
(C) Because she wrote a book about the town of Danton
(D) Because she is a frequent user of the library's computers

165. What is most likely true about Ms. Gonzalez?

(A) She is a retired librarian.
(B) She has applied for a job at the library.
(C) She owns a book scanner.
(D) She is a resident of Danton.

166. What current project is the Danton Public Library trying to complete?

(A) Purchasing new books
(B) Replacing old computers
(C) Transferring books to electronic format
(D) Reorganizing the nonfiction section

167. In which of the positions marked [1], [2], [3], and [4] does the following sentence best belong?

"It will require both financial resources from dedicated patrons and additional staff hours."

(A) [1]
(B) [2]
(C) [3]
(D) [4]

GO ON TO THE NEXT PAGE

```
👤—👤—👥 Live Chat
```

Maria Jacinto [10:24 A.M.]:
Good morning, everyone. I want to welcome Aika Okura to the chat.

Aika Okura [10:24 A.M.]:
Hi! I'm glad that my bookstore is able to cosponsor the writers' conference this year. It is a great new opportunity for us.

Maria Jacinto [10:25 A.M.]:
We are, too. We have expanded the conference to two days, so the additional sponsorship is a huge help. A larger conference means more sessions and additional hotel arrangements.

Arthur Rufo [10:26 A.M.]:
Speaking of the hotels… The Rowtown Hotel was great last year, but it is booked for the dates we need this time around. The Fairmount at Clark has availability for October 17 and 18, though. It might be better since they have a larger meeting space and more options for the buffet.

Maria Jacinto [10:28 A.M.]:
That sounds good. Can you send us the pricing details?

Arthur Rufo [10:29 A.M.]:
They can offer a special room rate for conference attendees, too. As soon as I have the details, I'll e-mail everyone.

Maria Jacinto [10:30 A.M.]:
Great. How are we doing with the keynote speaker?

Aika Okura [10:31 A.M.]:
Delora Lette has tentatively agreed.

Arthur Rufo [10:32 A.M.]:
Oh. I loved her latest mystery! I can see why it became a best seller so quickly.

Aika Okura [10:33 A.M.]:
Yes, she's great, and I've heard she's also a wonderful speaker. She has another engagement in October in London, and she wants to make certain she can do both events. She will confirm by the end of the week.

Maria Jacinto [10:34 A.M.]:
OK. It sounds like things are coming together. I'll check in again on Friday.

168. What is true about Ms. Okura?

    (A) She publishes novels.
    (B) She owns a business.
    (C) She has previously met Ms. Lette.
    (D) She has helped organize conferences.

169. What is indicated about the conference?

    (A) It will take place in London.
    (B) It has more than one sponsor.
    (C) It is being held for the first time.
    (D) It will offer discounted rates until Friday.

170. At 10:28 A.M., what does Ms. Jacinto mean when she writes, "That sounds good"?

    (A) She is pleased with the proposed conference site.
    (B) She thinks the cost of the hotel is reasonable.
    (C) She wants to join Mr. Rufo at the buffet.
    (D) She prefers the Rowtown Hotel.

171. Who most likely is Ms. Lette?

    (A) An event planner
    (B) A travel agent
    (C) An author
    (D) A bookseller

GO ON TO THE NEXT PAGE

Employee News

We would like to extend our congratulations to Alicia Portalska, who will be our new Vice President of Marketing from January 1. This follows last week's news of Vice President Louis Larson's retirement at the end of the year.

Ms. Portalska joined us as a trainee marketing assistant four years ago and was recently promoted to marketing director. We would like to thank Ms. Portalska for her dedication and outstanding contribution to the marketing department. Her work has had a significant impact on our sales figures. It is in part thanks to her tireless efforts that we have exceeded our sales targets this year. Congratulations, Ms. Portalska! Your example is an inspiration to us all.

172. What is the purpose of the article?

(A) To inform staff about sales targets
(B) To give notice of an employee's promotion
(C) To outline this year's marketing strategy
(D) To announce that an employee has received an award

173. What does the article indicate about Ms. Portalska?

(A) She is popular.
(B) She works hard.
(C) She is innovative.
(D) She lacks experience.

174. The word "outstanding" in paragraph 2, line 5, is closest in meaning to

(A) pending
(B) complete
(C) remarkable
(D) unexpected

175. What is indicated about this year's final sales figures?

(A) They were better than anticipated.
(B) They were the same as last year's figures.
(C) They were discussed at a recent staff meeting.
(D) They were announced at a ceremony on Friday.

GO ON TO THE NEXT PAGE

To:	Astrid Martin <amartin@elpost.com>
From:	Quail Airlines <reservations@quailairlines.com>
Subject:	Flight Confirmation
Date:	15 March

Dear Ms. Martin,

The flight information for the ticket you purchased today is below.

Traveler	**Flight Number**	**Seat**	**Confirmation Number**
Ms. Astrid Martin	QA566	18D	EV4363592

Date of Travel	**Departing**	**Arriving**
10 April	Brussels, Belgium, 10:35 A.M.	Toronto, Canada, 1:00 P.M.

Boarding Time: 9:35 A.M. to 10:05 A.M.

Baggage Reservation: 1 checked bag, 1 carry-on bag

On the day of travel, proceed to the Quail Airlines counter to receive your boarding pass and check in your baggage. As a Quail Travel Card member, you are allowed one checked bag and one carry-on bag free of cost. See the chart below for an explanation of baggage charges.

	1 bag	**2 bags**	**3 bags**	**4 bags**
Checked Bag	$0.00	$30.00	$60.00	$90.00
Carry-On	$0.00	–	–	–

In the event of an airline delay of more than three (3) hours, you may use your Quail Travel Card to enter our Quail Preferred Clubroom. There you may relax, use our high-speed wireless Internet service, and enjoy complimentary food and refreshments at our snack bar.

To: Astrid Martin
From: Quail Airlines Flight QA566
Date: 10 April, 6:00 A.M.

This text message alert is to inform you that your flight QA566 today to Toronto, Canada, has been delayed 4 hours due to poor weather conditions. Boarding will now begin at 1:35 P.M. We apologize for any inconvenience.

176. What is true about Ms. Martin?

(A) She is from Canada.
(B) She is flying with a group.
(C) She is taking a business trip.
(D) She is a Quail Travel Card member.

177. How much must Ms. Martin pay for her bags?

(A) $0.00
(B) $30.00
(C) $60.00
(D) $90.00

178. Why was the text message sent to Ms. Martin?

(A) To confirm her ticket purchase
(B) To notify her of a price increase
(C) To inform her of a time change
(D) To tell her what departure gate to use

179. What can Ms. Martin receive on April 10 ?

(A) A free travel bag
(B) A free snack
(C) A free seat upgrade
(D) A free flight reassignment

180. In the text message, the word "poor" in paragraph 1, line 3, is closest in meaning to

(A) bad
(B) weak
(C) little
(D) thick

TEST 10

To:	custserv@xanthusflowers.co.uk
From:	mnair@nortraxpetrol.co.uk
Date:	27 July
Subject:	Order #9871

Dear Sir or Madam:

On 24 July, I placed an online order for £180 for three arrangements of white roses and pink lilies on behalf of my company, Nortrax Petroleum. The flowers were meant to be delivered by 10 A.M. the following day for a company banquet that evening.

Unfortunately, the flowers did not arrive until noon. Moreover, the bouquets consisted of pink and white carnations. Worst of all, many of the flowers were either wilted or were shedding petals and thus could not be used to decorate the banquet room as planned. I was surprised and disappointed to be let down by Xanthus Flowers, a company we at Nortrax Petroleum have come to trust and depend on over the last five years.

Since the flowers were for a one-time event, a replacement order is not really an option. Consequently, I would like to receive a refund.

Thank you for your attention to this matter.

Sincerely,

Mindy Nair
Corporate Event Coordinator
Nortrax Petroleum

To:	mnair@nortraxpetrol.co.uk
From:	custserv@xanthusflowers.co.uk
Date:	28 July
Subject:	Order #9871

Dear Ms. Nair,

We sincerely apologize for the problems you recently experienced with your order. We have recently transitioned to a larger facility and have experienced a few challenges as we adjust. It is our goal to provide on-time delivery and high-quality flowers for every order. We regret that this order did not live up to our high standards.

A refund cheque in the amount of £180 has been issued to your company. Because we are at fault, we would like to offer you a 20% discount plus free delivery on your next order.

Thank you for being a loyal customer. We look forward to serving you again in the near future.

Regards,

Bill McCabe
Customer Service Manager

181. When did the banquet organized by Nortrax Petroleum take place?

(A) On July 24
(B) On July 25
(C) On July 27
(D) On July 28

182. What is NOT true about the flowers mentioned by Ms. Nair?

(A) Their condition was unacceptable.
(B) They were the wrong kind.
(C) They were too expensive.
(D) They were delivered late.

183. What is suggested about Ms. Nair?

(A) She works for an event-planning company.
(B) She would like to have flowers delivered monthly.
(C) She ordered more flower arrangements than she needed.
(D) She has done business with Xanthus Flowers in the past.

184. What does Mr. McCabe offer that Ms. Nair was not expecting?

(A) A discount on a future order
(B) Free delivery for all future purchases
(C) A refund for the entire cost of an order
(D) New flowers to replace some unsatisfactory ones

185. What is mentioned about Xanthus Flowers?

(A) It is known for its fast service.
(B) It is operating from a new location.
(C) It recently purchased delivery vehicles.
(D) It plans to expand its selection of flowers.

TEST 10

GO ON TO THE NEXT PAGE

http://www.singhsupplies.com

| Home | **About Us** | Products | Orders | Contact Us |

Singh Supplies LLC

Singh Supplies LLC is your leading source for shipping and packaging materials. Our founder, Chatar Singh, started the business more than 30 years ago, when he coined the company's motto, "Expect the best for less."

How do we, his children and grandchildren, make his pledge a reality today? We buy all materials in bulk and pass the savings along to our customers. You will receive the lowest prices and highest quality as well as the most attentive customer service in the shipping-supplies business.

✓ Each order is filled within 24 hours.
✓ You may phone, fax, e-mail, or text your order.
✓ Customer service agents are available 24 hours a day, 7 days a week.
✓ Five shipping centers in the Northeast minimize costs and shorten delivery times.

This is our satisfaction guarantee: If you are not completely satisfied, you may return your order within 10 days of purchase for a full refund. After 10 days you may return an order for a credit that is valid for up to one year. Please note that the cost of return shipping is the responsibility of the customer.

Singh Supplies LLC

Date: July 10   **Name:** Montjoy Antiques, attn. Shipping Department
Shipping address: 102 Danbury Street, Valleyville, New Hampshire 03038

Product number	Description	Quantity	Unit Price	Total Price
MB 01267	cardboard box (large)	80	1.75	140.00
MB 01257	cardboard box (medium)	200	1.50	300.00
MB 01268	reinforced crate	50	15.78	789.00
TR 01345	tape roll	30	2.90	87.00
BW 01456	bubble wrap roll	10	5.60	56.00
Thank you for your business!		Subtotal:		1372.00
		Delivery charge:		140.12
		Total:		**1512.12**

E-mail

To:	Jung Hee Kim <jhk@montjoyantiques.com>
From:	Francine Mayo <fmayo@montjoyantiques.com>
Date:	August 12
Subject:	Order problem

Hi, Jung Hee,

I just checked with our deliveries department and I am pleased that our July 10 order was delivered promptly by Singh Supplies as usual. However, now that we've finally moved the items into the warehouse, it appears we inadvertently ordered far too many of the sturdy crates. We use this item rarely, so it could take us years to go through this many. In addition, they're big, so we've had to stack several in the restoration department, where space is already at a premium. Could you contact Achint Singh today and find out if we can send half of them back? Please forward me any instructions he gives you and I'll take it from there.

Thank you!

Fran

---

186. What is indicated about Singh Supplies?

(A) It is a relatively new business.
(B) It is operated by members of a family.
(C) It ships its products all over the world.
(D) It manufactures the products that it sells.

187. Which aspect of business does the Web page emphasize?

(A) Attentive service to clients
(B) A wide selection of products
(C) Partnerships with other companies
(D) Conveniently located retail locations

188. In the e-mail, what does Ms. Mayo praise about Singh Supplies?

(A) It is easy to contact.
(B) It packs items securely.
(C) It delivers orders quickly.
(D) It sends product samples.

189. Which product does Ms. Mayo want to return?

(A) MB 01257
(B) MB 01268
(C) TR 01345
(D) BW 01456

190. How will Mr. Singh most likely respond to Ms. Kim's request?

(A) By sending Ms. Mayo additional items
(B) By apologizing to Ms. Kim for an error
(C) By issuing a credit to Montjoy Antiques
(D) By giving Montjoy Antiques a full refund

GO ON TO THE NEXT PAGE

Tolley Praises Local Farms

MANCHESTER (June 2)—Local horticulture expert Cassandra Tolley is scheduled to deliver a lecture Friday night at the Burton Auditorium in Manchester. The owner of Green Ridge Farm in nearby Windham County, Ms. Tolley will discuss the importance of supporting and promoting local farmers.

A strong advocate for small-scale farmers and a small-scale farmer herself, Ms. Tolley has traveled extensively over the past few years to deliver her message of "eating locally."

"If we make an effort to source our ingredients locally, we not only sustain and assist the local economy, we also encourage variety in the marketplace," says Ms. Tolley. "And that is beneficial to consumers."

"Everyone should spend their weekends browsing the regional farmers' markets," she adds. "It's the best place to get your groceries during the summer."

Friday night's lecture begins at 7 P.M. It is free, but seating is limited. Please arrive early. To view a comprehensive listing of statewide summer farmers' markets, visit www.vermontfarmersmarkets.org.

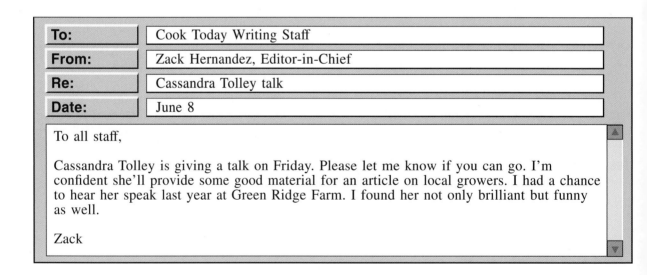

To:	Cook Today Writing Staff
From:	Zack Hernandez, Editor-in-Chief
Re:	Cassandra Tolley talk
Date:	June 8

To all staff,

Cassandra Tolley is giving a talk on Friday. Please let me know if you can go. I'm confident she'll provide some good material for an article on local growers. I had a chance to hear her speak last year at Green Ridge Farm. I found her not only brilliant but funny as well.

Zack

Features Outline for the August Issue of *Cook Today Magazine*		
Feature Title	**Topic**	**Writer**
Local Made Good	Sourcing and showcasing local producers and ingredients	Ira Newton
Herbs All Year	Growing and maintaining an indoor kitchen herb garden	Makalah Young
Vegan Delicious	Modern, nutritious, organic vegan recipes	Keyon Davis
Amazing August	A calendar of events in August	Jae-eun Park

191. What is the purpose of the article?

(A) To advertise a local business
(B) To discuss the local economy
(C) To promote an upcoming event
(D) To profile a new shopping market

192. What does Ms. Tolley encourage people to do?

(A) Visit her Web site
(B) Read her book
(C) Grow their own produce
(D) Shop at farmers' markets

193. What is indicated about Mr. Hernandez?

(A) He is a friend of Ms. Tolley's.
(B) He organized Ms. Tolley's talk.
(C) He has visited Ms. Tolley's business.
(D) He is selling tickets to Ms. Tolley's talk.

194. What featured article will help readers grow a garden inside their home?

(A) Local Made Good
(B) Herbs All Year
(C) Vegan Delicious
(D) Amazing August

195. Who most likely attended Ms. Tolley's talk?

(A) Mr. Newton
(B) Ms. Young
(C) Mr. Davis
(D) Ms. Park

GO ON TO THE NEXT PAGE

Madera Hotels Member Rewards

April Specials

Make a reservation by April 30 for a three-night or longer stay at any of our hotels between April 1 and August 31, and receive a choice of:

(1) 20 points per dollar spent + 500 bonus points
(2) $50 restaurant gift card for use at any Madera Hotel restaurants
(3) 40% discount off spa services during your stay
(4) A discount on a car rental booked at the same time as your stay

We appreciate our frequent customers and thank you for continuing to choose Madera Hotels.

Mr. Brian Carelli

815 Irving St.

New York, NY 10005

---

http://www.maderahotels/customersupport/form.com

Madera Hotels Member Rewards Customer Support:

Please complete this form with as much detail as possible so that we can better assist you.

Today's Date: July 14

Property Name: The Grand Madera   Reservation Number: XWQ43R2

Location: (select one) ☐ Denver ☒ Los Angeles ☐ New York ☐ Washington, DC

Hotel Stay Start Date: May 12

Name: Brian Carelli

Membership Number: B11932013

Email: bcarelli@pointinvesting.com

Phone Number: 555-0101

Comments/Concerns:

I recently took advantage of your April Specials when I booked a stay at the Los Angeles Grand Madera for May. I requested the bonus points offer when I made my reservation online, but when I received my June Member Rewards statement, I noticed that the points had not been applied to my account. Please let me know if I will still receive the bonus points. Thank you.

To:	Brian Carelli <bcarelli@pointinvesting.com>
From:	Oliver Beltran <obeltran@maderahotels.com>
Date:	July 16
Subject:	Your Inquiry - B11932013

Dear Mr. Carelli,

Thank you for being a valued member of the Madera Hotels Member Rewards program. We appreciate you choosing Madera for your business conferences and personal trips. I looked into your request, and it seems that you are correct; we did not credit your account with the bonus points for your stay. Instead, we sent the restaurant gift card to your business address. I apologize for this mistake and will credit your account right away. Also, to compensate for our mistake, I will double the offer.

Sincerely,

Oliver Beltran
Senior Manager, Customer Support
Madera Hotels

196. Why most likely did Mr. Carelli receive the postcard?

(A) He frequently reserves rooms at Madera Hotels.
(B) He rented a vehicle in May.
(C) He last visited a Madera Hotel in New York.
(D) He enjoys eating in hotel restaurants.

197. What is likely true about Mr. Carelli's hotel stay?

(A) It was for a conference.
(B) It included a spa visit.
(C) It was at least three nights long.
(D) It was paid for in advance.

198. According to the form, when did Mr. Carelli report an issue with his account?

(A) On April 1
(B) On May 12
(C) On June 30
(D) On July 14

199. What special April reward did Mr. Carelli mistakenly receive?

(A) One
(B) Two
(C) Three
(D) Four

200. What does Mr. Beltran offer to do?

(A) Upgrade a membership
(B) Change a reservation
(C) Give additional bonus points
(D) Schedule a business conference

Stop! This is the end of the test. If you finish before time is called, you may go back to Parts 5, 6, and 7 and check your work.

ANSWER SHEET

ETS TOEIC 토익 정기시험 기출문제집

수험번호

응시일자 : 20 년 월 일

성명	한글
	한자
	영자

Test 01 (Part 5~7)

101 102 103 104 105 106 107 108 109 110 111 112 113 114 115 116 117 118 119 120
121 122 123 124 125 126 127 128 129 130 131 132 133 134 135 136 137 138 139 140
141 142 143 144 145 146 147 148 149 150 151 152 153 154 155 156 157 158 159 160
161 162 163 164 165 166 167 168 169 170 171 172 173 174 175 176 177 178 179 180
181 182 183 184 185 186 187 188 189 190 191 192 193 194 195 196 197 198 199 200

Test 02 (Part 5~7)

101 102 103 104 105 106 107 108 109 110 111 112 113 114 115 116 117 118 119 120
121 122 123 124 125 126 127 128 129 130 131 132 133 134 135 136 137 138 139 140
141 142 143 144 145 146 147 148 149 150 151 152 153 154 155 156 157 158 159 160
161 162 163 164 165 166 167 168 169 170 171 172 173 174 175 176 177 178 179 180
181 182 183 184 185 186 187 188 189 190 191 192 193 194 195 196 197 198 199 200

ANSWER SHEET

ETS® TOEIC® 토익 정기시험 기출문제집

수험번호

응시일자 : 20   년   월   일

성명 한글 / 한자 / 영자

Test 03 (Part 5~7)

101	121	141	161	181
102	122	142	162	182
103	123	143	163	183
104	124	144	164	184
105	125	145	165	185
106	126	146	166	186
107	127	147	167	187
108	128	148	168	188
109	129	149	169	189
110	130	150	170	190
111	131	151	171	191
112	132	152	172	192
113	133	153	173	193
114	134	154	174	194
115	135	155	175	195
116	136	156	176	196
117	137	157	177	197
118	138	158	178	198
119	139	159	179	199
120	140	160	180	200

Test 04 (Part 5~7)

101	121	141	161	181
102	122	142	162	182
103	123	143	163	183
104	124	144	164	184
105	125	145	165	185
106	126	146	166	186
107	127	147	167	187
108	128	148	168	188
109	129	149	169	189
110	130	150	170	190
111	131	151	171	191
112	132	152	172	192
113	133	153	173	193
114	134	154	174	194
115	135	155	175	195
116	136	156	176	196
117	137	157	177	197
118	138	158	178	198
119	139	159	179	199
120	140	160	180	200

ANSWER SHEET

ETS® TOEIC® 토익 정기시험 기출문제집

수험번호

응시일자 : 20   년   월   일

성명 한글 / 한자 / 영자

Test 05 (Part 5~7)

101 102 103 104 105 106 107 108 109 110 111 112 113 114 115 116 117 118 119 120
121 122 123 124 125 126 127 128 129 130 131 132 133 134 135 136 137 138 139 140
141 142 143 144 145 146 147 148 149 150 151 152 153 154 155 156 157 158 159 160
161 162 163 164 165 166 167 168 169 170 171 172 173 174 175 176 177 178 179 180
181 182 183 184 185 186 187 188 189 190 191 192 193 194 195 196 197 198 199 200

Test 06 (Part 5~7)

101 102 103 104 105 106 107 108 109 110 111 112 113 114 115 116 117 118 119 120
121 122 123 124 125 126 127 128 129 130 131 132 133 134 135 136 137 138 139 140
141 142 143 144 145 146 147 148 149 150 151 152 153 154 155 156 157 158 159 160
161 162 163 164 165 166 167 168 169 170 171 172 173 174 175 176 177 178 179 180
181 182 183 184 185 186 187 188 189 190 191 192 193 194 195 196 197 198 199 200

ANSWER SHEET

ETS® TOEIC® 토익 정기시험 기출문제집

수험번호

응시일자 : 20 ___ 년 ___ 월 ___ 일

성명
- 한글
- 한자
- 영자

Test 07 (Part 5~7)

101 102 103 104 105 106 107 108 109 110 111 112 113 114 115 116 117 118 119 120
121 122 123 124 125 126 127 128 129 130 131 132 133 134 135 136 137 138 139 140
141 142 143 144 145 146 147 148 149 150 151 152 153 154 155 156 157 158 159 160
161 162 163 164 165 166 167 168 169 170 171 172 173 174 175 176 177 178 179 180
181 182 183 184 185 186 187 188 189 190 191 192 193 194 195 196 197 198 199 200

Test 08 (Part 5~7)

101 102 103 104 105 106 107 108 109 110 111 112 113 114 115 116 117 118 119 120
121 122 123 124 125 126 127 128 129 130 131 132 133 134 135 136 137 138 139 140
141 142 143 144 145 146 147 148 149 150 151 152 153 154 155 156 157 158 159 160
161 162 163 164 165 166 167 168 169 170 171 172 173 174 175 176 177 178 179 180
181 182 183 184 185 186 187 188 189 190 191 192 193 194 195 196 197 198 199 200

ANSWER SHEET

ETS® TOEIC® 토익 정기시험 기출문제집

수험번호

응시일자 : 20　　　년　　　월　　　일

성명	한글 / 한자 / 영자

Test 09 (Part 5~7)

101 102 103 104 105 106 107 108 109 110 111 112 113 114 115 116 117 118 119 120

121 122 123 124 125 126 127 128 129 130 131 132 133 134 135 136 137 138 139 140

141 142 143 144 145 146 147 148 149 150 151 152 153 154 155 156 157 158 159 160

161 162 163 164 165 166 167 168 169 170 171 172 173 174 175 176 177 178 179 180

181 182 183 184 185 186 187 188 189 190 191 192 193 194 195 196 197 198 199 200

Test 10 (Part 5~7)

101 102 103 104 105 106 107 108 109 110 111 112 113 114 115 116 117 118 119 120

121 122 123 124 125 126 127 128 129 130 131 132 133 134 135 136 137 138 139 140

141 142 143 144 145 146 147 148 149 150 151 152 153 154 155 156 157 158 159 160

161 162 163 164 165 166 167 168 169 170 171 172 173 174 175 176 177 178 179 180

181 182 183 184 185 186 187 188 189 190 191 192 193 194 195 196 197 198 199 200

ANSWER SHEET

ETS® TOEIC® 토익 정기시험 기출문제집

수험번호

응시일자 : 20   년   월   일

성 명	한글	
	한자	
	영자	

Test (Part 5~7)

101	ⓐⓑⓒⓓ	121	ⓐⓑⓒⓓ	141	ⓐⓑⓒⓓ	161	ⓐⓑⓒⓓ	181	ⓐⓑⓒⓓ
102	ⓐⓑⓒⓓ	122	ⓐⓑⓒⓓ	142	ⓐⓑⓒⓓ	162	ⓐⓑⓒⓓ	182	ⓐⓑⓒⓓ
103	ⓐⓑⓒⓓ	123	ⓐⓑⓒⓓ	143	ⓐⓑⓒⓓ	163	ⓐⓑⓒⓓ	183	ⓐⓑⓒⓓ
104	ⓐⓑⓒⓓ	124	ⓐⓑⓒⓓ	144	ⓐⓑⓒⓓ	164	ⓐⓑⓒⓓ	184	ⓐⓑⓒⓓ
105	ⓐⓑⓒⓓ	125	ⓐⓑⓒⓓ	145	ⓐⓑⓒⓓ	165	ⓐⓑⓒⓓ	185	ⓐⓑⓒⓓ
106	ⓐⓑⓒⓓ	126	ⓐⓑⓒⓓ	146	ⓐⓑⓒⓓ	166	ⓐⓑⓒⓓ	186	ⓐⓑⓒⓓ
107	ⓐⓑⓒⓓ	127	ⓐⓑⓒⓓ	147	ⓐⓑⓒⓓ	167	ⓐⓑⓒⓓ	187	ⓐⓑⓒⓓ
108	ⓐⓑⓒⓓ	128	ⓐⓑⓒⓓ	148	ⓐⓑⓒⓓ	168	ⓐⓑⓒⓓ	188	ⓐⓑⓒⓓ
109	ⓐⓑⓒⓓ	129	ⓐⓑⓒⓓ	149	ⓐⓑⓒⓓ	169	ⓐⓑⓒⓓ	189	ⓐⓑⓒⓓ
110	ⓐⓑⓒⓓ	130	ⓐⓑⓒⓓ	150	ⓐⓑⓒⓓ	170	ⓐⓑⓒⓓ	190	ⓐⓑⓒⓓ
111	ⓐⓑⓒⓓ	131	ⓐⓑⓒⓓ	151	ⓐⓑⓒⓓ	171	ⓐⓑⓒⓓ	191	ⓐⓑⓒⓓ
112	ⓐⓑⓒⓓ	132	ⓐⓑⓒⓓ	152	ⓐⓑⓒⓓ	172	ⓐⓑⓒⓓ	192	ⓐⓑⓒⓓ
113	ⓐⓑⓒⓓ	133	ⓐⓑⓒⓓ	153	ⓐⓑⓒⓓ	173	ⓐⓑⓒⓓ	193	ⓐⓑⓒⓓ
114	ⓐⓑⓒⓓ	134	ⓐⓑⓒⓓ	154	ⓐⓑⓒⓓ	174	ⓐⓑⓒⓓ	194	ⓐⓑⓒⓓ
115	ⓐⓑⓒⓓ	135	ⓐⓑⓒⓓ	155	ⓐⓑⓒⓓ	175	ⓐⓑⓒⓓ	195	ⓐⓑⓒⓓ
116	ⓐⓑⓒⓓ	136	ⓐⓑⓒⓓ	156	ⓐⓑⓒⓓ	176	ⓐⓑⓒⓓ	196	ⓐⓑⓒⓓ
117	ⓐⓑⓒⓓ	137	ⓐⓑⓒⓓ	157	ⓐⓑⓒⓓ	177	ⓐⓑⓒⓓ	197	ⓐⓑⓒⓓ
118	ⓐⓑⓒⓓ	138	ⓐⓑⓒⓓ	158	ⓐⓑⓒⓓ	178	ⓐⓑⓒⓓ	198	ⓐⓑⓒⓓ
119	ⓐⓑⓒⓓ	139	ⓐⓑⓒⓓ	159	ⓐⓑⓒⓓ	179	ⓐⓑⓒⓓ	199	ⓐⓑⓒⓓ
120	ⓐⓑⓒⓓ	140	ⓐⓑⓒⓓ	160	ⓐⓑⓒⓓ	180	ⓐⓑⓒⓓ	200	ⓐⓑⓒⓓ

Test (Part 5~7)

101	ⓐⓑⓒⓓ	121	ⓐⓑⓒⓓ	141	ⓐⓑⓒⓓ	161	ⓐⓑⓒⓓ	181	ⓐⓑⓒⓓ
102	ⓐⓑⓒⓓ	122	ⓐⓑⓒⓓ	142	ⓐⓑⓒⓓ	162	ⓐⓑⓒⓓ	182	ⓐⓑⓒⓓ
103	ⓐⓑⓒⓓ	123	ⓐⓑⓒⓓ	143	ⓐⓑⓒⓓ	163	ⓐⓑⓒⓓ	183	ⓐⓑⓒⓓ
104	ⓐⓑⓒⓓ	124	ⓐⓑⓒⓓ	144	ⓐⓑⓒⓓ	164	ⓐⓑⓒⓓ	184	ⓐⓑⓒⓓ
105	ⓐⓑⓒⓓ	125	ⓐⓑⓒⓓ	145	ⓐⓑⓒⓓ	165	ⓐⓑⓒⓓ	185	ⓐⓑⓒⓓ
106	ⓐⓑⓒⓓ	126	ⓐⓑⓒⓓ	146	ⓐⓑⓒⓓ	166	ⓐⓑⓒⓓ	186	ⓐⓑⓒⓓ
107	ⓐⓑⓒⓓ	127	ⓐⓑⓒⓓ	147	ⓐⓑⓒⓓ	167	ⓐⓑⓒⓓ	187	ⓐⓑⓒⓓ
108	ⓐⓑⓒⓓ	128	ⓐⓑⓒⓓ	148	ⓐⓑⓒⓓ	168	ⓐⓑⓒⓓ	188	ⓐⓑⓒⓓ
109	ⓐⓑⓒⓓ	129	ⓐⓑⓒⓓ	149	ⓐⓑⓒⓓ	169	ⓐⓑⓒⓓ	189	ⓐⓑⓒⓓ
110	ⓐⓑⓒⓓ	130	ⓐⓑⓒⓓ	150	ⓐⓑⓒⓓ	170	ⓐⓑⓒⓓ	190	ⓐⓑⓒⓓ
111	ⓐⓑⓒⓓ	131	ⓐⓑⓒⓓ	151	ⓐⓑⓒⓓ	171	ⓐⓑⓒⓓ	191	ⓐⓑⓒⓓ
112	ⓐⓑⓒⓓ	132	ⓐⓑⓒⓓ	152	ⓐⓑⓒⓓ	172	ⓐⓑⓒⓓ	192	ⓐⓑⓒⓓ
113	ⓐⓑⓒⓓ	133	ⓐⓑⓒⓓ	153	ⓐⓑⓒⓓ	173	ⓐⓑⓒⓓ	193	ⓐⓑⓒⓓ
114	ⓐⓑⓒⓓ	134	ⓐⓑⓒⓓ	154	ⓐⓑⓒⓓ	174	ⓐⓑⓒⓓ	194	ⓐⓑⓒⓓ
115	ⓐⓑⓒⓓ	135	ⓐⓑⓒⓓ	155	ⓐⓑⓒⓓ	175	ⓐⓑⓒⓓ	195	ⓐⓑⓒⓓ
116	ⓐⓑⓒⓓ	136	ⓐⓑⓒⓓ	156	ⓐⓑⓒⓓ	176	ⓐⓑⓒⓓ	196	ⓐⓑⓒⓓ
117	ⓐⓑⓒⓓ	137	ⓐⓑⓒⓓ	157	ⓐⓑⓒⓓ	177	ⓐⓑⓒⓓ	197	ⓐⓑⓒⓓ
118	ⓐⓑⓒⓓ	138	ⓐⓑⓒⓓ	158	ⓐⓑⓒⓓ	178	ⓐⓑⓒⓓ	198	ⓐⓑⓒⓓ
119	ⓐⓑⓒⓓ	139	ⓐⓑⓒⓓ	159	ⓐⓑⓒⓓ	179	ⓐⓑⓒⓓ	199	ⓐⓑⓒⓓ
120	ⓐⓑⓒⓓ	140	ⓐⓑⓒⓓ	160	ⓐⓑⓒⓓ	180	ⓐⓑⓒⓓ	200	ⓐⓑⓒⓓ

ANSWER SHEET

ETS® TOEIC® 토익 정기시험 기출문제집

수험번호

응시일자 : 20   년   월   일

성명: 한글 / 한자 / 영자

Test (Part 5~7)

101	ⓐ ⓑ ⓒ ⓓ	121	ⓐ ⓑ ⓒ ⓓ	141	ⓐ ⓑ ⓒ ⓓ	161	ⓐ ⓑ ⓒ ⓓ	181	ⓐ ⓑ ⓒ ⓓ
102	ⓐ ⓑ ⓒ ⓓ	122	ⓐ ⓑ ⓒ ⓓ	142	ⓐ ⓑ ⓒ ⓓ	162	ⓐ ⓑ ⓒ ⓓ	182	ⓐ ⓑ ⓒ ⓓ
103	ⓐ ⓑ ⓒ ⓓ	123	ⓐ ⓑ ⓒ ⓓ	143	ⓐ ⓑ ⓒ ⓓ	163	ⓐ ⓑ ⓒ ⓓ	183	ⓐ ⓑ ⓒ ⓓ
104	ⓐ ⓑ ⓒ ⓓ	124	ⓐ ⓑ ⓒ ⓓ	144	ⓐ ⓑ ⓒ ⓓ	164	ⓐ ⓑ ⓒ ⓓ	184	ⓐ ⓑ ⓒ ⓓ
105	ⓐ ⓑ ⓒ ⓓ	125	ⓐ ⓑ ⓒ ⓓ	145	ⓐ ⓑ ⓒ ⓓ	165	ⓐ ⓑ ⓒ ⓓ	185	ⓐ ⓑ ⓒ ⓓ
106	ⓐ ⓑ ⓒ ⓓ	126	ⓐ ⓑ ⓒ ⓓ	146	ⓐ ⓑ ⓒ ⓓ	166	ⓐ ⓑ ⓒ ⓓ	186	ⓐ ⓑ ⓒ ⓓ
107	ⓐ ⓑ ⓒ ⓓ	127	ⓐ ⓑ ⓒ ⓓ	147	ⓐ ⓑ ⓒ ⓓ	167	ⓐ ⓑ ⓒ ⓓ	187	ⓐ ⓑ ⓒ ⓓ
108	ⓐ ⓑ ⓒ ⓓ	128	ⓐ ⓑ ⓒ ⓓ	148	ⓐ ⓑ ⓒ ⓓ	168	ⓐ ⓑ ⓒ ⓓ	188	ⓐ ⓑ ⓒ ⓓ
109	ⓐ ⓑ ⓒ ⓓ	129	ⓐ ⓑ ⓒ ⓓ	149	ⓐ ⓑ ⓒ ⓓ	169	ⓐ ⓑ ⓒ ⓓ	189	ⓐ ⓑ ⓒ ⓓ
110	ⓐ ⓑ ⓒ ⓓ	130	ⓐ ⓑ ⓒ ⓓ	150	ⓐ ⓑ ⓒ ⓓ	170	ⓐ ⓑ ⓒ ⓓ	190	ⓐ ⓑ ⓒ ⓓ
111	ⓐ ⓑ ⓒ ⓓ	131	ⓐ ⓑ ⓒ ⓓ	151	ⓐ ⓑ ⓒ ⓓ	171	ⓐ ⓑ ⓒ ⓓ	191	ⓐ ⓑ ⓒ ⓓ
112	ⓐ ⓑ ⓒ ⓓ	132	ⓐ ⓑ ⓒ ⓓ	152	ⓐ ⓑ ⓒ ⓓ	172	ⓐ ⓑ ⓒ ⓓ	192	ⓐ ⓑ ⓒ ⓓ
113	ⓐ ⓑ ⓒ ⓓ	133	ⓐ ⓑ ⓒ ⓓ	153	ⓐ ⓑ ⓒ ⓓ	173	ⓐ ⓑ ⓒ ⓓ	193	ⓐ ⓑ ⓒ ⓓ
114	ⓐ ⓑ ⓒ ⓓ	134	ⓐ ⓑ ⓒ ⓓ	154	ⓐ ⓑ ⓒ ⓓ	174	ⓐ ⓑ ⓒ ⓓ	194	ⓐ ⓑ ⓒ ⓓ
115	ⓐ ⓑ ⓒ ⓓ	135	ⓐ ⓑ ⓒ ⓓ	155	ⓐ ⓑ ⓒ ⓓ	175	ⓐ ⓑ ⓒ ⓓ	195	ⓐ ⓑ ⓒ ⓓ
116	ⓐ ⓑ ⓒ ⓓ	136	ⓐ ⓑ ⓒ ⓓ	156	ⓐ ⓑ ⓒ ⓓ	176	ⓐ ⓑ ⓒ ⓓ	196	ⓐ ⓑ ⓒ ⓓ
117	ⓐ ⓑ ⓒ ⓓ	137	ⓐ ⓑ ⓒ ⓓ	157	ⓐ ⓑ ⓒ ⓓ	177	ⓐ ⓑ ⓒ ⓓ	197	ⓐ ⓑ ⓒ ⓓ
118	ⓐ ⓑ ⓒ ⓓ	138	ⓐ ⓑ ⓒ ⓓ	158	ⓐ ⓑ ⓒ ⓓ	178	ⓐ ⓑ ⓒ ⓓ	198	ⓐ ⓑ ⓒ ⓓ
119	ⓐ ⓑ ⓒ ⓓ	139	ⓐ ⓑ ⓒ ⓓ	159	ⓐ ⓑ ⓒ ⓓ	179	ⓐ ⓑ ⓒ ⓓ	199	ⓐ ⓑ ⓒ ⓓ
120	ⓐ ⓑ ⓒ ⓓ	140	ⓐ ⓑ ⓒ ⓓ	160	ⓐ ⓑ ⓒ ⓓ	180	ⓐ ⓑ ⓒ ⓓ	200	ⓐ ⓑ ⓒ ⓓ

Test (Part 5~7)

101	ⓐ ⓑ ⓒ ⓓ	121	ⓐ ⓑ ⓒ ⓓ	141	ⓐ ⓑ ⓒ ⓓ	161	ⓐ ⓑ ⓒ ⓓ	181	ⓐ ⓑ ⓒ ⓓ
102	ⓐ ⓑ ⓒ ⓓ	122	ⓐ ⓑ ⓒ ⓓ	142	ⓐ ⓑ ⓒ ⓓ	162	ⓐ ⓑ ⓒ ⓓ	182	ⓐ ⓑ ⓒ ⓓ
103	ⓐ ⓑ ⓒ ⓓ	123	ⓐ ⓑ ⓒ ⓓ	143	ⓐ ⓑ ⓒ ⓓ	163	ⓐ ⓑ ⓒ ⓓ	183	ⓐ ⓑ ⓒ ⓓ
104	ⓐ ⓑ ⓒ ⓓ	124	ⓐ ⓑ ⓒ ⓓ	144	ⓐ ⓑ ⓒ ⓓ	164	ⓐ ⓑ ⓒ ⓓ	184	ⓐ ⓑ ⓒ ⓓ
105	ⓐ ⓑ ⓒ ⓓ	125	ⓐ ⓑ ⓒ ⓓ	145	ⓐ ⓑ ⓒ ⓓ	165	ⓐ ⓑ ⓒ ⓓ	185	ⓐ ⓑ ⓒ ⓓ
106	ⓐ ⓑ ⓒ ⓓ	126	ⓐ ⓑ ⓒ ⓓ	146	ⓐ ⓑ ⓒ ⓓ	166	ⓐ ⓑ ⓒ ⓓ	186	ⓐ ⓑ ⓒ ⓓ
107	ⓐ ⓑ ⓒ ⓓ	127	ⓐ ⓑ ⓒ ⓓ	147	ⓐ ⓑ ⓒ ⓓ	167	ⓐ ⓑ ⓒ ⓓ	187	ⓐ ⓑ ⓒ ⓓ
108	ⓐ ⓑ ⓒ ⓓ	128	ⓐ ⓑ ⓒ ⓓ	148	ⓐ ⓑ ⓒ ⓓ	168	ⓐ ⓑ ⓒ ⓓ	188	ⓐ ⓑ ⓒ ⓓ
109	ⓐ ⓑ ⓒ ⓓ	129	ⓐ ⓑ ⓒ ⓓ	149	ⓐ ⓑ ⓒ ⓓ	169	ⓐ ⓑ ⓒ ⓓ	189	ⓐ ⓑ ⓒ ⓓ
110	ⓐ ⓑ ⓒ ⓓ	130	ⓐ ⓑ ⓒ ⓓ	150	ⓐ ⓑ ⓒ ⓓ	170	ⓐ ⓑ ⓒ ⓓ	190	ⓐ ⓑ ⓒ ⓓ
111	ⓐ ⓑ ⓒ ⓓ	131	ⓐ ⓑ ⓒ ⓓ	151	ⓐ ⓑ ⓒ ⓓ	171	ⓐ ⓑ ⓒ ⓓ	191	ⓐ ⓑ ⓒ ⓓ
112	ⓐ ⓑ ⓒ ⓓ	132	ⓐ ⓑ ⓒ ⓓ	152	ⓐ ⓑ ⓒ ⓓ	172	ⓐ ⓑ ⓒ ⓓ	192	ⓐ ⓑ ⓒ ⓓ
113	ⓐ ⓑ ⓒ ⓓ	133	ⓐ ⓑ ⓒ ⓓ	153	ⓐ ⓑ ⓒ ⓓ	173	ⓐ ⓑ ⓒ ⓓ	193	ⓐ ⓑ ⓒ ⓓ
114	ⓐ ⓑ ⓒ ⓓ	134	ⓐ ⓑ ⓒ ⓓ	154	ⓐ ⓑ ⓒ ⓓ	174	ⓐ ⓑ ⓒ ⓓ	194	ⓐ ⓑ ⓒ ⓓ
115	ⓐ ⓑ ⓒ ⓓ	135	ⓐ ⓑ ⓒ ⓓ	155	ⓐ ⓑ ⓒ ⓓ	175	ⓐ ⓑ ⓒ ⓓ	195	ⓐ ⓑ ⓒ ⓓ
116	ⓐ ⓑ ⓒ ⓓ	136	ⓐ ⓑ ⓒ ⓓ	156	ⓐ ⓑ ⓒ ⓓ	176	ⓐ ⓑ ⓒ ⓓ	196	ⓐ ⓑ ⓒ ⓓ
117	ⓐ ⓑ ⓒ ⓓ	137	ⓐ ⓑ ⓒ ⓓ	157	ⓐ ⓑ ⓒ ⓓ	177	ⓐ ⓑ ⓒ ⓓ	197	ⓐ ⓑ ⓒ ⓓ
118	ⓐ ⓑ ⓒ ⓓ	138	ⓐ ⓑ ⓒ ⓓ	158	ⓐ ⓑ ⓒ ⓓ	178	ⓐ ⓑ ⓒ ⓓ	198	ⓐ ⓑ ⓒ ⓓ
119	ⓐ ⓑ ⓒ ⓓ	139	ⓐ ⓑ ⓒ ⓓ	159	ⓐ ⓑ ⓒ ⓓ	179	ⓐ ⓑ ⓒ ⓓ	199	ⓐ ⓑ ⓒ ⓓ
120	ⓐ ⓑ ⓒ ⓓ	140	ⓐ ⓑ ⓒ ⓓ	160	ⓐ ⓑ ⓒ ⓓ	180	ⓐ ⓑ ⓒ ⓓ	200	ⓐ ⓑ ⓒ ⓓ

토익® 정기시험
기출문제집 1
1000
READING

정답 및 해설

101 (B)	**102** (C)	**103** (A)	**104** (D)	**105** (B)
106 (C)	**107** (A)	**108** (D)	**109** (C)	**110** (A)
111 (A)	**112** (C)	**113** (D)	**114** (A)	**115** (B)
116 (B)	**117** (A)	**118** (B)	**119** (A)	**120** (D)
121 (B)	**122** (D)	**123** (A)	**124** (C)	**125** (D)
126 (B)	**127** (A)	**128** (C)	**129** (D)	**130** (D)
131 (A)	**132** (C)	**133** (D)	**134** (C)	**135** (A)
136 (C)	**137** (A)	**138** (A)	**139** (B)	**140** (D)
141 (C)	**142** (B)	**143** (D)	**144** (A)	**145** (B)
146 (A)	**147** (B)	**148** (D)	**149** (B)	**150** (C)
151 (C)	**152** (B)	**153** (D)	**154** (A)	**155** (A)
156 (B)	**157** (B)	**158** (A)	**159** (C)	**160** (C)
161 (C)	**162** (B)	**163** (B)	**164** (C)	**165** (D)
166 (D)	**167** (A)	**168** (B)	**169** (A)	**170** (C)
171 (C)	**172** (B)	**173** (B)	**174** (A)	**175** (D)
176 (B)	**177** (A)	**178** (D)	**179** (B)	**180** (C)
181 (A)	**182** (B)	**183** (C)	**184** (C)	**185** (A)
186 (B)	**187** (C)	**188** (D)	**189** (C)	**190** (B)
191 (B)	**192** (D)	**193** (B)	**194** (C)	**195** (D)
196 (D)	**197** (B)	**198** (C)	**199** (A)	**200** (C)

PART 5

101 인칭대명사의 격 _ 목적격

해설 빈칸은 to help의 목적어 자리로, 보기 중 목적어 역할을 할 수 있는 대명사가 들어가야 한다. to help의 주체인 volunteers(자원봉사자들)가 도울 대상이 Ms. Durkin이므로, (B) her가 정답이다. (C) hers는 소유대명사로서 '그녀의 것'을 의미하기 때문에 문맥상 빈칸에 적절하지 않으며, 재귀대명사인 (D) herself는 목적어로 쓰일 경우 동사의 주체와 동일한 대상이어야 하는데, 해당 문장에서 to help의 주체는 volunteers이므로 (D) 역시 정답이 될 수 없다.

번역 더킨 씨는 직원 체력 단련 프로그램에서 그녀를 도와줄 자원봉사자들을 요청했다.

어휘 ask for ~를 요청하다 employee 직원 fitness 체력 단련

102 명사 자리 _ 목적어

해설 빈칸은 형용사 extensive의 수식을 받으며 동사 have의 목적어 역할을 하는 명사 자리이므로, (C) knowledge가 정답이다. (A) know는 동사, (B) known은 과거분사/형용사, (D) knowledgeable는 형용사이므로 품사상 빈칸에 적합하지 않다.

번역 라스너 전자 회사의 직원들은 현재 사용하는 하드웨어 시스템에 대한 폭넓은 지식을 보유하고 있다.

어휘 electronics 전자 장치, 전자 기술 extensive 폭넓은 current 현재의 knowledgeable 많이 아는

103 부사 어휘

해설 명사구 a year와 함께 동사 audits를 수식할 수 있는 부사가 들어가야 하며, 문맥상 '일 년에 한 번'이라는 내용이 되어야 자연스러우므로, (A) Once가 정답이다.

번역 일년에 한 번, 타린 산업 용품 회사는 자사의 모든 공장의 회계 장부를 감사한다.

어휘 industrial supply 산업 용품 (공급업) audit 회계를 감사하다 account (회계) 장부, 계좌 immediately 즉시 directly 즉시, 직접적으로

104 접속사 자리

해설 빈칸 앞뒤에 완전한 절이 왔으므로, 빈칸에는 두 절을 연결하는 접속사가 들어가야 한다. 문맥을 살펴보면 커피메이커가 파손된 것이 환불을 요청한 이유가 되므로, '~ 때문에'를 의미하는 부사절 접속사인 (D) because가 정답이다. (A) despite와 (C) concerning은 전치사로서 절을 이끌 수 없으므로 오답이다.

번역 팜 씨는 배송 받은 커피메이커가 파손되었기 때문에 환불을 요청했다.

어휘 refund 환불 receive 받다 damaged 파손된 despite ~에도 불구하고 concerning ~에 관한

105 전치사 어휘

해설 주어 Information을 수식하는 구를 이끌 전치사를 선택하는 문제이다. 문맥상 '로비에 있는 예술 작품에 관한 정보'라는 내용이 되어야 자연스러우므로, (B) about이 정답이다. 참고로, '~에 관한 정보'라는 표현에는 전치사 about과 on이 쓰이며, (C) upon은 on과 동의어이긴 하지만 '~에 관한'이라는 의미로는 쓰이지 않는다.

번역 로비에 있는 예술 작품에 관한 정보는 안내 데스크에서 구할 수 있다.

어휘 available 이용할 수 있는 reception desk 접수처, 프런트 except ~를 제외하고

106 부사 자리 _ 동사 수식

해설 빈칸은 조동사 can과 동사 see 사이에서 동사를 수식하는 부사 자리이므로, (C) easily가 정답이다. (A) ease는 동사/명사, (B) easy는 형용사, (D) easier는 형용사의 비교급이므로 품사상 빈칸에 적합하지 않다.

번역 제마 XTI 쌍안경을 이용하여, 사용자들은 100미터 넘게 멀리 떨어져 있는 물체를 쉽게 볼 수 있다.

어휘 binoculars 쌍안경 object 물체 ease 수월하게 하다; 용이함

107 형용사 어휘

해설 빈칸은 동명사 keeping의 목적어인 costs에 대해 설명하는 목적격 보어 자리로, 비용을 어떤 상태로 유지하는지 적절히 묘사하는 형용사가 들어가야 한다. 따라서 '(가격이 누구에게나) 적당한, 저렴한'이라는 의미의 (A) affordable이 정답이다. 참고로, keep은 「keep + 목적어 + 목적격 보어」 구조로 자주 쓰인다.

번역 물리치료 협회는 자격증 프로그램의 비용을 저렴하게 유지하려고 노력한다.

어휘 physical therapy 물리치료 association 협회
be committed to ~에 헌신[전념]하다 certification 증명(서)
permitted 허용된 cutting 예리한, 매서운 necessary 필요한

108 동사 자리

해설 주절에 동사가 보이지 않고 주어(Mr. Brennel)와 목적어(positions) 사이가 비어 있으므로, 빈칸에는 동사가 들어가야 한다. 따라서 보기 중 본동사 역할을 할 수 있는 (D) occupied가 정답이다. (A) occupation은 명사, (B) occupational은 형용사, (C) occupying은 준동사이므로 빈칸에 들어갈 수 없다.

번역 브레넬 씨는 사장이 되기 전에 회사의 다양한 분야에서 직책을 맡았다.

어휘 position 직위, 위치 various 다양한 occupation 직업, 재직
occupational 직업과 관련된 occupy 맡다, 차지하다

109 명사 어휘

해설 동사 submit 및 전치사구 to the book과 어울려 쓰이는 명사를 선택하는 문제로, 정답은 전치사 to와 함께 쓰여 '~에 대한 수정(사항), ~에서 수정한 사항'이라는 의미를 완성하는 (C) revisions이다. (D) suggestions도 문맥상 그럴듯해 보이지만, '제안(사항)'이라는 의미로 쓰일 경우 전치사 for나 about과 쓰이므로, 빈칸에 적절하지 않다.

번역 일정을 맞추기 위해, 편집자들은 작가들에게 책에 대한 모든 수정사항을 금요일까지 보내야 한다.

어휘 remain 유지하다 on schedule 일정[예정]대로 editor 편집자
submit 제출하다 author 작가

110 부사 자리 _ 명사구 강조

해설 빈칸은 명사구 industry professionals를 수식하는 자리로, 보기에서 명사(구)를 수식·강조할 수 있는 부사 중 하나를 선택해야 한다. 문맥상 '업계 전문가들만이 입장권을 구매할 수 있다'라는 내용이 되어야 자연스러우므로, (A) Only가 정답이다. (D) Quite는 명사를 수식할 때 「quite+한정사+명사」 형태로 쓰이며 '상당히, 굉장히'라는 의미를 나타내므로 빈칸에 적절하지 않다.

번역 업계 종사자들만이 쿠오 사진 박람회의 입장권을 구매할 수 있다.

어휘 industry 업(계), 산업 professional (전문직) 종사자, 전문가
be allowed to ~하는 것이 허용되다 purchase 구매하다

111 동사 어휘

해설 a trophy (for his performance)와 어울리는 동사를 선택하는 문제이다. '(성과를 보여) 연회에서 상을 받았다'라는 내용이 되어야 자연스러우므로, 정답은 '받아들였다, 수락했다'를 의미하는 (A) accepted이다. (B) congratulated와 (C) nominated는 목적어 자리에 사람이 와야 하며, (D) hoped가 '(명사)를 바라다'라는 의미로 쓰일 때는 전치사 for가 있어야 하므로, 모두 빈칸에 적절하지 않다.

번역 팜벡 연회에서 존스 씨는 올해 품질 개선 실행 계획 부문에서 그가 보인 성과로 상을 받았다.

어휘 banquet 연회, 만찬 performance 성과, 실적 quality-improvement 품질 개선 initiative (실행) 계획, (목표 달성을 위한) 활동 계획

112 형용사 자리 _ 보어

해설 빈칸은 동사 become의 보어 자리로, 명사 혹은 형용사가 들어갈 수 있다. 문맥상 '중요한 시장이 예측 가능해졌다'라는 내용이 되어야 자연스러우므로, '예측할 수 있는'이라는 의미의 형용사인 (C) predictable이 정답이다. 명사인 (B) prediction도 보어 역할을 할 수 있지만, 주어인 important market trends와 동격 관계가 성립되지 않으므로 정답이 될 수 없다.

번역 수토 씨는 데이터 분석 활용으로 중요한 시장 동향이 예측 가능해졌다고 주장한다.

어휘 claim 주장하다 market trend 시장 경향[동향] analysis 분석 predict 예측하다 prediction 예측, 예견 predictably 예상대로

113 전치사 어휘

해설 빈칸 앞의 the relationship 및 뒤따라 오는 명사구 salespeople and their customers와 어울리는 전치사를 선택하는 문제이다. 문맥상 '영업 사원과 고객 사이의 관계'라는 내용이 되어야 자연스러우므로, (D) between이 정답이다. between은 등위 접속사 and와 함께 「between A and B」의 구조로 자주 쓰이며, 'A와 B 사이에(의)'라는 의미를 나타낸다.

번역 그로머 컨설팅의 목표 중 하나는 영업 사원과 고객 사이의 관계를 증진하는 것이다.

어휘 enhance 향상하다, 증진하다 relationship 관계

114 동사 어형

해설 빈칸에 적절한 동사 형태를 고르는 문제이다. 문두에 '당신의 답변에 따라(Depending on your answers)'라는 내용이 왔으므로, 빈칸에는 '전화할 수도 있다'는 가능성을 나타내는 표현이 들어가야 자연스럽다. 따라서 (A) may call이 정답이다.

번역 설문 조사에 대한 귀하의 답변에 따라, 추가 정보를 수집하기 위해 저희가 전화를 드릴 수도 있습니다.

어휘 depending on ~에 따라 survey (설문) 조사 additional 추가의

115 부사절 접속사

해설 빈칸은 두 개의 완전한 절을 연결하는 부사절 접속사 자리이다. 문맥상 '젬버거가 새로운 가맹점을 열었을 때, 고객들은 무료 햄버거를 받았다'라는 내용이 되어야 자연스러우므로, '~할 때'라는 의미로 특정 시점을 나타내는 (B) When이 정답이다. (C) As if는 주로 주절 뒤에 위치하여 '마치 ~인 것처럼'이라는 뜻으로 쓰이므로 빈칸에 적절하지 않다.

번역　젬버거가 최근 새로운 가맹점을 열었을 때, 선착순 100명의 고객들이 무료 햄버거를 받았다.

어휘　newest 최신의　franchise 가맹점　customer 고객

116　명사 자리 _ 전치사의 목적어 _ 어휘

해설　빈칸은 전치사 in의 목적어 자리로, any의 수식을 받을 수 있는 명사가 들어가야 한다. 보기에서 명사인 (B) correspondence와 (D) correspondent 중 하나를 선택해야 하는데, '서신에 제품의 일련번호를 포함해 달라'라는 내용이 되어야 자연스러우므로, '서신, 편지'를 의미하는 (B) correspondence가 정답이다. (D) correspondent는 '특파원, 편지를 쓰는 사람'을 의미하는 사람 명사이므로 빈칸에 적절하지 않다.

번역　고객 서비스 부서와 주고받는 모든 서신에 귀하의 제품 일련번호를 포함해 주십시오.

어휘　include 포함하다　serial number 일련번호　department 부서

117　전치사 어휘

해설　빈칸 앞에 나온 명사 awareness와 어울리는 전치사를 선택하는 문제이다. awareness는 '의식, 인식'이라는 의미로 주로 전치사 of, about과 함께 쓰여 '~에 대한 의식[관심]'이라는 표현을 완성하므로, 정답은 (A) of이다.

번역　수상 경력에 빛나는 영화 〈바닷속 비밀〉은 해양 오염과 그것이 지구에 미치는 영향에 대한 의식을 고취한다.

어휘　award-winning 상을 받은　promote 고취하다, 홍보하다 pollution 오염　effect 영향, 결과

118　형용사 자리

해설　빈칸은 전치사 in과 promotional items 사이 자리이므로, 형용사 promotional을 수식하는 부사나 명사 items를 수식하는 형용사가 들어갈 수 있다. 보기에서 부사인 (A) personally와 과거분사형 형용사인 (B) personalized 중 하나를 선택해야 하는데, 문맥상 '맞춤형[맞춤화된] 홍보용 제품'이라는 의미가 되어야 자연스러우므로, (B) personalized가 정답이다. (A) personally는 '개인적으로, 개별적으로'라는 의미로 promotional(홍보의)을 수식하기에는 부적절하다.

번역　BYF사는 회사들이 자사 브랜드를 광고하는 데 도움이 될 수 있는 개별 맞춤형 홍보용 제품을 전문으로 한다.

어휘　specialize in ~을 전문으로 하다　advertise 광고하다 personality 성격, 개성　personalize (개인의 필요에) 맞추다

119　부사절 접속사

해설　빈칸은 완전한 두 절을 연결하는 접속사 자리로, (A) As long as와 (C) Not only 중 하나를 선택해야 한다. 빈칸 뒤 어순이 「주어+동사」이며 문맥상 '임차료 인상이 2퍼센트 이내인 한'이라는 조건을 나타내는 것이 자연스러우므로, (A) As long as가 정답이다. 참고로, (C) Not only가 문두로 와서 절을 이끌면 「Not only+(조)동사+주어」의 구조가 된다.

번역　임차료 인상이 2퍼센트 이내인 한, 셀윈 전력 공급사는 그 공간을 계속 임차할 것이다.

어휘　electrical 전기의　supply 공급　lease 임대하다, 임차하다 along with ~에 덧붙여　otherwise 달리, 그렇지 않으면

120　동사 어형 _ 태 _ 시제

해설　that절의 동사 자리에 적절한 어형을 선택하는 문제이다. 주어 procedures와 동사 perform의 관계를 생각해 보면 '절차가 진행되다'라는 수동태가 되어야 하며, 앞에 '정기적으로 회의한다(meets regularly)'라는 내용이 왔으므로 회의의 목적을 나타내는 부분에도 현재 시제가 쓰여야 자연스럽다. 따라서 (D) are being performed가 정답이다. 과거완료형인 (C) had been performed는 '(과거 이전에) 수행되었다'를 의미하므로 문맥상 부적절하다.

번역　벨튼 병원의 최고위 간부는 절차가 올바르게 진행되고 있는지 확인하기 위해 직원들과 정기적으로 회의를 한다.

어휘　chief of staff 최고위 간부, (병원) 진료부장　regularly 정기적으로　ensure 확실히 하다, 보장하다　procedure 절차

121　형용사 어휘

해설　빈칸 뒤의 명사구 department supervisor를 적절히 수식하는 형용사를 고르는 문제이다. 문맥상 '휴가 요청은 해당 부서장에게 해야 한다'라는 내용이 되어야 자연스러우므로, '적절한, 해당하는'이라는 의미의 (B) appropriate이 정답이다. 나머지 보기는 supervisor(관리자)를 수식하기에 적절하지 않다.

번역　모든 휴가 요청은 해당 부서장에게 해야 한다.

어휘　request 요청　time off 휴가　address (직접) 말하다, 신청하다 urgent 긴급한　subsequent 그 다음의　deliverable 배달 가능한

122　명사 자리 _ 복합명사 _ 어휘

해설　빈칸이 포함된 구(innovative ------- and shipping methods)가 전치사 thanks to의 목적어 역할을 하고 있는데, 이를 분석해 보면 등위 접속사 and를 사이에 두고 빈칸 및 shipping이 methods와 복합명사를 이루고 있음을 알 수 있다. 따라서 빈칸에는 '방법'과 어울리는 명사가 들어가야 하므로, '보존, 저장'이라는 의미의 (D) preservation이 정답이다. (A) preserves와 (C) preserve는 동사 외에도 '저장 식품'이라는 명사로 쓰일 수 있지만 문맥상 빈칸에 부적절하다.

번역　월드 피쉬 공급사는 혁신적인 보존 및 운송 방법 덕분에 가장 신선한 물고기를 배송한다.

어휘　deliver 배송하다, 제공하다　innovative 혁신적인　shipping 운송, 배송　method 방법

123　명사 어휘

해설　빈칸 앞 명사 budget과 복합명사를 이루는 단어를 고르는 문제이다. 보기 중 '예산'과 어울려 검토(review)할 대상이 될 만한 것은 '(자격) 요건'을 의미하는 (A) requirements뿐이다.

번역 회사 경영진들은 현재 재무 계획 부서가 제출한 연간 예산 요건을 검토하고 있다.

어휘 executive 경영진, 간부 review 검토하다 annual 연간의, 연례의 financial 재무(금융)의 delivery 배달 developer 개발(업)자 quality (자)질, 특성

124 부사 자리 _ 명사구 수식

해설 that절의 주어 Prasma Designs' win과 빈칸 뒤의 명사구 the result of fortunate timing이 동격 관계(프라스마 디자인즈의 수상 = 시기를 잘 탄 결과)이므로, 해당 절이 「주어＋be동사＋보어」 구조의 완전한 절임을 알 수 있다. 따라서 보기 중 부사인 (C) partly만이 빈칸에 들어갈 수 있다. 참고로, partly는 '어느 정도, 부분적으로'라는 의미로 명사구를 수식할 수 있다.

번역 심지어 최고경영자조차도 프라스마 디자인즈의 수상이 어느 정도는 시기를 잘 탄 결과라고 인정했다.

어휘 admit 인정하다 win 승리, 수상 fortunate 운 좋은

125 대명사 어휘

해설 목적격 관계대명사가 생략된 절(the focus group ～ session)의 수식을 받는 적절한 대명사를 고르는 문제이다. 문맥상 '포커스 그룹이 아침 시간에 논의했던 모든 것'이라는 내용이 되어야 자연스러우므로, (D) everything이 정답이다. (A) each(각각, 각자), (B) several(몇몇), (C) another(또 다른 사람[것])는 문장 내에 지칭하거나/대신하는 대상이 있어야 한다.

번역 싱 씨는 포커스 그룹이 아침 시간에 논의했던 모든 것을 기록했다.

어휘 take notes 기록하다, 받아 적다 discuss 논의하다 session (특정한 활동을 위한) 시간[기간]

126 부사 어휘

해설 빈칸 앞에 온 ranked third와 어울리는 부사를 선택하는 문제이다. 문맥상 '종합 3위를 차지했다'라는 내용이 되어야 자연스러우므로, '전체적으로'라는 의미의 (B) overall이 정답이다.

번역 작년에 타다카 컴퓨터 솔루션즈는 지역 수익 부문에서 종합 3위를 차지했다.

어휘 rank (등급·순위를) 차지하다, 매기다 regional 지역의 earnings 수익, 소득 consecutively 연속하여 generally 일반적으로

127 전치사 자리 _ 어휘

해설 빈칸 뒤에 명사구(the popularity of ～ speaker)와 콤마가 왔으므로, 빈칸에는 수식어구를 이끌 전치사가 들어가야 한다. 해당 구와 주절의 관계를 살펴보면, 인기(popularity) 때문에 생산량이 증가될 것이라는(production will be increased) 인과 관계가 성립되는 것을 알 수 있다. 따라서 '～의 결과로'라는 의미의 (D) As a result of가 정답이다. (A) On behalf of는 '～를 대신하여'라는 의미로 문맥상 어색하고, (B) Whether는 접속사, (C) Moreover는 접속 부사이므로 품사상 빈칸에 적절하지 않다.

번역 BPT39 무선 스피커가 인기를 끌게 됨에 따라, 다음 달부터 생산량이 5배 증가될 것이다.

어휘 wireless 무선(의) fivefold 5배로 increase 증가하다

128 관계대명사 _ 소유격

해설 뒤에 오는 절(offices ～ floor)을 이끌어 앞에 있는 명사구 the law firm을 수식하는 관계사를 고르는 문제이다. 해당 절의 주어인 offices가 선행사인 the law firm의 소유이므로, 소유격 관계대명사 (C) whose가 정답이다. 참고로, (A) how, (B) what, (D) wherever는 앞에 있는 명사를 수식할 수 없다.

번역 지포 프로퍼티는 3층에 사무실이 있는 법률 사무소와 막 임대 계약을 체결했다.

어휘 sign 서명하다, 계약하다 lease 임대, 임차 agreement 계약, 협정, 합의

129 형용사 어휘

해설 빈칸 뒤의 명사 events를 적절히 수식하는 형용사를 고르는 문제이다. '사건'이라는 단어 및 '원래(original) 예측과 수익이 많이 달라졌다'라는 문맥과 어울려야 하므로, '예기치 못한, 뜻밖의'라는 의미의 (D) Unforeseen이 정답이 된다.

번역 올해 있었던 예기치 못한 사건들로 인해 2분기와 3분기의 수익이 원래 예측했던 것과 상당히 달라졌다.

어휘 cause 야기하다 profit 수익 quarter 분기 differ 다르다 significantly 상당히 projection 예측 total 총, 전체의 marginal 미미한, 중요하지 않은 representative 대표하는

130 동사 어휘

해설 빈칸 뒤의 명사 input과 어울려 쓰이는 동사를 선택하는 문제이다. 빈칸 앞에서 일정이 연장되었다(was extended)고 하였고 to 이하가 연장의 목적을 나타내므로, 문맥상 '조언을 참작하기 위해'라는 내용이 되어야 자연스럽다. 따라서 '～을 참작하다, 감안하다'라는 의미의 (D) allow for가 정답이 된다.

번역 환경 위원회의 조언을 참작하기 위해 오솔길 조명 프로젝트의 일정이 연장되었다.

어휘 timeline 시간표 pathway 오솔길 lighting 조명 extend 연장하다 environmental 환경의 commission 위원회 use up 다 써버리다 believe in ～를 믿다 make into ～으로 만들다

PART 6

131-134 광고

> 여러분은 글로벌 스트렝스 짐의 30일 체험 기간에 저희의 강좌, 기구, 시설을 체험할 기회를 갖게 됩니다. [131]체험 기간 동안 이용료를 지불하실 필요가 없으며 계약서도 작성하지 않습니다. 손해 볼 위험이 전혀 없습니다! 등록을 위해 저희가 여러분의 연락처와 결제 정보를 요청하

긴 하지만, 여러분이 30일 ¹³²넘게 회원을 유지할 경우에만 요금 청구를 받으실 것입니다. 이 기간 내에 더 이상 글로벌 스트렝스의 회원이 되고 싶지 않으시면, ¹³³그냥 www.gsgym.com으로 저희 웹사이트를 방문하시기만 하면 됩니다. 멤버십 페이지에서 멤버십 ¹³⁴취소하기를 선택하시고 필요한 정보를 입력하세요. 너무나 간단합니다!

어휘 trial 체험, 시험 opportunity 기회 try out 시험해 보다 equipment 기구, 장비 facility 시설 risk-free 손해 볼 위험이 없는, 손해되지 않는 sign up 등록하다 details 세부 사항 charge 청구하다 within ~ 이내에 elect 선택하다

131 문맥에 맞는 문장 고르기

번역 (A) 체험 기간 동안 이용료를 지불하실 필요가 없으며 계약서도 작성하지 않습니다.
(B) 역도 수업은 현재 이용이 불가능합니다.
(C) 멤버십에 등록할 때 현금 보증금이 요구됩니다.
(D) 모든 질문은 customerservice@gsgym.com으로 이메일을 보내야 됩니다.

해설 빈칸 앞 문장에서 글로벌 스트렝스 짐의 30일 체험 기간에 강좌, 기구, 시설을 체험할 기회를 갖게 된다며 체험 기간(trial period)에 대해 홍보하고 있고, 뒤 문장에서는 손해 볼 위험이 없다(risk-free)는 내용이 왔다. 따라서 빈칸에는 체험 기간에 대한 추가 설명이 들어가야 자연스러우므로, (A)가 정답이다.

어휘 currently 현재 available 이용[사용] 가능한 deposit 보증금

132 전치사 어휘

해설 앞 문장에서 30일 체험 기간(30-day trial period) 내내 돈을 낼 필요가 없다(Throughout the trial, you pay nothing)고 했으므로, 해당 부분은 '30일 넘게 회원을 유지할 경우에만 요금 청구를 받게 될 것'이라는 내용이 되어야 자연스럽다. 따라서 '~을 초과하는, ~이 넘는'을 의미하는 (C) over가 정답이다.

133 부사 어휘

해설 동사 visit을 적절히 수식하는 부사를 선택하는 문제이다. 해당 부분은 더 이상 회원이 되고 싶지 않다면 웹사이트를 방문하라는 내용으로, 마지막에 이러한 절차가 아주 쉽다(that easy)는 것을 강조하고 있다. 따라서 '그냥, 간단히'를 의미하는 (D) simply가 빈칸에 가장 적절하다. (A) justly는 '정당하게', (B) regularly는 '정기적으로', (C) evenly는 '고르게'라는 뜻으로 문맥상 어울리지 않는다.

134 동사 어휘

해설 바로 앞 문장에서 더 이상 회원이 되고 싶지 않다면 웹사이트를 방문하라고 했으므로, 해당 부분은 '멤버십 페이지에서 멤버십 취소하기를 선택하라'라는 내용이 되어야 자연스럽다. 따라서 '취소하다'를 의미하는 (C) cancel이 정답이다. (A) extend는 '연장하다', (B) renew는 '갱신하다', (D) initiate는 '개시하다'라는 뜻으로 문맥상 빈칸에 부적절하다.

135-138 지침

한슨-로브스 사원 여러분은 병가를 낼 수 있으며, 건강상의 ¹³⁵이유로 인한 휴직 기간 동안 급여를 받을 것입니다. 급여 공제를 피하려면 질병 증빙 서류로 의사가 서명한 진단서를 제출¹³⁶해야 합니다. ¹³⁷해당 서류는 의사에게 진료받은 날짜, 직책에 해당하는 업무를 수행할 수 없다는 점을 증명하는 소견 및 예상 복귀일을 포함해야 합니다. 그러면 여러분의 상사가 해당 서류를 인사과로 전달할 것입니다. ¹³⁸한슨-로브스는 여러분의 의료 정보에 대한 개인 정보 보호를 보장합니다. 직원 의료 기록은 오직 해당 기록을 살펴볼 타당한 업무상의 이유가 있는 사람들만 열람할 수 있습니다.

어휘 be entitled to ~에게 자격이 주어지다 sick absence 병가 time off 휴식 deduction 공제(액) physician 의사 include 포함하다 statement 진술(서), 성명 certify 증명하다 duties 업무 supervisor 상관 forward 전달하다 access 접근하다, 이용하다 valid 유효한, 타당한

135 명사 어휘

해설 health와 복합명사를 이루며 문맥에 어울리는 명사를 고르는 문제이다. 문장 앞 부분에서 '여러분은 병가(sick absences)를 낼 자격이 있다'라고 하였으므로, 해당 부분은 '건강상의 이유로 인한 휴직 기간 동안 급여를 받게 될 것이다'라는 내용이 되어야 자연스럽다. 따라서 전치사 for와 함께 쓰여 '~의 이유로'라는 표현을 완성하는 (A) reasons가 정답이다. (B) origins는 '기원', (C) senses는 '감각', (D) contributions는 '기여'라는 뜻으로 문맥상 어울리지 않는다.

136 동사 어형_태_시제

해설 require가 '…에게 ~하도록 요청하다'라는 의미로 쓰일 때는 「require + 목적어 + to부정사」 구조를 이룬다. 그러나 여기서는 빈칸 뒤에 목적어가 없으며 주어가 소견서를 제출하도록 요청받는다, 즉 소견서를 제출해야 한다는 내용이므로, 수동태(be + required + to부정사)로 쓰여야 한다. 따라서 보기 (A) were required와 (C) are required 중 하나를 선택해야 하는데, 과거의 특정 사건이 아닌 회사의 일반적인 방침에 대해 설명하고 있으므로, 현재 시제인 (C) are required가 정답이다.

137 대명사 어휘

해설 빈칸은 동사 should include의 주어 자리로, 앞 문장에서 언급된 단수 명사구 a physician-signed note(의사가 서명한 진단서)를 대신하므로 (D) It이 정답이다.

138 문맥에 맞는 문장 고르기

번역 (A) 한슨-로브스는 여러분의 의료 정보에 대한 개인 정보 보호를 보장합니다.
(B) 결근에는 여러 이유가 있을 수 있습니다.
(C) 그런 다음 여러분은 의사의 진단서가 없는 이유를 설명해야 합니다.
(D) 여러분이 원래 배정받은 업무를 기록하세요.

해설 앞 문장에서 진료 기록이 담긴 서류가 인사과에 전달될 것이라고 했고, 뒤 문장에서 직원 의료 기록(Employee health records)은 타당한 이유를 가진 사람들만이 열람할 수 있다고 했으므로, 빈칸에는 의료 정보에 대한 취급 방침을 설명하는 내용이 들어가야 자연스럽다. 따라서 (A)가 정답이다.

어휘 ensure 보장하다 factor 요인 explain 설명하다 assign 배정하다

139-142 이메일

수신: fcontini@attmail.com
발신: btakemoto@arolischems.co.uk
날짜: 7월 15일
제목: 아롤리스에서 당신의 첫날

콘티니 씨께,

아롤리스 화학에 합류한 것을 환영합니다! 연구실 상근 조교 정규직을 **139수락해 주어** 고맙습니다. 우리는 8월 1일에 당신이 해리스 빌딩에 도착하기를 고대하고 있습니다. 안내 데스크로 와서 잭 맥놀란을 찾으세요. 그가 인사과 사무실로 당신과 **140동행할 것입니다.** 거기에서 직원 배지**141뿐만 아니라** 일을 시작하는 데 필요한 모든 서류도 받을 것입니다. 아롤리스의 레스터 구내는 규모가 크기 때문에 길 찾기가 어려울 수도 있음을 유의하세요. 구내 지도를 보면 다양한 건물의 위치를 찾는데 도움이 될 겁니다. **142우리 웹사이트에서 다운로드할 수 있습니다.**

질문이 있으면 주저 말고 저에게 연락 주세요.

브랜든 타케모토
인사과 관리 부장

어휘 full-time 상근의 permanent position 정규직 laboratory 실험실, 연구실 assistant 보조원, 조교 report to ~에 보고하다, ~로 출두하다 obtain 얻다 navigate 길을 찾다 orient 위치를 찾게 하다, ~를 적응시키다

139 동사 어휘

해설 앞 문장에서 회사에 합류한 것을 환영한다(Welcome to Arolis Chemicals)고 했으므로, 문맥상 조교직을 '수락해 주어 고맙다'라고 하는 것이 적절하다. 따라서 '받아들인 것, 수락한 것'을 의미하는 (B) accepting이 정답이다. (A) offering은 '제안한 것', (C) discussing은 '논의한 것', (D) advertising은 '광고한 것'이라는 의미로 앞뒤 내용과 어울리지 않는다.

140 동사 어형 _ 시제

해설 빈칸은 주어 He 뒤의 동사 자리이고, 앞뒤 문장으로 보아 입사 첫날, 즉 미래에 일어날 일에 대해서 설명하고 있으므로, '동행할 것이다'를 의미하는 (D) will accompany가 정답이다.

141 상관 접속사

해설 빈칸에는 두 개의 명사(구) employee badge와 documents를 연결할 수 있는 상관 접속사가 필요하다. 따라서 두 개의 명사(구)를 연결할 수 있는 (C) as well as가 정답이다. 나머지는 모두 부사로 접속사 역할을 할 수 없다.

142 문맥에 맞는 문장 고르기

번역 (A) 모든 서류에 서명하세요.
(B) 당신에게 교체품을 제공해 드리겠습니다.
(C) 공사가 내년에 완료될 것입니다.
(D) 우리 웹사이트에서 다운로드할 수 있습니다.

해설 바로 앞 문장에서 구내 지도(a campus map)를 보면 건물을 찾는 데 도움이 될 것이라고 했으므로, '웹사이트에서 다운로드할 수 있다'며 지도를 구할 수 있는 방법을 알려 주는 내용이 들어가야 자연스럽다. 따라서 (D)가 정답이다. 이 문장에서 one은 지도를 가리킨다.

143-146 기사

(4월 18일) – 이 지역에서 가장 큰 피칸 수출업체인 MKZ 식품 회사는 향후 수개월간 발송 화물이 상당히 증가할 것으로 예상한다. 이러한 **143예측**은 지역 내 피칸 농부들이 작년에 경작지를 20퍼센트 정도 확장했다는 사실에 기반한다. 카타리나 세일러 대변인에 따르면, 올해 MKZ의 수출은 어마어마한 양인 5만 미터톤에 달할 수 있다. **144이러한 수치는 회사 역사상 전례 없는 일이다.**

MKZ는 이 지역의 피칸 농장으로부터 수확량의 대부분을 사들이고, 전 세계 수출을 **145위해** 이를 가공한다. "지역 내 새로운 **146농업**용 부지의 이용 가능성이 성장 기회를 만들고 있습니다. 저는 MKZ가 정말 눈에 띄는 한 해를 보내게 될 것으로 믿습니다."라고 세일러 씨가 말했다.

어휘 exporter 수출업체 pecan (견과류) 피칸 outgoing (밖으로) 나가는 shipment 수송품 significantly 상당히 expand 확장하다 spokesperson 대변인 reach 도달하다 colossal 거대한 metric ton 미터톤(1,000킬로그램) figure 수치 yield 수확량 process (원자재·식품 등을) 가공(처리)하다 outstanding 뛰어난

143 명사 어휘

해설 앞 문장에 MKZ 식품 회사가 향후 몇 달간 발생할 일에 대해 예측한다(expects)는 내용이 왔으며, 빈칸 앞에 지시형용사 this가 있으므로, 해당 부분은 '이러한 예측이 ~라는 사실에 기반한다'라는 내용이 되어야 자연스럽다. 따라서 '예측, 예보'를 의미하는 (D) forecast가 정답이다. (A) cost는 '비용', (B) delay는 '지연', (C) decision은 '결정'이라는 의미로, 앞에 가리키는 대상이 없으므로 빈칸에 들어갈 수 없다.

144 문맥에 맞는 문장 고르기

번역 (A) 이러한 수치는 회사 역사상 전례 없는 일이다.
　　(B) 게다가, 세일러 씨는 경제학 분야에 상급 학위를 가지고 있다.
　　(C) 피칸은 비타민과 미네랄이 풍부하다.
　　(D) 그런데도, MKZ 주식은 최근 몇 년간 수익을 냈다.

해설 바로 앞 문장에서 '올해 수출량이 어마어마한 양인 5만 미터톤에 달할 수 있다(MKZ's exports could reach a colossal 50,000 metric tons this year)'라고 했으므로, 빈칸에는 이러한 수치에 대해 언급하는 문장이 들어가야 자연스럽다. 따라서 5만 미터톤을 '이러한 수치(Such a figure)'로 대체하며 '회사 역사상 전례 없는 일이다'라고 설명한 (A)가 정답이다.

어휘 unprecedented 전례 없는　advanced degree 상급 학위 (석사·박사)

145 전치사 어휘

해설 빈칸 뒤 export(수출)가 피칸을 구입하여 가공하는(processes) 목적에 해당하므로, 목적·이유를 나타내는 전치사 (B) for가 정답이다.

146 명사 자리 _ 어휘

해설 빈칸은 전치사의 목적어 자리로, 앞에 한정사(관사, 소유격 등)가 없으므로 복수명사 혹은 불가산명사가 들어가야 한다. 따라서 불가산명사로서 '새로운 농업용 부지의 이용 가능성'이라는 의미를 완성하는 (A) farming이 정답이다.

PART 7

147-148 문자 메시지

차키아 브라운 [오후 3시 32분]

안녕하세요, 지바. 지금 막 한사의 이사진과 회의했는데, 그들이 [147]시내 사옥 재설계를 위한 우리의 제안서에 관심을 보이네요. [147, 148]에이미 한이 추가 작업 샘플을 요청했는데, 적당한 포트폴리오가 저한테 없었어요. 지금 저는 다른 회의에 가는 중이니, 배달원 편으로 그녀에게 그레인저 센터 [148]파일 사본을 보내 주세요. 디자인 도면 전체를 포함해 주세요. 고마워요!

어휘 board of directors 이사진　proposal 제안(서)　head to ~로 향하다, ~에 가다

147 추론

번역 브라운 씨는 어디에서 일할 것 같은가?
　　(A) 회계 법인
　　(B) 건축 사무소
　　(C) 웹디자인 회사
　　(D) 마켓 리서치 회사

해설 한사의 시내 사옥 재설계를 위한 제안서(our redegisn proposal for their downtown office buildings)를 이미 제출했고, 에이미 한에게 포트폴리오(portfolio)를 보내 주라고 요청하는 것으로 보아, 브라운 씨 회사가 건물 디자인 관련 업무를 한다는 것을 추론할 수 있다. 따라서 (B)가 정답이다.

148 세부 사항

번역 지바가 요청받은 것은?
　　(A) 문자 메시지에 응답하기
　　(B) 포트폴리오 만들기
　　(C) 회의 잡기
　　(D) 작업 샘플 보내기

해설 후반부를 보면 에이미 한에게 배달원 편으로 그레인저 센터 파일 사본을 보내 달라고 요청했으므로, (D)가 정답이다.

> ▸ Paraphrasing　지문의 **have a messenger deliver a copy of the Grainger Centre files**
> → 정답의 **Send a work sample**

149-150 이메일

수신: 오크 레인 패션 계산원
발신: 제인 벤슨
날짜: 7월 8일
제목: 업데이트

[149]8월 1일부터, 오크 레인 패션은 원본 영수증이 있으며, 착용 흔적이 없고 손상되지 않은 의류의 반품 혹은 교환만 허용할 것입니다.

본 정보는 다음 주면 모든 계산대에 게시될 것입니다. 우리는 또한 기존 고객이 새로운 규정에 대해 알 수 있도록 이메일을 보낼 것입니다. [150]만약 고객이 영수증 없이 반품을 원한다면, 근무 중인 매니저에게 도움을 요청하세요. 협조 감사합니다.

제인 벤슨
영업부 이사

어휘 unworn 착용하지 않은　undamaged 손상되지 않은　receipt 영수증　post (안내문 등을) 게시[공고]하다　checkout counter 계산대　existing 기존의　be aware of ~를 알고 있다　on duty 근무 중인　operation 영업, 사업

149 주제 / 목적

번역 이메일의 목적은 무엇인가?
　　(A) 판매 보고서를 요청하기 위해
　　(B) 새로운 방침을 발표하기 위해
　　(C) 패션 트렌드를 논의하기 위해
　　(D) 곧 있을 할인 판매를 설명하기 위해

해설 첫 문장에서 8월 1일부터(Beginning August 1) 원본 영수증이 있는, 착용 흔적이 없고 손상되지 않은 의류의 반품 혹은 교환만을 허용할 것(Oak Lane Fashion ~ original receipt)이라며, 앞으로 새롭게 시행될 회사의 반품 및 교환 방침에 대해 계산원들에게 알리고 있다. 따라서 (B)가 정답이다.

150 세부 사항

번역 이메일에 따르면, 매니저들은 무엇을 할 것인가?

(A) 신상품을 어떻게 진열할지 결정하는 것
(B) 직원들이 금전 등록기를 사용하도록 훈련시키는 것
(C) 특별한 요구사항이 있는 고객들을 돕는 것
(D) 무슨 제품을 할인할지 결정하는 것

해설 후반부를 보면, 새로운 정책을 고지했음에도 불구하고 고객이 영수증 없이 반품을 원하면(If a customer wishes to make a return without a receipt) 근무 중인 매니저에게 도움을 요청하라고 했으므로, (C)가 정답이다.

151-152 웹페이지

https://www.carmontmedia.co.tt

카몬트 미디어의 문화

홈	프로그램	서비스	회사 소개	연락처

카몬트 미디어의 업무 문화는 임무 중심입니다. 우리는 사람들의 관심을 끄는 진실된 뉴스거리를 통해 청취자들의 마음을 풍요롭게 하는 공통의 목표를 공유하는 사람을 채용합니다. **151우리는 또한 트리니다드 및 토바고 청취자들의 견해를 반영할 다양한 직원들을 적극적으로 모집합니다. 151카몬트 미디어의 다양성은** 회사의 **152스타 팀들에게** 도움이 됩니다. 조직 내 모든 직위의 직원들로 구성된 **152이 팀들은 효율성 및 생산성 제고를 목표로 브레인스토밍 시간을 갖기 위해 정기적으로 회의합니다.** 카몬트 미디어는 전문적인 발전 기회를 제공하며 일과 생활의 균형을 장려합니다.

어휘 mission 임무 driven 중심의 common 공통의 enrich 풍요롭게 하다 engaging 관심[주의]를 끄는 recruit 모집하다 diverse 다양한 audience 청중 diversity 다양성 contribute to ~에 기여하다 composed of ~으로 구성된 organization 조직 brainstorming 브레인스토밍(창조적 집단 사고) session (특정 활동을 위한) 시간 improve 향상하다, 제고하다 efficiency 효율성 productivity 생산성 professional 전문적인, 직업상의 advancement 발전 encourage 장려하다

151 사실 관계 확인

번역 카몬트 미디어의 직원에 대해 언급된 것은?

(A) 다양한 부서에서 경험을 쌓는다.
(B) 조직을 위해 일하는 것을 즐긴다.
(C) 다양한 배경 출신이다.
(D) 채용 업체를 통해 모집된다.

해설 세 번째 문장에서 다양한 직원을 적극적으로 모집한다(We also actively recruit a diverse staff)고 했고, 이어지는 문장에서도 카몬트 미디어의 다양성(Carmont Media's diversity)을 언급했으므로, (C)가 정답이다.

어휘 various 다양한 recruit 모집하다

▸▸ Paraphrasing 지문의 **diverse** → 정답의 **a variety of**

152 세부 사항

번역 카몬트 미디어의 스타 팀들의 목적 중 하나는 무엇인가?

(A) 새로운 직원을 영입하는 것
(B) 프로젝트 자금을 마련하는 것
(C) 일과 생활의 균형을 장려하는 것
(D) 창의적인 해결책을 찾는 것

해설 스타 팀들은 효율성과 생산성 제고를 목표로 브레인스토밍 시간을 갖기 위해(to hold brainstorming sessions aimed at improving efficiency and productivity) 정기적으로 회의한다고 했으므로, (D)가 정답이다.

▸▸ Paraphrasing 지문의 **brainstorming**
→ 정답의 **Finding creative solutions**

153-154 문자 메시지

루이자 산토스	오전 9시 30분

켄지, 어디 있나요? **153입사 지원자들이 와 있어요.**

켄지 무로	오전 9시 31분

미안해요! 다리가 폐쇄되어서요. 제가 탄 버스가 우회해야 했어요. **15330분 후에 도착할 것 같네요. 저 없이 시작하세요.**

루이자 산토스	오전 9시 34분

알겠어요. 엘레나 크렌쇼부터 **153면접을 봐야겠네요.**

켄지 무로	오전 9시 34분

좋아요. 그녀가 다른 티셔츠 회사에서 일한 경험이 있는 사람이죠.

루이자 산토스	오전 9시 35분

네. 우리의 작은 회사가 이렇게나 성장해서 단지 주문을 처리하기 위해 누군가를 채용해야 한다는 게 믿어지세요?

켄지 무로	오전 9시 36분

제 말이요! 그럼 좀 있다 봐요.

어휘 candidate 후보자 detour 우회로 process 처리하다 order 주문

153 세부 사항

번역 무로 씨는 산토스 씨가 무엇을 하기를 원하는가?

(A) 주문을 처리하는 것
(B) 고용 결정을 내리는 것
(C) 회의 일정을 다시 잡는 것
(D) 입사 지원자와 이야기하는 것

해설 입사 지원자가 와 있다(The job candidates are here)는 산토스 씨의 말에 무로 씨가 본인 없이 시작하라(Please start without me)고 하자, 산토스 씨가 면접을 진행하겠다(I'm going to interview)고 했으므로, (D)가 정답이다.

어휘 reschedule 일정을 변경하다

154 의도 파악

번역 오전 9시 36분에 무로 씨가 "제 말이요"라고 쓸 때, 그 의도는 무엇인가?

(A) 그 역시 회사의 성장이 놀랍다.
(B) 급여가 더 높아야 한다고 생각한다.
(C) 크렌쇼 씨를 만난 적이 있다.
(D) 자신이 탄 버스가 30분 후에 도착할 것을 확신한다.

해설 I know는 본래 '맞아, 그래'라며 동의를 나타내는 표현이다. 앞에서 산토스 씨가 작은 회사가 성장해서 단지 주문 처리를 위해 사람을 고용한다는 게 믿어지냐(Can you believe ~ just to process orders?)며 놀라움을 표하자, 무로 씨가 본인도 믿기지 않는다며 똑같이 놀라움을 표현하는 것이다. 따라서 (A)가 정답이다.

155-157 회사 사보 내 기사

> **마크 챈들러가 돌아옵니다!**
>
> 행정 서비스부는 마크 챈들러 부국장의 본사 귀환을 환영합니다. 마크는 지난달에 오타와에 머물며 기업 정보 보안에 관한 상급 훈련에 참여했습니다. 기업 보안 훈련은 회사가 민감하고 기밀한 독점 정보를 보호할 수 있도록 해 줍니다.
>
> ^{155, 157}이 엄격한 코스를 성공적으로 수료한 회사 임원진 수가 증가하고 있는데, 마크가 이들 중 한 사람입니다. 훈련에는 60시간의 교육과 종합적인 필기 시험이 포함되어 있었습니다. 국립 기업 보안 담당자 협회의 회원인 ¹⁵⁶마크는 전자 서류를 안전하게 보관하는 소프트웨어를 개발하는 데 있어 그가 수행했던 역할로 해당 기관으로부터 공식적으로 공로를 인정받았습니다. ¹⁵⁵잘했어요, 마크!

어휘 administrative 관리[행정]의 division 부서 associate director 부책임자 advanced 고급의, 상급의 corporate 기업[회사]의 security 보안 safeguard 보호하다 confidential 기밀의 proprietary 전매의, 소유주의 executive 임원 rigorous 엄격한 recognize (공로를) 인정[표창]하다

---

155 주제 / 목적

번역 기사의 목적은 무엇인가?

(A) 직원의 성과를 인정하기 위해
(B) 새로운 직원을 소개하기 위해
(C) 어떤 정보가 기밀로 간주되는지 명시하기 위해
(D) 기업 보안의 어려움을 설명하기 위해

해설 본사로 귀환할 마크 챈들러가 성공적으로 훈련 과정을 수료(succesfully graduated from this rigorous course)하고 특정 기관에서 공로를 표창받았다(was formally recognized)며 그가 이루었던 성과에 대해 언급했고, 마지막 문장에서 '잘했어요, 마크!(Well done, Mark!)'라고 덧붙였으므로, (A)가 정답이다.

어휘 clarify 명확히 하다, 명시하다 challenge 난제, 도전

---

156 세부 사항

번역 챈들러 씨는 기업 보안을 어떻게 제고했는가?

(A) 회사의 보안 담당자를 훈련시켰다.
(B) 안전하게 서류를 보관하는 시스템을 고안하는 것을 도왔다.
(C) 새로운 안전 지침을 개발하는 것을 도왔다.
(D) 기업 보안을 전문으로 하는 직원들을 채용했다.

해설 기사의 후반부를 보면 마크가 전자 서류를 안전하게 보관하는 소프트웨어를 개발하는 데(in developing software that keeps electronic documents safe) 있어 그가 수행했던 역할로 공로를 인정받았다고 했으므로, (B)가 정답이다.

어휘 design 고안하다, 설계하다 assist 돕다 recruit 채용하다

> ▸▸ **Paraphrasing** 지문의 **software that keeps electronic documents safe** → 정답의 **a system for securely storing documents**

---

157 문장 삽입

번역 [1], [2], [3], [4]로 표시된 곳 중에서 다음 문장이 들어가기에 가장 적합한 곳은?

"훈련에는 60시간의 교육과 종합적인 필기 시험이 포함되어 있었습니다."

(A) [1]
(B) [2]
(C) [3]
(D) [4]

해설 주어진 문장의 주어인 훈련(The training)이 [1] 뒤에 나온 an advanced training session과 [2] 앞 문장에 나온 this rigorous course를 가리키며 이에 대해 설명하고 있으므로, [2]에 들어가야 글의 흐름이 자연스러워진다. 따라서 (B)가 정답이다.

어휘 comprehensive 종합적인, 포괄적인

158-160 카드

> ¹⁵⁸세상에서 가장 정교한 충전식 면도기인 메가그룸을 구매하신 것을 축하드립니다! 면도기를 최상의 상태로 유지하려면 매주 뜨거운 물 속에서 작동시켜 세척해 주세요. ¹⁵⁹한 달에 한 번 면도기를 분해하고 사용자 설명서에 나와 있는 대로 내부를 꼼꼼히 세척해 주세요. 면도기 윗부분은 설명서에 나열된 교체 부품으로 매년 교체되어야 합니다.
>
> 메가그룸 면도기는 수년간 수명이 지속되는 리튬 이온 배터리를 사용합니다. ¹⁶⁰면도기를 필요한 만큼 자주 충전하세요. 재충전하기 전에 완전히 방전시킬 필요는 없습니다. 다른 충전기 사용 시 품질 보증이 무효가 될 수 있으므로, 포함된 충전기만 사용하세요. 전체 지침 및 세부사항은 사용자 설명서에서 확인하실 수 있습니다.

어휘 rechargeable 재충전되는 shaver 면도기 disassemble 분해하다 internal 내부의 portion 부분 thoroughly 꼼꼼히 manual 설명서 replacement part 교체 부품 last 지속되다 charge 충전하다 discharge 방전하다 charger 충전기 void 무효로 하다 warranty (품질) 보증 instruction 지침 details 세부사항

158 추론 / 암시

번역 이 카드는 어디에서 찾아볼 수 있겠는가?

(A) 제품 상자 안
(B) 게시판
(C) 상점의 제품 진열대
(D) 잡지

해설 첫 문장에서 면도기 구매를 축하한다(Congratulations on purchasing ~ shaver!)면서 면도기를 최상의 상태로 유지하기 위한(To keep your shaver in top condition) 지침 사항을 알려 주고 있다. 따라서 해당 카드는 면도기를 구매한 사람을 대상으로 한다는 것을 알 수 있으며, 이러한 카드는 보통 제품이 담긴 상자에 들어 있으므로, (A)가 정답이다.

159 세부 사항

번역 면도기는 얼마나 자주 분해되어야 하는가?

(A) 매일
(B) 매주
(C) 매월
(D) 매년

해설 첫 단락 세 번째 문장에서 한 달에 한 번 면도기를 분해해(Once a month, disassemble the shaver) 내부를 꼼꼼히 세척하라고 했으므로, (C)가 정답이다.

▸▸ **Paraphrasing** 지문의 **Once a month** → 정답의 **Monthly**

160 사실 관계 확인

번역 면도기의 배터리에 대해 명시된 것은?

(A) 충전하기 전에 방전되어야 한다.
(B) 필요할 때마다 충전될 수 있다.
(C) 일주일 동안 충전을 유지할 수 있다.
(D) 다른 충전기로도 작동될 것이다.

해설 두 번째 단락을 보면 면도기를 필요한 만큼 자주 충전하라(Please charge the shaver as often as needed)고 했으므로, (B)가 정답이다. 재충전 전에 완전히 방전시킬 필요는 없다(It is not necessary ~ recharging it)고 하며 포함된 충전기만 사용하라(Use only the included charger)고 했으므로 (A), (D)는 명백한 오답이며, (C)는 언급된 바가 없으므로 정답이 될 수 없다.

어휘 run out 다 떨어지다

▸▸ **Paraphrasing** 지문의 **as often as needed**
→ 정답의 **whenever necessary**

161-163 웹페이지

http://www.diversifymuseum.org

다이버시파이 뮤지엄

비교 문화 역사 및 공예품 박물관
새로운 전시회 〈남미 예술〉을 발표하게 되어 자랑스럽습니다.

전시회는 박물관에서 진행 중인 전 세계 예술 프로그램의 일환으로 6월 7일에 개최될 것입니다. 박물관 입장료를 지불한 모든 박물관 이용객들은 전시회를 관람할 수 있습니다. **161전시회는 저명한 남미 예술가들의 고전 및 현대 미술 작품 전시를 특별히 포함할 예정입니다.**

1626주 간 진행되는 이번 전시회의 담당 큐레이터인 훌리오 까레라는 그의 방대한 전문 지식을 박물관으로 소환할 것입니다. **162올해 3월 박물관 경영진에 합류하기 전에, 까레라 씨**는 6년간 브라질 예술 협회의 큐레이터였고, 베네수엘라에 있는 예술 보존 센터인 센트로 드 라 이스토리아 델 아르떼에서 고대 공예품을 연구하는 데 3년을 보냈습니다.

〈남미 예술〉 전시회는 남미 6개국의 회화, 조각, 공예 도구, 의복, 장신구, 벽화, 토기를 포함할 것입니다. **163해당 국가 출신의 객원 예술가들이 7월 중 특정 날짜에 미술 워크숍을 제공할 것입니다.** 각 워크숍의 비용은 기본 입장료에 10파운드가 추가되며 기본적인 미술용품이 포함됩니다.

어휘 diversify 다양화하다 cross-cultural 비교 문화의
artifact 공예품 ongoing 진행 중인 patron 고객 feature
특징으로 삼다, 특별히 포함하다 contemporary 현대의
renowned 저명한 vast 방대한 expertise 전문 지식
ancient 고대의 preservation 보존 crafting 공예 jewellery
장신구 mural 벽화 clay 점토 pottery 도자기 select 선택된
admission 입장 supplies 용품

161 사실 관계 확인

번역 〈남미 예술〉 전시회에 대해 명시된 것은?

(A) 전 세계 예술 프로그램의 첫 전시회이다.
(B) 6월 말까지만 전시될 것이다.
(C) 신구 미술 둘 다를 포함한다.
(D) 벽에 거는 장식품과 벽화에 중점을 둔다.

해설 첫 단락의 세 번째 문장에서 전시회가 유명한 남미 예술가들의 고전 및 현대 미술 작품 전시(historical and contemporary artwork displays)를 특별히 포함한다고 했으므로, (C)가 정답이다.

▸▸ **Paraphrasing** 지문의 **historical and contemporary artwork**
→ 정답의 **old and new art**

162 세부 사항

번역 까레라 씨는 누구인가?

(A) 객원 예술가
(B) 예술 기자
(C) 자원봉사 투어 가이드
(D) 박물관 직원

해설 두 번째 단락에서 훌리오 까레라 씨가 이번 전시회의 큐레이터(The curator of the six-week exhibition, Julio Carrera)이며 올해 3월에 박물관 경영진에 합류했다(Before joining the museum's management in March of this year)고 했으므로, (D)가 정답이다.

163 세부 사항

번역 웹페이지에 따르면, 박물관 이용객들은 추가 비용으로 무엇을 할 수 있는가?

   (A) 남미에 관한 비디오 관람
   (B) 미술 수업 참가
   (C) 새로운 전시회 답사
   (D) 다가오는 전시회 후원

해설 마지막 단락을 보면 7월 중에 객원 예술가들이 미술 워크숍을 제공할 것(Visiting artists from these countries will provide art workshops)이며 각 워크숍의 비용은 기본 입장료에 10파운드가 추가된다(The cost for each workshop is £10 in addition to the regular admission)고 했으므로, (B)가 정답이다.

▸▸ **Paraphrasing**   지문의 art workshops → 정답의 an art class

164-167 온라인 채팅

> **올리버 코 (오전 10시 15분)**
> 아론과 데니스, 안녕하세요. ¹⁶⁴혹시 제 앞으로 온 소포가 있는지 아세요? 오늘 서류를 배송받기로 되어 있었는데, 실수로 다른 사람에게 발송되었을 수도 있거든요. 쉬란츠 팜 오가닉스에서 보낸 거고 긴급하다고 표시되어 있을 거예요.
>
> **아론 코스키넨 (오전 10시 17분)**
> 여기 안내 데스크에는 당신에게 온 게 없어요. ¹⁶⁵1층에 있는 인쇄소에 확인해 보는 게 어때요.
>
> **데니스 마토바 (오전 10시 18분)**
> ¹⁶⁶여기 우편물실에 쉬란츠 팜 오가닉스에서 보낸 소포가 있는데, 이름이 적혀 있지 않네요.
>
> **올리버 코 (오전 10시 18분)**
> 그게 저한테 온 게 틀림없어요. 송장 좀 다시 확인해 주시겠어요?
>
> **데니스 마토바 (오전 10시 19분)**
> 미안해요, ¹⁶⁶당신의 이름이 있네요. 너무 작아서 못 봤어요.
>
> **올리버 코 (오전 10시 20분)**
> 잘됐네요! ¹⁶⁷소포를 제 사무실로 올려 보내 주시겠어요?
>
> **데니스 마토바 (오전 10시 20분)**
> ¹⁶⁷그럴게요. 안 그래도 곧 위층으로 가려고 했어요.
>
> **올리버 코 (오전 10시 21분)**
> 좋아요, 도와주셔서 감사합니다.

어휘   be supposed to ~하기로 되어 있다   label 라벨을 붙이다, (라벨 등에 정보를) 적다   urgent 긴급한   ground floor 1층   delivery slip (택배) 송장

164 세부 사항

번역 왜 코 씨는 온라인 채팅을 시작했는가?

   (A) 그는 손상된 소포를 받았다.
   (B) 그는 곧 고객과 회의가 있다.
   (C) 그는 중요한 서류를 기다리고 있다.
   (D) 그는 잘못된 사람에게 물건을 배달시켰다.

해설 코 씨가 보낸 첫 메시지에서 본인 앞으로 온 소포가 있는지(if a package has arrived for me)를 물으며, 오늘 서류 배송을 받기로 되어 있다(I was supposed to get a delivery of some documents)라고 했으므로, (C)가 정답이다.

165 세부 사항

번역 코스키넨 씨가 하라고 추천하는 것은?

   (A) 쉬란츠 팜 오가닉스에 전화하기
   (B) 회의 장소 바꾸기
   (C) 안내 데스크에 가보기
   (D) 다른 장소를 확인하기

해설 코스키넨 씨가 10시 17분에 보낸 메시지를 보면 1층에 있는 인쇄소에 확인해 보라(You might want to check with the print shop)고 제안하고 있으므로, (D)가 정답이다.

166 의도 파악

번역 오전 10시 19분에 마토바 씨가 "미안해요"라고 쓸 때, 그 의도는 무엇인가?

   (A) 배달장을 분실했다.
   (B) 오늘 회사에 지각했다.
   (C) 코 씨가 다시 설명해 주기를 원한다.
   (D) 실수로 라벨을 잘못 읽었다.

해설 마토바 씨의 10시 18분 메시지에서 소포가 있는데 이름이 적혀 있지 않다(There's a package ~ but there's no name on it)고 했다가 10시 19분 메시지에서는 소포에 코 씨의 이름이 있는데(it does have your name on it) 너무 작아서 못 봤다(It was so small I didn't notice it)라고 했다. 따라서 마토바 씨가 본인의 실수를 인정하며 미안해서 한 말임을 알 수 있으므로, (D)가 정답이다.

어휘   misplace 잘못 두다, 둔 곳을 잊다

167 세부 사항

번역 마토바 씨는 소포를 어떻게 할 것인가?

   (A) 코 씨에게 가져간다.
   (B) 빠른 우편으로 발송한다.
   (C) 안내 데스크에 맡긴다.
   (D) 소포에서 물건을 꺼낸다.

해설 소포를 자신의 사무실로 올려 보내 달라(Could you have the package sent up to my office please?)는 코 씨의 부탁에 마토바 씨가 그러겠다(No problem)고 승낙하며 곧 위층으로 가려던 참(I'm going upstairs in a minute anyway)이라고 했으므로 소포를 직접 가져다 줄 것임을 알 수 있다. 따라서 (A)가 정답이다.

168-171 이메일

> 발신: 김원호
> 수신: 경영팀
> 날짜: 8월 12일
> 제목: 직원 만족 개선

경영팀에게:

향후 몇 개월에 걸쳐, 인사과는 경영팀과 함께 생산성 및 직원 만족 향상에 관해 다양한 논의를 할 것입니다.

¹⁶⁹직원들이 근무 시간의 전체 혹은 일부 동안 집에서 근무하도록 허용하는 재택근무는 온갖 방해로 가득한 사무실에서 완수하기 힘든 업무를 할 수 있도록 해주기 때문에 많은 회사들이 활용하고 있는 접근법입니다. ¹⁷⁰건물 구조 변경 프로젝트가 1월에 예정되어 있으니, 재택근무가 우리 회사에게도 좋은 해결책이 될지 가늠해 볼 기회를 가졌으면 합니다. 이 사안에 대한 최종 결정은 작업 공간이 재편성되는 방식에도 영향을 줄 것입니다.

^{168, 171}저는 여러분의 피드백을 요청하기 위해 이 글을 씁니다. 재택근무에 대해 어떠한 결정도 내려지지 않았다는 점에 유의하셔야 합니다. ¹⁷¹현 시점에서 인사과는 단순히 정보를 수집하고 있는 중입니다. 인사과 웹사이트에 있는 ¹⁶⁸재택근무 설문지를 작성해 주세요. 홈페이지의 왼쪽에 있는 링크를 찾으시면 됩니다.

미리 감사드리며, 질문 있으시면 제게 알려 주세요.

김원호
인사과장
GHTY 엔지니어링

어휘 engage with ~와 관계를 맺다 a variety of 다양한 productivity 생산성 telecommuting 재택근무 approach 접근(법) disruption 방해, 중단 reconfiguration 구조 변경 influence 영향을 주다 reorganize 재편성하다

---

168 주제 / 목적

번역 이메일은 왜 보내졌는가?

(A) 직원들에게 방침에 대해 상기시키기 위해
(B) 설문조사 참여를 요청하기 위해
(C) 다가오는 회의에 대해 논의하기 위해
(D) 직원들이 행사에 참석하도록 장려하기 위해

해설 이메일의 후반부에 팀의 피드백을 요청하기 위해 이 글을 쓴다(I am writing to ask for your feedback)면서, 재택근무 설문지를 작성해 줄 것(Please complete the telecommuting survey)을 요청하고 있으므로, (B)가 정답이다.

어휘 remind 상기시키다 participation 참여 encourage 장려하다

169 사실 관계 확인

번역 재택근무의 이점으로 언급된 것은?

(A) 직원들이 방해 받지 않고 일하도록 돕는다.
(B) 건물 내에 신입 직원들을 위한 공간을 내어 준다.
(C) 환경에 좋다.
(D) 회사 재정을 절약해 준다.

해설 두 번째 단락에서 재택근무는 온갖 방해로 가득한 사무실에서 완수하기 힘든 업무를 할 수 있도록(it allows employees to work on tasks that may be difficult to complete in an office full of disruptions) 해주기 때문에 많은 회사들이 활용하고 있는 접근법이라고 했으므로, (A)가 정답이다.

어휘 interruption 방해, 중단(시키는 것)

170 세부 사항

번역 회사가 새해에 하려고 계획하는 것은?

(A) 새로운 인사과 관리자를 고용하는 것
(B) 경영팀을 개편하는 것
(C) 건물의 배치를 변경하는 것
(D) 새 웹사이트를 선보이는 것

해설 두 번째 단락 두 번째 문장을 보면, 1월에 예정된 건물 구조 변경 프로젝트(the building reconfiguration project coming up in January)가 있다고 했으므로, (C)가 정답이다.

어휘 reorganize 재조직[재편성]하다, 개편하다 layout 배치

▶▶ Paraphrasing 지문의 the building reconfiguration
→ 정답의 Change the layout of its building

171 문장 삽입

번역 [1], [2], [3], [4]로 표시된 곳 중에서 다음 문장이 들어가기에 가장 적합한 곳은?

"재택근무에 대해 어떠한 결정도 내려지지 않았다는 점에 유의하셔야 합니다."

(A) [1]
(B) [2]
(C) [3]
(D) [4]

해설 주어진 문장은 재택근무에 대해 어떠한 결정도 내려지지 않았다는 점에 유의하라는 내용이므로, 재택근무에 관한 피드백을 요청한다(ask for your feedback)는 문장과 현재로서는 단순히 정보를 수집하고 있는(simply gathering information) 단계임을 알리는 문장 사이에 들어가야 흐름이 자연스럽다. 따라서 (C)가 정답이다.

172-175 행사 일정표

웁살라 국제 도서 박람회
¹⁷²9월 22-24일 • 베르글룬드 컨퍼런스 홀 • 웁살라, 스웨덴

¹⁷²9월 22일 금요일 일정

〈대중의 의견보다 깊이 생각하기〉
¹⁷²12:00 정오 – 오후 1시, 살롱 A
최신작 〈대중의 의견보다 깊이 생각하기〉의 홍보 투어 중인 작가 대미안 슈나우즈가 웁살라 국제 도서 박람회에 들러 자신의 최신 화두를 논하며 질문도 받고 책에 사인도 해 줍니다.

〈그래픽 디자인 입문 과정〉
¹⁷²오후 1시 30분–2시 30분, ¹⁷³시각 미디어 센터
¹⁷³전문 디지털 디자이너인 앨런 두벡과 이바넷 라카쎄가 유용한 기법들을 보여 주고 참가자들에게 직접 연습해 볼 기회를 제공합니다.

〈온라인 출판에 관한 세미나〉
¹⁷²오후 3시–4시 30분, 린드크비스트 강당
전자책과 오디오북을 인터넷에 출간하고 홍보하기. 발표자: 벤들러 출판의 편집장인 케네스 풀라스키와 벤들러 출판의 마케팅 매니저인 티나 사보나. ¹⁷⁴수반하는 모든 자료는 세미나 직전과 직후에 행사장에서 판매될 것입니다.

---

¹⁷²오후 5시-6시 30분, 210호

글을 읽고 쓰는 능력은 디지털 미디어에 의해 촉진되는가 아니면 저해되는가? 토론 사회자는 그렉 군나르손.

• 본 과정 및 기타 과정에 참석하려면 100크루나에 일일 입장권을 구입하세요.

• 어떠한 과정에도 예약이 필요하지는 않지만 ¹⁷⁵**좌석이 한정되어 있으므로 좌석을 확보하려면 예정된 시간보다 몇 분 일찍 오시기 바랍니다.** 또한 사진 촬영은 되지만, 비디오 녹화는 허용되지 않습니다.

• 베르글룬드 컨퍼런스 홀에 있는 몇몇 장소에서 식사 구매가 가능합니다. 숙소에 관한 정보는 저희 웹사이트 uibf.se/hotels에서 확인할 수 있습니다.

어휘 **outthink** ~보다 깊이[빨리] 생각하다, (상대를) 앞지르다 **introductory** 입문의 **present** 발표[제시]하다 **hands-on** 직접 해 보는 **release** 공개[발표]하다 **editor-in-chief** 편집장 **accompanying** 수반하는 **material** 자료 **venue** 장소, 행사장 **immediately** 즉시 **readership** 독자층 **literacy** 글을 읽고 쓰는 능력 **promote** 촉진하다 **inhibit** 저해하다 **moderate** 사회를 보다[조정하다] **purchase** 구입하다; 구입 **admission** 입장 **ensure** 확보하다 **permit** 허가하다 **accommodation** 숙소

172 추론 / 암시

번역 웁살라 국제 도서 박람회 첫날에 대해 암시된 것은?

(A) 출판업체 팀에 의해 준비되고 있다.
(B) 아침 시간에는 어떤 과정도 잡혀 있지 않다.
(C) 참석률이 가장 높을 것으로 기대된다.
(D) 슈나우즈 씨가 자신의 다음 책 주제를 발표할 것이다.

해설 웁살라 국제 도서 박람회의 기간은 9월 22일~24일이므로 9월 22일 금요일 일정표가 박람회의 첫날 일정표임을 추론할 수 있다. 일정표를 보면 모든 과정의 시간대가 낮 12시 이후이므로, (B)가 정답이다.

어휘 **publisher** 출판인[사] **attendance** 참석(률)

173 세부 사항

번역 도서 박람회 참가자들은 어디에서 상호적인 활동에 참여할 수 있는가?

(A) 살롱 A
(B) 시각 미디어 센터
(C) 린드크비스트 강당
(D) 210호

해설 그래픽 디자인 입문 과정(Introductory Course in Graphic Design)에서 발표자들이 유용한 기법들을 보여 주고 참가자들이 직접 연습할 기회도 제공한다(Professional digital designers ~ hands-on practice opportunities)고 했으므로, 이 과정에서 발표자와 참가자가 소통하는 상호적인 활동이 이루어진다는 것을 알 수 있다. 해당 강좌는 시각 미디어 센터(Visual Media Centre)에서 열린다고 나와 있으므로, (B)가 정답이다.

174 사실 관계 확인

번역 세미나에 수반되는 자료에 대해 언급된 것은?

(A) 현장에서 구매할 수 있다.
(B) 온라인에서 다운로드할 수 있다.
(C) 한정된 수만 구입 가능하다.
(D) 발표자에게 수문해야 한다.

해설 온라인 출판에 관한 세미나(Seminar on Online Publishing)에서 수반되는 모든 자료는 행사장에서 판매될 것(All accompanying materials will be sold at the venue)이라고 했으므로, (A)가 정답이다.

▸▸ **Paraphrasing** 지문의 **at the venue** → 정답의 **on-site**

175 세부 사항

번역 도서 박람회 참가자들이 하도록 권장되는 것은?

(A) 과정 후 질문하기
(B) 소셜 미디어에 사진 올리기
(C) 필요한 만큼 좌석 재배치하기
(D) 강좌를 위해 일찍 도착하기

해설 후반부에 두 번째 유의사항을 보면 좌석이 한정되어(seating is limited) 있으므로 좌석을 확보하려면(to ensure a seat) 예정된 시간보다 몇 분 일찍 도착할 것(please arrive a few minutes before the scheduled time)을 당부했으므로, (D)가 정답이다.

어휘 **rearrange** 재배열[배치]하다

▸▸ **Paraphrasing** 지문의 **arrive a few minutes before the scheduled time** → 정답의 **Arrive early**

176-180 웹페이지 + 이메일

http://www.mountainandforest.ca/custserv/shippinginfo

| 의류 | 장비 | **고객 서비스** | 회사 소개 |

마운틴 앤 포레스트 회사
고급 캠핑과 하이킹 장비의 선두 주자

일반적인 전자 주문 혹은 전화 주문품 대부분이 거의 즉시 처리되어 배송될 준비가 되어 있습니다. 주문 제작 및 개인 맞춤형 주문품은 배송되기 전 처리하는 데 5일까지 소요될 수 있습니다.

문의 사항이나 염려되는 점이 있으시면 고객 서비스 부서 service@mountainandforest.ca로 ¹⁷⁷**보내 주십시오**. 24시간 이내에 답변을 드리겠습니다.

배송 요금:

세금이 부과된 주문 비용	익일 배송 (1일)	특급 배송 (3일)	¹⁷⁶**기본** (6~8일)
25달러 미만	8달러	5달러	3달러
25달러-100달러	13달러	7달러	5달러
¹⁷⁹**100달러 이상**	18달러	¹⁷⁹**15달러**	무료

어휘 gear 장비 quality 질, 고급 electronic 전자의 custom 주문 제작한 personalized 개인 맞춤형의 processing 처리 direct 보내다 concern 우려(사항), 관심사 respond 응답하다 rate 요금 overnight 하룻밤 사이의, 익일의

수신: service@mountainandforest.ca
발신: jinheeshin@sharemail.ca
날짜: 1월 10일
제목: 주문 B75022

최근에 저는 180이번 주말 캠핑에 쓰려고 179등산화와 보온 재킷을 135달러에 주문했습니다. 구매 시 제가 받은 확인서에 따르면, 178제 주문품은 어제 도착해야 했습니다. 1793일 배송에 대한 추가 요금을 지불했기 때문에, 저는 제 주문품이 제때에 도착할 것으로 기대하고 있었습니다. 178그렇지 않았기 때문에, 저는 배송 비용에 대한 환불을 요청합니다. 또한, 180만일 제 주문품이 내일까지 배송되지 않을 경우, 지역 상점에서 비슷한 물건을 구매해야 할 것이므로 제 주문을 취소해 주세요.

신진희

어휘 hiking 도보 여행, 등산 thermal 보온성이 좋은 intended 의도된 confirmation 확인 in a timely fashion 시기 적절하게

176 사실 관계 확인

번역 웹페이지에서, 마운틴 앤 포레스트의 배송에 대해 명시된 것은?

(A) 25달러 미만의 주문 건은 기본 배송이 무료이다.
(B) 일부 배송은 도착하는 데 8일까지 걸릴 수 있다.
(C) 배송 비용은 주문품의 총 무게에 달려 있다.
(D) 주문 제작 제품은 기본 배송이 되지 않는다.

해설 웹페이지에 있는 배송 요금표의 기본 배송(Standard)란에 배송 기간이 6일~8일이라고 나와 있으므로, (B)가 정답이다. 25달러 미만의 주문에 대해 기본 배송은 3달러를 내야 하므로 (A)는 명백한 오답이며, 다른 보기에 대한 내용은 언급되지 않아 사실 여부를 알 수 없으므로 정답이 될 수 없다.

어휘 eligible ~할 자격이 있는, ~할 수 있는

177 동의어 찾기

번역 웹페이지에서 두 번째 단락 1행의 "direct"와 의미상 가장 가까운 것은?

(A) (~에게) 보내다   (B) 감독하다
(C) 처방하다   (D) 다루다

해설 지문에서 direct는 '(메시지 등을) ~에게 보내다'는 뜻으로 쓰였다. 따라서 보기 중 '(~에게) 보내다'라는 의미로도 쓰이는 (A) address 가 정답이다.

178 주제 / 목적

번역 이메일의 목적은 무엇인가?

(A) 새로운 서비스 방침을 제안하기 위해
(B) 주문 포장 실수에 대해 문의하기 위해
(C) 개인 맞춤형 제품을 요청하기 위해
(D) 배송 문제를 알리기 위해

해설 이메일의 두 번째 문장을 보면 주문품이 어제 도착해야 했는데(my order should have arrived yesterday) 그렇지 않았다(it has not)고 하며 환불을 요청하고(I am requesting a refund of the shipping cost) 있으므로, (D)가 정답이다.

어휘 policy 정책, 방침 inquire 묻다, 알아보다

179 연계

번역 신 씨는 배송에 얼마를 지불했는가?

(A) 5달러
(B) 8달러
(C) 15달러
(D) 18달러

해설 이메일 초반부에서 신 씨는 등산화와 보온 재킷을 135달러에 주문했으며(placed an order for $135 for hiking boots and a thermal jacket) 3일 배송에 대한 추가 요금을 지불했다(I paid an additional fee for three-day shipping)고 했다. 웹페이지의 배송 요금표를 보면 100달러 이상 주문 건에 대한 3일 배송(Express shipping, 3 days) 요금이 15달러이므로, (C)가 정답이다.

180 세부 사항

번역 이메일에 따르면, 신 씨는 왜 지역 상점에 가기로 결심할 수도 있는가?

(A) 더 낮은 가격에 제품을 구입하기를 기대한다.
(B) 자신의 동네에 있는 업체를 지원하고 싶어 한다.
(C) 특정 날짜 전에 물건을 받아야 한다.
(D) 더 다양한 스포츠웨어를 찾길 바란다.

해설 신 씨는 이번 주말 캠핑에 쓰려고(for a camping trip this weekend) 물건을 샀기 때문에, 물건이 내일까지 배송되지 않을 경우(if my order has not been delivered by tomorrow) 지역 상점에서 구매해야 한다(I will have to purchase similar items at a local shop)며 주문을 취소해 달라고 했다. 따라서 (C)가 정답이다.

181-185 일정표 + 이메일

<table>
<tr><td colspan="2" align="center">무역 및 산업을 위한 협회 *(STI)
"직업 훈련에 있어 원격 교육의 역할"
아부다비 시티 대학, 18110월 11-13일</td></tr>
<tr><td colspan="2" align="center">초안: 18110월 11일 수요일 일정</td></tr>
<tr><td>오전 7:30–9:00</td><td>학회 등록</td></tr>
<tr><td>오전 9:00–9:10</td><td>환영 및 개회사: 야스민 알 가우드, 학회 의장</td></tr>
<tr><td>오전 9:15–10:00</td><td>181개회 기조 연설: 아유미 무라카미, STI 회장</td></tr>
<tr><td>오전 10:05–10:50</td><td>발표 제목 알 수 없음: 대표 선정 예정, 야운데 농업 대학, 카메룬</td></tr>
<tr><td>오전 10:55–11:40</td><td>182혁신적인 온라인 자원: 치아 포 쳉, 타이베이 비즈니스 경영 대학, 대만</td></tr>
<tr><td>오전 11:45–오후 1:20</td><td>점심 식사 (터쿼즈 센터, 중앙 캠퍼스)</td></tr>
<tr><td>오후 1:30–2:15</td><td>영화 산업의 원격 교육: 스코틀랜드 대표 선정 예정</td></tr>
</table>

| 오후 2:20 – 3:05 | ¹⁸⁴교육 과정 내용 품질 향상: 안드레이 두르첸코, 모스크바 저널리즘 아카데미, 러시아 |
| 오후 3:10 – 4:00 | 학습자 지원 시스템: 마르셀 페랄타, 소아 치과 대학, 아순시온, 파라과이 |

어휘 distance education 원격 교육 draft 초안 conference (대규모) 회의, 학회 registration 등록 remark 발언 keynote address 기조 연설 representative 대표, 대리인 agriculture 농업 resource 자원 institute 기관, 협회 pediatric dentistry 소아 치과학

발신: 아유미 무라카미 〈amurakami@sti.org〉
수신: 야스민 알 가우드 〈yasmin.algaood@cuad.ac.ae〉
제목: 회신: 학회 수요일 일정 초안
날짜: 8월 25일

안녕하세요, 야스민

요청하신 대로, 수요일 임시 학회 일정표에 아직 비어 있던 ¹⁸³자리를 채웠습니다. 스코틀랜드의 알반 뷰캐넌 박사는 자국에 있는 영화 아카데미들에서 원격 교육이 실행되고 있기 때문에 그에 대해 강연하고 싶다고 합니다. 또한, 야운데에 있는 제 연락책이 마리-테레즈 창고우 씨가 학교 대표가 될 거라고 말해 주었습니다.

¹⁸⁴안드레이 두르첸코 씨는 자신이 총회에서 빠지게 되었다고 알려 왔습니다. ¹⁸⁵그를 대신할 같은 학교의 멜리나 바키토바 씨가 곧 그녀의 발표 제목을 보낼 것입니다.

아울러 저는 아부다비에 수요일 오전 6시에 도착할 예정입니다. 그렇게 하면 제 발표를 준비할 시간이 충분할 것입니다.

아유미

어휘 as per ~에 따라 slot 시간, 자리 tentative 임시의 eager 간절히 바라는 practice 실행하다 withdraw 취소하다, 철회하다 replacement 대신할 사람, 후임자

181 사실 관계 확인

번역 무라카미 씨에 대해 명시된 것은?

(A) 학회 첫날에 연설할 것이다.
(B) 최근에 STI 회장으로 선출되었다.
(C) 질문에 답변할 시간이 될 것이다.
(D) 오후에 발표하기로 되어 있다.

해설 학회의 기간은 10월 11일~13일(11-13 October)이고 일정표는 10월 11일 수요일(Schedule for Wednesday, 11 October)에 대한 것이므로, 제시된 일정표가 컨퍼런스 첫날 일정임을 알 수 있다. 일정표에 따르면 오전 9시15분 ~ 10시에 아유미 무라카미 STI 회장이 개회 기조 연설(Opening Keynote Address)을 한다고 나와 있으므로, (A)가 정답이다.

182 세부 사항

번역 경영학 분야의 전문가는 언제 연설하는가?

(A) 오전 10시 5분
(B) 오전 10시 55분
(C) 오후 2시 20분
(D) 오후 3시 10분

해설 일정표에 따르면 오전 10시 55분 ~ 11시 40분에 타이베이 비즈니스 경영 대학(Business Management Institute)의 치아 포 쳉이 혁신적인 온라인 자원에 대해 강연한다고 나와 있으므로, (B)가 정답이다.

183 동의어 찾기

번역 이메일에서 첫 번째 단락 1행의 "slots"와 의미상 가장 가까운 것은?

(A) 예약
(B) 기계
(C) 빈자리
(D) 건물

해설 지문에서 slots는 '(명단·프로그램 등에 들어가는) 자리(시간·틈)'라는 뜻으로 쓰였다. 따라서 보기 중 '빈자리'라는 의미로도 쓰이는 (C) openings가 정답이다.

184 연계

번역 어떤 발표가 취소되어야 하는가?

(A) 혁신적인 온라인 자원
(B) 영화 산업의 원격 교육
(C) 교육 과정 내용 품질 향상
(D) 학습자 지원 시스템

해설 이메일 두 번째 단락에서 안드레이 두르첸코 씨가 컨퍼런스에서 빠지게 되었다고 알려 왔다(Mr. Andrei Durchenko has informed ~ conference)고 했고, 일정표를 보면 그는 교육 과정 내용 품질 향상에 대해 강의하기로 되어 있었으므로, (C)가 정답이다.

185 세부 사항

번역 이메일에 따르면, 무라카미 씨는 무슨 정보를 받을 예정인가?

(A) 발표 제목
(B) 대체 연사의 이름
(C) 목요일 컨퍼런스 일정
(D) 뷰캐넌 씨의 연락처

해설 이메일의 두 번째 단락 마지막 문장에서 학회에서 빠지기로 한 안드레이 두르첸코 씨를 대신할 멜리나 바키토바 씨(His replacement from the same school, Ms. Melina Vakhitova)가 곧 그녀의 발표 제목을 보낼 것(will submit the title of her presentation shortly)이라고 했으므로, 무라카미 씨가 멜리나 바키토바 씨의 발표 제목을 기다리고 있음을 알 수 있다. 따라서 (A)가 정답이다.

186-190 이메일 + 명단 + 기사

발신: mstoch@hesidionclinic.com
수신: lstawinski@nostilde.com
날짜: 3월 20일
제목: 헤시디온 클리닉의 건강 인식의 날

스타윈스키 씨께,

헤시디온 클리닉의 장기 환자로서 저희 병원을 애용해 주신 것에 감사드리는 의미에서, ¹⁸⁶4월 10일 토요일에 본원에서 개최 예정인 우리 병원의 건강 인식의 날에 귀하를 초대하게 되어 기쁩니다. 우리 지역 사회의 건강에 대한 인식을 고취시키고자 고안된 다양한 활동을 제공할 예정이니, ¹⁸⁶귀하께서 참석해 주시면 좋겠습니다. ¹⁸⁷3월 31일까지 본

이메일에 답변을 주셔서 이 특별한 행사에 등록하시면, 깜짝 혜택으로 병원에 제시할 수 있는 코드를 받게 되실 것입니다.

마틴 스토크, 홍보 부장, 헤시디온 클리닉

어휘 awareness 인식, 관심 appreciation 감사 loyalty 충성(심) promote 고취하다 community 지역사회 present 제시하다 benefit 혜택

헤시디온 클리닉 건강 인식의 날, 4월 10일
업무 및 책임

• 홍보: 마틴 스토크
• 광고: 아딜렌 워커
• 발표: 질리안 오팔라 (영양), 랜스 버호벤 (체력 단련)
• **190어린이 건강 게임: 수잔 하야시**
• 건강 검진/강의: 앤 스필레인, 라미 알-아라즈, 커트 인, 티에리 도마스

어휘 task 과업, 일 responsibility 책무, 책임 nutrition 영양 checkup 점검

헤시디온 클리닉의 건강의 날

샤이 헤르조그 작성, 4월 10일

헤시디온 클리닉은 지난 토요일에 성공적인 건강 인식의 날을 주최했다. 이 행사는 지난 15년 동안 병원을 성원해 준 지역 사회에 감사하기 위한 방편으로 열렸다. 헤시디온 클리닉의 환자들과 일반 대중들 모두 많이 참석했다.

참가자들은 다양한 발표에 참여했고 모두가 행사 후원업체들로부터 무료 물병, 메모지와 기타 물품들을 받았다. **187스페셜 코드를 제시한 참가자들은 병원 의사들로부터 무료 건강 검진을 제공받았다.**

행사가 진행되는 동안, 티에리 도마스 박사의 창구에는 긴 줄이 늘어섰다. "저는 오늘 피부 관리와 눈 관리 기술의 발전에 대해 알고 싶어서 왔어요. **188하지만 충치 예방법과 구강 건강 개선법에 대한 도마스 박사의 강의에서 가장 도움이 되는 정보를 얻었답니다.**"라고 참가자인 리아나 스타윈스키가 말했다.

189가장 인기 있는 행사는 영양사인 질리안 오팔라의 건강한 식습관에 대한 발표였다. 슈퍼 푸드에 대한 최신 정보를 들으려고 100명 이상의 사람들이 모여들었는데, 그들 중 다수는 은퇴한 사람들이었다. 오팔라 씨가 참가자들의 계속되는 질문에 대답하느라 행사는 예상했던 것보다 두 배 가까운 시간이 걸렸다.

190어린이들은 일반 건강과 위생에 관한 질문들이 포함된 건강 퀴즈 대회에 즐겁게 참여했다. 대회 승자들은 게임 진행자로부터 장난감과 수료증을 받았다. 행사가 매우 성공적이어서 헤시디온 클리닉의 이사 랜스 버호벤은 벌써 이 행사를 연례 행사로 만들 것을 고려 중이다.

어휘 host 주최하다; 진행자 support 지원[지지]하다 general 일반적인 attendee 참석자 participate in ~에 참여하다 a variety of 다양한 sponsor 후원자 participant 참가자 complimentary 무료의 physical 신체의 physician 의사

---

sizable 꽤 큰 form 형성되다 advance 발전 prevent 예방하다 cavity 충치 oral 구강의 nutritionist 영양사 retiree 은퇴자 flock 모이다 steady 꾸준한 stream 흐름, 연속 involve 포함하다, 수반하다 hygiene 위생 certificate 증명서[자격증]

186 세부 사항

번역 스타윈스키 씨는 무엇을 하라고 권장받는가?

(A) 설문지를 작성할 것
(B) 행사에 갈 것
(C) 몇몇 활동을 준비할 것
(D) 스토크 씨를 만날 것

해설 이메일 첫 단락에서 4월 10일 토요일에 개최될 예정인 병원의 건강 인식의 날에 스타윈스키 씨를 초대하게 되어(to invite you to our clinic's Health Awareness Day) 기쁘다며 참석해 주면 좋겠다(We would be delighted to see you attend)고 했으므로, (B)가 정답이다.

187 연계

번역 일부 참가자들은 어떻게 무료 건강 점검을 받았는가?

(A) 병원이 문을 열 때 도착함으로써
(B) 도마스 박사의 강의에 참석함으로써
(C) 스토크 씨의 이메일에 답변함으로써
(D) 대회에서 우승함으로써

해설 스토크 씨가 보낸 이메일 마지막 문장에서 3월 31일까지 답변을 해서(by responding to this e-mail by March 31) 행사에 등록하면 코드를 받게 될 것(will receive a code to present at the clinic)이라고 했고, 기사의 두 번째 단락 마지막 문장에서 스페셜 코드를 제시한 참가자들은 병원 의사들로부터 무료 건강 검진을 제공받았다(Participants who provided a special code were offered a complimentary physical checkup)고 했으므로, (C)가 정답이다.

어휘 competition (경연) 대회, 시합

188 추론 / 암시

번역 도마스 박사는 무엇을 전문으로 할 것 같은가?

(A) 피부 　　　　(B) 귀
(C) 눈 　　　　(D) 치아

해설 기사의 세 번째 단락에서 충치 예방법과 구강 건강 개선법에 대한 도마스 박사의 강의(Dr. Daumas' talk about how to prevent cavities and improve oral health)에서 가장 도움이 되는 정보를 얻었다고 리아나 스타윈스키가 말한 것으로 보아, 도마스 박사는 치과 전문의임을 추론할 수 있다. 따라서 (D)가 정답이다.

189 사실 관계 확인

번역 식품에 관한 발표에 대해 명시된 것은?

(A) 촬영되었다.
(B) 연기되었다.
(C) 많은 관심을 끌었다.
(D) 은퇴한 병원 직원이 발표했다.

해설 기사의 네 번째 단락에서 가장 인기 있는 행사는 영양사인 질리안 오팔라의 건강한 식습관에 대한 발표였다(By far the most popular event was ~ healthy eating habits)고 했으므로, (C)가 정답이다.

▶▶ Paraphrasing 지문의 the most popular
→ 정답의 attracted a lot of attention

190 연계

번역 누가 수료증을 배포했겠는가?

(A) 스토크 씨　　　　(B) 하야시 씨
(C) 스필레인 씨　　　(D) 버호벤 씨

해설 기사의 마지막 단락에서 어린이들이 건강 퀴즈 대회(a health contest)에 참여했고 대회 승자들은 게임 진행자로부터 장난감과 수료증을 받았다(The winners received toys and certificates from the game host)고 했는데, 명단에 어린이 건강 게임(Kid's Health Game)은 수잔 하야시가 담당한다고 나와 있으므로, (B)가 정답이다.

191-195 안내책자 + 후기 + 이메일

싱가포르에서 비즈니스를 공부하세요

¹⁹²싱가포르 비즈니스 스쿨*(SBS)은 싱가포르 금융 지구의 중심에 위치합니다. ¹⁹¹저희는 학생들이 대학원에 진학할 수 있도록 준비시키는 것을 목표로 하는 다양하고 질 높은 강좌들을 제공합니다. 강의 시간 사이에 여러분은 도시를 탐험할 수 있고 사업 인맥을 구축할 수 있습니다. 저희는 금융, 경제 및 국제 마케팅과 같이 내용 기반 수업뿐만 아니라 이력서와 자기 소개서 작성을 포함한 대학원 지원서 준비에 관한 수업도 제공합니다.

저희는 수천 명의 학생들이 전 세계의 대학원 과정에 입학하는 것을 도왔습니다. 저희는 ¹⁹⁴오토 드라이브 코리아의 재무 담당 최고책임자인 디아라 로드스와 쿠알라룸푸르 유니온 렌더스의 부회장 파라 완 씨 등 다수의 유명 시간강사진을 자랑합니다. 인상적인 강사진 및 개설 과정에 대한 추가 정보를 원하시거나 온라인 등록을 하시려면 www.sbs.edu.sg로 저희 웹사이트를 방문하세요.

어휘 district 구역 a range of 다양한 graduate school 대학원 explore 탐사하다 cultivate 구축하다 application 지원(서) CV 이력서(= curriculum vitae) statement 성명(진술)서 high-profile 세간의 주목을 끄는 instructor 강사 expert 전문가 faculty 강사[교수]진, 학부 enroll 등록하다

---

http://www.sbs.edu.sg/reviews

| 홈 | 강의 | **후기** | 연락처 |

우리 학생들의 목소리

6월 3일 아츠시 코시 작성

저는 SBS에서 금융 과정을 들었어요. 제가 지금 영국에서 다니고 있는 학교는 학사 학위를 취득하는 동안 듣지 않았던 필수 이수 과목이 있어

서, 8주 코스가 편리했어요. 하지만 저는 근처의 높은 집세를 감당할 수 없었기 때문에 통학을 해야 했는데, ¹⁹²그 지역은 교통 체증이 심해요. ¹⁹⁵SBS가 학교에 학생들을 위한 기숙사를 마련했으면 합니다. 강의의 질은 훌륭했어요. ¹⁹⁴제 강사 선생님은 디아라 로드스 씨였습니다. ¹⁹³짧은 시간 동안 다양한 주제를 다루느라 강의 내내 서두르시는 경향은 있었지만, 읽기 자료와 선생님의 실전 경험 설명으로부터 정말 많은 것을 배웠어요. 선생님께서 비즈니스 문제를 해결하신 방식은 제 대학원 면접 동안 영감의 원천이었고, 지금 수업에도 도움이 되고 있어요.

어휘 prerequisite 전제 조건, 필수 과목 degree 학위 convenient 편리한 afford 여유가 되다 rent 집세 commute 통근[통학]하다 dormitory 기숙사 instruction 가르침, 교육 superb 훌륭한 lecturer 강사 rush 서두르다 reading 독서, 읽기 자료 source 원천 inspiration 영감

수신: atsushi.koshi@scholarmail.co.uk
발신: lsommersell@sbs.edu.sg
제목: 귀하의 후기
날짜: 8월 15일

코시 씨께,

귀하의 피드백에 감사드립니다. 귀하만 이 특정 문제에 대해 의견을 내신 것은 아닙니다. ¹⁹⁵참고로 알려 드리면, 본교는 귀하의 건의에 따라 본 건을 처리할 계획입니다. 이르면 1월 1일부터 본교의 강좌를 수강하는 학생들은 이 새로운 혜택을 누릴 수 있게 될 것입니다. 본교에서 강좌 수강을 고려하고 있는 주변 분들에게 이 점을 꼭 언급해 주시기 바랍니다.

로리 소머셀

어휘 particular 특정한 concern 우려, 걱정 address (문제 등을) 다루다 recommendation 건의, 권고 advantage 이점

191 추론 / 암시

번역 안내책자는 누구를 대상으로 하는가?

(A) 비즈니스 전문가들　　(B) 예비 대학원생들
(C) 일을 구하고 있는 강사들　(D) 작가 지망생들

해설 첫 번째 단락의 두 번째 문장에서 학생들이 대학원에 갈 수 있도록 준비시키는 것을 목표로 하는 다양하고 질 높은 강좌들을 제공한다(offer a range of high-quality courses aimed at preparing students for graduate school)고 했으므로, (B)가 정답이다.

어휘 professional 전문가, 전문직 종사자 potential ~할 가능성이 있는, 잠재적인 employment 직장, 취업 aspiring 장차 ~이 되려는

192 연계

번역 SBS에 대해 명시된 것은?

(A) 분주한 지역에 위치해 있다.
(B) 재정 지원을 제공한다.
(C) 인턴십 기회를 제공한다.
(D) 취업 알선 서비스를 제공한다.

해설 안내책자에 싱가포르 비즈니스 스쿨(SBS)이 싱가포르 금융 지구의 중심에 위치(The Singapore Business School is located in the heart of Singapore's financial district)한다고 나와 있는데, 코시 씨의 후기를 보면 그 지역은 교통 체증이 심하다(the traffic in that area is terrible)고 했으므로, (A)가 정답이다.

어휘 financial assistance 재정 지원 employment-assistance service 취업 알선 서비스

193 세부 사항

번역 코시 씨가 자신의 강사에 대해 언급한 것은?

(A) 많은 독서량을 요구했다.
(B) 수업 주제를 빠른 속도로 다루었다.
(C) 예시를 거의 들지 않았다.
(D) 수업 참여를 북돋았다.

해설 후기의 중반부를 보면 디아라 로데스 선생님이 짧은 시간 동안 다양한 주제를 다루느라(discussing a wide range of topics in a small amount of time) 강의 내내 서두르는 경향이 있었다(she tended to rush through lectures)고 했으므로, (B)가 정답이다. 읽기 자료와 실전 경험 설명(her descriptions of real-world experiences)으로부터 많은 것을 배웠다고 했으므로 (C)는 명백한 오답이고, (A), (D) 역시 언급된 바가 없으므로 정답이 될 수 없다.

194 연계

번역 코시 씨의 강사는 강의를 하지 않을 때는 어디에서 일하는가?

(A) SBS
(B) 싱가포르 금융 지구에 있는 은행
(C) 오토 드라이브 코리아
(D) 쿠알라룸푸르 유니온 렌더스

해설 후기 중반부에서 코시 씨가 자신의 강사 선생님이 디아라 로드스 씨(My lecturer was Diara Rhodes)라고 했는데, 안내책자의 두 번째 단락을 보면 디아라 로드스 씨가 오토 드라이브 코리아의 재무 담당 최고책임자(Diara Rhodes, chief financial officer of Auto Drive Korea)라는 것을 알 수 있으므로, (C)가 정답이다.

195 연계

번역 SBS는 어떻게 코시 씨의 불만을 처리할 것인가?

(A) 더 많은 강사진을 고용함으로써
(B) 강의 시간을 줄임으로써
(C) 교통수단 선택 사항을 추가함으로써
(D) 캠퍼스에 학생 기숙사를 지음으로써

해설 이메일에서 코시 씨의 건의에 따라 문제를 처리할 계획(we plan on addressing it by following your recommendation)이라고 했는데, 코시 씨가 작성한 후기를 보면 SBS가 학교에 학생들을 위한 기숙사를 마련했으면 한다(I wish SBS offered a dormitory for students at the school)고 제안했으므로, (D)가 정답이다.

▶▶ Paraphrasing 지문의 a dormitory for students
→ 정답의 student housing

196-200 광고 + 지원서 + 편지

상근직 부조리사 구함

더 델핀 스트리트 그릴은 1924년 이래로 뉴올리언스에서 영업해 온 유명 식당입니다. **196**저희는 총 주방장의 감독 하에 엄선된 볶음 요리와 소스를 준비할 부조리사를 구하고 있습니다. **197**이상적인 후보자는 최소한 1년의 관련 조리 경력이 있거나 확실히 자리잡은 레스토랑에서 2년의 견습 기간을 마친 사람이어야 합니다. 전통적인 케이준 스타일 요리뿐 아니라 혁신적인 요리를 준비할 수 있는 능력이 입증되어야 합니다. 지원하려면, www.delphinestreetgrill.com/careers를 방문하세요.

어휘 full-time 상근의 line cook (특정 요리[라인] 담당) 부조리사 high-profile 유명한, 세간의 주목을 받는 select 엄선된 sautéed (기름에 재빨리) 볶은 supervision 감독, 관리 executive chef 총 주방장 ideal 이상적인 candidate 지원자, 후보자 apprenticeship 견습(기간, 직) well-established 확실히 자리잡은 demonstrated 입증된 innovative 혁신적인 cuisine 요리

---

www.delphinestreetgrill.com/careers/line_cook/apply

이름: 앤톤 호앙
이메일: antonh94@textmail.com
전화번호: 504.555.0177
관련 교육: **198**조리학 준학사, 부드로 커뮤니티 칼리지

현 고용주/직함: 리버 페리 카페, 부조리사   고용 기간: 6개월
전 고용주/직함: 호텔 르느와르, 견습생   **197**고용 기간: 2년
200전 고용주/직함: 피카드 씨푸드, 인턴   **197**고용 기간: 3개월
이력서: ☑ 첨부함
추천인 명단: ☑ 첨부함

자기소개서:

저는 더 델핀 스트리트 그릴의 부조리사직에 매우 관심이 있습니다. 지난 6개월 동안, **197**저는 전통적인 케이준 식사를 제공하는 카페에서 부조리사로 근무했습니다. 카페가 최근에서야 문을 열었기 때문에, 저는 거의 모든 메뉴 준비를 책임지고 있습니다. 저는 스타 요리사인 유제니 미로네 곁에서 일하며 유명한 호텔 르느와르에서의 견습 기간을 마쳤습니다. 또한, **197, 198**테드 오버벡*(부드로 커뮤니티 칼리지에 계신 제 멘토이자 강사님) 씨가 확인해 줄 수 있듯이, 저는 창의적이고 새로운 조리법을 개발할 수 있습니다. 실제로, **197, 198**저는 대학에 다니는 동안 제가 공들여 만든 베트남식 샌드위치 조리법으로 우수 혁신상을 수상했고, 그 샌드위치는 현재 대학 구내식당의 메뉴에 있습니다.

[지원서 제출]

어휘 associate degree 준학사 (2년제 대학) culinary 요리의 reference 추천서[인] traditional 전통적인 celebrity 유명 인사 instructor 강사 confirm 확인해 주다 develop 개발하다 creative 창의적인 recipe 조리법 innovation 혁신 craft 공들여 만들다

196 사실 관계 확인

번역 부조리사직에 대해 명시된 것은?

(A) 2년짜리 계약이다.
(B) 심야 근무를 요구한다.
(C) 견습생 감독을 포함한다.
(D) 한정된 수의 요리를 준비한다.

해설 광고의 두 번째 문장에서 총 주방장의 감독 하에 엄선된 볶음 요리와 소스를 준비할 부조리사를 구하고 있다(We are seeking a line cook to prepare select sautéed items and sauces)고 했으므로, 부조리사가 한정된 수의 요리를 준비한다는 것을 알 수 있다. 따라서 (D)가 정답이다.

▶▶ **Paraphrasing** 지문의 **select** → 정답의 **a limited variety of**

197 연계

번역 호앙 씨에 대해 사실인 것은?

(A) 여러 레스토랑에 구직 중이다.
(B) 해당 일자리의 요건을 충족한다.
(C) 미로네 씨와 TV 출연을 한 적이 있다.
(D) 베트남에 있는 요리 학교에서 가르쳤다.

해설 광고 중반부에서 이상적인 후보는 최소한 1년의 조리 경력(at least one year of related cooking experience)이 있거나 확실히 자리잡은 레스토랑에서 2년의 견습 기간(a two-year apprenticeship in a well-established restaurant)을 마친 사람이어야 하고, 전통적인 케이준 스타일 요리뿐 아니라 혁신적인 요리를 준비할 수 있는 능력(ability to prepare innovative dishes

as well as classic Cajun-style cuisine)이 입증되어야 한다고 했다. 호앙 씨의 지원서와 자기소개서를 보면 2년의 견습 기간(Hotel Lenoir, Apprentice — Time employed: Two years)을 마쳤으며, 케이준 스타일 요리를 할 수 있고(I have been the line cook for a café serving traditional Cajun meals), 혁신적인 요리를 준비할 능력(Ted Overbeck can confirm, I am able to develop creative new recipes)도 증명할 수 있으므로, 구인 광고에서 요구하는 조건을 충족한다고 볼 수 있다. 따라서 (B)가 정답이다.

198 세부 사항

번역 오버벡 씨는 누구인가?

(A) 총 주방장
(B) 부책임자
(C) 요리 강사
(D) 식당 주인

해설 조리를 전공한 호앙 씨의 지원서 중반부를 보면 테드 오버벡 씨가 자신의 멘토이자 부드로 커뮤니티 칼리지의 강사(my mentor and instructor at Boudreau Community College)라고 했으므로, (C)가 정답이다.

199 추론 / 암시

번역 부드로 커뮤니티 칼리지에 대해 암시된 것은?

(A) 요리상을 수여한다.
(B) 무료 요리 워크샵을 제공한다.
(C) 구내식당에 새 요리사가 필요하다.
(D) 유명 요리사를 초청 연사로 초대한다.

해설 지원서에서 호앙 씨가 자신이 대학에 다니는 동안 베트남식 샌드위치 조리법으로 우수 혁신상을 수상(I was awarded the Excellence in Innovation Prize for a Vietnamese-style sandwich recipe)했고, 그 샌드위치는 현재 대학 구내식당의 메뉴에 있다(on the menu at the college's cafeteria)고 했으므로, 호앙 씨가 다녔던 부드로 커뮤니티 칼리지는 학생의 요리를 선정해 상을 수여하고 수상작을 학교 내 식당의 메뉴로 활용하고 있음을 알 수 있다. 따라서 (A)가 정답이다.

200 연계

번역 리오우 씨는 어디에서 일할 것 같은가?

(A) 리버 페리 카페
(B) 호텔 르느와르
(C) 피카드 씨푸드
(D) 더 델핀 스트리트 그릴

해설 편지를 보면 호앙 씨의 3개월 인턴십을 지도했던 사람이 유명 요리사 사빈 리오우 씨(Sabine Riou, the renowned chef who supervised his three-month internship)라는 것을 알 수 있고, 지원서에 호앙 씨가 피카드 씨푸드에서 3개월 인턴십을 수료했다(Previous employer/title: Picard Seafood, Intern / Time employed: Three months)고 나와 있으므로, 리오우 씨는 피카드 씨푸드에서 근무한다는 것을 추론할 수 있다. 따라서 (C)가 정답이다.

기출 TEST 2

101 (B)	102 (C)	103 (D)	104 (A)	105 (C)
106 (B)	107 (C)	108 (D)	109 (B)	110 (A)
111 (A)	112 (C)	113 (B)	114 (A)	115 (A)
116 (C)	117 (B)	118 (D)	119 (D)	120 (D)
121 (C)	122 (C)	123 (B)	124 (D)	125 (A)
126 (B)	127 (A)	128 (C)	129 (B)	130 (A)
131 (A)	132 (B)	133 (D)	134 (C)	135 (D)
136 (A)	137 (B)	138 (A)	139 (C)	140 (B)
141 (B)	142 (A)	143 (A)	144 (C)	145 (C)
146 (B)	147 (B)	148 (A)	149 (D)	150 (A)
151 (A)	152 (B)	153 (A)	154 (B)	155 (D)
156 (A)	157 (C)	158 (C)	159 (B)	160 (D)
161 (D)	162 (D)	163 (A)	164 (C)	165 (D)
166 (A)	167 (B)	168 (A)	169 (D)	170 (C)
171 (C)	172 (C)	173 (B)	174 (D)	175 (A)
176 (A)	177 (C)	178 (B)	179 (C)	180 (C)
181 (D)	182 (A)	183 (D)	184 (C)	185 (C)
186 (A)	187 (B)	188 (D)	189 (D)	190 (C)
191 (C)	192 (D)	193 (A)	194 (D)	195 (B)
196 (B)	197 (C)	198 (D)	199 (C)	200 (A)

PART 5

101 인칭대명사의 격 _ 소유격

해설 빈칸은 전치사 with의 목적어 역할을 하는 명사구 marketing team을 한정 수식하는 자리이므로, 소유격 인칭대명사인 (B) her가 정답이다.

번역 카펜터 씨는 그녀의 마케팅 팀과 함께 회의에 참석할 예정이다.

어휘 attend 참석하다 conference (대규모) 회의

102 전치사 어휘

해설 빈칸 뒤의 기간을 나타내는 명사구 the last ten years와 어울려 쓰이는 전치사를 선택하는 문제이다. 지난 10년간 발생한 일에 대해 설명하는 내용이므로, '(특정 기간) 동안, ~ 중에'라는 의미의 전치사 (C) During이 정답이다.

번역 지난 10년간 베이 시티의 인구는 약 27퍼센트 증가했다.

어휘 population 인구

103 명사 자리 _ 동격

해설 빈칸 앞에 사람 이름(Alan Schmit)과 콤마가 있고 뒤에는 전치사 of가 이끄는 수식어구가 있으므로, 빈칸에는 앨런 슈미트와 동격 관계를 이루는 명사가 들어가야 한다. 따라서 '수상자'라는 의미의 (D) winner가 정답이다.

번역 놀 병원 간호 부문의 지도자상 수상자인 앨런 슈미트를 축하해 주세요.

어휘 nursing 보육, 간호

104 부사 자리 _ 어휘

해설 빈칸은 미래 진행형 동사인 will be opening을 수식하는 부사 자리로, 문맥상 '곧 대규모 시설을 열 예정이다'라는 의미가 되어야 자연스럽다. 따라서 '곧'이라는 의미의 (A) soon이 정답이다. (B) such는 한정사/대명사이므로 품사상 오답이고, (C) ever는 '언젠가, 언제나, 도대체' 등의 의미로 쓰이는 부사로 빈칸에 들어갈 경우 문장이 부자연스러워진다. (D) like는 부사로 쓰일 경우 조동사와 be동사 사이에 위치할 수 없으므로 정답이 될 수 없다.

번역 아일랜드 최대의 소프트웨어 생산업체가 곧 코크에 대규모 시설을 열 예정이다.

어휘 facility 시설

105 부사 자리 _ 동사 수식

해설 빈칸은 동사구 has been in high demand를 수식하는 부사 자리이다. 따라서 부사인 (B) later와 (C) lately 중 하나를 선택해야 하는데, 문맥상 '수요가 최근 높아지고 있다'라는 내용이 되어야 자연스러우므로, '최근'이라는 의미의 (C) lately가 정답이 된다.

번역 애쉬번 은행의 온라인 서비스에 대한 수요가 최근 높아지고 있다.

어휘 demand 수요 lateness 늦음, 지각 latest 최신의, 가장 최근의

106 명사 어휘

해설 빈칸은 동사구 can help의 주어 역할을 하는 명사 자리로, 빈칸 뒤 전치사구 of videos to electronic press releases의 수식을 받는다. 따라서 해당 전치사구와 가장 잘 어울리는 명사를 선택해야 한다. 문맥상 '동영상을 인터넷 보도 자료에 추가하는 것'이라는 내용이 되어야 자연스러우므로, 전치사 to와 함께 자주 쓰여 '~에 추가(된 것)'라는 표현을 완성하는 (B) addition이 정답이다.

번역 동영상을 인터넷 보도자료에 추가하면 기업들이 자사의 제품을 선보이는 데 도움이 될 수 있다.

어휘 electronic 전자의, 온라인의 press release 보도 자료 showcase 선보이다; 공개 행사 content 내용 promotion 홍보, 승진

107 동사 어형 _ 태

해설 빈칸은 주어 updates 뒤에 나오는 동사 자리이다. 따라서 능동태 동사 (A) have need와 수동태 동사 (C) are needed 중 하나를 선택해야 하는데, updates는 필요한 대상이므로, (C) are needed가 정답이 된다. 참고로, 동명사/현재분사인 (B) needing과 to부정사 (D) to be needed는 동사 자리에 들어갈 수 없다.

번역 현 씨는 업데이트가 필요한지 확인하기 위해 교육용 매뉴얼을 검토하고 있다.

어휘 review 검토하다

108 전치사 어휘

해설 빈칸은 뒤에 오는 명사구 the doors를 목적어로 취하는 전치사 자리이며, 빈칸을 포함한 전치사구가 동사 exit을 수식하고 있다. 따라서 exit 및 door와 가장 잘 어울리는 전치사를 선택해야 한다. 문맥상 '아래층에 있는 문으로 나가세요'라는 내용이 되어야 자연스러우므로, '~을 통과하여, ~을 통해'라는 의미의 (D) through가 정답이다.

번역 강당을 나갈 때는 아래층에 있는 문으로 나가세요.

어휘 auditorium 강당   exit 나가다

109 명사 자리 _ 동사의 목적어

해설 빈칸은 타동사 include의 목적어 역할을 하는 명사 자리이므로, 명사인 (B) representatives가 정답이다. (A) represents와 (D) represent는 동사, (C) represented는 동사/과거분사(형용사)로 품사상 빈칸에 적합하지 않다.

번역 올해의 시나리오 경연 대회 심사위원에는 하노비 스튜디오즈 직원들이 포함되어 있다.

어휘 screenplay (영화) 시나리오, 대본   competition 경연 대회   representative 대표, 직원

110 형용사 어휘

해설 빈칸 뒤의 명사 experience를 적절히 수식하는 형용사를 선택하는 문제이다. '경력을 자세히 서술한(detailing) 이력서를 첨부했다'라는 내용의 문장이므로, 빈칸에 '많은, 폭넓은'이라는 의미의 형용사가 들어가야 자연스럽다. 따라서 (A) extensive가 정답이다.

번역 호텔 업계에서 쌓은 폭넓은 경력을 상세히 기록한 이력서를 첨부했습니다.

어휘 extensive 폭넓은, 광범위한   punctual 시간을 지키는   prospective 장래의, 유망한   accepted 용인된, 인수가 끝난

111 분사구문

해설 빈칸 앞 부사절 접속사 when은 완전한 절이나 주어가 생략된 분사구문을 이끌 수 있다. 빈칸 뒤에 주어가 없으므로 현재분사 (A) revising과 과거분사 (C) revised 중에 하나를 선택해야 하는데, 생략된 주어인 you가 revise의 주체가 되며 뒤에 목적어 역할을 하는 명사구 the document가 있으므로, 능동의 의미를 나타내는 현재분사 (A) revising이 정답이다.

번역 문서를 수정할 때는 카마시 씨 이름의 철자를 잊지 말고 확인하세요.

어휘 revise 수정하다

112 명사절 접속사

해설 빈칸은 뒤에 오는 완전한 절을 이끄는 접속사 자리이다. 빈칸을 포함한 절이 to ask의 목적어 역할을 하므로, 빈칸에는 명사절 접속사가 들어가야 한다. 따라서 '~인지 (아닌지)'라는 의미의 명사절 접속사인 (C) whether가 정답이다. 참고로, 부사절 접속사 (A) although와 (B) since가 이끄는 부사절은 수식어 역할을 하므로 빈칸에 들어갈 수 없다.

번역 주민들은 개발업자들이 역사 지구를 보존할지 여부를 문의하기 위해 시청을 방문했다.

어휘 resident 주민   preserve 보존하다   historic properties 역사 지구[지역]

113 형용사 자리 _ 최상급

해설 빈칸에는 최상급 표현 the most와 함께 쓰일 수 있는 형용사 혹은 부사가 들어가야 하는데, 빈칸 뒤에 명사나 형용사가 아닌 목적격 관계대명사가 생략된 관계사절이 왔다. 따라서 관계사절의 선행사인 명사가 생략된 것임을 알 수 있으므로, 명사를 수식할 수 있는 형용사인 (B) innovative가 정답이다. 참고로, 명사가 생략 가능한 이유는 앞에 advertising campaign이 명시되어 있어 명사 없이도 '우리가 본 광고 캠페인 중 가장 혁신적인 것'이라는 의미를 파악할 수 있기 때문이다. 만일 빈칸에 부사가 들어갈 경우 뒤에 부사의 수식을 받는 형용사가 와야 한다.

번역 포드 그룹이 제안한 광고 캠페인은 지금까지 우리가 본 것 중 가장 혁신적입니다.

어휘 proposed 제안된   innovative 혁신적인

114 부사 어휘

해설 빈칸 뒤 형용사 complete을 적절히 수식하는 부사를 선택하는 문제이다. complete이 '완성된'이라는 의미이므로, 빈칸에는 완성된 정도를 나타내는 부사가 들어가야 자연스럽다. 따라서 '거의'라는 의미의 (A) almost가 정답이다. (D) yet은 '아직'이라는 의미로 부정문과 쓰이거나 「be/have+yet+to부정사」 구조로 쓰이므로, 빈칸에는 적절하지 않다.

번역 솔레이 조경은 체리 힐 단지의 디자인이 거의 완성되었다고 발표했다.

어휘 landscaping 조경

115 인칭대명사의 격 _ 주격

해설 빈칸은 that절의 동사인 (should) be given의 주어 자리이다. 따라서 주격 인칭대명사 (A) he와 소유대명사 (C) his 중 하나를 선택해야 하는데, 책임이 주어지는 대상이 문장의 주어인 Daniel Nishida이므로, (A) he가 정답이다.

번역 비품 담당 최고 책임자인 다니엘 니시다 씨는 모든 송장을 승인하는 임무를 달라고 요청했다.

어휘 supply 공급(물)   responsibility 책임   approve 승인하다

116 동사 어휘

해설 빈칸 뒤에서 목적어 역할을 하는 명사구 a new facilities director와 가장 잘 어울리는 타동사를 선택해야 한다. 문맥상 '새로운 시설 부장을 채용하다'라는 내용이 되어야 자연스러우므로, '채용하다'라는 의미의 (C) recruit가 정답이다. (B) compete는 '경쟁하다'라는 의미의 자동사로 목적어를 취할 수 없고, (A) resume은 '재개하다', (D) conduct는 '수행하다, ~를 안내하다'라는 뜻으로 문맥상 어색하므로 정답이 될 수 없다.

번역 3월 말 쿠마르 씨의 은퇴에 대비해, 카록스사는 새로운 시설 부장을 채용해야 할 것이다.

어휘 in preparation for ~에 대비해 retirement 은퇴 facility 시설

어휘 eliminate 제거하다 rarely 드물게, 좀처럼 ~ 않고 seek 구하다 expert 전문가의; 전문가

117 부사 자리 _ 과거분사 수식

해설 빈칸은 부사 very의 수식을 받는 동시에 과거분사 acknowledged 를 수식하는 부사 자리이므로, '호의적으로, 좋게'라는 의미의 부사인 (B) favorably가 정답이다. (A) favor는 명사/동사, (C) favorable 은 형용사, (D) favored는 동사/형용사로 모두 품사상 빈칸에 적합하지 않다.

번역 립튼 그룹의 마케팅 계획에 대한 그 팀의 기여는 굉장히 호의적으로 인정을 받았다.

어휘 contribution 기여 acknowledge 인정하다 favor 호의, 부탁; 호의를 보이다, 찬성하다 favorable 호의적인, 찬성하는 favored 호의를 사고 있는, 혜택을 받는

118 전치사 어휘

해설 빈칸은 뒤에 오는 동명사구 receiving the engineering award 를 목적어로 취하는 전치사 자리이며, 빈칸을 포함한 전치사구가 콤마 뒤 주절을 수식하고 있다. 따라서 빈칸에는 '상을 받은 것'과 '오랜 멘토들에게 감사를 표했다'를 적절히 연결해 주는 전치사가 들어가야 한다. 문맥상 '공학상을 받자마자, 감사를 표했다'라는 내용이 되어야 자연스러우므로, 동명사와 쓰여 '~하자마자'라는 표현을 완성하는 (D) Upon이 정답이다.

번역 공학상을 받자마자, 권 씨는 오랜 멘토들에게 잊지 않고 감사를 표했다.

어휘 make a point of (의도적으로, 공을 들여) ~를 하다

119 형용사 어휘

해설 빈칸 뒤 명사 qualifications를 적절히 수식하는 형용사를 선택하는 문제이다. 자격 요건 목록을 보고 본인이 필요한(necessary) 학력 및 경력을 갖추고 있는지 확인하라는 내용이므로, 빈칸에는 '필수적인' 이라는 의미의 형용사가 들어가야 자연스럽다. 따라서 (D) essential 이 정답이다.

번역 필수 자격 요건 목록을 읽고 귀하가 그 직책에 필요한 교육과 경력을 갖추었는지 확인하십시오.

어휘 qualification 자격 (요건) ensure 확실히 하다, 보장하다 position 직책 slight 약간의, 가벼운 equal 동등한 obliged 고마워하는, 의무감을 느끼는

120 등위 접속사

해설 빈칸 뒤 완전한 절을 이끄는 접속사 자리이다. 빈칸 앞 절이 판단의 근거(소프트웨어 도구를 선택하는 것은 간단하지 않다)를, 빈칸이 포함된 절이 판단(전문가의 조언을 구하는 것이 중요하다)을 나타내며 대등한 관계를 이루고 있다. 따라서 '그래서, 그러므로'라는 의미의 등위 접속사인 (D) so가 정답이다.

번역 컴퓨터 바이러스를 제거하는 최고의 소프트웨어 도구를 고르는 일은 좀처럼 간단하지 않으므로, 전문가의 조언을 구하는 것이 중요하다.

121 전치사 자리

해설 빈칸은 뒤에 오는 동명사구 reviewing any more loan applications를 목적어로 취하는 전치사 자리이므로, '~ 전에'라는 의미의 전치사인 (C) before가 정답이다. 참고로, before가 접속사로 쓰였고 뒤에 주어가 생략된 분사구문(reviewing)이 온 구조로 볼 수도 있다. 부사절 접속사인 (A) now that 및 (B) as though는 뒤에 「주어＋동사」가 와야 하므로 정답이 될 수 없다.

번역 델가도 씨는 더 이상의 대출 신청서를 검토하기 전에 대출 담당자 전원과 회의를 하고 싶어 한다.

어휘 loan 대출, 융자 application 신청(서), 지원(서)

122 명사 어휘

해설 빈칸은 동사 has의 목적어 역할을 하는 명사 자리로, 전치사구 as a business-friendly environment의 수식을 받고 있다. 문맥상 '기업 친화적인 환경으로 명성을 떨치고 있다'라는 내용이 되어야 자연스러우므로, '명성, 평판'이라는 의미의 명사인 (C) reputation이 정답이다. 참고로, reputation은 전치사 for나 as와 함께 자주 쓰인다.

번역 시더 브랜치 힐은 효율적인 인허가 및 기타 법적 절차를 제공하는 기업 친화적인 환경으로 명성을 떨치고 있습니다.

어휘 reputation 명성 environment 환경 efficient 효율적인 licensing 인허가 legal 법적인 procedure 절차 prediction 예측 courtesy 예의 statement 성명, 진술

123 to부정사 _ 부사적 용법

해설 빈칸 앞에 완전한 절이 왔고, 뒤에 동사(perfect)와 목적어인 「소유격＋명사(their performance)」가 있으므로, 빈칸에는 절과 동사구를 연결할 수 있는 표현이 들어가야 한다. 문맥을 살펴보면 연기를 완벽하게 하는 것이 추가 리허설의 목적이 되므로, 동사원형과 함께 쓰여 '~하기 위해'라는 의미를 완성하는 (B) in order to가 정답이다. (A) considerably와 (C) nevertheless는 부사이므로 빈칸에 들어갈 수 없고, (D) as a result of 뒤에는 목적어 역할을 하는 동명사가 와야 하므로 역시 오답이다.

번역 배우들은 마지막 장면에서 연기를 완벽하게 하기 위해 추가 리허설을 했다.

어휘 perfect 완벽하게 하다; 완벽한 performance 공연, 연기 considerably 상당히 nevertheless 그럼에도 불구하고

124 동사 어휘

해설 빈칸 뒤의 명사구 the organization's rapid growth와 어울려 쓰이는 동사를 선택하는 문제이다. 빈칸이 포함된 to부정사구가 연구소 규모를 늘리는 목적을 나타내고 있으므로, 문맥상 '빠른 성장을 수용하기 위해'라는 내용이 되어야 자연스럽다. 따라서 '수용하다'라는 의미의 (D) accommodate가 정답이다.

번역 RZT 테크놀로지는 조직의 빠른 성장을 수용하기 위해 토론토 연구소의 규모를 두 배로 늘릴 예정이다.

어휘 laboratory 연구실, 실험실 accommodate 수용하다, 맞추다 organization 조직, 단체 assign 할당하다, 배당하다 investigate 조사하다

125 형용사 자리 _ 주격 보어

해설 빈칸은 주어 Smithton Electronics' second quarter를 설명하는 주격 보어 자리로, 형용사나 명사가 들어갈 수 있다. 문맥상 '스미스턴 전자의 2분기 수익이 좋지 않았지만'이라는 내용이 되어야 자연스러우므로, '수익이 있는'이라는 의미의 형용사인 (A) profitable이 정답이다. 명사인 (C) profitability도 보어 역할을 할 수 있지만, '수익성'이라는 뜻으로 주어와 동격 관계가 성립되지 않으므로 정답이 될 수 없다. 참고로, '이득을 얻다, 이익을 주다'라는 의미의 동사 profit의 현재분사인 (B) profiting은 목적어를 취하거나 전치사와 쓰여야 한다.

번역 스미스턴 전자의 2분기 수익이 좋지 않았지만, 회사는 연구에 많은 돈을 투자할 계획이다.

어휘 profitable 수익이 나는 sum 돈, 합계 research 연구 profitably 이익이 되게, 유익하게

126 명사 어휘

해설 빈칸은 전치사구 because of의 목적어 역할을 하는 명사 자리로, 뒤에 오는 전치사구 to the airport의 수식을 받는다. 따라서 to the airport와 어울려 쓰이며 호텔이 회의에 이상적인 장소인 이유를 나타내는 명사가 들어가야 하므로, '인접함'이라는 의미의 (B) proximity가 정답이 된다.

번역 윌리엄스포트 호텔은 공항과 가까워 회의에 이상적인 장소이다.

어휘 venue 장소 proximity to ~에 인접함, 가까움 achievement 성취, 업적 competence 역량 exception 예외

127 관계대명사 _ 소유격

해설 뒤에 오는 절(responsibilities ~ payroll forms)을 이끌어 앞에 있는 명사 employees를 적절히 수식하는 관계사를 고르는 문제이다. 빈칸 뒤에 명사가 왔으며, 해당 절의 주어인 respnosibilities가 선행사인 employees와 '직원들의 책임'이라는 소유 관계를 나타내므로, 소유격 관계대명사인 (A) whose가 정답이다.

번역 두 번째 교육 세션은 임금 대장 처리를 담당하는 직원을 대상으로 합니다.

어휘 session (특정 활동을 하는) 기간, 시간 employee 직원 responsibility 책임, 책무 payroll 급여 총액

128 부사절 접속사

해설 빈칸은 부사 poorly를 수식하면서, 뒤따르는 완전한(the high-speed printer ~ functioning)을 이끄는 접속사 자리이므로, '아무리 ~해도'라는 의미로 접속사 역할을 할 수 있는 (C) However가 정답이다. (A) Rather, (B) Seldom, (D) Thoroughly는 절을 이끌 수 없으므로 빈칸에 들어갈 수 없다.

번역 고속 프린터가 비록 제대로 작동하지는 않지만, 여전히 우리의 목적에 적합한 복사본은 만들고 있다.

어휘 function 작동하다, 기능하다 adequate 적합한 thoroughly 철저하게

129 동사 어휘

해설 빈칸은 will be와 함께 수동태를 이루는 과거분사 자리로, 부사 finally와 전치사구 at a product exhibition의 수식을 받는다. 따라서 이들과 가장 잘 어울리는 동사를 선택해야 한다. 문맥상 '카메라가 제품 전시회에서 마침내 공개된다'라는 내용이 되어야 자연스러우므로, '공개된'이라는 의미의 (B) unveiled가 정답이다.

번역 대망의 웨카 2XG 디지털 카메라가 8월 16일 제품 전시회에서 마침내 공개됩니다.

어휘 long-awaited 오래 기다렸던, 대망의 reduce 줄이다 resolve 결심하다, 해결하다

130 동사 어형 _ 태

해설 빈칸은 주어 Northeast Community Finance와 목적어 an online system 사이의 동사 자리이다. 따라서 문장에서 동사 역할을 할 수 있는 능동태 동사 (A) has implemented와 수동태 동사 (D) is implemented 중에 하나를 선택해야 하는데, 주어가 동사 implement(시행하다)의 주체이므로, (A) has implemented가 정답이 된다.

번역 노스이스트 커뮤니티 파이낸스는 지점의 서비스 라인을 축소하기 위해 온라인 시스템을 시행했다.

어휘 implement 시행하다 shorten 줄이다, 축소하다 location 지점, 위치

PART 6

131-134 광고

가든 쉐이드 나무 조경

가든 쉐이드는 규모에 상관없이 모든 정원에 어울리는 나무 조경과 울타리를 제작합니다. 당사의 디자인은 소규모 도시 정원들뿐만 아니라 건축가와 부동산 개발업자들이 의뢰하는 대규모 프로젝트까지도 **131탈바꿈시켜 왔습니다.** **132당사는 대부분의 프로젝트에 자체 묘목장의 나무를 사용합니다.** 하지만 어떤 묘목장도 모든 종과 크기의 나무를 제공할 수 없습니다. 따라서 가든 쉐이드는 당사에 필요한 나무를 제공할 **133준비가 되어 있는** 많은 전문 재배자들과 긴밀한 관계를 형성하고 있습니다. 이러한 공급원 덕분에 당사는 모든 **134주문**을 완수하는 데 필요한 다양성을 갖추고 있습니다. 다시 말해, 여러분이 꿈꾸는 조경 디자인이 무엇이든 간에 당사는 그 꿈을 실현할 수 있습니다.

어휘 landscape 조경 hedge 울타리, 담 suit 어울리다 transform 변형시키다, 전환하다 urban 도시의 commission 의뢰하다, 주문하다 architect 건축가 property developer 부동산 개발업자 nursery 묘목장 resource 자원, 공급원

131 동사 어휘

해설 주어인 designs 및 목적어인 small urban gardens as well as large-scale projects와 어울려 쓰이는 동사를 선택하는 문제이다. 조경 디자인이 소규모 정원 및 대규모 프로젝트에 할 수 있는 행위를 묘사하는 동사가 빈칸에 들어가야 자연스러우므로, '탈바꿈시키다, 변형시키다'라는 의미의 (A) transformed가 정답이다.

어휘 relate 관련시키다   collect 모으다, 징수하다, 모금하다   plant 심다

132 문맥에 맞는 문장 고르기

번역 (A) 당사는 조경에 관한 귀하의 질문에 답하기 위해 여기 있습니다.
(B) 당사는 대부분의 프로젝트에 자체 묘목장의 나무를 사용합니다.
(C) 일부 나무는 특별한 생장 요건이 필요합니다.
(D) 일반적인 조건이라면 묘목의 보증 기간은 1년입니다.

해설 빈칸 뒤 문장에서 '하지만, 어떤 묘목장도 모든 종과 크기의 나무를 제공할 수 없습니다(However, no single nursery ~ all species and sizes)'라며 나무 제공, 즉 프로젝트에 나무를 사용하는 데 있어서의 한계점을 언급했으므로, 빈칸에도 이와 관련된 내용이 언급되어야 문맥상 자연스럽다. 따라서 대부분의 프로젝트에 자체 묘목장의 나무를 사용한다는 내용의 (B)가 정답이다.

어휘 requirement 요건   nursery stock 묘목   guarantee 보증하다

133 형용사 자리 _ 관계대명사 + be동사 생략

해설 many specialist growers ~ we need까지 전치사 with의 목적어 역할을 하는데, 여기서 specialist growers가 빈칸 뒤 to provide(제공하다)의 주체가 되므로, 빈칸 이하가 specialist growers를 수식한다는 것을 알 수 있다. 이는 주격 관계대명사와 be동사가 생략된 구조로, 빈칸에는 형용사, 현재분사, 혹은 과거분사가 들어갈 수 있다. 따라서 보기 중 「be동사+ ~ +to부정사」 구조로 쓰여 '~할 준비가 되다'라는 의미를 완성하는 (D) ready가 정답이 된다. 최상급인 (C) readiest는 '가장 신속한, 가장 손쉬운'이라는 의미로 문맥상 적절하지 않다.

어휘 readiness 준비가 되어 있음, 신속, 용이   ready 준비가 된; 준비시키다

134 명사 어휘

해설 빈칸은 to complete의 목적어 역할을 하는 명사 자리로, complete 및 문맥과 적절히 어울리는 명사가 들어가야 한다. 뒤에 In other words(다시 말해)로 시작하는 문장에서 '꿈꾸는 조경 디자인이 무엇이든 간에(whatever your landscape design dream (is 생략)), 당사는 그 꿈을 실현할 수 있습니다(we can make it happen)'라고 했으므로, 빈칸이 포함된 부분 역시 이와 비슷한 내용(모든 주문을 이행할 수 있다)이 되어야 한다. 따라서 '주문'이라는 의미인 (C) order가 정답이다.

어휘 survey (설문) 조사; 조사하다

135-138 이메일

수신: 직원
발신: 에이미 헨위드
날짜: 1월 15일
제목: 신나는 소식

직원 여러분께,

멋진 한 해를 선사해 줘서 고마워요! 못 들으셨다면, 헨위드 홈 서플라이는 올봄에 두 번째 매장을 [135]열 예정입니다. 이번에 추가되는 소매점은 더비셔에 있는 애버턴 파크웨이와 서튼 애비뉴 모퉁이에 있는 쇼핑센터에 위치하게 됩니다.

4월 1일[136]까지 계산원 및 영업직 지원서를 접수할 예정입니다. 인사부장이 4월 2일부터 4월 6일까지 지원자의 자격 요건을 검토하고 [137]교육은 일주일 후에 시작됩니다. [138]관심을 가질만한 친구들과 이 소식을 자유롭게 공유하세요.

에이미 헨위드, CEO
헨위드 홈 서플라이

어휘 additional 추가의   retail 소매의; 소매   application 지원(서), 신청(서)   personnel 인사부, 인력   review 검토하다   qualification 자격 (요건)

135 동사 어휘

해설 빈칸은 our second store를 목적어로 취하는 동사 자리로, store 및 문맥에 어울리는 동사가 들어가야 한다. 뒤 문장의 주어인 '이번에 추가되는 소매점(This additional retail site)'이 our second store를 가리키므로, 해당 부분은 '열 예정이다'라는 내용이 되어야 자연스럽다. 따라서 (D) opening이 정답이다.

어휘 renovate 개조하다   expand 확장하다

136 전치사 어휘

해설 빈칸은 1 April을 목적어로 취하는 전치사 자리이며, 빈칸을 포함한 전치사구가 동사구 will be accepting을 수식하고 있다. 따라서 날짜 및 accept와 어울리는 전치사를 선택해야 한다. 문맥상 '4월 1일까지 접수할 예정이다'라는 내용이 되어야 자연스러우므로, 정답은 '~까지'라는 의미의 (A) until이다. (B) following은 '~ 후에, ~에 따라', (C) according to는 '~에 따라, (D) for는 '~를 위해, ~ 동안'이라는 의미로 빈칸에 적절하지 않다.

137 명사 자리 _ 어휘

해설 빈칸은 동사구 is scheduled to begin의 주어 역할을 하는 명사 자리로, 문맥에 어울리는 명사가 들어가야 한다. 앞 절에서 인사부장이 지원자(applicants)의 자격 요건을 검토할 예정이라고 했으므로, 해당 부분은 '교육이 예정되어 있다'라는 내용이 되어야 자연스럽다. 따라서 (B) training이 정답이다. (A) trainer는 '교육 담당자', (C) train은 '기차, 무리'라는 의미로 문맥상 적절하지 않다.

138 문맥에 맞는 문장 고르기

번역 (A) 관심을 가질만한 친구들과 이 소식을 자유롭게 공유하세요.
(B) 모든 자료를 받았는지 확인하세요.
(C) 아직 회신을 기다리신다면 헨우드 홈 서플라이에 문의하세요.
(D) 공사로 인해 정문 진입이 차단됩니다.

해설 빈칸 앞 부분에서 계산원 및 영업직 지원서를 받을 예정(We will be accepting applications ~ 1 April)이라며 관련 정보를 알려 주었으므로, 빈칸에는 이 소식(this news)을 다른 사람들에게 공유하라는 내용이 들어가야 자연스럽다. 따라서 (A)가 정답이다.

어휘 material 자료, 재료 response 응답, 회신 access 입장, 접근 construction 공사

139-142 기사

아몬, 그레넬 시의 음악 학교에 기부하다

브렌다 아몬 씨의 대변인은 이 피아니스트가 그레넬 시립 음악원의 확장을 위해 상당액을 기부했다고 139**확인해 주었다.** "그녀의 후한 지원이 없었다면, 앞으로 있을 본원의 개조 계획에 제약이 있었을 것입니다."라고 시설 계획 책임자인 마크 디아즈 씨가 말했다.

140**그 프로젝트는 예산 삭감으로 연기되었었다.** 이제, 141**기존** 음악원의 남쪽 끝에 새로운 부속 건물이 건설될 것이다. 완공되면 700석 규모의 음악당, 최첨단 녹음실, 새로운 교수실 및 행정실 등을 자랑하게 된다. 또한, 개인 연습실이 현재 학생 라운지 142**근처에** 위치하게 될 것이다.

어휘 sizeable 꽤 큰, 상당한 donation 기부 expansion 확장, 확대 conservatory 음악[예술] 학교, 음악원, 온실 generous 후한, 관대한 support 지원 limited 제한된 renovation 개조 boast 자랑하다 state-of-the-art 최첨단의 faculty 교수진 administrative 행정의 additionally 게다가, 또한 adjacent to ~에 가까운 current 현재의

139 동사 어형_시제

해설 빈칸은 주어 A spokesperson (for Brenda Amon)의 동사 자리로, that절을 목적어로 취하고 있다. that절의 동사가 과거 시제(made)이며, 문맥상 '(과거에) 기부했다는 것을 확인해 주었다'라는 내용이 되어야 자연스러우므로, 현재완료인 (C) has confirmed가 정답이다. 참고로, 과거에 발생한 일이더라도 현재까지 영향을 미치는 결과에 대한 소식이라면 현재완료를 사용할 수 있으며, 특히 기사에서 자주 나타난다.

어휘 confirm 확인해 주다, 확정하다

140 문맥에 맞는 문장 고르기

번역 (A) 아몬 씨의 음악원 공연은 훌륭했다.
(B) 그 프로젝트는 예산 삭감으로 연기되었었다.
(C) 지난 몇 년간 등록 학생이 감소했다.
(D) 원래의 음악원은 기숙사로 개조되고 있다.

해설 빈칸 앞에서 아몬 씨의 후원이 없었다면 앞으로 있을 개조 계획에 제약이 있었을 것(Without her generous support ~ going forward)이라고 했지만 빈칸 뒤에 이제 새로운 부속 건물이 건설될 예정(Now, a new wing ~ conservatory)이라는 내용이 왔으므로, 빈칸에는 재정 문제와 관련된 내용이 들어가는 것이 자연스럽다. 따라서 (B)가 정답이다.

어휘 performance 공연 outstanding 훌륭한 budget 예산 cut 삭감 enrollment 등록 decrease 감소하다 convert 바꾸다, 전환하다

141 형용사 어휘

해설 명사 conservatory를 적절히 수식하는 형용사를 선택하는 문제이다. 빈칸을 포함한 전치사구(on the ~ conservatory)는 새로운 부속 건물(a new wing)의 위치를 나타내므로 '기존 음악원의 남쪽 끝에'라는 의미가 되어야 자연스럽다. 따라서 '기존의, 현재 사용되는'이라는 의미의 (B) existing이 정답이다.

어휘 temporary 임시의, 일시의 corrected 수정된 proposed 제안된

142 전치사 자리_어휘

해설 빈칸은 명사구 the current student lounge를 목적어로 취하는 전치사 자리이며, 빈칸을 포함한 부분이 동사구 will be located를 수식하고 있다. 따라서 건물 및 located(~에 위치한)와 어울려 쓰이는 전치사를 선택해야 하므로, 보기 중 '인접한, 근접한'이라는 의미의 형용사를 포함하여 위치를 묘사하는 (A) adjacent to가 정답이다.

143-146 이메일

날짜: 1월 11일
수신: 미첼 파커 〈mparker@allmail.co.za〉
발신: 이네즈 로파로 〈ilofaro@daqtex.co.za〉
제목: 제품 리콜

파커 씨께,

최근에 닥텍스 미니-V 카메라를 143**구입해** 주셔서 감사합니다. 당사는 최근 이 제품을 구입한 모든 고객에게 연락하여 특정 모델이 수리를 위해 회수되고 있다는 사실을 알리고 있습니다. 이 모델들은 빛을 디지털로 전환할 수 있게 해주는 전자 칩에 결함이 있습니다. 144**이 결함은 결국 이미지 선명도에 지장을 주게 됩니다.** 카메라 하단에 있는 일련 번호를 확인하여 고객님의 카메라에 문제가 있는지 145**확인하십시오.** 문자 TVX로 끝나는 경우 수리가 필요합니다. 닥텍스는 미니-V를 본사로 반송하는 데 드는 배송비를 전액 지불할 예정입니다. 또한 무료로 146**그것을** 수리해 드릴 것입니다.

감사합니다.

이네즈 로파로, 고객 서비스 담당
닥텍스 인더스트리즈

어휘 recent 최근의 contact 연락하다 repair 수리 enable 가능하게 하다 conversion 전환 faulty 결점이 있는 shipping cost 배송비 in addition 또한 free of charge 무료로

143 명사 어휘

해설 형용사 recent와 전치사구 of the Daqtex Mini-V camera의 수식을 받는 명사를 선택하는 문제이다. 바로 뒤 문장을 보면 카메라(=this product)를 구입한 모든 고객에게 연락하고 있다(We are contacting everyone who has recently bought this product)고 했으므로, 해당 문장은 '구매해 주셔서 감사하다'라는 내용이 되어야 자연스럽다. 따라서 '구입'이라는 의미의 (A) purchase가 정답이다.

어휘 purchase 구매(품); 구매하다 review 비평, 검토 demonstration 시연

144 문맥에 맞는 문장 고르기

번역 (A) 앞으로 오랫동안 이 제품을 즐기시기 바랍니다.
    (B) 그것은 설명서의 문제 해결 부분에서 다뤄집니다.
    (C) 이 결함은 결국 이미지 선명도에 지장을 주게 됩니다.
    (D) 일부 구형 모델에는 이 특별한 기능이 없습니다.

해설 빈칸 앞 문장에서 빛을 디지털로 전환할 수 있게 해주는 전자 칩에 결함이 있다(the electronic chip that enables the digital conversion of light is faulty)며 특정 모델의 문제점을 언급했으므로, 빈칸에는 이 결함(This defect)이 제품에 미치는 영향과 관련된 내용이 들어가야 자연스럽다. 따라서 (C)가 정답이다.

어휘 cover (주제 등을) 다루다 troubleshooting 문제 해결, 고장 수리 defect 결함 eventually 결국에는 interfere with ~을 방해하다, ~에 지장을 주다 clarity 선명함 feature 특징 unavailable 이용할 수 없는

145 동사 어형 _ 명령문

해설 빈칸은 주어 you가 생략된 명령문의 동사자리이므로, 원형인 (C) verify가 정답이다. 동사 (B) verified와 (D) verifies 앞에는 주어를 생략할 수 없고, (A) verification은 명사로 품사상 적합하지 않다.

어휘 verification 확인, 조회 verify 확인하다, 검증하다

146 대명사 어휘

해설 동사 will repair의 목적어로 적절한 대명사를 선택하는 문제이다. 앞에서 파커 씨가 구매한 Mini-V camera의 제품 일련 번호가 TVX로 끝날 경우 수리가 필요하다(a repair will be required)며 카메라 반송비(shipping costs for sending your Mini-V back to us)를 회사에서 부담하겠다고 했으므로, 빈칸이 포함된 부분은 카메라를 무상 수리해 줄 것이라는 내용이 되어야 자연스럽다. 따라서 'your Mini-V'를 대신하는 3인칭 단수 대명사인 (B) it이 정답이다.

PART 7

147-148 공지

패스티스트 플릿

서비스를 평가하시고 무료 여행에 당첨되세요!

[148]당사 웹사이트 www.fastestfleet.com/feedback을 방문해 5분짜리 설문지를 작성해 주세요. [147]미국 대륙 내 어디든 갈 수 있는 10회 무료 왕복 버스 여행에 당첨될 수 있습니다!

18세 이상만 참가 가능합니다. 패스티스트 플릿으로 여행한 경험이 있는 고객들만 응모할 수 있습니다.

어휘 fleet 선단, 함대 fill out 작성하다 questionnaire 설문지 round-trip 왕복 여행의 destination 목적지 continental 대륙의 participate 참가하다 previously 이전에 be eligible to ~할 자격이 되다

147 추론 / 암시

번역 공지는 어디에서 볼 수 있겠는가?
    (A) 공항   (B) 버스 터미널
    (C) 기차역   (D) 여객선 터미널

해설 첫 번째 단락에서 설문 조사에 응하면 미국 대륙 내 어디든 갈 수 있는 10회 무료 왕복 버스 여행에 당첨될 수 있다(You could win one of 10 FREE round-trip bus trips ~ United States)고 했으므로, 버스 이용객을 대상으로 한 공지라는 것을 알 수 있다. 따라서 (B)가 정답이다.

어휘 ferry 여객선

148 세부 사항

번역 고객들은 무엇을 하도록 요청받는가?
    (A) 의견 제공하기   (B) 왕복 티켓 구입하기
    (C) 할인 이용하기   (D) 고객 보상 프로그램 가입하기

해설 첫 번째 단락에서 회사의 웹사이트를 방문해 5분짜리 설문지를 작성해 달라(Visit our Web site ~ and fill out the 5-minute questionnaire)고 요청했으므로, 정답은 (A)이다.

어휘 take advantage of ~을 이용하다 customer loyalty program 고객 보상 프로그램

▶▶ Paraphrasing 지문의 **fill out the 5-minute questionnaire** → 정답의 **Provide feedback**

149-150 온라인 채팅

대니얼 매더 (오전 9시 38분)
안녕 수, 오늘 집에서 일하세요?

수전 말디니 (오전 9시 39분)
아니요, 하지만 외부 회의 중이에요. 무슨 일이에요?

대니얼 매더 (오전 9시 41분)

149부장님께서 일부 계약서를 기록용으로 복사해 두라고 요청하셨어요.
150깜박하고 집에 프린터 카드를 두고 왔어요. 당신 것 좀 빌릴 수 있을까요?

수전 말디니 (오전 9시 42분)

물론이죠. 150제 책상 위 명함꽂이에 있어요.

대니얼 매더 (오전 9시 55분)

좋아요, 다 했어요. 고마워요! 책상 위에 도로 갖다 놓았어요.

어휘 off-site (특정 장소에서) 떨어진 contract 계약
agreement 합의, 계약 business card 명함

149 세부 사항

번역 매더 씨에게 부여된 일은?

(A) 계약서 보내기
(B) 복사기 수리하기
(C) 직원 출석 확인하기
(D) 일부 문서 복사하기

해설 매더 씨의 오전 9시 41분 메시지를 보면, 부장이 일부 계약서를 복사해 두라고 요청했다(The manager asked me to make hard copies of some contract agreements)고 했으므로, (D)가 정답이다.

▶ Paraphrasing   지문의 some contract agreements
→ 정답의 some documents

150 의도 파악

번역 오전 9시 42분에 말디니 씨가 "물론이죠"라고 쓸 때, 그 의도는 무엇인가?

(A) 매더 씨에게 카드를 빌려줄 수 있다.
(B) 사무실로 돌아올 것이다.
(C) 부장에게 연락할 것이다.
(D) 자신이 계약서를 복사할 수 있다.

해설 매더 씨가 오전 9시 41분에 깜박하고 집에 프린터 카드를 두고 왔다(I forgot my printer card at home)며 말디니 씨의 카드를 빌릴 수 있는지(Could I borrow yours?) 물었고, 이에 대해 말디니 씨가 '물론이죠(Sure thing)'라고 대답한 것이므로, 매더 씨에게 카드를 빌려줄 수 있다는 의도로 말한 것임을 알 수 있다. 따라서 정답은 (A)이다.

151-152 회람

회람

수신: 웨스트하우저 연구소 직원
발신: 지역 담당 책임자
날짜: 3월 22일
주제: 휴식 시간 음료

151지금부터 직원들은 당사 간이 주방에서 이용할 수 있는 뜨거운 음료의 비용을 지불해야 합니다. 본인이 마신 커피나 차 한 잔당 50센트를 남겨 주시기 바랍니다. 이 금액은 건물 옆 카페에서 지불하는 금액보다 훨씬 적다는 것을 유념해 주십시오.

음료를 준비할 때마다, 152지불금을 싱크대 옆 조리대 위에 있는 표시된 통에 두세요. 예전처럼 다양한 고급 차와 커피 공급품들이 제공되며, 제품들은 매달 재입고됩니다. 모든 사람이 하루 중일 편리한 위치에서 뜨거운 음료를 계속 즐길 수 있도록 이해해 주시면 감사하겠습니다.

어휘 beverage 음료 immediately 즉시 contribute 주다, 기부하다 available 이용할 수 있는 kitchenette 간이 주방 amount 금액, 양 a variety of 다양한 restock 보충하다 conveniently 편리하게

151 주제 / 목적

번역 회람의 목적은?

(A) 새 규정 설명하기
(B) 장시간 휴식 막기
(C) 예산 관련 최신 정보 제공하기
(D) 직원 불만 해소하기

해설 첫 번째 단락에서 지금부터(Beginning immediately) 간이 주방에서 이용할 수 있는 뜨거운 음료의 비용을 지불해야 한다(contribute toward the cost of hot beverages available in our kitchenette)고 했으므로, 기존과 다른 새 정책을 설명하기 위한 회람이라는 것을 알 수 있다. 따라서 (A)가 정답이다.

어휘 discourage 말리다, 좌절시키다 budget 예산 address 처리하다 complaint 불만 (사항)

152 세부 사항

번역 직원들은 무엇을 하도록 요청 받는가?

(A) 자신이 마실 음료 갖고 출근하기
(B) 통에 요금 넣기
(C) 비품 요청하기
(D) 간이 주방 깨끗이 정돈하기

해설 두 번째 단락의 첫 번째 문장을 보면, 지불금을 조리대 위에 있는 표시된 통에 넣어 달라(just place your payment in the marked can on the counter)고 했으므로, (B)가 정답이다.

▶ Paraphrasing   지문의 the marked can → 정답의 a container

153-155 공지

밀워키 현대 미술관 방문객들에게 알림

4월 1일부터 6월 30일까지 진행되는 현대 미술가 전시회를 위한 공간을 준비하는 관계로 미챔 룸이 임시 폐쇄됩니다.

153다시 오셔서 이 대망의 전시회를 감상하시기 바랍니다. 이 전시회에는 154샐리 아코스타, 프랭크 켐버, 킴벌리 홍, 마틸다 브릴랜드와 같이 호평 받고 있는 해외 미술가들의 회화, 조각, 멀티미디어 작품이 특별히 전시됩니다. 155주목할 작품은 신예 시어도어 카모디의 조각품 컬렉션으로, 〈아일랜드 아츠 크로니컬〉의 명망 있고 존경 받는 비평가 이선 러너는 이 컬렉션을 "10년 만의 가장 흥미진진한 데뷔"라고 일컬었습니다.

153전시 화가 및 작품에 대한 자세한 정보는 www.milwaukee-modernart.org에서 확인할 수 있습니다. 아니면 다가오는 모든 행사에 관한 소식을 전하는 저희 미술관 앱을 다운로드하십시오.

> 어휘 temporarily 일시적으로, 임시로 anticipated 기대하던, 대망의 sculpture 조각(품) acclaimed 호평을 받고 있는 dub 일컫다, 별명을 붙이다 decade 10년 renowned 유명한 critic 비평가, 평론가

153 사실 관계 확인

번역 미술관에 관해 명시된 것은?

(A) 웹사이트에서 다가오는 전시회를 홍보하고 있다.
(B) 조각품 전시회로 유명하다.
(C) 4월에 개조 공사로 문을 닫을 예정이다.
(D) 다가오는 전시회는 미술관 회원에게 무료이다.

해설 공지 초반부에서 현대 미술가 전시회(Modern Artist Showcase)를 감상하러 오라고(return to experience this much-anticipated exhibit) 권한 뒤, 두 번째 단락 후반부에서 전시 화가 및 작품에 대한 자세한 정보는 웹사이트에서 확인할 수 있다(More information ~ can be found at www.milwaukeemodernart.org)고 했다. 따라서 (A)가 정답이다.

▸▸ Paraphrasing 지문의 at www.milwaukeemodernart.org
→ 정답의 on its Web site

154 세부 사항

번역 브릴랜드 씨는 누구인가?

(A) 기자
(B) 미술가
(C) 미술관 큐레이터
(D) 미술 평론가

해설 두 번째 단락의 첫 번째 문장을 보면, 호평 받고 있는 해외 미술가들(acclaimed international artists) 중 한 사람으로 마틸다 브릴랜드를 예로 들고(such as ~ Matilda Breeland) 있으므로, (B)가 정답이다.

155 세부 사항

번역 러너 씨에게 찬사를 받은 사람은?

(A) 아코스타 씨
(B) 켐버 씨
(C) 홍 씨
(D) 카모디 씨

해설 두 번째 단락의 중반부에서 신예 시어도어 카모디의 조각품 컬렉션을 주목할 작품(Of note is newcomer Theodore Carmody's sculpture collection)이라고 소개하며, 이선 러너가 이 컬렉션을 '10년 만의 가장 흥미진진한 데뷔'라고 일컬었다(that was dubbed "most exciting debut of the decade" by Ethan Lerner)고 했으므로, (D)가 정답이다.

156-157 양식

작업 지시서 변경

종합 건설업자(계약 업체):

하워드 클라이버, 머크레스트 건설
106 피켄스 웨이, 콜럼버스, 오하이오 주 43211

부동산 소유주: 오스카 코프랜드, 866 앤델 로드, 콜럼버스, 오하이오 주 43215

공사 시작일: 7월 10일
157공사 종료일: 7월 15일

계약 업체는 계약서에서 다음 사항들을 변경하십시오:
추가/삭제 작업 명세:
156고객이 주방 수납장 외에도 조리대와 수도꼭지를 공급한다. 따라서 총 공사비는 설치비만 포함되도록 수정된다.

기존 계약 금액: 3,496달러

이전 계약에서 순 삭감액: -2,412달러

변경 승인에 따른 총 공사비: 1,084달러

수정된 결제 일정:
총 공사비의 15퍼센트(162달러)는 계약 업체를 확보하기 위해 선불로 지급하고 공사 시작일에 222달러를 지불하며 **157**완공 시 잔금(700달러)을 지불한다.

수락합니다:

계약 업체: 하워드 클라이버

부동산 소유주: 오스카 코프랜드

> 어휘 be instructed to ~하도록 지시 받다 description 설명 supply 공급하다 countertop 조리대, 작업대 faucet 수도꼭지 adjust 수정하다 installation 설치 net 순, 에누리 없는 reduction 삭감, 축소 due (돈을) 지불해야 하는 upfront 선불의, 선불로 remainder 남은 것, 잔금 completion 완료

156 세부 사항

번역 공사비가 수정된 이유는?

(A) 고객이 모든 자재를 제공한다.
(B) 고객이 경쟁 업체의 가격과 맞추기를 원한다.
(C) 계약 업체가 조리대를 잘못 설치했다.
(D) 계약 업체가 인건비를 과다 산정했다.

해설 추가/삭제 작업 명세(Description of Work Added/Deleted) 부분에서 고객이 주방 수납장 외에도 조리대와 수도꼭지를 공급하게(Client will now be supplying ~ the kitchen cabinets) 되어 총 공사비는 설치비만 포함되도록 수정된다(the total project cost will be adjusted to only include the cost of installation)고 했으므로, (A)가 정답이다.

어휘 material 재료, 자재 competitor 경쟁자[사] overestimate 과대평가하다, 부풀리다

157 추론 / 암시

번역 7월 15일 코프랜드 씨는 클라이버 씨에게 얼마를 주겠는가?

(A) 162달러   (B) 222달러
(C) 700달러   (D) 1,084달러

해설 상단에 7월 15일이 공사 종료일(Project End Date)이라고 나와 있고, 수정된 결제 일정(Revised Payment Schedule) 부분에서 완공 시 잔금 700달러를 지급한다(the remainder ($700) is due upon project completion)고 했으므로, (C)가 정답이다.

158-160 이메일

수신: 달리야 파와르 〈dpawar@bronsonco.ca〉
발신: 애나 본델 〈abondell@noaaa.com〉
제목: 정보
날짜: 8월 25일

파와르 씨께:

158북미 건축가 협회의 회원 자격을 유지해 주셔서 감사드립니다. 연례 총회 사전 등록이 9월 15일에 마감됨을 상기시켜 드리고자 합니다. 올해 총회에는 100회 이상의 회의, 전시장, 특별 워크숍이 열립니다.

159(D)사전 등록 시 정규 등록비에서 30달러를 절감할 수 있습니다. 동시에, 159(A),(C)단체 시티 투어와 VIP 연회에도 사전 등록하실 수 있는데, 이 행사들은 인원이 빨리 찹니다. 160온라인으로 등록하시려면 당사 웹사이트를 방문하십시오. 그곳에서 전체 회의 일정표도 볼 수 있습니다. 전화로 등록하고 싶으면 1-249-555-0177로 연락 주십시오. 회원님의 회원 번호를 준비해 주시기 바랍니다.

멕시코시티에서 뵙기를 고대합니다!

애나 본델 드림
회원 담당자

어휘 architect 건축가 association 협회 preregistration 사전 등록 annual 연례의 conference (대규모) 회의, 학회 registration fee 등록비 sign up 등록하다 in advance 사전에, 미리 banquet 연회

158 추론 / 암시

번역 파와르 씨의 직업은 무엇이겠는가?

(A) 건축가   (B) 작가
(C) 여행사 직원   (D) 회의 주최자

해설 첫 번째 단락의 '북미 건축가 협회의 회원 자격을 유지해 주셔서 감사드립니다(Thank you for your continued membership in the North American Architects Association)'라는 인사말을 통해 파와르 씨가 건축가임을 추론할 수 있으므로, (A)가 정답이다.

159 사실 관계 확인

번역 총회 사전 등록의 혜택이 아닌 것은?

(A) 멕시코시티 관광
(B) 호텔 객실 업그레이드
(C) 만찬 참가
(D) 등록비 할인

해설 두 번째 단락의 '사전 등록 시 정규 등록비에서 30달러를 절감할 수 있다(Preregistration will save you $30 off the regular registration fee)'에서 (D)를, '단체 시티 투어와 VIP 연회도 사전 등록할 수 있다(you'll be able to sign up in advance for a group tour of the city and for the VIP Banquet)'에서 (A), (C)를 확인할 수 있다. 그러나 호텔 객실 업그레이드는 언급된 바가 없으므로, (B)가 정답이다.

160 문장 삽입

번역 [1], [2], [3], [4]로 표시된 곳 중에서 다음 문장이 들어가기에 가장 적합한 곳은?

"그곳에서 전체 회의 일정표도 볼 수 있습니다."

(A) [1]
(B) [2]
(C) [3]
(D) [4]

해설 주어진 문장에서 '그곳에서 전체 회의 일정표도 볼 수 있다(You will also find the complete conference program there)'라고 했으므로, 부사 there가 가리키는 장소와 그곳에서 할 수 있는 일을 언급한 문장이 앞에 와야 한다. [4] 앞에서 온라인으로 등록하려면 당사 웹사이트를 방문하라(Visit our Web site to register online)고 하며 there에 해당하는 장소인 웹사이트와 그곳에서 온라인 등록이 가능하다는 것을 제시했으므로, (D)가 정답이다.

어휘 complete 완전한, 전체의 program (행사) 프로그램, 일정표

161-164 온라인 채팅

파일	지금 만나기	도구	도움

커트 웨버 (오후 4시 30분)
161일 마치고 5시 30분쯤 제이크와 함께 요기 좀 할까요. 같이 가고 싶은 사람 있나요?

다비 에이브릴 (오후 4시 31분)
글쎄요. 저는 중간 연도 보고서 관련해서 해야 할 일이 있어서요. 161어디로 갈 거예요?

커트 웨버 (오후 4시 32분)
163슬레이트 로드에 새로 생긴 멕시코 식당에 가 볼까 해요. 162오초 코로나스라는 곳이에요.

팀 폭스 (오후 4시 33분) 운이 없네요. 162, 163거기 며칠 전에 문 닫았어요.
커트 웨버 (오후 4시 34분) 아쉽네요. 거기 참 좋다고 하던데.
팀 폭스 (오후 4시 36분) 모퉁이에 있는 로터스 타코스는 어때요? 금요일에 항상 스페셜 메뉴가 있어요.
커트 웨버 (오후 4시 37분) 좋을 것 같네요. 제이크, 로터스 타코에 갈까요?
다비 에이브릴 (오후 4:38분) 164좋아요. 하지만 저는 6시쯤 되어야 도착할 거예요.
제이크 리바스 (오후 4시 39분) 좋아요. 그리고 다비, 보고서용으로 수정된 수치 방금 보냈어요.
어휘 　grab a bite 간단히 먹다, 요기하다　care to + 동사원형 ～하고 싶어 하다, ～하는 데 관심이 있다　figure 수치

161　주제 / 목적

번역　글쓴이들은 무엇을 논의하고 있는가?

　　(A) 회사 연회 장소
　　(B) 음식이 가장 괜찮은 식당
　　(C) 오초 코로나스 메뉴
　　(D) 저녁 먹을 곳

해설　웨버 씨의 오후 4시 30분 메시지 '일 마치고 5시 30분쯤 제이크 와 함께 요기 좀 할까 해요(Jake and I are grabbing a bite to eat after work, around 5:30). 같이 가고 싶은 사람 있나 요?(Anyone care to join us?)'와 에이브릴 씨의 오후 4시 31분 메 시지 '어디로 가요?(Where are you planning to go?)'를 시작으 로, 대화 전반에서 퇴근 후 간단히 식사할 장소에 대해 논의하고 있음 을 알 수 있다. 따라서 (D)가 정답이다.

162　세부 사항

번역　폭스 씨가 오초 코로나스에 관해 제공한 정보는?

　　(A) 사람들이 그에게 그곳을 추천했다.
　　(B) 대체로 금요일 일찍 문을 연다.
　　(C) 음식이 정통 요리가 아니다.
　　(D) 더 이상 영업하지 않는다.

해설　웨버 씨가 오후 4시 32분 메시지에서 오초 코로나스(Ocho Coronas)를 언급하자 그 다음 메시지에서 폭스 씨가 '거기 며칠 전에 문 닫았어요(The place closed a few days ago)'라며 정보를 제공 했으므로, (D)가 정답이다.

어휘　recommend 추천하다　「not very + 형용사」 전혀 ～가 아닌 authentic 진짜의[정통의], 믿을 만한　in business 영업[사업]을 하는

> ▸▸ Paraphrasing　지문의 **That place closed**
> 　　　　　　　　　→ 정답의 **It is no longer in business.**

163　의도 파악

번역　오후 4시 34분에 웨버 씨가 "아쉽네요"라고 쓴 이유는 무엇이겠는가?

　　(A) 새로운 식당에 가보고 싶었다.
　　(B) 폭스 씨는 프로젝트를 완료할 수 없다.
　　(C) 슬레이트 로드는 너무 멀다.
　　(D) 일정이 겹친다.

해설　웨버 씨가 오후 4시 32분 메시지에서 슬레이트 로드에 있는 멕시 코 식당에 갈 생각(We're thinking of trying the new Mexican place on Slate Road)이라고 했는데, 이에 대해 폭스 씨가 그 식당 이 문을 닫았다(That place closed)고 하자 좋은 평을 많이 들었다 (I heard great things about it)며 아쉬움을 표현했다. 따라서 웨 버 씨가 새로 생긴 식당에 가고 싶어 했음을 추론할 수 있으므로, (A) 가 정답이다.

> ▸▸ Paraphrasing　지문의 **the new Mexican place**
> 　　　　　　　　　→ 정답의 **a new restaurant**

164　세부 사항

번역　에이브릴 씨는 어떻게 하기로 결정하는가?

　　(A) 인근 식당 알아보기　　　(B) 내일 야근하기
　　(C) 동료들과 함께 식사하기　　(D) 사무실로 음식 배달 시키기

해설　에이브릴 씨의 오후 4시 38분 메시지 '좋아요. 하지만 저는 6시쯤 되 어야 도착할 거예요(OK, but I won't be able to get there till about six)'를 통해 그가 퇴근 후 저녁 식사에 참석하기로 결정했음을 알 수 있다. 따라서 (C)가 정답이다.

165-167 편지

〈멀티내셔널 보이스 매거진〉 사서함 17999 그린레인 오클랜드 1546 3월 22일 투아타 웨히 16 페이지 스트리트 웰링턴 6023 웨히 씨께, 165, 1663월 25일에 귀하의 〈멀티내셔널 보이스 매거진〉 3개월 시험 구 독이 만료됩니다. 165이 생생한 뉴스 자료를 계속 받아 보시려면, 본 편 지에 동봉된 우편 요금 지급필 갱신 카드를 작성해 이달 말 이전에 저희 에게 우편으로 보내 주십시오. 3개월, 6개월, 1년 또는 2년 구독 중에 서 선택하실 수 있습니다. 2년 구독이 가장 실속 있다는 점을 반드시 유 념하십시오. 또한 1년 및 2년 옵션에는 "올해의 주목할 인물" 특별판이 포함되어 있습니다. 〈멀티내셔널 보이스 매거진〉을 선택해 주신 데 대해 다시 한 번 감사 드립니다. 저희는 뉴질랜드의 관점에서 세계 정세에 대한 최고의 논평 을 제공하기 위해 계속 노력하고 있습니다. 167의견을 주시려면 www. mvmagazine.co.nz를 방문하여 온라인 의견 양식을 작성해 주십 시오.

에스텔 피어슨, 고객 서비스 담당

165 주제 / 목적

번역　웨히 씨에게 편지를 보낸 이유는?

(A) 납부 연체를 알리기 위해

(B) 환불을 제공하기 위해

(C) 새로운 서비스를 홍보하기 위해

(D) 재구독을 상기시키기 위해

해설　첫 번째 단락의 '3월 25일에 귀하의 〈멀티내셔널 보이스 매거진〉
3개월 시험 구독이 만료됩니다(On 25 March, your three-month
trial subscription ~ will expire)'와 '이 생생한 뉴스 자료를 계속
받아 보려면(To continue to receive this vital news resource)'
이라는 문구를 통해 잡지의 재구독을 독려하기 위한 편지임을 알 수
있으므로, (D)가 정답이다.

어휘　promote 홍보하다　resubscribe 재구독하다

> ▶▶ Paraphrasing　지문의 To continue to receive this vital
> news resource → 정답의 to resubscribe

166 세부 사항

번역　웨히 씨는 〈멀티내셔널 보이스 매거진〉을 약 얼마 동안 받아 보았는가?

(A) 3개월

(B) 6개월

(C) 1년

(D) 2년

해설　첫 번째 단락에서 3월 25일에 웨히 씨의 〈멀티내셔널 보이스 매
거진〉 3개월 시험 구독이 만료된다(your three-month trial
subscription ~ will expire)고 했으므로, (A)가 정답이다.

167 세부 사항

번역　웨히 씨가 하도록 권고 받은 일 한 가지는?

(A) 피어슨 씨에게 직접 전화하기

(B) 의견 제공하기

(C) 행사 참석하기

(D) 주소 확인해 주기

해설　두 번째 단락 후반부에서 의견을 주려면(To provide your
feedback) 웹사이트를 방문하여 온라인 의견 양식을 작성해 달
라(please visit www.mvmagazine.co.nz and fill out our
online comment form)고 요청했으므로, (B)가 정답이다.

어휘　confirm 확인해 주다, 확인하다

> ▶▶ Paraphrasing　지문의 provide your feedback
> → 정답의 Offer his opinion

168-171 이메일

발신: info@morganairportshuttle.com

수신: tgrant@tivimail.com

제목: 회신: 차내 여행 가방

날짜: 1월 19일

그랜트 씨께:

169문의 감사합니다. 저희 보관소에 고객님이 말씀하신 설명과 일치하는
여행 가방이 많이 있지만, 고객님이 소유자임을 표시한 이름표가 붙어
있는 가방은 찾지 못했습니다. 171고객님께서 620 베이커 스트리트로
오셔서 현장에서 가방을 찾으셔야 합니다. 168, 170공항 터미널에서 고객
님의 버스가 몇 시에 출발했는지 알려 달라는 요청을 받으시게 되거나,
더 나은 경우로, 아직 표를 갖고 계시다면 표를 제시해 달라는 요청을 받
으실 것입니다.

저희는 매일 오전 6시부터 오후 10시까지 문을 엽니다. 171지체하지 마
시기 바랍니다. 운전 기사들이 발견하는 물품 수가 많아서 당사는 보관
시간을 7일로 한정할 수밖에 없으며, 그 이후에는 해당 물품을 폐기합
니다.

지나 스타이너 드림
168모건 공항 셔틀

168 세부 사항

번역　스타이너 씨는 어디에서 일하는가?

(A) 교통 서비스 회사

(B) 보험회사

(C) 자동차 대여 회사

(D) 여행사

해설　첫 번째 단락의 '공항 터미널에서 버스가 몇 시에 출발했는지(what
time your bus left the airport terminal)', 두 번째 단락의
'당사의 운전 기사(our drivers)', 그리고 서명의 '모건 공항 셔틀
(Morgan Airport Shuttle)'을 통해 스타이너 씨가 공항 셔틀 버스
회사에서 근무한다는 것을 알 수 있다. 따라서 (A)가 정답이다.

169 추론 / 암시

번역　그랜트 씨는 무엇에 관해 문의했겠는가?

(A) 예약 옵션　　　　(B) 화물 제한

(C) 여행 경비　　　　(D) 분실물

해설　첫 번째 단락의 '문의 감사합니다(Thanks for your inquiry)'와 '고
객님이 소유자임을 표시한 이름표가 붙어 있는 가방은 찾지 못했습니
다(we have not found one bearing a name tag identifying
you as the owner)'를 통해 그랜트 씨가 분실한 여행 가방에 대해
문의했음을 추론할 수 있다. 따라서 (D)가 정답이다.

어휘　limitation 제한, 한계

170 세부 사항

번역 그랜트 씨는 어떤 정보를 제공하라고 요청받을 것인가?

(A) 주소 (B) 전화번호
(C) 출발 시간 (D) 최종 목적지

해설 첫 번째 단락 후반부에서 그랜트 씨가 탔던 버스가 공항 터미널에서 몇 시에 출발했는지 알려 달라(to indicate what time your bus left the airport terminal)고 하거나 아직 표를 갖고 있는 경우 표를 제시하라(to present your ticket)는 요청을 받게 될 것이라고 했으므로, (C)가 정답이다.

어휘 destination 목적지

▸▸ Paraphrasing 지문의 what time your bus left the airport terminal → 정답의 His departure time

171 세부 사항

번역 그랜트 씨가 하도록 요청받은 일은?

(A) 할인 이용하기
(B) 결제 방식 비교하기
(C) 가능한 한 빨리 사무실 방문하기
(D) 전자 티켓 출력하기

해설 첫 번째 단락 중반부에서 그랜트 씨가 현장에 와서 가방을 찾아야 한다(You will need to come over and find yours on-site)고 했고, 두 번째 단락 초반부에서 지체하지 말라(Please do not delay)고 했으므로, (C)가 정답이다.

어휘 take advantage of ~를 이용하다

▸▸ Paraphrasing 지문의 come over and find yours on-site at 620 Baker St. → 정답의 Visit the office
지문의 do not delay
→ 정답의 as soon as possible

172-175 기사

초대형 크레인으로 건설한 웅장한 다리

마셔 브루노 작성

3월 14일

5년 전, 마샬 산맥 기슭에 위치한 스톤웰 시는 스톤웰 강을 가로지르는 다리를 건설하는 데 자금을 조달하기로 결정했다. ^{174(A)}이 다리는 도시에 절실히 필요한 북부 경로로 계획되었다. 4년이 소요될 것으로 예상되었던 이 사업은 3년이 채 되지 않아 완공되었다. ¹⁷⁵이 프로젝트가 효율적이었던 것은 전적으로 영국에 본사를 둔 로손웍스가 제조한 두 대의 RWC451 크레인 덕분이었다.

동일한 타워 크레인 두 대는 건설 회사인 레딩 빌더스 소유였다. ¹⁷²크레인 한 대는 강의 남쪽 둑에서 조립되었고 다른 한 대는 스톤웰 강 중앙에 있는 콘크리트 주탑 위에 설치되었다. 물에 띄운 바지선 위에 있는 또 다른 크레인을 사용해야 했으므로 두 번째 크레인 조립에 특히 어려움이 있었다.

¹⁷³"대형 프로젝트에는 공식 건설 일정에 방해가 될 수 있는 뜻밖의 수정 사항이 생기기 마련입니다." 레딩 빌더스의 수석 엔지니어인 로저 리가 말했다. 이번 경우에는, 다리를 주탑에 연결하는 금속 고정체가

너무 작다고 판단되었다. 새로운 고정체들의 무게는 22톤이었는데, 이는 RWC451 크레인이 안전하게 들어올릴 수 있는 무게였다. 엔지니어들은 안전성을 한층 높이기 위해 기존의 크레인을 강화했고, 이들은 잘 작동했다.

현재, 엽서에 나올 만한 이 다리는 스톤웰의 자랑거리로, 보행자, 등산객, 방문객을 위한 전망대가 특징이며, 이 전망대는 산악 지대가 내려다보이는 각 교각 아래쪽에 있다. 건설 자재와 색상은 주변 환경과 아름답게 조화를 이루고 있다. ^{174(C)}교각, 전망대, 난간을 포함한 모든 디자인 요소들이 자연 경관을 보완하여, ^{174(B)}등산객부터 이 다리를 정기적으로 이용하게 된 트럭 운전사까지 모든 사람들에게 큰 인기를 얻고 있다.

어휘 situated at ~에 위치하고 있는 finance 재정[자금]을 대다; 자금 efficiency 효율(성), 능률 directly 바로, 전적으로 attributable to ~에 기인하는 manufacture 제조하다 identical 동일한 assemble 조립하다 bank 둑 assembly 조립 challenging 힘든, 도전적인 float (물 위에) 떠 있다 barge 바지선 unforeseen 예측하지 못한, 뜻밖의 adjustment 수정 (사항), 조정 disrupt 방해하다 weigh 무게가 ~이다 capacity 용량, 수용력, 능력 reinforce 강화하다 perform 수행하다 pedestrian 보행자 pier 교각, 기둥 environment 환경 railing 난간 complement 보완하다

172 사실 관계 확인

번역 크레인에 관해 언급된 것은?

(A) 로손웍스 소유이다.
(B) 스톤웰 다리 프로젝트를 위해 특별히 디자인되었다.
(C) 스톤웰 다리 건설 현장에서 조립되었다.
(D) 무게가 22톤이 넘는다.

해설 두 번째 단락을 보면, 크레인 한 대는 강의 남쪽 둑에서 조립되었고(One crane was assembled ~ the river) 다른 한 대는 스톤웰 강 중앙에 있는 콘크리트 주탑 위에 설치되었다(the other one was placed ~ in the center of the Stonewell River)고 했으며, 두 번째 크레인 조립에 특히 어려움이 있었다(The assembly of the second crane was particularly challenging)고 했으므로, 모두 스톤웰 다리 건설 현장에서 조립되었음을 알 수 있다. 따라서 (C)가 정답이다.

어휘 specifically 특별히

173 사실 관계 확인

번역 리 씨가 언급한 것은?

(A) 그의 전문 분야는 다리 건설이다.
(B) 스톤웰 다리 같은 프로젝트에는 언제나 문제가 생긴다고 생각한다.
(C) 예산상의 이유로 스톤웰 다리 프로젝트를 늦추었다.
(D) 수석 엔지니어로 처음 맡은 프로젝트가 스톤웰 다리이다.

해설 세 번째 단락을 보면 로저 리(Roger Lee) 씨가 대형 프로젝트(large project)에는 공식 건설 일정에 방해가 될 수 있는 뜻밖의 수정 사항(unforeseen adjustments that may disrupt an official construction schedule)이 생기기 마련이라고 했으므로, (B)가 정답이다.

어휘 specialty 전공, 전문 분야

> **▸▸ Paraphrasing** 지문의 **Any large project**
> → 정답의 **projects like the Stonewell Bridge**
> 지문의 **require unforeseen adjustments**
> → 정답의 **present problems**

174 추론 / 암시

번역 스톤웰 다리에 관해 암시된 것이 아닌 것은?

(A) 시내에서 북부로 나가는 출구를 제공한다.
(B) 보행자와 차량 모두를 위해 고안되었다.
(C) 자연 환경과 어울리도록 디자인되었다.
(D) 당초 예상보다 작업자가 더 많이 필요했다.

해설 첫 번째 단락의 '이 다리는 도시에 절실히 필요한 북부 경로로 계획되었다(It was planned as a much-needed northern route for the town)'에서 (A)를, 마지막 단락의 '교각, 전망대, 난간을 포함한 모든 디자인 요소들이 자연 경관을 보완하여(All design elements ~ complement the natural landscape), 등산객부터 이 다리를 정기적으로 이용하게 된 트럭 운전사까지 모든 사람들에게 큰 인기를 얻고 있다(making the bridge a hit with everyone from hikers to the truck drivers ~ route)'에서 (B), (C)를 추론할 수 있다. 그러나 예상보다 더 많은 작업자가 필요했다는 내용은 암시된 바가 없으므로, (D)가 정답이다.

어휘 setting 배경, 환경   estimate 측정하다, 예측하다

> **▸▸ Paraphrasing** 지문의 **northern route**
> → 보기 (A)의 **a northward exit**
> 지문의 **from hikers to the truck drivers**
> → 보기 (B)의 **for both pedestrians and vehicles**
> 지문의 **complement the natural landscape**
> → 보기 (C)의 **blend with the natural setting**

175 문장 삽입

번역 [1], [2], [3], [4]로 표시된 곳 중에서 다음 문장이 들어가기에 가장 적합한 곳은?

"4년이 소요될 것으로 예상되었던 이 사업은 3년이 채 되지 않아 완공되었다."

(A) [1]
(B) [2]
(C) [3]
(D) [4]

해설 주어진 문장이 프로젝트의 완공 기간이 예상했던 것보다 단축되었다는 내용이므로, 앞 또는 뒤 문장에서 이와 관련된 내용이 언급되어야 한다. [1] 뒤에서 '이 프로젝트가 효율적이었던 것은 영국에 본사를 둔 로손웍스가 제조한 두 대의 RWC451 크레인 덕분이었다(The efficiency of the project was directly attributable to two RWC451 cranes, ~ England)'라며 기간을 단축할 수 있었던 이유를 밝히고 있으므로, (A)가 정답이다. 참고로, 완공 기간이 단축된 것을 'The efficiency of the project'라고 표현했다.

176-180 회람 + 일정표

수신: 압살롬 앤 트위그 법률 사무소 직원
발신: 샤나 몽고메리, 사무장
제목: 3월 계획
발신일: 2월 12일
첨부: 일정표

176여러분 대부분이 알고 계시겠지만 3월 첫 주 일정이 좀 힘들 것 같습니다. 작업자들이 페인트칠을 다시 하고, 카펫과 오래된 가구를 교체할 수 있도록 여러 방과 사무실을 일정 기간 동안 비워 두어야 합니다. **179** 작업에 영향을 받는 직원은 방 작업 일정 전날 오후 3시까지 "모든" 사무용품을 상자에 포장해야 합니다(첨부된 일정표를 참조하세요). 작업자 두 팀이 현장에 배치될 예정이므로, 한 번에 방 하나 이상을 비워야 합니다. 월요일에 작업하기로 되어 있는 방은 2월 27일 금요일 오후까지 짐을 싸서 비워야 합니다.

상자가 제공될 겁니다. 작업자들이 치울 수 있도록 여러분의 상자를 방에 두면 됩니다. **177**작업이 완료되면 작업자들이 해당 사무실에 상자들을 다시 갖다 놓을 수 있도록 상자에 이름과 사무실 번호를 표시해 주십시오.

작업자들이 사무실에 있는 동안 여러분은 업무를 계속할 수 있도록 준비해 주십시오. **178**일주일 내내 회의실(409호)을 사무 공간으로 사용할 수 있을 것입니다. 선택 가능한 또 다른 사항은 하루나 이틀 동안 재택근무를 할 수 있도록 상사에게 허가를 요청하는 것입니다.

이러한 일시적인 불편을 참아 주시길 바라며, 기타 문의사항이나 우려되는 점이 있으면 주저하지 마시고 저에게 연락 주십시오.

어휘 vacate 비우다   replace 교체하다   affected 영향을 받는   attached 첨부된   on-site 현장의, 건물 내의   remove 옮기다, 제거하다   make arrangements 준비하다   assignment 임무, 과제   permission 허가   supervisor 상사   telecommute 재택근무를 하다   patience 인내심   temporary 일시적인, 임시의   inconveniences 불편   hesitate 망설이다

작업 일정표 - 3월 2일부터 3월 6일까지		
3월 2일 월요일	401호 (회의실)	403호 (앨리 스티븐스 & 매트 빌)
3월 3일 화요일		
1793월 4일 수요일	402호 (**179**마를린 애즈베리 & 루크 로)	408호 (회의실)
3월 5일 목요일		
3월 6일 금요일	407호 (정리)	404호 (**180**엘리엇 하그버그 & 애나 켈러)

176 주제 / 목적

번역 직원들에게 회람을 보낸 이유는?

(A) 임박한 보수 작업에 대해 주의를 환기시키기 위해
(B) 회사가 이전 예정이라는 것을 알리기 위해
(C) 새로운 작업장 시설에 관한 의견을 요청하기 위해
(D) 건물 관리에 대한 그들의 불만을 해소하기 위해

해설 회람 초반부의 '여러분 대부분이 알고 계시겠지만 3월 첫 주 일정이 좀 힘들 것 같습니다(As most of you are aware, ~ March)'와 '작업자들이 페인트칠을 다시 하고, 카펫과 오래된 가구를 교체할 수 있도록 여러 방과 사무실을 일정 기간 동안 비워 두어야 합니다(Various rooms and offices ~ replace old furniture)'를 통해 사무실 보수 작업에 대해 상기시키며 관련 정보를 제공하는 회람임을 알 수 있다. 따라서 (A)가 정답이다.

어휘 alert 주의를 환기시키다, 알리다 renovation 개조, 보수 relocate 이전하다 maintenance 관리, 유지·보수

▶▶ Paraphrasing 지문의 to repaint, recarpet, and replace old furniture → 정답의 renovations

177 세부 사항

번역 직원들은 무엇을 하라고 지시받는가?

(A) 일찍 출근하기
(B) 매니저와 회의 일정 잡기
(C) 어떤 사무용품이 자신들의 것인지 표시하기
(D) 온라인에서 연락 정보 수정하기

해설 회람의 두 번째 단락에서 작업이 완료되면 작업반이 해당 사무실에 상자들을 다시 갖다 놓을 수 있도록 상자에 이름과 사무실 번호를 표시해 달라(Please label them with your name and office number ~ complete)고 지시했으므로, (C)가 정답이다.

어휘 report for work[duty] 출근하다, 출근해서 보고하다 indicate 표시하다, 명시하다

▶▶ Paraphrasing 지문의 label them with your name and office number → 정답의 Indicate which office supplies are theirs

178 사실 관계 확인

번역 409호에 관해 언급된 것은?

(A) 화상 회의용으로 쓸 수 있다.
(B) 직원들이 모여 일할 수 있다.
(C) 일정 회의가 열린다.
(D) 그곳에 있는 가구를 잠시 치울 것이다.

해설 회람의 세 번째 단락에서 409호 회의실을 일주일 내내 사무 공간으로 사용할 수 있다(The conference room (Room 409) will remain available to be used as a workspace)고 했으므로, (B)가 정답이다.

▶▶ Paraphrasing 지문의 as a workspace → 정답의 for work

179 연계

번역 애즈베리 씨는 언제 자신의 사무실을 비울 준비를 해야 하는가?

(A) 2월 12일
(B) 2월 27일
(C) 3월 3일
(D) 3월 4일

해설 회람의 첫 번째 단락에서 작업에 영향을 받는 직원은 방 작업 일정 전날 오후 3시까지 모든 사무용품을 상자에 포장해야 한다(need to box up all their office items by 3 P.M. on the day before their room is scheduled for work)며 작업 일정 전날까지 방을 비울 것을 요청했다. 작업 일정(WORK SCHEDULE)을 보면 애즈베리 씨의 사무실은 3월 4일 수요일에 작업을 시작한다는 것을 확인할 수 있다. 따라서 전날인 3월 3일까지 사무실을 비워야 하므로, (C)가 정답이다.

180 추론 / 암시

번역 하그버그 씨에 관해 암시된 것은?

(A) 동료와 함께 사무실을 쓴다.
(B) 3월 5일 외부 근무 예정이다.
(C) 부서장이다.
(D) 회의실 사용을 요청했다.

해설 일정표를 보면 엘리엇 하그버그와 애나 캘러가 404호를 함께 사용한다는 것을 추론할 수 있으므로, (A)가 정답이다.

181-185 전단지 + 양식

리브로 농장

신선한 유기농 농산물—우리 농장에서 여러분의 가정까지

181퀘벡 주 브로몽에 있는 리브로 농장에서 지역 사회의 후원을 받는 농업 프로그램에 여러분을 초대합니다. 회원들은 1826월부터 11월까지 재배 기간 동안 신선한 농장 농산물을 즐기게 됩니다.

팜셰어를 신청하고 아래 혜택을 누리십시오:

• 182저희 농장 직원이 수확해서 여러분이 저희 창고에서 가져가실 수 있도록 준비된 30종 이상의 제철 채소, 과일, 허브
• 184직접 수확할 수 있는 딸기, 사과 등 다양한 과일
• 조리법, 농장 소식, 183(A)농장 소식지가 있는 회원 전용 웹사이트 이용 권한
• 183(C)연례 여름 음악 축제 등의 농장 행사 할인. 행사는 보통 15달러이지만 회원은 10달러 지불.

회원은 일주일에 한 번 농장에서 자신의 몫을 가져 갑니다. 전체 지분은 시즌당 700달러이며 185절반 지분은 350달러입니다. 절반 지분인 경우 매주 농산물의 절반을 받습니다. 다른 혜택은 모두 같습니다.

저희 농장 농산물은 살충제나 제초제를 쓰지 않고 재배하며 183(B)천연 비료만 사용합니다. 자세한 정보를 원하시거나 회원 등록을 하시려면 저희 웹사이트 www.livroufarm.ca를 참조하십시오.

어휘 produce 농산물 participate in ~에 참가하다 community 지역 사회 agriculture 농업 sign up for ~을 신청하다 harvest 수확하다 barn 헛간, 광 access 접근, 이용(권한) recipe 조리법 annual 연례의 typically 보통 share 지분, 몫 benefit 혜택 pesticide 살충제 herbicide 제초제 fertilizer 비료

```
http://www.livroufarm.ca
```

리브로 농장

회원	홈	위치	후기

184이름: 줄리엔 버나드

주소: 78 도리언 스트리트, 브로몽, QC J2L 2K7

수거 희망일 1순위: 목요일 ☒ 금요일 ☐ 토요일 ☐ 일요일 ☐

수거 희망일 2순위: 목요일 ☐ 금요일 ☒ 토요일 ☐ 일요일 ☐

지분율: 전체 ☐   **185절반** ☒

유의: 수거 시간은 오후 3시부터 오후 6시까지입니다.

회원님 가정의 다른 구성원들의 이름도 적어 주십시오. 본인 외에 이 인원들만 회원님의 주별 지분을 수거할 수 있습니다.

이름: 마르고 버나드, 로랑 버나드

다음 페이지의 결제 정보로 가시려면 여기를 클릭하세요.

어휘   individual 개인, 사람   household 가정   permit 허락하다

181 주제 / 목적

번역   전단지의 목적은?

(A) 농장 축제에 사람들 초대하기
(B) 지역 봉사 활동 기회 홍보하기
(C) 건강한 섭식을 위한 조리법 공유하기
(D) 농장 프로그램 광고하기

해설   전단지 첫 번째 단락의 '퀘벡 주 브로몽에 있는 리브로 농장에서 지역 사회의 후원을 받는 농업 프로그램에 여러분을 초대합니다(Livrou Farm ~ community-supported agriculture program)'라는 문구를 통해 농장 프로그램을 홍보하는 전단지임을 알 수 있다. 따라서 (D)가 정답이다.

어휘   community service 지역 사회 봉사 활동

▸▸ Paraphrasing   지문의 agriculture program
→ 정답의 farm program

182 추론 / 암시

번역   리브로 농장 직원들에 관해 암시된 것은?

(A) 6월부터 11월까지 농장 농산물을 수확한다.
(B) 1주일에 한 번 농장 웹사이트를 갱신한다.
(C) 농장 생산물을 이용해 식사를 만든다.
(D) 몇몇 지역 시장에서 농장 생산물을 판매한다.

해설   전단지 첫 번째 단락의 '6월부터 11월까지 재배 기간 동안(during our growing season from June to November)'과 두 번째 단락의 '저희 농장 직원이 수확한 30종 이상의 제철 채소, 과일, 허브(More than 30 varieties of in-season vegetables, fruits, and herbs, harvested by our farm staff)'를 통해 직원들이 6월부터 11월까지 농작물을 수확한다는 것을 추론할 수 있다. 따라서 (A)가 정답이다.

▸▸ Paraphrasing   지문의 farm staff
→ 질문의 workers at Livrou Farm
지문의 in-season vegetables, fruits, and herbs, harvested by our farm staff
→ 정답의 farm produce

183 사실 관계 확인

번역   리브로 농장에 관해 명시된 것이 아닌 것은?

(A) 소식지를 발행한다.
(B) 천연 비료를 쓴다.
(C) 음악 공연을 주최한다.
(D) 요리 교실을 제공한다.

해설   전단지 두 번째 단락의 '농장 소식지(a farm newsletter)'에서 (A)를, 두 번째 단락의 '연례 여름 음악 축제 등의 농장 행사 할인(Discounts on events at the farm, such as the annual summer music festival)'에서 (C)를, 마지막 단락의 '천연 비료만 사용합니다(we use only naturally occurring fertilizers)'에서 (B)를 확인할 수 있다. 그러나 요리 교실을 제공한다는 내용은 언급되지 않았으므로, (D)가 정답이다.

▸▸ Paraphrasing   지문의 naturally occurring fertilizers
→ 보기 (B)의 natural fertilizers
지문의 the annual summer music festival
→ 보기 (C)의 musical performances

184 연계

번역   버나드 씨의 회원 자격에 관해 사실인 것은?

(A) 일요일에 자신의 농산물을 수거해야 한다.
(B) 자신의 농장 지분을 수거할 수 있는 유일한 사람이다.
(C) 자신의 과일을 직접 수확할 수 있다.
(D) 자신의 채소를 심고 재배할 수 있을 것이다.

해설   양식을 보면 버나드 씨가 리브로 농장의 팜셰어 프로그램에 가입했다는 것을 알 수 있고, 전단지에 나온 회원 혜택에 직접 수확할 수 있는 딸기, 사과 등 다양한 과일(a selection of pick-your-own strawberries, apples, and other fruits)이 있는 것으로 보아, 그가 자신의 과일을 직접 수확할 수 있다는 것을 알 수 있다. 따라서 (C)가 정답이다. 전단지 세 번째 단락에서 일주일에 한 번(once a week) 자신의 지분을 수거해 갈 수 있다고 했는데, 양식을 보면 버나드 씨는 1지망을 목요일, 2지망을 금요일로 선택했으며 이후 일요일에 수거해야 한다는 조건이나 상황은 언급되지 않았으므로, (A)는 정답이 될 수 없다. 또한 양식에 본인을 제외한 다른 가족 구성원(other individuals in your household)도 농산물을 수거해 갈 수 있다고 했으므로 (B)는 명백한 오답이다. 마지막으로, 전단지 두 번째 단락에서 채소는 농장 직원이 수확한다(harvested by our farm staff)고 했고 채소 재배에 관한 내용은 별도로 언급되지 않았으므로, (D) 역시 정답이 될 수 없다.

185 연계

번역   버나드 씨는 회비로 얼마를 지불해야 하는가?

(A) 10달러   (B) 15달러
(C) 350달러   (D) 700달러

해설 양식을 보면 버나드 씨의 지분율(Size of share)이 절반(Half)에 해당한다는 것을 알 수 있다. 회원 가입을 위해 지불해야 하는 금액은 전단지에서 확인할 수 있는데, 전단지 세 번째 단락에서 절반 지분은 350달러(a half-size share is $350)라고 했으므로, (C)가 정답이다.

186-190 광고 + 광고 + 이메일

---

http://www.communitylinkforum.org/burlingtonermont

벌링턴에서 직장인 아파트 구함

호르헤 얀센 〈jjanssen@blitzer.com〉

주제: 부동산과 주택

날짜: 6월 23일

186벌링턴에 새 직책을 수락해서 근무를 시작하는 8월 15일 이전에 도심 인근으로 이사를 가야 합니다. 단출하고 깨끗한 침실 1개짜리 임대물을 찾고 있지만 가격에 따라 더 넓은 곳도 괜찮습니다. 친구나 가족을 접대할 수 있도록 외부 좌석이 있는 편안한 곳이면 더 좋겠습니다. 차를 가지고 있긴 하지만 대중교통 이용이 수월했으면 합니다. **187공과금을 포함해 주거비 전체에 쓸 수 있는 예산이 매달 1,400달러 정도 됩니다.**

어휘 accept (직책 등을) 수락하다 relocate 이사하다, 이전하다 rental 임대(물) entertain 접대하다, 즐겁게 하다 appreciate 고마워하다, 환영하다 access 접근(성) public transportation 대중교통 budget 예산 cover (비용 등을) 감당하다, (~하기에 돈이) 되다

---

http://www.communitylinkforum.org/burlingtonermont

벌링턴 아파트 임대함

엘러위즈 맥마흔 〈mcmahonrental@hmail.com〉

주제: 부동산과 주택

날짜: 6월 23일

이 침실 2개짜리 아파트의 대대적인 수리가 끝나면 가장 먼저 임차하십시오. **190이 아파트는 8월 1일이면 입주가 가능할 것입니다.** 깨끗하고 현대적인 외관, 집 전체에 새로 깐 바닥, 그리고 완전히 새로운 가전을 갖출 예정입니다. 이 아파트는 도심에 위치하며, 덴턴 대학교까지 버스로 10분이 채 안 걸리므로 학생들에게 좋습니다. 시 교통국에서 스티커를 받으면 노상 주차가 가능합니다. **188고양이나 소형견은 허용될 수도 있지만 조건이 있으므로 문의하시기 바랍니다.** **187임차료 1,400달러에는 상하수도, 쓰레기 수거, 일반적인 건물 관리 비용이 포함됩니다. 전기와 천연가스는 임차인이 부담합니다.** 임대 계약과 동시에 1개월분의 임차료에 해당하는 금액을 1회 보증금으로 납부해야 합니다.

어휘 completion 완료 extensive 대규모의, 폭넓은 property 부동산, 건물 anticipate 예상하다 appliance 가전제품 decal 스티커 potentially 아마도 permit 허용하다 condition 조건 inquire 문의하다 sewer 하수 garbage 쓰레기 upkeep 관리 tenant 세입자 security deposit 보증금

수신: 엘러위즈 맥마흔 〈mcmahonrental@hmail.com〉

발신: 호르헤 얀센 〈jjanssen@blitzer.com〉

제목: 아파트

날짜: 6월 24일

맥마흔 씨께,

communitylinkforum.org에 올리신 임대 게시물을 보았습니다. 설명을 보면 바로 제가 찾던 아파트 같습니다. **189아파트를 보고 싶은데 마침 이번 주 내내 벌링턴에 있습니다.** 벌링턴에서 보내는 마지막 날이 6월 30일 일요일입니다. **190그 아파트가 제게 적합하다면, 사용 준비가 될 바로 그날 이사하고 싶습니다.** 타이밍이 딱 맞을 것 같군요! 곧 연락 주십시오.

감사합니다.

호르헤 얀센
(802) 555-0122

어휘 notice 알아채다, 주목하다 description 묘사, 설명 eager 간절히 바라는 suit 어울리다, 적합하다

186 세부 사항

번역 얀센 씨가 이사하려는 이유는?

(A) 새 일을 시작하기 위해
(B) 고향으로 돌아가기 위해
(C) 시간제로 공부하기 위해
(D) 은퇴 생활을 시작하기 위해

해설 첫 번째 광고에서 얀센 씨는 벌링턴에 새 직책을 수락해서(I accepted a new position in Burlington) 근무를 시작하는 8월 15일 이전에 도심 인근으로 이사를 가야 한다(need to relocate ~ August 15)고 했으므로, (A)가 정답이다.

> ▸▸ Paraphrasing   지문의 accepted a new position
>   → 정답의 begin a new job

187 연계

번역 부동산의 어떤 면이 얀센 씨가 선호하는 조건과 맞지 않는가?

(A) 위치
(B) 월 비용
(C) 주차 가능 여부
(D) 크기

해설 첫 번째 광고의 마지막 문장을 보면 얀센 씨가 공과금을 포함해 주거비 전체에 쓸 수 있는 예산이 매달 1,400달러 정도(I have a budget of around $1,400 monthly ~ including utilities)라고 했는데, 두 번째 광고의 후반부를 보면 1,400달러의 임차료에는 상하수도, 쓰레기 수거, 일반적인 건물 관리(water, sewer, garbage pickups, and general upkeep of the property)만 포함되고 전기와 천연가스 같은 공과금은 세입자가 지불해야 한다(Electricity and natural gas will be the responsibility of the tenant)고 했다. 따라서 얀센 씨가 바라던 월 비용 조건과 맞지 않으므로, (B)가 정답이다.

188 사실 관계 확인

번역 맥마흔 씨는 어떤 상황에서 추가 정보가 필요하다고 언급하는가?

(A) 인테리어 변경을 선호할 때
(B) 임차인이 보증금을 지불하려고 할 때
(C) 아파트 수리가 필요할 때
(D) 실내에서 애완동물을 키우려고 할 때

해설 두 번째 맥마흔 씨의 광고 중반부를 보면, 고양이나 소형견은 허용될 수도 있지만 조건이 있으므로 문의 바란다(Cats or small dogs are potentially permitted, ~, so please inquire)고 되어 있다. 따라서 세입자가 애완동물을 키우려고 할 경우 추가 정보를 요청할 것임을 알 수 있으므로, (D)가 정답이다.

> ▸ **Paraphrasing** 지문의 **please inquire**
> → 질문의 **need additional information**
> 지문의 **Cats or small dogs** → 정답의 **pet**

189 주제 / 목적

번역 얀센 씨가 이메일을 보낸 이유는?

(A) 임대 계약 조건에 동의하기 위해
(B) 주택 광고의 세부사항을 변경하기 위해
(C) 아파트의 특징에 관해 문의하기 위해
(D) 부동산을 보러 갈 약속을 잡기 위해

해설 이메일의 세 번째 문장에서 아파트를 보고 싶다(I'm eager to look over the apartment)며 마침 이번 주 내내 벌링턴에 있다(I just happen to be in Burlington all this week)고 했으므로, 아파트를 보러 갈 약속을 잡기 위해 이메일을 보냈다는 것을 알 수 있다. 따라서 (D)가 정답이다.

어휘 terms (계약) 조건   contract 계약   residential 주택의   arrangement 준비, 계획   property 부동산

> ▸ **Paraphrasing** 지문의 **look over the apartment**
> → 정답의 **view a property**

190 연계

번역 얀센 씨는 언제부터 그 집에서 살고 싶어 하는가?

(A) 6월 24일
(B) 6월 30일
(C) 8월 1일
(D) 8월 15일

해설 이메일에서 얀센 씨는 아파트 사용 준비가 되는 바로 그 날에 이사하고 싶다(I'd want to move in the same day that it's expected to be available)고 했는데, 두 번째 광고의 초반부를 보면 8월 1일에 입주가 가능할 예정(This property is anticipated to be move-in ready on August 1)이라고 했으므로, (C)가 정답이다.

> ▸ **Paraphrasing** 지문의 **want to move in** → 질문의 **wish to start living in the residence**

191-195 제품 설명서 + 고객 후기 + 온라인 응답

> **키친웨어 유토피아 만능 조리 기구 – 모델 C3**
> 이제 다른 만능 조리 기구를 살 필요가 없으실 겁니다! 당사에서 [191(D)] **가장 많이 팔리는 모델인 C3**은 고품질 플라스틱과 세척이 쉬운 스테인리스(강철)로 제조되었습니다.
>
> **특징:** 독특한 칼날 디자인과 강력한 모터로 [191(B)]**모든 규모의 분주한 식당에 이상적인** 전문가급 가전입니다.
>
> **보증:** 모든 부품과 서비스를 7년 동안 보장하는 품질 보증서가 포함되어 있으며, 이는 [191(A)]**당사 만능 조리 기구가 오래 갈 것이라고 여러분을 안심시켜 드리는 것입니다.**
>
> 특별 구매가: 319.00달러/[193]KU 클럽 회원: 299.00달러

어휘 food processor 만능 조리 기구   blade (칼)날   warranty 품질 보증(서)   labor 노동(력)   reassurance 안심시키는 것[말], 재보증   purchase 구매(품); 구매하다

> www.kitchenwareutopia.com/C3/reviews/454
>
> **평점:** ★★★★★
> **후기:** 이 제품은 정말 좋아요! 요식업자로 일하고 있어서 아주 다양한 만능 조리 기구를 써 봤습니다. 지금까지 제가 본 제품 중 키친웨어 유토피아의 C3이 최고입니다. 모터도 아주 강력하고 다양한 날과 세팅이 있어서 매우 다양한 용도로 쓸 수 있습니다. 세팅도 아주 간단합니다. 비싸지만 투자할 가치가 충분한데, [193]저는 로열티 클럽 회원이라 가격이 적당했습니다. [194]유일한 불만이 있다면 꽤 무거워서 기대한 만큼 운반이 쉽지 않습니다. [192]하지만 대체로 이 제품에 정말 만족합니다.
>
> 엘리 펄스 3월 27일 게시

어휘 caterer 요식업체, 음식 공급업체   extremely 지극히, 매우   versatile 다용도의, 다재 다능한   straightforward 간단한, 쉬운   reasonable (가격이) 합리적인   portable 휴대가 쉬운   exceptionally 유난히, 특별히

> C3 만능 조리 기구에 만족하셨다니 아주 기쁩니다. 고객 만족은 당사의 첫 번째 우선 사항입니다. 고객님의 불만 사항에 답변하고 우려 사항에 [195]관해 제안하고자 합니다. [194]고객님 직종에 쓰시기에는 C2 조리 기구가 더 적합한 듯합니다. C2는 C3와 모터 크기는 같지만 전체적으로 C3보다 훨씬 작습니다. 하지만 이 모델은 C3보다 조금 더 비쌉니다. www.kitchenwareutopia.com/C2를 방문하시면 제품 설명서를 보실 수 있습니다.
>
> 키친웨어 유토피아 고객 서비스부 3월 28일 게시

어휘 satisfaction 만족   priority 우선 사항   suggestion 제안   regarding ~에 관한   suited 적합한, 어울리는   needs 필요한 것, 요구   slightly 약간   description 설명, 묘사

191 사실 관계 확인

번역 C3 만능 조리 기구의 특징으로 제품 설명서에 언급된 내용이 아닌 것은?

(A) 내구성이 뛰어나다.
(B) 업소 주방에 적합하다.
(C) 경쟁사 만능 조리 기구보다 크다.
(D) 인기 있는 모델이다.

해설 제품 설명서 세 번째 단락의 '당사 만능 조리 기구가 오래 간다는 것 (our food processor will last a long time)'에서 (A)를, 두 번째 단락의 '모든 규모의 분주한 식당에 이상적인(ideal for busy restaurants of any size)'에서 (B)를, 첫 번째 단락의 '가장 많이 팔리는 모델 C3(Our best-selling model, the C3)'에서 (D)를 확인할 수 있다. 그러나 경쟁사의 기구와 크기를 비교한 내용은 없으므로, (C)가 정답이다.

어휘 durable 내구성이 있는, 오래가는   suitable 적합한
commercial 상업적인   competitor 경쟁사[자]

▶▶ **Paraphrasing**   지문의 last a long time
→ 보기 (A)의 very durable
지문의 ideal for busy restaurants
→ 보기 (B)의 suitable for commercial kitchens
지문의 best-selling → 보기 (D)의 popular

192 사실 관계 확인

번역 고객 후기에 명시된 것은?

(A) C3에는 상세한 설명서가 제공된다.
(B) 펄스 씨는 구매품에 만족한다.
(C) 키친웨어 유토피아의 고객 서비스는 아주 훌륭하다.
(D) 사용자들은 C3 세척을 어려워한다.

해설 펄스 씨가 작성한 고객 후기를 보면 대체로 C3 제품에 굉장히 만족한다(Overall, though, I'm exceptionally satisfied with this product)고 했으므로, (B)가 정답이다.

어휘 instructions 설명(서)

▶▶ **Paraphrasing**   지문의 satisfied with this product
→ 정답의 pleased with his purchase

193 연계

번역 펄스 씨에 관해 암시된 것은?

(A) 만능 조리 기구에 299달러를 지불했다.
(B) 조리 기구의 몇 가지 옵션 부품을 구입했다.
(C) 3월 27일 대규모 행사에 음식을 조달했다.
(D) 전에는 만능 조리 기구를 써 본 적이 없다.

해설 고객 후기에서 펄스 씨는 자신이 로열티 클럽 회원(I'm a loyalty club member)라고 했는데, 제품 설명서에 따르면 KU 클럽 회원은 299.00달러(KU Club Members: $299.00)에 제품을 구매할 수 있다고 했으므로, 펄스 씨가 299달러를 지불했음을 추론할 수 있다. 따라서 (A)가 정답이다.

194 연계

번역 펄스 씨에게 더 적합한 조리 기구로 C2를 추천한 이유는 무엇이겠는가?

(A) 저렴하다.
(B) 식기 세척기로 세척할 수 있다.
(C) 조립이 쉽다.
(D) 가볍다.

해설 펄스 씨가 고객 후기에 조리 기구가 꽤 무거워서 자신이 기대한 만큼 운반이 쉽지 않은 것(it's very heavy and therefore not as portable as I'd hoped)이 유일한 불만(My only complaint)이라고 하자, 이에 대해 고객 서비스가 온라인 응답에서 C2 제품을 추천하며 전체적으로 C3보다 훨씬 작다(it is much smaller than the C3 in general)는 근거를 들었다. 따라서 (D)가 정답이다.

▶▶ **Paraphrasing**   지문의 better suited to your professional
needs → 질문의 more suitable for Mr. Perles
지문의 much smaller → 정답의 lightweight

195 동의어 찾기

번역 온라인 응답에서 첫 번째 단락 3행의 "regarding"과 의미상 가장 가까운 것은?

(A) ~을 맡으며   (B) ~에 관하여
(C) ~와 비교하여   (D) 감탄하며

해설 "regarding"을 포함한 부분은 '우려 사항에 관해 제안하고자 합니다(provide a suggestion regarding your concerns)'라는 의미로, 여기서 regarding은 '~에 관해'라는 뜻으로 쓰였다. 따라서 '~에 관하여 ~에 대한'이라는 의미의 (B) about이 정답이다.

196-200 기사 + 일정표 + 새 소식

멘트 홀에서 피아섹 컵 결승전이 열리다

현재 대대적인 개조 공사 중인 멘트 홀이 오는 6월 바르샤바에서 열리는 피아섹 컵 배구 선수권 대회 결승전을 주최할 준비를 하고 있다. 비록 이번 공사가 한동안 진행되어 오고 있지만, 공사가 완공되는 데 경제적 동기가 된 것은 이 선수권 대회를 주최할 기회였다. 시 관계자들은 건설이 예정대로 진행되고 있으며 선수권 대회 결승전 훨씬 이전에 완료될 것이라고 확인해 주었다.

멘트 홀은 전국에서 유일하게 피아섹 컵 행사를 한 번도 개최하지 않은 주요 경기장이기 때문에 홀 소유주들은 이번 해 결승전 개최지로 선정된 것에 자부심을 느꼈다. ¹⁹⁸**이 결승전이 새롭게 단장된 홀의 개시를 알릴 것이다.** 이 행사는 수많은 배구 팬을 ¹⁹⁶**끌어모을 것으로 예상되며** 주최측은 멘트 홀이 행사에 부응하리라 확신한다. ¹⁹⁷**멘트 홀은 관중 1만 9천 명을 수용할 수 있어 기존의 2배에 이르는 규모가 될 것이다.**

어휘 currently 현재   undergo 겪다, 받다   extensive 대규모의, 폭넓은   opportunity 기회   host 주최하다, 개최하다   incentive 장려책   official 관계자, 공무원   confirm 확인해 주다   progress 진행되다   inaugurate 개시를 알리다, 시작하다   refurbish 새로 꾸미다   draw 끌다, (사람을) 모으다   organizer 주최자, 조직자   spectator 관중   previous 이전의, 과거의

피아섹 컵 배구 선수권 대회			
준준결승전			
²⁰⁰베네수엘라 – 호주 **6월 10일, 오후 3시 로아브 경기장, 비드고슈치**	폴란드 – 프랑스 6월 10일, 오후 6시 팀파니 홀, 카토비체	브라질 – 미국 6월 11일, 오후 3시 폴라나 센터, 크라쿠프	쿠바 – 이집트 6월 11일, 오후 6시 미스트시 경기장, 브로츠와프
준결승전			
6월 10일 경기 승자 6월 13일, 오후 3시 팀파니 홀, 카 토비체		6월 11일 경기 승자 6월 13일, 오후 3시 폴라나 센 터, 크라쿠프	
결승전			
¹⁹⁸**6월 16일, 오후 6시 멘트 홀, 바르샤바**			
주의: ¹⁹⁹**결승전 티켓이 빠른 속도로 판매되고 있으므로 준결승전 이후 까지 주문을 미루지 마십시오.** 예약석만 가능, 일반석 없음. 환불 불가.			
어휘 reserved 예약된 general admission 일반석 refund 환불			

새 소식 할락스 라디오 108.3 FM
스포츠 – 배구, 6월 10일
오후 3시, ²⁰⁰베네수엘라가 준결승전 진출 자격을 놓고 호주와 겨룬다. ²⁰⁰초빙 아나운서는 지난해 우승팀인 캐나다의 코치로 있다가 은퇴한 **빈 코트 씨이다.**
오후 6시 개최국 팀인 폴란드가 프랑스와 대결한다. 이 경기는 제레미 보스코 씨가 생중계한다.
어휘 take on ~와 대결하다 qualification 자격 face off 대결할 준비를 하다 cover 보도[방송]하다

196 동의어 찾기

번역 기사에서 두 번째 단락 7행의 "draw"와 의미상 가장 가까운 것은?

(A) 홍보하다
(B) 유치하다
(C) 그리다
(D) 제거하다

해설 "draw"를 포함한 부분은 결승전이 수많은 배구 팬을 끌어모을 것
이 예상된다는 내용으로, 여기서 draw는 '끌어모으다, 운집시키
다'라는 뜻으로 쓰였다. 따라서 '유치하다, 끌어모으다'라는 의미의
(B) attract가 정답이다.

197 세부 사항

번역 멘트 홀에서 무엇이 변경될 예정인가?

(A) 소유주
(B) 티켓 가격
(C) 좌석수
(D) 위치

해설 기사의 마지막 단락에서 멘트 홀은 관중 1만 9천 명을 수용할 수 있어
(Seating 19,000 spectators) 기존의 2배에 이르는 규모가 될 것
이다(Ment Hall will be double its previous size)라고 했으므
로, (C)가 정답이다.

198 연계

번역 새 개최지에서 첫 번째 게임이 열리는 시기는?

(A) 6월 10일
(B) 6월 13일
(C) 6월 14일
(D) 6월 16일

해설 기사의 후반부에서 결승전이 새롭게 단장된 (멘트) 홀의 개시를 알릴
것(The final game will inaugurate the refurbished hall)이
라고 했으므로, 이 경기장에서 첫 번째로 열릴 경기가 결승전이라는
것을 알 수 있다. 경기 일정은 일정표에서 확인할 수 있는데, 결승전
(Final Game)이 6월 16일 오후 6시에 멘트 홀에서 개최될 예정이
라고 했으므로, (D)가 정답이다.

199 세부 사항

번역 일정표에서 사람들에게 하라고 권고되는 일은?

(A) 사용하지 않을 예정인 티켓 환불 요청하기
(B) 준결승 직후 티켓 주문하기
(C) 가능한 한 빨리 결승전 티켓 구매하기
(D) 결승전에 일찍 도착하기

해설 일정표의 주의(NOTE) 부분을 보면, 결승전 티켓이 빠른 속도로 판
매되고(Tickets for the final game are selling fast) 있으니 준
결승전 이후까지 주문을 미루지 말라(don't wait until after the
semifinal games to order)며 티켓 구매를 서두를 것을 조언하고
있으므로, (C)가 정답이다.

> ▸▸ Paraphrasing 지문의 **don't wait**
> → 정답의 **as soon as possible**

200 연계

번역 코트 씨는 어디에서 중계할 것인가?

(A) 비드고슈치
(B) 카토비체
(C) 크라쿠프
(D) 브로츠와프

해설 새 소식의 첫 번째 단락에서 베네수엘라가 준결승전 진출을 놓고 호주
와 겨룬다(Venezuela will take on Australia for qualification
to the semifinals)며 빈 코트 씨가 초빙 아나운서(Our guest
announcer will be Vin Cote)라고 했다. 경기 장소가 나온 일정표
를 보면 베네수엘라-호주의 준준결승전(Quarterfinal Games)이 비
드고슈치의 로아브 경기장(Loave Arena, Bydgoszcz)에서 개최될
것이라고 되어 있으므로, (A)가 정답이다.

101 (B)	**102** (A)	**103** (A)	**104** (C)	**105** (D)
106 (C)	**107** (A)	**108** (C)	**109** (B)	**110** (A)
111 (B)	**112** (A)	**113** (A)	**114** (D)	**115** (C)
116 (D)	**117** (C)	**118** (D)	**119** (D)	**120** (C)
121 (D)	**122** (C)	**123** (A)	**124** (B)	**125** (B)
126 (D)	**127** (D)	**128** (B)	**129** (D)	**130** (A)
131 (C)	**132** (A)	**133** (B)	**134** (D)	**135** (A)
136 (D)	**137** (D)	**138** (A)	**139** (D)	**140** (B)
141 (D)	**142** (A)	**143** (A)	**144** (C)	**145** (B)
146 (C)	**147** (A)	**148** (B)	**149** (C)	**150** (D)
151 (B)	**152** (C)	**153** (A)	**154** (B)	**155** (B)
156 (A)	**157** (D)	**158** (A)	**159** (D)	**160** (B)
161 (C)	**162** (A)	**163** (A)	**164** (C)	**165** (B)
166 (D)	**167** (B)	**168** (C)	**169** (A)	**170** (B)
171 (D)	**172** (B)	**173** (A)	**174** (A)	**175** (C)
176 (D)	**177** (B)	**178** (B)	**179** (D)	**180** (A)
181 (B)	**182** (C)	**183** (D)	**184** (B)	**185** (A)
186 (B)	**187** (D)	**188** (A)	**189** (D)	**190** (C)
191 (B)	**192** (D)	**193** (C)	**194** (B)	**195** (A)
196 (A)	**197** (D)	**198** (B)	**199** (C)	**200** (B)

PART 5

101 명사 자리 _ 동사의 목적어 _ 어휘

해설 빈칸은 정관사 the와 전치사 of 사이 자리로, 동사 marked의 목적어 역할을 하는 명사가 들어가야 한다. 문맥상 '사무소의 개관을 기념했다'라는 내용이 되어야 자연스러우므로, '개관, 개장'을 의미하는 (B) opening이 정답이다. (A) opens, (C) opened는 동사, (D) openly는 부사이므로 빈칸에 들어갈 수 없다.

번역 요크 개발 공사는 테이프 절단식으로 포드 로드 사무소의 개관을 기념했다.

어휘 mark 기념하다, 표시하다   ribbon-cutting ceremony 테이프 절단식

102 부사 어휘

해설 빈칸 뒤 형용사 helpful을 적절히 수식하는 부사를 선택하는 문제이다. helpful이 '도움이 되는'이라는 의미이므로, 빈칸에는 호텔 직원이 얼마나 도움이 되었는지 묘사하는 부사가 들어가야 자연스럽다. 따라서 '꽤, 상당히'라는 뜻의 (A) quite이 정답이다. 참고로, quite은 '완전히, 전적으로'라는 의미를 나타낼 수도 있다. (B) enough도 정도를 나타내는 부사로 쓰일 수 있지만 형용사 뒤에 위치해야 하므로 정답이 될 수 없다. (C) far는 비교급 형용사 및 부사를 강조하는 부사이다.

번역 비스마르크 호텔 직원들은 우리가 머무는 동안 꽤 도움이 되었다.

103 형용사 자리 _ 명사 수식

해설 빈칸은 명사 merger를 수식하는 형용사 자리로, 형용사 역할을 할 수 있는 과거분사 (A) proposed와 현재분사 (D) proposing 중 하나가 들어가야 한다. merger는 '합병'이라는 뜻으로 동사 propose (제안하다)의 대상이 되므로, 수동의 의미를 내포하는 과거분사 (A) proposed가 정답이 된다. 참고로, (B) proposal은 '제안(서)', (C) proposition은 '제의, 진술'이라는 의미로 merger 앞에 위치하여 복합명사를 이룰 수 없으며, proposal은 merger 뒤에 위치할 경우 가능하다.

번역 루오 씨가 제안된 윌슨-픽 사와의 합병으로 초래될 수 있는 몇 가지 결과에 대해 설명할 것이다.

어휘 explain 설명하다   consequence 결과   merger 합병   propose 제안하다

104 명사 어휘

해설 빈칸 앞 명사 survey와 복합명사를 이루어 동사 will be released 의 주어 역할을 하는 명사를 선택하는 문제이다. 문맥상 '설문 조사 결과가 발표될 것이다'라는 내용이 되어야 자연스러우므로, '결과'라는 의미의 (C) results가 정답이다.

번역 스프링데일 슈퍼마켓 설문 조사 결과는 평가 후 일주일 뒤에 발표될 것이다.

어휘 survey (설문) 조사; 조사하다   release 발표하다, 공개하다   evaluate 평가하다

105 부사 자리 _ 동사 수식

해설 빈칸은 more와 함께 자동사 operates를 수식하는 부사 자리이므로, '빠르게'라는 의미의 부사 (D) quickly가 정답이다. (A) quickest 는 최상급 형용사, (B) quickness는 명사, (C) quick은 형용사로, 모두 품사상 빈칸에 적합하지 않다.

번역 새 프린터는 이전 모델보다 더 빨리 작동합니다.

어휘 operate 작동하다, 운영하다   previous 이전의, 과거의

106 인칭대명사의 격 _ 주격

해설 help가 동사, members가 목적어, find (quality merchandise) 가 목적격 보어인 문장으로, 빈칸에는 동사 help의 주어 역할을 하는 대명사가 들어가야 한다. 따라서 주격 인칭대명사인 (C) we가 정답이다.

번역 이곳 뱅가드 바잉 클럽에서, 저희는 회원들이 가능한 한 최저 가격으로 양질의 상품을 찾을 수 있도록 도와 드립니다.

어휘 quality 양질의, 고급의; 품질   merchandise 상품

107 부사 어휘

해설 빈칸 뒤에 오는 전치사구 in time for summer vacations를 적절히 수식하는 부사를 선택하는 문제이다. 문맥상 '여름 휴가철에 딱 맞춰'라는 내용이 되어야 자연스러우므로, '딱, ~하는 바로 그 순간에'라는 의미의 (A) just가 정답이 된다.

번역 경영진은 모든 영업 사원이 여름 휴가철에 딱 맞춰 올해 보너스를 받게 된다고 발표했다.

어휘 management 관리(자), 경영(자) announce 발표하다
receive 받다

108 재귀대명사 _ 동사의 목적어

해설 consider가 동사, 빈칸이 목적어, to be traditional artists 가 목적격 보어인 문장으로, 빈칸에는 consider의 목적어로서 traditional artists와 동격 관계를 이루는 복수 명사가 들어가야 한다. 따라서 '그들 자신'이라는 의미로 목적어 역할을 할 수 있는 재귀대명사 (C) themselves가 정답이다.

번역 〈플로리다 디지털 디자이너 매거진〉에 따르면, 많은 그래픽 디자이너들이 스스로를 전통적인 예술가라고 생각하지 않는다고 한다.

어휘 magazine 잡지 consider 생각하다, 고려하다 traditional 전통적인, 인습적인

109 동사 어휘

해설 빈칸 뒤 전치사 to와 어울려 쓰이는 자동사를 선택해야 한다. 문맥상 '호텔의 9홀 골프장으로 이어진다'라는 내용이 되어야 자연스러우므로, '~로 이어지다, ~로 통하다'라는 의미의 (B) leads가 정답이다. (A) prepares는 자동사로 쓰일 때 주로 전치사 for와 함께 쓰이고, 타동사인 (C) presents와 (D) takes는 전치사 없이 바로 목적어를 취하므로 빈칸에 부적절하다.

번역 얕은 연못을 가로지르는 나무 다리는 호텔의 9홀 골프장으로 이어진다.

어휘 wade (얕은 물 속을 맨발로) 첨벙거리며 다니다 pond 연못
prepare 준비하다

110 동사 어형 _ 태

해설 빈칸은 주어 A special sale on stationery의 동사 자리이다. 따라서 문장의 동사 역할을 할 수 있는 (A) was announced, (B) announced, (C) was announcing 중 하나를 선택해야 하는데, 주어인 A special sale은 동사 announce(발표하다)의 대상이 되므로, 수동태 동사인 (A) was announced가 정답이다. 능동태 동사인 (B) announced 및 (C) was announcing 뒤에는 목적어가 와야 하므로 빈칸에 들어갈 수 없다.

번역 어제 라이트 씽즈 웹사이트에서 문구류 특별 할인 판매가 발표되었다.

어휘 stationery 문구류

111 부사 어휘

해설 빈칸은 전치사구 upon pickup과 함께 동사 is refrigerated를 수식하는 부사 자리이다. 뒤에 '부패를 방지하기 위해(to prevent spoilage)'라는 목적이 나오므로, 해당 부분은 '인수 즉시 냉장된다'라는 내용이 되어야 자연스럽다. 따라서 '즉시, 지체 없이'라는 의미의 (B) promptly가 정답이다.

번역 고카고 트럭킹에 의해 운반되는 모든 농산물은 부패를 방지하기 위해 인수 즉시 냉장된다.

어휘 produce 농산물, 생산물 transport 수송하다; 운송(업)
refrigerate 냉장하다 prevent 방지하다 spoilage 부패
lately 최근에 potentially 잠재적으로, 어쩌면

112 형용사 자리 _ 명사 수식

해설 빈칸은 most와 함께 최상급을 이루어 명사 sculptures를 수식하는 형용사 자리이므로, '혁신적인'이라는 의미의 형용사인 (A) innovative 가 정답이다. (B) innovation은 명사, (C) innovatively는 부사, (D) innovate는 동사로, 모두 품사상 빈칸에 적합하지 않다.

번역 페레라 박물관은 루시아 알메이다의 가장 혁신적인 조각품들을 전시할 계획이다.

어휘 exhibit 전시하다 sculpture 조각(품) innovative 혁신적인
innovation 혁신 innovatively 혁신적으로 innovate
혁신[쇄신]하다

113 전치사 어휘

해설 빈칸 뒤의 on Sundays와 어울리는 전치사를 선택하는 문제이다. 앞에 출납 창구가 매일(daily) 오전 8시부터 오후 4시까지 열려 있다는 내용이 왔으므로, 빈칸이 포함된 부분은 '일요일은 제외하고'라는 의미가 되어야 자연스럽다. 따라서 '~을 제외하고'라는 뜻의 (A) except 가 정답이다.

번역 은행 출납 창구는 일요일을 제외하고 매일 오전 8시부터 오후 4시까지 열려 있다.

어휘 cashier window 출납 창구

114 동사 어휘

해설 빈칸은 주어 Inventory control and warehousing strategies의 동사 자리로, 전치사구 within the responsibilities의 수식을 받는다. 빈칸 뒤에 목적어가 없으므로 자동사가 들어가야 하며, 문맥상 '재고 관리 및 입고 전략은 공급망 관리자의 책임에 속한다'라는 내용이 되어야 자연스러우므로, '~에 속하다'라는 의미의 (D) fall이 정답이다. (A) have 및 (B) cover는 타동사로 뒤에 바로 목적어가 와야 하므로 오답이며, (C) mark는 자동사로 쓰일 경우 '자국[흔적]이 생기다'라는 뜻이므로 문맥상 빈칸에 적합하지 않다.

번역 재고 관리 및 입고 전략은 공급망 관리자의 책임에 속한다.

어휘 inventory 재고(품) warehousing 창고 저장[관리], 입고
strategy 전략 responsibility 업무, 책임 supply chain
공급망

115 명사절 접속사

해설 빈칸 이하가 to figure out의 목적어 역할을 하고 있으며, 빈칸 뒤에 동사(would best suit)와 목적어(your company's needs)만 왔다. 따라서 빈칸에는 해당 절의 주어 역할을 하는 동시에 불완전한 절을 이끄는 명사절 접속사가 들어가야 하므로, (C) which가 정답이 된다. 참고로, (A) when, (B) why, (D) where 모두 명사절 접속사로 쓰일 수 있지만, 뒤에 절이 올 경우 모든 요소를 갖춘 완전한 절이 와야 한다.

번역 현재 이용 가능한 모든 트럭 모델 중에서 어떤 것이 귀사의 요구에 가장 적합할지 알아내기가 어려울 수 있습니다.

어휘 available 이용할 수 있는, 구할 수 있는 figure out 알아내다, 이해하다 suit 어울리다, 적합하다

116 명사 어휘

해설 빈칸은 전치사 in의 목적어 역할을 하는 명사 자리로, 빈칸 뒤 to부정사구의 수식을 받고 있다. '~에 전적인 신뢰를 표현했다(expressed complete faith)'라는 내용이 앞에 있으므로, 빈칸에는 긍정적인 평가의 대상이 되는 명사가 들어가야 한다. 따라서 '제시간에 제품을 배송하는(to deliver the product on time) 역량'이라는 의미를 완성하는 (D) ability가 정답이다.

번역 CEO 요시로 카사이 씨는 제시간에 제품을 배송하는 페어웨이 해양의 역량을 전적으로 신뢰한다고 밝혔다.

어휘 faith 신뢰 ability 능력, 역량 deliver 배달하다, 인도하다 measure 조치, 척도

117 전치사 어휘

해설 빈칸은 접속사 and로 이어진 동명사 구문(attending information sessions and working closely with assigned mentors)을 목적어로 취하는 전치사 자리이며, 빈칸을 포함한 전치사구가 동사 alternate를 수식하고 있다. 따라서 '교대가 되다'라는 뜻의 alternate와 가장 잘 어울리는 전치사를 선택해야 하므로, (C) between이 정답이다. 'alternate between A and B'는 'A와 B를 번갈아 가며 하다, A와 B 사이를 오가다'라는 의미이다. 참고로, alternate는 타동사로도 쓰일 수 있으며 이때는 뒤에 바로 목적어가 온다.

번역 더윈 증권에서 연수생들은 정보 세션에 참석하고 배정된 멘토들과 긴밀하게 협력하는 일을 계속 번갈아 하게 된다.

어휘 trainee 연수생, 수습 직원 assigned 배정된, 할당된

118 명사 자리 _ 동사의 목적어 _ 어휘

해설 빈칸은 동사 had의 목적어 역할을 하는 명사 자리로, 빈칸 앞 no의 수식을 받는다. 명사인 (C) objects와 (D) objection 중에 하나를 선택해야 하는데, 문맥상 '반대하지 않았다'라는 내용이 되어야 자연스러우므로, '반대, 이의'라는 의미의 (D) objection이 정답이 된다. 동명사인 (B) objecting은 일반적인 행위로서의 '반대하는 것'을 나타내며, 소유(had)의 대상이 되기에는 부자연스러우므로 정답이 될 수 없다.

번역 아스트리드 바레토 부사장은 자신이 최고 대표이사직 후보로 고려되는 것에 반대하지 않았다.

어휘 object 사물, 물건 objection to ~에 대한 반대 position 직위

119 형용사 어휘

해설 빈칸은 주격 관계대명사 who의 선행사인 Belinda McKay fans를 보충 설명하는 형용사 자리로, 빈칸 뒤 전치사 to와 함께 쓰이는 형용사가 들어가야 한다. 해당 문장은 팬들이 작가의 최신 자서전을 보면 놀랄 것(will be surprised)이라는 내용으로, 책에 팬들을 놀라게 할 만한 변화가 있음을 시사하고 있다. 따라서 빈칸에는 전치사 to와 함께 쓰여 '~에 익숙한'이라는 의미를 나타내는 (D) accustomed가 들어가야 자연스럽다.

번역 작가의 딱딱한 문체에 익숙한 벨린다 맥케이 팬들은 그녀의 최근 자서전을 보면 놀랄 것이다.

어휘 formal 격식을 차린, (문체 등이) 딱딱한 biography 자서전 fortunate 운 좋은 readable 읽기 쉬운 comparable 비슷한

120 부사 자리 _ 과거분사 수식 _ 어휘

해설 빈칸은 형용사 역할을 하는 과거분사 known and respected를 수식하는 부사 자리이다. 따라서 보기 중 부사인 (B) wider, (C) widely, (D) wide 중 하나를 선택해야 하는데, 문맥상 '널리 알려지고 존경받는'이라는 내용이 되어야 자연스러우므로, '널리(다양한 장소에, 많은 사람들에게)'라는 의미의 (C) widely가 정답이다. wide는 부사로 쓰일 때 '완전히, 활짝, 넓게'라는 뜻으로 주로 물리적인 정도를 나타낸다.

번역 동남아시아 비즈니스 총회에는 이 지역 각국에서 온 널리 알려지고 존경받는 지도자들이 특별히 참석한다.

어휘 feature 특별히 포함하다; 특징 region 지역

121 전치사 어휘

해설 빈칸은 명사구 the high cost of fuel을 목적어로 취하는 전치사 자리이며, 빈칸을 포함한 전치사구가 뒤에 나오는 주절을 수식하고 있다. 따라서 전치사구와 주절의 내용을 자연스럽게 이어주는 전치사를 선택해야 한다. 문맥을 살펴보면, '높은 연료비(the high cost of fuel)'가 '더 작고 더 효율적인(smaller, more efficient) 자동차를 구매한다'의 원인이 되므로, '~ 때문에'라는 의미의 (D) Because of가 정답이 된다.

번역 높은 연료비 때문에 소비자들은 더 작고 더 효율적인 자동차를 구매하고 있다.

어휘 fuel 연료 customer 소비자 efficient 효율적인 instead of ~ 대신에 as well as ~뿐만 아니라

122 동사 어형 _ 시제

해설 빈칸은 주어 Bellworth Medical Clinic의 동사 자리로, 빈칸을 포함한 절이 전치사구 Over the past ten years(지난 10년 동안)의 수식을 받고 있다. 따라서 빈칸에는 과거부터 현재까지의 일을 나타낼 때 쓰이는 현재완료시제가 들어가야 자연스러우므로, (C) has hired가 정답이다.

번역 지난 10년 동안 벨워스 병원은 모든 보안 요구사항에 응하기 위해 애틀란 프로텍션 요원들을 고용했다.

어휘 hire 고용하다 security 보안, 안전

123 명사 어휘

해설 빈칸은 동사 will make의 목적어 역할을 하는 명사 자리로, 빈칸 뒤 to부정사구의 수식을 받고 있다. 따라서 make 및 to deliver the package와 어울리는 명사를 선택해야 한다. 문맥상 '소포를 배달하려는 세 번의 시도를 해보다'라는 내용이 되어야 자연스러우므로, make와 함께 '시도하다'라는 표현을 완성하는 (A) attempts가 정답이다.

번역 운전 기사는 소포를 세 번 배달해 보고 안 되면 당사의 보관소로 반송할 것이다.

어휘 deliver 배달하다 package 소포 warehouse 창고, 보관소 attempt 시도 pursuit (복수형으로) 일[활동], 취미 aim 목표

124 형용사 자리 _ 명사 수식

해설 빈칸은 소유격 관계대명사 whose와 관계사절에서 주어 역할을 하는 명사 effort 사이 자리이므로, effort를 수식해 주는 형용사가 들어가야 한다. 따라서 '집단의, 단합된'이라는 의미의 형용사인 (B) collective가 정답이다. 해당 절에 이미 동사(has resulted)가 있으므로 (A) collect와 (C) collects는 정답이 될 수 없으며, '수집가'를 뜻하는 명사 (D) collector는 effort와 복합명사를 이룰 수 없으므로 빈칸에 들어갈 수 없다.

번역 리버사이드 전 직원에게 축하를 보냅니다. 여러분의 단합된 노력으로 폐기물 처리 비용이 20퍼센트나 절감되었습니다.

어휘 employee 직원 collective 집단의, 공동의 effort 노력 reduction 감소 waste disposal 폐기물 처리

125 부사절 접속사

해설 빈칸 앞뒤에 완전한 절이 있으므로, 빈칸에는 두 개의 절을 연결하는 접속사가 들어가야 한다. 문맥을 살펴보면, 빈칸 이하의 절(we have finished ~ work)이 먼저 일어날 일에 대한 내용이고, 주절(Andrzej Ptak's photography Web site ~ online)이 그 다음에 일어날 일에 대한 내용임을 알 수 있다. 따라서 '일단 ~하면'이라는 의미의 부사절 접속사인 (B) once가 정답이다. 참고로, (A) how는 접속사 역할을 할 경우 명사절을 이끈다.

번역 우리가 안드레이 프탁의 작품을 정리하고 목록 작성을 끝내고 나면, 그의 사진 웹사이트를 온라인에서 볼 수 있을 것이다.

어휘 organize 정리하다 catalog 목록을 작성하다; 목록

126 형용사 자리 _ 목적격 보어

해설 동사가 found, 목적어가 it, ------ to use가 목적격 보어인 절이다. it이 가리키는 것은 the Sunbell XC2 mobile phone이며, 빈칸 이하가 이 휴대폰이 어떤지를 설명해 주고 있다. 따라서 to부정사의 수식을 받아 '사용하기에 편리한'이라는 의미를 완성하는 형용사 (D) convenient가 정답이다.

번역 선벨 XC2 휴대폰을 조기 구매한 사람들에게 받은 초기 의견을 보면 그것이 사용하기에 편리했다는 것을 알 수 있다.

어휘 initial 처음의, 초기의 indicate 나타내다, 시사하다 find ~라고 생각하다[여기다], ~을 알게 되다 convenient 편리한

127 부사절 접속사

해설 빈칸 뒤에 완전한 절과 콤마가 왔으며 빈칸을 포함한 절이 주절(the contractor ~ a shower)을 수식하는 역할을 하므로, 빈칸에는 부사절 접속사가 들어가야 한다. 문맥상 '욕실 공간이 제한되어 있음에도, 세면대 두 개와 샤워기 하나를 넣었다'라는 내용이 되어야 자연스러우므로, 양보의 의미를 나타내는 부사절 접속사 (D) Even though가 정답이다.

번역 비록 욕실 공간이 제한되어 있었지만, 하청업체는 세면대 두 개와 샤워기 하나 넣는 데 성공했다.

어휘 limited 제한된 contractor 계약자, 하청업체 manage to + 동사원형 (가까스로) ~하다 so that ~하기 위해

128 동사 어휘

해설 빈칸 뒤 목적어 as much market-research data as possible과 가장 잘 어울리는 동사를 선택해야 한다. 문맥상 '가능한 한 많은 시장 조사 데이터를 수집하다'라는 내용이 되어야 자연스러우므로, '(자료를) 모으다'라는 의미의 (B) compile이 정답이다.

번역 직원들은 광고 캠페인을 기획하기 전에 가능한 한 많은 시장 조사 데이터를 수집해야 한다.

어휘 compile 엮다, 모으다 advertising campaign 광고 캠페인 equip 장비를 갖추다 endorse (상품을) 홍보하다, 승인하다 compose 구성하다

129 부사절 접속사

해설 빈칸 뒤에 완전한 절과 콤마가 왔으며 빈칸을 포함한 절이 주절(the Barstow Company ~ as well)을 수식하는 역할을 하므로, 빈칸에는 부사절 접속사가 들어가야 한다. 문맥상 '국경일이 목요일이 될 때마다 금요일도 쉴 수 있게 해 준다'라는 내용이 되어야 자연스러우므로, '~할 때마다'라는 의미의 부사절 접속사 (D) Whenever가 정답이다. (A) Even 및 (C) Nearly는 부사로서 품사상 빈칸에 들어갈 수 없으며, (B) For는 이유를 나타내는 접속사로 쓰이는 경우 주절 뒤에 위치해야 하므로 정답이 될 수 없다.

번역 국경일이 목요일이 될 때마다 바스토우 사는 직원들이 금요일도 쉴 수 있게 해 준다.

어휘 national holiday 국경일 fall on (날짜가) ~이다

130 형용사 어휘

해설 빈칸은 주어 역할을 하는 명사 materials를 수식하는 형용사 자리이므로, materials와 가장 잘 어울리는 형용사가 들어가야 한다. 문맥상 '강좌의 보충 자료'라는 의미가 되어야 자연스러우므로, '보충의, 추가의'라는 뜻의 (A) Supplementary가 정답이다.

번역 상급 페르시아어 강좌의 보충 자료에는 오디오 CD와 DVD가 포함됩니다.

어휘 advanced 상급의, 고급의 consequential ~에 따른 persistent 끈질긴 cooperative 협조하는

PART 6

131-134 기사

(9월 3일)—5년 전 브라이언 트랑 씨는 루레이 플레이스 30번지에 '트랑즈 비스트로'라는 자신의 식당을 개업하기 위해 5년 임차 계약을 체결했다. 처음 2년 간은 운영이 꽤 131**힘들었다고** 트랑 씨는 인정한다. "저희는 베트남 중부 지방의 매운 음식을 제공합니다." 그가 설명한다. "요리가 생소한 허브와 매운 맛에 바탕을 두고 있기 132**때문에** 처음에는 장사가 잘 안 됐어요. 손님들의 인기를 끄는 데 시간이 꽤 걸렸죠." 하지만 트랑 씨는 음식이 인기를 끌 것이라고 확신했고, 그의 생각이 맞았다. 133**이제 트랑즈 비스트로에 예약하려면 일주일 전에 해야 한다.** 트랑 씨는 또 다시 5년 임차 계약서에 서명했고, 내년에 공간을 134**개조할** 계획이다.

> 어휘 admit 시인하다, 인정하다 operation 영업 region 지역 cuisine 요리 unfamiliar 낯선 confident 확신하는, 자신하는 popularity 인기 in advance 앞서, 미리

131 형용사 어휘

해설 빈칸은 주어 the first two years of operation을 보충 설명하는 주격 보어 자리로, 처음 2년간 운영이 어땠는지 적절히 묘사하는 형용사가 들어가야 한다. 뒤에 나오는 문장에서 '처음에는 장사가 잘 안 됐어요(We didn't do well at first)'라고 했으므로, '힘든, 도전적인'이라는 의미의 (C) challenging이 정답이 된다.

어휘 competitive 경쟁력 있는, 뒤지지 않는 potential 잠재적인 rewarding 보람 있는, 수익이 나는

132 부사절 접속사

해설 빈칸 뒤 완전한 절(the cuisine ~ flavors)을 이끄는 접속사 자리이며, 빈칸을 포함한 절이 앞에 있는 완전한 절을 수식하고 있으므로, 빈칸에는 부사절 접속사가 들어가야 한다. 따라서 (A) because와 (B) unless 중 하나를 선택해야 하는데, 생소한 허브와 매운 맛에 바탕을 두고 있는 요리(the cuisine is ~ hot flavors)가 처음에 장사가 잘 되지 않았던(We didn't do well at first) 원인이 되므로, '~ 때문에'라는 의미의 (A) because가 정답이다. 참고로, (C) despite는 전치사, (D) besides는 전치사/부사로 절을 이끌 수 없다.

어휘 unless ~하지 않는 한, ~하지 않으면 despite ~에도 불구하고 besides ~에 더하여, 게다가, 또한

133 문맥에 맞는 문장 고르기

번역 (A) 원래 후에 출신인 트랑 씨는 5살 때 가족과 함께 런던으로 왔다.
(B) 이제 트랑즈 비스트로에 예약하려면 일주일 전에 해야 한다.
(C) 이런 상황이 그리 오래 지속될 것 같지는 않았다.
(D) 식당은 3월에 이전할 예정이다.

해설 빈칸 앞 문장에서 트랑 씨가 음식이 인기를 끌 것이라고 확신했으며(Mr. Trang was confident the food would gain in popularity) 그의 생각이 맞았다(he was correct)고 했으므로, 빈칸에는 인기에 따른 결과 혹은 이와 관련된 구체적인 사례를 제시하는 것이 문맥상 자연스럽다. 따라서 (B)가 정답이다.

어휘 relocate 이전하다

134 to부정사 _ 명사적 용법

해설 빈칸은 명사구 the space를 목적어로 취하는 동시에 동사 is planning의 목적어 역할을 하는 자리이므로, to부정사만이 들어갈 수 있다. 따라서 (D) to renovate가 정답이다. 참고로, 타동사 plan은 명사 혹은 to부정사를 목적어로 취한다.

어휘 renovate 개조하다

135-138 설명서 발췌

본 설명서는 말란타 설비의 재고 관리에 대한 지침을 제공합니다. 당사의 선진 제조 공정은 135**정확한** 재고 관리에 좌우됩니다. 재고의 흐름을 면밀하게 유지해야만 비용을 최소화할 수 있고 신속한 발송이 136**가능합니다.** 이러한 목표를 달성하기 위해서는 재고 부족을 방지해야 합니다. 주문이 이루어지는 시점에 재고가 정확한 위치에 있을 때 기본 운송비 및 예상 시간 범위 내에서 배송이 이루어집니다. 137**하지만 이는 예상치 못한 재고 부족이 발생하면 불가능합니다.** 따라서 본 설명서의 절차는 항상 충실하게 138**이행되어야** 합니다.

> 어휘 inventory 재고(품) advanced 선진적인, 고급의 manufacturing procedure 제조 공정 depend on ~에 좌우되다, ~에 달려 있다 accurate 정확한 precise 정밀한 minimize 최소화하다 ensure 보장하다 prompt 신속한, 즉각적인 avoid 피하다, 방지하다 shortage 부족 stock 재고(품) estimated 예상된, 예측된 faithfully 충실하게 implement 실행하다, 이행하다

135 형용사 어휘

해설 빈칸 뒤 명사구 inventory control을 적절히 수식하는 형용사를 선택하는 문제이다. 빈칸 뒤 문장에서 '재고의 흐름을 면밀하게 유지해야만(Only by maintaining a precise flow of inventory)'이라는 특정 조건을 언급했으므로, 빈칸에는 precise와 유사한 의미의 형용사가 들어가야 자연스럽다. 따라서 '정확한, 정밀한'이라는 의미의 (A) accurate이 정답이다.

어휘 seasonal 계절의, 계절적인 expensive 비싼 industrialized 산업화된

136 도치

해설 Only by maintaining a precise flow of inventory와 같이 only가 이끄는 부사구(절)가 강조되어 문장 앞에 나올 경우, 주절의 주어와 (조)동사가 도치된다. 문장의 동사가 be동사이므로, 「be동사＋주어＋~」 순이 되어야 한다. 따라서 (D) are we able to가 정답이다.

137 문맥에 맞는 문장 고르기

번역 (A) 고객님을 위해 비용을 계산했습니다.
(B) 배송은 최소 2주가 소요됩니다.
(C) 유감스럽게도, 일부 품목은 현재 재고가 없습니다.
(D) 하지만 이는 예상치 못한 재고 부족이 발생하면 불가능합니다.

빈칸 앞 문장에서 주문이 이루어지는 시점에 재고가 정확한 위치에 있을 때(When stock is in the correct location ~ ordered) 기본 운송비 및 예상 시간 범위 내에서 배송이 이루어진다(shipments are made ~ time frames)고 했으므로, 이와 관련된 내용이 빈칸에 들어가야 한다. 따라서 보기 중 재고가 있는 경우와 상반되는 내용, 즉 재고 부족이 발생할 경우를 묘사한 (D)가 들어가야 글의 흐름이 자연스러워진다. 여기서 this는 앞 문장의 주절(shipments are made ~ time frames)을 가리키는 지시대명사이다.

어휘 calculate 계산하다 delivery 배송 unfortunately 아쉽게도, 안타깝게도 currently 현재 in stock 재고가 있는 unexpected 예상치 못한 occur 발생하다

138 동사 어휘

해설 빈칸은 must be와 결합하여 주어 the procedures in this manual의 동사 역할을 하는 과거분사 자리로, 부사 faithfully의 수식을 받고 있다. 따라서 procedures 및 faithfully와 어울려 쓰이는 동사를 선택해야 한다. 앞에서 재고 부족을 방지해야 한다(we must avoid shortages)고 하며 재고 관리가 잘 되는 경우와 재고 부족이 발생하는 경우를 차례로 언급했으므로, 빈칸이 포함된 부분은 '그러므로 설명서에 나온 절차가 충실하게 이행되어야 한다'라는 내용이 되어야 자연스럽다. 따라서 '실행된, 이행된'을 의미하는 (A) implemented가 정답이다.

어휘 reproduce 복제하다 correct 수정하다 record 기록하다

139-142 이메일

수신: 앨런 포토 〈aporto@silverwing.ky〉
발신: 터크만 요금 청구 담당 〈billing@tuchmans.ky〉
제목: 자동 결제
날짜: 2월 19일

포토 씨께,

최근 터크만의 자동 결제 시스템에 139가입하신 것을 축하드립니다. 이 편리한 청구 시스템에 등록해 주셔서 감사합니다. 자동 결제는 고객님의 다음 청구 주기에 맞춰 3월 1일에 시작됩니다. 140고객님께서는 더 이상 우편으로 청구서를 받지 않으실 것입니다. 고객님의 명세서는 전자 우편으로 전달되며 납입금은 지정된 고객님의 은행 계좌에서 인출됩니다. 자금이 인출되는 계좌를 141변경할 수 있습니다. 저희 웹사이트 https://www.tuchmans.ky의 '내 계정' 섹션에 로그인하고 자동 결제를 선택한 다음 지시에 따라 대체 계좌 정보를 입력하시면 됩니다. 터크만의 자동 결제를 이용하는 데 142어려움이 있으시면 고객 서비스부에 문의하십시오.

터크만 청구 부서

어휘 recent 최근의 enrollment 등록, 가입 sign up for ~에 신청[가입]하다 convenient 편리한 billing system 결제 시스템 payment 지불(금) statement 명세서, 전표 electronically 전자적으로, 컴퓨터로 deduct 공제하다 designated 지정된 withdraw 인출하다 instruction 지시, 설명 alternate 대체의, 번갈아 나오는

---

139 명사 자리 _ 전치사의 목적어

해설 빈칸은 전치사 on의 목적어 역할을 하는 명사 자리로, 형용사 recent의 수식을 받는다. 따라서 '등록, 가입'이라는 의미의 명사인 (D) enrollment가 정답이다. (A) enroll, (B) enrolled, (C) enrolls는 동사로 품사상 오답이다.

140 문맥에 맞는 문장 고르기

번역 (A) 저희 요금 청구 담당 직원이 기꺼이 도와 드립니다.
　　 (B) 고객님께서 더 이상 우편으로 청구서를 받지 않으실 것입니다.
　　 (C) 오랜 고객 여러분께 감사드립니다.
　　 (D) 당사의 특가품을 이용하십시오.

해설 빈칸 앞 문장에서 자동 결제는 다음 청구 주기에 맞춘 3월 1일에 시작된다(Your automatic payments ~ on 1 March)고 했고, 뒤 문장에서 명세서는 전자 우편으로 전달된다(Your statements will come to you electronically)며 새로운 수령 방식을 제시했다. 따라서 빈칸에 자동 결제의 시작으로 인해 기존의 방식(우편)으로 명세서를 받지 않게 될 것이라는 내용이 들어가야 자연스러우므로, (B)가 정답이다.

어휘 clerk 직원 appreciate 감사하다 take advantage of ~을 이용하다 special offer 특가품, 파격 할인 제품

141 동사 어휘

해설 목적어 the account (from which the funds are withdrawn) 및 문맥에 어울리는 동사를 선택하는 문제이다. 뒤에 나오는 문장에서 '지시에 따라 대체 계정 정보를 입력하세요(follow the instructions ~ alternate account information)'라며 계좌 정보 수정 방식을 설명하고 있으므로, 빈칸이 포함된 부분은 '계좌를 변경할 수 있다'라는 내용이 되어야 자연스럽다. 따라서 (D) change가 정답이다.

어휘 own 소유하다 settle 처리하다 open (계좌를) 개설하다

142 명사 자리 _ 동사의 목적어

해설 빈칸은 동사 have의 목적어 역할을 하는 명사 자리이다. 빈칸이 포함된 부분은 '자동 결제를 이용하는 데 있어 어려움이 있으면'이라는 내용으로, 불특정한 문제나 어려움이 생기는 경우를 나타내고 있다. 따라서 (A) any difficulties가 정답이다. (C) the difficulty는 특정 문제(~하는 것의 어려움)를 지칭할 때 쓰이므로 빈칸에 적절하지 않다.

143-146 편지

12월 12일

레니 하우
222 이스턴 대로
포트 더글러스, 퀸스랜드 4877

하우 씨께,

어윈 지역 협회는 1월 10일 오후 1시부터 8시까지 펀 파크에서 열리는 여름 행사인 파크 페스트를 ¹⁴³**발표하게 된 것**을 기쁘게 생각합니다. 파크 페스트는 다양한 가족 친화적인 활동과 오후 6시에 제공되는 맛있는 야외 만찬을 선보입니다. 1인당 10달러의 참가비가 있습니다. 수익금은 ¹⁴⁴**주로** 공원 개선 프로젝트에 쓰일 예정입니다. 계약 업체를 고용해 공원 부지의 경관을 조성할 계획이며, 일부 금액은 광고 캠페인에 사용될 것입니다.

아주 재미있는 행사가 될 ¹⁴⁵**것입니다**. ¹⁴⁶귀하께서 참석하실 수 있기를 바랍니다.

페이 메이슨-존스
어윈 지역 협회 이사

어휘 **neighbourhood** 지역, 이웃 (사람들) **association** 협회 **feature** 특별히 포함하다; 특징 **numerous** 수많은 **proceeds** 수익금 **primarily** 주로, 우선 **enhancement** 강화, 증진 **contractor** 계약자, 하청업체 **landscape** 조경하다; 조경 **portion** 부분 **advertising campaign** 광고 캠페인

143 동사 어휘

해설 빈칸은 to부정사의 동사원형 자리로, 명사(구) a summer event를 목적어로 취한다. 따라서 a summer event와 어울리는 동사를 선택해야 한다. 해당 편지는 앞으로 열릴 여름 행사를 알리는 내용이므로, '발표하다'라는 의미의 (A) announce가 빈칸에 들어가야 가장 자연스럽다.

어휘 **admit** 시인하다, 인정하다 **recall** 기억하다 **state** 진술하다

144 부사 어휘

해설 주어 The proceeds(자금) 및 동사구 go towards a park enhancement project와 어울려 쓰이는 부사를 선택하는 문제이다. 그 다음 문장을 보면 공원 개선 프로젝트(a park enhancement project)의 일환으로 공원 부지의 경관을 조성하는(landscape the park grounds) 한편 일부 기금을 광고 캠페인에 사용한다(while a smaller portion ~ advertising campaign)고 했으므로, 공원 개선 프로젝트가 수익금의 주된 사용처임을 알 수 있다. 따라서 '주로'라는 의미의 (C) primarily가 정답이다.

어휘 **entirely** 전적으로

145 동사 어형 _ 수일치 _ 시제

해설 빈칸은 단수 주어 This event의 동사 자리이다. 따라서 (B) promises와 (D) promised 중 하나를 선택해야 하는데, 앞에서 행사가 1월 10일에 개최될 예정(to be held ~ on 10 January)이라고 했으므로, 현재 시제인 (B) promises가 정답이 된다. 동명사/현재분사 (C) promising은 단독으로 문장의 동사 역할을 할 수 없으므로 빈칸에 들어갈 수 없다.

146 문맥에 맞는 문장 고르기

번역 (A) 쓰레기를 전부 처리하시면 도움을 주실 수 있습니다.
(B) 공원은 75년 전에 조성되었습니다.
(C) 참석하실 수 있기를 바랍니다.
(D) 펀 파크는 해마다 2만 명의 방문객을 유치합니다.

해설 빈칸 앞 문장에서 '아주 재미있는 행사가 될 것입니다(This event promises to be great fun)'라고 했으므로, 빈칸에는 행사 참여를 독려하는 내용이 들어가야 문맥상 자연스럽다. 따라서 (C)가 정답이다.

어휘 **dispose of** ~을 처리하다 **rubbish** 쓰레기 **establish** 설립하다 **attract** 유치하다

PART 7

147-148 양식

라스티코 사원증
신청서

¹⁴⁷새 라스티코 사원증을 받으시려면 아래 양식을 작성해 주십시오. ¹⁴⁸펜으로만 쓰십시오. 정자로 기재해 주시기 바랍니다.

이름 로라 콘스탄티니   부서 고객 지원부
사원 번호 <u>2378</u>   라스티코 입사일 <u>2월 10일</u>

¹⁴⁷이전 사원증이 ☑ 만료되었다 ☐ 분실되었다 ☐ 파손되었다
(신규 신청은 빈칸으로 남겨두십시오.)

제출 <u>8월 2일</u>   서명 콘스탄티니

어휘 **application** 신청, 지원 **fill out** 작성하다 **print** 인쇄체로 쓰다, 정자로 쓰다 **division** 부서 **expire** 만료되다 **submit** 제출하다

147 세부 사항

번역 콘스탄티니 씨가 양식을 작성한 이유는?
(A) 자신의 신용카드 요금을 승인하기 위하여
(B) 회사에서 새로운 부서로 배정받기 위하여
(C) 증서 갱신을 요청하기 위하여
(D) 장비 분실을 보고하기 위하여

해설 상단의 '새 라스티코 사원증을 받으시려면(To receive a new Lastico employee badge) 아래 양식을 작성해 주십시오(please fill out the following form)'와 하단의 '이전 사원증이 만료되었다(My previous badge expired)'를 통해 콘스탄티니 씨가 사원증 갱신을 요청하기 위해 양식을 작성했음을 알 수 있다. 따라서 (C)가 정답이다.

어휘 **authorize** 승인하다, 허가하다 **assign** 배정하다, 할당하다 **renewal** 갱신 **equipment** 장비

▸▸ Paraphrasing   지문의 **employee badge**
                  → 정답의 **a document**

148 세부 사항

번역 어떤 지시 사항이 포함되어 있는가?

(A) 양식을 보낼 곳
(B) 양식 작성 방법
(C) 신청서 제출 시기
(D) 첨부할 문서

해설 첫 번째 단락에서 펜으로만 쓰라(Write in pen only)고 했고 정자로 기재해 달라(PRINT clearly)고 하며 작성 방법을 지시하고 있으므로, (B)가 정답이다.

어휘 attach 첨부하다

149-150 광고

```
★★★★★★★★★
구인

149더 골든 라군은 몬테고 베이에서 18년째 영업해 오고 있습니다. 저희는 수상 경력이 있는 식당으로 카리브해 전역에서 명성이 높습니다. 현재 종업원 자리에 공석이 있습니다. 직무는 고객 주문 접수, 음식 및 음료 제공, 계산서 준비, 결제 대금 받기를 포함합니다. 경력은 선호 사항이지만 필수 요건은 아닙니다. 저희는 높은 시급과 탄력근무제를 제공합니다. 150이력서와 취업 추천서 세 부를 지참하여 방문하셔서 지원하시기 바랍니다.

더 골든 라군
샤인 킨카이드, 매니저
135 콘체르티나 드라이브
몬테고 베이, 자메이카
영업 시간: 월요일-금요일, 오전 11시-오후 11시
토요일과 일요일, 정오-오후 10시
★★★★★★★★★
```

어휘 serve (음식 등을) 제공하다, (손님의) 시중을 들다 reputation 명성 span 걸치다, 미치다 currently 현재 vacancy 빈자리, 결원 beverage 음료 itemized 항목[품목]별로 구분된 hourly rate 시급 flexible 탄력적인, 유연한 in person 직접[몸소] supply 제공하다, 주다 reference 추천서, 추천인

149 사실 관계 확인

번역 더 골든 라군에 관해 언급된 것은?

(A) 일요일에는 문을 닫는다.
(B) 정기적으로 공석이 있다.
(C) 10년 넘게 영업하고 있다.
(D) 18년 전에 킨카이드 씨가 매입했다.

해설 첫 번째 문장에서 더 골든 라군이 몬테고 베이에서 18년째 영업을 하고 있다(The Golden Lagoon has been serving Montego Bay for 18 years)고 했으므로, (C)가 정답이다.

어휘 regularly 정기적으로 in business 영업[운영] 중인 decade 10년

▶▶ Paraphrasing 지문의 **has been serving**
→ 정답의 **has been in business**
지문의 **for 18 years**
→ 정답의 **for over a decade**

150 사실 관계 확인

번역 지원자에 관해 언급된 것은?

(A) 고정된 일정에 따라 근무할 것이다.
(B) 지원 신청을 하려면 식당에 가야 한다.
(C) 과거 식당에서 일한 경험이 있어야 한다.
(D) 자메이카 음식 요리법을 배울 것이다.

해설 광고의 마지막 문장에서 직접 방문해서 지원하라(Apply in person)며 이력서와 추천서 세 부를 가져와야 한다(supplying a résumé and three employment references)고 했으므로, (B)가 정답이다.

어휘 fixed 고정된 dish 요리

▶▶ Paraphrasing 지문의 **Apply** → 정답의 **to file their job request**
지문의 **in person**
→ 정답의 **must go to the restaurant**

151-152 이메일

```
수신: 직원
발신: 아스타 린드스트롬
제목: 주의
날짜: 4월 11일

전 직원에게:

151보수가 완료되는 동안 내일 오전 8시부터 톨리버 빌딩이 일시적으로 단수된다는 것을 다시 한 번 말씀드립니다. 건물에서 근무하는 직원 대다수가 외부에서 실시하는 소프트웨어 교육에 참석하기 때문에 영향을 받지 않을 것으로 알고 있습니다.

내일 톨리버에서 근무 예정인 분들을 위해 말씀 드리자면, 힐크레스트 수도국이 4시간 이상 단수되지는 않을 것이라고 약속했습니다. 이 시간 동안 전 직원에게 로비에서 병에 든 물을 무료로 제공합니다. 152물 공급이 재개될 때까지 구내식당은 문을 닫습니다. 물이 나올 때 식사 서비스와 음식 판매가 다시 시작됩니다. 불편을 끼쳐 드려 죄송합니다.

아스타 린드스트롬
시설 관리부장
```

어휘 reminder 상기시켜 주는 것, 주의 temporarily 임시로, 일시적으로 shut off 멈추다 repair 수리 complete 완료하다 affect 영향을 주다 assure 안심시키다, 장담하다 complimentary 무료의 meal 식사 resume 재개하다 apologize for ~에 대해 사과하다 inconvenience 불편

151 세부 사항

번역   내일 무슨 일이 발생하는가?

(A) 새 컴퓨터가 도착할 것이다.
(B) 보수 작업이 있을 것이다.
(C) 새로운 고용 정책이 시행될 것이다.
(D) 교육 장소가 발표될 것이다.

해설   첫 번째 단락 초반부에서 보수가 완료되는 동안(while repairs are completed) 내일 오전 8시부터 톨리버 빌딩이 일시적으로 단수된다(the water ~ tomorrow at 8 a.m.)고 했으므로, 보수 작업이 진행된다는 것을 알 수 있다. 따라서 (B)가 정답이다.

어휘   maintenance 유지·보수, 관리   policy 정책   take effect 효력이 발생하다, 시행되다

▸▸ **Paraphrasing**   지문의 repairs → 정답의 Maintenance work

152 사실 관계 확인

번역   오전에 직원들이 톨리버 빌딩에서 할 수 없는 것은?

(A) 새 소프트웨어 사용
(B) 병에 든 물 마시기
(C) 음식 구매하기
(D) 로비 지나가기

해설   오전에 단수가 될 예정이라고 했고, 두 번째 단락 후반부에서 물 공급이 재개될 때까지 구내식당이 문을 닫는다(The cafeteria will remain closed ~ again)며 물이 나올 때 식사 서비스와 음식 판매가 다시 시작된다(At that point meal service and food sales will resume)고 했으므로, 직원들은 음식을 구매할 수가 없다. 따라서 (C)가 정답이다.

153-154 문자 메시지

> **니콜 페르난데스 [오후 12시 23분]**
> 태드, ¹⁵³나 다음 주 월요일에 애머스트에 간다고 말하려고 문자해요.
>
> **태드 예이츠 [오후 12시 25분]**
> 무슨 일이에요?
>
> **니콜 페르난데스 [오후 12시 26분]**
> ¹⁵³애머스트 사무소에서 교육을 요청했어요. 그쪽 강사가 예기치 않게 출장을 가야 해서 대신할 사람이 필요하대요.
>
> **태드 예이츠 [오후 12시 26분]**
> ¹⁵⁴비행기표는 예약했어요?
>
> **니콜 페르난데스 [오후 12시 27분]**
> 이렇게 급하게는 못하죠. ¹⁵⁴운전해서 가요.
>
> **태드 예이츠 [오후 12시 28분]**
> 그렇군요, 잘 다녀와요!
>
> **어휘**   instructor 강사   unexpected 예상치 못한   substitute 대안, 대리; 대신하다   manage to (간신히) ~ 해내다   on short notice 갑자기, 충분한 예고 없이

153 세부 사항

번역   다음 월요일에 페르난데스 씨는 무엇을 할 것인가?

(A) 교육 과정 가르치기
(B) 강사 만나기
(C) 휴가 떠나기
(D) 일자리 지원하기

해설   페르난데스 씨가 오후 12시 23분 메시지에서 다음 주 월요일에 애머스트에 간다(I'll be in Amherst next Monday)고 했고, 그 다음 26분 메시지에서 '애머스트 사무소에서 교육을 요청했다(Our Amherst office requested a training session)'라며 그날 하게 될 업무를 밝혔으므로, (A)가 정답이다.

▸▸ **Paraphrasing**   지문의 a training session
→ 정답의 a training course

154 의도 파악

번역   오후 12시 27분에 페르난데스 씨가 "이렇게 급하게는 못하죠"라고 쓸 때, 그 의도는 무엇인가?

(A) 제시간에 도착하지 못할 것이다.
(B) 비행기로 이동하지 않을 것이다.
(C) 초청을 수락할 수 없다.
(D) 돈을 지불할 수 없다.

해설   예이츠 씨가 오후 12시 26분에 비행기표 예약을 했는지(Did you manage to book a flight?) 묻자 페르난데스 씨가 '이렇게 급하게는 못하죠(Not on such short notice)'라고 답한 후, 운전해서 간다(I'll drive)고 했다. 따라서 시간상 비행기표 예약이 불가능하여 항공편으로 갈 수 없다는 것을 나타내고 있으므로, (B)가 정답이다.

어휘   accept 수락하다

155-157 이메일

> 수신: 제이크 테라 〈jtaera@tritmail.com〉
> 발신: 나탈리 새터 〈nsatter@coldings.com〉
> 제목: 정보
> 날짜: 9월 30일
> 첨부: 📎 콜딩스 1
>
> 테라 씨께:
>
> 콜딩스 홈 스토어 가족이 되신 것을 환영합니다! ¹⁵⁵귀하께서는 영업 사원으로 채용되셨습니다. 교육은 10월 8일 오전 8시 30분에 크로스빌 가 42번지에 있는 오클랜드 매장에서 시작합니다. 콜딩스 홈 스토어 팀원으로 오리엔테이션을 시작하려면 인사과에 보고하십시오. ¹⁵⁶당사와 함께하는 첫 2주 동안에는 팀 활동 및 콜딩스 홈 스토어에 근무하면서 얻을 수 있는 많은 혜택에 대해 알게 되실 겁니다. 근무 시간은 오전 8시 30분부터 오후 5시까지입니다. ¹⁵⁶교육을 마친 후에는 다른 근무조에 배정되실 수 있으며 유연 연차제, 병가, 직원 할인 등의 혜택을 받으실 수 있습니다.
>
> ¹⁵⁷영업 사원직을 수락할 의사가 있음을 나타내는 첨부 문서에 서명하고 반송해 주십시오. 궁금하신 내용이 있거나 안내가 필요하시면 알려 주십시오. 10월 8일 오클랜드 매장에서 뵙기를 고대합니다.

나탈리 새터

인사 담당자

> 어휘 sales associate 영업 사원 team approach 팀 활동, 팀 접근 방식 benefit (회사에서 주는) 수당, 혜택 assign 배정하다 be eligible for ~의 자격이 되다 flexible 유연한, 탄력적인 willingness 의향 directions 안내, 조언

155 주제 / 목적

번역 이메일의 목적은?

(A) 직원에게 감사하기 위하여

(B) 직업 관련 정보를 제공하기 위하여

(C) 새로운 규정을 설명하기 위하여

(D) 특별 할인 행사를 알리기 위하여

해설 첫 번째 단락에서 테라 씨가 영업 사원으로 채용되었다(You have been hired as a sales associate)는 소식을 알리며 해당 단락 전반에서 교육, 업무 시간, 직원 혜택 등의 정보를 제공하고 있으므로, 채용에 따른 직업 관련 정보를 제공하기 위한 이메일임을 알 수 있다. 따라서 (B)가 정답이다.

156 추론 / 암시

번역 새터 씨에 따르면 2주 후에 무슨 일이 있겠는가?

(A) 테라 씨의 근무 일정이 변경될 수도 있다.

(B) 테라 씨가 다른 지점으로 전출될 수도 있다.

(C) 회사에서 테라 씨에게 새로운 업무를 교육할 수도 있다.

(D) 회사에서 테라 씨에게 새로운 혜택에 관한 정보를 우편으로 보낼 수도 있다.

어휘 transfer 이동하다, 이동시키다

해설 첫 번째 단락 중반부에서 첫 2주 동안(first two weeks) 교육을 받으면서 오전 8시 30분부터 오후 5시까지 근무하게 된다고 했는데, 그 다음 문장에서 교육 후에는 다른 근무조에 배정될 수 있다(After training, you might be assigned to a different work shift)고 했으므로, 테라 씨의 근무 일정이 변경될 수도 있다는 것을 추론할 수 있다. 따라서 (A)가 정답이다.

> ▸▸ Paraphrasing 지문의 might be assigned to a different work shift
> → 정답의 work schedule might change

157 세부 사항

번역 새터 씨가 이메일과 함께 보낸 것은?

(A) 매장 배치도

(B) 행사 일정

(C) 혜택 일람표

(D) 고용 계약서

해설 두 번째 단락의 '영업 사원직을 수락할 의사가 있음을 나타내는 첨부 문서에 서명하고 반송해 주십시오(Please ~ the attached document indicating your willingness to accept the position as sales associate)'라는 문구를 통해 새터 씨가 고용 계약서를 첨부했음을 알 수 있다. 따라서 (D)가 정답이다.

> ▸▸ Paraphrasing 지문의 attached
> → 질문의 send with the e-mail
> 지문의 document indicating your willingness to accept the position
> → 정답의 employment agreement

158-160 보도 자료

> | 즉시 보도용 | 연락처: 데스몬드 호크스, 홍보실 |
> | | 전화: (02) 5555 6506 |
> | | 이메일: dhawkes@carlisle.org.au |
>
> **시드니 칼라일 미술관에서 열리는**
> **새 전시회**
>
> 시드니 (6월 3일)—¹⁵⁸칼라일 미술관의 최신 전시회, 〈딥 워터즈〉가 6월 15일에 개최된다. 이번 전시회에서는 전 세계에 있는 대양의 아름다움과 광활함을 묘사한 사실주의 회화 및 추상화 38점을 선보인다. ¹⁵⁹모두 시드니를 중심으로 활동하는 호주 화가들의 작품으로 비평가들의 극찬을 받은 유화 작가 해럴드 번스타인의 작품 6점도 포함된다.
>
> 전시회는 7월 15일까지 열릴 예정이다. 입장권 가격은 10달러이다. 미술관 방문객들은 화요일, 수요일, 목요일에는 오전 9시부터 오후 4시까지, 금요일과 토요일에는 오후 2시부터 오후 9시까지 전시회를 관람할 수 있다. 전시회가 열리는 동안 매일 적어도 화가 1명이 출연해 창작 과정에 관한 방문객의 질문에 답할 예정이다. 번스타인 씨는 6월 30일에만 만날 수 있다.
>
> ¹⁶⁰7월 23일에는 이 전시회가 멜버른의 뮤리엘 미술관에서 열리며, 대양을 주제로 한 멜버른 화가들의 그림들도 컬렉션에 추가될 예정이다.

> 어휘 exhibition 전시회 realist (미술·예술 분야) 사실주의의 abstract 추상적인 portray 묘사하다, 그리다 vastness 광활함 critically acclaimed 비평가들의 극찬을 받은 present (~에) 참석한, 있는 available (사람이) ~할 시간이 있는

158 주제 / 목적

번역 보도 자료의 목적 중 하나는 무엇인가?

(A) 곧 있을 미술품 전시회 광고

(B) 구매 가능한 그림 홍보

(C) 미술관 소유주 소개

(D) 새 미술관 개관 발표

해설 첫 번째 단락의 '칼라일 미술관의 최신 전시회, 〈딥 워터즈〉가 6월 15일에 개최된다(The Carlisle Art Museum's latest exhibition, *Deep Waters*, will open on 15 June)'라는 문구를 통해 보도 자료의 목적 중 하나가 새로 시작할 전시회를 홍보하기 위함이라는 것을 알 수 있다. 따라서 (A)가 정답이다.

어휘 publicize 홍보하다 profile (인물을) 소개하다

159　세부 사항

번역　번스타인 씨는 누구인가?

(A) 미술 평론가
(B) 미술관 관장
(C) 홍보 전문가
(D) 미술가

해설　첫 번째 단락의 마지막 문장에서 전시 작품 중에는 비평가들의 호평을 받은 유화 작가 해럴드 번스타인의 작품 6점도 포함된다(among them ~ oil painter Harold Bernstein)고 했으므로, 번스타인 씨가 미술가라는 것을 알 수 있다. 따라서 (D)가 정답이다.

>> **Paraphrasing**　　지문의 oil painter → 정답의 artist

160　추론 / 암시

번역　멜버른에서 열리는 전시회에 관해 암시된 것은?

(A) 저녁 시간에만 일반 대중에게 공개된다.
(B) 시드니 전시회보다 더 많은 그림이 포함된다.
(C) 화가들이 회화 기법을 시연한다.
(D) 대양 그림뿐만 아니라 풍경화도 포함된다.

해설　보도 자료 첫 번째 단락에서 시드니에서 열릴 예정인 〈딥 워터스〉 전시회를 소개했는데, 세 번째 단락에 동일한 전시회가 7월 23일에 멜버른의 뮤리엘 미술관에서 열릴 예정(the exhibition will open ~ in Melbourne)이며 컬렉션에 멜버른 작가들의 작품도 추가될 것이라(paintings from Melbourne artists will be added to the collection)고 했으므로, 시드니 전시회보다 더 많은 그림이 전시된다는 것을 알 수 있다. 따라서 (B)가 정답이다.

어휘　demonstration 시연　landscape 풍경　in addition to ~에 더하여

161-163　이메일

발신: evaluation@crawforddds.com
수신: trosinsky@mailssen.com
제목: 크로포드 디자인 대회
날짜: 4월 2일

로진스키 씨께,

¹⁶¹크로포드 디자인 스튜디오 어워즈 콘테스트에 응모해 주셔서 감사합니다. 오늘 총 9장의 사진과 18페이지의 설명서 파일을 포함하는, "낡은 렉스토 공장 복원"이라는 제목이 붙여진 귀하의 프로젝트를 받았습니다. ¹⁶³귀하의 제출물은 추가 절차를 위해 전달되었으며, 응모 번호 P1298이 지정되었습니다. 귀하의 응모작과 관련하여 당사에 문의하실 때 이것을 사용하시기 바랍니다.

이제 귀하의 프로젝트는 당사의 사내 전문가 및 외부 디자이너로 구성된 심사위원단이 검토할 예정입니다. ¹⁶²당사 웹사이트의 기본 메뉴에 있는 "처리 중인 제출물" 링크를 통해 응모작 진행 현황을 확인할 수 있습니다.

문의 사항이 있으시면 언제든 저희에게 전화 주십시오.

크로포드 디자인 스튜디오 드림

어휘　description 묘사, 설명　submission 제출(물)　forward 전달하다　processing 처리　assign 배정하다　consist of ~으로 구성되다　in-house 사내의　expert 전문가　status 상태　process 처리하다　hesitate 주저하다, 망설이다

161　주제 / 목적

번역　이메일의 목적은?

(A) 분실 문서 보고
(B) 건설비 문의
(C) 자료 수령 확인
(D) 추가 사진 요청

해설　첫 번째 단락에서 로진스키 씨에게 크로포드 디자인 스튜디오 어워즈 콘테스트에 응모해 주어 감사하다(Thank you for entering the Crawford Design Studio Awards Contest)고 인사한 후 사진(photographs)과 설명서 파일(description file)을 포함한 프로젝트를 받았다(we received your project)고 확인해 주었으므로, (C)가 정답이다.

어휘　missing 분실된　inquire 문의하다　confirm 확인해 주다　receipt 수령　materials 자료　additional 추가의

162　세부 사항

번역　로진스키 씨가 온라인으로 하라고 권고 받은 사항은?

(A) 콘테스트 규정 읽기
(B) 지도와 길 안내 입수하기
(C) 연락 정보 수정하기
(D) 제출물 진행 현황 파악하기

해설　두 번째 단락 후반부에서 스튜디오 웹사이트의 기본 메뉴에 있는 "처리 중인 제출물" 링크를 통해 응모작 진행 현황을 확인할 수 있다(check on the status of your entry ~ in our Web site's Main Menu)고 했으므로, (D)가 정답이다.

어휘　obtain 입수하다, 얻다　progress 진행, 경과

>> **Paraphrasing**　　지문의 Web site → 질문의 online
지문의 check on the status of your entry → 정답의 Track the progress of her submission

163　문장 삽입

번역　[1], [2], [3], [4]로 표시된 곳 중에서 다음 문장이 들어가기에 가장 적합한 곳은?

"귀하의 응모작과 관련하여 당사에 문의하실 때 이것을 사용하시기 바랍니다."

(A) [1]
(B) [2]
(C) [3]
(D) [4]

해설 주어진 문장에서 '귀하의 응모작과 관련하여 문의할 때 이것을 사용하기 바란다(Please use it ~ regarding your entry)'라고 했으므로, 앞 문장에 '이것(it)'이 가리키는 대상이 있어야 하며, 이는 문의 시 사용할 수 있는 것이어야 한다. 첫 번째 단락의 마지막 문장에서 로진스키 씨의 제출물에 응모 번호 P1298이 지정되었다(Your submission ~ has been assigned the entry number P1298)라고 했으므로, 이 내용 다음에 주어진 문장이 들어가야 글의 흐름이 자연스러워진다. 따라서 (B)가 정답이다.

164-167 기사

5월 5일—[164]보스턴 법률 회사 워너 앤 아네스가 필라델피아 법률 회사 해밀턴 존스와 합병하여 워너, 해밀턴, 앤 어소시에이츠를 설립할 예정이라고 오늘 아침 발표했다. 이번 합병으로 이 회사는 655명 이상의 변호사를 거느린 미국 북동부 지역의 가장 큰 법률 회사가 될 것이다.

"기업 문화와 철학이 비슷하며 경영 상태가 양호한 두 회사로서는 반가운 합병입니다." 과거 워너 앤 아네스의 공동이사였던 안드레아 워너 씨가 말했다. 그는 워너, 해밀턴, 앤 어소시에이츠의 대표 이사를 맡을 예정이다. "우리의 결합된 전문성으로 워너, 해밀턴, 앤 어소시에이츠는 의뢰인들에게 훨씬 더 높은 수준의 상담과 서비스를 제공하는 독보적 위치에 서게 될 겁니다. [165]우리는 보스턴과 필라델리아에서 계속 영업하기를 바라며 앞으로 12개월 안에 하트포드에도 사무소를 열게 되기를 기대합니다."

보도 자료에 따르면, [166]워너 씨는 노동자의 권리, 동일 임금, 그리고 사회 정의와 관련된 중요한 소송에서 전국의 의뢰인들을 대변함으로써 주목을 받았다.

이 회사는 자사의 현 변호사 및 직원들을 계속 고용할 예정이며, 보도자료에 따르면 "[167]원활한 이행을 보장하기 위해 각 회사의 대표이사들로 구성된 경영진을 결합할 것"이라고 한다.

어휘 merge 합병하다 attorney 변호사 merger 합병, 통합 philosophy 철학 codirector 공동 이사 partner 공동 경영자, (법조계) 파트너 변호사 expertise 전문 지식, 전문 기술 uniquely 특별하게, 독보적으로 press release 보도 자료, 언론 발표 garner 얻다, 모으다 attention 주목 representation 대변 prominent 두드러진, 유명한 expect 예상하다, ~할 셈이다 seamless 끊김 없는, 매끄러운 transition 전환, 이행, 과도기

164 주제 / 목적

번역 기사를 작성한 이유는?

(A) 저명한 변호사의 경력을 소개하기 위해
(B) 법률 서비스를 홍보하기 위해
(C) 두 회사의 합병에 대해 이야기하기 위해
(D) 회사의 이전을 알리기 위해

해설 첫 번째 단락에서 보스턴 법률 회사 워너 앤 아네스가 필라델피아 법률 회사 해밀턴 존스와 합병하여 워너, 해밀턴, 앤 어소시에이츠를 설립할 예정이라고 오늘 아침 발표했다(Boston law firm Warner and Arnes ~ that it is merging with the Philadelphia law firm Hamilton Jones to create Warner, Hamilton, and Associates)고 했고, 기사 전반에 걸쳐 관련 내용에 대해 서술하고 있으므로, (C)가 정답이다.

어휘 promote 홍보하다 relocation 이전

165 세부 사항

번역 워너, 해밀턴, 앤 어소시에이츠는 무엇을 할 계획인가?

(A) 변호사 추가 고용
(B) 3번째 도시로 확장
(C) 경영진 교체
(D) 필라델피아 사무소 폐쇄

해설 두 번째 단락에 나온 안드레아 워너 씨의 인터뷰 내용을 보면, 합병 후 보스턴과 필라델피아에서 계속 영업하기를 바라며(We look forward to continuing our practices in Boston and Philadelphia) 앞으로 12개월 안에 하트포드에도 사무소를 열게 되기를 기대한다(expect to open yet another office in Hartford within the next twelve months)고 했으므로, (B)가 정답이다.

▸▸ Paraphrasing 지문의 open yet another office in Hartford → 정답의 Expand to a third city

166 추론 / 암시

번역 워너 씨에 관해 암시된 것은?

(A) 하트포드가 주 활동 무대이다.
(B) 곧 은퇴할 계획이다.
(C) 가끔 무료 법률 상담을 제공한다.
(D) 전국적으로 잘 알려져 있다.

해설 세 번째 단락에서 워너 씨가 노동자의 권리, 동일 임금, 그리고 사회 정의와 관련된 중요한 소송(prominent cases involving workers' rights, equal pay, and social justice)에서 전국의 의뢰인들을 대변해 주목을 받았다(Ms. Warner has garnered attention through her representation of clients across the country)고 했으므로, 그녀가 전국적으로 유명하다는 것을 추론할 수 있다. 따라서 (D)가 정답이다.

▸▸ Paraphrasing 지문의 has garnered attention → 정답의 is well-known
지문의 across the country → 정답의 nationally

167 동의어 찾기

번역 네 번째 단락 4행의 "seamless"와 의미상 가장 가까운 것은?

(A) 하나로
(B) 문제 없이
(C) 근거리에서
(D) 서두르지 않고

해설 "seamless"를 포함한 부분은 이행을 위해(to ensure a seamless transition) 각 회사의 대표이사들로 구성된 경영진을 결합할 것이라는 내용으로, 여기서 seamless는 '원활한, 매끄러운'이라는 뜻으로 쓰였다. 따라서 '문제 없이'라는 의미의 (B) without problems가 정답이다.

168-171 이메일

수신: maria_bellandini@pweb.net

발신: thomas.mclaren@delicatessenmag.com

날짜: 10월 2일 화요일

제목: 음식 사진 기사

벨란디니 씨께:

〈델리카트슨 잡지〉 다음 호에 게재될 예정이던 귀하의 기사에 관해 알려드릴 소식이 있습니다. 어제 주요 광고주가 본사와의 계약을 취소했다는 것을 알게 되었고, 그에 따라 저희는 발간 예정인 호의 페이지 수를 줄여야 합니다. 대단히 안타까운 일이지만, ¹⁶⁸이 광고가 없으면 잡지를 현재의 형태로 출판할 수 있는 충분한 자금 여력이 저희에게는 없습니다.

^{170(A)}독자들이 이탈리아에서의 귀하의 경험에 대해 즐겨 읽는다는 사실을 알고 있습니다. ¹⁶⁹음식 사진 작가로 일하는 것에 대한 8페이지 분량의 기사는 훌륭하지만, 더 얇아진 호에 맞추기 위해서는 30퍼센트 정도를 줄여야 합니다. ^{170(C), 171}저희 잡지의 다음 호에 기사가 게재되는 것에 동의하시기를 진심으로 바라지만, 나중에 전체 기사를 출판하는 것을 선호하신다 해도 이해합니다. 하지만 잡지 산업이 늘 안정적인 사업은 아니기 때문에 ^{170(C)}나중에 귀하의 이야기를 실을 지면이 있을지 알 수 없다는 점을 말씀드리고 싶습니다. 물론, 이것은 귀하의 선택이며 어떤 결정을 내리시든 그 결정을 존중하겠습니다.

^{170(D), 171}어떻게 하기를 원하시는지 최대한 빨리 알려 주십시오. 기사 편집에 동의하신다면, 월요일까지 새로 고친 글이 필요합니다.

토마스 맥라렌, 편집장

어휘 regarding ~에 관한 publish 발간하다, 발행하다 advertiser 광고주 contract 계약 reduce 줄이다 upcoming 다가오는 extremely 지극히 unfortunate 불행한 ad 광고(= advertisement) current 현재의 slim 얇은 stable 안정적인 edit 편집하다

168 추론 / 암시

번역 〈델리카트슨 잡지〉에 관해 암시된 것은?

(A) 다른 잡지와 합병할 계획이다.

(B) 직원은 구독료가 할인된다.

(C) 자금을 광고에 의존한다.

(D) 필자들에게 장기 계약을 제공한다.

해설 첫 번째 단락의 마지막 문장에서 광고가 없으면 잡지를 현재의 형태로 출판할 수 있는 충분한 자금 여력이 없다(we just do not have enough money without these ads ~ format)고 했으므로, 잡지 발행에 필요한 자금을 광고에 의존한다는 것을 추론할 수 있다. 따라서 (C)가 정답이다.

어휘 merge 합병하다 subscription 구독 long-term 장기의

> ▶ Paraphrasing 지문의 do not have enough money without these ads → 정답의 relies on advertisements for funding

169 추론 / 암시

번역 벨란디니 씨는 기사를 어떻게 수정하겠는가?

(A) 길이를 줄인다.

(B) 주제를 바꾼다.

(C) 정보를 보충한다.

(D) 음식 사진을 더 많이 넣는다.

해설 두 번째 단락에서 벨란디니 씨가 쓰는 8페이지 분량의 기사가 훌륭하지만(While your eight-page story ~ excellent), 더 얇아진 호에 들어가려면 30퍼센트 정도 줄여야 한다(it will need to be cut by about thirty percent)고 했으므로, 벨란디니 씨가 기사를 수정한다면 길이를 줄일 것임을 추론할 수 있다. 따라서 (A)가 정답이다.

> ▶ Paraphrasing 지문의 be cut by about thirty percent → 정답의 making it shorter

170 사실 확인 문제

번역 맥라렌 씨가 벨란디니 씨에게 암시하지 않은 것은?

(A) 그녀의 이전 기사들은 호평을 받았다.

(B) 그녀의 기사를 다른 잡지에 제출해야 한다.

(C) 추후 그녀의 기사 전체가 출판되지 않을 수 있다.

(D) 그녀의 결정을 그에게 알려야 한다.

해설 두 번째 단락의 '독자들이 이탈리아에서의 귀하의 경험에 대해 즐겨 읽습니다(readers have enjoyed reading about your experiences in Italy)'에서 (A)를, '나중에 전체 기사를 출판하는 편을 선호하신다 해도 이해합니다(I will understand ~ the article published in full at a later time)' 및 '앞으로 귀하의 이야기를 실을 지면이 있을지 알 수 없습니다(I do not know if there will be space for your story in the future)'에서 (C)를, 마지막 단락의 '어떻게 하기를 원하시는지 최대한 빨리 알려주십시오(Please let me know ~ what you would like to do)'에서 (D)를 확인할 수 있다. 그러나 그녀가 기사를 다른 잡지에 제출해야 한다고 제안하지는 않았으므로, (B)가 정답이다.

> ▶ Paraphrasing 지문의 readers have enjoyed reading → 보기 (A)의 were well liked
> 지문의 let me know what you would like to do → 보기 (D)의 notify him of her decision

171 문장 삽입

번역 [1], [2], [3], [4]로 표시된 곳 중에서 다음 문장이 들어가기에 가장 적합한 곳은?

"물론, 이것은 귀하의 선택이며 어떤 결정을 내리시든 그 결정을 존중하겠습니다."

(A) [1]

(B) [2]

(C) [3]

(D) [4]

해설 주어진 문장에서 '이것은 귀하의 선택이며(this is your choice) 어떤 결정을 내리든 그 결정을 존중하겠습니다(I will respect whatever decision you make)'라고 했으므로, 이 문장 전에 결정을 내릴 사항이 언급되어야 한다. [4] 앞 부분을 보면, '다음 호에 기사가 게재되는 것에 동의하시기를 진심으로 바라지만(Although I sincerely hope ~ your article published in our upcoming issue), 나중에 전체 기사를 출판하는 것을 선호하신다 해도 이해합니다(I will understand ~ the article published in full at a later time)'라며 기사를 줄여서 다음 호에 게재할지, 나중에 전체 기사로 출판할지 두 가지 선택권을 제시하고 있다. 또한 [4] 뒤에서 결정을 재촉하고 있으므로, (D)가 정답이다.

172-175 문자 메시지

델로이 게로우 (오후 1시 29분):

안녕하세요, 치체스터 씨. ¹⁷²회사 이름 마그나룩과 로고가 있는 티셔츠 10벌을 더 주문하고 싶어요. 스몰 사이즈 4벌, 미디엄 사이즈 2벌, 라지 사이즈 4벌이 필요합니다. 금요일까지 납품해 주실 수 있을까요?

니나 치체스터 (오후 1시 32분):

오늘로부터 이틀 뒤네요. ¹⁷⁴속달 주문료 75달러가 추가됩니다.

델로이 게로우 (오후 1시 34분):

수수료를 내지 않으려면 어떻게 해야 하죠?

니나 치체스터 (오후 1시 36분):

¹⁷⁴표준 5일 생산 옵션을 선택하시면 됩니다. 다음 주 월요일에 주문품이 준비됩니다.

델로이 게로우 (오후 1시 38분):

어쩔 수 없네요. ¹⁷³,¹⁷⁴이번 금요일부터 근무를 시작하는 직원들이 있는데 그쪽은 오전 8시에 문을 여니까 그 시간에 셔츠를 가지러 가도 될까요?

니나 치체스터 (오후 1시 39분):

주문품 수거 시간은 대체로 오후 1시부터지만 오전 8시까지 준비해 놓을게요.

델로이 게로우 (오후 1시 41분):

고마워요. 실은 제 비서가 가지러 갈 거예요.

니나 치체스터 (오후 1시 42분):

괜찮아요. ¹⁷⁵로고를 다시 이메일로 보내 주시겠어요? 로고를 저장해 두었던 컴퓨터가 고장이 나서 수리를 기다리고 있어요.

델로이 게로우 (오후 1시 44분):

¹⁷⁵그럴게요. 고마워요, 당신이 갖고 있는 저희 신용카드 정보로 결제해 주세요.

어휘 feature 특별히 포함하다 fill an order (주문한 제품을) 납품하다 rush-order 급한 주문 see to it 확실하게 하다, 확실히 ~하게 하다 assistant 비서 crash 고장 나다 repair 수리

172 추론 / 암시

번역 치체스터 씨가 일하는 회사에 관해 암시된 것은?

(A) 현재 라지 사이즈 셔츠 재고가 없다.
(B) 이전에 게로우 씨에게 납품한 적이 있다.
(C) 대량 주문은 할인해 준다.
(D) 매일 저녁 문을 연다.

해설 게로우 씨가 오후 1시 29분에 보낸 '회사 이름 마그나룩과 로고가 있는 티셔츠 10벌을 더 주문하고 싶어요(we'd like to order another 10 shirts, ~ its logo)'라는 메시지를 통해 치체스터 씨의 회사가 이전에 게로우 씨의 주문을 처리한 적이 있음을 추론할 수 있다. 따라서 (B)가 정답이다.

어휘 in stock 재고가 있는

173 세부 사항

번역 게로우 씨가 새 셔츠를 주문하는 이유는?

(A) 추가로 직원을 채용했다.
(B) 예상했던 것보다 더 많이 판매되었다.
(C) 회사 로고가 바뀌었다.
(D) 현재 사용하는 스타일이 낡았다.

해설 게로우 씨의 오후 1시 38분 메시지를 보면 이번 금요일부터 근무를 시작하는 직원들이 있다(we have employees starting this Friday)고 했으므로, 신입 직원들을 위해 셔츠를 주문했다는 것을 알 수 있다. 따라서 (A)가 정답이다.

어휘 anticipate 예상하다 outdated 낡은, 구식인

174 의도 파악

번역 오후 1시 38분에 게로우 씨가 "어쩔 수 없네요"라고 쓸 때, 그 의도는 무엇인가?

(A) 속달 주문료 75달러를 지불할 것이다.
(B) 자신의 비서에게 도와 달라고 할 것이다.
(C) 오후 1시에 치체스터 씨를 만날 것이다.
(D) 표준 생산 옵션을 선택할 것이다.

해설 게로우 씨가 오후 1시 34분에 속달 주문료(a $75 rush-order fee)를 내지 않을 방법을 물어보자 치체스터 씨가 표준 5일 생산 옵션을 선택하면 된다(By choosing the standard 5-day production option)고 하며 다음 주 월요일에 주문이 준비될 것(Your order would be ready Monday of next week)이라고 했다. 이에 대해 게로우 씨가 금요일부터 근무를 시작하는 직원이 있어(we have employees starting this Friday) 어쩔 수 없다고 한 것이므로, 그가 속달 주문료 75달러를 지불하여 제품을 일찍 받고자 한다는 것을 추론할 수 있다. 따라서 (A)가 정답이다.

175 추론 / 암시

번역 게로우 씨는 다음에 무엇을 하겠는가?

(A) 치체스터 씨에게 결제 정보를 제공한다.
(B) 치체스터 씨와 회의 일정을 잡는다.
(C) 치체스터 씨에게 이메일을 보낸다.
(D) 치체스터 씨의 컴퓨터를 수리한다.

해설 치체스터 씨가 오후 1시 42분 메시지에서 로고를 다시 이메일로 보내 달라(Could you please e-mail me your logo again?)고 요청했고, 이에 대해 게로우 씨가 오후 1시 44분 메시지에서 '그럴게요 (Will do)'라고 응답했다. 따라서 게로우 씨가 이메일로 로고를 보낼 것임을 추론할 수 있으므로, (C)가 정답이다.

176-180 이메일 + 공지

수신: staffmailinglist@coltonmedical.org
발신: 멜빈 마이어스 〈mmyers@coltonmedical.org〉
날짜: 6월 10일
제목: 주차 구역 재배정

동료 여러분께:

6월 18일 콜튼 의학 영양 센터 신관에서 작업팀이 공사를 시작한다는 것을 모두에게 다시 한 번 알려드립니다.

176, 179 6월 15일부터 공사 완료가 예상되는 8월 20일까지 F와 G 주차 구역이 폐쇄됩니다. 177 현재 F와 G 구역에 주차를 배정받은 직원들은 임시 '고객' 주차 스티커를 받게 되며, 고객 주차장에 주차해야 합니다. 시설 관리 사무소에서 오늘 오후 4시 전에 직원 우편함에 스티커를 넣어 둘 예정입니다. 스티커는 자동차 운전석 옆 유리창에 붙여야 합니다.

F와 G 주차 구역으로 가는 출입구 도로를 폐쇄해 공사장 접근 도로를 만들어질 예정입니다. 178 이로 인해 경비동과 연못으로 가는 길도 막히게 됩니다. 하지만 이 곳으로 가는 임시 대체 진입로를 만들 예정입니다. 178 과도한 교통량을 방지하려면 꼭 필요한 경우에만 이 장소들을 방문해 주세요. 본관 입구에 있는 안내소는 공사 기간에도 계속 개방됩니다.

주차 스티커 관련해서 궁금한 내용이 있으시면 바로 저에게 이메일을 보내 주세요.

멜빈 마이어스
시설 관리부

어휘 construction 건설, 공사 nutrition 영양 effective ~부터 시행[발효]되는 currently 현재 assign 배정하다 temporary 임시의 garage 주차장, 차고 property 부동산, 건물 maintenance 관리, 유지·보수 vehicle 차량 access 진입, 접근 security 보안, 안전 alternative 대안이 되는 eliminate 없애다 excessive 과도한 absolutely 반드시, 절대적으로

콜튼 의대 캠퍼스 안내소에 오신 것을 환영합니다
들어가시기 전에 수속을 밟으십시오.

직원 여러분께 알립니다:
179 F와 G 주차 구역이 9월 10일까지 폐쇄됩니다

평소 이 구역을 이용하는 직원으로 임시 주차 스티커를 받지 못한 분은 경비실에서 요청하십시오. 유효한 출입 카드 및 사원증이 필요합니다.

180 모든 통로, 임시 휴게소, 공사용 텐트를 포함해 인도 부근에 주차된 차는 즉시 견인됩니다. 유리창에 스티커를 붙이지 않고 주차장에 주차

한 차량 소유주에게는 하루에 25달러의 벌금이 부과됩니다.

경비원들이 도와 드리겠습니다.

어휘 proceed 진행하다, 계속하다 normally 평소, 보통 request 요청하다 valid 유효한 immediately 즉시 tow 견인하다 pedestrian 도보의; 보행자 fine 벌금을 부과하다; 벌금

176 세부 사항

번역 주차 구역이 폐쇄되고 있는 이유는?

(A) 재포장되고 있다.
(B) 고객용으로 따로 남겨 두고 있다.
(C) 주차 구역에서 야외 행사가 열릴 예정이다.
(D) 공사가 시작될 예정이다.

해설 이메일의 두 번째 단락에서 6월 15일부터 공사 완료가 예상되는 8월 20일까지 F와 G 주차 구역이 폐쇄된다(parking areas F and G will be closed until August 20, when construction is expected to be completed)고 했으므로, (D)가 정답이다.

어휘 resurface (도로 등의 표면을) 재포장하다 reserve (자리 등을) 따로 잡아두다

177 세부 사항

번역 이메일에 따르면 임시 주차 스티커를 받을 사람은?

(A) 의대 캠퍼스를 방문하는 사람
(B) 평소 F와 G 구역에 주차하는 사람
(C) 평소 주차장에 주차하는 사람
(D) 시설 관리소에 주차 스티커를 요청하는 사람

해설 이메일의 두 번째 단락에서 현재 F와 G구역에 주차를 배정받은 직원들(Staff currently assigned to park in areas F and G)은 임시 '고객' 주차 스티커(temporary "guest" parking stickers)를 받게 된다고 했으므로, (B)가 정답이다.

▶ Paraphrasing 지문의 be given → 질문의 receive
지문의 Staff currently assigned to park
→ 정답의 Anyone who usually parks

178 세부 사항

번역 직원들이 경비동 방문을 자제해야 하는 이유는?

(A) 방문객들이 연못을 즐기기 위해
(B) 해당 구역에 차량을 줄이기 위해
(C) 경비원이 교통량을 점검할 수 있도록 하기 위해
(D) 방문객들이 안내소에 갈 수 있도록 하기 위해

해설 이메일의 세 번째 단락에서 공사장 접근 도로로 인해 경비동에 가는 길도 막히게 된다(This will also block access to the security building)며 과도한 교통량을 방지하기 위해(To help eliminate excessive traffic) 꼭 필요한 경우에만 해당 장소를 방문해 달라고 했으므로, (B)가 정답이다.

> ▸ Paraphrasing   지문의 visit ~ only when absolutely
> necessary → 질문의 limit their visits
> 지문의 To help eliminate excessive traffic
> → 정답의 So that fewer cars will be in the
> area

179 연계

번역 6월 10일에 이메일이 발송된 뒤 변경된 것은?

(A) 폐쇄될 주차 구역
(B) 직원이 차를 주차해야 하는 장소
(C) 주차 스티커를 붙여야 하는 곳
(D) 일부 주차 구역이 폐쇄되는 기간

해설 이메일의 두 번째 단락에서 8월 20일까지 F와 G 주차 구역이 폐쇄된다(parking areas F and G will be closed until August 20)고 했는데, 공지 상단을 보면 9월 10일까지 폐쇄된다(PARKING AREAS F & G CLOSED UNTIL SEPTEMBER 10)고 나와 있다. 따라서 이메일이 발송된 후 주차 구역 폐쇄 일정이 변경되었음을 알 수 있으므로, (D)가 정답이다.

180 추론 / 암시

번역 공지에 따르면 직원의 차가 견인될 수도 있는 이유는 무엇인가?

(A) 통로 부근에 주차된 경우
(B) 방문객 구역에 주차된 경우
(C) 주차 스티커를 붙이지 않은 경우
(D) 8월 20일 이후 주차장에 주차된 경우

해설 공지의 두 번째 단락에서 모든 통로, 임시 휴게소, 공사용 텐트를 포함해 인도 부근에 주차된 차는 즉시 견인된다(Cars will be immediately towed away if parked next to pedestrian areas, including all walkways, ~ tents)고 했으므로, (A)가 정답이다.

181-185 설문 조사 + 이메일

설문지

잠시 시간을 내셔서 우드러프즈에서의 쇼핑 경험에 관한 설문지를 작성해 주시기 바랍니다. 각 항목의 오른편에 5점 만점으로 귀하의 의견을 표시하십시오. (1 = 전혀 그렇지 않다, 2 = 그렇지 않다, 3 = 의견 없음, 4 = 그렇다, 5 = 매우 그렇다)

매장이 깨끗했고 외관이 잘 정리되어 있었다. □1 □2 □3 ■4 □5
181내 사이즈의 품목이 다양하게 구비되어 있었다.
　　　　　　　　　　　　　　　□1 □2 □3 □4 ■5
181내가 사용할 수 있는 탈의실이 있었다. □1 □2 □3 □4 ■5
184영업 사원들이 정중하고 친절했다.　□1 ■2 □3 □4 □5
182타 매장에 비해 물품의 가격이 적절하게 책정되었다.
　　　　　　　　　　　　　　　□1 □2 □3 □4 ■5
우드러프즈에서의 쇼핑이 대체로 만족스럽다. □1 □2 □3 ■4 □5

이번 구매에 쓴 금액: $60
나이 (선택): □16-25　□26-35　■36-45
　　　　　　　□46-55　□56-65　□66+
성명 (선택): 칸스웨일러 토레스
이메일 (선택): catorres81@aumail.co.au

어휘　survey (설문) 조사; 조사하다　indicate 표시하다, 나타내다
scale (측정용) 등급, 척도　statement 진술, 주장　organized
정돈된　appearance 외관　courteous 공손한　attentive 주의
깊은, 친절한　compared to ~와 비교하여

발신: 고객 서비스부 〈custserv@woodruff.co.au〉
수신: 칸스웨일러 토레스 〈catorres81@aumail.co.au〉
날짜: 4월 27일, 금요일 오후 2시 40분
제목: 설문 조사
첨부: 🔗 할인권

토레스 씨께:

고객님께서 시간을 내어 우드러프즈에서의 최근 경험에 대한 설문지를 작성해 주신 데 대해 감사드립니다. **185이는 저희들의 서비스 품질을 높이는 데 도움이 되기 때문에, 저희는 많은 분들이 시간을 내서 저희에게 의견을 주신 데 대해 183감사하고 있습니다.**

우드러프즈에서의 고객님의 쇼핑 경험이 대체로 긍정적임을 알게 되어 기뻤습니다. **184그러나 설문 조사에 응한 고객 중 꽤 많은 분들이 지적하신 부분을 고객님께서도 불만족스러워하신 데 대해 송구하게 생각합니다.** 저희가 설문 조사 결과를 심각하게 받아들이고 있음을 고객님께 알려 드리고 싶습니다. **184곧 교육을 통해 해당 부분을 개선할 계획입니다.**

전 분야에서 높은 수준을 충족하지 못한 데 대한 사과의 의미로, 클라크스빌에 있는 저희 매장 세 곳에서 향후 구매 시 사용 가능한 15퍼센트 할인권(유효 기간 1년)을 첨부해 드립니다. 앞으로도 고객님을 모실 수 있기를 바랍니다.

마리에타 파산테

어휘　appreciate 감사하다　improve 개선하다　overall
전반적인　positive 긍정적인　dissatisfaction 불만족
significant 중요한, 커다란　proportion 비율, 부분　respond
to ~에 응답하다　take A seriously A를 심각하게 받아들이다
apology 사과　voucher 상품권, 할인권　purchase 구매(품);
구매하다　good 유효한

181 세부 사항

번역 우드러프즈의 업종은?

(A) 컴퓨터 소프트웨어 회사
(B) 의류 매장
(C) 핸드폰 서비스 공급업자
(D) 컨설팅 회사

해설 설문 조사 항목 중 '내 사이즈의 품목이 다양하게 구비되어 있었다 (There was a wide selection of items in my size)'와 '내가 사용할 수 있는 탈의실이 있었다(There were dressing rooms ~ to use)'라는 문구를 통해 우드러프즈가 의류 매장임을 알 수 있다. 따라서 (B)가 정답이다.

182 추론 / 암시

번역 우드러프즈에 관한 설명 중 토레스 씨는 어떤 것에 동의하겠는가?

(A) 토레스 씨의 집과 가깝다.
(B) 직원이 많다.
(C) 비교적 저렴하다.
(D) 타 업체보다 늦게까지 영업한다.

해설 설문 조사의 다섯 번째 항목인 '타 매장에 비해 물품의 가격이 적절하게 책정되었다(The items were priced well compared to other stores)'라는 진술에 대해 '5 = 매우 그렇다(5 = Strongly Agree)'라고 응답했으므로, (C)가 정답이다.

> ▸▸ Paraphrasing   지문의 **priced well compared to other stores** → 정답의 **relatively inexpensive**

183 동의어 찾기

번역 이메일에서 첫 번째 단락 2행의 "appreciate"와 의미상 가장 가까운 것은?

(A) 증가하다
(B) 주문하다
(C) 이해하다
(D) 소중하게 여기다

해설 "appreciate"가 포함된 부분은 '아주 많은 분들이 시간을 내서 의견을 주신 데 대해 감사하고 있다(We appreciate that so many people took the time to provide us with feedback)'라는 내용으로, 여기서 appreciate는 '감사하다, 가치를 인정하다'의 의미로 쓰였다. 따라서 '소중하게 여기다'라는 의미의 (D) value가 정답이다.

184 연계

번역 우드러프즈가 계획하고 있는 일은 무엇이겠는가?

(A) 직원들이 고객들에게 더 친절하고 도움이 될 수 있게 교육하기
(B) 매장을 더 깨끗하게 하고 더 잘 정리하기
(C) 클라크스빌에 추가 지점 열기
(D) 설문지를 작성한 모든 고객에게 할인권 제공하기

해설 이메일의 두 번째 단락에서 설문 조사에 응한 고객들 중 상당수가 지적한 부분을 토레스 씨도 불만족스러워(you shared one area of dissatisfaction ~ the survey)해서 송구하게 생각한다고 하며 곧 교육을 통해 해당 부분을 개선할 계획(We plan to improve this area with training soon)이라고 했다. 설문 조사 항목 중에서 토레스 씨가 동의하지 않은 진술은 '영업 사원들이 정중하고 친절했다 (The salespeople were courteous and attentive to me)'이므로, 우드러프즈가 직원들을 교육할 계획임을 알 수 있다. 따라서 (A)가 정답이다.

어휘 organized 정돈된 additional 추가의

> ▸▸ Paraphrasing   지문의 **training** → 정답의 **Teach**
> 지문의 **courteous and attentive**
> → 정답의 **friendly and helpful**

185 추론 / 암시

번역 설문지에 관해 암시된 것은?

(A) 많은 고객이 작성했다.
(B) 파산테 씨가 만들었다.
(C) 회사 웹사이트에서 볼 수 있다.
(D) 1년 동안 사용되었다.

어휘 accessible 접근 가능한, 이용 가능한

해설 이메일의 첫 번째 단락에서 아주 많은 인원이 시간을 내서 의견을 준 것(so many people took the time to provide us with feedback)에 대해 감사하고 있다고 했으므로, 설문 조사에 많은 고객이 참여했다는 것을 추론할 수 있다. 따라서 (A)가 정답이다.

186-190 청구서 + 이메일 + 이메일

맥기븐 도매

1486 베덴 트레일, 브램턴, 온타리오 L6R 2K7

905-555-0158 • www.mcgivernwholesale.ca

주문자: 데사우나즈 크리에이션즈
주문 날짜: 10월 12일

품목	189(A)품목명	수량	단가	금액
14L	3m 테이블보, 크림색	4	26.00달러	104.00달러
17P	25cm 큰 접시, 담청색	40	4.40달러	176.00달러
18S	50cm 접시, 흰색	20	7.95달러	159.00달러
187 21G	187 350ml 물잔, 호박색	40	3.25달러	130.00달러
			소계	569.00달러
			세금 (통합소비세)	73.97달러
			배송비	30.00달러
			총계	672.97달러

청구서 수령 즉시 결제 바랍니다.

어휘 wholesale 도매; 도매의 goblet 손잡이 없는 잔 HST 통합소비세(= Harmonized Sales Tax)

수신: 피트 맥기븐 〈pete.mcgivern@mcgivernwholesale.ca〉
발신: 데사우나 쟈크 〈deshaunajacques@deshaunascreations.ca〉
제목: 10월 주문품
날짜: 10월 17일

맥기븐 씨께,

186 10월 주문품을 받았는데, 몇 가지 문제가 있었습니다. 40개 대신 20개의 정찬용 접시를 받았고 187 손잡이가 없는 물잔 7개는 유리에 금이 간 상태로 도착했습니다. 최근 운송 업체를 교체했나요?

189(C)저는 귀사가 영업을 시작한 5년 전부터 단골이었는데, 이전에는 주문품에 아무런 문제가 없었습니다. 그건 그렇고, **189(A)**제가 오늘 아침 근처 살렉스 카페의 사장인 에드 살렉과 이야기를 나눴습니다. 그는 자신이 귀사에서 받은 마지막 배송에도 과실이 있었다고 말하더군요.

186언제 제 주문품을 바로잡아 주시겠어요? 다음 주에 파티가 3건 있어서 빨리 이 상품들이 필요합니다.

데샤우나 쟈크

어휘 crack 균열; 금 가다 carrier 운송 회사 recently 최근
incidentally 그런데, 그건 그렇고 mention 언급하다, 말하다
delivery 배송(품) fix 바로잡다

수신: 데샤우나 쟈크 〈deshaunajacques@deshaunascreations.ca〉
발신: 피트 맥기븐 〈pete.mcgivern@mcgivernwholesale.ca〉
제목: 회신: 10월 주문품
날짜: 10월 17일

쟈크 씨께,

고객님과 살렉 씨의 주문품에 대해 대단히 죄송하게 생각합니다. 살렉 씨께는 오늘 사과 **188**드릴 생각입니다. 저희 회사의 귀중한 고객이신데 그렇게 형편없는 배송품을 받으셨다니 당황스럽습니다. 저희가 **189(B)** 새 창고로 이전하는 중이라 제가 기대했던 만큼 일이 순조롭게 진행되지 않았습니다. 아무튼 최대한 빨리 보상해 드리고 싶습니다. 과실을 바로잡기 위해 물건을 주문했으며, **190**다음 배송품에 15퍼센트 할인 혜택을 드리고자 하니 이를 받아주시기 바랍니다. 주문하실 때 코드 15D를 사용하시면 됩니다.

이번 건을 바로잡기 위해 제가 할 수 있는 일이 있으면 알려 주시기 바랍니다.

피트 맥기븐

어휘 extend one's apology 사과하다 valued 소중한
embarrassed 당황스러운 shipment 배송(품) warehouse
창고 regardless 여하튼, 개의치 않고 make amends 보상하다
place an order 주문하다

---

186 주제 / 목적

번역 첫 번째 이메일을 보낸 이유는?

(A) 고객의 의견을 요청하기 위해
(B) 문제 해결책을 찾기 위해
(C) 상품에 대해 환불을 요청하기 위해
(D) 식기류 주문을 취소하기 위해

해설 첫 번째 이메일 첫 번째 단락의 '10월 주문품을 받았는데 몇 가지 문제가 있었습니다(I received my October order, but there were some errors)'와 세 번째 단락의 '언제 제 주문품을 바로잡아 주시겠어요?(How soon can you fix my order?)'를 통해 문제 해결을 요청하는 이메일임을 알 수 있다. 따라서 (B)가 정답이다.

187 연계

번역 파손된 상태로 받은 품목은?

(A) 14L
(B) 17P
(C) 18S
(D) 21G

해설 첫 번째 이메일의 첫 번째 단락에서 손잡이 없는 물잔 7개가 유리에 금이 간 상태로 도착했다(seven water goblets arrived with cracks in the glass)고 했고, 청구서를 보면 물잔의 품목이 21G이라는 것을 알 수 있다. 따라서 (D)가 정답이다.

▸▸ Paraphrasing 지문의 **arrived with cracks**
→ 질문의 **was received damaged**

188 동의어 찾기

번역 두 번째 이메일에서 첫 번째 단락 1행의 "extend"와 의미상 가장 가까운 것은?

(A) 제공하다
(B) 늦추다
(C) 계속하다
(D) 증가하다

해설 "extend"가 포함된 문장은 '살렉 씨께는 오늘 사과 드릴 생각입니다 (I will extend my apology to him today)'라는 의미로, 여기서 extend는 '주다, 베풀다'의 뜻으로 쓰였다. 따라서 '제공하다'라는 의미의 (A) offer가 정답이다.

189 연계

번역 맥기븐 도매에 관해 명시되지 않은 것은?

(A) 식당과 거래한다.
(B) 시설의 위치를 바꾸는 중이다.
(C) 5년째 영업하고 있다.
(D) 가격표를 수정하고 있다.

해설 청구서에 나온 맥기븐 도매의 판매 품목과 첫 번째 이메일에 언급된 쟈크 씨의 문제(I received 20 dinner plates instead of 40, ~) 및 살렉스 카페 사장이 겪은 문제(his last delivery from you had some mistakes)에서 (A)를 확인할 수 있다. 그리고 맥기븐 씨가 보낸 두 번째 이메일을 보면 새 창고로 이전하는 중이라(We are ~ moving to a new warehouse)고 했으므로 (B)도 사실이다. (C)는 쟈크 씨가 보낸 첫 번째 이메일의 '귀사가 영업을 시작한 5년 전부터 단골이었는데(I ~ since you opened five years ago)'라는 문구를 통해 확인할 수 있다. 그러나 가격표를 수정하고 있다는 내용은 언급되지 않았으므로, (D)가 정답이다.

어휘 facility 시설 operate 영업[운영]하다 revise 수정하다

▸▸ Paraphrasing 지문의 **in the middle of moving to a new warehouse** → 보기 (B)의 **changing the location of a facility**
지문의 **since you opened five years ago** → 보기 (C)의 **has been operating for five years**

190 세부 사항

번역 맥기븐 도매는 쟈크 씨에게 무엇을 제공할 예정인가?

(A) 배송비 환불
(B) 식탁보 한 상자 추가
(C) 다음 주문품 가격 할인
(D) 수정된 청구서

해설 맥기븐 씨가 보낸 이메일의 첫 번째 단락 후반부를 보면, 쟈크 씨가 다음에 주문할 때 배송품에서 15퍼센트 할인(a 15 percent discount on your next shipment)을 받기 바란다고 했으므로, (C)가 정답이다.

어휘 rebate 환불, 리베이트

▸▸ Paraphrasing 지문의 a 15 percent discount on your next shipment
→ 정답의 A reduced price on her next order

191-195 양식 + 공지 + 이메일

레드포드 건설   192, 193**날짜: 3월 15일**

450 마틸다 드라이브   비용 견적 번호: 50190

렉싱턴, 켄터키 40502

수신자: 제니 최, 518 버팔로 스프링스 로드

작성자: 가브리엘 누네스

193내역	수량	비용
191무광 세라믹 바닥 타일 (단가 2.49달러/타일)	400	996.00달러
프리미엄 밝은 백색 시멘트풀 (단가 32.99달러/갤런)	5	164.95달러
사전 작업, 설치 및 청소 인건비 (단가 35달러/시간)	16	560.00달러
견적 총액 1,720.95달러		
192모든 견적은 별도의 언급이 없는 한 1개월간 유효합니다.		

어휘 description (상세) 내역, 설명 preparation 준비 installation 설치 estimate 견적(서), 추정 valid 유효한 unless otherwise specified 별도의 언급이 없는 한

렉싱턴 시 신규 조례

1933월 30일 부로, 모든 건설사는 각 고객을 위해 개조 작업을 시작하기 전에 건축 허가(주거용 건물 100달러; 상가 건물 300달러)를 받아야 합니다. 건축 공사 지원서를 작성하려면 859-555-0103으로 시청에 연락하십시오.

어휘 ordinance 법령, 조례 permit 허가(증) residential 주거의 commercial 상업의 renovation 개조 application 신청(서)

수신: 가브리엘 누네스 ⟨gnunez@reddfordcon.com⟩
발신: 제니 최 ⟨jchoi86@citymail.com⟩
날짜: 4월 2일 금요일, 오전 10시 12분
제목: 허가

누네스 씨께,

191귀사와 194계약을 맺고자 하는 제 193식당 작업과 관련하여 메일 드립니다. 1914월 10일에 작업을 시작했으면 하는데 보내주신 견적서를 보고 나니 계산해주신 총 비용에 대한 궁금증이 생겼습니다. 구체적으로, 작업에 필요한 허가 비용도 견적에 넣으신 건가요? 제 동료가 그러는데 지난달부터 시행된 조례에 따르면 개조 작업은 모두 건축 허가를 받아야 한다고 합니다. 195저는 지난해 귀사가 했던 193거실 카펫 설치와 페인트칠이 정말 마음에 들었고 기왕이면 아는 회사와 작업하고 싶습니다. 하지만 제 예산이 빠듯해서 전체 작업비에서 건축 허가 비용을 고려해야 합니다. 가능한 한 빨리 저에게 연락 주시겠습니까?

제니 최 드림

어휘 concerning ~에 관하여 contract 계약하다 estimate 견적(액): 어림잡다 calculation 계산 specifically 특히 take into account 고려하다 permit 허가(증) colleague 동료 go into effect 발효하다, 실시되다 install 설치하다 tight budget 빠듯한 예산

191 연계

번역 4월 10일 최 씨는 누네스 씨가 어떤 일을 해주기를 바라는가?

(A) 가구 배송
(B) 타일 설치
(C) 거실 카펫 청소
(D) 식당 벽 페인트칠

해설 최씨가 누네스 씨에게 보낸 이메일을 보면 4월 10일에 자신의 식당(dining room)에 작업을 시작했으면 한다(I'd like work to begin on April 10)고 했는데, 해당 작업을 위한 견적서(양식)를 보면 내역에 무광 세라믹 바닥 타일(Unglazed ceramic floor tiles)과 설치 인건비(Labor for ~ installation)가 나와 있다. 따라서 (B)가 정답이다.

192 세부 사항

번역 4월 15일 후에 일어날 일은?

(A) 최 씨의 지원서가 검토된다.
(B) 최 씨가 최종 청구서를 받는다.
(C) 시의 신규 조례가 시행된다.
(D) 비용 견적이 무효가 된다.

해설 양식을 보면 견적서 발급일이 3월 15일(Date: March 15)인데, 마지막 줄에 모든 견적은 별도의 언급이 없는 한 1개월간 유효하다(All estimates are valid for one month)고 했으므로, 4월 15일에는 해당 견적이 무효가 됨을 알 수 있다. 따라서 (D)가 정답이다.

193 연계

번역 최 씨의 견적에 얼마가 추가되겠는가?

(A) 32.99달러
(B) 35.00달러
(C) 100.00달러
(D) 300.00달러

해설 공지에서 3월 30일 부로(As of March 30) 개조 작업 시작 전에 건축 허가를 받아야 하는(all construction companies ~ a renovation project) 조례가 시행된다고 했고, 이 소식을 동료로부터 들은 최 씨가 해당 비용이 견적 총액에 포함된 건지(does your estimate take into account any permits ~ job?) 누네스 씨에게 이메일로 문의했다. 견적서를 보면 작성일이 3월 15일이고 내역(Description)에 허가 비용에 대한 언급이 없으므로, 해당 비용이 반영되지 않았을 것이라고 보는 것이 타당하다. 이메일에서 최 씨가 식당(dining room)과 거실(living room)을 언급한 것으로 보아 주거용 건물에 개조 작업을 한다는 것을 알 수 있고, 공지를 보면 주거용 건물(residential buildings)을 위한 허가를 받으려면 100달러를 지불해야 한다고 나와 있다. 따라서 (C)가 정답이다.

194 동의어 찾기

번역 이메일에서 첫 번째 단락 1행의 "contract"와 의미상 가장 가까운 것은?

(A) 줄이다
(B) 고용하다
(C) 모으다
(D) 구매하다

해설 "contract"를 포함한 문장은 '귀사와 계약을 맺고자 하는 제 식당 작업과 관련하여 이메일을 드립니다'라는 의미로, 여기서 contract는 '계약을 맺다'라는 뜻으로 쓰였다. 따라서 '고용하다, 의뢰하다'라는 의미의 동사 (B) retain이 정답이다.

어휘 reduce 줄이다 retain 유지하다, 보유하다, 고용하다, 의뢰하다 purchase 구매하다; 구매(품)

195 사실 관계 확인

번역 최 씨가 레드포드 건설에 관해 명시한 것은?

(A) 이전에 작업을 의뢰한 적이 있다.
(B) 그들과의 약속 일정을 다시 잡아야 한다.
(C) 가격이 너무 비싸다고 생각한다.
(D) 타일을 너무 많이 샀다고 생각한다.

해설 최 씨가 보낸 이메일의 후반부를 보면 지난해 누네스 씨의 회사가 했던 거실 카펫 설치와 페인트 칠이 정말 마음에 들었다(I really liked the job you did ~ last year)고 했으므로, 이전에도 작업을 의뢰한 적이 있음을 알 수 있다. 따라서 (A)가 정답이다.

196-200 기사 + 이메일 + 문자 메시지

〈카디프 데일리 타임스〉

단신—3월 20일

196, 198올해 초 보도된 바와 같이 골드 케틀 식료품이 카디프에 지역 유통 센터를 추가로 개장할 예정이다. 현장 지반 상태와 관련한 예상치 못한 문제로 공사가 일시 연기된 바 있다. 그러나 문제는 해결되었고 6월이면 4만 제곱미터에 이르는 센터가 전면 운영된다. **198**개장은 6월 4일로 예정되어 있다. 창고에는 냉동 또는 냉장 보관되어야 하는 식품을 저장할 수 있는 최첨단 장비를 갖춘 특별 구역이 있다. 이 부지에는 적재 구획과 사무실도 포함될 예정이다.

운영 부장인 마일스 짐러에 따르면, 유통 센터가 400개 이상의 새 일자리를 창출할 것으로 예상된다고 한다. 프로젝트 규모 및 **197**범위 때문에 창고 적재자, 운전 기사에서 사무직에 이르기까지 다양한 직업이 필요하게 된다.

어휘 additional 추가의 regional 지역의 distribution 유통, 배포 postpone 연기하다 unanticipated 예상하지 못한 related to ~와 관련된 resolve 해결하다, 결정하다 operational 운영되는, 영업하는 state-of-the-art 최첨단의 equipment 장비 loading bay 적재 구획 vice president 부(서)장, 부사장 scope 범위 clerical 사무원의

수신: 마일스 짐러 〈msimler@goldkettle.co.uk〉
발신: 라디카 바랄 〈rbaral@goldkettle.co.uk〉
제목: 안내
198날짜: 6월 26일
첨부: 알림 비교

마일스 씨께:

198이달 초 개장식에 저를 태워다 주셔서 감사합니다. 그렇게 준비가 잘 된 행사를 본 적이 없습니다. 행사를 개최한 핑 첸에게 감사의 표시로 뭔가를 보내야 합니다.

이제 카디프 센터를 연 지 몇 주가 되었으니 직원들의 휴대폰에 자동 알림을 전송하는 업체를 고용하는 것을 고려해 봐야 할 것 같습니다. 이 서비스를 사용하면 직원들에게 신속하게 메시지를 발송할 수 있고 배송 오류를 방지할 수 있을 것입니다. **199**콜스 포 유의 고객 서비스 부서에서 일하는 사람을 알고 있습니다. 이 회사도 괜찮지만, 레이븐 노티피케이션즈 역시 괜찮아 보이고 비용이 더 저렴합니다. 어떤 회사를 이용할지 결정하는 데 도움을 드리기 위해 두 회사에 대한 정보를 첨부했습니다. 어떻게 생각하시는지 저에게 알려 주십시오.

라디카 바랄

어휘 notification 알림, 통보 give a lift 태워다 주다 appreciation 감사 organise 조직하다, 개최하다 prevent 막다, 방지하다 shipment 수송(품) contact 연락책 rate 가격, 비용 attach 첨부하다

---

¹⁹⁹**레이븐 노티피케이션즈** 오전 11시 43분

골드 케틀 직원 여러분께—화요일 도착 예정이던 냉동 제품 배송품이 수요일에나 도착할 예정입니다. 카디프 유통 센터에서 화요일 저녁 초과 근무를 자원했던 직원들이 필요하지 않게 되었습니다. 하지만 수요일 밤에는 철야 근무를 도와줄 추가 인력이 필요합니다. ²⁰⁰**이 시간에 추가 근무하실 분은 인사과의 베카 존스턴에게 연락하십시오.**

어휘 volunteer 자원하다; 자원자

---

196 주제 / 목적

번역 기사의 목적은?

(A) 지역 프로젝트에 관한 최신 정보 제공
(B) 최첨단 창고 장비에 대한 설명
(C) 직원 추가 채용 계획이 있는 지역 업체에 대한 보도
(D) 건설 프로젝트 상의 어려움 설명

해설 기사 첫 번째 단락에서 올해 초 보도된 바와 같이(As reported earlier this year) 골드 케틀 식료품이 카디프에 지역 유통 센터를 추가로 개장할 예정(Gold Kettle Grocery is opening an additional regional distribution centre in Cardiff)이라고 하며, 기사 전반에서 이 프로젝트에 관련된 최신 정보를 다루고 있다. 따라서 (A)가 정답이다.

어휘 encounter (위험·곤란 등에) 직면하다

▸▸ **Paraphrasing**   지문의 regional → 정답의 local

---

197 동의어 찾기

번역 기사에서 두 번째 단락 4행의 "scope"와 의미상 가장 가까운 것은?

(A) 보는 데 사용되는 도구
(B) 평가
(C) 완료 시간
(D) 범위

해설 "scope"를 포함한 부분은 '프로젝트 규모 및 범위 때문에 다양한 직업이 필요하게 된다(Because of the size and scope of the project, a variety of jobs will be needed)'라는 의미로, 여기서 scope는 '범위'라는 뜻으로 쓰였다. 따라서 '정도, 범위'라는 의미의 (D) extent가 정답이다.

어휘 instrument 도구   evaluation 평가

---

198 연계

번역 카디프 유통 센터에 관해 무엇이 사실이겠는가?

(A) 식품 저장에 문제가 있다.
(B) 개장식이 성공적이었다.
(C) 짐러 씨가 최근 그곳에서 일했다.
(D) 바랄 씨는 유통 센터의 서비스에 불만이 있었다.

해설 기사의 첫 번째 단락에서 '유통 센터의 개장이 6월 4일로 예정되어 있다(The grand opening ~ the fourth of June)'라고 했는데, 바랄 씨가 6월 26일에 보낸 이메일에서 짐러 씨에게 개장식에 태워다 줘서 감사하다(Thanks for giving me a lift to the grand opening earlier this month)고 한 것으로 보아 바랄 씨가 유통 센터의 개장식에 참석했다는 것을 알 수 있다. 바랄 씨가 '그렇게 준비가 잘 된 행사를 본 적이 없다(I do not believe I have ever seen such a well-planned event)'라고 했으므로, 개장식이 성공적이었음을 알 수 있다. 따라서 (B)가 정답이다.

▸▸ **Paraphrasing**   지문의 well-planned → 정답의 successful

---

199 연계

번역 짐러 씨가 선택한 회사는?

(A) 바랄 씨가 아는 사람이 일하는 회사
(B) 고객 서비스 담당자들이 가장 믿음직한 회사
(C) 경쟁사보다 비용이 저렴한 회사
(D) 철야 콜 센터가 있는 회사

해설 이메일 두 번째 단락의 중·후반부에서 바랄 씨는 자신이 아는 사람이 고객 서비스부에서 일하고 있는 콜스 포 유(I have a contact ~ Calls For You)와 더 저렴한 비용을 제시한 레이븐 노티피케이션즈(Raven Notifications ~, and their rates are lower)에 관한 정보를 짐러 씨에게 보내며 어떻게 생각하는지 알려 달라고 했다. 문자 메시지를 보면 알림을 보낸 회사가 레이븐 노티피케이션즈라고 나와 있으므로, 짐러 씨가 경쟁사보다 비용이 저렴한 업체를 선택했다는 것을 알 수 있다. 따라서 (C)가 정답이다.

어휘 representative 직원   competitor 경쟁자, 경쟁사

---

200 세부 사항

번역 문자 메시지에서 추가 근무를 원하는 직원들에게 요구하는 것은?

(A) 화요일 밤에 도착하기
(B) 인사과에 연락하기
(C) 일할 수 있는 시간을 메시지로 회신하기
(D) 다른 유통 센터로 가기

해설 메시지 후반부에서 수요일 밤(Wednesday night)에 추가 근무(working additional hours)를 할 사람은 인사부 베카 존스턴에게 연락하라(please contact Becca Johnson in Human Resources)고 했으므로, (B)가 정답이다.

▸▸ **Paraphrasing**   지문의 Human Resources
→ 정답의 the personnel office

101 (B)	102 (C)	103 (D)	104 (B)	105 (A)
106 (C)	107 (A)	108 (D)	109 (C)	110 (C)
111 (B)	112 (D)	113 (A)	114 (D)	115 (A)
116 (C)	117 (C)	118 (B)	119 (D)	120 (B)
121 (D)	122 (C)	123 (A)	124 (D)	125 (B)
126 (C)	127 (A)	128 (D)	129 (B)	130 (D)
131 (A)	132 (B)	133 (B)	134 (D)	135 (D)
136 (C)	137 (A)	138 (D)	139 (C)	140 (A)
141 (D)	142 (B)	143 (A)	144 (D)	145 (A)
146 (C)	147 (A)	148 (B)	149 (C)	150 (B)
151 (D)	152 (B)	153 (C)	154 (B)	155 (C)
156 (B)	157 (C)	158 (C)	159 (B)	160 (B)
161 (D)	162 (B)	163 (C)	164 (B)	165 (A)
166 (C)	167 (B)	168 (D)	169 (B)	170 (A)
171 (A)	172 (D)	173 (A)	174 (A)	175 (B)
176 (D)	177 (B)	178 (A)	179 (B)	180 (A)
181 (B)	182 (A)	183 (C)	184 (D)	185 (C)
186 (B)	187 (A)	188 (A)	189 (D)	190 (B)
191 (B)	192 (C)	193 (A)	194 (C)	195 (D)
196 (C)	197 (B)	198 (D)	199 (A)	200 (D)

PART 5

101 인칭대명사의 격 _ 소유격

해설 빈칸은 주어 역할을 하는 명사 documents를 한정 수식하는 자리이므로, 소유격 인칭대명사인 (B) her가 정답이다. 참고로, all이 명사를 수식하는 경우 「all+(the/소유격 인칭대명사)+(형용사)+명사」의 구조로 쓰인다.

번역 지역 관리자가 내일 도착하므로, 그녀의 서류가 모두 준비되었는지 확인하시기 바랍니다.

어휘 regional 지역의   ensure 확실히 하다

102 부사 어휘

해설 빈칸 앞 과거 시제 동사(was constructed) 및 nearly 200 years와 어울리는 부사를 선택하는 문제이다. 문맥상 '약 200년 전에 지어졌다'라는 내용이 되어야 자연스러우므로, 과거 시제와 함께 쓰여 '(얼마의 시간) 전에'라는 의미를 나타내는 (C) ago가 정답이다.

번역 역사적인 월드리지 건물은 약 200년 전에 건축되었다.

어휘 construct 건축하다   nearly 약, 거의

103 동사 자리

해설 Consumers가 주어, 빈칸이 동사인 문장이므로, 보기 중 본동사 역할을 할 수 있는 (D) responded가 정답이 된다. (A) responding은 동명사/현재분사로 문장에서 동사 역할을 할 수 없으며,

(B) response는 명사, (C) responsively는 부사로 품사상 빈칸에 적합하지 않다.

번역 소비자들은 샌웰 페인트가 개발한 새로운 색상에 열띤 반응을 보였다.

어휘 consumer 소비자   respond 반응하다, 응답하다
enthusiastically 열광적으로

104 형용사 어휘 _ 과거분사

해설 빈칸 뒤 명사 files를 적절히 수식하는 과거분사를 선택하는 문제이다. 문맥상 '첨부된 파일은 고용 계약서와 회사에 관한 정보를 포함한다'라는 내용이 되어야 자연스러우므로, '첨부된, 부착된'을 의미하는 (B) attached가 정답이 된다. 참고로, '이해관계가 있는'이라는 의미의 (C) interested는 party, group 등 사람을 나타내는 명사를 수식하는 데 쓰인다.

번역 첨부된 파일에는 귀하의 고용 계약서와 당사에 대한 정보가 들어 있습니다.

어휘 contain 포함하다, 들어 있다   employment contract 고용 계약
directed 지시된, 규제된   connected 관련이 있는, 연결된

105 부사 자리 _ 동사 수식

해설 동사(submit)와 목적어(each reimbursement request)를 갖춘 완전한 구조의 명령문이므로, 빈칸에는 submit을 수식하는 부사가 들어가야 한다. 따라서 '따로, 분리하여'라는 의미의 부사인 (A) separately가 정답이다. (B) separateness는 명사, (C) separates는 동사, (D) separate는 동사/형용사로, 품사상 빈칸에 적합하지 않다.

번역 모든 환급 요청은 지난달 회람에 설명된 대로 종류별로 분리하여 제출하십시오.

어휘 submit 제출하다   reimbursement 환급, 상환
separateness 분리, 단독   separate 분리하다; 분리된

106 부사절 접속사

해설 빈칸 뒤 완전한 절을 이끄는 접속사 자리이다. 문맥을 살펴보면, 빈칸을 포함한 절이 앞에 있는 주절을 수식하고 있으므로, 빈칸에는 부사절 접속사가 들어가야 한다. 따라서 '~ 동안에'를 의미하는 부사절 접속사 (C) while이 정답이다. 접속사 (A) whether는 or not과 결합해야만 부사절을 이끌 수 있고, (B) except와 (D) during은 전치사로서 완전한 절을 이끌 수 없으므로 오답이다.

번역 정비사들이 차량 수리를 완료하는 동안 고객께서는 안내실에서 대기하시면 됩니다.

어휘 reception area 접수처, 안내실   mechanic 정비사   complete 완료하다

107 명사 자리 _ 직접 목적어

해설 빈칸 앞 '주다, 수여하다'라는 의미의 동사 grant는 능동태일 때 「grant+간접목적어(~에게)+직접목적어(~를)」의 구조로 쓰일 수 있다. 해당 문장은 이 구조가 수동태로 변환된 것으로, 간접목적어가 주어가 되었으므로 빈칸에는 능동태 구조에서 직접목적어였던 명사가 들어가야 한다. 따라서 (A) admission이 정답이 된다.

번역 출입증이 없는 사람은 회의장 입장이 허용되지 않습니다.

어휘 grant 주다, 수여하다, 허가하다 admission 입장 admit 입장을 허락하다, 받아들이다

108 전치사 어휘

해설 빈칸 뒤 명사구 Albright Bank를 목적어로 취하는 전치사 자리로, 빈칸을 포함한 전치사구가 동사구 set up an online account를 수식하고 있다. 따라서 빈칸에는 '올브라이트 은행'과 '온라인 계정을 만들다'를 적절히 연결하는 전치사가 들어가야 한다. 문맥상 '올브라이트 은행에서 온라인 계정을 만들다'라는 내용이 되어야 자연스러우므로, '~와, (회사 등의) 서비스를 이용하는'이라는 의미의 (D) with가 정답이다.

번역 결제일이 되었을 때 전자 알림을 받으려면 올브라이트 은행에서 온라인 계정을 만드십시오.

어휘 reminder 알림, 상기시켜 주는 것 payment 결제, 납부 due 지불 기일이 된 account 계정, 계좌

109 부사 자리 _ 형용사 수식

해설 빈칸은 뒤에 오는 형용사 refundable을 수식하는 부사 자리이므로, '완전히, 충분히'를 의미하는 부사 (C) fully가 정답이다. (A) fullest는 최상급, (B) fuller는 비교급, (D) full은 원급 형용사로, 모두 품사상 빈칸에 적합하지 않다.

번역 등록비는 회의 날짜 2주 전까지 전액 환불 가능합니다.

어휘 registration fee 등록비 refundable 환불 가능한 prior to ~ 전에

110 동사 어휘

해설 빈칸은 has been과 함께 수동태를 이루는 과거분사 자리로, 주어인 All identifying information 및 문맥과 어울리는 동사를 선택해야 한다. 뒤에 나온 '교육 목적으로 사용될 수 있도록(so that ~ training purposes)'이라는 내용으로 미루어 보았을 때, 해당 부분은 이를 위해 '개인 식별 정보(identifying information)가 제거되었다'라는 내용이 되어야 자연스럽다. 따라서 has been과 함께 '제거되었다'라는 표현을 완성하는 (C) removed가 정답이다.

번역 불만사항을 적은 이 편지를 교육 목적으로 사용하기 위해 개인 식별 정보를 모두 제거했습니다.

어휘 identify (신원 등을) 알아보게 하다 complaint 불만사항 produce 생산하다 extend 확장하다 resolve 해결하다, 결정하다

111 전치사 자리 _ 어휘

해설 빈칸은 명사구 this time을 목적어로 취하는 전치사 자리로, 빈칸을 포함한 전치사구가 뒤에 나오는 동사 will have acquired를 수식하고 있다. 따라서 this time next year 및 미래완료 시제(will have p.p.)와 어울리는 전치사를 선택해야 한다. 문맥상 '내년 이맘때면 자회사 두 곳을 인수할 것이다'라는 내용이 되어야 자연스러우므로, '~쯤에는'이라는 의미의 (B) By가 정답이 된다.

번역 내년 이맘때면 라크뷰 테크놀로지는 새로운 자회사 두 곳을 인수할 것이다.

어휘 acquire 인수하다 subsidiary 자회사; 부수적인

112 명사 어휘

해설 빈칸은 전치사 for의 목적어 역할을 하는 명사 자리로 greater than ten의 수식을 받고 있고, 빈칸을 포함한 전치사구가 주어인 Table reservations를 수식해 주고 있다. 따라서 이 두 표현과 어울리는 명사가 빈칸에 들어가야 한다. 문맥상 '10인을 초과하는 단체(들)의 테이블 예약'이라는 내용이 되어야 자연스러우므로, '단체(들)'를 의미하는 (D) parties가 정답이다.

번역 10인을 초과하는 단체의 테이블 예약은 적어도 하루 전에 해야 합니다.

어휘 reservation 예약 at least 적어도 in advance 사전에, 미리

113 형용사 자리

해설 빈칸은 명사구 weather conditions를 수식하는 형용사 자리이므로, 보기에서 형용사 역할을 할 수 있는 현재분사 (A) worsening과 최상급 형용사 (D) worst 중에 하나를 선택해야 한다. 최상급인 (D) worst는 한정사(관사, 소유격 등) 없이 명사를 수식할 수 없기 때문에 빈칸에 들어갈 수 없고, 문맥상 '악화되는 날씨'라는 내용이 되어야 자연스러우므로 (A) worsening이 정답이 된다.

번역 기상 악화로 인해 오늘 밤 하얼빈 공원에서 열리는 콘서트가 취소되었다.

어휘 weather condition 기상 worsen 악화되다 cancel 취소하다

114 전치사 어휘

해설 빈칸은 명사구 team leaders를 목적어로 취하는 전치사 자리로, 자동사 rely와 함께 쓰이는 전치사가 들어가야 한다. 따라서 rely와 함께 '~에 의존하다'라는 표현을 완성하는 (D) upon이 정답이다. 참고로, 전치사 on 또한 rely와 어울려 쓰인다.

번역 알-오마니 씨는 직원 인센티브 프로그램을 개발하는 데 있어서 팀장들에게 의존할 것이다.

어휘 incentive 장려책, 유인책

115 명사 자리 _ 복합명사 _ 수 일치

해설 빈칸 앞에 명사(Survey), 뒤에 동사(analyze)가 있으므로, 빈칸에는 survey와 복합명사를 이루는 명사나 동사를 수식할 수 있는 부사가 들어갈 수 있다. 그러나 부사가 들어갈 경우 주어와 동사의 수 일치가 이루어지지 않으므로, 동사 analyze와 수가 일치하는 복수명사가 들어가야 한다. 따라서 '기술자들'을 의미하는 (A) technicians가 정답이 된다. (D) technicality는 '전문적 사항, 세부 조항' 등의 의미로 동사 analyze(분석하다)의 주체가 될 수 없고 수도 일치하지 않으므로 빈칸에 들어갈 수 없다.

번역 측량사는 지면 위아래의 토지 구획을 분석한다.

어휘 survey technician 측량사 analyze 분석하다 layout (지면) 구획, 배치 technically 기술적으로 technical 기술적인

116 to부정사 관용 표현

해설 빈칸에는 동사원형 assemble과 결합하여 뒤에 나오는 주절을 수식하는 표현이 들어가야 한다. 따라서 동사원형과 함께 쓰여 '~하기 위해'라는 목적을 나타내는 (C) In order to가 정답이다. (A) For the purpose of, (B) To be sure, (D) For example 뒤에는 동사원형이 바로 올 수 없다.

번역 게센 제품을 조립하려면 먼저 사용 설명서를 모두 읽고 필요한 도구를 모두 모으십시오.

어휘 assemble 조립하다 instructions (제품) 사용 설명서 required 필수의, 요구되는 tool 도구

117 to부정사 _ 명사적 용법

해설 Online shoppers (who ~ orders)가 주어, tend가 동사인 문장으로, 빈칸에는 명사(the business, low ratings)를 목적어로 취하는 동시에 tend의 목적어 역할도 하는 준동사가 들어가야 한다. '~하는 경향이 있다'라는 의미의 타동사 tend는 to부정사를 목적어로 취하므로, (C) to give가 정답이다.

번역 주문품을 오래 기다린 경험이 있는 온라인 쇼핑객들은 해당 기업체에게 낮은 평점을 주는 경향이 있다.

어휘 wait 기다리기, 대기 rating 평점, 평가

118 명사 어휘

해설 빈칸은 동사 will begin의 주어 역할을 하는 명사 자리로, 전치사구 of the new Delran train station의 수식을 받는다. 문맥상 '새 델란 기차역 건설이 시작될 것이다'라는 내용이 되어야 자연스러우므로, 빈칸에는 '건설, 건축'이라는 의미의 명사가 들어가야 한다. 따라서 (B) Construction이 정답이다.

번역 새 델란 기차역 건설은 9월 말에 시작될 것이다.

어휘 association 협회, 연합 violation 위반, 위배 comprehension 이해

119 형용사 자리 _ 주격 보어

해설 The computing power (of the new laptop)가 주어, is가 동사, 빈칸이 보어인 문장이다. 따라서 보어 역할을 할 수 있는 명사 (C) comparison과 형용사 (D) comparable 중에서 하나를 선택해야 한다. 빈칸 뒤에 전치사 to 및 비교 대상((that of 생략) any desktop computer)이 왔으므로, '~와 비슷한, 비교할 만한'이라는 의미의 형용사인 (D) comparable이 정답이 된다. (C) comparison은 '비교'라는 뜻으로 주어인 the computing power와 동격 관계를 이루지 않으므로 빈칸에 들어갈 수 없다. 참고로, (B) comparing이 현재분사로 쓰일 경우에는 타동사로서 목적어를 취해야 한다.

번역 새 노트북의 처리 성능은 동일한 가격대의 데스크톱 컴퓨터와 비슷하다.

어휘 computing power (컴퓨터) 처리 성능 compare 비교하다

120 부사 자리 _ 현재분사구 수식

해설 빈칸은 allowing 이하의 현재분사구를 수식하는 부사 자리이므로, '이리하여, 따라서'라는 의미의 부사 (B) thus가 정답이다. (A) that, (C) which, (D) so that은 「현재분사＋목적어」 앞에 올 수 없다.

번역 최근 들어 유이니 히시모토 박사가 자신의 병원에 다른 의사를 추가하여 더 많은 환자들이 진료 받을 수 있게 되었다.

어휘 recently 최근 practice (변호사·의사 등의) 개업, 개업 장소

121 동사 어휘

해설 빈칸 뒤 목적어 its superior reputation과 어울리는 동사를 선택하는 문제이다. 문맥상 '사장의 지도력 덕분에(thanks to the leadership of its president) 높은 명성을 얻었다'라는 내용이 되어야 자연스러우므로, '얻었다, 받았다'를 의미하는 (D) earned가 정답이 된다. 참고로, '명성을 얻다'라는 표현에는 동사 earn, win, gain, acquire가 자주 쓰인다.

번역 그라덴 호텔은 사장인 마샤 클레멘테의 지도력 덕분에 높은 명성을 얻었다.

어휘 reputation 명성 practice 연습하다, 실행하다 treat 대하다,

122 부사 어휘

해설 빈칸 앞 최상급 표현 his most exciting (one/novel 생략)과 어울리는 부사를 선택하는 문제이다. '지금까지 (그의 소설 중) 가장 흥미진진한 소설'이라는 의미가 되어야 자연스러우므로, '지금[이제]까지'라는 의미로 최상급을 강조하는 (C) yet이 정답이다. (D) very는 「the/소유격＋very＋최상급」의 구조로 최상급을 강조하므로 빈칸에 들어갈 수 없다.

번역 아키 가츠로의 최신 소설은 그의 소설 중 가장 흥미진진하며 분명 라딘 북스의 베스트셀러 목록에 오를 것이다.

어휘 make ~에 이르다, 오르다

123 부사 자리 _ 전치사구 수식

해설 빈칸은 Thanks to chef pastry chef Ana Villagra를 수식하는 부사 자리로, 라우두치스 레스토랑이 가장 인기 있는 식당이 된(has become a favorite) 데 있어 아나 빌라그라의 기여도가 차지하는 비율을 나타내는 부사가 들어가야 자연스럽다. 따라서 '주로, 대체로'라는 의미의 (A) largely가 정답이다.

번역 주로 제과제빵 요리사인 아나 빌라그라 덕분에 라우두치스 레스토랑은 지역 고객들에게 가장 인기 있는 식당이 되었다.

어휘 favorite 가장 좋아하는 것; 가장 좋아하는 local 지역의 patron 고객, 단골

124 명사 어휘

해설 동사 acknowledge 및 빈칸을 수식하는 to부정사구(to provide a safe workplace for our employees)와 적절히 어울리는 명사를 선택하는 문제이다. 직원들에게 안전한 일터를 제공하는 것은 회사의 '의무'라고 할 수 있으므로, '의무, 책임'이라는 의미의 (D) obligation이 정답이다.

번역 크린텍 매뉴팩처링은 당사 직원들에게 안전한 일터를 제공할 의무가 있음을 인정합니다.

어휘 acknowledge 인정하다 workplace 일터 assumption 가정, 추측 valuation 평가 perception 인식

125 부사절 접속사

해설 빈칸 뒤에 완전한 절과 콤마가 왔으므로 빈칸에는 접속사가 들어가야 한다. 주절을 보면 지역 사회의 반응이 '그래도(still)' 그를 감동시켰다고 했으므로, 빈칸이 이끄는 절은 '도노반 씨가 자선 행사의 성공을 예상했었지만'이라는 내용이 되어야 자연스럽다. 따라서 '비록 ~일지라도, ~이긴 하지만'이라는 의미의 부사절 접속사 (B) Although가 정답이 된다. (A) Whenever는 '~할 때마다'라는 의미로 문맥상 어색하며, (C) Even so와 (D) In spite of는 절을 이끌 수 없으므로 빈칸에 들어갈 수 없다.

번역 자선 행사가 성공할 것이라고 예상하기는 했지만, 그래도 도노반 씨는 지역 사회의 반응에 감동받았다.

어휘 charity 자선 response 반응 community 지역 사회 overwhelm (감정적으로) 압도하다, 놀래키다

126 형용사 어휘

해설 빈칸 뒤 명사구 calendar updates를 적절히 수식하는 형용사를 선택하는 문제이다. 약속을 놓치지 않게 도와주는 일정 업데이트의 특징을 묘사하는 형용사가 들어가야 자연스러우므로, '지속적인, 계속적인'이라는 의미의 (C) continual이 정답이다

번역 이 무료 모바일 앱은 지속적인 일정 업데이트를 제공하므로 영업사원들은 약속을 절대 놓치지 않을 것입니다.

어휘 appointment 약속 casual 평상시의, 격식을 차리지 않는 equal 동등한, 동일한 eventual 최종적인, 궁극적인

127 부정대명사

해설 빈칸은 although가 이끄는 절의 주어 자리이므로, 보기 중 주절의 주어(senior managers)를 적절히 대신하는 대명사를 선택해야 한다. 두 절 사이에 양보·대조의 접속사인 although(그러나, 하지만)가 있으므로, 빈칸에는 Most senior managers와 상반되는 의미의 대명사가 들어가야 한다. 따라서 (A) one이 정답이다. 참고로, '서로'라는 의미의 (B) one another와 (C) each other는 주어 자리에 들어갈 수 없고, (D) other는 대명사로 쓰일 경우 others 혹은 the other(s)의 형태가 되어야 한다.

번역 대다수 고위 간부들은 건축가의 사무실 배치안을 승인했지만, 한 사람이 비용에 대해 우려를 표명했다.

어휘 approve 승인하다 architect 건축가 concern 우려, 걱정

128 상관 접속사

해설 빈칸은 not only와 짝을 이루어 to perform general office duties와 to support an ongoing special project를 연결하는 접속사 자리이므로, (A) but also가 정답이다. 「not only A but also B」는 'A뿐만 아니라 B도'라는 의미를 나타낸다. (C) other than은 '~ 이외에, ~가 아닌'이라는 의미로 문맥상 빈칸에 부적절하다.

번역 그린빌 도서관은 일반 사무 업무를 수행할 뿐만 아니라 진행 중인 특별 프로젝트를 지원할 사무 보조원을 채용했다.

어휘 perform 수행하다 support 지원하다 ongoing 진행 중인

129 동사 어형_시제

해설 주절에 있는 동사의 시제를 선택하는 문제이다. if절에서 현재 시제(are made)를 사용해 미래에 가능한 일(특정 조건)을 나타내고 있으므로, 주절도 미래와 관련된 내용이 되어야 자연스럽다. 따라서 (B) will be continued가 정답이다.

번역 기존 사무실을 개조한다면 폴리키 그룹과의 임대 계약은 지속될 것이다.

어휘 modification 개조, 수정 existing 기존의

130 동사 어휘

해설 빈칸 뒤 목적어 a summary (with a list of recommendations)와 어울리는 동사를 선택하는 문제이다. 문맥상 '건의 사항 목록이 있는 요약본을 발행한다'라는 내용이 되어야 자연스러우므로, '발행하다, 발표하다'라는 의미의 (D) issues가 정답이다.

번역 라젠 어소시에이츠는 모든 감사에 있어 일종의 관례로서 건의 사항 목록이 있는 요약본을 발행합니다.

어휘 issue 발행하다 recommendation 권장, 추천 routine 통상적인, 정례적인 audit 감사 realize 깨닫다, 실현하다 induce 유도하다, 초래하다 cause 야기하다

PART 6

131-134 이메일

발신: 시설부

수신: 전 직원

제목: AC 문제

날짜: 2월 4일

장비 계약 업체인 토로노 판금이 내일 아침 건물 뒤쪽에 있는 냉각기 울타리에 대한 작업을 시작합니다. 계약 업체는 냉난방 장비의 내부 작동을 ¹³¹더 잘 보호하기 위해 강철 덮개를 설치할 예정입니다.

기술자들이 건물에 계속 드나들면서 대형 기계 부품과 연장을 카트로 나르는 모습을 보시게 될 것입니다. 이번 공사가 진행되면서 소음이 발생할 것이므로 인내심을 갖고 기다려 주시기를 당부 드립니다. ¹³²또한 여러분은 노상 주차 공간을 찾아야 할 수도 있습니다. 진입로 대부분이 계약 업체의 운반차들로 ¹³³가로막혀 있을 것입니다. ¹³⁴작업은 오후 2시에 마칠 예정입니다.

호르헤 카레라스, 시설 부장

어휘 facilities 시설 equipment 장비 contractor 계약
업체 be scheduled to + 동사원형 ～할 예정이다 chiller
냉각기 enclosure 울타리, 둘러쌈 rear 뒤쪽 install 설치하다
technician 기술자 repeatedly 계속, 반복하여 cart (수레나
차량으로) 운반하다 associated with ～와 관련된 patience 인내
driveway 진입로

131 부사 어휘

해설 빈칸은 to부정사의 동사원형 protect를 수식하는 부사 자리이며, 빈
칸을 포함한 to부정사구가 동사 will be installing을 수식하고 있
다. 문맥상 '더 잘 보호하기 위해 설치할 예정이다'라는 내용이 되어야
자연스러우므로, (A) better가 정답이다.

132 접속부사

해설 빈칸 앞뒤 문장을 의미상 연결하는 접속부사를 선택하는 문제이다. 빈
칸 앞 문장에서 공사 관련 소음 문제(There will be some noise
associated with this project)를, 빈칸 뒤에서 주차 문제(you
should probably look for on-street parking)를 언급했으므로,
빈칸에는 유사한 내용을 연결하는 접속부사가 들어가야 글의 흐름이
자연스러워진다. 따라서 '또한'이라는 의미의 (B) Also가 정답이다.
(A) As a result는 '결과적으로', (C) Nevertheless는 '그럼에도 불
구하고', (D) However는 '하지만'이라는 의미로 모두 문맥상 적절하
지 않다.

133 동사 어형 _ 시제

해설 적절한 동사의 시제를 선택하는 문제이다. 지문 전반에서 앞으로 있을
공사 작업에 대해 안내하며 현재 시제와 미래 시제를 함께 사용했다.
빈칸이 포함된 부분은 추후 발생할 수 있는 문제(진입로 차단)에 대한
내용이므로, 미래 시제가 쓰여야 자연스럽다. 따라서 (B) will block
이 정답이다.

134 문맥에 맞는 문장 고르기

번역 (A) 새 시설에 대한 의견을 보내 주십시오.
(B) 유지 관리 문제에 대해 알려 드리려고 편지를 씁니다.
(C) 오히려, 그들은 이 계약에서 저의 첫 번째 선택이 아니었습니다.
(D) 작업은 오후 2시에 마칠 예정입니다.

해설 빈칸 앞에서 공사 진행과 관련된 문제점을 언급했으므로, 공사 진행과
관련된 내용이 이어지는 것이 문맥상 자연스럽다. 따라서 (D)가 정답
이다.

어휘 suggestion 의견, 제안 maintenance (건물) 유지 관리, 정비
be expected + to동사원형 ～할 예정이다

135-138 이메일

수신: 멜리나 라모스 산도발
발신: welcome@sourcework.ca

날짜: 10월 25일
제목: 등록 완료

산도발 씨께,

선도적인 온라인 경력 매칭 서비스인 소스 워크 일자리 네트워크에 오
신 것을 환영합니다. 귀하의 주소, 경력, 선호 사항들이 저희 데이터베
이스에 135등록되었습니다. 이 정보는 136귀하와 같은 구직자를 찾고
있는 고용주를 식별하는 데 사용됩니다. 귀하는 앞으로 해당 지역 일자
리에 관한 알림을 정기적으로 받게 됩니다.

137당사는 개인 정보를 중시합니다. 따라서 귀하의 이름이나 주소를 누
구와도 공유하지 않을 것입니다. 언제든지 당사에서 수신한 이메일의
맨 아래에 있는 링크를 선택하여 이메일 설정을 취소하거나 변경하실
수 있습니다.

138가입해 주셔서 감사합니다. 질문이나 의견이 있으시면 언제든지 연
락 주십시오.

소스 워크 팀

어휘 leading 선도적인 preference 선호 identify 식별하다,
찾다 job candidate 구직자 periodic 정기적인 notification
알림, 통지 unsubscribe 취소하다 register 등록하다, 신청하다

135 동사 자리 _ 태

해설 Your e-mail address, work experience, and preferences
가 주어, 빈칸이 동사인 문장이므로, 보기 중 능동태 동사 (B) are
recording과 수동태 동사 (D) have been recorded가 빈칸에 들
어갈 수 있다. 문맥상 주어가 동사 record(기록하다)의 대상이 되므
로, 수동태인 (D) have been recorded가 정답이 된다.

136 인칭대명사

해설 빈칸은 전치사 like의 목적어 역할을 하는 자리이며, 빈칸을 포함한
전치사구가 명사 job candidates를 수식하고 있다. 빈칸 뒤 문장
에서 '귀하는 일자리에 관한 알림을 정기적으로 받게 된다(you will
receive periodic notifications about open positions)'라고 했
으므로, 이메일의 수신자인 산도발 씨도 구직자임을 알 수 있다. 따
라서 '귀하와 같은 구직자들'이라는 내용이 되어야 자연스러우므로,
(C) you가 정답이다.

137 문맥에 맞는 문장 고르기

번역 (A) 당사는 개인 정보를 중시합니다.
(B) 완벽한 직장을 찾는 일은 어려울 수 있습니다.
(C) 당사 일자리 데이터베이스는 매주 업데이트됩니다.
(D) 최근 귀하의 이력서를 검토했습니다.

해설 빈칸 뒤 문장에서 '그러므로, 이름이나 주소를 누구와도 공유하지
않을 것입니다(Therefore, we will not share your name or
address with anyone)'라고 했으므로, 빈칸에서 먼저 이름이나 주
소와 같은 개인 정보를 공유하지 않는 이유를 언급하는 것이 문맥상
자연스럽다. 따라서 (A)가 정답이다.

138 동사 어휘

해설 첫 번째 문장에서 온라인 경력 매칭 서비스인 소스 워크 일자리 네트워크에 온 것을 환영한다(Welcome to ~ the leading online career matching service)고 했으므로, 산도발 씨가 온라인 경력 매칭 서비스에 가입했다는 것을 알 수 있다. 따라서 '가입한 것, 등록한 것'이라는 의미의 (D) registering이 정답이다.

어휘 invest 투자하다 attend 참석하다 compete 경쟁하다

139-142 회람

> 발신: 누라 시몰라, 운영 담당 부사장
> 수신: 전 직원
> 날짜: 2월 8일
> 주제: 급여 변경
>
> 3월 15일부터, 우리는 현재 시행 중인 몇 가지 급여 처리 절차에 영향을 미칠 새로운 급여 서비스를 사용합니다. 첫째, 주급 명세서는 금요일이 아닌 목요일에 발송됩니다. 계좌 입금 급여 역시 하루 139**일찍** 처리됩니다. 둘째, 계좌 입금 급여에 대한 급여 명세서는 더 이상 이메일로 발송되지 않습니다. 대신, 직원들은 급여 계정에 온라인으로 접속하면 해당 정보를 140**볼** 수 있을 것입니다.
>
> 다른 절차는 동일하게 유지됩니다. 모든 근무 시간 기록 카드는 계속해서 월요일 오후 6시까지 경리부로 제출해야 합니다. 141**예전의 근무 시간 기록 카드 양식도 여전히 유효합니다.** 업데이트된 전체 급여 절차 지침 목록은 3월 1일 혹은 그 이전에 모든 직원에게 142**배포될 예정입니다.** 그 전에 문의가 있으면 내선 번호 **5810으로** 리온티 벨루소프 씨에게 문의하십시오.

어휘 employee 직원 affect 영향을 미치다 current 현재의 process 절차, 과정 direct-deposit (급여) 계좌 입금 pay stub 급여 명세서 payroll department 급여 지급 부서, 경리부 access 접속하다; 접속, 접근 valid 유효한 instruction 지침, 설명 procedure 절차 distribute 배포하다 ext. 내선 번호(= extension)

139 부사 어휘

해설 a day와 함께 동사 will be processed를 적절히 수식하는 부사를 선택하는 문제로, 해당 문장에 있는 부사 also와 그 앞 문장이 문제 해결의 단서가 된다. 앞 문장에서 주급 명세서가 금요일 대신 목요일(Thursday instead of Friday)에, 즉 기존보다 하루 일찍 발송된다고 했으므로, 빈칸이 포함된 문장은 '계좌 입금 급여 역시 하루 더 일찍 처리될 것이다'라는 내용이 되어야 자연스럽다. 따라서 '더 일찍'이라는 비교급 부사인 (C) earlier가 정답이다.

140 동사 어휘

해설 목적어 역할을 하는 명사구 this information 및 문맥과 어울리는 동사를 선택하는 문제이다. 급여 명세서를 이메일로 보내진 않지만, 그 대신(Instead) 다른 방법(accessing their payroll accounts online)을 사용하면 관련 정보를 확인할 수 있다고 안내하고 있으므로, '보다'를 의미하는 (A) view가 정답이다.

어휘 reject 거부하다

141 문맥에 맞는 문장 고르기

번역 (A) 날짜와 시간 변경에 유의하십시오.
(B) 대다수 직원이 오전 8시에 근무를 시작합니다.
(C) 경리부는 운영되지 않습니다.
(D) 예전의 근무시간 기록 카드 양식도 여전히 유효합니다.

해설 빈칸 앞에서 다른 절차는 동일하게 유지된다(Other processes will remain the same)고 했고, 그 다음에 카드를 계속해서 월요일 오후 6시까지 경리부로 제출해야 한다(All time cards will continue ~ at 6:00 P.M.)며 동일하게 유지되는 절차를 구체적으로 언급했다. 따라서 빈칸에도 이와 관련된 내용이 들어가야 문맥상 자연스러우므로, (D)가 정답이다.

어휘 operational 운영의

142 동사 자리 _ 시제 _ 태

해설 A complete, updated list가 주어, 빈칸이 동사인 문장이다. 문맥상 변경 사항이 적용된 지침 목록이 추후 배포될 것이므로 미래 시제가 쓰여야 하며, 주어 list가 동사 distribute(배포하다)의 대상이 되므로 수동태 문장이 되어야 한다. 따라서 (B) will be distributed가 정답이 된다. 참고로, (D) distributing은 동명사/현재분사로 문장에서 동사 역할을 할 수 없다.

143-146 기사

> **켄트론의 맛있는 간식**
>
> 켄트론 소유인 그루바토 젤라토는 미국에 이민 온 이탈리아 이민자인 루치아노 알지에리 씨가 커버비 애비뉴에 있는 143**공장**을 매입했던 2010년에 설립되었다. 그 건물은 이전에 홉스카치 아이스크림사가 있던 곳으로 알지에리 씨는 이전의 홉스카치 직원들을 많이 고용할 수 있었다. 144**숙련된** 아이스크림 제조자들에게 젤라토 제조법을 가르치는 일은 쉬웠다.
>
> 알지에리 씨는 자신의 제품을 145**만들기 위해** 가문의 오래된 조리법으로 시작했다. 그런 다음 과일과 견과류를 특이하게 조합하고 비법 재료까지 더해 맛을 돋우었다. 146**그 결과 다채롭고 만족스러운 맛의 배합이 탄생했다.**
>
> 현재 켄트론 지역에는 3개의 지점이 있다. 주민들은 이런 보물을 갖게 되어 정말 행운이다!

어휘 treat 간식 found 설립하다 immigrant 이민자 factory 공장 previously 이전에, 과거에 house 수용하다 experienced 숙련된, 노련한 crafter 제조자, 만드는 사람 enhance 향상하다, 강화하다 flavor 맛 ingredient 재료 resident 주민 gem 보물

143 명사 어휘

해설 빈칸 앞 동사 bought의 목적어 역할을 하는 명사를 선택하는 문제이다. 뒤에 나오는 문장에서 그 건물은 이전에 홉스카치 아이스크림사가 있던 곳(The building had previously housed the Hopscotch Ice Cream Company)이라며 매입한 건물을 설명하고 있으므로, 빈칸에는 이를 구체적으로 명시하는 명사가 들어가야 문맥상 자연스럽다. 따라서 '공장'이라는 의미의 (D) factory가 정답이다.

144 형용사 자리 _ 명사 수식

해설 빈칸은 동명사 Teaching의 목적어인 명사구 ice-cream crafters(아이스크림 제조자들)를 수식하는 형용사 자리이다. 따라서 명사(구) 앞에 위치하여 사람을 적절히 묘사하는 형용사가 빈칸에 들어가야 하므로, '숙련된, 경험이 많은'이라는 의미의 과거분사 (D) experienced가 정답이다. 참고로, (C) experiencing은 현재분사로서 명사를 수식할 경우 명사 뒤에 위치하여 '(~를) 경험하는'이라는 뜻을 나타낸다.

145 to부정사 _ 부사적 용법

해설 빈칸은 명사구 his product를 목적어로 취하면서 뒤에 나오는 주절을 수식하는 부사와 같은 역할을 한다. 따라서 to부정사인 (A) To create가 정답이 된다. (B) Creates와 (C) Had created는 동사, (D) Creation은 명사로, 품사상 빈칸에 들어갈 수 없다.

146 문맥에 맞는 문장 고르기

번역 (A) 바나나 호두는 조금 더 비싸다.
(B) 일부는 여전히 홉스카치 아이스크림을 선호한다.
(C) 그 결과 다채롭고 만족스러운 맛의 배합이 탄생했다.
(D) 시식해 보시고 의견 주십시오.

해설 빈칸 앞 문장에서 과일과 견과류를 특이하게 조합하고 비법 재료까지 더해 맛을 돋우었다(He then enhanced the flavor ~ fruits and nuts)며 제품의 맛을 위한 노력을 언급했으므로, 빈칸에는 이러한 노력에 따른 결과를 제시하는 문장이 들어가야 자연스럽다. 따라서 (C)가 정답이다.

PART 7

147-148 공지

맛보세요! 나누세요! 당첨되세요!

147이곳 사와디 월드 비스트로에서는, 재능 있는 요리사들이 전 세계의 맛있는 특별 요리를 선사함으로써 여러분에게 세계를 안겨 드립니다. 이제 버튼만 클릭하면 여러분의 식사 경험을 전 세계와 공유할 수 있습니다!

148요리 사진을 찍어 저희 웹사이트에 올리시기만 하면 됩니다. 100달러 상품권을 탈 수 있는 기회에 자동으로 응모됩니다.

무엇을 망설이십니까?

www.sawadeeworldbistro.com/tastesharewin

어휘 bistro (소규모) 식당 talented 재능 있는 serve (음식 등을) 제공하다 flavorful 맛 좋은 automatically 자동적으로

---

147 추론 / 암시

번역 공지는 어디에서 볼 수 있겠는가?

(A) 식당 벽   (B) 요리책 뒷면
(C) 사진 잡지 표지   (D) 주방용품 매장 문

해설 첫 번째 단락의 '이곳 사와디 월드 비스트로(Here at Sawadee World Bistro)에서는, 재능 있는 요리사들이 전 세계의 맛있는 특별 요리를 선사함으로써 여러분에게 세계를 안겨 드립니다(our talented chefs ~ by serving flavorful specialties from around the globe)'라는 문구를 통해 식당에서 볼 수 있는 공지임을 추론할 수 있다. 따라서 (A)가 정답이다.

어휘 supply 용품

148 세부 사항

번역 독자들이 경연에 참가하는 방법은?

(A) 후기 작성하기
(B) 조리법 만들기
(C) 기부하기
(D) 사진 제출하기

해설 두 번째 단락에서 요리 사진을 찍어서 웹사이트에 올리면(Just take a picture of your meal and post it on our Web site) 100달러 상품권을 탈 수 있는 기회에 자동으로 응모된다(You will be automatically be entered ~ a $100 gift card)고 했으므로, (D)가 정답이다.

▶▶ **Paraphrasing** 지문의 be entered to a chance to win
→ 질문의 enter a contest
지문의 take a picture of your meal and post it on our Web site
→ 정답의 submitting a photograph

149-150 문자 메시지

수잔 롤린스 (오전 10시 12분)
149방금 그린우드 레인에 있는 밀러 씨의 주택을 위한 당신의 설계 초안을 훑어보았어요. 다 괜찮아 보이는데 특히 주방과 주 거실 공간이 좋네요. 유일한 걱정이 있다면 유리 일광욕실의 실현 가능성입니다. 유리 방은 종종 예산을 초과하죠.

마일스 하트 (오전 10시 15분)
고객들이 일광욕실을 넣어 달라고 계속 요청했어요. 그들이 자금을 충당할 방법을 찾을 겁니다.

수잔 롤린스 (오전 10시 17분)
이 안을 확정하기 전에 자금이 준비될지 확실히 알아봐야 돼요. 그 사이 150이 추가 사항을 제외한 새로운 설계도를 만들 수 있을까요?

마일스 하트 (오전 10시 18분)
문제 없어요. 150지금 만들게요. 오늘 이따가 밀러 씨 가족과 예산에 대해 논의하기 위해 연락할 참이었어요.

어휘 preliminary 예비의, 임시의 concern 우려, 걱정 practicality 실현 가능성, 현실성 sunroom 일광욕실 budget 예산 finance 자금을 충당하다; 재원 come up with 생산하다, 내놓다

---

149 추론 / 암시

번역 작성자들은 어디에서 일하겠는가?

  (A) 은행
  (B) 유리 공장
  (C) 건축사 사무소
  (D) 인테리어 생활용품 매장

해설 롤린스 씨는 오전 10시 12분 메시지에서 밀러 씨의 주택을 위한 하트 씨의 설계 초안을 훑어보았다(I just looked through your preliminary design plans ~)고 한 후, 특히 주방과 주 거실 공간(especially the kitchen and main living area)의 작업을 칭찬했다. 따라서 작성자들이 건축사 사무소에 근무한다는 것을 추론할 수 있으므로, (C)가 정답이다.

150 의도 파악

번역 오전 10시 18분에 하트 씨가 "문제 없어요"라고 쓸 때, 그 의도는 무엇인가?

  (A) 프로젝트가 충분히 예산 범위 내에 있다.
  (B) 기꺼이 대체안을 만들 것이다.
  (C) 오늘 이따가 밀러 씨 가족을 만날 수 있다.
  (D) 밀러 씨 가족이 제안에 찬성했다.

해설 롤린스 씨가 오전 10시 17분 메시지에서 추가 사항을 제외한 새로운 설계도를 만들어 달라(can you come up with a new design that leaves off this addition?)고 요청을 했다. 이에 대해 하트 씨가 '문제 없어요(Shouldn't be a problem)'라고 응답한 후, '지금 만들겠다(I'll work on it now)'고 했으므로, 그가 기꺼이 대체안을 만들 것임을 알 수 있다. 따라서 (B)가 정답이다.

어휘 alternate 대체의

151-152 설명서

```
          베리타 모델 JX41Ci – 사용 설명서

• 전선 코드가 엉키지 않았는지 확인한 후 가까운 벽에 부착된 콘센트
  에 플러그를 꽂는다.

• ¹⁵²기계 위에 있는 다이얼을 이용해 적절한 설정(바닥, 털이 짧은 카
  펫, 털이 긴 카펫)을 선택한다.

• ¹⁵²손잡이 아래쪽에 있는 전원 버튼을 눌러 기계를 켠다. ¹⁵¹한 지점
  에서 2~3회를 천천히 계속 굴려 먼지와 부스러기를 빨아들인다.

• 구석이나 닿기 힘든 곳에 아직 부스러기가 남아 있다면 알맞은 부가
  장치를 연결한 다음 해당 부분에 사용한다.
```

어휘 ensure 확실히 하다 untangle (엉킨 것을) 풀다 outlet 콘센트 appropriate 알맞은, 적절한 steadily 계속, 지속적으로 debris 부스러기, 잔해 attachment 부가 장치 specified 명시된

151 세부 사항

번역 설명서에 따르면 기계의 용도는?

  (A) 음식 조리
  (B) 난방
  (C) 포장
  (D) 청소

해설 세 번째 항목에서 한 지점에서 2~3회를 계속 굴려 먼지와 부스러기를 빨아들인다(Run slowly and steadily over an area ~ to pick up dirt and debris)고 했으므로, 청소를 위한 기계임을 알 수 있다. 따라서 (D)가 정답이다.

> ▶▶ **Paraphrasing** 지문의 **to pick up dirt and debris**
> → 정답의 **Cleaning**

152 세부 사항

번역 사용자가 기계 사용 전에 매번 해야 하는 일은?

  (A) 기계 부가 장치 모두 연결하기
  (B) 기계 조절 장치 조정하기
  (C) 기계 부품 모두 청소하기
  (D) 기계 예열하기

해설 두 번째 항목 '기계 위에 있는 다이얼을 이용해 적절한 설정을 선택한다(Choose the appropriate setting ~ by using the dial on top of the machine)'와 세 번째 항목 '기계를 켠다(Turn the machine on)'를 통해 기계 사용 전에 매번 조절 장치를 조정해야 한다는 것을 알 수 있다. 따라서 (B)가 정답이다.

어휘 adjust 조정하다, 조절하다

> ▶▶ **Paraphrasing** 지문의 **Turn the machine on**
> → 질문의 **using the machine**
> 지문의 **Choose the appropriate setting by using the dial**
> → 정답의 **Adjust the machine's controls**

153-154 문자 메시지

발신: 마리아 바야르디	오후 8시 45분	555-0112

수신: 스티브 타키프

안녕하세요, 스티브. ¹⁵³비행편이 취소되어서 내일 오전 비행기를 타요. ¹⁵⁴전 씨가 우리 시설을 둘러보는 것도 내일 오전이에요. 당신이 전 씨를 안내해 주시겠어요? 그가 우리 입고 절차를 보고 싶어 해요. 그는 오전 10시에 도착할 예정이고, 우리측에서 점심 식사를 준비해요. 회의 관련 정보와 일정은 내 책상 위 파일 폴더에 있어요. 궁금한 것 있으면 전화하세요. 고마워요!

어휘 facility (특정 목적을 위한) 시설 warehousing 입고, 창고 저장 procedure 절차

153 주제 / 목적

번역 바야르디 씨가 타키프 씨에게 문자를 보낸 이유는?

(A) 그가 탄 비행기가 언제 도착하는지 알아보려고
(B) 창고로 가는 길을 물어보려고
(C) 최신 정보를 주려고
(D) 약속을 취소하려고

해설 항공편이 취소되어 내일 오전 비행기를 탈 것(My flight was canceled, and the new one is tomorrow morning)이라는 변동 사항을 알리며 타키프 씨에게 업무 관련 정보를 주고 있다. 따라서 (C)가 정답이다.

154 세부 사항

번역 바야르디 씨가 타키프 씨에게 요청한 일은?

(A) 점심 준비하기
(B) 안내하기
(C) 행사 일정 조정하기
(D) 전 씨에게 전화하기

해설 타키프 씨에게 전 씨가 시설을 둘러보는 게 내일 오전(Mr. Zhen's tour of our facility is also tomorrow morning)이라고 알려 준 후 그를 안내해 줄 것(Can you show him around?)을 요청했다. 따라서 (B)가 정답이다.

어휘 reschedule 일정을 조정하다

> ▶▶ Paraphrasing 지문의 show him around
> → 정답의 Give a tour

155-157 이메일

수신: 보 샤오
발신: 데이비드 모리소
날짜: 5월 16일
제목: 주문 번호 3A556

샤오 씨께,

155최근 Yippee.com에서 구매해 주신 데 대해 진심으로 감사드립니다! 당사와 거래해 주셔서 고맙습니다. 저희는 저희가 신뢰하고 직접 사용하는 고품질 제품만 판매하는 것을 자랑스럽게 생각합니다. 또한 고객님에게 최고의 고객 서비스를 제공하는 것에 대해 자부심을 갖고 있습니다.

155, 157고객님의 구매에 대해 감사를 표하기 위해 다음 주문에서 무료 배송뿐 아니라 15퍼센트 할인 혜택을 제공해 드리고자 합니다. 주문을 하시려면 당사 웹사이트 www.yippee.com을 방문하세요. 할인을 받으시려면 주문서를 작성할 때 코드 XB84RD를 사용하십시오. 157이 할인은 이메일 발신일로부터 60일 이후 만료됩니다.

최고의 서비스를 제공하기 위한 지속적인 노력의 일환으로, Yippee.com에서는 고객님들의 의견을 상시 요청합니다. 156그러니 www.yippee.com/survey를 방문해 고객 만족도 설문 조사서를 작성해 주시기 바랍니다.

155다시 한 번 감사드립니다.

데이비드 모리소

고객 서비스 담당 부서장

Yippee.com

어휘 recent 최근의 purchase 구매(품); 구매하다 grateful 감사하는 offer 제공하다; 할인 free shipping 무료 배송 expire 만료되다 routinely 일상적으로, 정기적으로 customer-satisfaction 고객 만족도 survey (설문) 조사서 vice president 부(서)장, 부사장

155 주제 / 목적

번역 이메일의 주요 목적은?

(A) 환불 제공하기
(B) 정보 명확히 밝히기
(C) 감사 표하기
(D) 신제품 광고하기

해설 첫 번째 단락에서 구매에 대해 감사 인사(Thank you very much for your recent purchase)를 한 후, 두 번째 단락에서 감사의 표시(To say thank you for your purchase)로 할인 혜택을 제공했고, 다시 한 번 감사드린다(Thank you again)며 메일을 마무리했다. 따라서 (C)가 정답이다.

어휘 clarify 명확하게 하다 appreciation 감사, 감상

156 세부 사항

번역 샤오 씨가 요청받은 일은?

(A) 축하 행사 참석하기
(B) 회사 서비스 평가하기
(C) 60일 이내에 이메일 보내기
(D) 곧 개업 예정인 신규 매장 방문하기

해설 세 번째 단락에서 웹사이트를 방문해 고객 만족도 설문 조사서를 작성해 달라(we invite you to visit ~ to complete our customer-satisfaction survey)고 요청했으므로, (B)가 정답이다.

어휘 celebratory 축하하는, 기념하는 evaluate 평가하다

> ▶▶ Paraphrasing 지문의 complete our customer-satisfaction survey
> → 정답의 Evaluate a company's service

157 문장 삽입

번역 [1], [2], [3], [4]로 표시된 곳 중에서 다음 문장이 들어가기에 가장 적합한 곳은?

"할인을 받으시려면 주문서를 작성할 때 코드 XB84RD를 사용하십시오."

(A) [1]
(B) [2]
(C) [3]
(D) [4]

해설 주어진 문장에서 할인을 받으려면 주문서를 작성할 때 특정 코드를 사용하라(Please use code ~ to receive the discount)고 했으므로, 이 앞에 할인에 대해 먼저 언급한 문장이 있어야 한다. [3] 앞 문장에서 15퍼센트 할인 혜택을 제안(offer you 15% off your next order)했고, 뒤 문장에서 할인의 유효 기간(This offer expires ~ this e-mail)을 안내했으므로, 이 사이에 주어진 문장이 들어가야 글의 흐름이 자연스러워진다. 따라서 (C)가 정답이다.

어휘 complete 완료하다, (빠짐 없이) 작성하다, 기입하다

158-160 광고

> 존 청의 집수리
>
> 중요하지 않은 일은 없다 • 인가받은 보험 가입 업체 • 무료 견적
>
> ➤ ¹⁵⁹⁽ᶜ⁾카펫, 타일, 목재 바닥 설치 및 제거
> ➤ ¹⁵⁹⁽ᴰ⁾문 설치 및 창문 교체
> ➤ ¹⁵⁹⁽ᴬ⁾데크와 현관 공사 및 수리
> ➤ 주방 조리대 및 수납장 설치
> ➤ 소규모 배관 및 전기 작업
>
> ¹⁵⁸적절한 비용으로 양질의 작업을 원하시면 910-555-0148로 전화 주십시오. 전화를 받지 않으면 메시지를 남겨 주십시오. 다음날 연락 드리겠습니다. ¹⁶⁰요청 시 추천서 제공 가능합니다.

어휘 licensed 인가 받은 insured 보험에 가입된 estimate 견적(서) laying 놓기, 설치하기 removal 제거 installation 설치 replacement 교체 repair 수리; 수리하다 porch 현관 countertop 조리대 plumbing 배관 (작업) affordable (가격이) 적당한, (대부분이 살 수 있을 만큼) 저렴한 reference 추천서 available 이용할 수 있는 upon request 요청 시

158 사실 관계 확인

번역 청 씨에 관해 명시된 것은?
(A) 최근 창업했다.
(B) 직원을 채용하고 있다.
(C) 그가 제시한 비용이 적정하다.
(D) 시간제로 일한다.

해설 마지막 단락의 '적절한 비용으로 양질의 작업을 원하시면(For high-quality work at affordable prices)'이라는 문구를 통해 그가 제시한 비용이 적정하다는 것을 알 수 있으므로, (C)가 정답이다.

어휘 reasonable 비싸지 않은, 합리적인

▸▸ Paraphrasing 지문의 affordable prices
→ 정답의 rates are reasonable

159 사실 관계 확인

번역 청 씨가 할 수 있는 작업으로 언급되지 않은 것은?
(A) 현관 수리
(B) 집 페인트칠
(C) 바닥재 교체
(D) 새 창문 설치

해설 작업 사항 세 번째 항목의 '현관 공사 및 수리(Construction and repair of ~ porches)'에서 (A)를, 첫 번째 항목의 '목재 바닥 설치 및 제거(Laying and removal of ~ wood flooring)'에서 (C)를, 두 번째 항목의 '창문 교체(Installation of ~ replacement windows)'에서 (D)를 확인할 수 있다. 그러나 페인트칠에 대한 언급은 없으므로, (B)가 정답이다.

어휘 fix 수리하다 replace 교체하다

▸▸ Paraphrasing 지문의 repair of porches
→ 보기 (A)의 Fixing porches
지문의 Laying and removal of wood flooring
→ 보기 (C)의 Replacing floor coverings
지문의 Installation of replacement windows
→ 보기 (D)의 Putting in new windows

160 세부 사항

번역 광고에 따르면 고객이 요구할 수 있는 것은?
(A) 타일 및 카펫 샘플
(B) 다른 고객의 추천서
(C) 급한 작업 시 작업 인원 증가
(D) 대규모 작업 할인

해설 마지막 문장에서 요청 시 추천서를 제공한다(References available upon request)고 했으므로, (B)가 정답이다.

어휘 recommendation 추천(서)

▸▸ Paraphrasing 지문의 upon request → 질문의 ask for
지문의 References
→ 정답의 Recommendations

161-163 기사

> **워싱턴 주, 자체 사과 소개 예정**
>
> 〈월간 농업〉 줄리아 리차드
>
> ¹⁶¹지난달 스케일스 대학교 과학자들은 워싱턴 주 농부들이 상표권을 갖게 될 최초의 사과인 "샤이너 크리스프" 개발을 완료했다고 보고했다. 소비자들은 이르면 내년에 첫 샤이너 크리스프를 구매할 수 있을 것으로 보인다.
>
> 사과 품종 개량가들은 특히 레즈와 쥬시즈 같은 전통적인 사과 품종들과의 경쟁에서 앞서 나가기 위해 새로운 사과를 개발한다. ¹⁶³새 과일은 반복해서 맛 테스트를 거쳐야 하므로 개발 과정에 상당한 돈과 시간이 투자된다. 다시 말해, 이런 신품종 사과들은 인기 있는 맛과 높은 수익을 염두에 두고 만들어진다. ¹⁶²레즈와 쥬시즈는 파운드 당 평균 1.29달러인데 반해 (아주 인기가 높은 브랜버스, 허니 스위츠 같은) 신품종 사과들은 적어도 3배 이상 벌어들인다.
>
> 이렇게 신품종이 추가되면 시장에도 장기적으로 큰 영향을 미친다. 20년 전에는 레즈와 쥬시즈가 사과 총 판매량의 50퍼센트 이상을 차지했는데, 지금은 시장에서 25퍼센트에도 못 미친다. 사과 품종 개발가들이 차기 인기 사과를 내놓기 위해 경쟁하는 것은 전혀 놀랄 일이 아니다!

161 주제 / 목적

번역 기사의 목적은?

(A) 샤이너 크리스프 가격에 대한 의견 제공하기
(B) 스케일스 대학교 학생 모집하기
(C) 사과 산업의 가격 차이 상세히 설명하기
(D) 신품종 사과 개발 알리기

해설 첫 번째 단락에서 '스케일스 대학교 과학자들이 워싱턴 주 농부들이 상표권을 갖게 될 최초의 사과를 개발했다고 보고했다(Scientists at Scales University reported ~ that they have completed the development of ~ the first apple that Washington state farmers will have trademarked all to themselves)'라고 한 후, 기사 전반에서 관련 내용을 서술하고 있다. 따라서 신품종 사과의 개발을 알리기 위한 기사임을 알 수 있으므로, (D)가 정답이다.

어휘 explanation 설명

▸▸ Paraphrasing 지문의 the development of the "Shiner Crisp," the first apple
→ 정답의 the design of a new apple

162 사실 관계 확인

번역 기사에 따르면 레즈와 쥬시즈에 관해 사실인 것은?

(A) 특이하게 워싱턴 주에 상표권이 있다.
(B) 허니 스위츠보다 저렴하다.
(C) 최근 판매량이 증가했다.
(D) 대학교 소속 과학자들이 재배했다.

해설 두 번째 단락에서 레즈와 쥬시즈는 파운드 당 평균 1.29달러인 데 반해(Whereas Reds and Juiceys average $1.29 per pound) 허니 스위츠 같은 신품종 사과들은 적어도 3배 이상 벌어들인다(new types of apples (such as ~ Honey-Sweets) are raking in at least three times as much)고 했으므로, 레즈와 쥬시즈가 허니 스위츠에 비해 저렴하다는 것을 알 수 있다. 따라서 (B)가 정답이다.

어휘 uniquely 독특하게, 특이하게 breed 재배하다; 품종

163 문장 삽입

번역 [1], [2], [3], [4]로 표시된 곳 중에서 다음 문장이 들어가기에 가장 적합한 곳은?

"다시 말해, 이런 신품종 사과들은 인기 있는 맛과 높은 수익을 염두에 두고 만들어진다."

(A) [1]
(B) [2]
(C) [3]
(D) [4]

해설 주어진 문장이 '다시 말해(In other words)'라는 표현을 사용하여 앞에 언급된 내용을 부연 설명하고 있으므로, 해당 문장과 비슷한 내용이 언급된 부분을 찾아야 한다. [3] 앞 문장에서 새 과일은 반복해서 맛 테스트를 거쳐야 하므로 개발 과정에 상당한 돈과 시간이 투자된다(The development process involves a considerable investment of time and money ~ their new fruits)고 했는데, 이를 바꿔 말하면, 상당한 시간과 금액을 투자하여 맛이 좋고(big flavor) 높은 수익(big profits)을 가져다 줄 과일을 개발한다고도 할 수 있다. 또한 [3] 뒤 문장에서 새로운 품종의 사과가 가져오는 수익을 언급했으므로, 이 사이에 주어진 문장이 들어가야 글의 흐름이 자연스러워진다. 따라서 (C)가 정답이다.

164-167 이메일

수신: 테레사 펄 〈tpearle@praguequarterly.cz〉
발신: 마레크 쿠벡 〈mkoubek@bistrokoubek.cz〉
제목: 보도 자료
날짜: 3월 15일

펄 씨께,

저희가 아까 나누었던 통화에 따라, 164제가 새로 개업한 식당인 비스트로 쿠벡과 관련된 보도 자료를 아래와 같이 보내 드립니다. 귀사의 잡지에 이 내용을 게재하겠다고 제안해주신 것에 대해 다시 한 번 감사드립니다. 귀사가 잡지를 발행하는 프라하 내에서 영어를 사용하는 지역사회가 성장하고 있다는 귀하의 견해를 듣게 되어 흥미로웠습니다. 식당이 체코 시민들뿐만 아니라 프라하에 거주하거나 방문하는 미국인들과 다른 외국인들에게도 165인기를 끌면 좋겠습니다.

마레크 쿠벡 드림

즉시 보도용: 체코-미국 식당 신장개업

프라하 (3월 15일)—프라하 1구역 브이 첼니치 가 437블록 4번 빌딩 (우편번호: 110 00)에 위치한 비스트로 쿠벡이 5월 21일 금요일 오후 6시부터 파티와 함께 개업을 축하한다.

소유주이자 주방장인 마레크 쿠벡 씨에 따르면 이 식당은 검보, 잼발레이아 등과 같이 루이지애나 주 뉴올리언스에서 인기 있는 메뉴에 체코 전통 요리를 결합한 케이준-체코 퓨전 요리를 주로 제공할 예정이라고 한다.

166개업 행사 기간에는 무료 시식 및 시음이 가능하지만 정식 식사 주문은 불가능하다. 5월 22일부터 정규 영업 시간은 오후 5시부터 자정까지이며 매일 영업한다. 메뉴는 www.bistrokoubek.cz에서 확인할 수 있다.

167(A)주방장인 쿠벡 씨는 16살까지 프라하에 살다가 가족과 뉴올리언스로 이주했으며, 167(C)거기서 아버지가 식당을 열었다. 그곳에서 그는 주방에서 일하며 루이지애나 요리 학교에 다녔다. 졸업 후에는 크레슨트 시티 이터리에 주방장으로 채용되어 167(D)독특한 메뉴와 플레이팅 능력으로 주요 상을 네 차례 수상했다. 그는 자신의 어린 시절 고향으로 돌아와 두 문화의 음식 유산을 프라하 식당 고객들과 공유하게 되어 기쁨을 감추지 못하고 있다.

어휘 press release 보도 자료 community 지역 사회 publication 발행(물), 출간(물) cater (서비스를) 제공하다 reside 거주하다 feature 특별히 포함하다, ~를 특징으로 삼다 cuisine 요리 complimentary 무료의 beverage 음료 operation 영업, 운영 flair 재능 culinary 요리의 heritage 유산

164 주제 / 목적

번역 쿠벡 씨가 펄 씨에게 이메일을 보낸 이유는?

(A) 파티에 초대하기 위해
(B) 기사 내용을 제공하기 위해
(C) 새로운 웹사이트 개설을 알리기 위해
(D) 글 편집에 도움을 요청하기 위해

해설 첫 번째 단락에서 자신이 새로 개업한 식당인 비스트로 쿠벡의 보도 자료를 아래에 첨부한다(please find the press release for my new restaurant, ~ below)며 잡지 게재를 제안해 줘서 고맙다(Thank you again ~ in your magazine)고 했으므로, 쿠벡 씨가 잡지에 실릴 보도 자료를 제공하기 위해 펄 씨에게 이메일을 보냈음을 알 수 있다. 따라서 (B)가 정답이다.

어휘 content 내용 launch 개시, 출시 request 요청하다
assistance 도움 edit 편집하다

165 동의어 찾기

번역 첫 번째 단락 4행의 "appeal to"와 의미상 가장 가까운 것은?

(A) 마음을 끌다
(B) 함께하다
(C) 득을 보다
(D) 부탁하다

해설 "appeal to"를 포함한 부분은 식당이 체코 시민뿐만 아니라 프라하에 거주하거나 프라하를 방문하는 미국인과 외국인들에게도 인기를 끌면 좋겠다고 희망하는 내용으로, 여기서 appeal to는 '~의 마음을 끌다, ~의 흥미를 일으키다'라는 의미로 쓰였다. 따라서 '마음을 끌다, 끌어들이다'라는 뜻의 (A) attract가 정답이 된다.

166 사실 관계 확인

번역 5월 21일 행사에 관해 명시된 것은?

(A) 오후 5시에 시작한다.
(B) 몇 사람만 초대받았다.
(C) 모든 품목은 무료로 제공될 것이다.
(D) 티켓 소지 고객만 입장할 수 있다.

해설 세 번째 단락에서 개업 행사 기간에 무료 시식 및 시음이 가능하다(Complimentary samples and beverages ~ during the grand opening event)고 했으므로, (C)가 정답이다.

어휘 patron 고객, 손님

> ▶ Paraphrasing 지문의 Complimentary samples and beverages will be available → 정답의 All items will be served free of charge

167 사실 관계 확인

번역 쿠벡 씨에 관해 언급되지 않은 것은?

(A) 프라하에서 자랐다.
(B) 유럽에서 여행을 많이 다녔다.
(C) 아버지의 식당에서 일했다.
(D) 요리상을 몇 차례 수상했다.

해설 보도 자료 마지막 단락의 '주방장인 쿠벡 씨는 16살까지 프라하에 살았다(Chef Koubek lived in Prague until age sixteen)'에서 (A)를, '아버지가 식당을 열었다(where his father opened a restaurant)'와 '그곳에서 그는 주방에서 일했다(There, he worked in the kitchen)'에서 (C)를, '독특한 메뉴와 플레이팅 능력으로 주요 상을 네 차례 수상했다(he earned four major awards for his unique menus and flair for meal presentation)'에서 (D)를 확인할 수 있다. 그러나 그가 유럽에서 여행을 다녔다는 내용은 언급되지 않았으므로, (B)가 정답이다.

어휘 extensively 널리, 광범위하게

> ▶ Paraphrasing 지문의 lived in Prague until age sixteen → 보기 (A)의 grew up in Prague
> 지문의 earned four major awards for his unique menus and flair for meal presentation → 보기 (D)의 has won several cooking prizes

168-171 온라인 채팅

피터 하러 [오전 9:30]	모두들 안녕하세요. ¹⁶⁸금요일 편집 회의에서 검토할 원고를 읽느라 모두 바쁘시니 짧게 할게요.
코라 그랜트 [오전 9:31]	회의 시간을 바꿨던가요?
피터 하러 [오전 9:32]	여전히 2시죠, 그렇죠?
메일리 슈 [오전 9:32]	네. ¹⁶⁹처음에는 오전에 할까 이야기했는데 제가 10시에 약속이 있어서요.
피터 하러 [오전 9:33]	그렇군요. 해결되어서 기쁘네요. 광의 생각을 같이 나누고 싶어요. 광, 설명해 주시겠어요?
광 천 [오전 9:35]	그러죠. ¹⁷⁰고객들에게 매달 소식지를 이메일로 받도록 신청하라고 독려하면 어떨까요? 특별 판촉이나 도서 나눔 콘테스트에 관한 정보를 포함하는 거죠. 우리 저자 몇 분에게 가끔 글을 쓰게 할 수도 있고요.
코라 그랜트 [오전 9:36]	맞아요. 저자들이 자신의 작품에 관해 알려주거나, 좋아하는 책에 관해 이야기할 수도 있겠어요.
메일리 슈 [오전 9:37]	좋은 생각이에요! 요즘에는 업계에서 이런 일이 점점 인기예요. 게다가 무료 도서를 받을 수 있는 기회는 사람들이 언제나 좋아하죠.
피터 하러 [오전 9:38]	음, 우리가 예산이 적은 소규모 출판사라는 점 명심하세요. 여러분 중 이 아이디어 진행해 볼 사람 있나요?
광 천 [오전 9:39]	제가 제안하는 거니까 제가 해야 할 것 같아요. ¹⁷¹메일리가 도와줄래요?
메일리 슈 [오전 9:40]	¹⁷¹물론이죠.
피터 하러 [오전 9:41]	좋아요. 모두들 감사합니다. 모두 금요일에 봅시다.

168   추론 / 암시

번역   온라인 채팅에 참여한 사람들은 누구이겠는가?

(A) 마케팅 회사 직원들
(B) 지역 신문사 기자들
(C) 회의 발표자들
(D) 출판사 동료들

해설   하러 씨가 오전 9시 30분 메시지에서 편집 회의에서 검토할 원고를 읽느라 모두 바쁠 테니 짧게 이야기하겠다(I'll make this brief ∼ reading the manuscripts for the editorial meeting)고 했으므로, 대화 참여자가 출판사에서 근무하는 사람들임을 추론할 수 있다. 따라서 (D)가 정답이다.

어휘   publishing 출판(업)

169   의도 파악

번역   오전 9시 33분에 하러 씨가 "해결되어서 기쁘네요"라고 쓸 때, 그 의도는 무엇인가?

(A) 원고가 모두 배당되었다.
(B) 회의 시간이 합의되었다.
(C) 약속이 취소되었다.
(D) 새로운 업무 규정을 따랐다.

해설   슈 씨가 오전 9시 32분 메시지에서 처음에는 회의를 오전에 할까 했는데(At first we talked about having it in the morning) 자신이 10시에 약속이 있어서(but I have an appointment at 10:00) 2시로 최종 결정이 되었다고 했다. 이에 대해 하러 씨가 '해결되어서 기쁘네요(I'm glad we got that sorted out)'라고 응답한 것이므로, 회의 시간이 합의되었음을 알 수 있다. 따라서 (B)가 정답이다.

어휘   policy 정책, 규정

170   세부 사항

번역   천 씨는 어떤 프로젝트를 진행하게 되는가?

(A) 소식지 개발
(B) 예산안 수정
(C) 서평 작성
(D) 상담란 작성

해설   천 씨가 오전 9시 35분 메시지에서 고객들에게 매달 소식지를 이메일로 받도록 신청하라고 독려할 것(encourage our customers to sign up to receive a newsletter)과 뉴스 레터에 특별 판촉이나 도서 나눔 콘테스트에 관한 정보를 포함할 것(include information about our special promotions or book giveaway contests)을 제시했다. 이후 하러 씨가 9시 38분 메시지에서 누가 이 아이디어를 진행할 것인지(Would one of you like to get this idea off the ground?) 묻자 9시 39분 메시지에서 천 씨가 자신이 하겠다(I suppose I should)고 했다. 따라서 (A)가 정답이다.

어휘   revise 수정하다   review (책 등에 대해) 논평하다   advice column (신문 등의) 상담란, 상담 코너

171   세부 사항

번역   슈 씨가 동의한 일은?

(A) 동료 돕기
(B) 일정 변경
(C) 저자 인터뷰
(D) 출장

해설   천 씨가 오전 9시 39분 메시지에서 메일리 슈 씨의 도움을 요청(Maybe Meili would help?)했고, 이에 대해 그녀가 오전 9시 40분 메시지에서 긍정의 응답(Of course)을 했으므로, (A)가 정답이다.

▶▶ **Paraphrasing**   지문의 **help** → 정답의 **Assist**

172-175   문서

해즈웰 타이어사 정비 보증서

해즈웰 타이어사는 여러분이 타이어를 믿고 원하는 곳에 가신다는 것을 알고 있습니다. 그런 이유로 당사는 여러분이 구매하신 당사의 모든 타이어에 대해 평생 정비 보증을 제공합니다. 타이어 점검, 위치 교환, 수리를 무료로 보장합니다.

점검: 서비스 팀이 공기압을 점검하고 필요시 공기를 주입하며, 타이어의 접지면이 닳으면 알려 드립니다.

위치 교환: 주기적으로 차량 타이어의 위치를 교환하는 것이 중요합니다. 저희 팀이 30분 이내에 이 서비스를 ¹⁷²시행할 수 있습니다.

수리: 타이어에 펑크가 나면 저희 팀이 최선의 노력을 다해 손상된 곳을 수리해 드립니다. ¹⁷³타이어 수리가 불가능하면 새 타이어를 구매하실 때 정가에서 20퍼센트 할인해 드립니다.

정규 영업 시간에 차량을 가져오시면 여러분이 금방 다시 운행하실 수 있도록 친절한 서비스 직원이 도와 드리겠습니다. 예약은 필요 없습니다. ¹⁷⁴타이어 구매 영수증만 보여 주십시오. 최초 구입자가 사용하는 타이어의 수명이 다할 때까지 서비스를 보증하며, 다른 차량 및 소유자에게 양도할 수 없습니다.

저희는 여러분의 만족을 최우선으로 합니다. 경쟁 업체들과 달리 당사는 단순히 타이어 판매만 하지 않습니다. 지역 내 가족 경영 업체로서, 30년 간 ¹⁷⁵당사는 탁월한 서비스를 제공해 고객들과 지속적인 관계를 맺어 왔습니다. 저희와 거래해 주셔서 감사합니다.

어휘   maintenance 정비, 유지 관리   warranty 보증(서)   lifetime 평생의   inspection 점검, 조사   rotation (타이어) 위치 교환   repair 수리; 수리하다   pressure 압력   inflate 공기를 주입하다, 부풀리다   tread 접지면   vehicle 차량   periodically 주기적으로   flat tire 펑크 난 타이어   transferrable 양도할 수 있는   priority 우선 사항   competitor 경쟁업체, 경쟁자   outstanding 탁월한

172 동의어 찾기

번역 세 번째 단락 2행의 "perform"과 의미상 가장 가까운 것은?

(A) 접대하다
(B) 운영하다
(C) 묘사하다
(D) 완료하다

해설 "perform"을 포함한 문장은 '30분 이내에 교체 서비스를 시행할 수 있다(Our team can perform this service for you in less than half an hour)'라는 의미로, 여기서 perform은 '수행하다, 완수하다'라는 뜻으로 쓰였다. 따라서 '완료하다'라는 의미의 (D) complete가 정답이 된다.

173 세부 사항

번역 문서에 따르면 해즈웰 타이어사는 언제 할인을 제공하는가?

(A) 고객이 교체 타이어를 구입할 때
(B) 서비스가 30분 이상 걸릴 때
(C) 회사가 특별 할인 행사를 하는 날
(D) 고객이 차량 한 대 이상에 쓸 타이어를 구매할 때

해설 네 번째 단락의 '수리(Repair)' 항목에서 타이어 수리가 불가능하면(If the tire can't be repaired) 새 타이어를 구매할 때 정가에서 20퍼센트 할인해 준다(we'll offer you 20 percent off ~ when you purchase a new tire)고 했으므로, (A)가 정답이다.

어휘 replacement 교체

> ▸▸ **Paraphrasing** 지문의 **offer you 20 percent off the regular price** → 질문의 **provide a discount**
> 지문의 **purchase a new tire** → 정답의 **buys a replacement tire**

174 세부 사항

번역 보증 서비스를 받으려면 고객은 무엇을 가지고 있어야 하는가?

(A) 타이어 구매 증빙 자료
(B) 과거 점검 인증 서류
(C) 보증서 1부
(D) 예정된 약속

해설 다섯 번째 단락을 보면 보증 서비스를 받기 위해서는 정규 영업 시간에 차를 가져오면 된다(Bring in your vehicle during regular business hours)고 했으며, 이때 타이어 구매 영수증을 보여 달라(Just show the receipt from your tire purchase)고 했으므로, (A)가 정답이다.

어휘 proof 증거, 증빙 자료   documentation 입증 서류, 기록

> ▸▸ **Paraphrasing** 지문의 **the receipt from your tire purchase** → 정답의 **Proof of tire purchase**

175 추론 / 암시

번역 해즈웰 타이어사에 관해 암시된 것은?

(A) 다른 타이어 매장보다 가격이 저렴하다.
(B) 고객과의 좋은 관계를 중시한다.
(C) 판매하는 타이어를 제조한다.
(D) 국제 기업이다.

해설 마지막 단락에서 '여러분의 만족을 최우선으로 합니다(Your satisfaction is our top priority)'라고 하며, 탁월한 서비스를 제공해 고객들과 지속적인 관계를 맺어 왔다(we have developed lasting relationships with our customers ~ service)고 덧붙였으므로, 고객과의 관계를 중시한다는 것을 추론할 수 있다. 따라서 (B)가 정답이다.

어휘 emphasize 강조하다, 중시하다   manufacture 제조하다   corporation 기업, 회사

> ▸▸ **Paraphrasing** 지문의 **lasting relationships with our customers** → 정답의 **good customer relations**

176-180 이메일 + 기사

수신: 마이클 카일로 〈mkaelo@hawthorneclinic.bw〉
발신: 소피 타바도 〈sthabado@Gaboronestar.bw〉
날짜: 2월 20일
제목: 주제: 행사
첨부: 𝕌 저녁과 점심 메뉴 선택 사항

카일로 씨께:

¹⁷⁶귀하의 행사를 위해 가보로네 스타 호텔을 고려해 주셔서 감사합니다. 귀하의 문의와 관련하여 답변을 드리자면, ¹⁷⁸저희 호텔에는 대규모 단체를 수용할 수 있는 4개의 연회장인 주피터 홀, 새턴 홀, 넵튠 홀, 비너스 홀이 있습니다. 각각 400명, 300명, 200명, 100명의 고객을 수용할 수 있습니다.

¹⁷⁷점심 및 저녁 식사 메뉴를 첨부했습니다. 하지만 특정 요청이 있으시면 기꺼이 협조해 드리겠습니다. 자리에 앉아서 드시는 식사 또는 뷔페 스타일의 서비스를 준비해 드릴 수 있습니다. 또한 업무 프레젠테이션이나 축하 행사를 위한 시청각 장비도 제공합니다.

추가 정보가 필요하면 알려 주십시오.

소피 타바도, 행사 부장

어휘 regarding ~에 관한   inquiry 문의   accommodate 수용하다   respectively 각각   specific 특정한, 구체적인   audiovisual 시청각의

가보로네 타임스
5월 20일

지역 소식

5월 15일 패트릭 마탐보 박사의 가족, 친구, 동료는 6월 1일자로 은퇴하는 그를 축하하기 위해 가보로네 스타 호텔에 모였다. 179(C)**마탐보 박사는 20년 동안 호손 시티 대학교 인근에 있는 호손 병원의 원장으로 재직했다.** 178**박사의 안녕을 기원하기 위해 참석한 180여 명의 사람들** 중에는 그의 친절함과 전문성을 입증하는 예전 환자들두 몇몇 있었다.

마탐보 박사는 지역 자선 행사에서도 친숙한 얼굴인데, 179(D)**특히 많은 지역 학교를 위해 모금을 도왔다.** 179(A)**당장에 그가 세운 계획은 아내인 앨리샤 마탐보 씨와 한 달간 크루즈 여행을 떠나는 것이다.**

마탐보 씨는 은퇴하긴 하지만 180**고문으로 병원 업무에 계속 관여할 예정이다.** 호손 병원 이사회는 신임 원장 선임을 승인했으며 이번 주 후반에 발표될 예정이다.

어휘   retirement 은퇴   take effect 발효하다   well-wisher 행복을 비는 사람   attest to 입증하다, 증언하다   honoree 영예를 받는 사람, 수상자   charity 자선 (단체)   in particular 특히   raise money 모금하다   immediate 당장의   retire 은퇴하다   approve 승인하다   board of trustees 이사회

176   주제 / 목적

번역   타바도 씨가 이메일을 보낸 이유는?
(A) 새 호텔을 홍보하기 위해
(B) 호텔 특별 할인을 제공하기 위해
(C) 행사 참석을 확정하기 위해
(D) 정보 요청에 응하기 위해

해설   이메일 첫 번째 단락에서 행사를 위해 가보로네 스타 호텔을 고려해 주어 감사하다(Thank you for considering the Gaborone Star Hotel for your event)고 인사한 후 카일로 씨의 문의와 관련하여 (Regarding your inquiry) 정보를 제공하고 있으므로, (D)가 정답이다.

어휘   promote 홍보하다   confirm 확인해 주다, 확정하다   attendance 참석

▸▸ Paraphrasing   지문의 your inquiry
→ 정답의 a request for information

177   세부 사항

번역   이메일과 함께 전달된 것은?
(A) 행사 무도회장 사진
(B) 식사 선택 사항에 관한 정보
(C) 호텔 서비스 목록
(D) 음향 장비 주문서

해설   이메일의 두 번째 단락에서 점심 및 저녁 식사 메뉴를 첨부했다(I've attached some lunch and dinner menu options)고 했으므로, (B)가 정답이다.

▸▸ Paraphrasing   지문의 attached
→ 질문의 sent with the e-mail
지문의 lunch and dinner menu options
→ 정답의 meal choices

178   연계

번역   축하 행사는 어디에서 열렸겠는가?
(A) 주피터 홀
(B) 새턴 홀
(C) 넵튠 홀
(D) 비너스 홀

해설   기사의 첫 번째 단락 후반부에서 약 180명이 박사의 안녕을 기원하기 위해 참석했다(Among the nearly 180 well-wishers in attendance)며 참석 인원을 언급했다. 연회장 이름과 수용 가능 인원은 이메일 첫 번째 단락에 나와 있는데, 네 개의 연회장(Jupiter, Saturn, Neptune, and Venus) 중 약 180명이 참석한 행사에 적절한 장소는 200명을 수용할 수 있는 넵튠 홀이므로, (C)가 정답이다.

179   사실 관계 확인

번역   마탐보 박사에 관해 언급되지 않은 것은?
(A) 레저 여행을 계획하고 있다.
(B) 20년 전에 호손 시로 이사 왔다.
(C) 의료 시설 책임자였다.
(D) 많은 지역 학교를 도왔다.

해설   기사 두 번째 단락의 '당장에 그가 세운 계획은 아내인 앨리샤 마탐보 씨와 한 달간 크루즈 여행을 떠나는 것이다(His immediate plans ~ vacation on a cruise ship)'에서 (A)를, 첫 번째 단락의 '마탐보 박사는 20년 동안 호손 병원의 원장으로 재직했다(For twenty years, Dr. Matambo ~ the director of the Hawthorne Clinic)'에서 (C)를, 두 번째 단락의 '많은 지역 학교를 위해 모금을 도왔다(he has helped ~ many area schools)'에서 (D)를 확인할 수 있다. 그러나 호손 시로 20년 전에 이사 왔다는 내용은 언급되지 않았으므로, (B)가 정답이다.

▸▸ Paraphrasing   지문의 a month-long vacation on a cruise ship → 보기 (A)의 leisure travel
지문의 the director of the Hawthorne Clinic → 보기 (C)의 in charge of a medical facility
지문의 many area schools → 보기 (D)의 many local schools

180   세부 사항

번역   기사에 따르면 마탐보 박사는 무엇을 할 계획인가?
(A) 전문적 활동 유지
(B) 취미에 더 많은 시간 할애하기
(C) 강의하기
(D) 후임자 면접하기

해설   기사의 마지막 단락에서 '그가 고문으로 병원 업무에 계속 관여할 예정이다(he will remain involved with the clinic as a consultant)'라고 했으므로, (A)가 정답이다.

어휘   remain 계속 ~이다   replacement 후임자, 대체하는 사람[것]

▸▸ Paraphrasing   지문의 remain involved with the clinic as a consultant
→ 정답의 Remain professionally active

수신: 빈센트 라이스터 〈vreister@hexagonmail.com〉

발신: 플로렌스 장 〈fzhang@zhtours.com.hk〉

제목: ¹⁸⁴홍콩 여행

날짜: 5월 3일

첨부: 📎 여행 일정표

라이스터 씨께:

¹⁸¹여행에 관해 장 홍콩 여행사에 문의해 주셔서 감사합니다. 그리고 칭찬해 주신 것도 감사드립니다. ^{182, 183}귀하의 동업자인 브라운 씨가 지난달 저희 크리에이티브 HK 관광 프로그램에 만족하셨고, 귀하께 저희 서비스를 추천하셨다는 소식을 듣게 되어 매우 기쁩니다.

¹⁸⁴5월 24일 주간에 이 도시를 짧게 방문하시는 동안 많은 관광 프로그램이 예정되어 있습니다. 이메일을 통해 ¹⁸⁵귀하가 역사적인 유적지 관람에 가장 관심이 있다는 것을 알게 되었습니다. 귀하가 특별히 좋아할 만한 선택 사항이 몇 가지 있습니다. 첨부된 일정표에서 보시듯이, ¹⁸⁵그 관광 프로그램 중 하나는 이미 예약이 다 찼습니다. 다른 관광 프로그램에서 자리를 확보하시려면 곧 예약하시기 바랍니다. 확정하시는 대로 바로 자리를 예약하겠습니다. 답신 기다리겠습니다.

플로렌스 장, 장 홍콩 여행사

어휘 compliment 칭찬 recommend 추천하다 gather (수집한 정보에 따라) 알다, 이해하다 secure 확보하다

장 홍콩 여행사 – 5월 투어

아래 관광 및 기타 관광에 관한 자세한 내용은 www.zhtour.com.hk를 방문하세요.

날짜	관광 프로그램	주요 경유지	시간/기간	가격(US$)	남은 자리
5월 25일	쇼핑객을 위한 HK	✓ 홍콩 몰 ✓ 홍콩 시장	오전 9시 –오후 3시 (6시간)	45.00달러	*4자리 남음*
5월 26일	¹⁸³크리에이티브 HK	✓ 영상 자료 보관소 ✓ ¹⁸³현대미술관	정오 12시 –오후 5시 (5시간)	45.00달러	*3자리 남음*
5월 27일	¹⁸⁵HK 역사 (중심 지구)	✓ 로판 사원 ✓ 비숍 하우스 ✓ 황후 부두	오전 10시 –오후 2시 (4시간)	45.00달러	¹⁸⁵*매진*
5월 28일	HK 아웃도어즈	✓ 카오룽 공원 ✓ 청샤 해변	오후 1시 –오후 6시 (5시간)	35.00달러	*3자리 남음*
5월 30일	¹⁸⁵HK 역사 (리다오 구)	✓ 틴하우 사원 ✓ 응하우 사원 ✓ 유후이 사원	오전 10시 –오후2시 (4시간)	50.00달러	¹⁸⁵*2자리 남음*

---

181 주제 / 목적

번역 이메일의 목적은?

(A) 추천하기

(B) 회사 서비스에 관한 문의에 답하기

(C) 신규 고객을 위해 여행 일정 수정하기

(D) 예약 확인하기

해설 이메일 첫 번째 단락의 '여행에 관해 장 홍콩 여행사에 문의해 주셔서 감사합니다(Thank you for your inquiry about tours with Zhang Hong Kong Tours, Inc)'라는 문구를 통해 여행 문의에 응답하기 위한 이메일임을 알 수 있으므로, (B)가 정답이다.

어휘 referral 소개, 추천 itinerary 여행 일정표

> ▸▸ Paraphrasing 지문의 your inquiry about tours with Zhang Hong Kong Tours, Inc → 정답의 a question about a company's service

182 세부 사항

번역 라이스터 씨가 장 홍콩 여행사에 대해 듣게 된 경위는?

(A) 동료

(B) 여행사

(C) 광고

(D) 인터넷 검색

해설 이메일의 첫 번째 단락을 보면 라이스터 씨의 동업자인 브라운 씨가 그에게 장 홍콩 여행사의 서비스를 추천했다(your business partner, Mr. Brown, ~ recommended our services to you)는 것을 알 수 있다. 따라서 (A)가 정답이다.

> ▸▸ Paraphrasing 지문의 your business partner → 정답의 a colleague

183 연계

번역 브라운 씨는 여행에서 무엇을 보았겠는가?

(A) 시장

(B) 사원

(C) 그림

(D) 공원과 해변

해설 이메일 첫 번째 단락에서 브라운 씨가 지난달 크리에이티브 HK 관광 프로그램에 만족했다(your business partner, Mr. Brown, was satisfied with our Creative HK tour)고 했는데, 일정표를 보면 크리에이티브 HK에는 영상 자료 보관소(Film Archive)와 현대미술관(Gallery of Modern Art)이 포함되어 있다. 따라서 브라운 씨가 현대미술관에서 그림을 보았다고 추론할 수 있으므로, (C)가 정답이다.

184 추론 / 암시

번역 라이스터 씨에 관해 암시된 것은?

(A) 예산이 빠듯하다.

(B) 곧 창업할 예정이다.

(C) 중국 요리에 관심이 있다.

(D) 잠시 홍콩에 머무를 것이다.

해설 이메일의 제목 '홍콩 여행(Hong Kong Tour)'과 두 번째 단락의 '5월 24일 주간에 이 도시를 짧게 방문하시는 동안(during your short visit to our city during the week of 24 May)'이라는 문구에서 라이스터 씨가 홍콩에 짧게 머무를 예정임을 추론할 수 있다. 따라서 (D)가 정답이다.

어휘 budget 예산 temporarily 일시적으로, 임시로

> ▶ Paraphrasing 지문의 **your short visit to our city**
> → 정답의 **will be in Hong Kong temporarily**

185 연계

번역 장 씨에 따르면 라이스터 씨에게 가장 적합한 여행은?

(A) HK 아웃도어즈
(B) 쇼핑객을 위한 HK
(C) HK 역사 (리다오 구)
(D) HK 역사 (중심 지구)

해설 이메일의 두 번째 단락에서 라이스터 씨가 역사적인 유적지 관람에 관심이 가장 많다(you are most interested in viewing historical landmarks)는 것을 알고 있다며 관련 관광 프로그램 중 하나가 예약이 찼으니(one of those tours is already fully booked) 다른 하나를 예약하려면(to secure a place on the other tour) 서두르라고 조언했다. 일정표를 보면, 역사 관련 프로그램(HK History) 중 자리가 남은 프로그램은 5월 30일의 'HK 역사(리다오 구)'이므로, (C)가 정답이다.

186-190 웹페이지 + 이메일 + 이메일

---

http://www.aeolusovens.com/commercial

| 홈 | 설명서 | 서비스 | 후기 |

아이올로스 제트베이크 3 컨벡션 오븐

이 고성능 업소용 오븐은 순환하는 뜨거운 공기를 이용해 음식을 골고루 그리고 효율적으로 익힙니다.

특징:
- 융통성 있는 사용자 설치 가능 옵션
- 187(B)넓은 내부 공간 – 깊이 104센티미터
- 187(C)11개의 다른 위치에 놓을 수 있는 조리판 5개
- 떼어낼 수 있는 바퀴
- 187(D)밝은 내부 LED 조명
- 187(A)팬 모드 선택 가능

어휘 convection (열 등의) 대류 high-yield 고성능의, 고수익의 commercial 업소용의, 상업의 evenly 골고루, 균등하게 efficiently 효율적으로 feature 특징 flexible 융통성 있는 spacious 넓은 removable 떼어낼 수 있는 lighting 조명

발신: 알도 카스트로 〈aldoc@businessdining.com〉
수신: 〈customerservice@aeolusovens.com〉
제목: 온도 문의

날짜: 5월 1일

담당자님께,

아이올러스 제트베이크 3에 대한 몇 가지 의견을 나누고 싶습니다. 188당사는 오스틴 시내 레드 엄브렐라 콤플렉스에 위치한 업체들을 위해 식사 서비스를 운영하고 있습니다. 저희는 지난달에 아이올러스 제트베이크 3를 구입했습니다. 이 오븐은 지금까지 저희가 접한 오븐 중 가장 효율적인 오븐으로, 187(B)대용량에 조리 시간도 빠릅니다. 저희 직원들은 매일 많은 인원을 위한 식사를 준비하므로 이 점은 매우 186중요합니다. 187(D)조명이 훌륭해서 187(C)한 번에 조리판을 3개 이상 사용해도 무엇을 요리하고 있는지 쉽게 볼 수 있습니다. 그런데 189저희 고객들이 가장 선호하지만 만들기 어려운 크로아상은 제대로 구워지지 않고, 저희 제과제빵사는 정확한 온도 설정을 찾지 못하고 있습니다. 그리고 왜 바퀴 위에 제품이 있는 걸까요? 제품이 무거운 데다 주방에서 이리저리 옮길 필요도 없는데 바퀴가 불필요하게 공간을 차지합니다. 저는 정확히 저희가 뭘 잘못하고 있는지 모르겠습니다. 어떻게 하면 더 효과적으로 빵을 구울 수 있는지 가능한 한 빨리 알려 주시기 바랍니다.

신속히 회신해 주시면 감사하겠습니다.

알도 카스트로

어휘 temperature 온도 by far 지금까지 efficient 효율적인 encounter 접하다, 마주치다 capacity 용량, 수용 능력 critical 매우 중요한 tricky 어려운 unnecessarily 불필요하게 incorrectly 틀리게

발신: 아이리스 마츠 〈imartz@aeolusovens.com〉
수신: 알도 카스트로 〈aldoc@businessdining.com〉
제목: 귀하의 문의
날짜: 5월 5일

카스트로 씨께,

최근에 아이올러스 제트베이크 3에 대한 이메일을 보내 주셔서 감사합니다. 189제가 추측하기로는 고객님께서 겪고 있는 문제는 당사의 대다수 모델에 기본으로 설치된 1.0 제어판과 관련이 있습니다. 이것은 패널 2.0과 호환되는데, 이 제어판에는 열 순환 팬을 세 가지 모드로 설정하는 기능이 포함되어 있어 더욱 정교한 조정이 가능합니다. 고객님께 무료로 한 개를 보내드리겠습니다. 190배송 주소와 오븐의 일련 번호를 기입하신 후 회신해 주시기 바랍니다. 일련 번호는 뒷면의 검사필증 바로 아래 있습니다.

구매해 주셔서 감사합니다!

아이리스 마츠
고객 관리

어휘 related to ~와 관련된 standard 일반적인, 표준의 interchangeable 호환[교체] 가능한 adjustment 조정 feature 기능 without charge 무료로 back 뒷면 inspection certificate 검사필증

186 동의어 찾기

번역 첫 번째 이메일에서 첫 번째 단락 4행의 "critical"과 의미상 가장 가까운 것은?

(A) 판단의
(B) 중요한
(C) 위험한
(D) 뜻밖의

해설 "critical"을 포함한 부분은 대용량에 조리 시간이 빠른 것(large capacity and rapid cooking times)이 업무상 매우 중요하다는 내용으로, 여기서 critical은 '중요한'이라는 뜻으로 쓰였다. 따라서 (B) important가 정답이다.

187 연계

번역 웹페이지에 열거된 오븐의 특징 중 카스트로 씨의 이메일에서 언급되지 않은 것은?

(A) 팬 모드 설정 기능
(B) 넓은 내부 공간
(C) 여러 개의 조리판 사용
(D) 밝은 내부 LED 조명

해설 첫 번째 이메일 네 번째 줄의 '대용량(with its large capacity)'에서 (B)를, 여섯 번째 줄의 '한 번에 조리판을 3개 이상 사용해도(even with three or more racks in use at once)'에서 (C)를, 다섯 번째 줄의 '조명이 훌륭하다(The lighting is great)'에서 (D)를 확인할 수 있다. 따라서 웹페이지에서 열거된 특징 중 하나이지만 이메일에서는 언급되지 않은 (A)가 정답이다.

어휘 spacious 넓은

▶▶ Paraphrasing 지문의 Selectable fan modes
→ 정답의 Ability to select fan modes
지문의 its large capacity
→ 보기 (B)의 Spacious interior
지문의 three or more racks in use
→ 보기 (C)의 Use of multiple racks

188 세부 사항

번역 카스트로 씨의 회사는 무엇을 하는가?

(A) 업체 직원을 위한 식사 준비
(B) 음식 서비스 장비 디자인
(C) 지역 식당에 제빵류 납품
(D) 온라인 음식 잡지 발행

해설 카스트로 씨가 보낸 이메일을 보면, 두 번째 문장에서 자신의 회사가 업체들을 위해 식사 서비스를 운영하고 있다(Our company runs the dining service for the businesses)고 했으므로, (A)가 정답이다.

어휘 equipment 장비 supply 공급하다, 납품하다

▶▶ Paraphrasing 지문의 runs the dining service for the businesses → 정답의 Prepare meals for business employees

189 연계

번역 마츠 씨가 카스트로 씨에게 이메일을 보낸 이유는?

(A) 오븐 바퀴 제거 방법에 관한 정보를 제공하려고
(B) 설치 문제를 해결하는 방법을 안내하려고
(C) 요리 세미나에 도움을 요청하려고
(D) 빵 굽기 문제에 관한 해결책을 제공하려고

해설 첫 번째 이메일에서 카스트로 씨가 크로아상이 제대로 구워지지 않고(our croissants ~ are not turning out right), 제과제빵사가 정확한 온도 설정을 찾지 못하고 있다(our pastry chef can't ~ find the right temperature settings)는 문제점을 언급했고, 어떻게 하면 더 효과적으로 빵을 구울 수 있는지 알려 달라(Please let me know ~ how we can bake more effectively)고 요청했다. 이에 대해 두 번째 이메일에서 마츠 씨가 문제의 원인(the trouble ~ is related to the 1.0 control panel)을 알려 주며 문제를 해결할 수 있는 부품(panel 2.0)을 보내 주겠다(I will ship one to you)고 했으므로, (D)가 정답이다.

어휘 guidance 지도, 안내 address (문제를) 다루다, 해결하다 assistance 도움

190 세부 사항

번역 마츠 씨가 카스트로 씨에게 요청한 일은?

(A) 부품 보내기
(B) 제품 정보 보내기
(C) 온라인 출처 참고하기
(D) 후속 후기 작성하기

해설 마츠 씨가 보낸 이메일 후반부를 보면, 카스트로 씨에게 배송 주소와 오븐의 일련 번호를 적어 회신해 달라(Please reply with your shipping address and the serial number of your oven)고 요청했으므로, (B)가 정답이다.

▶▶ Paraphrasing 지문의 the serial number of your oven
→ 정답의 some product information

191-195 이메일 + 웹페이지 + 이메일

수신: jacknajarian@sellomail.com
발신: guestservices@pamakanihotel.com
제목: 서핑 강습
날짜: 5월 10일

나자리안 씨께,

191주변에 있는 서핑 스쿨을 추천해 줄 수 있는지 저희 파마카니 호텔에 메일을 주셔서 감사합니다. 저희 호텔에서 몇 걸음 떨어진 해변에 라울로아 서프 스쿨(www.lauloasurfschool.com)이 있다는 것을 아신다면 기뻐하시리라 생각됩니다. 비용이 192적절하고, 강습도 꽤 훌륭합니다. 193저는 굉장히 유명한 알라나 카파쿠에게 4시간 동안 직접 강습을 받았으므로 개인적으로 그 스쿨을 추천해 드릴 수 있습니다.

6월 4일 고객님이 도착하실 때 고객님과 따님을 맞게 되기를 고대합니다. 체류 전이나 체류 중에 추가 문의 사항이나 필요한 것이 있으시면 알려 주시기 바랍니다. 저희가 도와 드리겠습니다.

어휘 fair 타당한, 적당한 recommend 추천하다 legendary 전설적인, 아주 유명한

---

http://www.lauloasurfschool.com/lessons

라울로아 서프 스쿨

- **2495 케카우 로드, 호놀룰루, 하와이 96815**
- **808-555-0142**

단체 강습

초급 및 중하급 서퍼를 위한 수업. 단체 강습은 강사 3명과 최대 12명의 수강생으로 구성됩니다. 단체가 아니신 경우, 저희가 고객님을 위해 단체를 구성해 드립니다.

- 2시간 강습 / 1인당 75달러
- 최소 13세 이상이어야 함.

가족 및 친구 강습

초급부터 중상급 서퍼까지를 위한 수업. 4인 이하. 강사 1인의 전담 지도를 원하는 수강생들을 위한 강습입니다. 일반 단체 강습보다 서핑할 기회가 더 많습니다.

- 2시간 강습 / 1인당 100달러
- 최소 13세 이상이어야 함.

개인 강습

초급부터 상급까지 모든 레벨을 위한 수업. 강사가 1대1로 전담하여 가르치므로 서핑 방법에 관해 배우고 싶은 것은 무엇이든 배울 수 있습니다.

- 2시간 강습 / [194]1인당 125달러
- [194]안전상의 이유로 13세 미만 어린이는 개인 강습 요망.

전문 강습

[193]상급 서퍼를 위한 수업. [193]전직 프로 서퍼인 알라나 카파쿠에게 고급 기술을 배우세요. 알라나는 10년 이상 프로 경기에서 참가했습니다. 그녀의 수강생 중에는 유명한 영화배우들도 있습니다!

- 1대1 4시간 강습 / 1인당 200달러
- 최소 13세 이상이어야 함.

모든 서핑 강습에 포함: 보호용 래쉬가드, 리프 슈즈, 보드 리쉬, 서핑보드 대여.

어휘 intermediate 중급의, 중간의 consist of ~로 구성되다 instructor 강사 advanced 고급의, 상급의 compete (경기 등에) 참가하다, 경쟁하다 protective 보호하는, 보호(용)의

수신: information@lauloasurfschool.com
발신: jacknajarian@sellomail.com
제목: 서핑 강습
날짜: 6월 17일

안녕하세요,

---

[194]12살 딸과 함께 하와이를 방문한 주간에 제 딸이 받았던 훌륭한 서핑 강습에 대해 아이를 대신해 감사를 표하고자 메일을 씁니다. [195]다시 방문하게 되면 그때는 다른 강습권도 구매해서 딸과 함께 등록해 둘이 같이 서핑하는 법을 더 배우자고 딸에게 벌써 이야기했습니다.

다시 한 번 감사드립니다. 어서 빨리 그곳에 다시 가서 라울로아 서프 스쿨에서 함께 해변과 파도를 즐기고 싶습니다.

잭 나자리안

어휘 on behalf of ~을 대신[대표]하여 purchase 구매하다 sign up 등록하다, 신청하다

191 주제 / 목적

번역 마니보그 씨가 첫 번째 이메일을 쓴 이유는?

(A) 예약 확인
(B) 문의 답변
(C) 추천 받기
(D) 강사 소개

해설 나자리안 씨에게 보낸 이메일의 첫 번째 단락에서 주변에 있는 서핑 스쿨을 추천해 줄 수 있는지 메일을 주어 고맙다(Thank you for writing to us ~ to ask if we could recommend a surfing school nearby)고 인사한 후, 라울로아 서프 스쿨을 추천해 주고 있다. 따라서 추천 요청 문의에 응답하기 위한 이메일임을 알 수 있으므로, (B)가 정답이다.

어휘 obtain 받다, 획득하다

▸▸ **Paraphrasing** 지문의 **to ask if we could recommend a surfing school nearby** → 정답의 **an inquiry**

192 동의어 찾기

번역 첫 번째 이메일에서 첫 번째 단락 4행의 "fair"와 의미상 가장 가까운 것은?

(A) 관대한
(B) 객관적인
(C) 적당한
(D) 가벼운

해설 "fair"를 포함한 부분은 '비용이 적절하다(The prices are fair)'라는 의미로, 여기서 fair는 '(가격이) 적당한, 괜찮은'이라는 뜻으로 쓰였다. 따라서 '적당한, 합리적인'이라는 의미의 (C) reasonable이 정답이다.

193 연계

번역 마니보그 씨에 관해 무엇이 사실이겠는가?

(A) 상급 수준 서퍼이다.
(B) 파마카니 호텔 고객 서비스 팀장이다.
(C) 이전에 라울로아 서프 스쿨에서 일했다.
(D) 나자리안 씨 가족의 가까운 친구다.

해설 첫 번째 이메일의 첫 번째 단락에서 마니보그 씨는 자신이 알라나 카 파쿠에게 4시간 동안 직접 강습을 받았다(Having taken a 4-hour lesson with ~ Alana Kapaku myself)고 했다. 웹페이지에 나온 강습 안내문을 보면, 전문 강습(Professional Lesson)은 상급 서퍼(For advanced surfers)를 대상으로 하며 전직 프로 서퍼인 알라나 카파쿠에게 고급 기술을 배우는(Learn advanced techniques from ~ Alana Kapaku) 강좌라고 했으므로, 마니보스 씨가 상급 수준의 서퍼라는 것을 추론할 수 있다. 따라서 (A)가 정답이다.

194 연계

번역 나자리안 씨는 딸의 강습을 위해 얼마를 지불했는가?

(A) 75달러
(B) 100달러
(C) 125달러
(D) 200달러

해설 두 번째 이메일을 보면 나자리안 씨의 딸이 12살(my 12-year-old daughter)이라는 것을 알 수 있고, 웹페이지를 보면 13살 미만의 아이들은 안전상의 이유로 개인 강습만 등록할 수 있다(For safety reasons, children under 13 years old require a private lesson)고 했으므로, 그녀가 개인 강습을 수강했음을 알 수 있다. 웹페이지에 나와 있는 개인 강습 등록비는 1인당 125달러이므로, (C)가 정답이다.

195 사실 관계 확인

번역 나자리안 씨와 딸에 관해 명시된 것은?

(A) 카파쿠 씨와 해변에서 만났다.
(B) 매년 하와이로 휴가 여행을 간다.
(C) 파마카니 호텔에 다시 머물 계획이다.
(D) 같이 서핑 강습을 받기를 기대한다.

해설 두 번째 이메일의 첫 번째 단락에서 다시 방문하게 되면 그때는 다른 강습권도 구매해서 딸과 함께 등록해 둘이 같이 서핑하는 법을 더 배울 것(when we visit again, I'll purchase another lesson and even sign up with her this time, so we can both learn more about how to surf)이라는 계획을 밝혔으므로, (D)가 정답이다.

196-200 기사 + 기사 + 프로그램 공지

팝 슈퍼스타 귀향

라퐁 (5월 23일)—소니아 베니테스가 모든 것이 시작된 곳으로 돌아와 그것을 되돌려준다. 이 국제적인 팝 슈퍼스타는 6월 2일 시작되는 롱로드 투어에 라퐁에서의 무료 콘서트를 추가했다고 발표했다. 베니테스는 7월 17일 라퐁에서 공연할 예정이다.

올렌더 인근에서 태어난 베니테스는 다섯 살 때 가족과 함께 라퐁으로 이주했다. 198그녀는 재스퍼 고등학교를 졸업했는데, 14살 때 학교 장기자랑 무대에 처음 올라 상을 타면서 동급생들과 교사들의 주목을 받았다. 이후 전문 경력을 쌓기 시작해 5개 대륙을 다니며 전 세계에서 수백만 명의 팬을 확보했다.

베니테스는 자신의 매니저인 제레미 햄프턴이 196시카고에서 공연 후 사흘간의 휴식 기간이 있다고 하자 라퐁에서의 콘서트를 추가하기로 결정했다. "우리 둘 모두에게 분명했어요." 자신의 로스앤젤레스 녹음실에서 전화를 걸어 온 베니테스가 말했다. "196라퐁에서 그렇게 가까운 곳에서 사흘이 비는데 공연을 안 한다는 건 생각할 수도 없어요. 매우 쉬운 결정이었죠."

197유일한 어려움은 베니테스의 고향 팬들을 모두 수용할 수 있는 장소를 찾는 일이었다. 도시에서 가장 큰 극장도 1,200석밖에 되지 않는다. 라퐁의 시장인 엘리스 스완슨이 기발한 해결책을 생각해 냈다. "그가 야외 콘서트를 제안했습니다." 베니테스가 말했다. "경기장이 아니라 도시 외곽 지역 농장입니다. 그렇게 하면 참석 가능한 인원에 제한이 없을 것입니다. 드넓은 벌판 한가운데 그냥 무대를 세울 겁니다."

지역 라디오 DJ 테일러 웬델은 콘서트에 8천여 명의 팬이 모일 것으로 예상한다.

"소니아가 이곳에서 얼마나 인기가 있는지와 콘서트가 무료라는 점을 감안하면 적게 잡은 겁니다." 웬델이 말한다. "기억에 남을 행사가 될 겁니다."

어휘 embark 시작하다 continent 대륙 obvious 분명한, 뻔한 venue 장소 accommodate 수용하다 local 지역의 estimate 예측하다 conservative (숫자 등을) 적게 잡은, 보수적인 memorable 기억에 남을, 기억할 만한

베니테스, 수많은 군중 앞에서 공연하다

라퐁 (7월 18일)—어젯밤 킹엄 힐스 팜 들판에서 열린 소니아 베니테스의 귀향 콘서트는 그야말로 장관이었다. 1만여 명의 군중이 12년 만에 처음으로 라퐁에 돌아온 고향의 영웅을 즐겁게 환영했다. 199베니테스는 평상시 2시간 분량의 노래에 8곡을 더 부름으로써 공연을 한 시간 더 연장해 멋진 볼거리를 제공했다.

(기억에 남는 순간들이 많았지만) 그날 저녁 가장 기억에 남는 순간은 200또 다른 라퐁 출신이자 6살 때부터 소니아의 친구인 피아니스트 제너비브 파커가 무대에 합류한 순간이었다. 파커는 베니테스만큼 유명하지는 않지만 베니테스만큼 뛰어난 음악가로, 비엔나에서 클래식 피아노를 공부하고 비엔나 순회 오케스트라와 함께 국제 순회 공연을 했다.

어휘 nothing short of 굉장히 ~한, 거의 ~나 마찬가지인 phenomenal 경이로운, 놀랄만한 quite a/an (+ 명사) 대단한 extend 연장하다 equally 동등하게, 마찬가지로 accomplished 뛰어난, 완성된

소니아 베니테스 라퐁 공연
특별 공지

킹엄 힐스 팜은 소니아 베니테스의 귀향 콘서트를 개최하게 되어 자랑스럽게 생각합니다. 아래에 열거된 목록은 소니아가 오늘밤 공연하게 될 곡들로 소니아와 라퐁 지역 주민들에게 특별한 의미가 있습니다.

"나비 노래"	소니아가 처음 작곡한 곡으로 11살 때 자매와 함께 작곡
"강변의 식사"	라퐁을 가로지르는 월턴 강에 관한 노래로 재스퍼 고등학교 합창단이 코러스
198"하나의 아침"	198고등학생 시절 첫 공연 때 소니아가 부른 노래
200"모두 웃다"	200어린 시절 친구의 피아노 반주에 맞추어 소니아가 부름

어휘 significance 의미, 중요성 composition 작곡, 작품 backing vocal 백그라운드 보컬, 코러스 choir 합창단 accompany 동반하다, (피아노로) 반주하다

196 추론 / 암시

번역 라퐁에 관해 암시된 것은?

(A) 시장이 신임이다.
(B) 베니테스가 태어난 곳이다.
(C) 시카고 인근에 위치한다.
(D) 순회 콘서트에서 첫 번째 경유지가 될 것이다.

해설 첫 번째 기사의 세 번째 단락에 나온 베니테스의 인터뷰를 보면, 시카고 공연 후 사흘간의 휴식 기간이 주어질 것(a three-day break after a show in Chicago)이기 때문에 시카고와 굉장히 가까운 라퐁에서 공연을 안 한다는 것은 생각할 수 없었다(To be so close to Lafont ~ and not do a show would be unthinkable)고 했으므로, 라퐁이 시카고 인근에 위치한다는 것을 추론할 수 있다. 따라서 (C)가 정답이다.

▸▸ Paraphrasing 지문의 **be so close to**
→ 정답의 **is located near**

197 세부 사항

번역 첫 번째 기사에 따르면 콘서트에서 어떤 문제가 해결되어야 했는가?

(A) 추가로 음악가들 찾기
(B) 충분히 넓은 장소 구하기
(C) 가능한 날짜 결정하기
(D) 적정한 티켓 가격 설정하기

해설 네 번째 단락에서 콘서트 개최에 있어서 유일한 어려움은 베니테스의 고향 팬들을 모두 수용할 수 있는 장소를 찾는 일(The only challenge was finding a venue that would accommodate all of Benitez' hometown fans)이라고 했으므로, (B)가 정답이다.

어휘 determine 결정하다 affordable (가격이) 적당한, (대부분이 살 수 있을 만큼) 저렴한

▸▸ Paraphrasing 지문의 **finding a venue that would accommodate all of Benitez' hometown fans**
→ 정답의 **Locating a large enough space**

198 연계

번역 곡 "하나의 아침"에 관해 명시된 것은?

(A) 라퐁에서의 생활에 관한 곡이다.
(B) 대개 합창단과 함께 공연한다.
(C) 라디오에서 연주된 베니테스 씨의 첫 번째 곡이었다.
(D) 장기자랑에서 베니테스 씨가 부른 노래이다.

해설 프로그램 공지에서 '하나의 아침(A Single Morning)'은 베니테스 씨가 고등학생 시절 첫 공연 때 부른 노래(Sung by Sonia at her first-ever performance during high school)라고 설명했다. 해당 공연 관련 내용은 첫 번째 기사에서 확인할 수 있는데, 두 번째 단락을 보면 그녀가 재스퍼 고등학교 장기자랑에서 처음으로 무대에 올라 상을 탔다(winning the school-wide talent show ~ the first time she ever set foot on a stage)고 했으므로, 이 노래가 장기자랑 무대에서 부른 노래임을 알 수 있다. 따라서 (D)가 정답이다.

199 세부 사항

번역 베니테스 씨의 평상시 콘서트와 라퐁 콘서트가 다른 점은?

(A) 한 시간 더 길었다.
(B) 낮에 열렸다.
(C) 참석자들이 경기장에 착석했다.
(D) 비엔나 순회 오케스트라가 오프닝 공연을 했다.

해설 두 번째 기사의 첫 번째 단락을 보면, 베니테스 씨가 라퐁 콘서트에서는 평상시 2시간 분량의 노래에 곡을 추가하여 공연을 한 시간 더 연장했다(Benitez ~ extending her usual two-hour set of songs by another hour)고 했으므로, (A)가 정답이다.

어휘 attendee 참석자

▸▸ Paraphrasing 지문의 **extending by another hour**
→ 정답의 **an hour longer**

200 연계

번역 파커 씨가 연주한 곡은?

(A) "나비 노래"
(B) "강변의 식사"
(C) "하나의 아침"
(D) "모두 웃다"

해설 두 번째 기사의 두 번째 단락에서 베니테스 씨와 6살부터 친구였던 피아니스트 제너비브 파커가 그녀의 무대에 합류했다(Benitez was joined onstage by pianist Genevieve Parker, ~ friend of Sonia's since the age of six)고 했는데, 프로그램 공지를 보면 소니아 베니테스 씨가 어린 시절 친구의 반주에 맞춰(Sonia will be accompanied by a childhood friend on the piano) 부른 노래가 '모두 웃다'임을 알 수 있다. 따라서 (D)가 정답이다.

101 (B)	102 (B)	103 (A)	104 (A)	105 (C)
106 (A)	107 (D)	108 (B)	109 (A)	110 (C)
111 (B)	112 (C)	113 (A)	114 (D)	115 (D)
116 (C)	117 (D)	118 (B)	119 (A)	120 (C)
121 (A)	122 (D)	123 (C)	124 (B)	125 (B)
126 (C)	127 (B)	128 (A)	129 (C)	130 (D)
131 (C)	132 (A)	133 (D)	134 (D)	135 (A)
136 (D)	137 (C)	138 (B)	139 (D)	140 (B)
141 (A)	142 (D)	143 (C)	144 (A)	145 (A)
146 (B)	147 (B)	148 (C)	149 (D)	150 (D)
151 (B)	152 (A)	153 (D)	154 (B)	155 (D)
156 (D)	157 (D)	158 (C)	159 (B)	160 (C)
161 (B)	162 (D)	163 (A)	164 (A)	165 (D)
166 (D)	167 (A)	168 (C)	169 (B)	170 (C)
171 (D)	172 (C)	173 (A)	174 (D)	175 (C)
176 (A)	177 (D)	178 (D)	179 (C)	180 (B)
181 (B)	182 (D)	183 (B)	184 (C)	185 (D)
186 (B)	187 (D)	188 (C)	189 (B)	190 (A)
191 (D)	192 (D)	193 (A)	194 (B)	195 (A)
196 (C)	197 (A)	198 (D)	199 (B)	200 (D)

PART 5

101 전치사 자리 _ 어휘

해설 빈칸 앞에 완전한 절이 왔고 뒤에는 명사구 her innovative ideas가 있으므로, 보기에서 전치사인 (B) for와 (D) across 중 하나를 선택해야 한다. 문맥상 '혁신적인 아이디어로 여러 개의 상을 수상했다'라는 내용이 되어야 자연스러우므로, '~으로'라는 의미로 이유나 원인을 나타내는 전치사 (B) for가 정답이다.

번역 틸링해스트 씨는 혁신적인 아이디어로 여러 개의 상을 수상했다.

어휘 award 상, 상품; (상을) 주다 innovative 혁신적인

102 동사 어휘

해설 해당 문장은 '물건을 -------하는 데 적절한 기술을 사용하면 허리 부상의 위험을 크게 줄일 수 있다'라는 내용이므로, 빈칸에 허리 부상을 야기할 수 있는 행위를 묘사하는 동사가 들어가야 자연스럽다. 따라서 '들어올리다'라는 의미의 (B) lift가 정답이다.

번역 물건을 들어올릴 때 적절한 기술을 사용하면 허리 부상의 위험을 크게 줄일 수 있다.

어휘 proper 적당한, 적절한 technique 기술, 기법 drastically 엄청나게, 급진적으로 reduce 줄이다, 감소시키다 back injury 허리 부상 damage 손상[피해]을 입히다 attract 끌어들이다, 관심을 끌다

103 형용사 자리 _ 명사 수식

해설 빈칸은 명사구 health guidelines를 수식하는 형용사 자리이므로, '현지의, 지역의'라는 의미의 형용사인 (A) local이 정답이 된다. (B) locals는 명사, (C) locally는 부사, (D) localize는 동사이므로 품사상 빈칸에 적합하지 않다.

번역 론데일에 있는 식당들은 현지의 보건 지침을 모두 준수해야 한다.

어휘 guideline 지침, 수칙 locals 지역 주민(들) locally 지역적으로 localize 국한하다, ~의 위치를 알아내다

104 형용사 어휘

해설 빈칸에는 to부정사구와 함께 쓰여 Sinee's Catering에 대해 묘사하는 형용사가 들어가야 한다. 문맥상 '특별 행사에 정말 맛있는 음식을 배달할 준비가 되어 있다'라는 내용이 되어야 자연스러우므로, '준비가 된, 기꺼이 ~하는'이라는 의미의 (A) ready가 정답이다. 「be동사+ready+to부정사」는 '~할 준비가 되다'라는 의미로 자주 쓰이는 표현이니 암기해 두자.

번역 시니스 케이터링은 여러분의 특별 행사에 정말 맛있는 음식을 배달해 드릴 준비가 항상 되어 있습니다.

어휘 catering 음식 공급(업) deliver 배달하다, 전해 주다 outstanding 뛰어난, 탁월한 skillful 능숙한, 숙련된 complete 완전한, 완벽한; 완료하다

105 형용사 자리 _ 어휘

해설 빈칸은 명사 way를 수식하는 형용사 자리로, 보기 중 형용사인 (B) practicing과 (C) practical이 들어갈 수 있다. 문맥상 '경제 성장을 지원하는 실질적인 방법'이라는 내용이 되어야 자연스러우므로, '실제의, 실질적인'이라는 의미인 (C) practical이 정답이 된다. (B) practicing은 '개업하고 있는, (종교) 실천적인'이라는 의미로 사람을 나타내는 명사를 수식하므로 빈칸에 적절하지 않다. (D) practically는 부사이므로 품사상 오답이며, '연습'을 뜻하는 명사 (A) practice는 way와 복합명사를 이룰 수 없으므로 빈칸에 들어갈 수 없다.

번역 루드로우 시의 경제 성장을 지원하는 실질적인 방법은 지역 업체에서 물건을 구입하는 것이다.

어휘 economic growth 경제 성장 area (특정) 지역 business 사업(체) practice 실행, 관행, 연습; 연습하다 practically 사실상, 실질적으로

106 명사 자리 _ 전치사의 목적어

해설 appliance -------이 전치사 of의 목적어 역할을 하고 있으며, A record number of(기록적인 숫자의, 유례 없이 많은 숫자의)라는 수량 표현의 수식을 받고 있으므로, 빈칸에는 복수 가산 명사가 들어가야 한다. 따라서 정답은 (A) shipments이다. (B) shipping은 불가산 명사, (C) shipment는 단수 명사이므로 정답이 될 수 없다.

번역 유례 없이 많은 가전 제품이 지난달 리스항에 입항했다.

어휘 record 기록적인, 유례 없는 appliance 가전 제품, (가정용) 전기 기구 shipment 선적 (화물), 우송물 shipping 발송, 배송

107 명사 어휘

해설 빈칸에는 「a ------- of」 형태로 쓰이며 동사인 are assigned 및 전치사 of의 목적어인 positions와 어울리는 명사가 들어가야 한다. '인턴 사원들이 점차 책임이 커지는 ------- 자리에 배정된다'라는 내용이므로, 보기의 명사를 하나씩 대입해 보면 a, of와 함께 쓰여 '일련의'라는 의미를 완성하는 (D) series가 가장 적절하다.

번역 슬로트 퍼블리싱에서 인턴 사원들은 점차 책임이 커지는 일련의 자리에 배치된다.

어휘 publishing 출판(업) be assigned to ~에 배치되다, ~에 할당되다 frequency 빈도, 빈발 shortage 부족

108 동사 자리 _ 수 일치 _ 태

해설 The conference fee가 주어, 빈칸이 동사인 문장이다. 주어가 단수이며 빈칸 뒤에 목적어 역할을 하는 명사 admittance가 있으므로, 능동태 단수 동사인 (B) includes가 정답이 된다. 참고로, 준동사(to부정사, 동명사, 분사)는 문장의 동사 역할을 할 수 없으므로 (D) including은 정답이 될 수 없다.

번역 학회비는 20개가 넘는 워크숍과 세미나 입장을 포함한다.

어휘 conference 회의, 학회 admittance 입장 include 포함하다

109 전치사 어휘

해설 빈칸 앞의 imported가 문제 해결의 단서로, 문맥상 '덴마크로부터 수입된 최고급 목공용 기계들'이라는 내용이 되어야 자연스럽다. 따라서 '~로부터, ~에서 온'이라는 의미로 출처나 장소를 나타내는 전치사 (A) from이 정답이 된다.

번역 고급 가구 제작자인 핀리 오르체타는 덴마크로부터 수입된 최고급 목공용 기계들을 사용한다.

어휘 cabinetmaker (고급) 가구 제작자[사] woodworking 목공용의 import 수입하다

110 부사 자리 _ 동사 수식

해설 빈칸 없이도 완전한 문장이므로, 빈칸에는 자동사 differ를 수식하는 부사가 들어가야 한다. 따라서 '크게, 대단히'라는 의미의 부사인 (C) greatly가 정답이다. 참고로, differ는 widely, significantly 등의 부사와 함께 자주 쓰인다.

번역 선임 호텔 매니저의 급여는 회사, 위치 및 경력에 따라 크게 다르다.

어휘 senior 선임의, 고위의 location 소재, 위치

111 부사 어휘

해설 동사 works (with)를 수식하는 적절한 부사를 선택하는 문제이다. 뒤에 오는 to부정사구가 '장기적인 제휴 관계를 확립하기 위해'라는 특정 목적을 나타내고 있으므로, 빈칸에는 이를 달성하기 위해 고객사들과 어떻게 협력하는지(work with)를 묘사하는 부사가 들어가야 자연스럽다. 보기를 하나씩 대입해 보면 '긴밀히, 밀접하게'라는 의미의 (B) closely가 가장 적절하다.

번역 팬텝 주식회사는 장기적인 제휴 관계를 확립하기 위해 고객사들과 긴밀히 협력한다.

어휘 customer 고객(사) establish 확립하다, 수립하다 long-term 장기적인 partnership 제휴 (관계), 협력 nearly 거의 recently 최근에 newly 최근에, 새로

112 부사 어휘

해설 빈칸은 형용사 effective를 수식하는 부사 자리로, 어느 정도로 효과적인지를 묘사하는 부사가 들어가야 한다. 문맥상 '매우 효과적인 것으로 입증되어 왔다'라는 내용이 되어야 자연스러우므로, '매우, 대단히'라는 의미의 (C) highly가 정답이다. 참고로, (A) far와 (D) much는 '훨씬 더, 아주'라는 뜻으로 주로 형용사의 비교급이나 「too + 형용사」를 수식한다.

번역 아달렛 농장만의 독특한 채소 관개 방식은 매우 효과적인 것으로 입증되었다.

어휘 unique 독특한, 유일한 irrigate 관개하다(물을 대다) effective 효과적인, 효력이 있는 correctly 올바르게, 정확히

113 전치사 자리 _ 어휘

해설 빈칸 뒤의 March 10과 어울려 쓰이는 전치사를 고르는 문제이다. 뒤에 연체료가 청구될(will be charged a late fee) 것이라는 내용이 왔으므로, 해당 부분은 '3월 10일 이후에 지불금을 납부하는 고객들'이라는 의미가 되어야 자연스럽다. 따라서 '~ 후에, ~ 뒤에'라는 뜻으로 시점을 나타내는 전치사인 (A) after가 정답이다. 참고로, (B) behind가 '~에 (뒤)늦은'라는 의미의 전치사로 쓰일 경우, 특정 시간을 나타내는 표현이 아닌 schedule, time 등과 같은 명사와 함께 쓰인다.

번역 3월 10일 이후에 지불금을 납부하는 고객들에게는 연체료가 청구될 것이다.

어휘 submit 제출하다 payment 지불금 charge 청구하다 late fee 연체료

114 동사 어휘

해설 해당 절의 수식을 받는 financial decisions 및 by의 목적어로 수동태에서 행위의 주체가 되는 employee opinions와 어울려 쓰이는 동사를 선택해야 한다. 직원들의 의견이 재무 의사 결정에 할 수 있는 행위를 생각해 보면, '영향을 주다'라는 동사가 가장 적절하므로, (D) influenced(영향을 받은)가 정답이다.

번역 조사 결과는 회사 간부들이 얼마나 자주 직원들의 의견에 영향을 받아 재무 의사 결정을 하는지 보여 준다.

어휘 poll 여론 조사, 투표(수) executive (회사) 간부, 임원 make a decision 결정하다 financial 재무의, 재정적인 opinion 견해, 의견 train 교육하다, 훈련하다 remind 상기시키다

115 부사 자리 _ 형용사 수식

해설 빈칸 뒤의 비교급 형용사 lower를 수식하는 부사 자리이므로, '상당히, 주목할 만하게'라는 의미의 부사인 (D) significantly가 정답이다. (A) more significant는 형용사의 비교급, (B) significant는 형용사, (C) significance는 명사이므로 품사상 빈칸에 적합하지 않다.

번역 테일러 시티 북스의 가격은 다른 온라인 서점보다 상당히 더 저렴하다.

어휘 significant 중요한, 상당한 significance 중요성, 의의

116 명사 어휘

해설 빈칸 뒤의 of this workshop과 어울려 쓰이며, be동사의 보어인 to 이하와 동격 관계를 이루는 명사를 선택해야 한다. '업계 지도자들이 신중한 재무 의사 결정을 내릴 수 있는 수단을 갖추도록 하는 것'은 워크숍의 '목적, 목표'라고 할 수 있으므로, 정답은 (C) aim이다.

번역 이 워크숍의 목적은 업계 지도자들이 신중한 재무 의사 결정을 내릴 수 있는 수단을 갖추도록 하는 것이다.

어휘 equip A with B A가 B를 갖게 하다 tool 수단, 도구
prudent 신중한, 분별 있는 guide 안내인, 안내(서)
experience 경험, 경력 aim 목적, 목표 solution 해결책, 해법

117 대명사

해설 빈칸은 to target의 목적어 자리로, 「------- of the+복수 명사」의 형태로 쓸 수 있는 대명사가 들어가야 한다. 문맥상 '세 개의 인구 집단 각각을 대상으로 하기 위해[대상으로 하는]'라는 내용이 되어야 자연스러우므로, '각각(의 것)'이라는 의미의 (D) each가 정답이 된다. (C) either도 「either of the+복수 명사」 형태로 쓰일 수 있으나, '~ 둘 중 하나, ~ 중 어느 한쪽'이라는 의미이므로 빈칸에 적절하지 않다.

번역 우리가 규정했던 세 개의 인구 집단 각각을 대상으로 하는 마케팅 캠페인이 고안되었다.

어휘 be designed to ~하기 위해 고안되다, ~하도록 설계[계획]되다
target ~을 대상으로 삼다, 목표로 하다 demographic 인구 집단, 인구 통계(학) identify 밝히다, 규정하다, 확인하다

118 부사절 접속사

해설 빈칸은 두 개의 완전한 절을 연결하는 부사절 접속사 자리이다. 해당 절에서 음식 비평가들이 ZJ's Bistro를 추천한다고 했으나 주절에서 대부분의 지역 주민들은 Dree's Café를 더 좋아한다고 했으므로, 빈칸에는 양보·대조의 의미를 지닌 접속사가 들어가야 한다. 따라서 '비록 ~할지라도'라는 의미의 (B) Although가 정답이다.

번역 비록 음식 비평가들이 지역 최고의 레스토랑으로 지제이스 비스트로를 추천하지만, 대부분의 지역 주민들은 드리스 카페를 더 좋아한다.

어휘 critic 비평가 bistro 비스트로, 작은 레스토랑 local 지역의, 현지의 resident 주민, 거주자

119 재귀대명사 _ 강조 용법

해설 빈칸 없이도 필요한 요소를 모두 갖추고 있는 완벽한 문장으로, '고객들은 맨 위쪽 선반에서 제품을 꺼내지 말고 직원들에게 도움을 요청해야 한다'라는 내용이다. 따라서 빈칸에는 주어를 강조하는 재귀대명사만이 들어갈 수 있으므로, '(그들이) 직접, 스스로'를 의미하는 (A) themselves가 정답이다. 참고로, (B) their own의 경우 '직접, 스스로'라는 의미가 되려면 앞에 전치사 on이 있어야 한다.

번역 그린 식료품점 고객들은 직접 맨 위쪽 선반에서 제품을 꺼내지 말고 직원들에게 도움을 요청해야 한다.

어휘 grocer 식료품점, 식료품 잡화상 assistance 도움, 지원
remove A from B A를 B에서 빼내다[제거하다]

120 형용사 어휘

해설 주어인 sales revenue(판매 수익) 및 목적어인 improvement(향상)와 어울려 쓰이는 형용사를 선택하는 문제이다. 문맥상 '판매 수익이 눈에 띄는 향상을 보였다'라는 내용이 되어야 자연스러우므로, '눈에 띄는, 현저한'이라는 의미의 (C) marked가 정답이다.

번역 스코벤트 프로덕츠의 판매 수익은 지난 분기 말에 눈에 띄게 향상되었다.

어휘 revenue 수익 improvement 향상, 진보, 개선 quarter
(4분의1) 분기 respective 각각의 diverse 다양한

121 형용사 자리 _ 명사 수식

해설 빈칸 뒤의 명사구 permit applications를 수식하는 형용사 자리이므로, '관련 있는, 적절한'이라는 의미의 형용사인 (A) relevant가 정답이다. (B) relevantly는 부사, (C) relevance와 (D) relevancies는 명사이므로 품사상 빈칸에 적절하지 않다.

번역 공사 현장에서 작업이 시작되기 전에 관련 허가 신청서가 처리되어야 한다.

어휘 construction site 공사 현장 permit application 허가 신청서 process 처리하다 relevantly 관련되어, 관련성 있게
relevance 관련성 relevancies 관련 있는 것들

122 명사 어휘

해설 빈칸 앞의 price와 함께 쓰여 주어 역할을 할 수 있는 명사를 선택하는 문제이다. 가격과 관련해서 시행되어야(be implemented) 할 것을 생각해 보면 '할인'이 가장 적절하므로, (D) reductions가 정답이 된다. 참고로, 문장의 동사가 insisted이기 때문에 that절의 동사는 should가 생략된 채 바로 be동사의 원형이 왔다.

번역 협상 동안에 뒤퐁 씨는 지체 없이 가격 할인이 시행되어야 한다고 주장했다.

어휘 negotiation 협상, 교섭 implement 시행하다, 실행하다
without delay 지체[지연] 없이 expectation 예상, 기대
institution 기관, 제도 sensation 느낌, 감각 reduction 감소, 할인

123 동사 자리 _ 시제

해설 Ms. Li가 주어, 빈칸이 동사인 문장으로, 보기 중 문장의 동사 역할을 할 수 있는 (C) will decide와 (D) has decided가 빈칸에 들어갈 수 있다. 전치사 수식어구 After the team meeting next week(다음 주 팀 회의 후에)이 미래를 나타내고 있으므로, (C) will decide가 정답이 된다. 참고로, needs는 whether가 이끄는 절의 동사이다.

번역 다음 주 팀 회의 후에 리 씨는 프로젝트 마감일을 변경할 필요가 있을지의 여부를 결정할 것이다.

어휘 deadline 마감일, 최종 기한

124 부사절 접속사

해설 빈칸에 알맞은 부사절 접속사를 고르는 문제이다. 문맥을 살펴보면, 제안서가 미완인(incomplete) 채 일정표도 불분명(unclear)했던 것이 거부된(was rejected) 원인이라고 보는 것이 타당하다. 따라서 '~ 때문에'라는 의미의 (B) Because가 정답이다.

번역 사우스사이드 도서관 정원에 대한 제안서는 미완인 채 일정표도 불분명했기 때문에 거부되었다.

어휘 proposal 제안(서) incomplete 미완의, 불충분한 unclear 불분명한 timetable 일정표, 시간표 reject 거부하다, 불합격 처리하다

125 to부정사

해설 As로 시작하는 부사절에 이미 동사(is set)가 있기 때문에, 보기 중 준동사(to부정사, 동명사, 분사)만이 빈칸에 들어갈 수 있다. 문맥상 임대 계약이 곧 만료될(expire) 예정이라는 내용이므로, be set과 함께 쓰여 '만료될 예정이다'라는 의미를 완성하는 (B) to expire가 정답이 된다. 참고로, 「be동사+set+to부정사」는 '~할 준비가 되어 있다, ~할 것 같다'라는 의미로도 쓰인다.

번역 스미스 그룹과의 임대 계약이 곧 만료될 예정이기 때문에, 조만간 비게 될 그 사무실 공간을 광고할 수 있다.

어휘 rental agreement 임대 계약(서) available 사용 가능한, 비어 있는 advertise 광고하다 expire 만료되다

126 전치사 어휘

해설 빈칸 뒤의 five business days와 어울려 쓰이는 전치사를 선택하는 문제이다. 문맥상 '영업일 기준으로 5일 이내에 배송될 것이다'라는 의미가 되어야 자연스러우므로, '~ 이내에'라는 의미의 (C) within이 정답이다. 참고로, (A) since가 '~ 이래로, ~부터'라는 의미로 쓰일 경우, 뒤에 기간이 아닌 특정 시점을 나타내는 표현이 온다.

번역 마티스 슈퍼스토어에서 2월 중에 구입하신 모든 가구는 영업일 기준으로 5일 이내에 배송될 것입니다.

어휘 purchase 구입하다 throughout ~ 동안 내내, 처음부터 끝까지 deliver 배달하다, 전해주다 business day 영업일, 평일

127 명사 자리 _ 전치사의 목적어

해설 빈칸은 전치사 with의 목적어 자리이므로, 목적어 역할을 할 수 있는 명사가 들어가야 한다. 따라서 '강조, 주안점'이라는 의미의 명사인 (B) emphasis가 정답이다. (A) emphatic은 형용사, (C) emphasize는 동사, (D) emphasized는 분사(형용사)이므로 품사상 빈칸에 적절하지 않다.

번역 부장은 주목할 만한 실적에 주안점을 둔 인사 고과 관련 자료를 제출했다.

어휘 present 제시하다, 제출하다 employee performance 인사고과, 직무 능력 평가 measurable 주목할 만한, 측정할 수 있는 achievement 업적, 성취한 것 emphatic 단호한, 강조하는 emphasize 강조하다

128 부사 어휘

해설 빈칸 뒤 were not familiar with를 수식하는 적절한 부사를 선택하는 문제이다. '새 소프트웨어 프로그램에 익숙하지 않았던 직원들조차 (나중에는) 그것이 사용하기 쉽다고 생각하게 되었다'라는 내용이므로, 빈칸에는 '처음에는, 초기에는'이라는 의미의 부사가 들어가야 자연스럽다. 따라서 (A) initially가 정답이다.

번역 처음에는 새 소프트웨어 프로그램에 익숙하지 않았던 직원들조차 그것이 사용하기에 쉽다고 생각하게 되었다.

어휘 employee 직원 be familiar with ~에 익숙하다, ~를 잘 알다 initially 처음에, 초기에 annually 매년, 1년에 한 번 successfully 성공적으로 inadvertently 무심코, 우연히

129 부사 자리 _ 동사 수식

해설 빈칸 뒤의 동사 approve를 수식하는 부사 자리이므로, '대개, 일반적으로'라는 의미의 부사인 (C) generally가 정답이다. (A) generalization은 명사, (B) generalize는 동사, (D) general은 형용사이므로 품사상 빈칸에 적절하지 않다.

번역 바쁘게 운영되는 몇 달 동안 관리자들은 일반적으로 직원들의 휴가를 승인하지 않으려고 한다.

어휘 supervisor 감독, 관리자 approve 승인하다, 받아들이다 time off 휴식, 휴가 peak 최고의, 최대의 operational 운영상의, 가동상의 generalization 일반화 generalize 일반화하다 generally 일반적으로 general 일반적인

130 동사 어휘

해설 현재분사 being 이하의 수식을 받는 three cities 및 빈칸 뒤에 있는 as the host와 어울려 쓰이는 동사(과거분사)를 선택하는 문제이다. 보기 중 「be동사+과거분사+as」 형태로 쓰일 수 있는 동사는 (B) categorized, (C) known, (D) considered인데, '차기(next) 총회 개최지로 고려되고 있는 세 개의 도시'라는 내용이 되어야 자연스러우므로, 정답은 (D) considered이다. 참고로, 'be known as'와 같은 표현은 완료된 상태를 나타내므로, 진행의 의미를 내포하는 현재분사로는 쓰이지 않는다.

번역 토론토는 세계 회계사 협회의 차기 총회 개최지로 고려되고 있는 세 개의 도시 중 하나이다.

어휘 host (행사·경기 등의) 개최지, 개최국 convention 회의, 총회 accountant 회계사 be categorized as ~로 분류되다 be known as ~로 알려져 있다

PART 6

131-134 공고

본사의 주 공장에 새로운 제조 장비 설치가 완료되었음을 알리게 되어 기쁩니다. 새로운 기계는 생산에 유연성을 부여함으로써 작업의 흐름을 **131향상시킬 것입니다. 132다양한** 크기의 혼합 탱크 6개로 소량 주문에

서 대량 주문에 이르기까지 광범위한 주문을 충족시킬 수 있을 것으로 예상합니다. 이러한 ¹³³업그레이드는 밤 매뉴팩처링이 향수 업계에서 계속 선두 자리를 지키게끔 해 주는 중요한 방법입니다.

¹³⁴모든 직원들은 이달 말까지 새로운 장비에 대한 교육을 받아야 합니다. 이 활동을 준비하고 있는 짐 마르텔이 곧 여러분에게 연락하여 자세한 내용을 알려 줄 것입니다.

어휘 installation 설치 manufacturing 제조(의) equipment 장비, 기기, 설비 plant 공장 complete 완료하다, 완공하다 work flow 작업 흐름 improve 개선하다, 향상시키다 flexibility 유연성 production 생산, 제작 a wide range of 광범위한, 다양한 ensure 확실하게 하다, 보장[보증]하다 fragrance 향기, 향수 organize 체계화하다, 조직하다 effort (조직적인) 활동, 노력

131 동사 어형 _ 시제

해설 앞 문장에서 현재완료 시제를 사용하여 새로운 제조 장비 설치가 완료되었다(has been completed)고 했으므로, 해당 문장은 새 기계 도입이 앞으로 가져올 장점에 대한 내용이 되어야 자연스럽다. 따라서 미래 시제인 (C) will improve가 정답이다.

132 형용사 자리 _ 명사 수식

해설 빈칸에는 sizes를 수식하는 형용사나 sizes와 복합명사를 이루는 명사가 들어갈 수 있다. 문맥상 '다양한 사이즈'라는 내용이 되어야 자연스러우므로, '가지각색의'라는 의미의 형용사인 (A) varying이 정답이 된다. (B) varies 및 (C) vary는 동사이므로 품사상 빈칸에 적절하지 않으며, '변화, 차이'를 의미하는 명사인 (D) variation은 size와 어울리지 않으므로 정답이 될 수 없다.

어휘 varying 다양한, 가지각색의 vary 다양하다

133 명사 어휘

해설 공장에 새로 설치한 제조 장비가 작업 흐름을 향상시킬 수 있으며 다양한 규모의 주문을 충족시킬 것으로 예상한다는 내용의 안내문이다. 따라서 이러한 변화를 가리키는 적절한 단어가 빈칸에 들어가야 하므로, '업그레이드, 향상'이라는 의미의 (D) upgrade가 정답이 된다.

어휘 proposal 제안, 제안서 contract 계약, 계약서 impression 인상, 생각

134 문맥에 맞는 문장 고르기

번역 (A) 관리자들은 어제 공장 견학을 완료했다.
(B) 안타깝게도, 설치 비용은 우리가 예상했던 것보다 훨씬 더 많이 소요되었다.
(C) 여러분이 알듯이 우리 업계는 점차 경쟁이 심해지고 있습니다.
(D) 모든 직원들은 이달 말까지 새로운 장비에 대한 교육을 받아야 합니다.

해설 빈칸 뒤 문장에서 이 활동을 준비하고 있는 짐 마르텔이 공지 대상자들에게 연락하여 자세한 내용을 알려 줄 것(Jim Martel, who is organizing this effort, will contact each of you soon with details)이라고 했으므로, 빈칸에는 그가 준비하고 있는 활동과 관련된 내용이 들어가야 글의 흐름이 자연스러워진다. 따라서 (D)가 정답이다.

어휘 supervisor 관리자, 상사 anticipate 예상하다, 기대하다 aware 알고 있는, 알아차린 increasingly 점차, 점점 competitive 경쟁적인, 경쟁력이 있는 personnel 직원(들)

135-138 웹페이지

www.kateweicommunications.com

여러분의 사업체를 광고하는 것은 복잡합니다. 신문이나 잡지는 ¹³⁵여전히 광고를 하기에 유용한 곳입니다. ¹³⁶하지만, 소셜 미디어 플랫폼이 훨씬 더 중요한 마케팅 수단이 되었습니다. 케이트 웨이 커뮤니케이션즈는 전통적인 수단과 최신 커뮤니케이션 플랫폼 두 가지 모두를 활용합니다. ¹³⁷저희는 여러분의 사업체를 위한 다양한 계획을 수립할 것입니다. 뛰어난 인쇄 서비스 외에도, 케이트 웨이 커뮤니케이션즈는 여러분이 온라인 진출을 ¹³⁸최대한 활용할 수 있게 도와 드릴 전문 지식을 갖추고 있습니다. 왜 망설이시나요? 오늘 여러분의 회사 이미지를 강화하고 싶으시면 수상 경력이 있는 당사를 선택하세요!

어휘 market (상품을) 내놓다, 광고하다 confusing 혼동을 주는, 복잡한 venue 장소, 개최지 platform 플랫폼(컴퓨터 사용의 기반이 되는 하드웨어·소프트웨어의 환경) critical 결정적인, 중요한 outlet 수단, 직판장 utilize 이용하다, 활용하다 traditional 기존의, 전통적인 exceptional 예외적인, 뛰어난 expertise 전문 지식[기술] presence 존재, (사업) 주둔, 진출 award-winning 수상한, 상을 받은 strengthen 강화하다, 증강하다

135 부사 어휘

해설 빈칸 뒤 형용사 useful을 적절히 수식하는 부사를 고르는 문제이다. (B) nowhere는 장소, (C) soon은 시간과 관련된 부사로 '유용한'을 수식하기에는 적절하지 않으므로, (A) still과 (D) evenly 중 하나를 선택해야 한다. 뒤 문장에서 소셜 미디어 플랫폼이 훨씬 더 중요한 (even more critical) 마케팅 수단이 되었다고 했으므로, 비교 대상이 되는 신문과 잡지도 '여전히 유용한 곳이다'라는 내용이 되어야 자연스럽다. 따라서 (A) still이 정답이다.

어휘 nowhere 어디에도 ~ 없다, 아무데도 ~ 않다 evenly 골고루, 균등하게

136 접속 부사

해설 빈칸 앞에는 신문이나 잡지가 여전히 광고를 하기에 유용한 곳 (useful venues)이라는 내용의 문장이 왔으며, 빈칸 뒤에는 소셜 미디어 플랫폼이 훨씬 더 중요한 마케팅 수단(even more critical marketing outlets)이 되었다는 내용의 문장이 왔다. 따라서 두 문장의 관계를 생각해 보면, 대조의 의미를 나타내는 (D) However가 빈칸에 들어가야 자연스럽다.

어휘 demonstrate 입증하다, 시범을 보이다

137 문맥에 맞는 문장 고르기

번역 (A) 마케팅 전문가들은 상충되는 조언을 합니다.
(B) 전통적인 방법이 가장 강한 영향력을 지닙니다.
(C) 저희는 여러분의 사업체를 위한 다양한 계획을 수립할 것입니다.
(D) 저희는 최근에 서비스 조건을 변경했습니다.

해설 바로 앞 문장에서 케이트 웨이 커뮤니케이션즈는 기존의 수단과 최신 커뮤니케이션 플랫폼 두 가지 모두를 활용한다(utilizes both traditional outlets and the latest communication platforms)고 했으므로, 빈칸에 들어갈 문장에서는 이 두 가지 수단을 사용하여 고객을 위해 할 수 있는 일을 언급하는 것이 자연스럽다. 따라서 (C)가 정답이다.

어휘 professional 전문가; 전문적인 conflicting 상충되는, 일치하지 않는 impact 영향 diverse 다양한 terms (계약·지불 등의) 조건

138 동사 어형 _ 원형부정사

해설 「help + 목적어(you) + 목적격 보어」의 구조로, help는 to부정사나 원형부정사를 목적격 보어로 취하는 동사이다. 따라서 보기 중 원형인 (B) optimize가 정답이 된다. (A) optimal은 형용사, (C) optimization은 명사, (D) optimum은 명사/형용사이므로, 품사상 빈칸에 적절하지 않다.

어휘 optimal 최적의 optimize 최대한 활용하다, 최적화하다 optimization 최적화 optimum 최적 조건; 최적의

139-142 이메일

수신: 에밀리 스완턴 〈eswanton@swantonfarmfeed.com〉
발신: 아놀드 한센 〈AHansen@poltonfairgrounds.org〉
제목: 폴턴 농장 박람회
날짜: 6월 2일

이 이메일은 귀사의 등록 영수증으로 사용될 수 있으며, **139또한** 7월 14일부터 7월 16일까지 열리는 제7회 연례 폴턴 농장 박람회에 귀사가 참가한다는 것을 확인해 주기도 합니다. 스완턴 팜 피드는 재차 참가하는 전시 업체이므로 할인된 금액에 **140임대** 공간을 이용하실 수 있습니다.

귀사의 공간을 준비할 때 새로운 요구 사항이 있다는 것을 숙지하시기 바랍니다. 올해, 모든 부스는 7월 13일 저녁 8시까지 완벽히 준비되어야 합니다. **141여기에는 쓰레기와 포장재를 치우는 것도 포함됩니다.** 탁자는 지난해와 마찬가지로 주최측에서 제공할 예정입니다.

저희 **142행사**에 다시 참여해 주셔서 다시 한 번 감사드립니다.

아놀드 한센, 부책임자
폴턴 카운티 농장 박람회

어휘 fair 박람회, 품평회 serve as (특정 용도로) ~로 사용될 수 있다 registration 등록, 신청 confirm 확인하다 participation 참여, 참가 annual 연례의, 해마다의 exhibitor 전시업체, 출품자 requirement 필요 조건, 자격, 요구 organizer 조직자, 주최자 assistant 보조의; 비서, 조수 coordinator 코디네이터, 책임자

139 등위접속사

해설 This e-mail이 주어이고, 두 개의 동사 serves와 confirms가 왔으므로, 빈칸에는 두 개의 동사를 적절히 연결하는 등위접속사가 들어가야 한다. 문맥상 '이메일이 등록 영수증으로 사용되며, 참가 확인도 해준다'라는 내용이 되어야 자연스러우므로, '또한'을 의미하는 (D) and also가 정답이다.

140 형용사 자리 _ 명사 수식

해설 빈칸에는 명사 space를 수식하는 형용사나 space와 복합명사를 이루는 명사가 들어갈 수 있다. 문맥상 '임대 공간'이라는 내용이 되어야 자연스러우므로, '임대의, 임차의'라는 의미의 형용사인 (B) rental이 정답이다. 참고로, rental은 명사로 '임대, 임대료, 임대물'이라는 뜻을 나타내기도 한다.

141 문맥에 맞는 문장 고르기

번역 (A) 여기에는 쓰레기와 포장재를 치우는 것도 포함됩니다.
(B) 음식을 판매하는 상인들의 수가 최근에 증가했습니다.
(C) 정확한 일정은 추후 공지 예정입니다.
(D) 라이브스톡 파빌리온은 남쪽 출구 옆에 위치할 것입니다.

해설 빈칸 바로 앞 문장에서 올해에 모든 부스는 7월 13일 저녁 8시까지 완벽히 준비되어야 한다(all booths must be completely ready)고 했으므로, 부스 준비와 관련된 내용이 이어지는 것이 자연스럽다. 따라서 (A)가 정답이다.

어휘 removal 제거, 없애기 trash 쓰레기 packing material 포장지, 포장 재료 vendor 행상인, 파는 사람

142 명사 어휘

해설 이메일 제목(Polton Farm Fair)이나 첫 단락의 첫 번째 문장(This e-mail serves as a receipt for your registration and also confirms your participation in ~ Farm Fair)을 통해, 농장 박람회에 참가하는 것에 대해 감사를 표하는 문장임을 알 수 있다. 따라서 Polton Farm Fair를 대체할 수 있는 단어인 (C) event가 정답이다.

어휘 discovery 발견 survey (설문) 조사 vote 투표, 표결

143-146 기사

스파클 프로 엔터프라이즈 미국 공장을 열다

전 세계 뉴스

맨체스터 (4월 10일)—벨기에에 본사를 둔 선도적인 세제 **143생산 업체**인 스파클 프로 엔터프라이즈가 영역을 확장하고 있다. 이 회사는 미국의 인디애나폴리스에 첫 번째 공장을 열었다. 40년이 넘는 기간 동안 스파클 프로는 가정용 세제 및 산업용 세제를 제조하고 유럽 전역의 소매점과 호텔 체인을 포함한 다양한 판매 업체에 이를 유통해 왔다. **144회사 웹사이트에 주요 판매 업체가 모두 정리되어 있다.**

인디애나폴리스 공장 시설이 완전히 가동되게 하려면 회사에서는 올해 말**145까지** 300명의 직원을 추가로 고용해야 할 것이다. 북미 사업 신임

이사인 이건 브레츠에 따르면, 스파클 프로는 아주 많은 인원의 직원들을 신속하게 교육시킬 수 있을 것이라고 자신한다. 브레츠 씨는 이런 요구를 충족시키는 데 큰 146어려움은 없을 것으로 예상하고 있다.

> 어휘 leading 일류의, 선도하는 expand 확장하다, 확대하다 territory 활동 범위, 영역, 분야 plant 공장 distribute (상품을) 유통하다, 배급하다 industrial 산업의 a wide range of 다양한, 광범위한 vendor 상인, 판매 업체 retail outlet (할인) 소매점 facility 시설 additional 추가의 capacity (공장·기계의) 생산 능력 director 이사 operations 영업, 사업 confident 확신하는, 자신만만한 personnel 직원(들) significant 중요한, 상당한 meet the needs 필요에 응하다, 요구를 충족시키다

143 명사 자리 _ 동격

해설 a leading Belgium-based ------- (of cleaning products)는 주어인 Sparkle Pro Enterprises와 동격이므로, 빈칸에는 명사가 들어가야 한다. 따라서 '생산 업체, 제조 업체'라는 의미의 명사인 (C) producer가 정답이다. (D) produce는 '생산하다'라는 동사 외에 명사로도 쓰일 수 있지만 '농산물, 생산물'이라는 의미이므로 문맥상 정답이 될 수 없다.

144 문맥에 맞는 문장 고르기

번역 (A) 수성 세제는 더 비싸졌다.
(B) 회사 웹사이트에 주요 판매 업체가 모두 정리되어 있다.
(C) 호텔은 대부분의 도시에서 편리한 위치에 있다.
(D) 다른 공장 시설들은 서서히 매각되었다.

해설 빈칸 앞 문장에서 스파클 프로가 유럽 전역의 소매점과 호텔 체인을 포함한 다양한 판매 업체에 가정용 세제 및 산업용 세제를 유통시켜 왔다(Sparkle Pro has been ~ to a wide range of vendors, including retail outlets and hotel chains)고 했으므로, 이 뒤에는 판매 업체와 관련된 내용이 이어지는 것이 문맥상 자연스럽다. 따라서 (B)가 정답이다.

어휘 water-based 수성의 conveniently 편리하게 gradually 점차, 서서히

145 전치사 어휘

해설 빈칸 뒤에 온 the end of this year와 함께 어울려 쓰이는 전치사를 선택하는 문제이다. 문맥상 '올해 말까지 직원을 추가로 고용해야 한다'는 내용이 되어야 자연스러우므로, '~까지, ~ 전에'라는 의미의 (A) by가 정답이다.

146 명사 어휘

해설 빈칸 앞 문장에서 추가로 고용할 300명의 직원들을 신속하게 교육시킬 수 있을 것이라고 자신한다(Sparkle Pro is confident that it will be able to train a large number of personnel quickly)고 했으므로, 빈칸이 포함된 부분은 '이런 요구를 충족시키는 데 큰 어려움은 없을 것으로 예상한다'는 내용이 되어야 자연스럽다. 따라서 '어려움, 난제'라는 의미의 (B) challenges가 정답이다.

어휘 decrease 감소 candidates 후보자, 지원자

PART 7

147-148 공고

> 공고
>
> 148크레스트뷰 대로의 보도가 다음 주에 보수될 예정입니다. 147, 148안전상의 우려로 1월 15일 월요일부터 1월 17일 수요일까지 퀸즈타운 파이낸셜 서비시즈(QFS) 건물의 정문 출입이 통제될 것입니다. QFS 직원들과 고객들은 시커모어 가에 있는 북쪽 출입구를 사용하시기 바랍니다. 2층에 있는 안내원에게 가시려면 북쪽 출입구 가까이에 있는 계단이나 엘리베이터를 이용하십시오.

> 어휘 sidewalk 인도, 보도 boulevard 대로 concern 걱정, 염려 inaccessible 접속[접근]할 수 없는 entrance 입구, 출입구 receptionist 접수원, 안내원 staircase 계단

147 주제 / 목적

번역 공고의 목적은 무엇인가?
(A) 특정 안전 수칙의 변경을 알리기 위해
(B) 입구의 임시 폐쇄를 발표하기 위해
(C) 새 엘리베이터 설치를 보고하기 위해
(D) 회사의 새로운 위치를 발표하기 위해

해설 두 번째 문장에서 1월 15일 월요일부터 1월 17일 수요일까지 퀸즈타운 파이낸셜 서비시즈(QFS) 건물의 정문 출입이 통제될 것(the front door ~ will be inaccessible from Monday, 15 January, to Wednesday, 17 January)이라고 한 후 관련 사항을 안내하고 있으므로, 입구의 임시 폐쇄를 발표하기 위한 공고임을 알 수 있다. 따라서 정답은 (B)이다.

어휘 safety regulations 안전 수칙[규정] temporary 임시의, 일시적인 closure 폐쇄, 폐점 entryway 입구(의 통로) installation 설치 disclose 발표하다, 공개하다

> ▸▸ Paraphrasing 지문의 the front door ~ will be inaccessible from Monday, 15 January, to Wednesday, 17 January → 정답의 the temporary closure of an entryway

148 추론 / 암시

번역 QFS 건물에 대해 암시된 것은?
(A) 많은 직원들이 그 건물에서 근무한다.
(B) 목요일에 다시 문을 열 것이다.
(C) 정문이 크레스트뷰 대로에 있다.
(D) 보수 공사가 1주일 이상 걸릴 예정이다.

해설 첫 번째와 두 번째 문장에서 크레스트뷰 대로의 보도가 보수될 예정(The sidewalk along Crestview Boulevard is scheduled to be repaired next week)이며, 안전상의 우려로 퀸즈타운 파이낸셜 서비시즈(QFS) 건물의 정문 출입이 통제될 것(the front door of the Queenstown Financial Services (QFS) building will be inaccessible)이라고 했으므로, QFS 건물의 정문이 크레스트뷰 대로에 있음을 추론할 수 있다. 따라서 (C)가 정답이다.

어휘 reopen 다시 열다, 재개하다   main entrance 정문, 중앙 출입구
renovation 수리, 개축, 개조

> ▸▸ Paraphrasing   지문의 front door → 정답의 main entrance

149-150 이메일

수신: 기업 자원팀
발신: 준코 시게노, 팀장
날짜: 1월 27일
제목: 지원 문제

안녕하세요, 팀원 여러분,

다음 주 전략 회의 시간에, ¹⁴⁹우리는 해외의 신규 소매점에서 근무하는 회사 직원들의 구체적인 요구 사항을 다룰 예정입니다. 우리의 목적은 직원 모두가 우리 제품을 광고하고 고객을 유지하는 데 있어서 완전히 숙련되도록 교육하는 것입니다. ¹⁵⁰그들이 국내 직원들과 필적할 수준이 될 수 있도록 교육과 물류 지원을 제공할 수 있는 최선의 방법에 대한 아이디어를 각자 두 개씩 발표할 수 있도록 준비해 주세요.

고마워요.

준코 시게노
팀장, 인테그라 옵틱스

어휘 corporate 기업의, 회사의 strategy 전략, 전술 session 시간, 기간 address (문제를) 다루다 specific 구체적인, 특정한 representative 직원 overseas 해외의 retail location 소매점 retention 유지 present 발표하다, 제시하다 logistical 수송의, 물류의 comparable 비교할 수 있는, 유사한 domestic 국내의 counterpart 대응 관계에 있는 사람, 상대

149 사실 관계 확인

번역 이메일에 따르면, 인테그라 옵틱스에 관해 사실인 것은?
(A) 교정 안경을 광고한다.
(B) 해외에 진출해 있다.
(C) 매장을 몇 군데 더 추가로 개설할 계획이다.
(D) 신제품 라인을 막 생산했다.

해설 첫 번째 문장에서 다음 주 전략 회의 시간에 해외의 신규 소매점에서 근무하는 회사 직원들의 구체적인 요구 사항(specific needs of our company representatives working at our new overseas retail locations)에 대해 다룰 예정이라고 했으므로, 인테그라 옵틱스가 해외에 진출해 있다는 것을 알 수 있다. 따라서 (B)가 정답이다.

어휘 corrective 교정의 eyewear 안경류 presence 주재, 주둔

> ▸▸ Paraphrasing   지문의 overseas retail locations
> → 정답의 an international presence

150 세부 사항

번역 시게노 씨가 직원들에게 요청한 것은?
(A) 제안서 평가
(B) 고객들에게 연락
(C) 교육 시간 참석
(D) 회의 준비

해설 세 번째 문장을 보면, 시게노 씨는 직원들에게 해외 직원들이 국내 직원들과 필적할 수준이 될 수 있도록 교육과 물류 지원을 제공할 수 있는 최선의 방법에 대한 아이디어를 두 개씩 발표할 수 있도록 준비해 오라(I'm requesting that each of you be ready to present two ideas on the best way to ~ domestic counterparts)고 했다. 따라서 (D)가 정답이다.

어휘 evaluate 평가하다 proposal 제안(서) contact 연락하다

> ▸▸ Paraphrasing   지문의 requesting → 질문의 ask

151-152 정보문

중요한 정보

프로엘링사는 고품질의, 조립이 쉬운 당사의 가구에 자부심을 느끼며, 귀하가 구매하신 제품에 완전히 만족하시기를 바랍니다.

제품을 조립하기 전에 부품 목록을 보시고 모든 부품들이 상자 안에 다 들어 있는지 반드시 확인하십시오.

¹⁵¹만약 구입하신 제품에 부품 또는 조립 장비가 없거나 배송 중에 제품이 파손된 경우에는 해당 제품을 구입하신 매장으로 반품하지 마십시오. 매장은 교체 부품을 갖추고 있지 않습니다. 대신, 저희에게 직접 연락을 주시면 저희 측에서 귀하가 필요한 품목(들)을 무료로 보내 드리겠습니다. 아래 방법으로 연락 주시면 됩니다.
- 온라인으로 교체 부품을 주문하시려면 www.froehlingco.com을 방문하십시오.
- parts@froehlingco.com으로 저희에게 이메일을 보내 주십시오.
- 혹은 ¹⁵²555-0128로 언제든 저희에게 전화 주십시오.

어휘 take pride in ~을 자랑스럽게 여기다 assemble 조립하다 purchase 구매; 구매하다 missing 잃어버린, 분실된 part 부품, 부속품 assembly 조립, 조립 부품 hardware 철물, 장비 damaged 파손된 stock (가게에 물품을) 사들이다, 비축하다 replacement 교체(품) free of charge 무료로

151 주제 / 목적

번역 정보문의 목적은 무엇인가?
(A) 고객들에게 제품 조립 설명서를 구할 수 있는 곳을 알려 주기 위해
(B) 고객들에게 구입품과 관련된 문제를 해결할 수 있는 방법을 알려 주기 위해
(C) 회사의 단골 고객에게 선물을 제공하기 위해
(D) 고객들이 가까운 소매점을 찾는 것을 도와주기 위해

해설 세 번째 단락에서 만약 부품 또는 조립 장비가 없거나 배송 중에
　　 파손되었다면(If your item is missing parts or assembly
　　 hardware, or if it has been damaged during shipping), 제품
　　 을 구입한 매장이 아니라 자신들에게 직접 연락을 주면 필요한 제품을
　　 무료로 보내 주겠다(contact us directly and we will send you
　　 the item(s) required free of charge)고 했다. 따라서 고객들에
　　 게 구입한 제품과 관련된 문제를 해결할 수 있는 방법을 알려 주기 위
　　 한 정보문임을 알 수 있으므로, (B)가 정답이다.

어휘 assembly instructions 조립 설명서 notify 알리다, 통지하다
　　 resolve (문제 등을) 해결하다 loyal customer 단골 고객
　　 retail store 소매점

152 추론 / 암시

번역 프로엘링사에 관해 암시된 것은?
　　 (A) 항시 대기 중인 고객 서비스 상담원이 있다.
　　 (B) 파손된 제품은 소매점에 반납할 것을 권장한다.
　　 (C) 재고를 파악하는 새로운 시스템을 갖추고 있다.
　　 (D) 각 주문품과 함께 제품 카탈로그를 제공한다.

해설 세 번째 단락 마지막 항목에서 555-0128로 언제든 전화하라
　　 (calling us anytime at 555-0128)고 했으므로, 항상 대기중인 고
　　 객 서비스 상담원이 있음을 알 수 있다. 따라서 (A)가 정답이다.

어휘 customer service representative 고객 서비스 상담원
　　 available 이용 가능한, (~할) 시간이 있는 retailer 소매점,
　　 소매업자 keep track of (상태의 진전이나 상황을) 계속 알고 있다,
　　 추적하다 inventory 재고(품), 재고 목록

▶▶ Paraphrasing　지문의 anytime → 정답의 at all times

153-154 문자 메시지

마리나 틴체바　　　 오전 9시 01분
안녕, 루이스. 153저 레스토랑에 있어요. 오후에 있을 결혼 피로연을 위
해 후식 테이블을 준비해야 하는데, 문이 잠겨 있고 전 열쇠를 집에 두
고 왔어요.

루이스 마차도　　　 오전9시 03분
하월 씨가 거기 있지 않아요? 154그녀는 보통 준비를 하기 위해 행사보
다 몇 시간 일찍 오거든요.

마리나 틴체바　　　 오전 9시 04분
알아요. 이건 말도 안 돼요. 당신은 오늘 늦게 오죠, 그렇죠?

루이스 마차도　　　 오전 9시 06분
네. 사실 153매니저 회의에 가고 있는 중이기는 하지만, 10분 후에 거기
에 가서 당신을 들여보내 줄 수 있어요.

마리나 틴체바　　　 오전 9시 07분
정말 고마워요! 바로 옆 카페에 있을게요.

어휘 set up 준비하다, 설치하다 banquet 연회, 피로연 show
up 나타나다 make sense 이치에 맞다, 이해되다 conference
회의, 회담

153 추론 / 암시

번역 마차도 씨는 누구일 것 같은가?
　　 (A) 카페 웨이터
　　 (B) 후식 요리사
　　 (C) 웨딩 플로리스트
　　 (D) 레스토랑 매니저

해설 문이 잠겨 레스토랑에 들어가지 못하는 틴체바 씨가 마차도 씨에게
　　 문제를 설명하자 마차도 씨가 오전 9시 6분 메시지에서 자신이 매
　　 니저 회의에 가고 있는 중(I'm on my way to a conference for
　　 managers)이지만 레스토랑에 잠깐 들러 틴체바 씨가 들어가게끔 해
　　 줄 수 있다(I can be there ~ to let you in)고 했다. 따라서 마차도
　　 씨가 레스토랑 매니저임을 추론할 수 있으므로, (D)가 정답이다.

154 의도 파악

번역 오전 9시 4분에 틴체바 씨가 '이건 말도 안돼요'라고 쓸 때, 그 의도는
　　 무엇인가?
　　 (A) 신부는 이미 그곳에 도착했어야 한다.
　　 (B) 그녀의 동료는 보통 일찍 도착한다.
　　 (C) 그녀는 잘못된 서류를 받았다.
　　 (D) 그녀는 열쇠가 어디에 있는지 알지 못한다.

해설 오전 9시 3분 메시지에서 하월 씨는 보통 준비하려고 행사 몇 시간
　　 전에 온다(She usually shows up hours ahead of an event
　　 to get things ready)고 하자, 틴체바 씨는 자신도 알고 있다고 하
　　 며 하월 씨가 레스토랑에 없는 것은 말이 안 된다(It doesn't make
　　 sense)고 했다. 따라서 틴체바 씨는 보통 일찍 도착하는 동료가 아직
　　 오지 않은 것을 믿을 수 없다고 말한 것이므로, (B)가 정답이다.

▶▶ Paraphrasing　지문의 shows up hours ahead of an event
　　　　　　　　　　→ 정답의 arrives early

155-157 브로셔 정보

155칼린 카운티를 방문할 예정이세요?
이 흥미로운 볼거리들을 놓치지 마세요!

155아베보 식물원
개관: 매일 오전 9시–오후 6시; 입장료 8달러
157걸 만이 보이는 근사한 전망을 갖춘 아베보 식물원은 지역의 풍요롭
고 다양한 식물에 대해 살펴보고 배울 수 있는 아름다운 장소입니다.

155레버 콘서트 홀
개관: 월요일부터 금요일 오전 10시부터 오후 4시까지 일반인에게
공개
저명한 건축가 앙 자오가 설계한 레버 콘서트 홀은 인상적인 건축 양식
을 갖추고 있어 방문할 만한 충분한 가치가 있습니다. 1인당 2달러로
안내원이 딸린 관광이 가능합니다.

155칼린 카운티 미술관
개관: 매일 오전 10시–오후 7시; 입장료 5달러

이 아름다운 미술관은 현지 예술가들의 작품에 중점을 둡니다. ¹⁵⁶**특별 전시품이 매달 순회 전시됩니다.**

¹⁵⁵**해양 박물관**
개관: 수요일부터 일요일까지 오전 9시–오후 4시; 입장료는 없지만 기부금은 환영. 해양 박물관은 인상적인 역사 공예품들을 소장하고 있어 지역의 해양 역사에 관해 배우기 좋은 장소입니다. ¹⁵⁷**이 박물관은 이스트 해변에 있는 폐선 위에 위치해 있습니다.**

어휘 botanical garden 식물원 admission 입장, 입장료 stunning 깜짝 놀랄 만한, 굉장히 아름다운 examine 살펴보다 abundant 풍부한, 많은 diverse 다양한 renowned 유명한, 저명한 architect 건축가 striking 인상적인, 두드러진 architecture 건축, 건축 양식 guided tour 안내원이 딸린 관광 available 이용할 수 있는 local 현지의, 지역의 exhibit 전시회 rotate 순환하다 maritime 해양의 donation 기부(금) impressive 인상적인 artifact 공예품 seafaring 항해, 바다 여행 retired ship 폐선

155 주제 / 목적

번역 정보문의 목적은 무엇인가?
(A) 행사 일정표를 제공하기 위해
(B) 주목할 만한 명소에 가는 길을 알려 주기 위해
(C) 현지 예술가들의 업적을 강조하기 위해
(D) 관광지를 설명하기 위해

해설 제목에서 '칼린 카운티를 방문할 예정이세요? 이 흥미로운 볼거리를 놓치지 마세요!(Visiting Carlin County? Don't miss these points of interest!)'라고 한 후, 본문에서 아베보 식물원(Avevo Botanical Garden), 레버 콘서트 홀(Rever Concert Hall), 칼린 카운티 미술관(Carlin County Museum of Art)과 해양 박물관(The Maritime Museum)에 대해 설명하고 있다. 따라서 관광지를 안내하기 위한 정보문임을 알 수 있으므로, (D)가 정답이다.

어휘 directions 길 안내 notable 주목할 만한, 중요한 landmark 랜드마크 highlight 두드러지게 하다, 강조하다 accomplishment 성취, 업적 tourist destination 관광지

156 사실 관계 확인

번역 칼린 카운티 미술관에 관해 언급한 것은?
(A) 월요일에는 휴관한다.
(B) 유명한 건축가가 설계했다.
(C) 전 세계의 소장품을 전시한다.
(D) 주기적으로 전시품을 바꾼다.

해설 특별 전시품이 매달 순회 전시된다(Special exhibits rotate monthly)고 했으므로, (D)가 정답이다.

어휘 feature 특집으로 꾸미다, 특별히 포함하다 periodically 주기적으로, 정기적으로

▸▸ Paraphrasing 지문의 rotate monthly
→ 정답의 changes ~ periodically

157 사실 관계 확인

번역 정보문에 따르면, 아베보 식물원과 해양 박물관의 공통점은 무엇인가?
(A) 두 곳 모두 소액의 입장료를 부과한다.
(B) 두 곳 모두 물가에 위치해 있다.
(C) 두 곳 모두 역사적인 공예품을 전시한다.
(D) 두 곳 모두 안내원이 딸린 관광을 제공한다.

해설 아베보 식물원은 걸 만이 보이는 근사한 전망을 갖춘(With stunning views of Gull Bay) 곳이라고 했으며, 해양 박물관은 이스트 해변에 있는 폐선 위에 위치해 있다(This museum is located on a retired ship on East Beach)고 했다. 따라서 아베보 식물원과 해양 박물관 둘 다 물가에 위치해 있음을 알 수 있으므로, (B)가 정답이다.

어휘 have ~ in common 공통으로 ~을 갖고 있다, ~가 공통점이다 charge 부과하다, 청구하다 admission fee 입장료 display 전시하다

158-160 기사

빙엄 출신이 상을 수상하다

티무르 카르도스 작성

10월 9일—빙엄 출신이 무역 단체인 철교 공사 협회(ACSB)에서 수여하는 올해의 공로상을 받았다. 66세인 스콧 무어 씨가 어제 노워크에서 열린 연례 ACSB 회의에서 이 상을 수상했다.

ACSB 보도 자료에 따르면, 이 상은 매년 '철강 산업 진보에 크게 기여한 사람'에게 주어진다. ACSB 대변인 코라 슈뢰더 씨는 "무어 씨는 일하지 않는 시간에도 우리 업계의 품질을 보장하는 데 기여했습니다. ¹⁵⁹지난 10년 동안 그는 ACSB가 철강 생산 기준 및 관행을 추적 관찰하고 개선하는 것을 돕는 데 헌신해 왔습니다. ¹⁵⁸올해에는 위원회 의장 직을 맡아 철교 공사에 사용되는 구조 강재에 대한 일련의 기준을 개선했습니다."라고 말했다.

무어 씨는 빙엄에서 태어나고 자랐으며, 빙엄 대학교에서 공학 학위를 받았다. 졸업 후 그는 빙엄의 새 청사를 건설하는 동안 공사 관리자로 근무했다. ¹⁶⁰그는 39년 전에 건물 관리자로 마셜 철강에 입사했으며, 결국 현재의 선임 프로젝트 엔지니어 자리에 올랐다.

어휘 native 원주민, 토박이 contributor 기여자, 공헌자 association 협회, 조합 construction 건설, 공사 organisation 조직, 기관 present an award 시상하다, 상을 주다 annual 연례의, 해마다의 press release 보도 자료 contribute 공헌하다, 기여하다 significantly 상당히, 주목할 만하게 betterment 진보, 향상 steel industry 철강 산업, 철강업계 spokesperson 대변인 devote 헌신하다 spare time 일하지 않는 시간 ensure 보장하다, 반드시 ~하게 하다 decade 10년 dedicate oneself to ~에 전념하다, 헌신하다 monitor 관찰하다, 감시하다 refine 세련되게 하다, 개선하다 practice 관행, 관례 chair 의장직을 맡다, (회의를) 주재하다 committee 위원회 structural steel 구조 강재 engineering degree 공학 학위 supervisor 감독, 관리자 ultimately 궁극적으로, 결국

158 추론 / 암시

번역 무어 씨에 관해 암시된 것은?

(A) 강철 사용에 대한 기준을 높이는 작업을 이끌었다.
(B) 새로운 유형의 다리를 설계했다.
(C) 슈뢰더 씨와 함께 위원회에서 일한다.
(D) ACSB로부터 여러 상을 수상했다.

해설 두 번째 단락에서 무어 씨가 올해 위원회 의장직을 맡아(chaired a committee) 철교 공사에 사용되는 구조 강재에 대한 일련의 기준을 개선했다(created an improved set of standards for structural steel used in the construction of bridges)고 했으므로, (A)가 정답이다.

어휘 effort (조직적인) 활동[작업], 노력

> ▸ Paraphrasing 지문의 created an improved set of standards → 정답의 raise standards

159 세부 사항

번역 기사에 따르면 10년 전에 무슨 일이 있었는가?

(A) 무어 씨가 노워크로 이사했다.
(B) 무어 씨가 ACSB를 돕기 시작했다.
(C) ACSB가 회원 자격 요건을 수정했다.
(D) ACSB가 처음 시상을 했다.

해설 두 번째 단락에서 무어 씨가 지난 10년 동안 ACSB가 철강 생산 기준과 관행을 추적 관찰하고 개선하는 것을 돕는 데 헌신해 왔다(For the past decade, he has dedicated himself to helping the ACSB)고 했으므로, 그가 10년 전에 ACSB를 돕기 시작했다는 것을 알 수 있다. 따라서 (B)가 정답이다.

어휘 revise 수정하다, 바꾸다 requirement 필요 조건, 자격

> ▸ Paraphrasing 지문의 the past decade → 질문의 ten years ago

160 세부 사항

번역 마셜 철강에서 무어 씨의 첫 번째 일자리는 무엇이었는가?

(A) 선임 프로젝트 엔지니어   (B) 회사 대변인
(C) 공사 관리자   (D) 건물 관리자

해설 세 번째 단락 마지막 문장에서 무어 씨는 39년 전에 건물 관리자로 마셜 철강에 입사했다(He joined Marshall Stell 39 years ago as a building supervisor)고 했으므로, (D)가 정답이다.

161-164 웹페이지

http://www.goldendayimages.com

골든 데이 스톡 사진

귀사의 자료에 스톡 이미지를 사용하면 귀사의 소통 능력을 크게 개선할 수 있으며, 외부 고객과의 소통 능력뿐만 아니라 직원과의 소통 능력도 향상시킬 수 있습니다. 잘 선택한 이미지는 ¹⁶¹⁽ᴬ⁾**내부 의사소통에 있어 직원의 참여를 높이는 것부터** ¹⁶¹⁽ᶜ⁾**잠재 고객의 관심을 끌고**

¹⁶¹⁽ᴰ⁾**문서를 읽는 독자들이 복잡한 내용을 더 잘 이해할 수 있도록 돕는 것에 이르기까지 많은 기능을 할 수 있습니다.**

¹⁶²**골든 데이의 이미지는 전 세계 독창적인 기고자들의 네트워크를 통해 얻기 때문에 저희의 작품 목록은 방대할 뿐만 아니라 아주 다양합니다.** 귀사의 규모나 위치와 상관없이, 또한 거래 상대가 누구든 간에 여러분의 메시지를 강화할 수 있는 완벽한 사진을 찾으실 것입니다.

저희의 월 구독료는 여러분이 다운로드하는 이미지의 수량과 ¹⁶³**해상도**에 따라 49달러에서 495달러에 이릅니다. 일단 이미지를 다운로드하면 사용에는 제한이 없습니다.

저희의 신규 가입 특별 할인 기회를 놓치지 마십시오. ¹⁶⁴**신규 가입 구독자들은 6개월 동안 추가 비용 없이 저희 브랜딩 전문가들의 상담 자문을 받을 수 있습니다!** 저희 전문가들이 여러분의 고객을 대상으로 하는 모든 자료를 응집력 있게 만들 수 있도록 도와드리고 귀사를 돋보이게 해줄 것입니다.

어휘 significantly 상당히, 주목할 만하게 external 외부의 function 기능, 작용 engagement 참여, 개입 potential client 잠재 고객 document 문서, 서류 contributor 기고가, 기여자 diverse 다양한 do business 거래하다, 사업하다 enhance 늘리다, 강화하다 subscription 정기 구독 resolution 해상도 introductory offer 신규 가입 할인, 출시 기념 특별가 subscriber 가입자, 구독자 qualify for ~의 자격이 있다 consultation 상담, 자문 branding (마케팅 전략) 브랜딩, 브랜드 상품화 expert 전문가 at no extra cost 추가[별도] 비용 없이 cohesive 응집력 있는, 화합하는 stand out 눈에 띄다, 빼어나다

161 사실 관계 확인

번역 광고에서 스톡 이미지를 사용하는 이유로 언급되지 않은 것은?

(A) 직원들이 사보를 읽도록 권장하기 위해
(B) 현 고객들이 회사의 브랜드에 계속 관심을 갖게 하기 위해
(C) 새 고객을 유치하기 위해
(D) 서면 정보를 명확히 하는 것을 돕기 위해

해설 첫 번째 단락 마지막 문장에서 잘 선택한 이미지는 내부 의사소통에 있어 직원의 참여를 높여 주고(increasing employee engagement with internal communications), 잠재 고객의 관심을 끌고(catching the attention of potential clients), 문서를 읽는 독자들이 복잡한 내용을 더 잘 이해할 수 있도록 돕는다(helping readers of documents better understand complex ideas)고 했다. 따라서 언급되지 않은 (B)가 정답이다.

어휘 company newsletter 회사 사보, 회보 attract 유치하다, 끌어들이다 clarify 명백히 하다

> ▸ Paraphrasing 지문의 increasing employee engagement with internal communications
> → 보기 (A)의 To encourage employees to read company newsletters
> 지문의 catching the attention of potential clients
> → 보기 (C)의 To attract new customers
> 지문의 helping readers of documents better understand complex ideas → 보기 (D)의 To help clarify written information

162 세부 사항

번역 광고에 따르면 골든 데이의 이미지가 특별한 이유는 무엇인가?

(A) 일반적으로 제공되는 것보다 사이즈가 더 크다.
(B) 유명한 사진 작가들의 작품이다.
(C) 다국적 기업에 의해 이용된다.
(D) 전 세계에서 공급된다.

해설 두 번째 단락 첫 문장에서 골든 데이의 이미지는 전 세계의 독창적인 기고자들을 통해 얻기(Golden Day's images come from a unique international network of contributors) 때문에 아주 방대하며 다양하다(our selection is not only large but also truly diverse)고 했으므로, (D)가 정답이다.

어휘 multinational company 다국적 기업

> ▸▸ Paraphrasing 지문의 come from a unique international
> network → 정답의 are sourced from all over
> the world

163 동의어 찾기

번역 세 번째 단락 1행의 "resolution"과 의미상 가장 가까운 것은?

(A) 상세함의 정도
(B) 협의서
(C) 주제
(D) 목적의 확고함

해설 the quantity and resolution of the images는 '이미지의 수량 또는 해상도'라는 의미로, 여기서 resolution은 '해상도, 선명도'를 뜻한다. 따라서 '상세함의 정도'를 의미하는 (A) level of detail이 정답이다.

어휘 statement of agreement 협의서   subject matter 주제, 소재
firmness 확고함, 단단함

164 세부 사항

번역 골든 데이는 신규 고객들에게 무엇을 제공하고 있는가?

(A) 무료 마케팅 조언
(B) 구독료 할인
(C) 제한된 시간 내에 별도 사진집 접속
(D) 신규 잠재 고객에게 소개

해설 마지막 단락 첫 문장에서 신규 가입 구독자들은 추가 비용 없이 브랜딩 전문가들의 상담 자문을 받을 수 있다(first-time subscribers qualify for consultations with our branding experts)고 했으므로, (A)가 정답이다.

어휘 access 접속, 접근

> ▸▸ Paraphrasing 지문의 first-time subscribers
> → 질문의 new customers
> 지문의 at no extra cost → 정답의 Free

165-167 기사

우리는 제대로 하고 있다

아리엘 가번 작성

서스턴 (11월 8일)—[165]중부 대서양 호텔 협회에서 실시한 최근의 연구에 따르면, 우리 지역의 해변 관광 산업이 지난여름에 대폭 성장했으며, 호텔 산업은 작년보다 올해 더 큰 수익을 거두었다. [167]여름 성수기 동안 호텔 이용률은 평균 94퍼센트였다. 이는 불과 77퍼센트였던 작년 여름 평균에서 상당히 증가한 수치였다.

[166(B)]작년 봄 서스턴에서는 지역 내 최대 호텔인 더 글래스턴이 개업했다. 이 새 호텔은 여름 내내 거의 매 주말마다 만원이었다. 주중의 이용률 역시 기대 이상이었다.

[166(B)]호텔 매니저인 아니카 바스티양은 "관광객들은 24시간 제공되는 식사 메뉴, 인근 해변까지의 무료 셔틀, 무료 와이파이 등을 포함한 다양한 편의 시설을 아주 좋아했습니다. 사실, 많은 관광객들이 이미 내년 여름을 위해 객실을 예약했습니다."라고 말했다.

[166(A)]서스턴은 지역 내에서 가장 인기 있는 관광지가 되었으며, 최대 경쟁 상대인 델마이어 해변보다 대략 20퍼센트나 더 많은 해변 피서객들을 끌어들였다. [166(C)]전문가들은 이를 증가하는 서스턴 내의 할인점, 전반적으로 더 저렴한 물가, 그리고 풍부한 새 레스토랑, 호텔 및 지역 행사 때문이라고 여긴다. 관광객들은 해변을 찾는 성수기 이후에도 계속해서 이 지역을 방문하며, 호텔 객실에 더 오래 머문다.

어휘 conduct 수행하다, 실시하다   association 협회
significantly 상당히, 주목할 만하게   industry 산업   profit 수익, 이익   occupancy 점유(율), 이용(율); 수용 능력   peak 최고의, 최대의; 성수기   at full capacity 수용인원이 다 찬, 완전히 가동하여   exceed 초과하다, 능가하다   an array of 다수의, 각양각색의   amenities 오락 시설, 편의 시설   reserve 예약하다   tourist destination 관광지   competitor 경쟁 상대   expert 전문가   attribute A to B A를 B의 원인으로 돌리다   overall 전반적으로, 종합적으로   an abundance of 많은, 풍부한   community 지역 사회, 공동체   prime 최고의, 주요한

165 주제 / 목적

번역 기사의 목적은 무엇인가?

(A) 새로운 호텔 개장을 알리기 위해
(B) 현지 관광 산업에 대한 정보를 제공하기 위해
(C) 호텔 산업의 취업 기회를 논의하기 위해
(D) 두 곳에 위치한 해변의 질을 비교하기 위해

해설 첫 단락 첫 번째 문장에서 '우리 지역의 해변 관광 산업이 지난여름에 대폭 성장했으며(tourism at our beaches improved significantly this past summer) 호텔 산업은 작년보다 올해 더 큰 수익을 거두었다(the hotel industry showed greater profits this year than last)'라고 한 후 기사 전반에서 관련 내용을 설명하고 있다. 따라서 현지 관광 산업에 대한 정보 제공을 목적으로 하는 기사임을 알 수 있으므로, (B)가 정답이다.

166 사실 관계 확인

번역 서스턴에 대해 명시되지 않은 것은?

(A) 서스턴의 해변은 델마이어 해변보다 더 인기가 있다.
(B) 바스티앙 씨는 새 호텔에서 근무하고 있다.
(C) 아주 다양한 행사를 개최한다.
(D) 최근에 주말 동안 해변 대청소를 했다.

해설 네 번째 단락의 '서스턴은 지역 내에서 가장 인기 있는 관광지(the most popular tourist destination)가 되었으며 경쟁 상대인 델마이어 해변보다 20%퍼센트나 더 많은 해변 피서객들을 끌어들였다(with about 20 percent more beachgoers than the Delmire shore)'에서 (A)를 확인할 수 있다. 또한 두 번째 단락에서 작년 봄 서스턴 지역 내 최대 호텔인 더 글래스턴이 개업했다(Sustern saw the opening of the area's largest hotel, The Glaston, last spring)고 했는데, 세 번째 단락을 보면 호텔의 매니저가 바스티앙 씨(The hotel's manager, Anika Bastien)라는 것을 알 수 있으므로 (B) 역시 사실이다. 마지막으로, 네 번째 단락의 후반부에서 풍부한 지역 행사(an abundance of ~ community events)가 있다고 했으므로 (C)도 언급된 사실이다. 따라서 언급되지 않은 (D)가 정답이다.

어휘 employ 고용하다, 채용하다   a wide variety of 아주 다양한 cleanup 대청소

167 문장 삽입

번역 [1], [2], [3], [4]로 표시된 곳 중에서 다음 문장이 들어가기에 가장 적절한 곳은?

"이는 불과 77퍼센트였던 작년 여름 평균에서 상당히 증가한 수치였다."

(A) [1]
(B) [2]
(C) [3]
(D) [4]

해설 주어진 문장에서 지시대명사 this를 사용하여 '이는 77퍼센트에서 상당히 증가한 수치였다'라고 설명했으므로, 이 문장 앞에 77퍼센트보다 더 높은 수치가 언급되어야 한다. [1] 앞 문장을 보면, 여름 성수기 동안 호텔 이용률이 평균 94퍼센트였다(Hotel occupancy averaged 94 percent during the peak summer months)고 했으므로, 이 뒤에 주어진 문장이 들어가야 글의 흐름이 자연스러워진다. 따라서 (A)가 정답이다.

168-171 이메일

수신: 전 직원
발신: 제시카 페리
제목: 회의
날짜: 7월 19일
첨부 파일: 🖉 워크숍 신청서

안녕하세요, 여러분,

¹⁶⁹제4회 연례 호주 전국 영업 및 마케팅 컨퍼런스(ANSMC)가 11월 18일부터 22일까지 이곳 퍼스에서 열릴 예정입니다. 컨퍼런스 주최측

에서는 지역 마케팅 전문가들에게 기조 연설을 하거나, 워크숍을 진행하거나 전시회장에서 근무해 달라고 도움을 요청했습니다.

¹⁶⁹최고경영자인 마틴 휴즈 씨는 우리가 이 좋은 기회를 활용해 휴즈 오스트레일리아 마케팅이 전국 무대에서 두각을 나타내기를 원합니다.

¹⁷⁰이는 분명 우리의 고객층을 늘리는 데 도움이 될 것입니다. 휴즈 씨는 성공적인 마케팅 캠페인 제작을 위해 설문 조사를 활용하는 것에 대한 기조 연설을 하기로 동의했습니다. 저는 전시회장에 설치할 우리 회사의 부스를 디자인하고 있습니다. 도와주실 의향이 있으면, 7월 23일 다음 주 화요일 오후 2시에 C556실에서 열릴 예정인 기획 회의에 참석해 주세요.

^{168, 171}워크숍을 진행할 의사가 있으면 첨부된 제안서 양식을 작성하셔서 7월 26일까지 제게 다시 보내 주십시오. 그렇게 해주시면 워크숍 주제가 겹치지 않도록 하는 데 도움이 될 것입니다. 혼자 발표해도 되고 파트너와 함께 발표해도 됩니다. 워크숍에 관한 아이디어는 7월 29일에 열릴 부장 회의에서 논의 후 승인될 것입니다.

감사합니다.

제시카

어휘 attachment 첨부 파일   application 신청(서) conference 회의, 회담   take place (행사가) 열리다, 개최되다 organizer 주최자, 조직자   specialist 전문가   keynote speech 기조 연설   exhibition hall 전시회장   chief executive officer 최고경영자(= CEO)   take advantage of ~을 이용하다, 활용하다   achieve 달성하다   visibility 가시성, 눈에 잘 보임 expand 늘리다, 확장하다   client base 고객층   attached 첨부된 proposal 제안(서)   approve 승인하다

168 주제 / 목적

번역 이메일의 목적은 무엇인가?

(A) 직원들에게 컨퍼런스 등록을 상기시키기 위해
(B) 기한을 놓친 데 대해 사과하기 위해
(C) 직원들에게 신청서를 제출하도록 요청하기 위해
(D) 마케팅 설문 조사에 응답하도록 요청하기 위해

해설 첫 번째 단락에서 ANSMC 주최측에서 지역 마케팅 전문가들에게 기조 연설을 하거나, 워크숍을 진행하거나 전시회장에서 근무해 달라고 도움을 요청했다(Conference organizers ~ to help out by giving a keynote speech, leading a workshop, or working in the exhibition hall)고 했고, 세 번째 단락에서 워크숍을 진행할 의사가 있으면(If you would like to lead a workshop) 첨부된 제안서 양식을 작성하여 7월 26일까지 제출해 달라(please complete the attached proposal form and return it to me by 26 July)고 요청했다. 따라서 (C)가 정답이다.

어휘 register for ~에 등록하다   apologize for ~에 대해서 사과하다 deadline 마감(일), 최종 기한   submit 제출하다

▸▸ **Paraphrasing**   지문의 **complete the attached proposal form and return it to me** → 정답의 **submit an application**

169 추론 / 암시

번역 휴즈 오스트레일리아 마케팅에 관해 암시된 것은?

(A) ANSMC를 개최한다.
(B) 퍼스에 위치해 있다.
(C) 4년 동안 성업해 왔다.
(D) 호주 전역에서 고객에게 서비스를 제공한다.

해설 첫 번째 단락에서 제시카 페리 씨가 ANSMC의 주최지를 '이곳 퍼스 (here in Perth)'라고 했고, 두 번째 단락을 보면 제시카 페리 씨의 회사가 휴즈 오스트레일리아 마케팅임을 알 수 있으므로, (B)가 정답이다.

어휘 be in business 영업 중이다, 성업 중이다

170 세부 사항

번역 이메일에 따르면, 휴즈 씨가 직원들이 ANSMC에 참가하기를 원하는 이유는 무엇인가?

(A) 새로운 마케팅 전략을 배울 수 있어서
(B) 설문 조사 결과를 공유할 수 있어서
(C) 새 고객을 유치할 수 있어서
(D) 휴즈 씨의 기조 연설을 들을 수 있어서

해설 두 번째 단락을 보면, 휴즈 씨가 직원들이 ANSMC에 참가하여 휴즈 오스트레일리아 마케팅이 전국 무대에서 두각을 나타내기를 원한다(want us ~ to achieve visibility on a national stage)며, 이는 분명 고객층을 늘리는 데 도움이 될 것(It is sure to help us to expand our client base)이라고 했으므로, (C)가 정답이다.

어휘 strategy 전략 attract 끌어들이다, 유치하다

> ▸▸ **Paraphrasing** 지문의 expand our client base
> → 정답의 attract new clients

171 문장 삽입

번역 [1], [2], [3], [4]로 표시된 자리 중 다음 문장이 들어가기에 가장 적절한 곳은?

"그렇게 해주시면 워크숍 주제가 겹치지 않도록 하는 데 도움이 될 것입니다."

(A) [1]
(B) [2]
(C) [3]
(D) [4]

해설 주어진 문장에서 '그렇게 하면 워크숍 주제가 겹치지 않도록 하는 데 도움이 될 것'이라고 했으므로, 이 앞에는 워크숍 주제가 겹치지 않도록 하는 방안에 관련된 내용이 와야 한다. [4] 앞 문장에서 첨부된 워크숍 제안서 양식을 작성해서 7월 26일까지 다시 보내 달라(please complete the attached proposal form ~ 26 July)고 했으므로, 이 뒤에 주어진 문장이 들어가야 글의 흐름이 자연스러워진다. 따라서 (D)가 정답이다.

172-175 온라인 채팅

> **알베르토 오반도 [오전 11시 15분]**
> 172우리가 지난주에 회의했을 때, 레드몬즈에 납품할 상자와 다른 포장재 생산은 거의 끝나가고 있었죠. 라니, 지금은 어느 정도 진척이 되었나요?
>
> **라니 베르마 [오전 11시 16분]**
> 173냉장고와 식기 세척기 상자는 수요일에 레드몬즈 창고에 도착하기로 되어 있었는데, 눈보라 때문에 배송 일정이 많이 지연되었어요.
>
> **알베르토 오반도 [오전 11시 17분]**
> 175이런 상황을 그들에게 말했나요?
>
> **스테이시 파이퍼 [오전 11시 18분]**
> 할게요. 175하지만 운전 기사들로부터 소식을 기다리고 있던 중이에요. 조지, 도와줄 수 있어요?
>
> **조지 켈러만 [오전 11시 19분]**
> 17510분 전에 그들과 이야기했어요. 이제 다시 운행할 수 있다고 하니, 고작 하루 늦어진 거예요. 그들(=레드몬즈)은 이번 주말 전에 모든 것을 받을 거예요.
>
> **스테이시 파이퍼 [오전 11시 21분]**
> 174알겠어요. 아무리 늦어도 금요일까지 배송될 거라고 말할게요.
>
> **라니 베르마 [오전 11시 22분]**
> 어쨌든 소형 가전 제품 포장재는 눈보라 전에 배송했으니, 대형 상자만 영향을 받게 됩니다.
>
> **알베르토 오반도 [오전 11시 23분]**
> 172계약에 따르면 우리는 소형 포장재만이 아니라 레드몬즈의 전 제품에 대한 포장 재료를 제공해야 해요. 꼭 수정된 일정대로 진행하도록 합시다.

어휘 production 생산 packaging 포장, 포장재 dishwasher 식기 세척기 warehouse 창고 on the road 도로를 주행할 수 있는, 통행 중인 at the very latest 아무리 늦어도 material 재료 appliances 가전 제품 contract 계약(서); 계약하다

172 추론 / 암시

번역 사람들은 어떤 종류의 사업체에서 근무할 것 같은가?

(A) 레스토랑 공급품 회사
(B) 가전 제품 수리점
(C) 포장재 제조 업체
(D) 가구 배송 서비스

해설 11시 15분 메시지에서 오반도 씨는 지난주에 레드몬즈에 납품할 상자와 다른 포장재 생산은 거의 끝나가고 있었다(production was nearly finished on the boxes and other packaging for Redmond's)며 현재의 진행 상황을 물었다(where are we now?). 또한 11시 23분 메시지에서는 소형 포장재만이 아니라 레드몬즈의 전 제품에 대한 포장 재료를 제공해야 한다(provide packaging materials for all of Redmond's products, not just the smaller ones)는 계약 조건을 언급했다. 따라서 대화 참가자들이 포장재 제조 업체에 근무한다는 것을 추론할 수 있으므로, (C)가 정답이다.

173 주제 / 목적

번역 사람들은 어떤 문제에 대해 논의하고 있는가?

(A) 배송이 지연되었다.
(B) 창고 문이 닫혀 있다.
(C) 주문이 잘못되었다.
(D) 운전기사가 출근하지 않았다.

해설 11시 16분 베르마 씨의 메시지에서 원래 수요일에 냉장고와 식기 세척기 상자가 레드몬즈 창고에 도착하기로 되어 있었는데((The refrigerator and dishwasher boxes ~ on Wednesday), 눈보라 때문에 배송 일정이 지연되었다(the snowstorm ~ backed up our delivery schedule)고 했으므로, (A)가 정답이다.

어휘 report for work 출근하다

> ▸▸ **Paraphrasing** 지문의 backed up our delivery schedule → 정답의 A shipment was delayed.

174 추론 / 암시

번역 파이퍼 씨는 다음에 무엇을 할 것 같은가?

(A) 배송 취소
(B) 계약서 서명
(C) 운전 기사에게 전화하기
(D) 고객에게 연락하기

해설 11시 21분 메시지에서 파이퍼 씨는 아무리 늦어도 금요일까지 배송될 거라고 레드몬즈에 말하겠다(I'll tell them to expect delivery by Friday at the very latest)고 했으므로, (D)가 정답이다.

> ▸▸ **Paraphrasing** 지문의 tell them → 정답의 Contact the client

175 의도 파악

번역 11시 18분에 파이퍼 씨가 '도와줄 수 있어요?'라고 말할 때, 그 의도는 무엇인가?

(A) 켈러만 씨가 상자를 실어야 한다고 생각한다.
(B) 켈러만 씨가 창고까지 차를 가지고 가야 한다.
(C) 켈러만 씨가 배송 정보를 알려 주기를 원한다.
(D) 켈러만 씨가 운전 기사들에게 비용을 지불하길 기대한다.

해설 11시 17분 메시지에서 오반도 씨가 배송 문제를 레드몬즈에 말했는지(Have you told them this?) 묻자, 파이퍼 씨는 운전 기사들로부터 소식을 기다리고 있던 중(I was waiting to hear from the drivers)이라고 하며 켈러만 씨에게 도와줄 수 있는지 물었다. 그러자 11시 19분에 켈러만 씨가 10분 전에 그들과 이야기했다(I spoke with them ten minutes ago)며 현재 상황을 알려 주었다. 따라서 켈러만 씨가 배송 관련 정보를 알려 주길 바라며 한 말임을 알 수 있으므로, (C)가 정답이다.

어휘 load (차나 배 등에) 짐을 싣다

176-180 전단지 + 이메일

제17회 PAGA 연례 식물 및 원예 박람회, ¹⁷⁸7월 10일-13일
스타키 컨벤션 센터, 피츠버그, 펜실베이니아

¹⁷⁶피츠버그 지역 정원 협회(PAGA)가 정원 전시회를 지원할 기업을 초대합니다. 지난해 정원 전시회에는 거의 4만 명의 방문객들이 참가했습니다. 이 전시회는 가정 원예사들 및 야외 활동을 좋아하는 사람들에게 다가갈 수 있는 비용 대비 효과적인 방법이며, 귀사의 상업적 성과를 높여 드립니다.

¹⁷⁶PAGA는 아래와 같이 기업의 후원 정도에 따라 이에 상응하는 혜택을 제공합니다. (¹⁷⁷문의 사항이 있으시면 925-555-0412번으로 PAGA 행사 책임자인 카리타 아라곤 씨에게 연락 주시기 바랍니다. 등록하시려면 sponsors@paga.org로 이메일을 보내시면 됩니다.)

워크숍 후원사—1,250달러 귀사의 대표가 행사 두 번째 날에 열릴 예정인 워크숍의 발표자(들)를 소개하는 영광을 얻게 됩니다.	가방 후원사—3,500달러 모든 방문객에게 나누어 줄 천 가방에 귀사의 엠블럼이 부착됩니다.
충전소 후원사—2,000달러 ¹⁸⁰전시장에 여덟 곳의 모바일 장치 충전소가 설치되며, 그 옆에 후원사의 서명이 게시됩니다.	전체 프로그램 후원사—5,000달러 ¹⁷⁸박람회 개막 첫날 밤에 열리는 PAGA 축하 연회에 귀사의 경영진 두 분이 참석할 수 있습니다.

어휘 annual 연례의 botanical 식물의 horticultural 원예의, 원예학의 expo 박람회 association 협회 exhibition 전시(회) cost-effective 비용 대비 효과적인 enthusiast 열광자, ~를 좋아하는 사람 enhance 증대시키다, (정도를) 높이다, 강화하다 performance 실적, 업무 능력 corporate 기업의, 회사의 sponsorship 후원 corresponding (~에) 해당[상응]하는 inquiry 질문, 문의 coordinator 책임자, 진행자 register 등록하다 patron 후원자 representative 대표, (대표하는) 직원 presenter 발표자, 사회자 conduct 실시하다, 행하다 charging station 충전소 emblem 엠블럼, 상징, (그림이나 문자로 된) 표지 fabric 직물, 천 distribute 배포하다, 나누어주다 executive 간부, 임원 banquet 연회

발신: caragon@paga.org
수신: mkee@wimosol.com
날짜: 5월 15일
제목: 감사합니다

키 씨에게,

와이어리스 모니터링 솔루션즈를 피츠버그 지역 정원 협회(PAGA) 박람회의 후원사로 등록해 주셔서 감사합니다. ¹⁷⁹귀사의 후원은 올해 행사를 개최하는 것뿐만 아니라 원예에 대한 관심을 이끌어내는 데도 도움이 됩니다.

¹⁸⁰귀사의 기부금 2천 달러가 처리되었습니다. 또한, 별도의 추가 비용 없이 저희 박람회 가방 후원에 상응하는 혜택을 제공해 드리겠습니다.

이 제의는 PAGA와 PAGA 프로그램을 오랫동안 지원해 주신 것에 대한 감사의 표시입니다. 홍보용 제품을 완성하려면 귀사의 로고 이미지를 저희에게 보내 주십시오.

카리타 아라곤, PAGA 행사 책임자

> 어휘 generate 만들어 내다, 발생[창출]시키다 contribution 기부(금) process 처리하다 additionally 게다가, 이밖에 at no additional cost 추가 비용 없이 token 표시, 징표 appreciation 감사, 고마움 long-standing 오랫동안 지속되어 온, 다년간의 finalize 마무리짓다, 완성하다 promotional 홍보용의, 판촉의

176 주제 / 목적

번역 전단의 목적은 무엇인가?
(A) 행사 참여에 대한 혜택을 홍보하기 위해
(B) 행사 개최 비용 내역을 공개하기 위해
(C) 모금 캠페인의 재정적 성공에 대해 보고하기 위해
(D) 지역 주민들이 자연 보호 프로젝트에 함께하도록 권장하기 위해

해설 첫 번째 단락에서 PAGA가 정원 전시회를 지원할 기업을 초대한다(The Pittsburgh Area Garden Association (PAGA) invites companies to support its garden exhibition)고 했고, 두 번째 단락에서 기업의 후원 정도에 따라 그에 상응하는 혜택을 제공한다(PAGA ~ offer the following levels of corporate sponsorship with corresponding benefits)며 후원 금액별 혜택을 설명하고 있다. 따라서 (A)가 정답이다.

어휘 participate in ~에 참여하다, 참가하다 breakdown 분석, 내역 fund-raising 모금의 preservation 보존[보호]

▸▸ Paraphrasing 지문의 corresponding benefits → 정답의 the benefits of participating in an event

177 세부 사항

번역 전단에 따르면 언제 PAGA 사무실에 전화를 걸어야 하는가?
(A) 기부금을 처리할 수 없을 때
(B) 대금을 받지 못할 때
(C) 추가 정보가 필요할 때
(D) 후원 수준을 변경할 때

해설 두 번째 단락을 보면, 문의 사항이 있을 시 925-555-0412번으로 행사 책임자인 카리타 씨에게 연락하라(For inquiries, contact Ms. Carita Aragon, PAGA's Event Coordinator, at 925-555-0142)고 했으므로, (C)가 정답이다.

▸▸ Paraphrasing 지문의 For inquiries → 정답의 additional information

178 세부 사항

번역 7월 10일에 무슨 일이 있을 것인가?
(A) 지난해 박람회 참석 인원을 발표할 것이다.
(B) 모바일 기기 충전소를 설치할 것이다.
(C) 워크숍이 진행될 것이다.
(D) 공식 만찬이 열릴 것이다.

해설 전단지 제목(PAGA's Seventeenth Annual Botanical and Horticultural Expo, July 10-13)에서 7월 10일은 제17회 PAGA 연례 식물 및 원예 박람회가 열리는 첫날임을 알 수 있고, General Program Patron 항목을 보면 박람회 첫날 밤에 PGAG 축하 연회(the PAGA Gala Banquet on the opening night of the expo)가 열릴 것임을 알 수 있다. 따라서 (D)가 정답이다.

어휘 attendance figures 참석자 수 release 공개하다, 발표하다 install 설치하다

▸▸ Paraphrasing 지문의 the PAGA Gala Banquet on the opening night → 정답의 A formal dinner

179 추론 / 암시

번역 PAGA의 행사에 관해 암시된 것은?
(A) 피츠버그 시 정부에서 일부 기금을 댔다.
(B) 매년 다른 장소에서 열린다.
(C) 원예에 대한 열정을 고취하고자 한다.
(D) 매년 4만 명 이상의 방문객을 유치한다.

해설 이메일 첫 단락에서 와이어리스 모니터링 솔루션즈의 후원이 올해 행사를 개최하는 것뿐만 아니라 원예에 대한 관심을 이끌어내는 데도 도움이 된다(Your sponsorship not only helps to ~ to generate interest in gardening)고 했다. 따라서 PAGA의 행사는 원예에 대한 열정을 고취하고자 개최되는 것을 알 수 있으므로, (C)가 정답이다.

어휘 partially 부분적으로 fund 자금을 조달하다[대다] promote 촉진하다, 증진하다 enthusiasm 열의, 열정 attract 유치하다

▸▸ Paraphrasing 지문의 generate interest in gardening → 정답의 promote enthusiasm for gardening

180 연계

번역 와이어리스 모니터링 솔루션즈에 대해 명시되지 않은 것은?
(A) 회사명이 컨벤션 센터의 다양한 장소에 전시될 것이다.
(B) 전시장에 무선 모니터링 장치를 설치할 것이다.
(C) 다양한 행사에서 PAGA의 전시회를 후원해 왔다.
(D) 기념품 가방에 회사의 로고가 표시될 것이다.

해설 이메일의 두 번째 단락 첫 문장에서 와이어리스 모니터링 솔루션즈가 2천 달러를 기부했음을(Your contribution of $2,000 has been processed) 알 수 있으며, 전단지에서 2천 달러를 기부하는 충전소 후원사(Charging Station Patron-$2,000) 항목을 보면 후원사의 서명이 전시장 내 여덟 곳의 모바일 장치 충전소 옆에 게시될 것(eight mobile-device charging stations in the exhibition hall, each with a sponsor sign next to it)이라고 했으므로, (A)는 사실이다. 또한 그 다음 문장에서 PAGA를 오래 후원한 것에 대한 감사의 표시(a token of our appreciation for the long-standing support of PAGA and its programs)로 방문객들에게 나눠줄 가방에 회사의 엠블럼을 새길 수 있게 해준다(offering you sponsorship of our expo bags)고 했으므로, (C)와 (D)의 내용도 확인할 수 있다. 그러나 와이어리스 모니터링 솔루션즈가 전시장에 모바일 장치 충전소를 설치할 것이라는 내용은 언급되지 않았으므로, (B)가 정답이다.

어휘 feature (특별히) 포함하다, 특징을 이루다 souvenir 기념품, 선물

---

https://www.buyforbusiness.com/projectors0102

바이 포 비즈니스 미니프로젝터 후기

콜리어프로사의 HJ6 미니프로젝터

[181]HJ6는 최고급 미니프로젝터로, 콜리어프로에 익숙한 사용자들에게는 전혀 놀라운 일이 아니다. 기존과 다를 바 없이, 이 회사는 프로젝터를 거의 어디든 쉽게 가지고 다닐 수 있도록 하기 위해 비용을 아끼지 않았다. 프로젝터는 가볍고, 리모컨과 삼각대가 포함된 휴대용 케이스와 함께 제공된다. 내장된 램프는 같은 사이즈의 다른 프로젝터보다 훨씬 더 밝다. [182]이 밝기 때문에, HJ6는 우리가 실험해 본 모든 미니프로젝터들 중에서 가장 선명한 이미지를 영사한다.

[184]HJ6의 가장 큰 결점은 스피커이다. 다른 기능의 우수성을 고려해 봤을 때, 스피커 소리는 기대한 만큼 크지 않다. 쉽게 다양한 스피커에 플러그를 연결할 수 있다. 그러나 이것은 미니프로젝터이며 사이즈가 작기 때문에 강의실이나 대규모 회의실에서 프레젠테이션을 할 때에는 탁월한 선택이 될 수 없다.

전반적으로 이것은 여행자들에게 환상적인 프로젝터이고, 그래서 우리는 이 제품을 추천한다. 하지만 이 제품은 신형 모델이며, 소비자 가격이 상당히 비싸다. 즉시 구입하지 말고 잠시 미루는 것이 최선일 수도 있다. [183]프로젝터프로가 다음 달에 피코 P17 프로젝터를 출시할 예정이므로, 경쟁력을 유지하기 위해 HJ6의 가격이 인하될 수도 있다.

어휘 top-of-the-line 최고급품의, 최신식의 spare no expense 비용을 아끼지 않다 internal 내장된, 내부의 project 영사하다, 투사하다 superiority 우수성 feature 기능, 특징 overall 전체적으로, 종합적으로 sticker price 표시 가격, 소비자 가격 hold off 연기하다, 지체시키다 competitive (품질·가격 따위가) 경쟁력이 있는, (남에게) 뒤지지 않는

---

https://www.buyforbusiness.com/projectors0103

바이 포 비즈니스 미니프로젝터 후기

엑설런트로닉스사의 포켓 미니 C

포켓 미니 C는 믿을 수 있는 프로젝터이며 많은 돈을 쓰고 싶지 않은 사람들이 구입하기에 좋은 제품이다. 다른 경쟁 제품들과 마찬가지로 가볍고 소형이다. [185]우리가 가장 깊은 인상을 받은 기능은 배터리인데, 그것은 최고 6시간까지 지속될 수 있으며 이는 우리가 사용해 본 다른 배터리식 프로젝터들보다 훨씬 더 오래가는 것이다.

저렴한 가격에서 예상할 수 있는 몇 가지 결점이 있다. 포트가 불편한 곳에 있으며, 메뉴 구성이 헷갈려서 프로젝터 설치가 쉽지 않다. [184]오디오 음량도 제한적이어서, 볼륨을 크게 하면 소리가 불분명하게 들릴 수 있다. 하지만 전반적으로 가성비가 좋은 쓸만한 미니프로젝터이다.

어휘 reliable 믿을 수 있는, 신뢰할 수 있는 competitor 경쟁업체, 경쟁자 compact 소형의 downside 결점, 약점 budget (값이) 싼; 예산 awkward 불편한, 어색한, 적합하지 않은 set up 설치하다 straightforward 간단한, 손쉬운 capability 용량, 성능 muffled (소리를) 낮춘 듯한, 불분명한 decent 만족스러운, 괜찮은 reasonable (가격이) 적당한, 비싸지 않은

---

181 추론 / 암시

번역 콜리어프로에 대해 암시된 것은?

(A) 〈바이 포 비즈니스〉 소유이다.
(B) 고급 전자 제품을 제조한다.
(C) 신생 기업이다.
(D) 출장객들에게 할인을 제공한다.

해설 첫 번째 후기의 첫 단락에서 HJ6는 최고급 미니프로젝터인데(The HJ6 is a top-of-the-line miniprojector), 콜리어프로에 익숙한 사용자들에게는 전혀 놀라운 일이 아니라고(which is no surprise to those familiar with Collierpro) 했다. 따라서 콜리어프로는 고급 전자 제품을 제조한다는 것을 추론할 수 있으므로, (B)가 정답이다.

▸▸ Paraphrasing   지문의 top-of-the-line → 정답의 high-quality
지문의 miniprojector → 정답의 electronics

---

182 사실 관계 확인

번역 HJ6 미니프로젝터의 특징으로 언급된 것은?

(A) 피코 P17보다 더 저렴하다.
(B) 여분의 전선이 함께 제공된다.
(C) 충전용 배터리를 갖추고 있다.
(D) 아주 선명한 이미지를 보여 준다.

해설 첫 번째 후기의 첫 단락에서 HJ6는 실험해 본 모든 미니프로젝터들 중에서 가장 선명한 이미지를 영사한다(the HJ6 was able to project the sharpest picture)고 했으므로, (D)가 정답이다.

어휘 spare 예비의, 여분의 power cord 전선 rechargeable battery 충전지

▸▸ Paraphrasing   지문의 project the sharpest picture
→ 정답의 produces a very clear image

---

183 세부 사항

번역 고객들이 HJ6 미니프로젝터를 구입하기 전에 기다려야 하는 이유는 무엇인가?

(A) (HJ6) 모델의 기능이 곧 업데이트될 것이다.
(B) 곧 프로젝터가 더 저렴해질 수도 있다.
(C) 기계의 경미한 문제가 곧 수리될 것이다.
(D) 다른 기업에서 프로젝터의 제조 업체를 곧 매입할 것이다.

해설 첫 번째 후기의 마지막 단락에서 다음 달에 피코 P17 프로젝터가 출시될 것(Projectopro will introduce the Pico P17 projector next month)이므로, 경쟁력을 유지하기 위해 HJ6의 가격이 인하될 수도 있다(the HJ6's price may drop in order to remain competitive)고 했다. 따라서 (B)가 정답이다.

어휘 manufacturer 제조업체, 생산자

▸▸ Paraphrasing   지문의 the HJ6's price may drop
→ 정답의 The projector might become less expensive

184 연계

번역 두 프로젝터가 공통으로 받은 비판은 무엇인가?

(A) 너무 무겁다.
(B) 설치하기에 쉽지 않다.
(C) 음향 장치가 제대로 작동하지 않는다.
(D) 영상이 충분히 크기 않다.

해설 첫 번째 후기의 두 번째 단락에서 HJ6의 가장 큰 결점은 스피커(The major weakness of the HJ6 is its speakers)이며, 스피커 소리가 기대한 만큼 크지 않다(They are not nearly as loud as one would expect)고 했다. 두 번째 후기의 두 번째 단락에서는 포켓 미니 C의 오디오 음량이 제한적이어서 볼륨을 크게 하면 소리가 불분명하게 들릴 수 있다(when the volume is turned up, the audio can sound muffled)고 했다. 따라서 두 프로젝터 모두 음향 장치가 좋지 않다는 평을 받았으므로, (C)가 정답이다.

어휘 criticism 비평, 비난 work 작동하다 projection (투사된) 영상

> ▸▸ **Paraphrasing** 지문의 its speakers / The audio capabilities → 정답의 Their sound systems

185 세부 사항

번역 두 번째 후기에 따르면, 포켓 미니 C의 가장 좋은 점은 무엇인가?

(A) 디자인이 매력적이다.
(B) 다른 프로젝터보다 휴대가 더 용이하다.
(C) 다른 프로젝터보다 포트가 더 많다.
(D) 배터리가 오랫동안 지속된다.

해설 두 번째 후기 첫 단락에서 가장 깊은 인상을 받은 기능은 배터리(The feature we were most impressed with is its battery)라고 하며, 최고 6시간까지 지속되고(it can run for up to six hours) 다른 배터리식 프로젝터들보다 훨씬 더 오래가는 것(which is much longer than the other battery-powered projectors)이라고 했다. 따라서 (D)가 정답이다.

어휘 attractive 매력적인, 인기를 끄는 last 지속되다, 계속되다

> ▸▸ **Paraphrasing** 지문의 The feature we were most impressed with → 질문의 the best feature

186-190 이메일 + 이메일 + 양식

발신: 앨런 그래디 〈agrady@st.pro.com〉
수신: 제이코 네베스 〈owner@neveslocal.com〉
날짜: 8월 7일 월요일 오전 9시 31분
제목: 계약 추가 조항

네베스 씨께,

주택 공사 관련 진행 상황에 대한 논의를 위해 전화 주셔서 감사합니다. **186, 187우리가 나눈 대화를 요약하면, 9월 22일까지 지연된다고 할지라도 제 아파트 임차 계약이 만료되는 10월 10일 이전에 제가 그 집에 입주할 수 있도록 준비되어야 합니다. 190우리가 논의한 현황 보고서에** 관해 좀 더 생각해 보았는데, 일주일에 두 번이 가장 좋을 것 같습니다. **186제가 이번 주에 서명하여 승인할 수 있도록 귀하가 계약서에 이러한 변경 사항을 기록해 주실 것으로 알고 있겠습니다.**

늘 드리는 말씀이지만, 이번 공사에 세심한 주의를 기울여 주셔서 감사합니다.

앨런 그래디

어휘 contract 계약(서) addendum (계약 등의) 추가 조항 progress 진행 상황, 진척 construction 건설, 공사 summarize 요약하다, 개괄하다 lease 임대, 임차 expire (기간이) 만료되다 status report 현황 보고(서) document 기록하다; 문서, 서류 sign off on (서명을 하여) ~을 승인하다

발신: 제이코 네베스 〈owner@neveslocal.com〉
수신: 앨런 그래디 〈agrady@st.pro.com〉
날짜: 8월 7일 월요일 오후 4시 16분
제목: 회신: 계약 추가 조항
첨부: ⬛ 추가 조항

그래디 씨에게,

우리가 논의한 6월 5일자 계약에 대한 수정안을 **188작성해서** 이 메시지에 첨부했습니다. **189최근 날씨가 좋지 않아 지연되었지만**, 많이 늦어지지는 않았습니다. 프로젝트 마감이 다가오니 많은 부분을 곧 하나로 합쳐야 합니다. 힘이 닿는 한 계속 상황을 알려 드리겠습니다만, 늘 그렇듯 저의 최우선 사항은 작업 자체를 잘 마무리하는 것입니다.

186서류에 이견이 없으시면 서명하셔서 제게 사본을 한 부 보내 주시기 바랍니다. 186저희가 귀하에게 서비스를 제공하는 방식에 대해 문의 사항이나 염려되는 부분이 있으시면 언제든 저나 에반 바우르콧에게 연락 주십시오.

제이코 네베스

어휘 attachment 첨부 (파일) draw up (문서를) 작성하다 revision 수정, 개정 attach 첨부하다 set back 지연시키다 come together 모이다, (하나로) 합치다 to the best of ~하는 한, ~이 미치는 한 priority 우선 사항, 우선(권) acceptable to ~에게 만족스러운 hesitate to ~하는 것을 망설이다[주저하다] contact 연락하다

계약 추가 조항

1. **1897월 24일부터 7월 28일까지 불가피한 상황으로 인해 수행이 불가능했던 작업 때문에** 전체 공사 완공일이 9월 17일에서 9월 22일로 변경될 예정이다. 해당 변경 사항으로 인해 발생한 어떠한 추가 인건비도 '의뢰인'에게 청구하지 않는다. 건축 허가 연장으로 인한 모든 비용은 '계약 업체'에서 지불한다.

2. 즉시 효력을 발하는 사항으로, **1908월 12일 월요일부터 '계약 업체'** 에서는 (이미 초래되었거나 앞으로 예상되는 모든 지연을 포함하는) 완료된 작업에 대한 보고서를 주 1회 제출한다.

어휘 unavoidable 피할 수 없는, 불가피한 completion date
완공일, 완성일 charge 청구하다; 청구 금액, 비용 labor cost
인건비 extension 연장, 연기 building permit 건축 허가(서)
effective immediately 즉시 효력이 발생하는 contractor 계약
업체, 하청 업체 incur 초래하다, 자초하다 anticipate 기대하다,
예상하다

186 세부 사항

번역 그래디 씨는 누구인가?

(A) 네베스 씨의 사업 파트너
(B) 네베스 씨의 의뢰인
(C) 바우르콧 씨의 비서
(D) 바우르콧 씨의 법률 고문

해설 두 번째 이메일의 두 번째 단락을 보면, 네베스 씨가 그래디 씨에게
자신들이 서비스를 제공하는 방식(how our business can serve
you)에 대해 문의 사항이나 염려되는 부분이 있으면 언제든 연락을
달라고 했으므로, 그래디 씨가 그의 의뢰인임을 알 수 있다. 따라서
(B)가 정답이다.

187 세부 사항

번역 10월에 무슨 일이 계획되어 있는가?

(A) 임대 기한이 연장될 것이다.
(B) 계약이 변경될 것이다.
(C) 공사 일정이 수정될 것이다.
(D) 집에 사람이 입주할 것이다.

해설 첫 번째 이메일의 두 번째 문장에서, 그래디 씨는 공사가 지연되더라
도 자신의 아파트 임차 계약이 만료되는 10월 10일 이전에 그 집에
입주할 수 있도록 준비되어야 한다(the house should be ready
for me to move into ~ on October 10)고 했으므로, 그래디 씨
가 10월에 입주할 계획임을 알 수 있다. 따라서 (D)가 정답이다.

어휘 extend 기한을 연장하다 occupy (건물을) 사용하다, 거주하다

▶ Paraphrasing   지문의 the house should be ready for me
to move into
→ 정답의 A house will be occupied.

188 동의어 찾기

번역 두 번째 이메일에서 첫 번째 단락 1행의 "drawn up"과 의미상 가장
가까운 것은?

(A) 올렸다
(B) 스케치했다
(C) 작성했다
(D) 똑바르게 했다

해설 have drawn up the revisions는 '수정안을 작성했다'는 의미로,
여기서 draw up은 '문서를 준비하다, 작성하다'라는 뜻으로 쓰였다.
따라서 '준비했다'라는 의미의 (C) prepared가 정답이다.

189 연계

번역 공사가 악천후의 영향을 받은 것은 언제였겠는가?

(A) 6월 5일
(B) 7월 24일
(C) 8월 12일
(D) 9월 22일

해설 두 번째 이메일 첫 단락에서 최근 날씨가 좋지 않아 공사가 지연되었
다(The recent bad weather set us back)고 했고, 계약 추가 조
항의 1번 항목에서 7월 24일부터 7월 28일까지 불가피한 상황으
로 인해(due to unavoidable circumstances from July 24 to
July 28) 공사를 할 수 없었다고 했으므로, 7월 24일부터 7월 28
일 사이에 악천후의 영향을 받았다는 것을 알 수 있다. 따라서 정답은
(B)이다.

190 연계

번역 계약서의 정보 중 그래디 씨가 요청한 것과 다른 것은 무엇인가?

(A) 보고 빈도
(B) 추가 인건비 청구
(C) 완공일
(D) 요구되는 허가서 개수

해설 첫 번째 이메일의 첫 단락에서 그래디 씨가 현황 보고서(status
reports)는 일주일에 두 번이 가장 좋을 것 같다(twice a week
would be best)고 했는데, 계약서 추가 조항의 2번 항목을 보면 계
약 업체에서는 완료된 작업에 대한 보고서를 주 1회 제출할 것(the
Contractor will submit a report of all work completed
once every week)이라고 했다. 따라서 (A)가 정답이다.

▶ Paraphrasing   지문의 twice a week / once every week
→ 정답의 The frequency

191-195 기사 + 이메일 + 이메일

추가 개선 작업

화요일 회의에서 엘던베리 시 의회는 투표를 통해 마을 시설에 추가할
작업에 대한 선택 사항을 조사하기로 했다. **191 찰스 그루버 서기관에
따르면, 엘던베리 주민 센터 보수 공사에 예산보다 비용이 적게 들었다.
따라서 의회는 남은 자금으로 할 수 있는 소소한 개량 공사 항목을 집계
해 보기로 결정했다.**

제안된 프로젝트에는 엘던베리 공공 도서관 입구의 지붕 추가, 웨스폴
공원의 조명 개선, 그리고 시청 바닥 교체가 포함된다. 그루버 씨에 따
르면 의회는 주민들에게 아이디어를 구할 예정이다. **193 관심 있는 사람
들은 3월 20일 화요일 오후 4시 의회 회의에서 자신들의 의견을 발표하
거나 3월 31일 전에 의회 사무실로 이메일을 보내면 된다.** 주민들의 의
견 수렴이 있고 난 후에, 기획 위원회는 시 의회가 논의할 최종 리스트
를 **192 제안할** 것이며, 이에 대한 결정은 4월 15일까지 내려질 것이다.

발신: mccaffrey32@citymail.co.uk
수신: towncouncil@eldonbury.org.uk
날짜: 3월 25일
제목: 추가 프로젝트

시 의회 의원 여러분께,

주민 센터 보수 공사 후 남은 자금을 사용할 방법에 대한 건의를 받고 있다는 기사를 읽었습니다. **193선약이 있어 의회 회의에는 참석할 수 없었습니다만**, 저는 공원의 조명을 늘리자는 의견을 지지하고자 합니다. 작업 가능한 다른 공사들에 비해 공사비가 적당한 한편, 개선된 조명은 웨스트폴 공원의 편리성을 제고할 것이며 특히 어두운 겨울에 많은 사람들에게 도움이 될 것입니다. **195조명이 밝고 잘 관리된 공원은 분명 시의 자랑거리가 될 것이며, 우리 모두 환영할 만한 것이 될 겁니다.** 의회에서 이 프로젝트를 신중히 고려해 주기를 바랍니다.

헤더 맥카프리

발신: sunil.pai@hgnetworks.co.uk
수신: towncouncil@eldonbury.org.uk
날짜: 3월 27일
제목: 도시 프로젝트

그루버 씨에게,

최근의 보수 공사가 완료되었고 예산도 남았다니 기쁩니다. **194주민 센터에서 모든 연령대의 시민들을 위한 활동을 후원하기는 하지만, 대개 청소년들과 자녀가 있는 부모들이 센터를 방문합니다.** 따라서 다음 공사는 엘던베리의 노년층이 종종 이용할 곳에 중점을 둘 것을 제안합니다.

도서관은 노인들이 자연스럽게 모일 수 있는 장소이며, 새로운 입구 통로는 비에 젖지 않는 안전한 곳이 되어 사람들이 이야기를 나누거나 교통편을 기다릴 수 있게 해줄 것입니다. 눈에 띄는 개선이 될 것이고, 주민 센터의 개선으로 별다른 혜택을 보지 못했다고 느끼는 시민들에게 박수를 받을 것 같습니다. **1954월에 투표가 진행될 때, 엘던베리의 모든 주민들이 고르게 혜택을 받을 수 있도록 이 제안을 고려해 주시기 바랍니다.**

감사합니다.

선일 배

191 세부 사항

번역 엘던베리 시에서 자금을 이용할 수 있는 이유는?

(A) 시 의회에서 공사를 취소했다.
(B) 시에서 세율을 올렸다.
(C) 시민 단체에서 돈을 기부했다.
(D) 먼저 이루어진 공사 비용이 예상보다 적게 들었다.

해설 기사문 첫 단락에서 찰스 그루버 서기관에 따르면 엘던베리 주민 센터 보수 공사에 예산보다 비용이 적게 들어(the renovation of the Eldonbury Community Centre came in well under budget) 남은 자금을 이용할 수 있다고 했으므로, (D)가 정답이다.

어휘 available 이용할 수 있는 tax rate 세율 donate 기부하다, 기증하다

▶▶ Paraphrasing 지문의 came in well under budget
→ 정답의 cost less than expected

192 동의어 찾기

번역 기사문에서 두 번째 단락 12행의 "put forth"와 의미상 가장 가까운 것은?

(A) 자라다   (B) 발휘하다
(C) 제안하다   (D) 요청하다

해설 the planning committee will put forth a final list는 '기획 위원회에서 최종 리스트를 제안할 것이다'라는 내용으로, 여기에서 put forth는 '제시하다, 제안하다'의 의미로 쓰였다. 따라서 (C) propose가 정답이다.

193 연계

번역 맥카프리 씨는 언제 약속이 있었는가?

(A) 3월 20일   (B) 3월 25일
(C) 3월 31일   (D) 4월 15일

해설 첫 번째 이메일 두 번째 문장에서 맥카프리 씨는 선약이 있어 의회 회의에는 참석할 수 없었다(Because of a previously scheduled appointment, I was not able to attend the council meeting)고 했는데, 기사문 두 번째 단락을 보면 의회 회의가 3월 20일에 열렸다(the council's meeting on Tuesday, 20 March, at 4:00 P.M.)는 것을 알 수 있다. 따라서 (A)가 정답이다.

194 사실 관계 확인

번역 배 씨가 이메일에서 엘던베리 주민 센터에 관해 언급한 것은?

(A) 대중 교통편 가까이에 위치해 있다.
(B) 주로 젊은 주민들이 이용한다.
(C) 주민 센터 건물은 이전에는 다른 용도로 쓰였다.
(D) 주민 센터 프로그램은 1년 내내 운영될 것이다.

해설 배 씨가 그루버 씨에게 보낸 이메일의 첫 번째 단락을 보면, 대개 청소년들과 자녀가 있는 부모들이 주민 센터를 방문한다(it is, for the most part, visited by adolescents and parents with children)고 했다. 따라서 (B)가 정답이다.

어휘 public transportation 대중 교통   resident 주민, 거주자   run 운영하다   year-round 일 년 내내

> ▸▸ **Paraphrasing** 지문의 adolescents and parents with children → 정답의 younger residents

195 연계

번역 맥카프리 씨와 배 씨는 어떤 점에서 의견을 같이할 것 같은가?

(A) 선정된 공사는 전체 지역 주민에게 혜택을 주어야 한다.
(B) 시에서 다음 공사에 가능한 적은 돈을 지출해야 한다.
(C) 시 의회는 일반 시민의 의견 수렴을 위해 마감일을 연장해야 한다.
(D) 도서관과 공원 이용자들이 협력해 돈을 모금해야 한다.

해설 첫 번째 이메일의 후반부에서 맥카프리 씨는 조명이 밝고 잘 관리된 공원은 모두가 환영할 만한 일이 될 것이라(A well-lit, nicely maintained park is ~ something we could all appreciate)고 했고, 두 번째 이메일의 후반부에서 배 씨는 엘던베리의 모든 주민들이 고르게 혜택을 받을 수 있도록(to balance the interests of all members of the Eldonbury public) 자신의 제안을 고려해 달라고 했다. 따라서 두 사람 다 주민 전체의 이익을 바라고 있음을 추론할 수 있으므로, (A)가 정답이다.

어휘 beneficial 유익한, 이익이 되는   extend (기한을) 연장하다   patron 후원자, 고객   raise (돈을) 모으다, 모금하다

196-200 양식 + 이메일 + 웹페이지

타하라 에어
지연 수하물 양식

타하라 에어 고객님께,

고객님의 수하물 도착이 지연되어 죄송하게 생각합니다. 고객님의 수하물을 추적하여 더 빨리 돌려 드릴 수 있도록 다음 세부 사항을 작성해 주십시오. ¹⁹⁶**수하물을 찾는 즉시 타하라 에어 직원이 고객님께 전화를 드릴 것입니다.** 고객님의 수하물이 사흘 넘게 발견되지 않는 경우, www.tahara-air.com/baggage를 방문해 추가 안내 사항을 확인해 주시기 바랍니다.

날짜: 10월 12일
이름: 마르제나 마제프스카
현지 주소: 호텔 단테, 루아 자우, 1300 리스본, 포르투갈
전화 번호: +44 1632812110
항공편명: J77FG2

지연 수하물 정보

	수량	기재 사항
☑ 여행용 가방	1	바퀴가 달린 소형 검은색 여행용 가방; 이름표에 '마르제나 마제프스카'라고 적혀 있음
☐ 배낭		

☐ 지갑		
¹⁹⁷☑ 상자	1	작은 판지 상자, '마르제나 마제프스카, 살토니 푸즈'라고 적혀 있음
☐ 기타		

어휘 luggage 수하물, 짐   track down ~을 추적하다[찾아 내다]   representative 직원   locate (위치를) 알아내다, 찾아내다   missing 잃어버린, 분실된   instruction 지시 사항, (사용) 설명서

발신: hgilbert@saltonifoods.co.uk
수신: mmajewska@saltonifoods.co.uk
제목: 회신: 소스 샘플
날짜: 10월 12일, 오후 2시 3분

마르제나에게,

당신의 수하물에 대한 소식을 듣게 되어 유감이에요. ¹⁹⁷**적어도 항공사에서 여행 가방이 어디에 있는지 찾긴 했네요.**

¹⁹⁷**언제 나머지 수하물이 발견되어 돌려받을 수 있을지 알 수 없으니, ¹⁹⁹익일 배송으로 샘플을 더 보내 드렸어요. ¹⁹⁸그러니 내일 있을 고객과의 회의에 빈손으로 가지 않아도 될 거예요.** 각각의 맛이 다섯 통씩 있고, 라벨이 붙어 있는 소스 두 병도 있습니다. BDW 택배사를 이용해 당신이 머물고 있는 호텔로 보냈어요. ²⁰⁰**소포는 오전 8시 30분까지 배송될 것이니 ¹⁹⁹11시 회의에서 발표할 때 소스 샘플과 포장을 보여 줄 수 있을 거예요.**

그럼 이만,

해리 길버트

어휘 determine 판단하다, 결정하다   overnight shipping 익일 배송   empty-handed 빈손인   packaging 포장

---

https://www.bdwshipping.co.uk/overnight

BDW SHIPPING
빠르고 믿을 수 있는 배송 회사

익일 배송품 제출
배송 정보:
발송지: 살토니 푸즈, 27 애스턴 스트리트, 옥스퍼드 OX1 1HD, UK
배송지: 호텔 단테, 루아 자우, 1300 리스본, 포르투갈
중량: 0.75kg
☐ 봉투   ☑ 상자   ☐ 고객 맞춤 포장

익일 배송 선택 사항:
²⁰⁰**BDW 익일 오전 8시 30분까지 배송   지금 배송하기 52파운드 이른 오전**

BDW 오전   익일 오전 11시까지 배송   지금 배송하기 45파운드
BDW 오후   익일 오후 2시까지 배송   지금 배송하기 39파운드
BDW 저녁   익일 저녁 8시까지 배송   지금 배송하기 31파운드

어휘 reliable 믿을 만한, 신뢰할 만한   corporation 기업, 회사

196 사실 관계 확인

번역 타하라 에어에 대해 명시된 것은?

(A) 고객은 모든 수하물에 이름표를 붙여야 한다.
(B) 사흘 안에 분실된 수하물을 돌려받을 수 있도록 보장한다.
(C) 수하물을 찾으면 마제프스카 씨에게 통지해 줄 것이다.
(D) 분실 수하물에 대해 마제프스카 씨에게 변제할 것이다.

해설 양식 첫 단락에서 수하물을 찾는 즉시 타하라 에어 직원이 마제프스카 씨에게 전화로 연락할 것(A Tahara Air representative will contact you ~ as soon as your luggage is located)이라고 했으므로, (C)가 정답이다.

어휘 notify 통지하다, 알리다   reimburse 환불하다, 변제하다

> ▸▸ Paraphrasing   지문의 contact you by phone
> → 정답의 notify Ms. Majewska
> 지문의 as soon as your luggage is located
> → 정답의 when her luggage is found

197 연계

번역 마제프스카 씨는 샘플을 어디에 포장했을 것 같은가?

(A) 상자
(B) 지갑
(C) 여행 가방
(D) 배낭

해설 양식을 보면 마제프스카 씨가 '마르제나 마제프스카, 살토니 푸즈'라고 적혀 있는 작은 판지 상자(small cardboard box with "Marzena Majewska, Saltoni Foods" written on it)를 잃어 버렸다고 표기했는데, 이메일을 보면 그녀가 여행 가방은 찾았으나(the airline has located your suitcase) 나머지 수하물, 즉 상자를 언제 돌려받을 수 있을지 알 수 없어(Since it's impossible ~ the rest of your luggage ~ returned) 길버트 씨가 샘플을 더 보내 주었음을 알 수 있다. 따라서 마제프스카 씨가 샘플을 상자에 넣었다고 추론할 수 있으므로, (A)가 정답이다.

198 추론 / 암시

번역 길버트 씨에 대해 암시된 것은?

(A) 포르투갈에서 고객을 만날 것이다.
(B) 종종 살토니 푸즈를 위해 출장을 간다.
(C) 타하라 에어 고객 서비스 직원이다.
(D) 고객들이 몇몇 제품을 검토하기를 원한다.

해설 길버트 씨가 보낸 이메일의 후반부를 보면, 마제프스카 씨가 고객과의 회의에 빈손으로 가지 않도록(you will not have to go empty-handed to tomorrow's meeting with the clients) 익일 배송으로 샘플을 더 보냈고, 오전 8시 30분까지 배송될 것이니 11시 회의에서 발표할 때 소스 샘플과 포장을 고객들에게 보여 줄 수 있을 것(you are sure to have the sauce samples and packaging to show ~ at 11)이라고 했으므로, (D)가 정답이다.

199 세부 사항

번역 이메일에 따르면 마제프스카 씨는 내일 오전 11시에 무엇을 할 것인가?

(A) 배송품 수령
(B) 프레젠테이션 하기
(C) 호텔 퇴실
(D) 자신의 왕복 항공편 확인

해설 길버트 씨가 보낸 이메일의 후반부를 보면, 내일 있을 11시 회의에서 발표할 때 소스 샘플과 포장을 고객들에게 보여 줄 수 있을 것(you are sure to have the sauce samples and packaging to show ~ at 11)이라고 했다. 따라서 마제프스카 씨가 내일 오전 11시에 프레젠테이션할 예정이라는 것을 알 수 있으므로, (B)가 정답이다.

> ▸▸ Paraphrasing   지문의 speak at the meeting
> → 정답의 Make a presentation

200 연계

번역 길버트 씨는 배송비로 얼마를 지불했는가?

(A) 31파운드
(B) 39파운드
(C) 45파운드
(D) 52파운드

해설 이메일 두 번째 단락의 후반부에서 길버트 씨가 보낸 소포가 오전 8시 30분까지 배송될 것(The package will be delivered by 8:30 a.m.)이라고 했다. 배송비는 웹페이지에서 확인할 수 있는데, 익일 오전 8시 30분까지 도착하는 BDW 이른 아침 배송 요금(BDW Early Morning)은 52파운드라고 나와 있으므로, (D)가 정답이다.

기출 TEST 6

101 (B)	102 (A)	103 (A)	104 (D)	105 (C)
106 (C)	107 (A)	108 (B)	109 (A)	110 (B)
111 (C)	112 (C)	113 (A)	114 (C)	115 (C)
116 (B)	117 (D)	118 (D)	119 (D)	120 (C)
121 (D)	122 (C)	123 (D)	124 (A)	125 (A)
126 (A)	127 (B)	128 (D)	129 (B)	130 (D)
131 (B)	132 (C)	133 (D)	134 (A)	135 (B)
136 (C)	137 (D)	138 (B)	139 (C)	140 (B)
141 (D)	142 (A)	143 (A)	144 (D)	145 (D)
146 (B)	147 (D)	148 (C)	149 (C)	150 (C)
151 (C)	152 (D)	153 (A)	154 (C)	155 (C)
156 (A)	157 (B)	158 (A)	159 (B)	160 (B)
161 (C)	162 (D)	163 (B)	164 (A)	165 (C)
166 (C)	167 (D)	168 (B)	169 (A)	170 (A)
171 (D)	172 (B)	173 (A)	174 (B)	175 (A)
176 (A)	177 (B)	178 (A)	179 (D)	180 (C)
181 (B)	182 (A)	183 (D)	184 (D)	185 (A)
186 (B)	187 (C)	188 (A)	189 (A)	190 (D)
191 (B)	192 (D)	193 (B)	194 (A)	195 (C)
196 (D)	197 (D)	198 (C)	199 (B)	200 (D)

PART 5

101 명사 자리 _ 동사의 목적어

해설 빈칸은 동사 has의 목적어 역할을 하는 명사 자리로, 전치사구 with 26 different food suppliers의 수식을 받고 있다. 문맥상 '26곳의 다양한 식품 납품 업체들과 계약을 맺고 있다'라는 내용이 되어야 자연스러우며, 납품 업체가 여러 곳이므로 계약(contract)도 여러 개가 되어야 한다. 따라서 복수형인 (B) contracts가 정답이 된다. 참고로, 빈칸 앞에 한정사(관사, 소유격 등)가 없으므로 단수 가산명사인 (C) contractor와 (D) contract는 빈칸에 들어갈 수 없다.

번역 제스퍼 어소시에이츠는 현재 26곳의 다양한 식품 납품 업체들과 계약을 맺고 있다.

어휘 currently 현재   contract 계약; 계약하다, 수축하다 contractor 계약자, 계약업체   supplier 공급자, 공급 업체

102 부사구 어휘

해설 빈칸 뒤 25 minutes prior to boarding their flight와 가장 잘 어울리는 부사구를 선택해야 한다. 문맥상 '비행기에 탑승하기 최소 25분 전에'라는 내용이 되어야 자연스러우므로, '적어도, 최소'라는 의미의 (A) at least가 정답이다.

번역 승객들은 비행기에 탑승하기 최소 25분 전에 탑승구에 도착해야 한다.

어휘 passenger 승객   prior to ~ 전에

103 인칭대명사의 격 _ 목적격

해설 빈칸은 「help + 목적어 + 목적격 보어」 구조의 목적어 자리로, 보기에서 목적어 역할을 할 수 있는 (A) you, (C) yours, (D) yourself 중 하나를 선택해야 한다. 보어가 묘사하는 행위(identify issues, predict trends, and improve business)에 있어서 델트란 분석 소프트웨어의 도움을 받을 수 있는 대상이 빈칸에 들어가야 하므로, 청자(혹은 일반 사람들)를 가리키는 (A) you가 정답이 된다.

번역 델트란 분석 소프트웨어는 귀하가 문제를 식별하고 추세를 예측하며 사업 실적을 개선하는 데 도움을 줄 수 있습니다.

어휘 analytics 분석(론)   identify 식별하다, 확인하다   predict 예측하다

104 동사 어휘

해설 빈칸 뒤 to부정사구 to purchase three new servers next year를 목적어로 취하며 문맥상 잘 어울리는 동사를 선택하는 문제이다. '내년에 서버 3대를 구입할 계획이다'라는 내용이 되어야 자연스러우므로, '계획하다'라는 의미의 (D) plans가 정답이다. 참고로, (A) announces와 (C) predicts는 to부정사구를 목적어로 취하지 않으며, (B) thinks는 to부정사와 쓰일 경우 '(기억을 살려) ~할 생각을 하다'라는 의미가 된다.

번역 기술부는 내년에 서버 3대를 구입할 계획이다.

어휘 purchase 구입하다

105 형용사 어휘

해설 빈칸 뒤 명사구 new efficiency expert를 수식하는 형용사를 고르는 문제로, 보기 중에서 '전문가'와 어울리는 단어를 선택해야 한다. 따라서 '뛰어난, 특출한'이라는 의미의 (C) exceptional이 정답이 된다. 참고로, 형용사는 여러 개가 나란히 올 수 있으며 사람에 대한 평가를 나타내는 형용사(뛰어난)가 단순 묘사를 하는 형용사(새로운)보다 앞에 위치한다.

번역 젠슨 모터스는 지난달에 뛰어난 경영 능률 전문가를 새로 고용했다.

어휘 efficiency 능률   expert 전문가   approximate 근사치인, 비슷한   angular 앙상한, 모난   eventual 궁극적인

106 명사 자리 _ 어휘

해설 빈칸에는 뒤에 오는 responsibilities를 수식하는 형용사나 responsibilities와 복합명사를 이루는 명사가 들어갈 수 있다. '원컬 씨의 ------ 책무에는 회계 감사(auditing)와 재무 검토(financial review)가 포함된다'라는 내용의 문장이므로, 빈칸에는 '회계'를 의미하는 명사가 들어가야 자연스럽다. 따라서 (C) accounting이 정답이다. 명사인 (A) accounts는 '계정, 계좌', 과거분사인 (B) accounted는 '간주되는', 형용사인 (D) accountable은 '책임이 있는'이라는 뜻으로 문맥상 빈칸에 부적절하다. 참고로, accounting은 종종 다른 명사와 함께 복합명사를 이룬다.

번역 원컬 씨의 회계 책무에는 대형 기업 고객에 대한 감사와 재무 검토가 포함됩니다.

어휘 responsibility 책임, 책무   auditing 감사

107 전치사 자리

해설 빈칸 앞에 완전한 절이 왔고 뒤에 명사구(a luncheon)가 있으므로, 빈칸에는 명사를 목적어로 취하는 전치사가 들어가야 한다. 따라서 '~에서'라는 의미의 전치사인 (A) at이 정답이다. 문장에 이미 동사(greeted)가 있기 때문에 (B) had는 빈칸에 들어갈 수 없고, (C) such는 한정사/대명사, (D) where는 접속사로 완전한 절과 명사를 이어주지 못하므로 정답이 될 수 없다.

번역 총리는 오늘 런던에서 열린 오찬에서 외국 외교관들을 맞았다.

어휘 prime minister 총리 diplomat 외교관

108 to부정사 _ 부사적 용법

해설 빈칸은 뒤에 오는 명사구 employee productivity를 목적어로 취하면서, 앞에 있는 동사구(offers incentives)를 수식하는 부사와 같은 역할을 한다. 따라서 '촉진하기 위해'라는 목적을 나타내어 동사구를 꾸며주는 to부정사 (B) to stimulate가 정답이다. 문장에 이미 동사(offers)가 있기 때문에 (A) stimulate, (C) will stimulate, (D) are stimulating은 빈칸에 들어갈 수 없다.

번역 오프토사의 경영진은 직원 생산성을 촉진하기 위해 인센티브를 제공한다.

어휘 stimulate 촉진하다, 자극하다 employee 직원 productivity 생산성

109 명사 어휘

해설 customer와 복합명사를 이루어 in response to의 목적어 역할을 하는 명사를 선택하는 문제이다. 문맥상 '고객의 요구에 부응하여'라는 내용이 되어야 자연스러우므로, '요구'라는 의미의 (A) demand가 정답이 된다.

번역 고객의 요구에 부응하여, 로페즈 내츄럴스는 유기농 비누 제품군을 발매할 예정이다.

어휘 in response to ~에 부응하여, ~에 대한 반응으로 release 발매하다, 발표하다 permit 허가(증) account 계좌, 계정

110 동사 어휘

해설 빈칸은 be동사(are)와 함께 수동태 동사를 이루는 과거분사 자리로, 부사 thoroughly와 to부정사구 to ensure they have no defects의 수식을 받고 있다. 문맥상 '결함이 없는지 확인하기 위해 철저히 점검을 받는다'라는 내용이 되어야 자연스러우므로, '점검받는'이라는 의미의 (B) inspected가 정답이 된다.

번역 컴퓨터는 공장에서 나가기 전에 결함이 없는지 확인하기 위해 철저히 점검을 받습니다.

어휘 thoroughly 철저하게 defect 결함 attach 첨부하다

111 동사 어휘

해설 빈칸은 전치사구 to business news and economic analysis와 결합하여 명사구 a new show를 수식하는 과거분사 자리이다. 문맥상 '비즈니스 뉴스와 경제 분석에 전념하는 새로운 프로그램'이라는 내용이 되어야 자연스러우므로, '전념하는, 헌신하는'이라는 의미의 (C) dedicated가 정답이 된다. 참고로, (A) allowed와 (B) prepared는 전치사 to와 함께 쓰이지 않는다.

번역 WRUZ 라디오는 비즈니스 뉴스와 경제 분석에 전념하는 새로운 프로그램을 방송할 예정이다.

어휘 analysis 분석

112 부사 자리 _ 동사 수식

해설 빈칸 앞 동사 met을 수식하는 부사 자리이므로, '자주'라는 의미의 부사 (C) frequently가 정답이다. (A) frequent는 형용사/동사, (B) frequenting은 동명사/현재분사, (D) frequented는 동사/과거분사로, 모두 품사상 빈칸에 적합하지 않다.

번역 오카다 씨는 철거 프로젝트를 논의하기 위해 건물 관리인과 자주 만났다.

어휘 demolition 철거, 해체 frequent 빈번한; 자주 다니다

113 동사 어휘

해설 목적어인 명사구 the job offer 및 빈칸을 수식하는 부사 politely와 가장 잘 어울리는 동사를 선택해야 한다. 문맥상 '일자리 제안을 정중히 거절했다'라는 내용이 되어야 자연스러우므로, '거절하다'라는 의미의 (A) declined가 정답이 된다.

번역 몬트리 씨는 바랜카 운송 회사의 일자리 제안을 정중히 거절했다.

어휘 politely 정중히 decrease 감소하다 prevent 막다 convert 전환하다

114 동사 어형 _ 조동사 뒤

해설 빈칸 앞에 조동사 must가 있으므로, 빈칸에는 동사원형이 들어가야 한다. 주어인 Written permission이 '얻다'를 뜻하는 동사 obtain의 대상이 되므로, 동사원형으로 시작하는 수동태 (C) be obtained가 정답이 된다.

번역 타보르사의 로고를 사용하기 전에 서면 허가를 얻어야 합니다.

어휘 permission 허가 obtain 얻다, 획득하다

115 부사절 접속사

해설 빈칸은 완전한 절(it is relatively small)을 이끄는 접속사 자리이며, 빈칸을 포함한 절이 뒤에 나오는 주절을 수식하고 있다. 따라서 '비록 ~일지라도'라는 의미로 부사절을 이끄는 접속사 (C) Although가 정답이 된다. (A) Reasoning의 경우, '판단하다, 추론하다'라는 의미의 동사 reason이 분사로 쓰여 that이 생략되었다고 가정하더라도 문맥상 어색하므로 정답이 될 수 없고, (B) Essentially는 부사, (D) Throughout은 전치사로 품사상 빈칸에 적합하지 않다.

번역 비교적 작지만, 진더 아파트의 피트니스 센터는 주민들에게 매우 인기가 높다.

어휘 relatively 비교적 reasoning 추리, 추론 essentially 근본적으로 throughout 내내, 도처에

116 부사 어휘

해설 빈칸 앞 동사 can be shared를 수식하는 부사를 선택하는 문제이다. 부사절의 주어 they가 주절의 주어인 All communications를 가리키므로, 통신이 공유되는 방식을 적절히 묘사하는 부사가 빈칸에 들어가야 자연스럽다. 따라서 '외부에, 외부적으로'라는 의미의 (B) externally가 정답이 된다.

번역 모든 통신은 홍보 책임자의 승인을 받아야 외부에 공유할 수 있습니다.

어휘 approve 승인하다   public relations 홍보   certainly 명백히
deeply 깊이, 매우   utterly 완전히, 전적으로

117 형용사 자리 _ 명사 수식

해설 빈칸은 industries를 수식해주는 표현인 「a ------- array of」에서 명사 array를 수식하는 형용사 자리이다. 따라서 '광범위한, 폭 넓은'이라는 의미의 형용사인 (D) wide가 정답이 된다. a wide array[range, variety] of는 자주 쓰이는 표현이니 암기하는 것이 좋다. (A) widely는 부사, (B) widen은 동사, (C) width는 명사로, 모두 품사상 빈칸에 적합하지 않다.

번역 다양한 산업에 정밀 용접 서비스를 제공해 온 미스톤 메탈웍스는 최근 퀘벡에서 서비스를 제공한 지 한 세기가 된 것을 축하했다.

어휘 precision 정밀, 정확   welding 용접   a wide array of 다양한, 다수의   recently 최근   widely 널리, 매우   widen 넓히다, 넓어지다   width 폭, 너비

118 명사 어휘

해설 「consider+목적어+목적격 보어」의 구조로, 빈칸에는 목적어인 명사 punctuality와 동격 관계를 이루는 명사가 들어가야 한다. 시간 엄수(punctuality)는 비서들이 가져야 할(for all his assistants to have) '특성'이라고 할 수 있으므로, (D) trait가 정답이 된다.

번역 김 씨는 시간 엄수가 그의 모든 비서들이 가져야 할 매우 중요한 특성이라고 생각한다.

어휘 punctuality 시간 엄수   crucial 매우 중요한   device 기기

119 동사 어휘

해설 빈칸 앞 has와 현재완료 동사를 이루는 과거분사 자리로, 목적어인 the importance of attracting new customers와 가장 잘 어울리는 동사를 선택해야 한다. 문맥상 '신규 고객 유치의 중요성을 강조했다'라는 내용이 되어야 자연스러우므로, '강조하다, 역설하다'라는 의미의 (D) emphasized가 정답이 된다.

번역 재무 담당 최고책임자는 다음 분기에 신규 고객을 유치하는 것이 중요하다고 강조했다.

어휘 quarter 분기   apply 적용하다   demand 요구하다
administer 관리하다

120 부사 자리 _ 동사 수식

해설 빈칸은 be동사(are)와 현재분사(ordering) 사이에서 동사를 수식하는 부사 자리이므로, '점점 더'라는 의미의 부사인 (C) increasingly

가 정답이다. (A) increasing은 동명사/현재분사, (B) increase는 명사/동사, (D) increased는 동사/과거분사로, 모두 품사상 빈칸에 적합하지 않다.

번역 슈어드 가구는 점점 더 많은 고객들이 온라인으로 가구를 주문하고 있기 때문에 일부 전시장을 폐쇄하고 있다.

121 전치사 자리

해설 빈칸 뒤 명사 construction을 목적어로 취하는 전치사 자리이므로, '~ 때문에'라는 의미의 전치사인 (D) Due to가 정답이 된다. (A) Now that, (B) While, (C) Even if는 모두 부사절 접속사로, 뒤에 주어와 동사를 갖춘 완전한 절이 나와야 한다.

번역 구도심 청사에서 진행 중인 공사로 인해 관광단은 현장에 들어갈 수 없을 것입니다.

어휘 construction 공사, 건설   in progress 진행중인

122 명사 어휘

해설 빈칸은 전치사 of의 목적어 역할을 하는 명사 자리로, 빈칸을 포함한 전치사구가 동사 will present의 목적어인 the results를 수식하고 있다. 따라서 results와 가장 잘 어울리는 명사를 선택해야 한다. 보기 중 결과가 나올 수 있는 행위를 나타내는 명사는 '조사'이므로, (C) investigation이 정답이 된다.

번역 몇몇 시추 기술 전문가들이 6월 23일에 조사 결과를 발표할 것이다.

어휘 expert 전문가   comprehension 이해   resolution 결정, 해결
specification 세목, 내역

123 형용사 어휘

해설 빈칸 뒤 명사 display를 적절히 수식하는 형용사를 선택하는 문제이다. to부정사구 to promote the newest book이 '최신 저서를 홍보하기 위해'라는 전시의 목적을 나타내므로, 빈칸에는 이를 달성하기 위한 전시 방식이나 규모를 설명하는 형용사가 들어가야 자연스럽다. 따라서 '거대한, 대량의'라는 뜻의 (D) massive가 정답이 된다.

번역 그 매장은 베스트셀러 추리 작가의 최신 저서를 홍보하기 위해 이를 대량으로 진열했다.

어휘 author 작가   default 내정 값의; 불이행; 이행하지 않다
grateful 감사하는   talented 재능이 있는

124 관계대명사 _ 주격

해설 빈칸은 주어가 없는 불완전한 절(attended yesterday's workshop)을 이끄는 접속사 자리이며, 빈칸부터 workshop까지가 people을 수식해 주고 있다. 따라서 빈칸에는 동사 attended의 주어 역할을 하며 두 절을 이어주는 접속사가 들어가야 하므로, 주격 관계대명사인 (A) who가 정답이 된다. (B) those는 대명사/한정사, (D) some은 대명사/한정사로 접속사 역할을 할 수 없고, 소유격 관계대명사인 (C) whose 뒤에는 명사가 와야 하므로 모두 빈칸에 들어갈 수 없다.

번역 어제 워크숍에 참석한 사람들 대다수가 이미 피드백을 제출했다.

어휘 attend 참석하다   submit 제출하다   feedback 피드백, 의견

TEST 6

125 부사 어휘

해설 빈칸에는 형용사 large를 뒤에서 수식할 수 있는 부사가 들어가야 한다. 따라서 '~할 만큼 (충분히)'이라는 의미의 부사인 (A) enough가 정답이다. (B) fully, (C) nearly, (D) well은 형용사를 뒤에서 수식할 수 없다.

번역 맛있고 건강에도 좋은 알프레디즈 비스트로의 토마토 샐러드는 주요리로 내놓아도 될 만큼 양이 많다.

어휘 tasty 맛있는 fully 완전히, 충분히 nearly 거의 well 잘, 아주

126 명사 자리 _ 수 일치

해설 빈칸은 동사 has garnered의 목적어 역할을 하는 명사 자리이다. 앞에 불가산명사를 수식하는 much가 있으므로, (A) interest가 정답이 된다. (C) interested는 동사/과거분사, (D) interesting은 형용사로, 품사상 빈칸에 적합하지 않다.

번역 자유 건축 엑스포에서 클라신 그룹의 부스는 많은 관심을 끌었다.

어휘 garner 모으다, 얻다 interest 관심, 흥미 interests 관심사

127 부사절 접속사 _ 어휘

해설 빈칸은 완전한 절을 이끄는 접속사 자리이다. 빈칸 이하의 절이 앞에 있는 완전한 절을 수식하고 있으므로, 빈칸에는 부사절 접속사가 들어가야 한다. 문맥상 '노트북 컴퓨터를 구입할 때마다 프린터 값을 25퍼센트 절약하라'라는 내용이 되어야 자연스러우므로, '~할 때마다, ~할 때는 언제나'를 의미하는 (B) whenever가 정답이 된다.

번역 디에고 전자에서 노트북 컴퓨터를 구입할 때마다 모든 프린터에 대해 25퍼센트를 절약하세요.

어휘 electronics 전자 기기 whereas 반면에 such as ~와 같은 seeing that ~인 것으로 보아

128 형용사 자리 _ 어휘

해설 빈칸은 명사구 five-step plan을 수식하는 형용사 자리이므로, 형용사 역할을 할 수 있는 현재분사 (A) managing과 형용사 (D) manageable 중 하나를 선택해야 한다. 문맥상 '실행 가능한 5단계 계획'이라는 내용이 되어야 자연스러우므로, '감당할 수 있는, 다루기 쉬운'이라는 의미의 (D) manageable이 정답이 된다. (A) managing은 '경영하는, 경영을 잘하는'이라는 의미로 주로 사람을 수식하며, (B) manageably는 부사, (C) manages는 동사이므로 모두 빈칸에 적합하지 않다.

번역 최근 채택된 정책은 실행 가능한 5단계 계획에 따라 회사의 부채를 구조조정한다.

어휘 adopt 채택하다 policy 정책 restructure 구조조정하다 debt 부채

129 부사절 접속사 _ 어휘

해설 빈칸은 완전한 절을 이끄는 접속사 자리이며, 빈칸을 포함한 절이 앞에 있는 완전한 절을 수식하고 있다. 따라서 빈칸에는 부사

절 접속사가 들어가야 한다. 문맥을 살펴보면 생산량이 증가한 것(production has increased)이 추가 채용을 해야 하는(needs to hire additional staff) 이유가 되므로, '~ 때문에'라는 의미의 부사절 접속사인 (B) since가 정답이 된다. (A) even though는 의미상 어색하고, (C) because of는 전치사, (D) therefore는 부사로 완전한 절을 이끌 수 없으므로 정답이 될 수 없다.

번역 생산량이 50퍼센트 증가했기 때문에 품질 보증부는 직원을 추가로 채용해야 한다.

어휘 assurance 보증, 보장 increase 증가하다

130 동사 어형 _ 조동사 뒤

해설 빈칸 앞에 조동사 cannot이 있으므로, 빈칸에는 동사원형이 들어가야 한다. 주어인 Your order가 '처리하다'를 뜻하는 동사 process의 대상이 되므로, 수동태 동사원형인 (B) be processed가 정답이 된다.

번역 저희가 대금을 완납받을 때까지는 귀하의 주문을 처리할 수 없습니다.

어휘 process 처리하다 receive 받다 full payment 완납, 전액 지급

PART 6

131-134 웹페이지

업체 이전은 언뜻 보면 [131]**복잡해** 보일 수도 있지만, 메스터 무버즈는 이 과정을 최대한 단순화하기 위해 귀사와 함께하겠습니다. 귀사가 사무실, 공장, 혹은 실험실을 도시 내에서 이동하는지 아니면 전국 단위로 이동하는지의 여부에 상관없이 저희는 귀사의 이전을 효율적으로 [132]**처리할 수 있는** 인력, 기술 그리고 자원을 보유하고 있습니다.

저희는 작고 파손되기 쉬운 물건들을 포장할 때 특별히 주의를 기울입니다. [133]**아울러**, 고객들에게 특별한 꼬리표를 제공함으로써 책상, 서류 보관함, 의자 같은 대형 물품들도 이사 준비가 되도록 만전을 기합니다. [134]저희 '이전 안내문'에 그것들을 올바르게 부착하는 방법이 설명되어 있습니다.

어휘 relocation 이전 complicate 복잡한, 어려운; 복잡하게 만들다 laboratory 실험실, 연구실 efficiency 효율, 능률 delicate 깨지기 쉬운, 섬세한

131 형용사 자리 _ 주격 보어

해설 빈칸은 주어 Commercial relocation을 보충 설명하는 주격 보어 자리이므로, 보기 중 명사인 (A) complication과 형용사인 (B) complicated가 들어갈 수 있다. 문맥상 '업체 이전이 복잡해 보인다'라는 내용이 되어야 자연스러우므로, 형용사 (B) complicated가 정답이 된다. (A) complication은 불가산명사로 쓰일 경우 '복잡(화)'라는 의미로, 주어와 동격 관계를 이루지 않으므로 빈칸에 들어갈 수 없다.

어휘 complication 복잡(화), 문제

132 to부정사 _ 형용사적 용법

해설 빈칸 앞에 주어(we), 동사(have), 목적어(the people, technology, and resources)를 갖춘 완전한 절이 왔고, to와 명사구 your move 사이에 빈칸이 있다. 문맥상 to 이하가 have의 목적어를 수식해주어 '이전을 효율적으로 처리할 수 있는 인력, 기술, 그리고 자원'이라는 내용이 되어야 자연스러우므로, 빈칸에는 to부정사를 완성하는 동사원형이 들어가야 한다. 따라서 (C) handle이 정답이다.

133 접속부사

해설 빈칸 앞 문장에서 작고 파손되기 쉬운 물건을 포장할 때 특별히 주의를 기울인다(We take special care when packing small and delicate objects)고 했고, 뒤 문장에서 대형 물품들도 이사 준비가 되도록 만전을 기한다(we make sure that large items are also ready for the move)고 했으므로, 빈칸에는 크고 작은 물품을 동시에 다룰 수 있음을 강조하는 접속부사가 들어가야 한다. 따라서 '동시에, 아울러'라는 의미의 (D) At the same time이 정답이 된다. (A) Rather는 '오히려', (B) In brief는 '간단히 말해서', (C) In other words는 '다시 말해서'라는 의미로 모두 문맥상 빈칸에 적절하지 않다.

134 문맥에 맞는 문장 고르기

번역 (A) 저희 이전 안내문에 그것들을 올바르게 부착하는 방법이 설명되어 있습니다.
(B) 귀하의 고용주가 언제 이사할지 귀하에게 말해 줄 것입니다.
(C) 저희는 빨리 움직이기 위해 이면도로로 이동합니다.
(D) 저희는 이삿짐 트럭 12대를 보유하고 있습니다.

해설 빈칸 앞 문장에서 특별한 꼬리표를 제공함으로써(by providing you with special tags) 대형 물품들도 이사 준비가 되도록 만전을 기한다고 했으므로, 빈칸에도 이와 관련된 내용이 들어가야 자연스럽다. 따라서 (A)가 정답이다. 여기서 them은 special tags를 가리킨다.

어휘 properly 제대로, 적절하게 affix 붙이다 back road 이면도로, 뒷길

135-138 설명서

> **구매 주문 지침**
>
> 메이플셰이즈 의료 센터는 회사 관련 업무에 필요한 상품 및 서비스를 구매할 수 있도록 특정 직원에게 권한을 부여합니다. ¹³⁵**특정 품목 또는 서비스**를 구매하려면 온라인 신청 양식을 작성하십시오. 양식을 사용하여 필요한 품목에 대한 설명을 ¹³⁶**제공하십시오.** 또한 해당 구매가 필요한 이유를 간략하게 설명해 주십시오. ¹³⁷**제시한 이유**가 차후 결정에 영향을 미칠 수 있다는 점을 유의하십시오. 고장 난 기기를 교체하는 요청이라면, 신청서를 제출하기 전에 그 문제에 대해 관리 부서 책임자인 로웬 씨에게 먼저 알리십시오. ¹³⁸그러한 조치가 타당한지의 여부를 그가 결정할 것입니다. 사무용품 및 장비 구입과 관련하여 궁금한 사항이 있으면 구매 부서에 문의하십시오.

어휘 purchase 구매(품); 구매하다 authorize 권한을 부여하다 specific 특정한 fill out 작성하다 description 설명, 묘사 briefly 간략하게 justification (타당한) 이유 subsequent 차후의, 이어지는 entail 필요로 하다 replace 교체하다 out of order 고장 난 attention 관심, 주의 submit 제출하다 related to ~와 관련된 office supplies 사무용품 equipment 장비

135 형용사 자리 _ 명사 수식

해설 빈칸 뒤 명사구 item or service를 수식하는 형용사 자리이므로, '특정한, 구체적인'이라는 의미의 형용사인 (B) specific이 정답이다. (A) specify는 동사, (C) specifics는 명사, (D) specifically는 부사로, 모두 품사상 빈칸에 적합하지 않다.

어휘 specify 명시하다 specifics 세부 사항 specifically 명확하게

136 동사 어휘

해설 빈칸은 to부정사의 동사원형 자리로, 명사구 a description of the item을 목적어로 취한다. 따라서 description 및 문맥에 어울리는 동사를 선택해야 한다. 앞 문장에서 필요한 상품과 서비스를 구매하려면 온라인 신청 양식을 작성하라(fill out the online request form)고 했으므로, 빈칸이 포함된 문장은 해당 양식을 사용하여 필요한 품목에 대한 설명(description)을 제공하라는 내용이 되어야 자연스럽다. 따라서 (C) provide가 정답이 된다.

137 명사 어휘

해설 앞 문장에서 구매품이 필요한 이유를 간략하게 설명해 달라(briefly explain why the purchase is necessary)고 요청했고, 해당 문장에서 'your -------'이 차후 결정에 영향을 미칠 수 있다고 했다. 따라서 빈칸에는 설명 혹은 해당 구매가 필요한 이유를 가리키는 명사가 들어가야 자연스러우므로, '(타당한) 이유, 명분'을 의미하는 (D) justification이 정답이다.

어휘 retirement 은퇴

138 문맥에 맞는 문장 고르기

번역 (A) 그는 가능한 모든 선택 사항들을 상세히 연구해 왔습니다.
(B) 그러한 조치가 타당한지의 여부를 그가 판단할 것입니다.
(C) 저희 사무실 건물 두 곳에 서비스를 제공하는 6명의 직원이 있습니다.
(D) 그것은 대체로 매달 유지됩니다.

해설 빈칸 앞 문장에서 고장 난 기기를 교체하는 요청이라면(If the request entails replacing a device that is out of order) 신청서를 제출하기 전에 관리 부서 책임자인 로웬 씨에게 해당 문제를 먼저 알리라(bring the matter to the attention of Mr. Rowen ~ before submitting the request)고 했으므로, 빈칸에는 이와 관련된 내용이 들어가야 글의 흐름이 자연스러워진다. 따라서 로웬 씨의 역할에 대해 설명한 (B)가 정답이다.

어휘 determine 판단하다, 결정[결심]하다 warranted 타당한, 인가받은 maintain 유지하다

139-142 회람

어휘 increased 늘어난, 증가한 contact 연락하다 maintenance 정비, 유지 보수 contractor 계약 업체, 계약자 repair 수리 alert 주의를 환기하다, 알리다 operational 작동하는 prolong 길어지다 apologize for ~에 대하여 사과하다 inconvenience 불편 appreciate 감사하다 patience 인내

139 전치사 어휘

해설 기간을 나타내는 명사구 the past week를 목적어로 취하는 전치사를 선택하는 문제이다. 문장에 과거부터 현재까지의 경험에 대해 말할 때 쓰이는 현재완료(have experienced)가 쓰였으므로, 빈칸이 포함된 부분은 '지난 한 주 동안'이라는 내용이 되어야 자연스럽다. 따라서 '~ 동안'이라는 의미의 (C) Over가 정답이 된다.

140 동사 자리 _ 시제

해설 빈칸은 주격 관계대명사 who가 이끄는 절의 동사 자리이며, 여기서 who는 Higwam, our elevator maintenance contractor를 가리킨다. 뒤에 나오는 문장에서 내일부터 이번 주말까지(beginning tomorrow and through the end of the week) 작업하는 히그웜 기술자들과 로비에서 마주칠 수 있다고 했으므로, 히그웜에서 미래에 수리(repairs)를 진행할 예정이라는 것을 알 수 있다. 따라서 (B) will be conducting이 정답이 된다.

141 명사 어휘

해설 앞 문장에서 내일부터 이번 주말까지(beginning tomorrow and through the end of the week) 수리가 진행된다고 했으므로, 대기 시간(prolonged wait times) 문제 역시 며칠간 지속될 것임을 알 수 있다. 따라서 (B) days가 정답이다.

142 문맥에 맞는 문장 고르기

번역 (A) 그 대신, 여러분은 건물 뒤쪽에 있는 서비스 엘리베이터를 이용하실 수 있습니다.
(B) 로비에서 일하는 작업자에게는 무료 다과를 제공할 예정입니다.
(C) 엘리베이터 수리는 비용이 많이 들 수 있으므로 여러분의 협조를 요청합니다.
(D) 지난달에도 B-레벨 엘리베이터의 서비스가 중단되었습니다.

해설 빈칸 앞 문장에서 '대기 시간이 길어질 수 있습니다(there may continue to be prolonged wait times)'라며 문제점을 언급했으므로, 이에 대한 해결책이나 대안과 관련된 내용이 이어지는 것이 문맥상 자연스럽다. 따라서 (A)가 정답이다.

어휘 alternatively 대신에, 양자택일로 rear 뒤쪽 complimentary 무료의 refreshments 다과 suffer (나쁜 일·고난 등을) 겪다 disruption 중단, 분열

143-146 기사

어휘 variety (식물 등의) 품종 pollinate 수분하다 crop 작물 withstand 견디다 temperature 온도 extended 장기간의, 길어진 equator 적도 exclusively 오로지, 배타적으로 spokesman 대변인 income 수입 reinvest 재투자하다 environmentally friendly 환경 친화적인

143 동사 자리 _ 수 일치

해설 빈칸은 주격 관계대명사 that의 동사 자리이다. 따라서 동사인 (A) tolerates와 (C) tolerate 중 하나를 선택해야 하는데, 선행사인 a new variety of organic wheat와 수가 일치해야 하므로 단수동사인 (A) tolerates가 정답이 된다.

어휘 tolerate (힘든 환경 등을) 견디다 tolerable 웬만한, 견딜 만한

144 명사 어휘

해설 문장의 주어인 It은 앞에서 언급한 '신품종 유기농 밀, GR-712(a new variety of organic wheat, GR-712)'를 가리키므로, 밀을 포함하는 상위어가 빈칸에 들어가야 자연스럽다. 따라서 '(농)작물'이라는 의미의 (D) crops가 정답이다.

어휘 fuel 연료 material 천, 직물, 재료 vehicle 차량

145 부사 자리 _ 전치사구 수식

해설 빈칸은 동사(focus) 뒤에서 전치사구 on rice production 을 강조하는 부사 자리이므로, '오직 ~만, 독점적으로'라는 의미의 부사인 (D) exclusively가 정답이 된다. (A) exclude는 동사, (B) exclusion은 명사, (C) exclusive는 형용사로 모두 품사상 빈칸에 적합하지 않다.

어휘 exclude 제외하다 exclusion 제외(되는 것), 차단 exclusive 독점적인, 배타적인

146 문맥에 맞는 문장 고르기

번역 (A) 이 지역은 8월과 9월에 비가 더 많이 온다.
 (B) 넨티크사는 이런 종류의 다양화가 더 큰 수익으로 이어질 것이라고 믿고 있다.
 (C) 새로운 종의 속명은 아직 정해지지 않았다.
 (D) 또한 이 합병은 넨티크사의 생산 과정 효율화에 도움이 될 것이다.

해설 빈칸 뒤 문장에서 '이렇게 추가된 수입은 더 좋은 기계에 재투자될 수 있다(This added income can, in turn, be reinvested in better machinery)'라며 수입 증가에 따른 혜택을 예측했으므로, 빈칸에서 먼저 수익에 관련된 내용을 언급하는 것이 문맥상 자연스럽다. 따라서 (B)가 정답이다.

어휘 rainfall 강우(량) diversification 다양화 profit 수익 merger 합병 streamline 간소화[능률화]하다

PART 7

147-148 문자 메시지

> **제인 에퀴 [오전 10시 41분]**
> 안녕하세요 마테오. 브라이언 재퍼스가 방금 전화해서 내일 가기로 한 유니언 스트리트 721번지 집 보기 계획을 취소했어요.
>
> **마테오 로드리게스 [오전 10시 42분]**
> 유감이네요. ¹⁴⁷그 아파트가 그 사람한테 안성맞춤인데요. 일정 다시 잡으셨나요?
>
> **제인 에퀴 [오전 10시 44분]**
> 네, 목요일이에요. ¹⁴⁷, ¹⁴⁸당신이 김 씨 가족에게 록리지 플레이스에 있는 부동산을 보여 주기 바로 전이에요. ¹⁴⁸두 곳의 위치가 서로 아주 가까워요.
>
> **마테오 로드리게스 [오전 10시 45분]**
> 좋아요. 오늘 김 씨와 시간 확정해 주실래요?
>
> **제인 에퀴 [오전 10시 47분]**
> 그럴게요.
>
> 어휘 walk-through 설명, (부동산) 점검, 확인 property 부동산, 건물 site 위치

147 추론 / 암시

번역 로드리게스 씨는 누구이겠는가?
 (A) 조경 설계사
 (B) 업무 비서
 (C) 인사 담당자
 (D) 부동산 중개업자

해설 로드리게스 씨의 오전 10시 42분 메시지 '그 아파트가 그 사람한테 안성맞춤인데요(That apartment is just right for him)'와 에퀴 씨의 오전 10시 44분 메시지 '당신이 김 씨 가족에게 록리지 플레이스에 있는 부동산을 보여 주기 바로 전이에요(just before you show the Rockledge Place property to the Kim family)'를 통해 로드리게스 씨가 부동산 중개업을 한다고 추론할 수 있다. 따라서 (D)가 정답이다.

어휘 administrative 행정(상)의, 경영(상)의

148 의도 파악

번역 오전 10시 45분에 로드리게스 씨가 "좋아요"라고 쓸 때, 그 의도는 무엇인가?
 (A) 자신의 업무 결과에 들떠 있다.
 (B) 회사의 새로운 위치에 기뻐한다.
 (C) 에퀴 씨의 업무 처리에 만족한다.
 (D) 재퍼스 씨에게 연락하는 데 관심이 있다.

해설 에퀴 씨의 오전 10시 44분 메시지 '김 씨 가족에게 록리지 플레이스에 있는 부동산을 보여 주기 바로 전이에요(just before you show the Rockledge Place property to the Kim family)'와 '두 곳의 위치가 서로 아주 가까워요(The two sites are very close to each other)'에 대해 '좋아요(Great)'라고 응답한 것이므로, 그가 에퀴 씨의 일정 조정에 만족한다는 것을 알 수 있다. 따라서 (C)가 정답이다.

149-150 공지

> **왈라비 데크**
> 퀸즐랜드 및 인근 지역 시공
>
> 새로운 목재 데크를 갖게 되신 것을 축하드립니다! 앞으로 몇 년 동안 목재 테크를 최상의 상태로 유지하려면 다음 도움말을 참고하세요.
>
> ✓ ¹⁵⁰⁽ᴬ⁾매년 자외선 방수제를 칠해 수분과 열기의 영향으로부터 데크를 보호하세요.
>
> ✓ ¹⁴⁹판자 사이 공간에 있는 먼지와 이물질을 제거하세요. 판자 주변 및 사이에 공기가 통해야 습기가 생기는 것을 방지할 수 있습니다.
>
> ✓ ¹⁵⁰⁽ᴮ⁾주기적으로 데크를 청소하세요. 부드러운 털이 달린 솔, 호스, 화학 성분이 없는 세제를 사용하여 마감재가 벗겨지지 않는 선에서 먼지를 닦아내세요.
>
> ✓ 물 얼룩과 곰팡이를 방지하세요. ¹⁵⁰⁽ᴰ⁾데크 표면 바로 위에 화분에 심은 식물이나 다른 무거운 물건을 올려 두지 마세요.

어휘 keep in top shape 최상의 상태로 유지하다 apply 칠하다, 바르다 annually 해마다 shield 보호하다 debris 이물질, 잔해 periodically 주기적으로 bristled 털이 많은 detergent 세제 stain 얼룩 mildew 곰팡이 surface 표면

149 사실 관계 확인

번역 판자에 관해 명시된 것은?

(A) 그늘진 곳에 설치해야 한다.
(B) 방수가 된다.
(C) 판자 사이에 공간이 있다.
(D) 퀸즐랜드에서만 판매된다.

해설 두 번째 도움말 항목에서 판자 사이 공간에 있는 먼지와 이물질을 제거하라(Keep the gaps between boards free of dirt and debris)고 했으므로, 판자 사이에 공간이 있음을 알 수 있다. 따라서 (C)가 정답이다.

▸▸ Paraphrasing 지문의 **the gaps between boards**
→ 정답의 **space between them**

150 사실 관계 확인

번역 데크 유지 관리를 위한 도움말로 언급되지 않은 것은?

(A) 방습 코팅 칠하기
(B) 정기적으로 표면 청소하기
(C) 화학 세제로 얼룩 제거하기
(D) 위에 식물 올려 두지 않기

해설 첫 번째 항목인 '매년 UV 방수제를 칠해 수분과 열기의 영향으로부터 데크를 보호하세요(Apply a coat of UV sealant ~ from the effects of moisture and heat)'에서 (A)를, 세 번째 항목인 '주기적으로 데크를 청소하세요(Wash the deck periodically)'에서 (B)를, 마지막 항목인 '데크 표면 바로 위에 화분에 심은 식물이나 다른 무거운 물건을 올려 두지 마세요(Do not allow potted plants ~ on the surface of the deck)'에서 (D)를 확인할 수 있다. 하지만 화학 세제로 얼룩을 제거하라는 내용은 언급되지 않았고, 화학 성분이 없는 세제(chemical-free detergent)를 사용하라고 했으므로, (C)가 정답이다.

어휘 resistant ~에 잘 견디는, ~를 방지하는

▸▸ Paraphrasing 지문의 **to shield the deck from the effects of moisture and heat**
→ 보기 (A)의 **weather-resistant**
지문의 **Wash the deck periodically**
→ 보기 (B)의 **Cleaning the surface regularly**
지문의 **Do not allow potted plants ~ to rest directly on the surface**
→ 보기 (D)의 **Keeping plants off the surface**

151-152 기사

햅켈 인더스트리즈, E&T 재활용 센터와 협업

6월 19일—컴퓨터 기술 회사인 햅켈 인더스트리즈는 E&T 재활용 센

터와 협업을 시작한다고 발표했다. 이 제휴를 통해 소비자들은 개인 비용을 들이지 않고 컴퓨터 장비를 수거 센터로 가져가기만 하면 재활용 책임을 이행할 수 있게 되었다.

"중고 컴퓨터가 폐기물을 급속히 증가하게 만드는 원인입니다." CEO 인디라 카푸르 씨가 말했다. "151컴퓨터 제품의 주요 생산업체로서 재활용할 수 있는 것을 재사용하고 중금속이 매립지에 들어가지 않도록 하는 것이 우리의 의무라고 생각합니다. 이것이 바로 우리가 이 계획을 추진하려고 노력한 이유입니다."

햅켈 인더스트리즈는 처음에 시험 삼아 두 곳의 E&T 수거지를 후원했고, 이 계획이 성공하면 연말까지 수거지 10곳을 더 추가하는 것을 목표로 하고 있다. 152이 계획에 대한 자세한 내용과 현재 수거지 및 제안된 수거지의 지도를 보려면 ETrecyclingcenter.com을 방문하면 된다.

어휘 recycling 재활용 responsibly 책임 있게 obligation 의무 landfill 매립지 prompt (결정을 내리도록) 유도하다 initiative 계획 proposed 제안된

151 세부 사항

번역 카푸르 씨에 따르면 그녀의 회사가 재활용 회사와 제휴한 이유는?

(A) 더 적당한 가격의 컴퓨터 제품을 생산하려고
(B) 정부의 환경 정책을 준수하려고
(C) 업계 선도자로서 책임을 다하려고
(D) 재정적으로 수익이 나는 기회를 추구하려고

해설 두 번째 단락에 나온 카푸르 씨의 인터뷰 내용을 보면, 컴퓨터 제품의 주요 생산자로서(As a major producer of computer products) 재활용할 수 있는 것을 재사용하고 중금속이 매립지에 들어가지 않도록 하는 것이 자신들의 의무라고 생각한다(we believe it is our obligation ~ the landfills)고 했다. 따라서 (C)가 정답이다.

어휘 affordable (가격이) 적당한 environmental 환경의 policy 정책, 규정 pursue 추구하다 rewarding 수익이 많이 나는, 보람있는 financial 재정의, 금융의

▸▸ Paraphrasing 지문의 **a major producer of computer products** → 정답의 **an industry leader**
지문의 **our obligation**
→ 정답의 **a responsibility**

152 사실 관계 확인

번역 수거지에 관해 언급된 것은?

(A) 예상만큼 쓸모가 없다.
(B) 더 이상 자원봉사자를 받지 않는다.
(C) 위생 요건이 매우 엄격하다.
(D) 위치는 온라인 지도에서 찾을 수 있다.

해설 마지막 단락에서 현재 수거지 및 제안된 수거지의 지도를 보려면 웹사이트를 방문하면 된다(for a map of current and proposed collection sites, visit ETrecyclingcenter.com)고 했으므로, (D)가 정답이다.

어휘 sanitary 위생의, 위생과 관련된

153-154 이메일

수신: 스탠 아냐티

발신: 스텔라 제랄디

날짜: 5월 1일

제목: 카페 마르티

스탠에게,

어제 당신의 매장에 전화를 걸어 제 빈티지 에스프레소 메이커에 대해 안드레와 이야기했습니다. 저는 그가 그렇게 오래된 기계의 교체 부품을 찾을 수 있었다는 것에 놀랐습니다. 그는 또한 더 이상 제조되지 않는 일부 부품도 다시 만들었습니다. ¹⁵⁴제조사의 명판을 거는 황동 거치대는 이탈리아에서 아직 도착하지 않은 듯합니다. 그것만 도착하면 복원이 완성될 수 있습니다.

앞서 논의한 바와 같이, 5월 7일까지 그 기계를 배달해 주십시오. 5월 8일에 카페 개업 10주년을 기념할 예정입니다. ¹⁵³그 에스프레소 기계는 항상 저희 가게의 중심이었습니다. 저희는 모든 광고에 그것을 사용합니다. ¹⁵⁴명판이 없더라도 이 빈티지 기계를 기념 행사에 사용해야 합니다.

스텔라

어휘 replacement 대체(품) apparently 아무래도 ~ 같은, 분명히 manufacturer 제조사 nameplate 명판 restoration 복원 deliver 배달하다 anniversary 주년, 기념일 centerpiece 중심적 존재, 주요 특징

---

153 사실 관계 확인

번역 에스프레소 기계에 관해 명시된 것은?

(A) 카페 마르티의 상징이다.

(B) 제대로 작동된 적이 없다.

(C) 스탠 아냐티가 설계했다.

(D) 10년 되었다.

해설 두 번째 단락의 '그 에스프레소 기계는 항상 저희 가게의 중심이었습니다(The espresso machine has always been our centerpiece)'와 '저희는 모든 광고에 그것을 사용합니다(We use it on all our advertising)'라는 문장을 통해 에스프레소 기계가 카페 마르티의 상징임을 알 수 있다. 따라서 (A)가 정답이다.

154 추론 / 암시

번역 황동 거치대에 관해 암시된 것은?

(A) 다시 디자인되었다.

(B) 다시 만들어야 한다.

(C) 황동 거치대가 없어도 기계는 작동할 수 있다.

(D) 이탈리아에 있는 제조업체가 황동 거치대를 엉뚱한 주소로 보냈다.

해설 첫 번째 단락에서 제조사의 명판을 거는 황동 거치대가 이탈리아에서 아직 도착하지 않은 것 같다(there is a brass holder ~ has not yet arrived from Italy)고 했는데, 두 번째 단락에서 명판이 없더라도 이 빈티지 기계를 기념 행사에 사용해야 한다(Even without the nameplate, I need to have this vintage machine working for our celebrations)고 했다. 따라서 황동 거치대가 없어도 기계

가 작동한다는 것을 추론할 수 있으므로, (C)가 정답이다.

어휘 function 작동하다, 기능하다

155-157 이메일

수신: 부서장들

발신: 마가렛 랭글리

날짜: 12월 27일

제목: 장기 부재중 인사말

첨부: 샘플 메시지 #5

부서장들께,

¹⁵⁵다가오는 휴일에 사무실이 문을 닫는 때를 대비하기 위해, 회사 정책에 따라 각 부서에서 음성 메시지 시스템의 기존 인사말을 장기 부재중 인사말로 바꾸어야 한다는 것을 다시 한 번 알려 드립니다. 다음 주에 발신 전화가 음성 메일로 전환되면 이 장기 부재중 인사말이 재생되어야 합니다. 이렇게 하려면 새로 녹음하고 시스템에 저장해서 금요일 업무 마감 시에 녹음이 활성화되도록 시스템을 프로그래밍하는 작업을 해야 합니다. 장기 부재중 인사말을 활성화하면, 휴일 동안 기존의 인사말이 중단될 것입니다.

¹⁵⁶첨부된 문서에는 녹음해야 할 인사말의 텍스트가 포함되어 있습니다. ¹⁵⁷우리가 이전에 사용한 것과 동일한 내용이지만, 늘 그렇듯이 현재의 업무 중단 일정을 반영하기 위해 날짜는 바뀌었습니다. 이 문서를 사용해 휴일 인사말을 녹음하십시오. 금요일 퇴근하기 전에 이를 반드시 활성화하기 바랍니다.

어휘 in preparation for ~에 대비하여 extended 길어진, 연장된 divert 전환하다 activate 활성화하다 override ~를 중단시키다, ~보다 우선하다 reflect 반영하다

---

155 주제 / 목적

번역 이메일의 주제는?

(A) 신설된 회사 방침

(B) 음성 메일 접근 방식 개선

(C) 휴일 업무 중단 관련 절차

(D) 기존 교대 일정표 변경

해설 첫 번째 단락에서 다가오는 휴일에 사무실이 문을 닫는 때를 대비하기 위해(In preparation for the upcoming holiday when offices will be closed) 회사 정책에 따라 각 부서에서 음성 메시지 시스템의 기존 인사말을 장기 부재중 인사말로 바꾸어야 한다는 것을 다시 한 번 알린다(I'd like to remind you that company policy requires ~ an extended-absence greeting)고 한 후, 관련 내용과 절차를 설명했다. 따라서 (C)가 정답이다.

어휘 established 설립된 improved 개선된 procedure 절차

▸▸ Paraphrasing 지문의 the upcoming holiday when offices will be closed → 정답의 a holiday closing

156 세부 사항

번역 첨부 파일로 포함된 것은?

(A) 소리 내어 읽을 대본
(B) 회사 행사를 발표하는 전단지
(C) 새 전화기 설치 설명서
(D) 녹음된 고객 통화 기록

해설 두 번째 단락에서 첨부된 문서에는 녹음할 인사말의 텍스트가 포함되어 있다(The attached document contains the text of the greeting you should record)고 했으므로, (A)가 정답이다.

> **Paraphrasing**   지문의 **The attached document**
> → 질문의 **an attachment**
> 지문의 **the text of the greeting you should record** → 정답의 **A script to be read aloud**

157 사실 관계 확인

번역 첨부 문서에 관해 이메일에 명시된 것은?

(A) 출판 준비가 되었다.
(B) 해마다 배포된다.
(C) 고객에게 배포된다.
(D) 신입사원만을 위한 것이다.

해설 두 번째 단락에서 첨부된 대본이 이전에 사용한 것과 같은 내용(This is the same text we have used in the past)이지만, 늘 그렇듯 현재의 업무 중단 일정을 반영하기 위해 날짜는 바뀌었다(as usual, the dates have been changed to reflect the current closure)고 했으므로, 해마다 날짜만 수정되어 배포된다는 것을 알 수 있다. 따라서 (B)가 정답이다.

어휘 intend 의도하다, (어떤 목적에) 쓰고자 하다

158-160 공지

킴포 마케팅 솔루션즈

킴포 마케팅 솔루션즈 이메일 소프트웨어를 구매해 주셔서 감사합니다. 이 제품이 귀하의 사업을 발전시키는 데 도움이 되리라 확신합니다.

158추가 보너스로 당사 전 제품에 대해 무료 교육이 제공됨을 알려 드리게 되어 기쁘게 생각합니다. 짧지만 효과적인 이 온라인 세미나는 당사 제품을 처음 쓰는 업체들이 이 소프트웨어를 최대한 활용할 수 있도록 해주는 좋은 기회입니다.

159강사들은 당사의 툴을 사용해 자신들의 사업을 160성장시켜 온 전문가들입니다. 세미나에 관한 더 자세한 내용을 알고 싶거나 세미나를 예약하고 싶으시다면 웹사이트 kimformarketingsolutions.com/seminarsignup을 방문하십시오.

어휘 confident 확신하는 effective 효과적인 utilize 활용하다 professional 전문가 reservation 예약

158 주제 / 목적

번역 공지의 목적 중 하나는 무엇인가?

(A) 고객에게 서비스에 관한 정보 제공하기
(B) 신제품 라인에 관해 이야기하기
(C) 마케팅 강사 소개하기
(D) 고객에게 다가오는 마감일 상기시키기

해설 두 번째 단락의 '당사 전 제품에 대해 무료 교육이 제공됨을 알려 드리게 되어 기쁘게 생각합니다(As an added bonus, we are pleased to announce that free training is offered for all of our products)'라는 문구를 통해 공지의 목적 중 하나가 고객에게 무료 교육에 관한 정보를 제공하기 위함이라는 것을 알 수 있다. 따라서 (A)가 정답이다.

> **Paraphrasing**   지문의 **that free training is offered for all of our products** → 정답의 **a service**

159 세부 사항

번역 공지에 따르면 강사들은 어떤 자격을 공통으로 갖고 있는가?

(A) 여러 해 동안 회사에서 일했다.
(B) 해당 이메일 소프트웨어의 숙련된 사용자들이다.
(C) 소프트웨어 설계에 참여했다.
(D) 마케팅 부서에서 일한다.

해설 두 번째 단락에서 온라인 세미나의 강사들은 킴포 마케팅 솔루션의 툴을 사용해 자신들의 사업을 성장시켜 온 전문가(Our instructors are professionals who have used our tools to grow their own businesses)라고 했으므로, 해당 이메일 소프트웨어의 숙련된 사용자임을 알 수 있다. 따라서 (B)가 정답이다.

어휘 participate 참석하다

> **Paraphrasing**   지문의 **professionals who have used our tools** → 정답의 **experienced users of the e-mail software**

160 동의어 찾기

번역 세 번째 단락 1행의 "grow"와 의미상 가장 가까운 단어는?

(A) 되다
(B) 확대하다
(C) 생산하다
(D) 움직이다

해설 "grow"를 포함한 부분은 '당사의 툴을 사용해 자신들의 사업을 성장시켜 온(have used our tools to grow their own businesses)'이라는 의미로, 여기서 grow는 '성장시키다, 키우다'라는 뜻으로 쓰였다. 따라서 '확대하다, 확장하다'라는 의미의 (B) expand가 정답이다.

161-163 기사

161요리사이자 라이프스타일 코치인 라나 왓슨 씨가 새로운 피부 관리 사업을 시작하면서 화장품 분야에 처음으로 진출을 시도한다고 발표했

다. ¹⁶²그녀의 서머 가든 피부 관리 제품군은 오직 유기농 성분으로만 제조한 제품으로 구성되며 식물, 과일, 채소에서 추출한 원료가 들어간다는 점이 특징이다.

¹⁶³"저는 제 식당에서 항상 가장 건강에 좋을 만한 음식을 제공해 왔습니다." 왓슨 씨가 말한다. "천연 재료는 안에서부터 우리의 건강과 아름다움을 키워 줍니다. 그런 다음 밖에서 안으로 피부에 영양을 공급하는 제품을 만드는 것이 맞는 것 같았어요. 제 피부 관리 제품군은 시금치, 오이 같은 음식에 있는 비타민과 단백질만을 활용하고 그것들을 결합하여 ¹⁶²인공 화학 물질이 없는 강력한 보습제와 세안제를 만듭니다."

서머 가든 제품들은 건성, 민감성, 또는 복합성 피부에 적합하며 올 9월부터 온라인 매장과 선정된 소매점에서 구매할 수 있다.

어휘 foray (다른 활동이나 업종에) 진출하려는 시도 consist of ~로 구성되다 solely 오직 ingredient 성분 feature 특별히 포함하다, 특징으로 삼다 extract 추출물 nourish 키우다, 증진하다 utilize 활용하다 artificial 인공의 suitable for ~에 적합한 sensitive 민감한 combination 혼합, 복합 select 선정된, 엄선된 retail store 소매점

161 주제 / 목적

번역 기사의 주제는?

(A) 지역 유기농장
(B) 온라인 쇼핑 추세
(C) 새로운 벤처 사업
(D) 기업 합병

해설 첫 번째 단락에서 요리사이자 라이프스타일 코치인 라나 왓슨 씨가 새로운 피부 관리 사업을 시작하면서 화장품 분야에 처음으로 진출을 시도(her first foray into cosmetics with the launch of a new skin care business)한다고 했으므로, 왓슨 씨의 새로운 사업 분야 진출을 알리기 위한 기사임을 알 수 있다. 따라서 (C)가 정답이다.

162 사실 관계 확인

번역 서머 가든 제품에 관해 명시된 것은?

(A) 모든 연령에 적합하다.
(B) 지금 구매할 수 있다.
(C) 상대적으로 저렴하다.
(D) 인공 성분이 없다.

해설 첫 번째 단락에서 서머 가든 피부 관리 제품군은 오직 유기농 성분으로만 제조한 제품으로 구성된다(Her Summer Garden skin care line consists solely of products made from organic ingredients)고 했고, 두 번째 단락 후반부에서 제품들에 인공 화학 물질이 없다(free from artificial chemicals)고 했으므로, (D)가 정답이다.

어휘 relatively 상대적으로, 비교적으로

▶▶ Paraphrasing 지문의 consists solely of products made from organic ingredients, free from artificial chemicals
→ 정답의 contain no artificial ingredients

163 문장 삽입

번역 [1], [2], [3], [4]로 표시된 곳 중에서 다음 문장이 들어가기에 가장 적합한 곳은?

"그런 다음 밖에서 안으로 피부에 영양을 공급하는 제품을 만드는 것이 맞는 것 같았어요."

(A) [1]
(B) [2]
(C) [3]
(D) [4]

해설 주어진 문장에 순서를 나타내는 부사 then이 있고, '그런 다음 밖에서 안으로 피부에 영양을 공급하는 제품을 만드는 것(to then create products to nurture our skin from the outside in)이 맞는 것 같았다'라고 했으므로, 이 앞에 이전 단계에 관한 내용이 들어가야 한다. 두 번째 단락을 보면 왓슨 씨가 자신은 항상 가장 건강에 좋을 만한 음식을 제공해 왔다(I've always served the healthiest possible food)며 천연 재료가 안에서부터 건강과 아름다움을 키워 준다(Natural ingredients nourish our health and beauty from the inside out)고 했으므로, 이 뒤에 주어진 문장이 들어가야 글의 흐름이 자연스러워진다. 따라서 (B)가 정답이다.

어휘 logical 타당한, (논리에) 맞는 nurture 영양을 공급하다, 보살피다

164-167 온라인 채팅

마리아 주카리니 오후 5시 30분 안녕하세요. ¹⁶⁴듀본빌 주민 대화방은 처음 이용해 봐요. 이웃분들 중에 도자기 타일 바닥 깔아 보신 분 계신가요?

유키우 왕 오후 5시 35분 안녕하세요, 마리아. 직접 하시려고요? ¹⁶⁵지난해 주방 바닥에 타일을 깔았는데 전부 제 손으로 했어요. 하지만 제 결정을 후회해요.

마리아 주카리니 오후 5시 37분 저는 돈을 아끼고 싶어서 전문가를 고용하고 싶지는 않아요. 하지만 전에 이런 작업을 혼자 힘으로 해 본 적은 없어요.

데니스 구르카 오후 5시 41분 집수리를 잘하는 사람이라면 동영상을 보거나 강습을 듣고 바닥 타일을 깔 수 있어요. 하지만 노력, 시간, 정밀함이 정말로 필요합니다.

유키우 왕 오후 5시 44분 제 경우에는 저희집 주방에 작업을 하기 전에 친구가 타일 작업하는 것을 도왔어요. 시작하기 전에 myhomefix.com에서 동영상도 몇 개 봤었죠. ¹⁶⁵하지만 앞으로는 전문가의 도움을 받을 겁니다.

유키우 왕 오후 5시 45분 데니스, 이 분야에 경험이 있나요? 마리아가 전문가 없이 이 작업을 처리할 수 있을까요?

마리아 주카리니 오후 5시 51분 흥미롭군요. 경험을 공유해 줘서 고마워요.

데니스 구르카 오후 5시 58분 ¹⁶⁶저는 바닥 시공 업체를 운영하고 있어요. 그녀가 할 수 있는지의 여부는 몇 가지 요인에 따라 달라집니다. 마리아, 타일을 자르고 배수구를 설치하거나 울퉁불퉁한 바닥을 고르게 펴야 하나요?

마리아 주카리니 오후 6시 06분 깨진 타일 몇 개만 교체하면 되지만 아마추어가 할 수 있는 일은 아닌 것 같네요. **167**데니스, 업체가 듀본빌에 있나요? 연락처 정보 좀 주시겠어요?

데니스 구르카 오후 6시 07분 **167**시 경계 바로 외곽에 있어요. 업체명은 플로어즈 포에버예요. 전화번호는 642-555-0143입니다.

> 어휘   community 주민, 지역 사회   regret 후회하다
> comfortable with ~을 쉽게 다룰 수 있는, 잘하는   prior to
> ~ 전에   tackle 해결하다, 다루다   factor 요인   drain 배수구
> flatten 평평하게 하다   uneven 울퉁불퉁한, 고르지 못한

164   추론 / 암시

번역   누구를 위한 대화방인가?

(A) 같은 도시에 사는 사람들
(B) 같은 온라인 강습을 듣는 사람들
(C) 대기업에서 함께 일하는 사람들
(D) 같이 여행을 계획하는 사람들

해설   주카리니 씨의 오후 5시 30분 메시지 '듀본빌 주민 대화방은 처음 이용해 봐요(This is my first time using the Dubonville community chat room)'에서 같은 도시에 사는 사람들이 참여하는 대화방임을 추론할 수 있다. 따라서 (A)가 정답이다.

어휘   attend 참석하다

165   의도 파악

번역   오후 5시 35분에 왕 씨가 "하지만 제 결정을 후회해요"라고 쓸 때, 그 의도는 무엇인가?

(A) 결국 돈을 아끼지 못했다.
(B) 전문가를 고용했어야 했다.
(C) 다른 타일을 선호했을 것이다.
(D) 주방을 개조할 필요가 없었다.

해설   왕 씨가 오후 5시 35분 메시지에서 '지난해 주방 바닥에 타일을 깔았는데 전부 제 손으로 했어요(I put in a tile floor ~ myself)'라고 한 후 자신의 결정을 후회한다고 했고, 그러고 나서 오후 5시 44분 메시지에서 앞으로는 전문가의 도움을 받을 것(In the future, I'd get professional help)이라고 했다. 따라서 주방 타일 작업에 전문가를 고용하지 않은 것을 후회하며 한 말임을 알 수 있으므로, (B)가 정답이다.

166   추론 / 암시

번역   구르카 씨에 관해 무엇이 사실이겠는가?

(A) 주카리니 씨의 동료이다.
(B) 자신의 집 타일을 깼다.
(C) 타일 시공 경험이 많다.
(D) myhomeifx.com에서 수강하고 있다.

해설   구르카 씨의 오후 5시 58분 메시지 '저는 바닥 시공 업체를 운영하고 있어요(I have my own flooring business)'를 통해 그가 타일 시공 경험이 많다는 것을 추론할 수 있다. 따라서 (C)가 정답이다.

167   추론 / 암시

번역   주카리니 씨는 다음에 무엇을 하겠는가?

(A) 세라믹 타일 사러 가기
(B) 타일 시공에 관한 동영상 찾아보기
(C) 깨진 타일 한 상자 반품하기
(D) 듀본빌 인근에 있는 업체에 연락하기

해설   주카리니 씨가 오후 6시 6분 메시지에서 구르카 씨에게 업체가 듀본빌에 있는지(is the business in Dubonville?) 물어보며 연락처 정보를 달라(Could you send me your contact information?)고 부탁하자, 구르카 씨가 오후 6시 7분 메시지에서 시 경계 바로 외곽에 있다(just outside the city limits)며 업체명과 번호를 알려 주었다. 따라서 주카리니 씨가 듀본빌 인근에 있는 구르카 씨의 업체에 연락할 것이라고 추론할 수 있으므로, (D)가 정답이다.

> ▶▶ Paraphrasing   지문의 outside the city limits
> 정답의 near Dubonville

168-171   이메일

> 수신: nora.simmons@heltlx.edu
> 발신: e.agbayani@periodicalquest.com
> 날짜: 2월 28일
> 제목: 피리어디컬 퀘스트
>
> 시몬스 씨께,
>
> **168, 169**신용 카드 만료로 인해 피리어디컬 퀘스트 3월 회비가 처리되지 못했음을 알려 드리는 서비스 메시지입니다. 서비스 중단을 피하기 위해서는 periodicalquest.com/useraccount를 방문하여 청구 정보를 업데이트하십시오. 어려움이 있으시다면 기꺼이 해당 절차를 안내해 드리겠습니다.
>
> 덧붙여 말씀드리면, **171**계정을 검토하면서 고객님께서 당사 서비스 전부를 이용하고 있지 않으시다는 것을 알게 되었습니다. 회원으로서 고객님께서는 3천 개가 넘는 학술지, 신문, 잡지로 구성된 당사의 장서에 온라인으로 무제한 접속하실 수 있습니다. 또한 **170**교수로서 강의 및 연구 목적으로 당사의 자료에서 도움을 받으실 수도 있습니다. 고객님께서 4개월 전에 저희 서비스에 가입할 때 프로필을 작성하지 않으신 것 같습니다. 잠시 짬을 내어 회원 선호 사항을 검토해 보시기 바랍니다. 저희는 고객님께서 피리어디컬 퀘스트가 제공하는 모든 혜택을 꼭 이용하셨으면 합니다.
>
> **171**고객님의 계정에 대해 문의 사항이 있으시면 언제든지 연락 주십시오. 회원권을 취소하는 데는 별도의 추가 작업이 필요하지 않습니다.
>
> 엘레나 아그바야니
> 피리어디컬 퀘스트

> 어휘   courtesy 서비스의, 무료의   process 처리하다   expired
> 만료된   disruption 중단   incidentally 그런데, 덧붙여 말하자면
> unlimited 무제한의   access 이용(권), 접근   additionally 또한,
> 게다가   benefit from ~의 도움을 받다, ~에서 이득을 취하다
> preference 선호 (사항)   take advantage of ~을 이용하다

168 세부 사항

번역 시몬스 씨가 연락을 받은 이유는?

(A) 새로운 서비스를 이용할 수 있다.
(B) 결제가 처리되지 않았다.
(C) 곧 주문품이 배송될 것이다.
(D) 기사가 수정되어야 한다.

해설 첫 번째 단락에서 신용 카드 만료로 인해 피리어디컬 퀘스트 3월 회비가 처리되지 못했음(your monthly Periodical Quest membership fee for March could not be processed)을 시몬스 씨에게 알려 주고 있으므로, (B)가 정답이다.

어휘 revise 수정하다

> ▸▸Paraphrasing 지문의 **your monthly Periodical Quest membership fee** → 정답의 **A payment**

169 사실 관계 확인

번역 피리어디컬 퀘스트에 관해 명시된 것은?

(A) 매월 이용료가 부과된다.
(B) 이제 소장 학술지가 두 배가 되었다.
(C) 웹사이트가 탐색하기 쉽다.
(D) 고객 지원팀을 24시간 이용할 수 있다.

해설 첫 번째 단락의 '신용 카드 만료로 인해 피리어디컬 퀘스트 3월 회비가 처리되지 않았다(your monthly Periodical Quest membership fee for March could not be processed)'라는 문장을 통해 매월 이용료를 지불해야 한다는 것을 알 수 있다. 따라서 (A)가 정답이다.

어휘 navigate 탐색하다

170 사실 관계 확인

번역 시몬스 씨에 관해 명시된 것은?

(A) 교육 분야에서 일한다.
(B) 최근 고객 서비스부에 이메일을 보냈다.
(C) 오랫동안 피리어디컬 퀘스트의 회원이었다.
(D) 피리어디컬 퀘스트의 회원 자격을 취소할 생각이다.

해설 두 번째 단락에서 '교수로서(as a professor) 강의 및 연구 목적으로 당사의 자료에서 도움을 받으실 수도 있습니다(you can also benefit from our resources for teaching and research purposes)'라고 했으므로, 수신인인 시몬스 씨가 교수임을 알 수 있다. 따라서 (A)가 정답이다.

> ▸▸Paraphrasing 지문의 **as a professor**
> → 정답의 **works in the field of education**

171 추론 / 암시

번역 아그바야니 씨는 누구이겠는가?

(A) 잡지 편집자
(B) 은행 직원
(C) 컴퓨터 프로그래머
(D) 계정 관리자

해설 두 번째 단락에서 시몬스 씨의 계정을 검토했다(reviewing your account)고 했으며, 마지막 단락에서 계정에 대해 문의 사항이 있으면 언제든지 연락을 달라(Feel free to contact me ~ regarding your account)고 했으므로, 발신자인 아그바야니 씨가 계정 관련 업무를 담당하고 있음을 추론할 수 있다. 따라서 (D)가 정답이다.

172-175 웹페이지

http://www.torontoconstructionshow.ca/magazine

| 연례 박람회 | **잡지** | 자주 묻는 질문 | 홈 |

〈월간 시멘트 & 건설〉은 토론토 건설 박람회 주최자들이 만듭니다. 이 잡지는 매달 온라인으로 발행됩니다. 175〈연례 박람회〉 특별판도 있습니다. 이것은 박람회에 등록한 모든 방문자에게 배포됩니다.

172〈월간 시멘트 & 건설〉은 업계 소식, 제품 후기, 무역 박람회 정보 등을 합쳐서 제공합니다. 즐거움을 주는 월간 칼럼은 업무 관련 조언에서 광고 전략까지 모든 사항을 다룹니다.

173올해 〈월간 시멘트 & 건설〉은 업계의 멘토들을 향한 저희의 존경심을 보여 드리기 위한 작업을 시작하려고 합니다. 저희는 회원들에게 조언자 역할을 탁월하게 수행했던 분들을 추천해 주실 것을 부탁드리고 있습니다. 추천 방식에 대한 정보는 아래 링크를 보십시오. 추천을 검토한 후 올해의 최고 멘토 다섯 분을 선정할 예정입니다. 174선정된 분들은 11월 3일 토론토 건설 박람회에서 특별상을 받게 됩니다. 그분들의 약력 및 사진은 〈월간 시멘트 & 건설〉 12월호에 게재됩니다.

링크

| 추천서 | 올해 발행된 호 | 자료실 (과거 발행된 호) |

어휘 organizer 주최자 entertaining 즐거움을 주는, 재미있는 strategy 전략 demonstrate 보여 주다 esteem 존경 nominate 추천[지명]하다

172 주제 / 목적

번역 웹페이지의 목적 중 하나는 무엇인가?

(A) 등록 절차 설명하기
(B) 컨벤션 일정 수정하기
(C) 제품 품평하기
(D) 업계 출판물 홍보하기

해설 두 번째 단락의 '〈월간 시멘트 & 건설〉은 업계 소식, 제품 후기, 무역 박람회 정보 등을 합쳐서 제공합니다(Cement & Construction Monthly offers a mix of industry news, product reviews, and trade show information)'와 '즐거움을 주는 월간 칼럼은 업무 관련 조언에서 광고 전략까지 모든 사항을 다룹니다(Entertaining monthly columns cover everything from job advice to advertising strategies)'라는 문구를 통해 웹페이지의 목적 중 하나가 〈월간 시멘트 & 건설〉을 홍보하기 위함이라는 것을 알 수 있다. 따라서 (D)가 정답이다.

어휘 registration 등록 trade 무역, (특정) 업계 publication 출판(물)

173 세부 사항

번역 새로운 특집으로 발표되고 있는 것은?

(A) 멘토들을 예우하기 위한 계획
(B) 온라인 토론 포럼
(C) 현장 취업 면접
(D) 월간 조언 칼럼

해설 세 번째 단락에서 올해에는 업계의 멘토들에 대한 존경심을 보여 주기 위한(to demonstrate our high esteem for mentors in the industry) 작업을 시작하려 한다고 했으므로, (A)가 정답이다.

▶▶ Paraphrasing 지문의 beginning a mission
→ 질문의 new feature
지문의 to demonstrate our high esteem for mentors → 정답의 to honor mentors

174 세부 사항

번역 11월 3일에 일어날 일은?

(A) 특별 뉴스 보도가 실릴 것이다.
(B) 상이 수여될 것이다.
(C) 선정 결과가 발표될 것이다.
(D) 사진 모음집이 전시될 것이다.

해설 세 번째 단락에서 선정된 멘토들은 11월 3일 토론토 건설 박람회에서 특별상을 받게 된다(These winners will receive a special award ~ on November 3)고 했으므로, (B)가 정답이다.

▶▶ Paraphrasing 지문의 will receive a special award
→ 정답의 Awards will be given out.

175 문장 삽입

번역 [1], [2], [3], [4]로 표시된 곳 중에서 다음 문장이 들어가기에 가장 적합한 곳은?

"이것은 박람회에 등록한 모든 방문자에게 배포됩니다."

(A) [1]
(B) [2]
(C) [3]
(D) [4]

해설 주어진 문장에서 '이것은 박람회에 등록한 모든 방문자에게 배포됩니다(This is distributed to all registered visitors to the show)'라고 했으므로, 이 앞에 단수 지시대명사 This가 가리키는 대상이 나와야 한다. [1] 앞 문장에서 '〈연례 박람회〉 특별판도 있습니다(There is also a special *Annual Show* print edition)'라며 배포될 만한 대상을 언급했으므로, (A)가 정답이다.

어휘 distribute 배포하다

176-180 양식 + 이메일

제62회 연례 샘스빌 홈 앤 가든 박람회
3월 31일부터 4월 2일까지, 샘스빌 회의장
전시 신청서

회사명: 카스티요 조경 디자인
연락처 이름: 발리아 카스티요
전화: 302-555-0198
이메일: vcastillo@castillold.com
웹사이트: www.castillold.com

전시 품목/서비스:
176당사에서 제공 가능한 실외 디자인 서비스의 사진, 도면, 그리고 모델을 전시하려고 합니다.

추가 정보 또는 요청 사항:
177저희 직원 한 명도 참가해서 자재 이송을 도울 예정이므로 두 번째 주차권 한 장을 요청합니다.

주의: 이 신청서는 계약서가 아니므로 박람회 부스를 확보해 드리지 않습니다. 공간은 선착순으로 이용할 수 있습니다. 178작성하신 신청서가 접수되면 근무일 기준으로 5일 이내에 진행자가 연락을 드려서 예약 및 대금을 확정합니다. 샘스빌 홈 앤 가든 회원에게는 결제 시 자동으로 할인이 적용됩니다. 문의 사항은 fli@samsvillehg.org로 전시회 주최자인 페이 리 씨에게 하십시오. 모든 신청서는 1월 31일이 마감입니다.

어휘 annual 연례의 exhibitor 전시자, 전시 업체 display 전시하다 attend 참석하다 transport 나르다, 운반하다 guarantee 보장하다 first-come basis 선착순으로 completed 작성된, 완료된 coordinator 진행자, 책임자 finalize 확정하다 organizer 주최자, 조직자 due ~할 예정인, ~하기로 되어 있는

수신: vcastillo@castillold.com
발신: rconway@samsvillehg.org
날짜: 1782월 1일
제목: 홈 앤 가든 박람회
첨부: 📎 계약서와 청구서

카스티요 씨께:

178회원님의 제62회 연례 샘스빌 홈 앤 가든 박람회 전시 신청서를 받았습니다. 179부스 공간에 대한 회원님의 계약서와 회원 할인가가 적용된 청구서를 첨부합니다. 계약서에 서명하시고 2월 10일까지 사본 1부를 보내 주십시오.

회원님의 예약에는 콘센트가 딸려 있고 칸막이가 있는 부스 한 곳, 회원님과 동료 1인의 전시자용 명찰, 그리고 두 번째 주차권에 대한 요청이 승인되어 무료 주차권 2장이 포함됩니다. 177통상적으로 주차권은 부스당 1장으로 제한되어 있지만, 180회원님께서는 오랜 회원이자 저희 행사의 전시자이므로 이번 경우는 예외로 하겠습니다.

회원님의 지속적인 참여와 성원에 감사드립니다.

라일란 콘웨이, 판매 업체 관리 담당
샘스빌 홈 앤 가든

176 세부 사항

번역 카스티요 씨는 박람회에 무엇을 가지고 갈 계획인가?

(A) 정원 사진
(B) 샘플 나무와 식물
(C) 샘플 프로젝트 견적서
(D) 원예 도구

해설 양식의 전시 품목/서비스(Items/services to be exhibited)란에
카스티요 씨가 자신의 회사(Castillo Landscpae Design)에서 제
공 가능한 실외 디자인 서비스의 사진, 도면, 그리고 모델을 전시할
것(I will display photographs ~ available outdoor design
services that my company offers)이라고 적었으므로, 조경
(landscape) 관련 사진을 가져갈 것임을 알 수 있다. 따라서 (A)가
정답이다.

▶▶ Paraphrasing 지문의 will display
→ 질문의 planning to bring to the show
지문의 photographs → 정답의 Pictures

177 연계

번역 통상적으로 부스 예약에 포함되는 것은?

(A) 전시자 서명
(B) 주차 허가증
(C) 연간 회원권
(D) 지역 판매 업체 안내 책자

해설 카스티요 씨가 양식의 추가 정보 또는 요청 사항(Additional
information or requests)란에 두 번째 주차권을 요청한다(I
would like to request a second parking pass)고 적었는데, 콘
웨이 씨가 보낸 이메일을 보면 통상적으로 주차권은 부스 당 1장으로
제한되어(Passes are typically limited to one per booth) 있지
만 카스티요 씨에게만 특별히 두 번째 주차권을 제공한다고 했다. 따
라서 부스 예약에 주차권 1장이 포함되어 있음을 알 수 있으므로, (B)
가 정답이다.

▶▶ Paraphrasing 지문의 parking pass → 정답의 parking permit

178 연계

번역 카스티요 씨는 언제 신청서를 제출했겠는가?

(A) 1월   (B) 2월
(C) 3월   (D) 4월

해설 양식의 주의(NOTE) 부분에서 작성된 신청서가 접수되면(Once your
completed application is received) 진행자가 근무일 기준으로
5일 이내에 연락을 해서 예약 및 대금을 확정한다(a coordinator
will contact you within five business days)고 했는데, 콘웨
이 씨가 신청서를 받았다(We have received your exhibitor

appplication)고 한 이메일의 날짜를 보면 2월 1일이라고 되어 있
다. 따라서 카스티요 씨가 1월에 신청서를 제출했다는 것을 추론할 수
있으므로, (A)가 정답이다.

179 추론 / 암시

번역 카스티요 씨에 관해 암시된 것은?

(A) 샘스빌 홈 앤 가든에서 근무한다.
(B) 샘스빌에서 10년째 살고 있다.
(C) 추가 콘센트를 요청했다.
(D) 부스 공간 요금으로 할인된 가격을 지불할 것이다.

해설 이메일의 첫 번째 단락에서 카스티요 씨가 예약한 부스 공간에 대한
계약서와 회원 할인가가 적용된 청구서를 첨부한다(I am attaching
~ your invoice at the discounted member rate)고 했으므로,
카스티요 씨가 할인된 금액을 지불할 것임을 추론할 수 있다. 따라서
(D)가 정답이다.

▶▶ Paraphrasing 지문의 the discounted member rate
→ 정답의 a reduced price

180 세부 사항

번역 콘웨이 씨가 카스티요 씨에게 예외를 적용해 준 이유는?

(A) 과거 행사 주최자이다.
(B) 박람회에 자주 참가한다.
(C) 추가 요금을 내는 데 동의했다.
(D) 아주 강렬한 지원서를 제출했다.

해설 이메일의 두 번째 단락 후반부에서 카스티요 씨가 오랜 회원이며 행사
전시자(a longtime member and exhibitor at our event)라서
이번 경우는 예외로 하겠다(we will make an exception in this
case)고 했으므로, 그녀가 박람회에 자주 참가했기 때문에 예외를 적
용해 주었음을 알 수 있다. 따라서 (B)가 정답이다.

▶▶ Paraphrasing 지문의 a longtime member and exhibitor at
our event
→ 정답의 often participates in the show

181-185 웹페이지 + 이메일

http://www.projectelements.com

팀 플랜	회사 소개	리소스	자주 묻는 질문

프로젝트 관리에 필요한 모든 것이 한 곳에, 모두 온라인으로.

프로젝트 엘리먼츠 LLC는 중소기업과 대기업 모두 사용할 수 있는 프
로젝트 관리 소프트웨어입니다. [181]당사의 전매 특허 소프트웨어가 귀
사에 속한 팀의 의사 소통, 일정 잡기, 정보 관리를 도우면서 처음부터
끝까지 귀사에 만족을 드리겠습니다.

팀 베이식

5인 팀은 베이식 솔루션으로 시작하십시오. 업무 관리, 파일 공유, 모바
일 접속을 간편하게 할 수 있습니다. 소정의 비용을 추가해 클라우드에
온라인 데이터 저장 공간 100기가바이트를 추가하십시오.

팀 크리에이티브

이 옵션은 최대 35인의 크리에이티브 전문가들로 이루어진 소규모 팀에 적합한 최상의 솔루션입니다. 팀 베이식의 모든 기능 외에도 동영상 편집 툴, 그래픽 디자인 소프트웨어, 300기가바이트의 클라우드 저장 공간 등 디자인에 필요한 모든 것을 획득하십시오.

팀 플레이어

최대 50인의 팀은 이 향상된 서비스로 탁월한 성과를 거둘 수 있습니다. 팀 베이식의 모든 기능에다가 팀을 위한 시간 계획표, 세컨드 파티 플랫폼과의 첨단 통합, 최대 400기가바이트의 클라우드 저장 공간까지 획득하십시오.

184팀 리더

이 옵션은 최대 100인의 팀에게 가장 좋습니다. 팀 플레이어의 모든 기능에 더해 향상된 개인 설정 옵션, 리소스 추적, 시간 추적, 500기가바이트의 클라우드 공간, 빠른 동영상 업로드로 원활한 팀 업무를 경험해 보세요.

확신이 더 필요하신가요? **182당사는 2년 연속으로 〈워크 위너 잡지〉가 수여하는 골드 스타 신생 기업상을 수상해 소프트웨어 품질을 인정받았습니다.** 프로젝트 엘리먼츠의 성공담을 더 들으시려면 회사 소개 탭에서 고객 추천글을 확인하세요.

어휘 proprietary 전매 특허인, 등록 상표가 붙은 accessibility 접속, 이용 at one's fingertips 손가락 끝에서, 간편하게 additional 추가의 excel 탁월하다, 능가하다 enhanced 향상된, 강화된 feature 기능 advanced 첨단의, 고급의 integration 통합 personalization 개인 설정, 개인 맞춤 seamless 원활한 convince 확신시키다, 설득하다 recognize (상으로) 표창하다, 인정하다 client testimonial 고객 추천글

수신: ebennis@projectelements.com
발신: jasbury@clarelcommunications.com
주제: 프로젝트 엘리먼츠 업그레이드
날짜: 12월 5일

베니스 씨께,

저는 클라렐 통신의 디지털 광고 담당 신임 이사입니다. 전임 이사인 로버트 러스트 씨가 프로젝트 엘리먼츠 플랫폼이 얼마나 유익한지 말해주었는데, **183클라렐이 현재 사용하고 있는 플랜을 바꿔야 할 가능성이 있어 이를 귀하와 함께 살펴보려고 합니다. 184우리는 현재 45명으로 이루어진 팀이지만 내년에 55명으로 성장하리라 예상합니다.** 이 팀은 저장 기능을 좋아하지만, 400기가바이트 이상의 저장 공간과 더 좋은 개인 설정 옵션이 있는 플랜에 관심이 있을 것입니다. **183저희의 요구 사항에 185딱 맞는 플랜이 있을까요?**

연락 기다리겠습니다.

줄리아 애즈버리
디지털 광고 담당 이사
클라렐 통신

어휘 valuable 소중한, 유익한 explore 살펴보다, 분석하다 potential 잠재적인, ~할 가능성이 있는 current 현재의, 기존의 presently 현재 anticipate 예상하다, 기대하다

---

181 추론 / 암시

번역 프로젝트 엘리먼츠 소프트웨어는 어디에 사용되겠는가?

(A) 온라인으로 제품 주문하기
(B) 팀으로서 협력하기
(C) 신입 관리자 교육하기
(D) 소셜 미디어 게시글 감시하기

해설 웹페이지 첫 번째 단락의 '당사의 전매 특허 소프트웨어가 귀사에 속한 팀의 의사 소통, 일정 잡기, 정보 관리를 도우면서 처음부터 끝까지 귀사에 만족을 드리겠습니다(Our proprietary software will serve you ~ helping your teams to communicate, schedule, and manage information)'라는 문구를 통해 팀으로 일할 때 사용되는 소프트웨어임을 추론할 수 있다. 따라서 (B)가 정답이다.

▸▸ Paraphrasing 지문의 **your teams to communicate, schedule, and manage information**
→ 정답의 **working together as a team**

182 사실 관계 확인

번역 프로젝트 엘리먼츠 LLC에 관해 사실인 것은?

(A) 업계에서 상을 받았다.
(B) 10년 넘게 영업하고 있다.
(C) 클라렐 통신을 매입했다.
(D) 기술 잡지를 발간한다.

해설 웹페이지의 마지막 단락에서 2년 연속으로 〈워크 위너 잡지〉가 수여하는 골드 스타 신생 기업상을 수상해 소프트웨어 품질을 인정받았다(We were recognized for our software quality with the Gold Star Start-Up Awards)고 했으므로, (A)가 정답이다.

183 주제 / 목적

번역 이메일을 보낸 이유는?

(A) 제품을 등록하려고
(B) 제품에 관한 기술적 도움을 요청하려고
(C) 제품 등록 문제를 설명하려고
(D) 제품 선택에 있어 조언을 구하려고

해설 이메일에서 클라렐이 현재 사용하고 있는 플랜을 바꿔야 할 가능성이 있어 베니스 씨와 함께 살펴보고 싶다(I want to explore with you a potential change in Clarel's current plan)며 팀의 요구 사항에 맞는 플랜이 있는지 문의(Is there a plan that will fit our needs?)하고 있으므로, 소프트웨어 선택에 있어 조언을 구하려고 보낸 메일임을 알 수 있다. 따라서 (D)가 정답이다.

184 연계

번역 베니스 씨는 어떤 제품을 추천하겠는가?

(A) 팀 베이식
(B) 팀 크리에이티브
(C) 팀 플레이어
(D) 팀 리더

해설　이메일에서 디지털 광고팀이 내년에 55명으로 성장하리라 예상한다 (anticipate growing to 55 members over the next year)며 400기가바이트 이상의 저장 공간과 더 나은 개인 설정 옵션이 있는 플랜에 관심이 있을 것(they would be interested in a plan with more than 400 GB and better personalization options)이라고 했다. 웹페이지의 제품 목록을 보면, '팀 리더(Team Leader)'에서 언급된 옵션들이 애즈버리 씨 팀의 요구 사항을 충족하므로, 베니스 씨가 '팀 리더(Team Leader)'를 추천할 것임을 추론할 수 있다. 따라서 (D)가 정답이다.

185 동의어 찾기

번역　이메일에서 첫 번째 단락 6행의 "fit"과 의미상 가장 가까운 단어는?

(A) 부응하다
(B) ~에 합의하다
(C) ~에 의존하다
(D) 조정하다

해설　"fit"을 포함한 문장은 '저희의 요구에 딱 맞는 플랜이 있을까요?(Is there a plan that will fit our needs?)'라는 의미로, 여기서 fit은 '적합하다, 맞다'라는 뜻으로 쓰였다. 따라서 '부응하다, 맞추다'라는 의미의 (A) match가 정답이다.

186-190 광고 + 이메일 + 양식

> ### *라이드-어웨이 비히클즈 여름 특가*
>
> **186 7월 한 달간 아일랜드를 여행하실 때**
> **요금*에서 15퍼센트를 절약하세요.**
>
> **189 소형차 21유로**
> 중형차 32유로
> 대형 세단 46유로
> 밴 52유로
>
> 020 917 1212로 전화하시거나
> www.ride-awayvehicles.co.ie에서 온라인으로 예약하세요.
>
> *186 광고에 제시된 가격은 자격이 있는 운전자를 대상으로 하는 일일 요금이며 부가가치세(VAT) 및 기본 보장 보험이 포함됩니다. 추가 요금이 적용될 수 있습니다. 자세한 내용은 라이드-어웨이 비히클즈 직원에게 문의하세요.

어휘　eligible 자격 있는 inclusive 포함한 protection plan 보험 representative 직원

> 수신: yayoiadachi@jrengineering.co.jp
> 발신: info@rideawayvehicles.co.ie
> 날짜: 7월 14일
> 제목: 예약 확인 - #122055
>
> 아다치 씨께,
>
> 고객님의 렌터카 예약이 확인되었습니다. 대여 조건에 따른 세부 정보는 다음과 같습니다.

> 187, 188 인수: 7월 21일 오전 9시, 아일랜드, 섀넌, 섀넌 공항, 라이드-어웨이 비히클즈
>
> 188 반납: 7월 29일 오후 5시, 아일랜드, 코크 시티, 코크 시티 센터, 라이드-어웨이 비히클즈
>
> 189 요금: 1일 21유로×8일 = 168유로 (주행 거리 무제한 및 내비게이션 시스템/GPS 포함)
>
> 모델: 콜라바 시사이더 또는 유사 차종
>
> **중요한 정보:** 운전자는 인수 시 유효한 운전면허증을 제시해야 합니다. 인수 또는 반납일, 시간, 장소 변경을 포함하여 예약 변경 시 추가 요금이 적용될 수 있습니다. 190 연료 탱크에 휘발유를 가득 채우지 않고 반납한 차량에 대해 연료비에 더해 25유로의 서비스 요금이 부과됩니다.
>
> 라이드-어웨이 비히클즈를 선택해 주셔서 감사합니다. 문의 사항은 020 917 1212로 전화 주십시오.

어휘　terms 조건 present 제시하다 valid 유효한 assess (요금 등을) 부과하다 fuel 연료

> **라이드-어웨이 비히클즈 반납 양식**
>
> 작성자: 헨리 리오던, 부팀장, 코크 시티 센터 지점
> 운전자 성명: 야요이 아다치
> 모델/번호판:
> 콜라바 시사이더, 161-C-45329
> 190 연료 탱크: 절반 채움
>
> 반납일/시간:
> 7월 29일, 오후 4시 40분
> 차량 상태: 파손 없음
> 주행 기록계 눈금값:
> 33,763킬로미터
>
> 야요이 아다치
> 운전자 서명

어휘　odometer 주행 기록계

186 주제 / 목적

번역　라이드-어웨이 비히클즈가 광고하고 있는 것은?

(A) 무료 대여일
(B) 할인된 일일 요금
(C) 더 큰 차량으로 무료 승급
(D) 추가 비용 면제

해설　광고 상단의 '7월 한 달간 아일랜드를 여행하실 때 요금에서 15퍼센트를 절약하세요(Save 15 percent off our rates ~ for travel within Ireland)'와 하단의 '광고에 제시된 가격은 일일 요금입니다(Price advertised is the daily rate)'라는 문구를 통해 일일 요금 할인 행사 광고임을 알 수 있다. 따라서 (B)가 정답이다.

어휘　waiver (권리 등의) 포기

> ▸▸ Paraphrasing　지문의 Save 15 percent off our rates, the daily rate → 정답의 A reduced daily rate

187 세부 사항

번역 7월 21일에 무슨 일이 있을 것인가?

(A) 판촉 기간이 끝난다.
(B) 확인서를 보낸다.
(C) 아다치 씨가 섀넌 공항에 올 것이다.
(D) 아다치 씨가 계약서에 운전자를 추가할 것이다.

해설 이메일을 보면 7월 21일 오전 9시(21 July, 9:00 A.M.)에 섀넌 공항에 있는 라이드-어웨이 비히클즈에서 아다치 씨가 차량을 인수(Pickup)할 것임을 알 수 있다. 따라서 (C)가 정답이다.

188 사실 관계 확인

번역 이메일에서 라이드-어웨이 비히클즈에 관해 명시된 것은?

(A) 여러 지점에서 운영한다.
(B) GPS 사용에 대해 요금을 부과한다.
(C) 1주일 이상 대여 시 할인을 적용한다.
(D) 예약을 확정하기 전에 요금을 받는다.

해설 아다치 씨의 차량 대여 조건을 보면, 차량 인수(Pickup)는 섀넌(Shannon)에 있는 라이드-어웨이 비히클즈에서, 반납(Drop-Off)은 코크 시티(Cork City)에 있는 라이드-어웨이 비히클즈에서 해야 한다고 나와 있다. 따라서 지점이 2개 이상임을 알 수 있으므로, (A)가 정답이다.

어휘 multiple 복수의, 다양한

189 연계

번역 아다치 씨는 어떤 차량을 대여했는가?

(A) 소형차
(B) 중형차
(C) 대형차
(D) 밴

해설 이메일에서 아다치 씨가 지불할 일일 요금이 21유로(Rate: €21/day×8 days = €168)라고 했는데, 광고를 보면 해당 금액이 소형차(Compact Car)를 위한 요금임을 알 수 있다. 따라서 (A)가 정답이다.

190 연계

번역 아다치 씨에 관해 암시된 것은?

(A) GPS를 받지 못했다.
(B) 차를 늦게 반납했다.
(C) 요청한 차를 받지 못했다.
(D) 서비스 요금 25유로가 부과될 것이다.

해설 이메일의 중요한 정보(Important Information) 부분에서 연료 탱크에 휘발유를 가득 채우지 않고 반납한 차량에 대해 연료비에 더해 25유로의 서비스 요금이 부과된다(A €25 service fee will be assessed for vehicles returned without a full tank of petrol)고 했는데, 아다치 씨의 차량 반납 양식을 보면 연료 탱크가 절반만 차 있다(Gas Tank: Half full)고 나와 있으므로, 그녀에게 25유로의 서비스 요금이 부과될 것임을 추론할 수 있다. 따라서 (D)가 정답이다.

191-195 제품 설명서 + 온라인 후기 + 온라인 답글

← →　http://www.stylero.com/printers/RD525

| 홈 | 컴퓨터 | 프린터 | 잉크 & 토너 | 액세서리 | 지원 |

제품: 스타일로 RD525, 3가지 기능 일체형 프린터

가격: 정가 120.00달러 현재 99.99달러 (특가 3월 1일부터 3월 15일까지 유효)

[192]구매 시 스타일로-01 (검정) 잉크 카트리지가 무료로 포함됩니다! 스타일로 컬러 잉크 카트리지는 별도 판매합니다.

[191]RD525는 당사에서 가장 인기 있는 모델 중 하나로, 무선 컬러 프린터, 스캐너, 복사기가 하나로 통합된 복합기입니다. 가정, 교실, 소규모 사무실에서 일상적으로 인쇄하는 데 적합합니다. 여러 브랜드의 잉크 카트리지와 호환 가능하지만 타사 제품보다 2배 오래 가는 당사 자체 스타일로-브랜드 잉크를 추천합니다. 7.95달러에 3년간 보증 혜택을 받을 수 있습니다.

어휘 complimentary 무료의　separately 분리하여, 따로
compatible 호환이 가능한　warranty 보증(서)

---

http://www.loveitornot.com/productreviews/stylero/RD525

(4월 3일) 저는 지난달에 재택 근무 사무실을 위해 스타일로 RD525를 구입했습니다. [194]저는 매주 여러날 밤에 집에서 디지털 사진 강좌를 여는데 제 강의를 듣는 수강생들의 작품을 위해 컬러 프린터를 바로 이용할 수 있어야 합니다. 복사기나 스캐너는 문제가 없고 [192, 193]인쇄물의 품질도 컬러와 흑백 모두 우수합니다. 하지만 때때로 프린터 기능이 지연되고 있습니다. 컴퓨터에서 인쇄물을 전송하는 시간과 실제 인쇄가 시작되는 시간 사이에 5분이 지체됩니다. 교실에서 바로 인쇄물이 필요할 때는 이 기기를 쓸 수 없습니다. 이걸 쓰게 되면 귀중한 강의 시간이 허비되거든요. 다른 프린터를 사거나 적어도 수리를 받을 수 있는 보증서를 구매할 걸 그랬어요!

알리샤 부와베흐

어휘 access 이용, 접근　feature 기능, 특징　device 장비
instant 즉시의, 즉각의

---

http://www.loveitornot.com/productreviews/stylero/RD525

(4월 5일) [194]교실에서 쓰려고 이 프린터를 구입했는데 부와베흐 씨가 설명한 것과 똑같은 문제를 발견했습니다. 하지만 비교적 쉽게 고칠 수 있습니다. 대다수 프린터는 인쇄 사이 사이에 에너지를 절약하기 위해 "절전 모드"에 들어갑니다. 절전 모드에 들어가기 전에 걸리는 시간이 너무 짧게 설정되어 있으면 매번 인쇄기 예열이 필요하게 되어 컴퓨터에서 사진을 전송하는 시간과 실제 인쇄 사이에 지체되는 시간이 생깁니다. [195]적어도 한 시간은 기다린 후에 절전에 들어가도록 절전 모드 기능을 조정하십시오. 사용법은 설명서에 나와 있습니다. 저는 항상 수업 몇 분 전에 프린터를 켜는데, 그러면 문제가 없습니다. 그것은 쉽게

조정할 수 있으며, 저는 RD525가 가격 대비 좋은 제품이라고 생각합니다.

안토니오 톰슨

191 사실 관계 확인

번역   스타일로 RD525에 관해 명시된 것은?

(A) 스타일로 브랜드 잉크가 필요하다.
(B) 복사기 기능도 한다.
(C) 한 달 동안 할인가에 판매되었다.
(D) 3월 15일 이후에 단종될 것이다.

해설   제품 설명서의 중반부를 보면 RD525가 가장 인기 있는 모델 중 하나로, 무선 컬러 프린터, 스캐너, 복사기가 하나로 통합된 복합기(The RD525 is ~ a wireless color printer, scanner, and photocopier in one)라고 했으므로, (B)가 정답이다.

어휘   function 기능하다   discontinue 중단하다

192 연계

번역   부와베흐 씨는 어디에 추가로 돈을 썼겠는가?

(A) 모니터
(B) 3년 보증
(C) 스캐너
(D) 컬러 잉크 카트리지

해설   제품 설명서에서 스타일로 컬러 잉크 카트리지는 별도 판매한다(Stylero color ink cartridges sold separately)고 했는데, 부와베흐 씨의 후기를 보면 인쇄물의 품질이 컬러와 흑백 모두 우수하다(the quality of the prints is excellent in both color and in black and white)고 나와 있으므로, 그녀가 컬러 잉크 카트리지를 별도로 구매했음을 추론할 수 있다. 따라서 (D)가 정답이다.

193 사실 관계 확인

번역   부와베흐 씨가 스타일로 RD525에 관해 언급한 것은?

(A) 내구성이 있다.
(B) 인쇄가 잘된다.
(C) 비싸다.
(D) 주기적으로 정비가 필요하다.

해설   부와베흐 씨가 작성한 후기를 보면 인쇄물의 품질이 컬러와 흑백 모두 우수하다(the quality of the prints is excellent in both color and in black and white)고 나와 있으므로, (B)가 정답이다.

어휘   durable 내구성 있는   maintenance 정비, 유지 보수

> ▸▸ Paraphrasing   지문의 the quality of the prints is excellent
> → 정답의 It produces good prints.

194 연계

번역   부와베흐 씨와 톰슨 씨에 관해 암시된 것은?

(A) 교사들이다.
(B) 스타일로 RD525를 반품했다.
(C) 사진을 좋아한다.
(D) 집에 프린터가 있다.

해설   후기에서 부와베흐 씨는 자신이 집에서 디지털 사진 강좌를 연다(I give digital photography lessons out of my home)고 했고, 온라인 답글에서 톰슨 씨는 자신의 교실에서 쓰려고 프린터를 구매했다(I bought this printer for my classroom)고 했다. 따라서 둘 다 가르치는 일을 한다고 추론할 수 있으므로, (A)가 정답이다.

195 세부 사항

번역   스타일로 RD525에 관해 톰슨 씨가 한 조언은?

(A) 사용 후 플러그를 뽑는다.
(B) 전원 버튼을 교체한다.
(C) 한 가지 기능을 조정한다.
(D) 한 시간 미리 켠다.

해설   온라인 답글에서 부와베흐 씨가 설명했던 문제를 언급하며 이를 해결하려면 적어도 한 시간은 기다린 후에 절전에 들어가도록 절전 모드 기능을 조정하라(adjust the sleep mode feature to wait at least an hour before going to sleep)고 조언했다. 따라서 (C)가 정답이다.

196-200 차트 + 고객 문의 + 고객 공지

바드슨 세탁기 시리즈

모델	적재 용량	196적재 문 위치	자동 세제통	애벌빨래 사이클
루트	9kg	196**전면**	있음	없음
제논	10kg	196**전면**	없음	없음
인디엄	12kg	196**전면**	있음	있음
197**머큐리**	14kg	196**전면**	있음	있음

주의: 적재 규모가 10킬로그램 이상인 바드슨 세탁기는 플럭스탯 물 절약 기술을 갖추고 있습니다.

바드슨 관련 문제

게시자: 패트리샤 캔턴

5개월 전 숙박 및 조식 제공 호텔에 사용하기 위해 바드슨 세탁기를 구입했습니다. 전반적으로 이 가전 제품의 기능에 만족합니다. 추가 헹굼 사이클은 세제에 들어 있는 화학 물질이나 향에 민감한 고객들에게 도움이 됩니다. 197일상적으로 나오는 분량의 침대보와 수건을 처리할 수 있는 용량이 가장 큰 세탁기가 필요했습니다. 198,200제 기계의 가장 큰

문제는 거슬리게 쾅쾅거리는 소리입니다. 투숙객이 기계를 사용할 때도 가끔 소리가 납니다. **¹⁹⁸투숙객들이 종종 식사를 하는 테라스 바로 옆에 세탁실이 있기 때문에 문제입니다.** 회사에 도움을 요청하는 메시지를 보내니 세탁통에 세탁물이 고르게 분포되어야 한다고 알려 주었습니다. 하지만 그건 문제의 원인이 아니었습니다. 소음을 어떻게 하면 없앨 수 있을까요?

> 어휘   appliance 가전   sensitive 민감한   chemicals 화학 물질   annoying 거슬리는   situated 위치한   patio 파티오, 테라스   evenly 고르게   distribute 분포하다   get rid of ~을 없애다

패티즈 B&B 투숙객 서비스:

주방:

오전 8시부터 9시 30분까지 제공되는 아침 식사를 테라스에서 드시면서 화창한 봄 날씨를 즐기세요. **¹⁹⁹커피와 차를 24시간 셀프 서비스로 제공합니다.** 가정용 커피메이커와 찻주전자는 가스레인지 옆에 있으며 비품은 근처에 있는 찬장에 보관되어 있습니다.

세탁실:

깨끗한 수건이 매일 제공되며 침대보는 매주 교체됩니다. 세탁기를 사용하려면 환경 보호 설정을 선택해 주세요. 선호하는 온도와 강도 설정을 선택하세요. **²⁰⁰세제를 추가할 때는 기계를 작동시키기 전에 세제통이 꽉 닫혔는지 반드시 확인하세요. 제대로 고정되지 않으면 헹굼 사이클 동안 열려서 거슬리는 소음이 날 수 있습니다.** 또한 세제에 민감하시다면 추가 헹굼 옵션을 추천합니다.

패트리샤 캔턴, 사장

> 어휘   temperature 온도   properly 적절히, 제대로   secure 고정시키다   bothersome 거슬리는, 성가신   sensitivity 민감함, 예민함

---

196   사실 관계 확인

번역   차트에 따르면 바드슨 세탁기의 모든 모델에 관해 사실인 것은?

   (A) 동일한 물 절약 기능을 사용한다.
   (B) 에너지 효율이 좋다.
   (C) 자동으로 세제가 나온다.
   (D) 가전제품 전면에 있는 문으로 세탁물을 넣는다.

해설   차트를 보면 모든 모델의 적재 문 위치(Loading Door Position)가 전면(Front)이라고 나와 있으므로, (D)가 정답이다.

197   연계

번역   캔턴 씨는 어떤 세탁기 모델을 구입했겠는가?

   (A) 루트   (B) 제논
   (C) 인디엄   (D) 머큐리

해설   캔턴 씨는 고객 문의에서 일상적으로 나오는 분량의 침대보와 수건을 처리할 수 있는 용량이 가장 큰 세탁기가 필요했다(I needed a washer with the largest capacity)고 했는데, 차트를 보면 적재 용량(Load Capacity)이 가장 큰 모델이 머큐리(Mercury)라고 나와 있다. 따라서 그녀가 이 모델을 구매했음을 추론할 수 있으므로, (D)가 정답이다.

---

198   세부 사항

번역   캔턴 씨의 문의에 따르면 언제 소음이 유난히 거슬리는가?

   (A) 자신이 세탁기를 사용할 때
   (B) 호텔 투숙객들이 자고 있을 때
   (C) 호텔 투숙객들이 식사를 하고 있을 때
   (D) 건조기도 함께 작동하고 있을 때

해설   캔턴 씨는 고객 문의에서 기계의 가장 큰 문제가 거슬리게 쾅쾅 거리는 소리(an annoying banging sound)라고 하며, 투숙객들이 종종 식사를 하는 테라스 바로 옆에 세탁실이 있기 때문에(because the laundry room is situated just off the patio where guests often dine) 문제가 된다고 했다. 따라서 (C)가 정답이다.

> ▸▸ Paraphrasing   지문의 **banging sound** → 질문의 **noise**
> 지문의 **dine** → 정답의 **are eating**

---

199   세부 사항

번역   공지에 따르면 언제든 고객이 이용할 수 있는 것은?

   (A) 깨끗한 수건
   (B) 따뜻한 음료
   (C) 점심 도시락
   (D) 객실 냉장고

해설   고객 공지의 주방(Kitchen) 부분을 보면, '커피와 차를 24시간 셀프 서비스로 제공합니다(We offer self-service for coffee and tea around the clock)'라고 했으므로, (B)가 정답이다.

> ▸▸ Paraphrasing   지문의 **offer ~ around the clock**
> → 질문의 **is available at any time**
> 지문의 **coffee and tea**
> → 정답의 **Hot beverages**

---

200   연계

번역   캔턴 씨는 문의에 대한 응답으로 어떤 조언을 받았겠는가?

   (A) 세탁기에 세탁물 너무 많이 넣지 않기
   (B) 항상 물 절약 설정 사용하기
   (C) 항상 추가 헹굼 기능 선택하기
   (D) 세제통이 꽉 닫혔는지 확인하기

해설   캔턴 씨는 고객 문의에서 거슬리게 쾅쾅거리는 소리(an annoying banging sound)를 없앨 방법을 알려 달라(How can I get rid of this noise?)고 요청했었다. 캔턴 씨가 작성한 공지의 세탁실(Laundry Room) 관련 부분을 보면, 기계를 작동시키기 전에 세제통이 꽉 닫혔는지 반드시 확인하라(make sure the detergent drawer is closed tightly before you start the machine)며 제대로 고정되지 않으면 헹굼 사이클 동안 거슬리는 소음이 날 수 있다(If not properly secured, it may ~ cause a bothersome noise)고 했다. 따라서 그녀가 회사로부터 세제통을 꼭 닫으라는 조언을 받았음을 추론할 수 있으므로, (D)가 정답이다.

> ▸▸ Paraphrasing   지문의 **the detergent drawer is closed tightly**
> → 정답의 **the soap drawer is firmly closed**

101 (A)	102 (D)	103 (B)	104 (D)	105 (C)
106 (B)	107 (D)	108 (B)	109 (A)	110 (C)
111 (D)	112 (D)	113 (C)	114 (D)	115 (D)
116 (D)	117 (D)	118 (D)	119 (C)	120 (C)
121 (A)	122 (A)	123 (C)	124 (B)	125 (B)
126 (C)	127 (D)	128 (D)	129 (A)	130 (A)
131 (A)	132 (D)	133 (C)	134 (D)	135 (B)
136 (C)	137 (D)	138 (B)	139 (D)	140 (B)
141 (A)	142 (B)	143 (C)	144 (A)	145 (B)
146 (D)	147 (B)	148 (B)	149 (B)	150 (A)
151 (C)	152 (C)	153 (B)	154 (A)	155 (C)
156 (B)	157 (A)	158 (B)	159 (D)	160 (A)
161 (B)	162 (A)	163 (A)	164 (C)	165 (B)
166 (B)	167 (C)	168 (C)	169 (D)	170 (B)
171 (B)	172 (B)	173 (B)	174 (A)	175 (C)
176 (B)	177 (C)	178 (C)	179 (D)	180 (A)
181 (C)	182 (B)	183 (C)	184 (A)	185 (D)
186 (B)	187 (C)	188 (A)	189 (B)	190 (A)
191 (B)	192 (D)	193 (C)	194 (A)	195 (C)
196 (D)	197 (D)	198 (A)	199 (C)	200 (B)

PART 5

101 인칭대명사의 격 _ 주격

해설 빈칸에는 are의 주어 역할을 하는 인칭대명사가 들어가야 한다. 문맥상 제품에 만족하지 않는(are not satisfied with an item) 주체와 반납하는(return it) 주체가 동일인이어야 하므로, 명령문(return ~)의 생략된 주어와 동일한 주격 인칭대명사 (A) you가 정답이다. 소유대명사인 (C) yours도 주어 자리에 들어갈 수 있지만, 해당 문장에서는 의미상 어색하므로 정답이 될 수 없다.

번역 제품에 만족하지 않으시면 구입 후 30일 이내에 전액 환불을 위해 제품을 반납해 주십시오.

어휘 full refund 전액 환불 purchase 구입, 구매

102 동사 어휘

해설 빈칸은 '아직 ~되지 않다'라는 의미의 「be+yet+to be p.p.」 구조를 완성하는 과거분사 자리로, 주어 The location과 가장 잘 어울리는 과거분사를 선택해야 한다. 문맥상 '장소가 아직 결정되지 않았다'라는 내용이 되어야 자연스러우므로, '결정된'이라는 의미의 (D) decided가 정답이다.

번역 다음달 온라인 게임 포럼이 열릴 장소는 아직 결정되지 않았다.

어휘 conclude 끝나다, 결론을 내리다 prevent 막다, 방지하다

103 형용사 자리 _ 주격 보어

해설 빈칸은 주어 Guests를 설명하는 주격 보어 자리이므로, 보기에서 형용사인 (A) impressive와 과거분사인 (B) impressed 중 하나를 선택해야 한다. 문맥상 '손님들은 테이블 장식에 감명을 받았다'라는 내용이 되어야 자연스러우며, 빈칸이 묘사하는 대상이 특정 감정을 느끼는 사람이므로, 과거분사인 (B) impressed가 정답이 된다. 참고로, impress가 '~에게 감명[감동]을 주다'라는 의미일 때는 진행형으로 쓰이지 않는다.

번역 손님들은 회사 연회용 테이블 장식에 깊은 인상을 받았다.

어휘 decoration 장식 banquet 연회

104 부사 어휘

해설 빈칸 뒤 형용사 effective를 적절히 수식하는 부사를 선택하는 문제이다. effective는 '효과적인, 유능한'이라는 의미이므로, 빈칸에는 주어인 The Schubert Company가 얼마나 유능한지를 묘사하는 부사가 들어가야 문맥상 자연스럽다. 따라서 '매우'라는 의미의 (D) very가 정답이다. (A) once는 '한때, 한 번', (C) early는 '일찍'이라는 의미로 문맥상 빈칸에 적절하지 않고, (B) far는 비교급 형용사 및 부사를 강조하는 부사이므로, 빈칸에 들어갈 수 없다.

번역 더 슈버트 컴퍼니는 발전소들이 이산화탄소 배출을 줄이도록 돕는 데 있어서 굉장히 유능하다.

어휘 effective 효과적인, 유능한 power plant 발전소 carbon dioxide 이산화탄소 emission 배출

105 동사 자리

해설 Mr. Hodges가 주어, 빈칸이 동사인 문장이므로, 보기 중 본동사 역할을 할 수 있는 (C) requests가 정답이다. 동명사/현재분사인 (A) requesting, to부정사인 (B) to be requested와 (D) to request는 문장에서 동사 역할을 할 수 없으므로 빈칸에 들어갈 수 없다.

번역 호지스 씨는 자원봉사자들에게 금요일까지 하녹 리버 청소를 돕는 일에 지원해 달라고 요청한다.

어휘 assist 돕다 request 요청하다

106 동사 어휘

해설 빈칸 뒤 목적어 the number of readers와 가장 잘 어울리는 동사를 선택하는 문제이다. 문맥상 '디지털 구독 옵션을 추가하여(by adding a digital subscription option) 구독자의 수를 늘렸다'라는 내용이 되어야 자연스러우므로, '늘렸다, 증가시켰다'라는 의미의 (B) increased가 정답이다.

번역 작년에 〈대전 영어 뉴스〉는 디지털 구독 옵션을 추가하여 구독자 수를 늘렸다.

어휘 subscription 구독(료)

107 명사 자리 _ 전치사의 목적어

해설 빈칸 앞 전치사 into의 목적어 역할을 하는 명사 자리이므로, 보기에서 명사인 (A) product, (B) producer, (D) production 중 하나를 선택해야 한다. 빈칸을 포함한 전치사구가 동사 can go를 수식하여 '제작에 들어가다'라는 내용이 되어야 문맥상 자연스러우므로, '생산, 제작'이라는 의미의 (D) production이 정답이 된다. 참고로, '생산자, 제작자'를 의미하는 (B) producer는 한정사(관사, 소유격 등) 없이 바로 빈칸에 들어갈 수 없고, (A) product는 일반적으로 가산명사로 쓰이며 특정 문맥에서 '상업 제품, 미용 제품'을 뜻하는 불가산명사로 쓰일 수 있으나, 빈칸에는 적절하지 않다. (C) productive는 형용사로 품사상 오답이다.

번역 업데이트된 디자인은 제작에 들어가기 전에 경영진의 승인을 받아야 한다.

어휘 go into production 생산을 개시하다   approve 승인하다

108 전치사 어휘

해설 빈칸은 명사구 the Xi'an Trade Tower를 목적어로 취하는 전치사 자리이며, 빈칸을 포함한 전치사구가 동사 will be held를 수식하고 있다. 따라서 빈칸에는 will be held와 장소를 나타내는 명사구 the Xi'an Trade Tower를 적절히 연결해 주는 전치사가 들어가야 한다. 문맥상 '시안 트레이드 타워에서 개최될 예정이다'라는 내용이 되어야 자연스러우므로, '~에(서)'라는 의미의 (B) at이 정답이다.

번역 경제 개발 정상 회담은 9월 22일에 시안 트레이드 타워에서 개최될 예정이다.

어휘 economic 경제의   summit 정상, 정상 회담

109 부사 자리 _ 형용사 수식

해설 빈칸은 형용사 responsible을 수식하는 부사 자리로, 악천후(Inclement weather)가 낮은 참석자 수에 얼마나 큰 원인이 되는지를 나타내는 부사가 빈칸에 들어가야 문맥상 자연스럽다. 따라서 '주로, 대체로'라는 의미의 (A) largely가 정답이다.

번역 토요일에 열렸던 엑스턴 뮤직 페스티벌의 참석자 수가 저조했던 것은 악천후가 주된 원인이었다.

어휘 inclement (날씨가) 좋지 못한, 혹독한   be responsible for ~에 책임이 있다, ~의 원인이 되다   turnout 참석자 수

110 등위 접속사

해설 빈칸 앞뒤 절을 자연스럽게 연결하는 접속사를 선택하는 문제이다. 문맥을 살펴보면, 빈칸 앞 절이 '다른 설문을 보내기에는 너무 이르다(it is too soon to send another one)'라는 판단에 대한 근거(최신 설문지가 지난주에 고객에게 전송되었다)를 나타내고 있다. 따라서 '그래서, 그러므로'라는 의미의 등위 접속사인 (C) so가 빈칸에 들어가야 자연스럽다. 부사절 접속사인 (A) when과 (B) since는 완전한 절을 이끌 수 있지만 문맥상 빈칸에 적절하지 않고, 부사인 (D) finally는 절을 이끌 수 없으므로 오답이다.

번역 우리의 최신 설문지가 지난주에 고객들에게 전송되었으니 다른 설문지를 보내기에는 너무 이르다.

111 수량 형용사 _ 수 일치

해설 빈칸은 뒤에 오는 단수 가산명사인 necklace를 한정 수식하는 자리이므로, 단수 가산명사와 수가 일치하는 수량 형용사 (D) Each가 정답이다. (C) All은 복수 가산명사 또는 불가산명사를 수식하므로 빈칸에 적절하지 않고, 부사절 접속사인 (A) Whenever와 부사인 (B) Also는 품사상 오답이다.

번역 길리스 디자이너스에서 배송되는 목걸이는 철저한 품질 검사를 거친다.

어휘 thorough 철저한   quality check 품질 검사

112 부사 어휘

해설 빈칸은 to부정사구(for her to be ~)와 함께 형용사 good을 뒤에서 수식하는 부사 자리이다. 문맥상 '이달의 직원상 대상으로 고려될 만큼 충분히 우수하다'라는 내용이 되어야 자연스러우므로, '충분히'라는 의미의 (D) enough가 정답이다. 참고로, 부사 enough는 항상 형용사, 부사, 동사 뒤에 위치한다.

번역 발데즈 씨의 판매 수치는 이달의 직원상 대상으로 고려될 만큼 충분히 우수하다.

어휘 award 상   forward (공간[시간]상) 앞으로   ahead (공간[시간]상) 앞에, 미리

113 재귀대명사

해설 빈칸 없이도 완전한 문장을 이루고 있으므로, 빈칸에는 '직접'이라는 의미로 행위의 주체를 강조하는 재귀대명사가 들어가야 한다. 문맥을 살펴보면, 집을 직접 설계하고(designed) 짓는(built) 행위의 주체는 집주인들(the homeowners)이므로 3인칭 복수 재귀대명사인 (C) themselves가 정답이 된다.

번역 아론 박의 새 저서에는 집주인들이 직접 설계하고 지은 집들의 사진이 실려 있다.

어휘 feature (특별히) 포함하다, 특징으로 삼다

114 형용사 어휘

해설 가주어(It)와 진주어(to hold its applause) 구문에서 주어를 묘사하는 형용사를 선택하는 문제이다. to부정사구의 의미상 주어인 청중(the audience)이 연사가 연설을 마칠 때까지 박수를 치지 않는 행위를 적절히 설명하는 단어가 빈칸에 들어가야 한다. 따라서 '관례의, 통상적인'이라는 의미의 (D) customary가 정답이다.

번역 연사가 끝마칠 때까지 청중이 박수를 치지 않는 것이 관례이다.

어휘 applause 박수   enthusiastic 열정적인   casual 격식을 차리지 않는   exclusive 배타적인, 독점적인

115 명사 자리 _ 전치사의 목적어

해설 빈칸은 전치사 Despite의 목적어 역할을 하는 명사 자리로, 뒤따르는 명사절(that Legend Air would perform ~ competition)과 동격 관계를 이루고 있다. 따라서 '(~할 것이라는) 예측(들)'이라는 의미의 명사인 (D) predictions가 정답이다. (A) predicted는 동사/과거분사, (B) predictable은 형용사, (C) predicts는 동사로 모두 품사상 빈칸에 적합하지 않다.

번역 레전드 에어는 가격이 더 저렴한 경쟁 업체의 등장으로 실적이 좋지 못할 것이라는 예측에도 불구하고 뛰어난 2분기 실적을 발표했다.

어휘 entry 등장 competition 경쟁, 경쟁 업체 post 발표하다 quarter 분기 earning 수익, 실적 predict 예측하다 predictable 예측할 수 있는

116 전치사(구) 어휘

해설 빈칸에 적절한 전치사(구)를 선택하는 문제이다. ------- retirement가 주어인 Mr. Nigam을 설명하는 주격 보어 역할을 하고 있으며, 문맥상 '니감 씨가 은퇴를 눈앞에 두고 있었다'라는 내용이 되어야 자연스러우므로, '~에 가까워진'이라는 의미의 (D) close to가 정답이다.

번역 사장에게서 새 공장의 보안팀장을 맡아 달라는 요청을 받았을 때 니감 씨는 은퇴를 눈앞에 두고 있었다.

어휘 retirement 퇴직, 은퇴 security 보안 facility 시설, 공장 nearby 인근의; 가까운 곳에

117 부사 자리 _ 과거분사 수식

해설 빈칸은 과거분사 prepared를 수식하는 부사 자리로, 문맥상 '세심하게 준비된 점심 및 저녁 식사'라는 내용이 되어야 자연스럽다. 따라서 '사려 깊게, 세심하게'라는 의미의 부사인 (D) thoughtfully가 정답이다. (A) thought는 명사/동사, (B) thoughtfulness, (C) thoughts는 명사로 품사상 빈칸에 적합하지 않다.

번역 메인 스트리트 레스토랑에서는 세심하게 준비한 점심 및 저녁 식사 메뉴를 제공한다.

118 부사 어휘

해설 빈칸에 적절한 부사를 선택하는 문제이다. 주절에서 현재완료(has been)를 사용하여 가자리언 씨가 언론 홍보 부서장(vice president of media relations)으로 임명되었다고 했으므로, 빈칸이 포함된 부분은 '예전에 우리의 홍보 부장이었던'이라는 내용이 되어야 자연스럽다. 따라서 '이전에, 예전에'라는 의미의 (D) Formerly가 정답이다.

번역 우리의 전임 홍보 부장이었던 가자리언 씨는 언론 홍보 부서장으로 임명되었다.

어휘 public relations 홍보 appoint 임명하다 vice president 부서장, 부사장 media relations 홍보 지원 sincerely 진심으로 immediately 즉시 solely 오로지, 단지

119 전치사 어휘

해설 빈칸은 명사 adolescents (worldwide)를 목적어로 취하는 전치사 자리이며, 빈칸을 포함한 전치사구가 보어인 (very) popular를 수식하고 있다. 따라서 빈칸에는 popular와 adolescents를 적절히 연결해 주는 전치사가 들어가야 한다. 문맥상 '전세계 청소년 사이에서 인기가 높아졌다'라는 내용이 되어야 자연스러우므로, '~ 사이에, ~ 중에'라는 의미의 (C) among이 정답이다. 참고로, (B) whereas는 접속사로, 뒤에 완전한 절이 와야 한다.

번역 케이팝 동영상은 전세계 청소년 사이에서 인기가 매우 높아졌다.

어휘 adolescent 청소년 whereas 반면에

120 부사 자리 _ 동사 수식

해설 빈칸은 동사 altered를 수식하는 부사 자리이므로, '빠르게'라는 의미의 부사인 (C) quickly가 정답이다. 형용사의 원급인 (A) quick과 최상급인 (B) quickest, 동사인 (D) quicken은 품사상 빈칸에 적합하지 않다. 참고로, 비격식체에서는 quick을 quickly 대신 부사로 사용할 수 있으나, 이 경우 움직임을 나타내는 동사 뒤에 위치한다.

번역 밀란테 슈즈는 최근의 경제 변화 이후 회사의 마케팅 전략을 발빠르게 변경했다.

어휘 alter 변경하다 strategy 전략 recent 최근의 shift 변화

121 등위 접속사

해설 빈칸 앞뒤 절을 자연스럽게 연결하는 접속사를 선택하는 문제이다. 앞 절(연례 보고서가 온라인에 게시되었다)과 뒤 절(이사실에서는 아직 인쇄본을 받지 못했다)이 서로 대조적인 내용을 나타내며, 대등한 관계를 이루고 있다. 따라서 '하지만, 그러나'라는 의미의 등위 접속사인 (A) but이 정답이다. (D) once도 접속사로 쓰이면 완전한 절을 이끌 수 있지만 '(일단) ~하면'이라는 의미이므로 문맥상 빈칸에 적절하지 않다.

번역 연례 보고서가 온라인에 게시되었지만 이사실에서는 아직 인쇄본을 받지 못했다.

어휘 post 게시하다

122 형용사 자리 _ 명사 수식

해설 빈칸은 관사 the와 명사 effects 사이 자리로, effects와 복합명사를 이루는 명사나 effects를 수식하는 형용사가 들어갈 수 있다. 문맥상 '수면의 긍정적인 효과에 대한 연구'라는 내용이 되어야 자연스러우므로, '좋은, 긍정적인'이라는 의미의 형용사인 (A) favorable이 정답이 된다. (B) favor와 (C) favors는 동사 이외에 명사로도 쓰이지만 effects와 복합명사를 이루지 않으며, 부사인 (D) favorably는 effects를 수식할 수 없다.

번역 하신 파리즈는 수면의 긍정적인 효과에 대한 연구를 베스트셀러로 만들어 냈다.

어휘 effect 효과, 영향

123 동사 어휘

해설 빈칸은 뒤에 오는 명사구 a yearly shutdown of its factory를 목적어로 취하는 현재분사 자리이며, 특정 목적을 나타내는 부사절(so that ~ efficiency)이 빈칸을 수식하고 있다. 따라서 빈칸에는 목적어 및 부사절과 가장 잘 어울리는 타동사가 들어가야 한다. 문맥상 '공장을 임시 휴업하여 안전 및 효율성 평가를 받을 수 있도록 한다'라는 내용이 되어야 자연스러우므로, '시행하고 있는'이라는 의미의 (C) implementing이 정답이다.

번역 윈스턴 컨테이너는 1년에 한 번씩 공장을 임시 휴업하여 안전 및 효율성 평가를 받을 수 있도록 한다.

어휘 shutdown 폐쇄, (임시) 휴업 evaluate 평가하다 efficiency 효율성 involve 수반하다

124 명사 어휘

해설 빈칸 앞 명사 plant와 복합명사를 이루어 동사 has의 목적어 역할을 하는 명사를 선택하는 문제로, 빈칸에는 식물 기록 보관소가 보유할 만한 대상을 나타내는 명사가 들어가야 자연스럽다. 따라서 '표본, 견본'이라는 뜻의 (B) specimens가 정답이다.

번역 지라드 식물 기록 보관소는 30만 점에 달하는 식물 표본을 보유하고 있으며, 모두 기록 용지에 깔끔하게 압착되어 있다.

어휘 neatly 깔끔하게 archival 기록의 authority 당국 founder 창립자 specifics 세부 사항

125 형용사 어휘

해설 빈칸 앞의 be동사 및 뒤에 나오는 to부정사구와 함께 쓰여 주어인 Hotels and universities를 적절히 설명하는 형용사를 선택해야 한다. 문맥상 '호텔과 대학은 중고 매트리스를 재활용할 수 있다'라는 내용이 되어야 자연스러우므로, '~할 수 있는, ~할 자격이 있는'이라는 의미의 (B) eligible이 정답이 된다.

번역 호텔과 대학은 시 재활용 프로그램을 통해 중고 매트리스를 재활용할 수 있다.

어휘 recycle 재활용하다 systematic 체계적인 familiar 익숙한

126 명사 자리 _ 동사의 주어

해설 빈칸에는 정관사 The 및 to부정사구(to review plans ~ Bridge)의 수식을 받으며 동사 will be scheduled의 주어 역할을 하는 명사가 들어가야 한다. 따라서 '공청회'라는 의미의 명사인 (C) hearing이 정답이다. (A) heard, (B) hears, (D) hear는 동사로 주어 자리에 들어갈 수 없으므로, 빈칸에 적합하지 않다.

번역 트런튼 브리지 교체 계획을 검토하는 공청회 일정이 곧 잡힐 것이다.

어휘 replace 교체하다 schedule 일정을 잡다 hearing 공판, 심리, 청력

127 부사절 접속사

해설 빈칸 뒤 분사구(reducing the impact on the environment)를 이끄는 동시에 앞에 있는 to부정사구(to optimize quality)를 수식하는 부사절 접속사 자리이다. 빈칸 앞 to부정사구(품질을 최적화하는 것)와 뒤따르는 분사구(환경에 미치는 영향을 줄이는 것)가 모두 이루고자 하는 목표를 나타내고 있으므로, '~와 동시에, ~하는 동안'이라는 의미의 (B) while이 정답이 된다. 참고로, 보기 중 주어와 be동사가 생략된 현재분사구를 이끌 수 있는 접속사는 while뿐이다.

번역 코복스사는 환경에 미치는 영향을 줄이는 동시에 품질을 최적화하는 것을 목표로 한다.

어휘 aim 목표하다 optimize 최적화하다 impact 영향 environment 환경

128 동사 어형 _ 시제

해설 빈칸에 적절한 동사의 시제를 선택하는 문제이다. 부사절 접속사 until(~할 때까지)이 이끄는 절에 과거 시제(went down)가 쓰였으므로, 주절에는 과거 이전에 발생한 일을 나타내는 시제가 쓰여야 한다. 즉, '지난달 현지 가격이 내려갈 때까지 시외에서 채소를 구매해 오고 있었다'라는 내용이 되어야 자연스러우므로, 과거완료 진행형인 (D) had been buying이 정답이 된다.

번역 그 식료품점은 지난달에 현지 가격이 내려갈 때까지 시 외곽에서 채소를 구매해 오고 있었다.

어휘 local 지역의, 현지의

129 to부정사 관용표현

해설 빈칸에는 동사원형 enter와 결합하여 앞에 있는 must have a valid ID card를 수식하는 표현이 들어가야 한다. 따라서 동사원형과 함께 쓰여 '~하기 위해'라는 목적을 나타내는 (A) in order to가 정답이다. 참고로, 부사절 접속사인 (B) as long as 뒤에는 동사원형이 바로 올 수 없고, 전치사인 (C) regarding 뒤에는 명사가 와야 한다. 부사인 (D) always는 동사원형인 enter를 수식할 수 있지만, 이렇게 될 경우 하나의 절에 두 개의 본동사가 있게 되므로 비문이 된다.

번역 올 허쉘 인더스트리즈 직원은 건물에 들어가려면 유효한 ID 카드를 소지해야 한다.

어휘 valid 유효한 regarding ~에 관해

130 명사 어휘

해설 빈칸은 cost와 함께 동사 factored의 주어 역할을 하는 명사 자리이며, 주어의 행위를 나타내는 동사 factored는 부사 equally와 전치사구 in choosing ~ as our main supplier의 수식을 받고 있다. 따라서 주요 공급 업체를 선정함에 있어 비용(cost)과 더불어 고려할 만한 사항을 나타내는 명사가 빈칸에 들어가야 자연스러우므로, '신뢰도, 확실성'이라는 의미의 (A) Reliability가 정답이 된다.

번역 우리의 주요 공급 업체로 캔타복스를 선택하는 데 있어서 신뢰도와 비용을 똑같이 고려했다.

어휘 factor 요인; 요인으로 작용하다 supplier 공급 업체 allowance 허용량 dependence 의존성 estimation 판단, 평가

PART 6

131-134 편지

PGD 예금주님께,

PGD 은행은 최고 수준의 고객 보안 및 서비스를 ¹³¹**제공하고자 노력하고 있습니다.** 이는 온라인 및 전화 서비스뿐 아니라 실제 지점에서도 마찬가지입니다. 저희 지점 세 곳은 모두 합쳐 40년 ¹³²**동안** 지역 사회의 자랑스러운 일원이 되어 왔습니다.

향후 더 나은 서비스로 고객님들을 도와 드리기 위해 저희 스미스빌 지점은 7월 8일부터 22일까지 보수 공사를 진행하며, 이 기간 동안 임시로 휴무합니다. ¹³³**이로 인해 불편을 끼쳐 드리게 되어 죄송합니다.** 그 동안 파인그로브와 브래드포드에 있는 타 지점 두 곳은 정상 영업¹³⁴**시간**을 유지합니다. 저희는 고객님의 의견을 소중히 반영하겠으며, 우려하시는 모든 사항에 최대한 신속히 답변해 드리겠습니다.

에드윈 첸, 업무 팀장
PGD 은행

어휘 account 계좌 strive to ~하고자 힘쓰다 security 보안 apply 적용되다 brick-and-mortar 소매의, 오프라인 거래의 branch office 지점 temporarily 임시로 renovation 개조, 보수 in the meantime 그 동안 regional 지역의 respond 반응하다, 응답하다 concern 우려, 관심사

131 to부정사 _ 부사적 용법

해설 빈칸은 명사구 the highest levels ~ service를 목적어로 취하는 동시에 자동사인 strives를 수식하는 자리이다. 따라서 '제공하기 위해'라는 의미로 목적을 나타내는 to부정사 (A) to provide가 정답이다. 분사인 (B) provided, (C) providing은 자동사 strives를 수식할 수 없고, to부정사의 수동형인 (D) to be provided는 목적어를 취할 수 없으므로 빈칸에 들어갈 수 없다.

132 전치사 어휘

해설 빈칸은 기간을 나타내는 명사구 a combined total of 40 years를 목적어로 취하는 전치사 자리이며, 빈칸을 포함한 전치사구가 현재완료 동사구 have proudly been a part of the community를 수식하고 있다. 따라서 이들을 적절히 연결해 주는 전치사를 선택해야 하므로, '~ 동안'이라는 의미로 현재완료와 자주 쓰이는 (D) for가 정답이 된다.

어휘 amid ~ 중에, ~로 에워싸인

133 문맥에 맞는 문장 고르기

번역 (A) 안타깝게도, 서비스가 제한됩니다.
(B) 그동안 PGD 은행을 신뢰해 주셔서 감사합니다.
(C) 이로 인해 불편을 끼쳐 드리게 되어 죄송합니다.
(D) 대로의 교통량이 최근 증가했습니다.

해설 빈칸 앞에서 스미스빌 지점이 보수 공사로 임시 휴무한다(our Smithville branch will be temporarily closed for

renovations)는 불편 사항을 언급했으므로, 빈칸에는 이에 대해 사과를 하거나 양해를 구하는 내용이 들어가야 문맥상 자연스럽다. 따라서 (C)가 정답이다. 참고로, (C)의 this는 앞 절을 가리킨다.

어휘 limit 제한하다 inconvenience 불편 boulevard 대로

134 명사 어휘

해설 빈칸 앞 business와 복합명사를 이루며 형용사 normal의 수식을 받는 명사를 선택하는 문제이다. 빈칸 앞 문장에서 스미스빌 지점이 임시 휴무한다(our Smithville branch will be temporarily closed)고 했으므로, 해당 문장은 '타 지점 두 곳은 정상 영업 시간을 유지한다'는 내용이 되어야 문맥상 자연스럽다. 따라서 business와 함께 '영업 시간'이라는 복합명사를 완성하는 (C) hours가 정답이다.

어휘 investment 투자

135-138 이메일

수신: 새뮤얼 아처슨 〈sarcherson@vona.co.uk〉
발신: 제임스 대러스 〈jdarrers@sky.co.uk〉
날짜: 1월 10일
제목: 원가 회계사직

아처슨 씨께,

오늘 제게 시간을 내 주셔서 감사했습니다. 함께 나눈 대화도 ¹³⁵**즐거웠고,** 저는 아직도 원가 회계사직에 큰 관심이 갑니다. 3차 및 최종 ¹³⁶**면접**을 보러 다시 올 수 있는 기회가 있었으면 좋겠습니다.

수년간의 제 회계 경력이 귀사에 도움이 될 것으로 확신합니다. 말씀드린 바와 같이 저는 지난 10년 동안 많은 업체들이 ¹³⁷**상당한** 금액을 절약하도록 도왔습니다. 저는 특히 업체의 일일 영업 활동을 분석하고 그들이 비용 대비 더 효율적인 방법을 찾을 수 있도록 도와주는 데 능숙합니다.

업무 시작이 가능한 날짜 관련 질문에 대해 확인해 보았습니다. ¹³⁸**2월 첫째 주 중에 일을 시작할 수 있습니다.** 빠른 시일 내에 연락 주시기 바랍니다.

제임스 대러스

어휘 remain ~한 상태로 남아 있다 opportunity 기회 confident 자신 있는 accounting 회계 adept 능숙한 analyse 분석하다 day-to-day operations 일일 영업 활동, 일상 업무 determine 알아내다, 결정하다 cost-effective 비용 대비 효율적인 regarding ~에 관해 potential 잠재적인, 가능성이 있는; 잠재력

135 동사 어형 _ 시제

해설 빈칸은 주격 인칭대명사 I의 동사 자리로, 빈칸 뒤 명사구 our conversation을 목적어로 취한다. 앞 문장에서 오늘 시간을 내주어 감사하다(Thank you for taking the time to meet with me today)고 했으므로, 빈칸에는 만나서 나눈 대화가 즐거웠다는 과거 시제 동사가 들어가야 문맥상 자연스럽다. 따라서 '즐겼다'라는 의미의 (B) enjoyed가 정답이 된다.

TEST 7

136 명사 어휘

해설 빈칸에 적절한 명사를 선택하는 문장이다. 앞 문장에서 아직도 원가 회계사직에 큰 관심이 간다(I remain very interested in the position of cost accountant)고 했으므로, 빈칸을 포함한 부분은 '3차 및 최종 면접을 볼 기회'라는 구직 절차와 관련된 내용이 되어야 자연스럽다. 따라서 '면접'이라는 의미의 (C) interviews가 정답이다.

어휘 revision 수정, 변경 promotion 승진 reception 접수처, 환영[축하] 연회

137 형용사 자리 _ 명사 수식

해설 빈칸은 불가산명사를 수식하는 표현인 「a ------- amount of」에서 명사 amount를 수식하는 형용사 자리이다. 따라서 '상당한'이라는 의미의 형용사인 (D) substantial이 정답이 된다. (A) substance는 명사, (B) substantiate는 동사, (C) substantially는 부사로, 모두 품사상 빈칸에 적합하지 않다.

어휘 substance 물질 substantiate 입증하다 substantially 상당히

138 문맥에 맞는 문장 고르기

번역 (A) 여쭤볼 질문이 네 가지 더 있습니다.
(B) 2월 첫째 주 중에 일을 시작할 수 있습니다.
(C) 제가 이 직책에 대한 잠재력이 있다고 확신합니다.
(D) 채용해 주셔서 감사합니다.

해설 빈칸 앞 문장에서 업무 시작이 가능한 날짜 관련 질문에 대해 확인해 보았다(I checked regarding your question about a potential start date)고 했으므로, 빈칸에는 이에 대한 구체적인 내용이 들어가야 문맥상 자연스럽다. 따라서 (B)가 정답이다.

어휘 additional 추가의

139-142 이메일

수신: 메이슨 우 〈mwu@wustudios.co.nz〉
발신: 트렌트 튜일로마 〈ttuiloma@canterburyairport.co.nz〉
제목: 캔터베리 공항 프로젝트
날짜: 7월 2일 월요일

우 씨께,

캔터베리 공항 재설계 프로젝트 컨설팅을 맡는 데 동의해 주셔서 감사합니다. **139귀하께서 지역 공항들에 하셨던 작업에 오랫동안 감탄해 왔습니다.** 그래서 저희 메인 터미널 개선에 대한 의견을 특히 듣고 싶습니다.

이번 주에 만나 뵐 수 있을까요? 제 사무실 근처에 **140훌륭한** 식당이 많이 있습니다. 이번 금요일에 시간이 되시면 컴버랜드 스트리트에 있는 셀리아 카페에서 만날 수 있습니다. 제 동료 몇 명이 **141자리를 함께 했으면** 하는데요. 그들은 공항 이용자들의 경험을 향상시킬 수 있는 방법을 **142논의하고** 싶어 할 겁니다.

답장 기다리겠습니다.

트렌트 튜일로마
캔터베리 공항 재설계 팀장

어휘 consult on ~에 대해 상담하다 particularly 특히, 특별히 be eager to ~하고 싶어 하다 available 시간이 있는 colleague 동료 appreciate 환영하다 enhance 향상하다 look forward to -ing ~하기를 고대하다

139 문맥에 맞는 문장 고르기

번역 (A) 도착하실 때 만나 뵐 수 있습니다.
(B) 비행 일정을 잡는 것은 꽤 어렵습니다.
(C) 귀하께서 지역 공항들에 하셨던 작업에 오랫동안 감탄해 왔습니다.
(D) 공항에는 여러 가지 식사 옵션이 있습니다.

해설 빈칸 앞 문장에서 공항 재설계 프로젝트 컨설팅을 맡는 데 동의해 주어 감사하다(Thank you for agreeing to consult on the Canterbury Airport redesign project)고 했고, 빈칸 뒤 문장에서 메인 터미널 개선에 대한 의견을 특히 듣고 싶다(I am particularly eager to hear your ideas about upgrading our main terminal)며 구체적인 컨설팅 내용을 언급했으므로, 빈칸에도 우 씨의 컨설팅 작업과 관련된 내용이 들어가야 문맥상 자연스럽다. 따라서 (C)가 정답이다.

어휘 tricky 까다로운, 힘든 admire 감탄하다, 존경하다

140 형용사 자리 _ 명사 수식

해설 빈칸은 수량 형용사 a number of와 명사 restaurants 사이에서 restaurants를 수식하는 형용사 자리이다. 따라서 '훌륭한, 우수한'이라는 의미의 형용사인 (B) excellent가 정답이다. (A) excel, (D) excelled는 동사, (C) excellently는 부사로 품사상 빈칸에 적합하지 않다.

어휘 excel 뛰어나다, 탁월하다

141 동사 어휘

해설 빈칸에 적절한 동사를 선택하는 문제이다. 앞 문장에서 카페에서 만날 것(we could meet at ~ Café)을 제안했으므로, 해당 문장은 '동료 몇 명이 우리와 자리를 함께했으면 한다'라는 내용이 되어야 문맥상 자연스럽다. 따라서 '함께하다, 합류하다'라는 의미의 (A) join이 정답이다.

어휘 remind 상기시키다, 다시 한 번 알려 주다 defend 방어하다, 수호하다

142 동명사 _ 동사의 목적어

해설 They가 주어, would appreciate가 동사인 문장으로, 빈칸에는 명사 ways를 목적어로 취하는 동시에 동사 appreciate의 목적어 역할을 하는 준동사가 들어가야 한다. '~를 감사하다, 환영하다'라는 의미의 타동사 appreciate는 명사나 동명사를 목적어로 취하므로, (B) discussing이 정답이다. (D) discussed가 과거분사로 명사 ways를 수식한다고 가정할 경우 문맥상 어색해지므로 (D)는 빈칸에 적절하지 않다.

143-146 기사

> 샤이어스베리 (2월 15일)—제2회 연례 샤이어스베리 영화 축제가 4월 18일에 시작되어 5주간 **143계속될 예정입니다.** 올해 상영작들은 북아메리카와 유럽 출품작에 국한되지 않으며, 아시아 및 남아메리카 **144영화들**도 상영할 예정입니다. 작년 축제에서 모두가 가장 좋아했던 특별 행사가 올해 재연되는데요. 감독과 시나리오 작가가 영화 최초 상영 후 질의응답 시간을 갖는 것입니다. 이 **145인기 높은** 행사를 놓치지 마세요. 입장권은 항상 빠르게 매진됩니다. **1463월 3일에 일반 대중에게 판매가 개시됩니다.** 샤이어스베리 영화 동호회 회원들은 우선 입장권을 지금 구매할 수 있습니다. 샤이어스베리 극장 매표소 또는 www.shiresberrytheater.com을 방문하세요.

> 어휘 annual 연례의 offering 제공되는 것, 내놓은 작품 be limited to ~로 국한되다 screenwriter 시나리오 작가 question-and-answer session 질의응답 시간 initial 최초의 sell out 매진되다 priority 우선권

143 동사 어형 _ 시제

해설 빈칸은 동사 begins와 함께 The second annual Shiresberry Film Festival의 동사 역할을 하는 자리로, 기간을 나타내는 전치사구 for five weeks의 수식을 받는다. 기사를 쓴 날짜가 2월 15일이고 행사 시작일이 4월 18일이므로, 해당 부분은 '5주간 계속될 예정입니다'라는 내용이 되어야 문맥상 자연스럽다. 따라서 미래를 나타내는 (C) will run이 정답이다.

144 명사 어휘

해설 빈칸에 적절한 명사를 선택하는 문제이다. 앞에서 '제2회 연례 샤이어스베리 영화 축제(The second annual Shiresberry Film Festival)'가 열릴 예정이라고 했으므로, 빈칸에는 영화제에서 보여 줄 만한 대상이 되는 명사가 들어가야 한다. 따라서 (A) movies가 정답이다.

145 형용사 어휘

해설 뒤에 오는 명사 event를 적절히 수식하는 형용사를 선택하는 문제이다. 앞에서 작년 축제 때 모두가 가장 좋아했던 특별 행사가 올해 재연된다(everyone's favorite feature from last year's festival will be back)고 한 후 그 행사를 자세히 설명(directors and screenwriters will hold question-and-answer sessions)하고 있으므로, 빈칸에 'everyone's favorite'과 비슷한 의미를 지닌 형용사가 들어가야 글의 흐름이 자연스러워진다. 따라서 '인기 있는'이라는 의미의 (B) popular가 정답이다.

어휘 political 정치적인 preliminary 예비의

146 문맥에 맞는 문장 고르기

번역 (A) 헌터 존스가 시상할 예정입니다.
(B) 개조 공사는 거의 완료되었습니다.
(C) 더 늦게 선보인 작품이 훨씬 더 성공적이었습니다.
(D) 3월 3일에 일반 대중에게 판매가 개시됩니다.

해설 빈칸 앞 문장에서 입장권은 항상 빠르게 매진된다(Tickets always sell out quickly)고 했고, 빈칸 뒤 문장에서 샤이어스베리 영화 동호회 회원들은 우선 입장권을 지금 구매할 수 있다(Shiresberry Film Club members can now purchase priority tickets)고 했으므로, 빈칸에도 입장권 구매와 관련된 내용이 언급되는 것이 문맥상 자연스럽다. 따라서 (D)가 정답이다.

어휘 present an award 시상하다 nearly 거의 complete 완료된

PART 7

147-148 광고

> **세드윅 일렉트로닉스 채용 행사**
>
> 3월 2일, 오전 10시–오후 5시
> 22 마이어 스트리트, 하노버, 펜실베니아 17331
>
> **148세드윅 일렉트로닉스가 펜실베이니아 주 하노버에 제조 공장을 신설할 예정이어서 147다수의 직원을 충원해야 합니다.** 당사는 직원들에게 훌륭한 업무 환경 및 복리 후생을 제공하고 있습니다.
>
> **148행사에 참석하셔서 랭커스터 공장 직원들의 경험담을 듣고, 147공석에 대해 알아보신 후 채용 담당자들과 이야기를 나눠 보세요.** 참석 여부는 통지하지 않으셔도 됩니다. 이력서 사본을 지참하십시오.

> 어휘 hiring 채용 manufacturing facility 제조 시설, 제조 공장 fill a position 자리를 채우다 environment 환경 open position 공석 recruiter 채용 담당자 RSVP (répondez s'il vous plait) 초대에 대한 회답; 회답하다

147 추론 / 암시

번역 광고는 누구를 위한 것인가?
(A) 채용 담당자
(B) 구직자
(C) 지역 업체 소유주
(D) 세드윅 일렉트로닉스 현 직원

해설 첫 번째 단락에서 다수의 직원을 충원해야 한다(we need to fill many positions)고 언급했고 두 번째 단락에서 공석에 대해 알아보고 채용 담당자들과 이야기를 나눠 볼 것(learn about the open positions, and speak with our recruiters)을 제안했으므로, 구직자를 위한 광고라는 것을 알 수 있다. 따라서 (B)가 정답이다.

148 사실 관계 확인

번역 세드윅 일렉트로닉스에 대해 명시된 것은?
(A) 본사를 이전할 예정이다.
(B) 신입 직원에게 교육 프로그램을 제공한다.
(C) 직원은 유니폼을 착용해야 한다.
(D) 소재지가 한 곳이 넘을 것이다.

해설 첫 번째 단락에서 펜실베이니아주 하노버에 제조 공장을 신설할
예정(opening a new manufacturing facility in Hanover,
Pennsylvania)이라고 했고, 두 번째 단락에서 랭커스터 공장 직원들
(employees from our Lancaster facility)이 채용 행사에 참여
한다는 것으로 보아 회사의 소재지가 두 곳 이상이 될 것임을 알 수 있
다. 따라서 (D)가 정답이다.

어휘 headquarters 본사 require 요구하다

149-150 공지

아구니 플러밍 서플라이 반품

^{149}3월 1일부터 고객 여러분께서는 아구니 플러밍 서플라이 전 지점에
서 온라인으로 구매하신 모든 제품을 반품하실 수 있습니다. $^{150(B)}$전액
환불을 받으시려면 구입 후 30일 이내에 반품이 이루어져야 하며 영수
증을 지참하셔야 합니다. 아울러 $^{150(D)}$상품은 원래의 포장 상태로 반품
되어야 하며, $^{150(C)}$모든 구성품이 다 들어 있어야 합니다. 30일이 경과
하면 환불은 매장 내 사용 가능한 포인트로만 제한됩니다. 결함이 있는
상품은 동일 제품으로만 교환 가능합니다.

어휘 plumbing 배관 return 반납, 반품; 반품하다 purchase
구매 complete refund 전액 환불 accompany ~를 동반하다,
수반하다 packaging 포장 component 구성 요소, 부품
include 포함하다 limit 제한하다 credit 크레딧, (현금처럼 쓸 수
있는) 포인트, (추가되는) 금액 defective 결함이 있는 exchange
교환하다

149 세부 사항

번역 3월 1일에 어떤 일이 있을 것인가?

(A) 수송품이 반환될 것이다.
(B) 새로운 정책이 실시될 것이다.
(C) 판촉 판매가 이뤄질 것이다.
(D) 고객 설문 조사가 발표될 것이다.

해설 첫 번째 문장에서 3월 1일부터(Beginning March 1) 아구니 플러밍
서플라이 전 지점에서 온라인으로 구매한 전 제품을 반품할 수 있다
(at all Aguni Plumbing Supply locations, customers will be
able to ~ return purchases made online)는 새로운 정책을 언
급했으므로, (B)가 정답이다.

어휘 shipment 수송품 policy 정책 go into effect 발효되다,
실시되다 promotional 홍보성의, 판촉의 publish 발표하다

150 사실 관계 확인

번역 전액 환불에 대한 요건이 아닌 것은?

(A) 원래 구매한 지점에서만 반품이 가능하다.
(B) 특정 기간 이내에만 반품이 가능하다.
(C) 제품의 모든 구성품을 반납해야 한다.
(D) 제품은 원래 포장 상태로 반납해야 한다.

해설 '구입 후 30일 이내에 반품이 이루어져야 한다(the return must
be made within 30 days of purchase)'에서 (B)를, '모든 구성
품이 다 들어 있어야 한다(all components must be included)'
에서 (C)를, '상품은 원래의 포장 상태로 반품되어야 한다(the

merchandise must be returned in the original packaging)'
에서 (D)를 확인할 수 있다. 그러나 원래 구매한 지점에서만 반품이
가능하다는 요건은 언급되지 않았으므로, (A)가 정답이다.

어휘 requirement 요구 조건 original 원래의 time frame 기간

▶ Paraphrasing 지문의 within 30 days of purchase
→ 보기 (B)의 within a certain time frame
지문의 all components must be included
→ 보기 (C)의 with all its components
지문의 the merchandise
→ 보기 (D)의 The item

151-152 정보문

스프링필드 지역 사회 학교
컴퓨터 과정

인터넷 보안
본 과정에서는 수강생들이 안전하게 웹을 탐색하는 데 필요한 모든 사
항을 가르칩니다.

코스 ID	강의 시간	강사	강의실
249800: 01	화요일 오후 5:30-7:30	패트릭 맥캔	211
249800: 02	^{152}토요일 오후 1:00-3:00	^{152}노라 패리드	166

스프레드시트 기초
^{151}본 과정에서는 온라인 스프레드시트의 기초를 가르칩니다. 수강생은
데이터를 정확하고 쉽게 계산하고 분석하는 데 필요한 효과적인 차트 생
성 방법을 학습하게 됩니다.

코스 ID	강의 시간	강사	강의실
225810: 01	목요일 오후 5:30-8:30	^{151}레미 샌더스	118
225810: 02	^{152}일요일 오후 1:00-4:00	^{152}노라 패리드	315

어휘 safety 안전, 보안 navigate (인터넷 등을) 돌아다니다,
탐색하다 effective 효과적인 calculate 계산하다 analyze
분석하다

151 추론 / 암시

번역 사람들은 왜 샌더스 씨가 가르치는 과정에 등록하겠는가?

(A) 웹사이트 디자인 연습을 위해
(B) 인터넷 검색 능력 향상을 위해
(C) 스프레드시트 생성에 대한 조언을 얻기 위해
(D) 인터넷에 광고하는 방법을 배우기 위해

해설 샌더스 씨가 가르치는 스프레드시트 기초(Spreadsheet Basics) 과
정에서 데이터를 정확하고 쉽게 계산하고 분석하는 데 필요한 효과적
인 차트 생성 방법(how to create effective charts ~ easily)을
학습할 수 있다고 했다. 따라서 (C)가 정답이다.

어휘 enroll in ~에 등록하다 improve 향상시키다

152 사실 관계 확인

번역 패리드 씨에 대해 명시된 것은?

(A) 아이들도 가르친다.
(B) 샌더스 씨의 상관이다.
(C) 주 2회 가르친다.
(D) 데이터 분석가로 일했었다.

해설 수업 시간표를 보면 패리드 씨가 토요일에는 인터넷 보안(Internet Safety) 과정을, 일요일에는 스프레드시트 기초(Spreadsheet Basics) 과정을 가르치는 것을 알 수 있다. 따라서 (C)가 정답이다.

어휘 supervisor 감독관, 상관   analyst 분석가

153-154 문자 메시지

샐리 위덤 (오후 4시 47분)
안녕하세요, 와키코. 방금 이곳 교토 매장에서 업무를 마쳤습니다. ¹⁵³내일 아침 11시 35분에 도쿄에 도착하는 기차를 탈 예정입니다. 당신이 있는 매장에 어떻게 가야 하나요?

와키코 오하라 (오후 4시 48분)
제 동료가 역으로 데리러 갈 수 있도록 할게요. ¹⁵⁴교토 매장은 어때요?

샐리 위덤 (오후 4시 49분)
¹⁵⁴교토 매장은 잘해 나가고 있어요. 본사에서 바라는 모든 것을 갖추고 있죠. 운동화와 샌들은 사양에 따라 진열되어 있고 판매 사원들은 친절하고 제품에 대해 잘 알고 있어요.

와키코 오하라 (오후 4시 51분)
저희 매장도 마음에 드실 거예요. 점심 식사 후 2시 정도에 방문하시겠어요?

샐리 위덤 (오후 4시 52분)
좋습니다. 내일 뵐게요.

어휘 associate 동료   athletic shoes 운동화   according to ~에 따라   specification 사양, 설명서   sales associate 판매원   knowledgeable 아는 것이 많은

153 주제 / 목적

번역 위덤 씨는 오하라 씨에게 왜 연락했는가?

(A) 매출액을 검토하기 위해
(B) 매장 방문 일정을 잡기 위해
(C) 직원 인사 고과에 대해 논의하기 위해
(D) 탑승이 가장 편리한 기차를 정하기 위해

해설 위덤 씨가 오후 4시 47분 메시지에서 내일 아침 11시 35분에 도쿄 도착하는 기차를 탈 예정(I'll be on the train ~ tomorrow morning)이라고 한 후, 기차역에서 오하라 씨의 매장까지 가는 방법을 문의(How should I get to your location?)했으므로, 매장 방문 일정을 잡기 위해 연락했음을 알 수 있다. 따라서 (B)가 정답이다.

어휘 sales figure 매출액   arrange 주선하다, 마련한다   performance review 인사 고과   determine 결정하다, 판단하다   convenient 편리한

154 의도 파악

번역 오후 4시 51분에 오하라 씨가 "저희 매장도 마음에 드실 거예요"라고 쓸 때, 그 의도는 무엇인가?

(A) 도쿄 매장이 회사 정책에 따라 운영되고 있다.
(B) 위덤 씨에게 필요한 운동화가 있을 것이다.
(C) 오하라 씨의 동료는 항상 시간을 잘 지킨다.
(D) 도쿄 매장은 유명한 음식점 옆에 있다.

해설 오하라 씨가 오후 4시 48분 메시지에서 교토 매장의 상황을 묻자(How do things look in Kyoto?), 위덤 씨가 오후 4시 49분 메시지에서 교토 매장은 잘해 나가고 있고(The Kyoto store is doing a great job), 본사에서 바라는 모든 것을 갖추고 있다(It has everything that we at the home office are looking for)며 칭찬했다. 이에 대해 오하라 씨가 '저희 매장도 마음에 드실 거예요(You should like things here, too)'라고 반응했으므로, 도쿄 매장 역시 본사의 정책에 따라 잘 운영되고 있다는 의도로 말한 것임을 추론할 수 있다. 따라서 (A)가 정답이다.

어휘 corporate 회사의   punctual 시간을 엄수하는

155-157 보고서

건축물: 블레인 리버 드로우브리지
위치: 리지라인 고속도로, 기점에서 147킬로미터 지점
주요 경간 소재: 철골보
소유주: 주 고속도로국
구조물 연식: 30년
¹⁵⁵보고서 작성자: 비비안 튤리오
일자: 10월 17일

비고:
¹⁵⁵본 교량은 전반적으로 구조적 이상이 없습니다. 아스팔트의 작은 균열에 대해 교통부에 알려 주십시오.

교량 구성 요소	등급	등급 설명
지지물	4	1 망가짐; 즉각 폐쇄 요망
타워	4	2 노후함; 곧 망가질 수 있음
¹⁵⁶도로 표면	¹⁵⁶3	3 노후화 징후가 보이나 용인 가능한 한도 내에서 기능함
배수 시설	4	4 작은 마모가 보임
안전벽	5	5 신축
¹⁵⁷인도/보도	¹⁵⁷6	¹⁵⁷6 해당 없음

어휘 structure 건축물   drawbridge 도개교   material 소재   complete 완료하다   overall 전체적으로   sound 이상 없는, 손상되지 않은   crack 금, 균열   component 구성 요소   rating 등급   element 요소   surface 표면   drainage 배수   barrier 장벽   sidewalk 보도   immediate 즉각적인   deteriorate 악화되다   acceptable 용인[허용] 가능한   parameter 한도, 변수   applicable 해당되는, 적용할 수 있는

155 추론 / 암시

번역 튤리오 씨는 무엇을 했겠는가?

(A) 수리하기
(B) 도급 업체 고용하기
(C) 검사 실행하기
(D) 건설 계획 승인하기

해설 보고서 작성자인 튤리오 씨(Report completed by: Vivian Tulio)가 비고란(Notes)에 전반적으로 교량에 구조적 이상이 없으며(The bridge is overall structurally sound), 아스팔트의 작은 균열에 대해서는 교통부에 알리라고(Inform Department of Transportation about small cracks in asphalt) 적었으므로, 튤리오 씨가 교량 검사를 실행했음을 추론할 수 있다. 따라서 (C)가 정답이다.

어휘 contractor 계약자[업체], 도급업자[체] inspection 검사 authorize 승인하다 construction 건설

156 세부 사항

번역 건축물의 어느 부분에 유지 보수가 가장 필요한가?

(A) 지지물
(B) 도로 표면
(C) 배수 시설
(D) 안전벽

해설 교량 구성 요소(Bridge component)의 등급(Rating)을 살펴보면, 도로 표면(Road surface)이 3등급으로 다른 부분들보다 낮은 등급을 받았으므로, 유지 보수가 가장 필요한 부분으로 볼 수 있다. 따라서 (B)가 정답이다.

어휘 maintenance 유지 보수

> ▶▶ Paraphrasing   지문의 **Bridge component**
> → 질문의 **part of the structure**

157 추론 / 암시

번역 블레인 리버 드로우브리지에 대해 사실인 것은?

(A) 보행 목적으로 만들어지지 않았다.
(B) 10월에 폐쇄될 예정이다.
(C) 필요한 신호 체계가 없다.
(D) 리지라인 고속도로에서 가장 오래된 교량이다.

해설 교량 구성 요소(Bridge component)에 등급을 매긴 부분을 보면, 인도/보도(Sidewalk or walkway)가 '해당 없음(Not applicable)'인 6등급으로 분류되었으므로, 교량이 보행 목적으로 만들어지지 않았다는 것을 추론할 수 있다. 따라서 (A)가 정답이다.

어휘 pedestrian 보행자 required 필요한 signage 신호 체계

> ▶▶ Paraphrasing   지문의 **Sidewalk or walkway**
> → 정답의 **pedestrian use**

158-160 기사

지하철 음향 시스템 개선 예정

보스턴 (4월 1일)—[158]운송 당국은 지하철 역 중 몇 곳의 구내방송 시스템을 재단장할 예정이라고 이번주에 밝혔다. 구내방송 시스템은 승강장 및 역내에서 통근자를 대상으로 방송하는 데 사용되고 있다.

이미 오래 전에 재단장이 이루어졌어야 했지만, 어쨌든 지역 통근자들은 이를 반기는 모습이다.

"[159]가장 자주 이용하는 몇 군데 역에서 방송을 알아듣기가 꽤 어려워요." 지난 18년간 거의 매주 출근길 지하철을 이용한 [159]이안 밀러 씨의 말이다. "[159]TV에서 관련 기사를 봤는데요, 이건 진작에 했어야 할 일이죠!"

현재 사용 중인 시스템 일부는 30년이 넘은 것들이다. 낡은 스피커, 전선, 마이크, 앰프 등이 새롭고 더 믿을 만한 기기로 교체될 예정이다. 공사는 10월에 완료되며 1,100만 달러 이상의 비용이 소요된다.

보스턴 지하철 시스템은 지난 몇 년간 [160]단계적으로 통합되었다. 녹색 노선의 기본 시설은 1890년대 후반 트레몬트 스트리트에서 처음 개통되었다. 이는 미국 최초로 만들어진 것이었다.

어휘 public address system 구내방송 시스템 selected 선별된 be scheduled to ~할 예정이다 refurbish 재단장하다 make an announcement 방송하다, 공지하다 commuter 통근자 overdue 훨씬 전에 했어야 할 frequently 자주, 빈번하게 about time 이미 했어야 했다 currently 현재 worn-out 낡은 wiring 전선 amplifier 앰프, 증폭기 replace 교체하다 reliable 믿을 만한 complete 완료하다 in stages 단계적으로 foundational 기본적인 component 구성 요소

158 주제 / 목적

번역 기사를 쓴 목적은?

(A) 지하철 승객이 어디서 정보를 찾을 수 있는지 알려 주기 위해
(B) 일부 지하철 역의 개선 사항을 알려 주기 위해
(C) 지하철 신규 호선 설립을 알리기 위해
(D) 지하철 시간표 변경 이유를 설명하기 위해

해설 첫 번째 단락에서 지하철 역 중 몇 곳의 구내방송 시스템을 재단장할 예정(The public address systems at selected subway stations are scheduled to be refurbished)이라고 했으므로, 일부 지하철 역의 개선 사항을 알리기 위한 기사임을 알 수 있다. 따라서 (B)가 정답이다.

어휘 clarify 명확하게 하다 describe 묘사하다, 설명하다 revise 변경하다

> ▶▶ Paraphrasing   지문의 **selected subway stations**
> → 정답의 **some subway stations**
> 지문의 **be refurbished**
> → 정답의 **improvements**

159 세부 사항

번역 밀러 씨는 계획에 대해 어떻게 생각하는가?

(A) 해당 프로젝트가 실패하기를 바란다.
(B) 비용에 대해 우려한다.
(C) 공사가 필요하지 않다고 확신한다.
(D) 이러한 변화를 기다려 왔다.

해설 세 번째 단락에서 밀러 씨는 몇 군데 역에서 방송을 알아듣기가 꽤 어렵다(It can be pretty difficult to understand announcements at some of the stations)며 문제 제기를 한 후, 음향 시스템 개선은 진작에 했어야 할 일이었다(all I can say is that it is about time)는 의견을 밝혔다. 따라서 그가 이러한 변화를 기다려 왔음을 알 수 있으므로, (D)가 정답이다.

어휘 be concerned about ~에 대해 우려하다

160 동의어 찾기

번역 다섯 번째 단락 2행의 "stages"와 의미상 가장 가까운 것은?

(A) 단계   (B) 현장
(C) 기차   (D) 승강장

해설 "stages"를 포함한 부분은 '지난 몇 년간 단계적으로 통합되었다(came together in stages over the course of several years)'라는 의미로, 여기서 stages는 '단계'라는 뜻으로 쓰였다. 따라서 비슷한 의미의 (A) steps가 정답이다.

161-163 이메일

> 수신: 전 직원
> 발신: 셀린 홍
> 날짜: 3월 25일
> 제목: 알림
>
> 직원 여러분께,
>
> **161, 163출장 경비 보고서에 관한 몇 가지 새로운 절차에 주목해 주시기 바랍니다.** 이 단계대로 하시면, 저희가 여러분의 비용 환급을 신속하게 처리해 드릴 수 있게 됩니다. 다음 달부터 업무 관련 식사 참석자 명단을 영수증과 함께 제출하셔야 합니다. 아울러 업무와 관련 없는 상품 및 활동의 영수증을 보고서에 포함시키지 않도록 하십시오. 마지막으로 **162저희 회계 소프트웨어가 여러분이 환급받으실 총액을 자동으로 계산할 것임을 유념하십시오. 소프트웨어가 이 작업을 할 수 있도록 영수증 사진을 업로드해주시기만 하면 됩니다.**
>
> 문의 사항에 기꺼이 답변해 드리겠습니다. 그런데 제가 금요일에 고객을 만나러 도쿄에 갈 예정이라 해당일에는 이메일 확인이 어렵습니다.
>
> 셀린 홍
> 인사부 차장
> 다토릭 시스템즈

어휘 draw one's attention ~의 주의를 끌다   procedure 절차   business trip 출장   expense 경비   accompany ~를 동반하다   attendee 참석자   accounting 회계   automatically 자동으로   calculate 계산하다   reimburse 배상하다, 변제하다

161 사실 관계 확인

번역 다토릭 시스템즈에 대해 명시된 것은?

(A) 업무상 저녁 식사에 허용되는 비용을 상향했다.
(B) 새로운 출장 경비 보고서 제출 절차를 채택할 예정이다.
(C) 여러 국가에 지점이 있다.
(D) 회사 기념 행사를 계획하고 있다.

해설 첫 번째 단락에서 출장 경비 보고서에 관한 몇 가지 새로운 절차(several new procedures regarding business trip expense reports)를 언급한 후 내달부터 적용되는 보고서 제출 관련 변경 사항을 설명했으므로, (B)가 정답이다.

어휘 increase 늘리다, 증가시키다   spending 지출   allow 허가하다   adopt 채택하다   hold 개최하다

162 세부 사항

번역 회계 소프트웨어를 언급한 이유는?

(A) 소프트웨어의 특별한 기능을 강조하기 위해
(B) 직원들에게 설치를 독려하기 위해
(C) 직원들의 소프트웨어 접속을 돕기 위해
(D) 교체 예정임을 언급하기 위해

해설 첫 번째 단락 후반부를 보면, 회계 소프트웨어가 환급받을 총액을 자동으로 계산할 것(our accounting software will now automatically calculate for you the total to be reimbursed)이라며 소프트웨어의 특별한 기능을 언급했으므로, (A)가 정답이다.

어휘 highlight 강조하다   capability 능력, 역량   install 설치하다   point out 지적하다, 언급하다   replace 교체하다

> ▸▸ Paraphrasing   지문의 **automatically calculate for you the total to be reimbursed**
> → 정답의 **a special capability**

163 문장 삽입

번역 [1], [2], [3], [4]로 표시된 곳 중에서 다음 문장이 들어가기에 가장 적합한 곳은?

"이 단계대로 하시면, 저희가 여러분의 비용 환급을 신속하게 처리해 드릴 수 있게 됩니다."

(A) [1]
(B) [2]
(C) [3]
(D) [4]

해설 주어진 문장에서 '이 단계대로 하시면(Following these steps)'이라고 했으므로, 앞에서 먼저 '이 단계(these steps)'와 관련된 내용이 언급되어야 한다. [1] 앞에서 출장 경비 보고서에 관한 몇 가지 새로운 절차(several new procedures regarding business trip expense reports)를 도입할 예정임을 밝혔고, [1] 뒤에서 구체적으로 각 단계를 설명하고 있으므로, 이 사이에 주어진 문장이 들어가야 글의 흐름이 자연스러워진다. 따라서 (A)가 정답이다. 참고로, 주어진 문장의 these steps는 new procedures regarding business trip expense reports를 가리킨다.

어휘 issue 발행하다, 지급하다   reimbursement 배상, 변제, 환급

164-167 기사

전자 상거래가 아프리카 패션업계에 길을 열어주다

아디스 아바바 (5월 6일)—¹⁶⁴**최근 패션 소비자로서 아프리카의 역할이 커지고 있다.** 이러한 동향은 전자 상거래의 출현에 크게 기인한다. 전자 상거래 덕분에 아프리카인들이 아프리카 대륙에 실재적으로 진출하지 않은 소매업체들로부터 의류를 구입할 기회를 얻게 된 것이다.

그런데 더욱 중요한 사실은 전자 상거래의 성장으로 인해 소규모 아프리카 디자이너들이 자신들의 의상을 전세계 소비자들에게 선보임으로써 패션 "제작자"로 부상했다는 점이다. ¹⁶⁶**점점과 롱가 같은 아프리카의 쇼핑 웹사이트들은 아프리카 디자이너들의 작품을 아프리카 대륙뿐 아니라 런던, 뉴욕 등 먼 곳에서도 구입할 수 있게 하고 있다.**

"아프리카 디자이너들이 마침내 눈에 띄게 되었습니다." 아프리카에서 급성장 중인 ¹⁶⁵운동용 신발업체인 아비 스포츠코어의 창립자마자 압셔의 말이다. "저희는 이곳 아프리카에서 훌륭한 디자인과 생산 역량을 항상 갖추고 있었습니다. 하지만 세계로 진출하기가 어려웠죠. 이제 매장보다 온라인에서 더 많은 매출액을 창출하고 있습니다."

¹⁶⁵, ¹⁶⁷압셔 씨는 자신의 회사를 세계적인 업체로 변모시키는 동시에, 자신의 본거지인 나즈렛 시에서 제품을 제조하는 데 따르는 이점을 계속 강조했다. 그 도시는 네 곳의 의류 공장을 자랑하는데, 올해 원지 근처에 다섯 번째 공장이 건립될 계획이다. 아프리카의 강점인 직물 분야와 혁신적인 디자인은 전통과 내구성을 결합했으며, 이러한 방식으로 압셔 씨의 회사와 같은 업체들이 대륙 너머로 눈을 돌릴 수 있게 되었다.

"에티오피아 및 아프리카 전역의 더 많은 도시에서 제조 역량이 향상되고 있어 세계 다른 곳에 진출하기가 더 쉬워질 겁니다."라고 압셔 씨는 말한다.

어휘 e-commerce 전자 상거래 open doors for ~에게 문[길]을 열어 주다, 성공할 기회를 마련해 주다 be on the rise 오르다, 증가하다 recent 최근의 emergence 부상 opportunity 기회 retailer 소매업자 physical 물리적인 presence 존재함, 주둔, 진출 continent 대륙 small-scale 소규모의 purchase 구매 gain visibility 가시성을 얻다, 눈에 보이게 되다 generate 발생시키다, 만들어 내다 transform 변형시키다 powerhouse 유력 집단 highlight 강조하다 advantage 이점 textile 직물 innovative 혁신적인 wearability 내구성 formula 공식

164 주제 / 목적

번역 기사의 주제는?

(A) 운동용 신발 마케팅의 새로운 동향
(B) 아프리카 의류 시장에서의 경쟁 심화
(C) 아프리카 패션업계의 최근 성장
(D) 아프리카 최대의 의류업체

해설 첫 번째 단락에서 최근 패션 소비자로서 아프리카의 역할이 커지고 있다(Africa's role as a consumer of fashion ~ on the rise in recent years)고 한 후 관련 내용을 서술하고 있으므로, 아프리카 패션업계의 최근 성장에 관한 기사임을 알 수 있다. 따라서 (C)가 정답이다.

어휘 competition 경쟁 recent 최근의

▸▸ Paraphrasing 지문의 on the rise in recent years → 정답의 Recent growth

165 사실 관계 확인

번역 아비 스포츠코어에 대해 명시된 것은?

(A) 온라인으로만 제품을 판매한다.
(B) 나즈렛에서 신발을 제조한다.
(C) 본사를 곧 이전할 예정이다.
(D) 에티오피아 최초의 신발업체다.

해설 네 번째 단락에서 신발 제조 회사인 아비 스포츠코어의 창립자 압셔 씨가 나즈렛 시에서 제품을 제조하는 데 따르는 이점을 계속 강조한다(highlight the advantages of manufacturing its products in ~ Nazret)고 했으므로, 아비 스포츠코어가 나즈렛에서 신발을 생산한다는 것을 알 수 있다. 따라서 (B)가 정답이다.

▸▸ Paraphrasing 지문의 its products → 정답의 its shoes

166 추론 / 암시

번역 점점과 롱가의 웹사이트에 대해 암시된 것은?

(A) 수제품만 판매한다.
(B) 전세계에서 주문을 받는다.
(C) 런던, 뉴욕으로 무료 배송을 제공한다.
(D) 소매점을 열 계획이다.

해설 두 번째 단락에서 점점과 롱가 같은 아프리카의 쇼핑 웹사이트들이 아프리카 디자이너들의 작품을 런던, 뉴욕 등 먼 곳에서도 구입할 수 있도록 하고 있다(African shopping Web sites like Jumjum and Longa are making the work of African designers available ~ as far away as London and New York)고 했으므로, 전세계에서 주문을 받는다고 추론할 수 있다. 따라서 (B)가 정답이다.

▸▸ Paraphrasing 지문의 are making ~ available for purchase → 정답의 receive orders
지문의 as far away as London and New York → 정답의 from around the world

167 문장 삽입

번역 [1], [2], [3], [4]로 표시된 곳 중에서 다음 문장이 들어가기에 가장 적합한 곳은?

"그 도시는 네 곳의 의류 공장을 자랑하는데, 올해 원지 근처에 다섯 번째 공장이 건립될 계획이다."

(A) [1]
(B) [2]
(C) [3]
(D) [4]

해설 주어진 문장에서 '그 도시는 네 곳의 의류 공장을 자랑한다(The city boasts four garment factories)'라고 했으므로, 앞에서 먼저 '그 시(The city)'의 구체적인 명칭과 제조 공장 관련 내용이 언급되어야 한다. [3] 앞에서 압셔 씨가 자신의 본거지인 나즈렛 시에서 제품을

제조하는 데 따르는 이점(the advantages of manufacturing its products in her home city of Nazret)을 강조한다고 했으므로, 이 문장 뒤에 주어진 문장이 들어가야 글의 흐름이 자연스러워진다. 따라서 (C)가 정답이다.

168-171 문자 메시지

> **개리 박 (오전 10시 23분)**
> 168몇 분 전에 9월 호 표지 디자인을 이메일로 보냈어요. 받으셨나요?
>
> **질 라일리 (오전 10시 26분)**
> 네, 169그런데 이게 최신 버전인가요? 169, 170바탕색을 더 밝게 해서 기사 제목이 더 잘 보이게 하도록 의견을 모았던 것 같은데요.
>
> **개리 박 (오전 10시 28분)**
> 169깜박했어요. 죄송합니다! 170최신 버전을 지금 다시 보낼게요.
>
> **질 라일리 (오전 10시 30분)**
> 지금 열고 있어요. 더 낫군요. 171그래픽 부서에 보내 견본 출력물을 요청할게요.
>
> **질 라일리 (오전 10시 35분)**
> 안녕하세요, 오제다 씨. 저희 새 표지 디자인이 완성됐습니다. 171언제 작업할 수 있으실 것 같습니까?
>
> **프랭크 오제다 (오전 10시 38분)**
> 지금 보내 주세요. 171점심 시간 지나고 승인받을 인쇄물을 준비하겠습니다.
>
> 어휘 issue 호 latest 최신의 background 배경 request 요청하다 approval 승인

168 추론 / 암시

번역 이 사람들은 어디에서 근무하겠는가?
(A) 서점
(B) 공공도서관
(C) TV 스튜디오
(D) 잡지 출판사

해설 박 씨가 오전 10시 23분 메시지에서 9월 호 표지 디자인을 라일리 씨의 이메일로 보냈다(I e-mailed you the cover design for our September issue)고 했고, 이후 해당 디자인에 관해 논의하고 있으므로, 이들이 잡지 출판사에 근무한다는 것을 추론할 수 있다. 따라서 (D)가 정답이다.

169 세부 사항

번역 박 씨는 왜 사과하는가?
(A) 파일을 잘못 보냈다.
(B) 이전 이메일 주소를 사용했다.
(C) 프로젝트 마감 시간을 맞추지 못했다.
(D) 중요한 문서를 분실했다.

해설 라일리 씨가 오전 10시 26분 메시지에서 박 씨가 보낸 파일이 최신 버전인지(is this the latest version?) 물은 후 바탕색을 더 밝게 해서 기사 제목이 더 잘 보이게 하자고 했던 일(we agreed that the background color should be lighter ~ visible)을 언급했고, 이에 대해 박 씨가 사과를 하며(sorry about that!) 다시 최신 파일을 보낸다고(I'm just now sending the file with the most recent version) 했다. 따라서 그가 파일을 잘못 보냈음을 알 수 있으므로, (A)가 정답이다.

어휘 apologize 사과하다 deadline 마감 시간

>> **Paraphrasing** 지문의 sorry → 질문의 apologize

170 의도 파악

번역 오전 10시 30분에 라일리 씨가 "더 낫군요"라고 쓸 때, 그 의도는 무엇인가?
(A) 예산이 더 적정하다.
(B) 색상이 더 낫다.
(C) 기사가 더 재미있다.
(D) 일정이 더 현실적이다.

해설 라일리 씨가 오전 10시 26분 메시지에서 박 씨가 보낸 파일이 최신 버전인지(is this the latest version?) 물은 후 바탕색을 더 밝게 해서 기사 제목이 더 잘 보이게 하자고 했던 일(we agreed that the background color should be lighter ~ visible)을 언급하자 박 씨가 다시 최신 파일(the file with the most recent version)을 보냈다. 파일을 받은 후 라일리 씨가 '더 낫군요(That's more like it)'라고 응답한 것이므로, 최신 버전의 색상이 더 낫다는 의도로 말한 것임을 추론할 수 있다. 따라서 (B)가 정답이다.

어휘 budget 예산 reasonable 합리적인, 적정한 realistic 현실적인

171 세부 사항

번역 오제다 씨는 오후까지 무엇을 할 것인가?
(A) 마케팅 계획 승인하기
(B) 견본 만들기
(C) 프린터 수리하기
(D) 동의서 복사하기

해설 라일리 씨가 오전 10시 30분 메시지에서 그래픽 부서에 표지를 보내 견본 출력물을 요청하겠다(I'll forward it to Graphics and request a sample printout)고 한 후, 오전 10시 35분 메시지에서 오제다 씨에게 언제 작업할 수 있는지(When do you think you'll have a chance to work on it?) 문의했다. 이에 대해 오제다 씨가 오전 10시 38분 메시지에서 점심 시간 지나고 승인받을 인쇄물을 준비하겠다(I'll have a print copy ready for your approval after lunch)고 응답했으므로, 그가 견본을 준비할 것임을 알 수 있다. 따라서 (B)가 정답이다.

어휘 approve 승인하다

172-175 편지

2월 8일

말라 셸비 씨
60 잘란 툰 라작
54200 쿠알라룸푸르

셸비 씨께,

172올해 스몰 비즈니스 챌린지 대회의 결선 진출자로 선정되셨음을 알려 드리게 되어 기쁩니다. 올해로 5년째인 본 대회는 젊은 기업가들이 출시한 혁신적인 제품 및 서비스를 주목받게 하기 위해 설립되었습니다. **173귀하가 개발하신 자선 단체와 자원봉사자를 연결하는 수단을 제공하는 웹 애플리케이션**은 저희 심사위원단으로부터 최고점 중 하나를 받았습니다.

다음 차수에서는 전문가로 구성된 심사위원단 앞에서 제품에 대해 직접 발표하시게 됩니다. 발표를 가장 잘한 3인은 자신의 사업체에 투자할 10,000링깃의 보조금을 각각 일시불로 지급받습니다.

sbc.org/competition을 방문하셔서 발표 개요 및 애플리케이션 사용법을 잘 174**보여 주는** 간단한 동영상, 본인의 여권용 사진을 제출해 주십시오. 175**필요 시 저희 웹사이트의 홍보 자료에 귀하의 성함과 사진을 사용할 수 있도록 동의서에 날인해 주셔야 합니다. 해당 자료 제출 기한은 3월 10일입니다.**

펠릭스 팡
스몰 비즈니스 챌린지 위원회장

어휘 be delighted to ~해서 기쁘다   nominate 후보자로 지명하다   finalist 결승전 진출자   competition 대회, 경기   highlight 강조하다   innovative 혁신적인   entrepreneur 기업가   provide 제공하다   charitable 자선의   organization 단체, 기관   volunteer 자원봉사자   judge 심사위원   participate in ~에 참가하다   presentation 발표, 설명   expert 전문가   one-time 일시불의   grant 보조금   invest 투자하다   outline 개요   illustrate 분명히 보여 주다   consent 동의서   promotional 홍보성의   submission 제출

172 주제 / 목적

번역 편지의 목적은?

(A) 행사 자원봉사자를 찾기 위해
(B) 대회 결승 진출자에게 통지하기 위해
(C) 업체 상담 서비스를 판매하기 위해
(D) 소기업 대출을 제공하기 위해

해설 첫 번째 단락의 '올해 스몰 비즈니스 챌린지 대회의 결선 진출자로 선정되었다는 것을 알려 드리게 되어 기쁩니다(We are delighted to inform you that you have been nominated as a finalist ~ this year)'라는 문구를 통해 대회 결승 진출자에게 통지하기 위한 편지임을 알 수 있다. 따라서 (B)가 정답이다.

어휘 seek 찾다   notify 알리다, 통지하다   consultation 상담   loan 대출

▸▸ Paraphrasing   지문의 to inform → 정답의 To notify
지문의 a finalist for the Small Business Challenge competition
→ 정답의 a contest finalist

173 추론 / 암시

번역 셸비 씨는 어떤 분야의 전문가이겠는가?

(A) 법
(B) 기술
(C) 금융
(D) 마케팅

해설 첫 번째 단락에서 편지 수신인인 셸비 씨가 개발한 웹 애플리케이션(The Web application that you developed)이 심사위원단으로부터 최고점 중 하나를 받았다고 했으므로, 그녀가 기술 분야 전문가임을 추론할 수 있다. 따라서 (B)가 정답이다.

어휘 specialize in ~를 전문으로 하다

174 동의어 찾기

번역 세 번째 단락 2행의 "illustrates"와 의미상 가장 가까운 것은?

(A) 보여 주다
(B) 번역하다
(C) 가볍게 해 주다
(D) 장식하다

해설 "illustrates"가 포함된 부분은 '애플리케이션 사용법을 잘 보여 주는 간단한 동영상(a brief video that clearly illustrates the use of your application)'이라는 의미로, 여기서 illustrates는 '(예를 들어) 보여 주다, 설명하다'라는 뜻으로 쓰였다. 따라서 '보여 주다, 나타내다'라는 의미의 (A) represents가 정답이다.

175 세부 사항

번역 셸비 씨는 3월 10일까지 무엇을 하도록 요청받았는가?

(A) 웹페이지 디자인 업데이트하기
(B) 발표하기
(C) 동의서에 날인하기
(D) 요금 지불하기

해설 마지막 단락에서 필요 시 셸비 씨의 이름과 사진을 웹사이트 홍보 자료에 사용할 수 있도록 3월 10일까지 동의서에 날인해 줄 것(You will also need to sign a consent form ~ on our Web site)을 요청했으므로, (C)가 정답이다.

어휘 fee 요금

▸▸ Paraphrasing   지문의 The deadline ~ is 10 March
→ 질문의 by March 10

176-180 이메일 + 영수증

수신: riedewald@parasur.net.sr
발신: client_services@mhf.ca
날짜: 4월 2일 오후 12시 21분
제목: 귀하의 의견

리데발트 씨께,

¹⁷⁶맥캔 홈 퍼니싱즈 (MHF) 설문 조사에 ¹⁷⁷응해 주셔서 감사합니다. 감사의 표시로 고객님의 계정에 보상 포인트를 적립해 드렸습니다. 소매점에서 판매되는 제품뿐 아니라 온라인 상품 구매 시에도 적용하실 수 있습니다. 단, 재고 정리 상품 및 15달러 이상 제품은 포인트로 구매하실 수 없습니다.

온라인 구매 시 보상 포인트를 사용하시려면 구매하시고 싶은 제품을 선택하신 다음 계산 단계로 넘어가십시오. 페이지 맨 아래쪽에서 "포인트 적용"을 선택하십시오. ¹⁸⁰적용된 포인트는 특별 할인으로 주문 영수증에 기재됩니다.

¹⁷⁸소매점 중 한 곳에서 보상 포인트를 사용하시려면 저희 웹사이트상의 계정에 로그인하시면 됩니다. "나의 보상" 페이지로 가신 다음 "쿠폰으로 출력하기"를 선택하십시오. 해당 쿠폰에는 바코드가 있어서 매장 계산대에서 스캔하실 수 있습니다.

맥캔 홈 퍼니싱즈 고객 서비스

어휘 furnishing 가구, 비품 fill out a survey 설문에 응하다 reward 보상 account 계정 apply 적용하다 purchase 구매 retail 소매 clearance 정리, 없애기 credit 크레딧, (현금처럼 쓸 수 있는) 포인트, (추가되는) 금액 check out 계산하다 appear 나타나다

온라인 주문 번호 1157	¹⁷⁹꽃무늬 담요
맥캔 홈 퍼니싱즈 매장	수량: 1
3월 19일 오전 11시 31분	가격: 25.00
¹⁸⁰손그림 액자	사진첩
수량: 1	수량: 1
가격: 10.00	가격: 34.00
특별 할인: -10.00	계절 상품 할인: -17.00
요트 도자기 머그	품목 합계: 62.00
수량: 4	배송: 무료
가격: 40.00	총액: 62.00
재고 정리 할인: -20.00	

어휘 quantity 양 shipping 배송

---

176 세부 사항

번역 이메일에 따르면 리데발트 씨는 어떻게 보상 포인트를 받았는가?

(A) 온라인 대회에서 우승했다.
(B) 고객 설문에 참여했다.
(C) 특정 금액을 지출했다.
(D) 제품을 환불했다.

해설 이메일의 첫 번째 단락에서 수신자인 리데발트 씨가 설문 조사에 응해 준 것(filling out the ~ survey)에 대한 감사의 표시로(To show our appreciation) 계정에 보상 포인트를 적립했다(we have added reward points to your account)고 했으므로, (B)가 정답이다.

▸▸ Paraphrasing 지문의 filling out the ~ survey → 정답의 participated in a customer survey

---

177 동의어 찾기

번역 이메일의 첫 번째 단락 1행의 "filling out"과 의미상 가장 가까운 것은?

(A) 비운 것
(B) 공급한 것
(C) 작성한 것
(D) 확장한 것

해설 "filling out"이 포함된 부분은 '설문 조사에 응해 주셔서 감사합니다 (Thank you for filling out the ~ survey)'라는 의미로, 여기서 filling out은 '(서류 등을) 완성한 것, 작성한 것'이라는 뜻으로 쓰였다. 따라서 (C) completing이 정답이다.

---

178 세부 사항

번역 고객들은 MHF 소매점에서 자신이 받은 보상 포인트를 어떻게 사용할 수 있는가?

(A) 계좌 번호를 입력해서
(B) 전화번호를 입력해서
(C) 쿠폰의 바코드를 스캔해서
(D) 고객 서비스 부서로 가서

해설 이메일의 마지막 단락에서 소매점중 한 곳에서 보상 포인트를 사용하려면(to use reward points at one of our retail locations) 웹사이트에서 쿠폰을 출력하면 된다(by logging in to your account on our Web site ~ select "Print as a coupon")고 했고, 그 쿠폰에 매장 계산대에서 스캔할 수 있는 바코드(a bar code that can be scanned at the store's checkout counter)가 있다고 했으므로, (C)가 정답이다.

▸▸ Paraphrasing 지문의 use reward points at one of our retail locations → 질문의 apply their reward points in an MHF retail store

---

179 사실 관계 확인

번역 영수증에 따르면 리데발트 씨에 대해 사실인 것은?

(A) 제품 배송비를 냈다.
(B) 제품을 저녁에 구입했다.
(C) 모두 합해 70달러 이상을 지불했다.
(D) 한 가지 제품만 정상가에 구입했다.

해설 영수증에 나온 제품 목록을 보면, 다른 제품은 모두 할인을 받았고 꽃무늬 담요(Floral Blanket)만 정상가(Price)인 25.00달러를 지불했다는 것을 확인할 수 있다. 따라서 (D)가 정답이다. 주문 시간이 오전 11시 31분이므로 (B)는 정답이 될 수 없고, 품목 합계(Item total)가 62.00달러이고 배송(Shipping)이 무료(free)라고 했으므로, (C)와 (A) 또한 오답이다.

어휘 delivery 배송, 배달 all combined 모두 합해서 regular price 정상 가격

180 연계

번역 리데발트 씨는 보상 포인트를 써서 어떤 제품을 구입했겠는가?

(A) 액자 (B) 도자기 머그
(C) 꽃무늬 담요 (D) 사진첩

해설 이메일의 두 번째 단락 후반부를 보면, 온라인 구매 시 적용된 포인트는 특별 할인으로 주문 영수증에 기재된다(The value of the applied credits ~ as a special discount)고 했는데, 영수증을 보면 손그림 액자(Hand-Painted Picture Frame) 밑에 특별 할인으로 10달러가 차감된 것을 확인할 수 있다. 따라서 (A)가 정답이다.

181-185 편지 + 주문서

투 스완 프레스

72 홀리웰 로드, 에딘버러 EH8 8PJ

12월 4일

앨버트 모렐로 씨
17 페이턴 애비뉴
킹스턴 5
자메이카, 서인도제도

모렐로 씨께,

181동봉한 〈우리 바다 이해하기〉에 대한 인세 지불금을 확인해 주시기 바랍니다. 182최근에 귀하의 저서 출판본 및 전자본 매출액과 귀하가 받으실 인세가 표시된 이메일을 받으셨을 겁니다.

183저희 투 스완 프레스가 10월에 UK 북 인더스트리에서 수여하는 올해의 출판사 상을 수상했음을 알려 드리게 되어 자랑스럽게 생각합니다. 5년 전 창립 이래 저희와 함께해 주신 저자 여러분께 감사를 드립니다.

184모든 투 스완 프레스 저자 분들은 저희 웹사이트에서 어떤 서적을 구매하시든 간에 40퍼센트의 할인을 적용받을 수 있습니다. 할인을 받으시려면 AUX1417 코드를 사용하시면 됩니다.

궁금하신 점이 있으시면 언제든 연락 주십시오.

사라 위클린
별첨

어휘 enclose 동봉하다 royalty 인세, 저작권 사용료 recently 최근에 sales figure 매출액 due 지불하기로 되어 있는 electronic 전자의 announce 발표하다, 알리다 author 저자 found 창립하다, 설립하다 be entitled to ~할 자격이 있다, ~할 권리가 있다 hesitate 주저하다

◀ ▶ https:www.twoswanpress.co.uk/orderconfirmation

주문해 주셔서 감사합니다!
18512월 특별 할인 - 35파운드 이상 주문 시 무료 배송

이름:	던컨 부스
이메일:	mbooth@silvertech.co.kr
구입일:	12월 12일
배송지:	던컨 부스 321 매슬린 스트리트 코트브리지 ML5 1LZ, 스코틀랜드, 영국

1 〈생활 속의 비즈니스〉 엘레인 슈일러 저	75.00파운드
184할인 적용 (AUX1417)	-30.00
185지불해야 할 금액	45.00파운드

신용카드 지불 ***5732

여러 건의 주문품은 하나의 소포로 합쳐질 수 있습니다. 귀하의 주문품이 배송되면 알려 드리겠습니다.

어휘 balance due 지불해야 할 금액 multiple 다수의 combine 결합하다 notify 알리다

181 주제 / 목적

번역 편지를 쓴 목적 중 하나는 무엇인가?

(A) 모렐로 씨에게 저서 집필을 요청하기 위해
(B) 동봉한 계약서에 대해 설명하기 위해
(C) 모렐로 씨에게 지불금에 관해 알리기 위해
(D) 인사 정책 업데이트에 대해 설명하기 위해

해설 편지의 첫 번째 단락에서 〈우리 바다 이해하기〉 인세 지불금을 동봉했다며 확인(Enclosed please find your royalty payment for *Understanding Our Oceans*)을 요청했으므로, 편지의 목적 중 하나가 모렐로 씨에게 지불금에 관해 알리기 위함이라는 것을 알 수 있다. 따라서 (C)가 정답이다.

어휘 personnel policy 인사 규정, 인사 정책

182 세부 사항

번역 모렐로 씨에게 보내는 이전 메시지에 포함된 것은?

(A) 잘못된 연락처
(B) 상세된 매출액
(C) 제안된 변경 사항 목록
(D) 전자책 링크

해설 첫 번째 단락에서 모리스 씨에게 '저서 매출액과 받게 될 인세가 표시된 이메일(an e-mail that listed the sales figures and the royalties due to you) 최근에 받았을 것이다'라고 했으므로, (B)가 정답이다.

어휘 incorrect 부정확한 detailed 상세한 suggest 제안하다 electronic book 전자책

▸▸ Paraphrasing 지문의 sales figures → 정답의 sales numbers

183 세부 사항

번역 투 스완 프레스에 대해 위클린 씨가 언급한 것은?

(A) 10월에 새로운 주소지로 이전했다.
(B) 5주년을 맞아 새로운 프로그램을 시작했다.
(C) 업계에서 주는 상을 받았다.
(D) 과학 서적 출판에 중점을 두기로 결정했다.

해설 편지의 두 번째 단락에서 투 스완 프레스가 10월에 UK 북 인더스트리에서 수여하는 올해의 출판사 상을 수상했다(Two Swan Press was given the Publisher of the Year Award by the UK Book Industry)고 했으므로, (C)가 정답이다.

어휘 anniversary 기념일 scientific 과학적인 publication 출판, 발행물

> ▶▶ **Paraphrasing** 지문의 **was given the Publisher of the Year Award by the UK Book Industry**
> → 정답의 **has won an industry award**

184 연계

번역 부스 씨에 대해 암시된 것은?

(A) 투 스완 프레스 저자이다.
(B) 〈생활 속의 비즈니스〉 저자이다.
(C) 모렐로 씨의 지인이다.
(D) 이전에 투 스완 프레스에서 제품을 구입했다.

해설 편지의 세 번째 단락에서 모든 투 스완 프레스 저자들은 웹사이트에서 어떤 서적을 구매하든 간에 40퍼센트의 할인을 적용받을 수 있고(All Two Swan Press authors are entitled to an author discount of 40 percent off), 할인을 받으려면 AUX1417 코드를 사용하라(Simply use the code AUX1417 for your discount)고 했다. 주문서를 보면, 부스 씨가 AUX1417 코드를 사용해 할인을 적용받았다(Discount Applied)는 것을 확인할 수 있으므로, 부스 씨가 투 스완 프레스 저자임을 추론할 수 있다. 따라서 (A)가 정답이다.

어휘 acquaintance 지인

185 사실 관계 확인

번역 주문에 대해 명시된 것은?

(A) 주문이 지연되었다.
(B) 아직 금액 지불이 되지 않았다.
(C) 여러 권의 책이 주문되었다.
(D) 무료 배송이 포함된다.

해설 주문서 상단을 보면 12월 특별 할인 행사(Special December Offer)로 35파운드 이상 주문 시 무료 배송(free shipping on all orders over £35) 혜택을 제공한다고 했는데, 부스 씨가 지불해야 할 금액(Balance Due)이 45파운드이므로 제품이 무료로 배송될 것임을 알 수 있다. 따라서 (D)가 정답이다.

186-190 이메일 + 양식 + 기사

수신: 전 직원

발신: 인사부

날짜: 6월 20일

제목: 멘토링 프로그램

첨부: ⬭ 지원서

186, 188브로드사이드 일렉트로닉스에서 근무한 기간이 18개월 미만인 직원 여러분께서는 최대 10명의 하급 직원들을 장기 근무한 회사의 전문 인력들과 연결해 주는 새로운 멘토링 프로그램에 참가 신청을 하실 수 있습니다. 본 프로그램의 목표는 하급 직원이 업무 기량을 닦고, 회사의 문화를 더욱 잘 이해하며, 목표가 더 명확한 진로를 개발할 수 있도록 하는 것입니다. 멘티는 업무 배정 및 업무 관련 관심 분야에 전적으로 기반하여 멘토에게 배정됩니다. 멘토와 멘티는 일 년 동안 매월 3~5시간 정도 서로 편한 시간에 만남을 갖게 됩니다.

본 프로그램에 참가하고 싶으시면 첨부된 지원서를 작성하셔서 7월 1일까지 t.wrigley@broadsideelec.com, 멘토링 프로그램 담당자 팀 리글리 씨 앞으로 보내 주십시오. **187**리글리 씨가 7월 15일까지 선정 결과를 통지할 것입니다.

어휘 application 지원서, 지원 attachment 첨부 apply 지원하다 maximum 최대 long-term 장기간의 sharpen 갈다, 날카롭게 하다 career path 진로 assign 배정하다, 할당하다 based on ~에 기반하여 strictly 엄격하게, 순전히 assignment 배정, 할당 professional 직업상의, 전문적인 mutually 상호간에, 서로 convenient 편리한 initiative (특정 목적 달성을 위한) 계획, 과정

188멘토링 프로그램 지원서

이름: **188**카라 드러몬드   내선번호: 144

부서: 영업

업무 관련 관심 분야:
189저는 해외 시장에 대해 학습하고 해외 시장에서 활용할 저의 영업 발표 능력을 개발하는 데에 가장 관심이 있습니다. 또한 일반적인 진로 지도에도 관심이 있습니다.

만남에 가장 좋은 근무일 및 시간:
월요일을 제외한 주중 오전 시간

어휘 extension 내선, 구내전화 division 부서, 분과 ability 능력 general 보통의, 일반적인 career guidance 진로 지도

브로드사이드사 소식지

멘토링 프로그램 결실을 보다

189장기 근속한 알레나 루소 영업 부서장은 인사 부장이 작년에 시작한 프로그램 내에서 경험이 부족한 직원들을 멘토링해 달라고 부탁해 왔을 때 큰 관심을 보였다. 그녀는 이러한 임무를 흔쾌히 수락했다. "**189, 190**드러몬드 씨와 함께한 후 제 자신의 업무에 더 큰 만족을 느꼈습니다. 이제 막 시작한 전문가 한 명에게 제가 도움을 주었으니까요. 제 초창기에

누군가 저를 돌봐 주는 사람이 있었으면 좋았을 텐데라고 생각할 뿐입니다." 루소 씨의 설명이다.

드러몬드 씨는 "영업을 더 잘하는 방법에 대한 조언이 필요했다"고 설명한다. 현재는 매출이 20퍼센트 상승했다고 말한다. 브로드사이드 일렉트로닉스가 제공하는 기회와 관리자가 되는 데 필요한 요소를 더 잘 이해하게 됐다고 한다. "¹⁹⁰루소 씨 덕분에 제 진로 목표를 분명히 할 수 있었고 매일 출근하면서 더 행복해집니다."

새로운 멘토십 파트너가 결성되고 있다. 관심 있는 사원은 인사부의 팀 리글리 씨에게 연락하면 된다.

> 어휘 long-time employee 장기 근속자 intrigue 큰 흥미를 불러일으키다 less experienced 경험이 부족한 accept 수락하다 assignment 과제, 임무 look out for ~를 돌보다 remark 진술하다 pointer 충고, 조언 sales pitch 판매를 위한 설득 offer 제공하다 require 요구하다 define 규정하다, 분명하게 하다 form 형성하다, 결성하다

186 사실 관계 확인

번역 멘토링 프로그램에 대해 이메일에서 명시된 것은?

(A) 업계 전체에서 인기가 많다.
(B) 참가자 수가 제한된다.
(C) 영업 부서 직원을 위해 만들어졌다.
(D) 참가자는 오리엔테이션에 참석해야 한다.

해설 이메일의 첫 번째 단락에서 최대 10명의 하급 직원들을 장기 근무한 회사의 전문인력들(a maximum of ten junior employees with long-term company veterans)과 연결해 주는 새로운 멘토링 프로그램이라고 했으므로, 참가자 수가 제한된다는 것을 알 수 있다. 따라서 (B)가 정답이다.

어휘 industry-wide 업계 전체에서 participant 참가자 be limited 제한되다 attend 참석하다

> ▸▸ Paraphrasing 지문의 a maximum of ten junior employees → 정답의 The number of participants is limited

187 추론 / 암시

번역 하급 직원들은 어떻게 선정되겠는가?

(A) 경영자 교육 그룹에서 선발된다.
(B) 경쟁 면접을 치른다.
(C) 리글리 씨가 평가한다.
(D) 지역 경영 대학원의 추천을 받는다.

해설 이메일의 마지막 단락에서 멘토링 프로그램 담당자인 리글리 씨가 선정 결과를 통지할 것(Mr. Wrigley will send notification of his selections)이라고 했으므로, 리글리 씨가 평가하여 선정한다는 것을 추론할 수 있다. 따라서 (C)가 정답이다.

어휘 management training 경영자 교육 undergo 겪다 competitive 경쟁적인 evaluate 평가하다 recommend 추천하다

188 연계

번역 드러몬드 씨에 대해 암시된 것은?

(A) 브로드사이드 일렉트로닉스에 근무한 기간이 18개월 미만이다.
(B) 다른 부서에서 막 이동했다.
(C) 긍정적인 연례 평가 결과를 받았다.
(D) 해외에서 성공적인 발표 사례가 다수 있었다.

해설 양식(MENTORING PROGRAM APPLICATION)을 보면 드러몬드 씨가 멘토링 프로그램에 지원했다는 것을 알 수 있다. 해당 프로그램 관련 내용은 이메일에서 확인할 수 있는데, 첫 번째 단락에서 브로드사이드 일렉트로닉스에 근무한 지 18개월 미만인 직원은 새로운 멘토링 프로그램 참가 신청을 할 수 있다(Employees ~ less than eighteen months are invited to apply to participate in a new mentoring program)고 했으므로, 드러몬드 씨의 근무 기간이 18개월 미만이라는 것을 추론할 수 있다. 따라서 (A)가 정답이다.

어휘 transfer 옮기다, 이동하다 positive 긍정적인 annual 연례의

> ▸▸ Paraphrasing have been with → 정답의 has worked at

189 연계

번역 루소 씨에 대해 사실인 것은 무엇이겠는가?

(A) 곧 은퇴를 계획하고 있다.
(B) 해외 영업 경험이 있다.
(C) 많은 후배 직원들을 멘토링했다.
(D) 최근 채용팀에 합류했다.

해설 기사의 첫 번째 단락에서 루소 씨가 경험이 부족한 직원들을 멘토링해 달라(mentoring a less experienced employee under a program)는 임무를 수락했고(accepted the assignment), 드러몬드 씨와 함께하게 되었다(working with Ms. Drummond)고 했다. 루소 씨의 멘토링 분야는 드러몬드 씨가 작성한 양식에서 확인할 수 있는데, 업무 관련 관심 분야(Professional areas of interest)에서 드러몬드 씨가 해외 시장에 대한 학습 및 해외 시장에서 활용할 자신의 영업 발표 능력 개발(learning about our market abroad and developing my sales-presentation abilities for these international markets)에 관심이 있다고 했으므로, 드러몬드 씨를 멘토링한 루소 씨가 해외 영업 경험이 있음을 추론할 수 있다. 따라서 (B)가 정답이다.

어휘 retire 퇴직하다, 은퇴하다 hiring 채용

190 세부 사항

번역 드러몬드 씨와 루소 씨가 모두 멘토링 프로그램을 통해 얻은 이익은?

(A) 직업 만족도 증가
(B) 빠른 승진
(C) 상여금
(D) 명확해진 진로 목표

해설 기사에서 루소 씨는 자신의 업무에 더 큰 만족을 느꼈다(I am more satisfied with my own duties)고 했고, 드러몬드 씨 또한 매일 출근하면서 더 행복해진다(I am a happier person when I arrive to work every day)고 했으므로, 멘토링 프로그램을 통해 업무에 대한 만족도가 증가했음을 알 수 있다. 따라서 (A)가 정답이다.

어휘 satisfaction 만족 promotion 승진

https://www.runklefencing.co.uk

| 홈 | 임시 | 주거용 | 상업용 |

임시 울타리 서비스

주택, 작업장, 특별 행사에 임시 울타리 설치가 필요하십니까? 저희 전문가 팀이 예약된 날짜와 시간에 철사로 엮은 울타리를 배송해서 설치해 드립니다. 더 이상 울타리가 필요치 않으면 저희가 해체해서 옮겨 드립니다. 주거용 및 상업용 울타리처럼 임시 울타리 역시 최상의 소재를 사용하는 최고의 제조 업체로부터 공수합니다. 당사의 울타리는 지역 주민과 업체들이 인정하는 깔끔하고 견고하며 전문적인 외관을 갖춘 제품입니다. 당사는 법적으로 필요한 모든 검사 및 증명서 교부 업무도 처리하고 있습니다.

가격 견적을 낼 준비가 되셨나요? 그렇다면 저희 온라인 견적 서비스를 통해 지금 바로 연락 주십시오. 저희가 정확한 견적을 제공할 수 있도록 다음의 정보를 꼭 알려 주시기 바랍니다.

1. ¹⁹³⁽ᴬ⁾선호하는 울타리 높이 (¹⁹¹일반적으로 현지 규정은 최고 3미터 높이까지 허용하고 있음을 알려 드립니다.)
2. ¹⁹³⁽ᶜ⁾둘러싸야 하는 구역의 둘레
3. ¹⁹³⁽ᴰ⁾필요한 출입구 개수
4. ¹⁹³⁽ᴮ⁾울타리를 설치해 두어야 하는 일수

어휘 temporary 임시의 residential 주거용의 commercial 상업용의 install 설치하다 residence 거주지, 주택 expert 전문가 booked 예약된 take down 해체하다 haul away 운반하다 obtain 얻다, 구하다 manufacturer 제조 업체 sturdy 견고한 appearance 외양 appreciate 진가를 인정하다 legally required 법적으로 필요한 inspection 검사 certification 증명, 증명서 교부 quote 견적 accurate 정확한 preferred 선호하는 regulation 규정 commonly 일반적으로 perimeter 주변, 둘레 enclose 둘러싸다 entrance 출입구

| 이름: | 마거리트 카하트 | 전화: (0117) 555-9102 |

설치 주소: 438 스트레트포드 웨이, 브리스톨 BS5 7TB
이메일: mcarhart@stockporteventcentre.co.uk
¹⁹⁴오늘 날짜: 8월 8일

울타리 세부 사항:

¹⁹²,¹⁹³⁽ᴬ⁾앞으로 2주 이내에 스톡포트 이벤트 센터 주변에 설치할 3미터 높이 임시 울타리가 필요합니다. ¹⁹²,¹⁹³⁽ᴮ⁾,¹⁹⁴8월 18일부터 30일까지 보수 공사를 진행하는 동안 일반인이 들어오지 못하게 막는 용도입니다. ¹⁹³⁽ᴰ⁾두 개의 문이 있어서 작업자와 차량이 드나들 수 있어야 합니다.

어휘 prevent A from B A가 B하지 못하게 막다 renovation 보수, 개조 vehicle 탈것, 차량

수신: mcarhart@stockporteventcentre.co.uk
발신: hmontalbo@runklefencing.co.uk
날짜: 8월 9일
제목: 견적 번호 080817
첨부: ⬦ fencequote_mcarhart

카하트 씨께

문의해 주셔서 감사합니다. 요청하신 작업 건은 첨부한 견적서를 확인해 주십시오. ¹⁹⁴3주 미만의 기간을 앞두고 통지하는 긴급 주문 건을 제외하고는 배송료가 추가로 포함되지 않습니다. 제공하신 정보를 바탕으로 대략적인 견적을 낸 것입니다. (0117) 555-2938로 전화하셔서 누락된 세부 사항을 알려 주시면 정확한 견적을 드릴 수 있습니다.

¹⁹⁵귀하의 주문 건에 비닐막 포함을 고려해 보시는 것이 어떨까 합니다. 비닐막은 울타리에 씌워진 채 고정되어 보행자들이 건설 현장을 볼 수 없도록 합니다. 관심이 있으시면 수정 견적에 포함해 드릴 수 있습니다.

하워드 몬탤보

어휘 enquiry 문의 attached 첨부된 estimate 견적 delivery 배송 at no further charge 추가 요금이 없는 notice 통지 rough estimate 어림 견적 accurate 정확한 wrap 싸다, 포장하다 fasten 조이다 pedestrian 보행자 revise 수정하다

191 사실 관계 확인

번역 웹사이트에서 3미터보다 높은 울타리에 대해 명시한 것은?
(A) 비닐로 만들어졌다.
(B) 대개 법으로 금지되어 있다.
(C) 특별 운송 수단을 필요로 한다.
(D) 제조 업체에서 직접 주문해야 한다.

해설 웹사이트 마지막 단락의 1번 항목에서 일반적으로 현지 규정은 울타리 높이를 최고 3미터까지 허용하고 있다(local regulations commonly allow a maximum height of three metres)고 했으므로, 3미터보다 높은 울타리는 법으로 금지된다는 것을 알 수 있다. 따라서 (B)가 정답이다.

어휘 prohibit 금지하다 transportation 운송, 교통편

▸▸ **Paraphrasing** 지문의 local regulations → 정답의 law
지문의 commonly → 정답의 usually

192 세부 사항

번역 양식에 따르면, 카하트 씨는 왜 임시 울타리를 설치해야 하는가?
(A) 대지 경계선을 표시하기 위해
(B) 전시회에 이목을 집중시키기 위해
(C) 특별 행사에 모인 관중을 통제하기 위해
(D) 일반인의 공사 현장 접근을 제한하기 위해

해설 온라인 양식에서 보수 공사를 진행하는 동안 일반인이 들어오지 못하게 막기 위해(to prevent the public from entering while we make renovations) 임시 울타리 설치가 필요하다고 했으므로, (D)가 정답이다.

어휘 property line 대지 경계선 draw attention to ～에 관심을 끌다 limit 제한하다

193 연계

번역   카하트 씨는 필요한 울타리에 대해 어떤 정보를 주지 않았는가?

(A) 세워야 하는 울타리 높이
(B) 울타리가 필요한 날짜
(C) 둘러쌀 구역의 둘레
(D) 필요한 출입구 개수

해설   카하트 씨는 온라인 양식에 8월 18일부터 30일까지(from 18 to 30 August) 3미터 높이 임시 울타리(a temporary three-metre-tall fence)를 설치하고 싶다고 하며, 두 개의 문이 필요하다(Two gates are needed)고 적었다. 이는 웹사이트에서 요청한 정보 항목 중 각각 4, 1, 3번에 해당한다. 따라서 2번 항목인 울타리가 둘러쌀 구역의 둘레(The perimeter of the area you need to enclose) 정보를 제공하지 않은 것이므로, (C)가 정답이다.

어휘   erect 세우다

> ▸▸ **Paraphrasing**   지문의 **The preferred height of your fence**
> → 보기 (A)의 **The height of the fence to be erected**
> 지문의 **The number of days the fence needs to be up** → 보기 (B)의 **The dates when the fence is needed**

194 연계

번역   카하트 씨의 울타리 프로젝트에 대해 암시된 것은?

(A) 배송료가 있을 것이다.
(B) 프로젝트에는 여러 곳의 현장에서의 작업이 포함된다.
(C) 울타리 설치에 추가 작업자를 채용해야 한다.
(D) 감독관이 프로젝트를 먼저 승인해야 한다.

해설   이메일의 첫 번째 단락에서 3주가 채 안 되는 기간을 앞두고 통지하는 긴급 주문 건을 제외하고는(unless a rush order—one providing less than three weeks' notice—is required) 배송료가 추가로 붙지 않는다고 했는데, 카하트 씨가 8월 8일에 작성한 온라인 양식을 보면 8월 18일부터 30일까지 보수 공사를 진행하는 동안(while we make renovations from 18 to 30 August) 설치할 울타리가 필요하다고 했다. 따라서 카하트 씨의 주문은 긴급 주문 건으로 분류되어 배송료가 청구될 것임을 추론할 수 있으므로, (A)가 정답이다.

어휘   inspector 감독관   approve 승인하다

195 세부 사항

번역   몬탈보 씨는 왜 막을 추가할 것을 권하는가?

(A) 소음 차단벽 역할을 한다.
(B) 먼지를 줄이는 데 도움이 된다.
(C) 시각적인 가림막 역할을 한다.
(D) 안전 환경을 향상시킨다.

해설   이메일의 마지막 단락에서 비닐막(a plastic curtain)은 보행자들이 건설 현장을 볼 수 없게 한다(hiding the construction site from the view of pedestrians)며 추가 설치 고려를 권하고 있다. 따라서 (C)가 정답이다.

어휘   barrier 벽   keep in ~를 억제하다   serve as ~의 역할을 하다

> ▸▸ **Paraphrasing**   지문의 **hiding the construction site from the view** → 정답의 **serves as a visual screen**

196-200 이메일 + 전단지 + 일정표

수신: 다니엘 로드리게스 페라이라
발신: 리비아 로메로
제목: 회사 야유회
날짜: ¹⁹⁷8월 5일

안녕하세요 다니엘 씨,

¹⁹⁷잘 적응하고 계시길 바랍니다. 지난 몇 주간 바쁘셨을 거라 생각합니다. ¹⁹⁶매년 이맘때 사무실 관리자가 보통 연례 야유회 준비를 시작합니다. ¹⁹⁷6월에 보신 면접에서 이를 언급했던 것 같군요. 예전에는 음악회에 가거나 지역에 있는 강 유람선 여행을 했습니다. 이러한 야유회는 언제나 사기 진작에 효과적이며, 모두가 이를 손꼽아 기다리고 있습니다.

¹⁹⁶올해는 스포츠 행사 입장권을 구하는 것이 좋을 것 같습니다. ²⁰⁰많은 직원들이 산호세 스탈링 야구팀의 팬인 것으로 압니다. 팀이 홈 경기를 하는 저녁 경기여야 합니다. ¹⁹⁹올해는 600달러의 예산이 있어요. 입장권 가격을 살펴보니 전 직원의 입장권을 구매하기에 딱 맞을 것 같습니다.

엘리제 씨가 도와 드릴 수 있을 겁니다. 야유회 준비를 종종 도왔거든요. 질문이 있으시면 저에게 알려 주세요.

리비아 로메로
총무부장, 로프트그렌 컨설팅

어휘   outing 야유회   settle in 적응하다   typically 보통, 일반적으로   arrange 준비하다, 마련하다   mention 언급하다   morale 사기   look forward to ~를 고대하다   budget 예산

산호세 스탈링과 함께하는 행사를 계획해 보세요!

¹⁹⁸10인 이상의 단체에게 입장권을 할인해 드립니다. 입장권을 더 많이 구매할수록 더 많은 금액을 절약할 수 있습니다. 가족 모임, 회사 야유회, 자선 단체 기금 마련 행사 등에 더할 나위 없이 완벽합니다! 주최자를 위한 무료 입장권, 식사 할인, 점수판에 단체명 게시 등 특전을 누려 보세요.

단체 입장권 가격

10장	130달러
30장	360달러
¹⁹⁹**50장**	**550달러**
70장	700달러

더 자세한 정보를 원하시면 grouptickets@sanjosestarlings.com 또는 408-555-0101로 연락하세요.

**산호세 스탈링
8월 일정표**

날짜	요일	시간	상대팀	홈/원정
8월 13일	일요일	오후 1시 05분	아스펜 마너크	홈
200 8월 15일	화요일	200 오후 7시 05분	아스펜 마너크	200 홈
8월 19일	토요일	오후 1시 05분	필립스버그 핀스트라이프	원정
8월 22일	화요일	오후 7시 05분	필립스버그 핀스트라이프	원정

www.sanjosestarlings.com/tickets에서 온라인으로 입장권을
구매하세요.

196 주제 / 목적

번역 로메로 씨는 왜 로드리게스 페라이라 씨에게 이메일을 보냈는가?

(A) 곧 있을 예산 삭감에 대해 이야기하기 위해
(B) 음악회에 초대하기 위해
(C) 그의 새 비서를 소개하기 위해
(D) 행사 준비를 요청하기 위해

해설 이메일의 첫 번째 단락에서 매년 이맘때 사무실 관리자가 보통 연례 야유회 준비를 시작한다(the office manager typically begins arranging our annual company outing)고 한 후, 두 번째 단락에서 올해는 스포츠 행사 입장권을 구하는 것이 좋을 것 같다(it would be a good idea to get tickets to a sporting event)며 준비와 관련된 사항을 안내하고 있으므로, 행사 준비를 요청하기 위한 이메일임을 알 수 있다. 따라서 (D)가 정답이다.

어휘 upcoming 곧 있을, 다가오는 budget cut 예산 삭감

197 추론 / 암시

번역 로드리게스 페라이라 씨에 대해 이메일에서 암시된 것은?

(A) 최근 산호세 스탈링 경기를 보러 갔다.
(B) 몇 주 후 휴가를 떠날 예정이다.
(C) 전문 파티 기획자이다.
(D) 최근 로프트그렌 컨설팅에서 근무를 시작했다.

해설 로프트그렌 컨설팅의 총무부장인 로메로 씨는 로드리게스 페라이라 씨에게 잘 적응하고 있길 바란다(I hope you are settling in well)는 인사말로 이메일을 시작한 후에 그가 6월에 보았던 면접(during your interview in June)을 언급했다. 이메일을 작성한 날짜를 보면 8월 5일이므로, 로드리게스 페라이라 씨가 최근에 회사에서 근무하기 시작했다는 것을 추론할 수 있다. 따라서 (D)가 정답이다.

어휘 attend 참석하다

198 세부 사항

번역 전단지에 따르면 단체 입장권 구매에 따른 혜택은?

(A) 입장권 가격 인하
(B) 무료 음식
(C) 앞줄 좌석
(D) 팀 로고가 그려진 티셔츠

해설 전단지 상단에서 10인 이상의 단체에게 입장권을 할인해 준다(Discounted tickets are available for groups of ten or more)고 했으므로, (A)가 정답이다.

어휘 reduce 감소시키다, 줄이다 seating 좌석

▸▸ **Paraphrasing** 지문의 **Discounted tickets**
→ 정답의 **Reduced ticket prices**

199 연계

번역 로프트그렌 컨설팅 직원은 몇 명이겠는가?

(A) 10
(B) 30
(C) 50
(D) 70

해설 이메일의 두 번째 단락을 보면, 올해 야유회에 600달러의 예산이 책정되었고(We have a budget of $600.00 this year) 전 직원의 입장권을 구매하기에 딱 맞을 것 같다(it seems ~ just enough to get a ticket for every staff member)고 했다. 인원에 따른 입장권 금액은 전단지에서 확인할 수 있는데, 600달러 예산에 가장 근접한 금액은 550달러이므로, 로프트그렌 컨설팅 직원이 50명임을 추론할 수 있다. 따라서 (C)가 정답이다.

200 연계

번역 로프트그렌 컨설팅 직원들은 며칠에 경기를 보러 가겠는가?

(A) 8월 13일
(B) 8월 15일
(C) 8월 19일
(D) 8월 22일

해설 이메일의 두 번째 단락에서 로메로 씨는 스포츠 행사 입장권 구매를 추천하면서 많은 직원들이 산호세 스탈링 야구팀의 팬이며(many staff members are fans of the San Jose Starlings baseball team) 팀이 홈경기를 하는 저녁 경기에 가야 한다(It should be an evening game when the team is playing at home)고 했다. 일정표를 보면 산호세 스탈링 야구팀이 저녁에 홈경기를 하는 날은 8월 15일이므로, 로프트그렌 컨설팅 직원들이 이날 경기를 보러 갈 것임을 추론할 수 있다. 따라서 (B)가 정답이다.

101 (D)	**102** (B)	**103** (C)	**104** (A)	**105** (A)
106 (D)	**107** (D)	**108** (B)	**109** (C)	**110** (A)
111 (B)	**112** (A)	**113** (C)	**114** (D)	**115** (A)
116 (B)	**117** (C)	**118** (C)	**119** (C)	**120** (D)
121 (D)	**122** (B)	**123** (B)	**124** (A)	**125** (A)
126 (B)	**127** (C)	**128** (C)	**129** (D)	**130** (C)
131 (A)	**132** (D)	**133** (A)	**134** (B)	**135** (B)
136 (D)	**137** (A)	**138** (C)	**139** (D)	**140** (C)
141 (A)	**142** (B)	**143** (B)	**144** (D)	**145** (A)
146 (A)	**147** (C)	**148** (C)	**149** (C)	**150** (D)
151 (C)	**152** (B)	**153** (D)	**154** (A)	**155** (B)
156 (A)	**157** (C)	**158** (C)	**159** (D)	**160** (C)
161 (C)	**162** (A)	**163** (B)	**164** (B)	**165** (C)
166 (B)	**167** (C)	**168** (C)	**169** (A)	**170** (D)
171 (C)	**172** (A)	**173** (C)	**174** (C)	**175** (B)
176 (A)	**177** (B)	**178** (A)	**179** (D)	**180** (C)
181 (D)	**182** (B)	**183** (C)	**184** (B)	**185** (C)
186 (C)	**187** (A)	**188** (C)	**189** (C)	**190** (B)
191 (A)	**192** (D)	**193** (A)	**194** (C)	**195** (D)
196 (A)	**197** (D)	**198** (B)	**199** (D)	**200** (D)

PART 5

101 명사 자리 _ 전치사의 목적어

해설 빈칸은 전치사 in의 목적어 역할을 하는 명사 자리이므로, '재정, 재무'라는 의미의 명사인 (D) finance가 정답이다. (A) financially는 부사, (B) financed는 동사/과거분사(형용사), (C) financial은 형용사로 모두 품사상 빈칸에 적합하지 않다.

번역 빌라누에바 씨는 기업 재무와 예산 책정 분야에 폭넓은 경력을 가지고 있다.

어휘 extensive 폭넓은 budget 예산을 책정하다 financially 재정적으로, 재정상 financial 금융[재무]의 finance 재원; 지금을 대다

102 부사 어휘

해설 동사 works를 적절히 수식하는 부사를 선택하는 문제이다. work가 '일하다'라는 의미이므로, 빈칸에는 어떻게 일했는지를 나타내는 부사가 들어가야 자연스럽다. 따라서 '열심히'라는 의미의 (B) hard가 정답이다. (A) bright는 '환히, 밝게', (C) tight는 '단단히, 꽉', (D) sharp는 '정각에'라는 의미로 빈칸에 적절하지 않다.

번역 루이스 씨는 아주 열심히 일했기 때문에 급여를 인상 받았다.

어휘 pay raise 급여 인상

103 부사 자리 _ 어휘

해설 빈칸 뒤 동사 offers를 적절히 수식하는 부사를 선택하는 문제이다. '고풍스러운 매력(old-fashioned charm)'이 가득할 뿐만 아니라 현대적인 편의 시설(modern conveniences)을 제공하기도 한다'라는 내용이 되어야 자연스러우므로, '또한, ~도'라는 의미의 (C) also가 정답이다. 참고로, (A) plus는 '~도 또한'이라는 의미이긴 하지만, 전치사나 접속사로 쓰이므로 빈칸에 적절하지 않다.

번역 고풍스러운 매력으로 가득한 브론스타드 여관은 현대적인 편의 시설을 제공하기도 한다.

어휘 old-fashioned 고풍스러운 convenience 편의 (시설)

104 전치사 어휘

해설 빈칸은 뒤에 나오는 명사구 a larger location을 목적어로 취하는 전치사 자리이며, 빈칸 이하의 전치사구가 동사 will be moving을 수식하고 있다. 따라서 빈칸에는 will be moving과 a larger location을 적절히 연결해 주는 전치사가 들어가야 한다. 문맥상 '더 넓은 장소로 이전할 예정이다'라는 내용이 되어야 자연스러우므로, '~로'라는 의미의 (A) to가 정답이다.

번역 프랭클린 서점은 다음 달에 퀸 스트리트에 있는 더 넓은 장소로 이전할 예정이다.

어휘 location 장소, 위치

105 부사 자리 _ 동사 수식

해설 빈칸 뒤 동사 considered를 수식하는 부사 자리이므로, '잠시'라는 의미의 부사인 (A) briefly가 정답이다. (B) briefs는 명사/동사, (C) briefing은 명사/동명사/현재분사, (D) briefed는 동사/과거분사(형용사)로 모두 품사상 빈칸에 적합하지 않다.

번역 마리나 호우 씨는 잠시 배우가 될까 생각하다가 대신 극본을 쓰기로 결심했다.

어휘 consider 고려하다, 생각하다 briefly 잠시, 간단히 brief 짧은; 업무 (지침서); ~에게 보고하다 briefing 브리핑, 정보[지시]

106 형용사 어휘

해설 전치사 for의 목적어 역할을 하는 명사 repairs를 적절히 수식하는 형용사를 선택하는 문제이다. 문맥상 '일반적인 수리에 대한 경제적인 해결책'이라는 내용이 되어야 자연스러우므로, '일반적인, 공동의'라는 의미의 (D) common이 정답이다.

번역 픽시트 타임 웹사이트에서 주택 소유자들은 일반적인 수리에 대한 경제적인 해결책을 찾을 것이다.

어휘 economical 경제적인 solution 해결책 repair 수리; 수리하다

107 부사 자리 _ 동사 수식

해설 빈칸은 수동태 동사인 was hired를 수식하는 부사 자리이므로, '원래'라는 의미의 부사인 (D) originally가 정답이다. (A) originality는 명사, (B) original은 명사/형용사, (C) originals는 명사로 모두 품사상 빈칸에 적합하지 않다.

번역 월터 키건 씨는 원래 영업 사원으로 채용되었지만 곧 마케팅부 부서장이 되었다.

어휘 department 부서 originality 독창성 original 독창적인, 원래의; 원본

108 전치사 자리

해설 빈칸 앞에 완전한 절이 왔고, 뒤에 명사구가 있으므로 빈칸에는 its rich culture를 목적어로 취하는 전치사가 들어가야 한다. 따라서 '~ 때문에'라는 의미의 전치사인 (B) because of가 정답이다. 접속사인 (A) provided that 뒤에는 완전한 절이, (D) how 뒤에는 완전한 절이나 to부정사가 와야 하고 (C) even은 형용사/부사/동사이므로, 모두 품사상 빈칸에 적합하지 않다.

번역 듀어 섬은 풍부한 예술 및 음악 문화 때문에 관광객들에게 인기가 높아졌다.

어휘 provided that 만일 ~이라면

109 동사 자리 _ 수 일치

해설 빈칸은 주어 Mr. Shang의 동사 자리이다. 따라서 미래 시제인 (C) will consider와 현재 시제인 (D) consider 중 하나를 선택해야 하는데, 주어인 Mr. Shang이 3인칭 단수이므로 (C) will consider가 정답이 된다. (D) consider는 수가 일치하지 않으므로 오답이며, 동명사/현재분사인 (A) considering과 to부정사인 (B) to consider는 문장의 동사 역할을 할 수 없으므로 빈칸에 들어갈 수 없다.

번역 상 씨는 그 제안을 좋아하지는 않지만 고려는 해 볼 것이다.

어휘 enthusiastic 열광적인

110 명사 어휘

해설 빈칸은 design과 복합명사를 이루어 동사 has been relocated의 주어 역할을 하는 명사 자리로, 빈칸 뒤 전치사구 of Tavalyo Toys의 수식을 받고 있다. 따라서 회사(Tavalyo Toys)에서 이전의 대상이 될 만한 대상을 나타내는 명사가 빈칸에 들어가야 하므로, '부서'라는 뜻의 (A) division이 정답이 된다.

번역 타바요 토이즈의 디자인 부서는 회사 본사로 이전되었다.

어휘 relocate 이전하다 headquarters 본사 specification 명세 allowance 허용량, 비용 construction 건설

111 형용사 자리 _ 명사 수식

해설 빈칸에는 명사 sites를 수식해 주는 형용사나 sites와 복합명사를 이루는 명사가 들어갈 수 있다. 문맥상 '역사적인 장소', 즉 '유적지'라는 내용이 되어야 자연스러우므로, '역사적인'이라는 의미의 형용사인 (B) historic이 정답이 된다.

번역 메릭 여행사는 상트페테르부르크 지역에 있는 국가적인 기념물과 다른 유적지를 둘러보는 관광 프로그램을 조직한다.

어휘 organize 조직하다 monument 기념물, 유적 historic site 유적지 historian 사학자 historically 역사상 histories (기록된) 역사(물)

112 상관접속사

해설 빈칸은 not only 및 as well과 짝을 이루어 두 개의 동사구 works with smartphones와 is waterproof를 연결하는 접속사 자리이다. 따라서 'A뿐만 아니라 B도'라는 의미의 상관접속사 「not only A but B (as well)」를 완성하는 (A) but이 정답이다. 참고로, 「not only A but (also) B」의 구조로도 쓰일 수 있다.

번역 MHS 무선 스피커는 스마트폰과 연동될 뿐 아니라 방수도 된다.

어휘 waterproof 방수의

113 인칭대명사 격 _ 소유격

해설 빈칸은 전치사 in의 목적어 역할을 하는 명사 departments를 한정 수식하는 자리이므로, 소유격 인칭대명사인 (C) their가 정답이다.

번역 부팀장들은 부서 내 일상적인 업무를 주로 담당한다.

어휘 largely 주로 responsible for ~을 담당하는, ~의 책임을 맡은 day-to-day 일상적인

114 부사 어휘

해설 빈칸 뒤 동사구 review the terms를 적절히 수식하는 부사를 선택하는 문제이다. 따라서 계약 조건을 검토하는 방식을 묘사하는 부사가 들어가야 자연스러우므로, '철저히'라는 의미의 (D) thoroughly가 정답이다.

번역 고객들은 서명하기 전에 헬스클럽 회원권 계약 조건을 철저히 검토해야 한다.

어휘 terms (계약 등의) 조건 smoothly 부드럽게, 순조롭게 probably 아마 legibly 읽기 쉽게

115 형용사 자리 _ 명사 수식

해설 빈칸은 명사 estimate 앞 자리로, '약간 적게 잡은 추정치'라는 의미를 완성하는 형용사가 들어가야 문맥상 자연스럽다. 따라서 '(실제보다 숫자·양을) 적게 잡은, 보수적인'이라는 의미의 형용사인 (A) conservative가 정답이다. (B) conservation은 '보존', (C) conservatism은 '보수성'이라는 의미의 명사로 estimate와 복합명사를 이루지 않으며, (D) conservatively(보수적으로, 줄잡아)는 부사로서 명사를 수식할 수 없으므로 빈칸에 들어갈 수 없다.

번역 우리는 다음 달에 얼마나 많은 관광객이 올지에 대해 추정치를 약간 적게 잡았다.

어휘 estimate 추정(치), 추산, 견적서

116 동사 어휘

해설 주어인 the workers at Loruja 및 목적어인 additional vacation time과 가장 잘 어울리는 타동사를 선택하는 문제이다. 문맥상 '직원들이 추가로 휴가를 얻게 된다'라는 내용이 되어야 자연스러우므로, '얻다, 벌다'라는 의미의 (B) earn이 정답이다.

번역 로루자 직원들은 입사 후 3년이 지나면 추가로 휴가를 얻게 된다.

어휘 employment 근무, 집무 additional 추가의 reserve 예약하다

117 명사절 접속사

해설 뒤에 오는 불완전한 절(has ~ the day)을 이끌며 해당 절에서 주어 역할을 할 수 있는 명사절 접속사를 고르는 문제로, (B) Who와 (C) Whoever 중 하나를 선택해야 한다. 빈칸부터 day까지가 문장의 주어 역할을 하는데, 문맥을 살펴보면 사무실 내 모두에게 해당될 수 있는 규칙에 대한 내용이므로 '누구든 일과가 끝날 때 시간이 있는 사람'이 주어가 되어야 자연스럽다. 따라서 (C) Whoever가 정답이다.

번역 누구든 일과가 끝날 때 시간이 있는 사람이 파일 캐비닛이 모두 잠겼는지 확인해야 한다.

어휘 lock 잠그다

118 전치사 어휘

해설 빈칸 뒤 명사 Asia를 목적어로 취하는 전치사 자리로, 빈칸을 포함한 전치사구가 promises next-day shipping을 수식하고 있다. 따라서 특정 장소(Asia) 및 배송(shipping)과 어울려 쓰이는 전치사를 선택해야 하는데, 문맥상 '아시아 전역에 익일 배송을 보장합니다'라는 내용이 되어야 자연스러우므로, '전역에, 도처에'라는 의미의 (C) throughout이 정답이 된다.

번역 노스 리버 린넨즈는 아시아 전역에 익일 배송을 보장합니다.

어휘 next-day shipping 익일 배송

119 분사구문

해설 빈칸에는 뒤에 나오는 주절을 수식하는 분사가 들어가야 하므로, 과거분사 (C) Discovered와 현재분사 (D) Discovering 중 하나를 선택해야 한다. 주절의 주어이자 분사구문의 생략된 주어인 the unpublished novel이 발견된 대상이므로, 수동의 의미를 나타내는 과거분사 (C) Discovered가 정답이 된다. 동사인 (A) Discover와 명사인 (B) Discovery는 부사와 같은 역할을 할 수 없으므로 빈칸에 적합하지 않다.

번역 지난해에 발견된 마틴 심 씨의 미출간 소설은 여러 출판사들로부터 집중적인 관심을 끌었다.

어휘 unpublished 출판되지 않은 attract 끌다 intense 집중적인, 강렬한 publishing company 출판사 discover 발견하다 discovery 발견

120 수량형용사

해설 빈칸 뒤 neighborhood를 적절히 수식하는 수량형용사를 선택하는 문제이다. 문맥상 특수 온라인 데이터 베이스를 사용하면 어떤 인근 지역을 선택하든 간에 그 지역의 부동산 목록을 검색할 수 있다는 내용이 되어야 자연스러우므로, '어떤 ~라도'라는 의미의 (D) any가 정답이 된다. 참고로, any는 '특정 범주 내에 있는 사람[것] 누구나[무엇이나]'를 뜻하기 때문에 문맥에 따라 '모든'이라고 번역될 수 있지만, '특정 범주 내에 있는 사람[것] 전부'를 가리키는 all과는 어감이 다르다. 또한 해당 문장에서처럼 neighborhood가 '(물리적인) 인근 지역'을 의미할 때는 가산명사로 쓰이므로 (A) other, (B) several, (C) all은 빈칸에 적절하지 않다.

번역 훈튼 부동산의 고객은 특수 온라인 데이터베이스를 사용해 모든 인근 지역의 부동산 목록을 검색할 수 있다.

어휘 realty 부동산 property 부동산, 건물 neighborhood 인근 지역, 이웃 (사람들)

121 명사 자리 _ 전치사의 목적어

해설 빈칸은 전치사 of의 목적어 역할을 하는 명사 자리로, 빈칸을 포함한 전치사구가 지시대명사 those(=hotels)를 수식하고 있다. 따라서 동명사인 (B) competing과 명사인 (D) competition 중 하나를 선택해야 하는데, 문맥상 '경쟁사의 호텔들'이라는 내용이 되어야 자연스러우므로, (D) competition이 정답이 된다. 참고로, competition은 '경쟁, 경연 대회' 이외에 '경쟁자, 경쟁 상대'라는 뜻으로도 쓰인다.

번역 우수한 서비스가 우리 호텔이 경쟁사의 호텔과 차별화되는 점이다.

어휘 exceptional 우수한 set A apart from B A를 B와 구별하다 compete 경쟁하다 competitive 경쟁력을 지닌, 경쟁하는

122 부사절 접속사

해설 빈칸 앞뒤에 완전한 절이 왔으며 빈칸 이하의 절이 앞에 있는 절을 수식하고 있으므로, 빈칸에는 두 절을 연결해 주는 부사절 접속사가 들어가야 한다. 문맥상 '속도가 느려지는 원인이 확인될 때까지'라는 내용이 되어야 자연스러우므로, (B) until이 정답이 된다. 참고로, 전치사인 (C) due to는 절을 이끌 수 없다.

번역 속도가 느려지는 원인이 확인될 때까지 인터넷 연결을 면밀히 관찰할 것이다.

어휘 closely 면밀히 monitor 감시하다, 관찰하다 source 원인, 출처 slowdown 감속, (경기) 부진 confirm 확인하다

123 형용사 자리 _ 명사 수식

해설 빈칸 앞 most와 함께 최상급을 이루어 명사 customers를 수식하는 형용사 자리이므로, '소중한, 귀중한'이라는 의미의 과거분사형 형용사인 (B) valued가 정답이다. (A) valuation은 명사, (C) value와 (D) values는 명사/동사로 품사상 빈칸에 적합하지 않다.

번역 지난 10년간 댄턴 운송의 가장 소중한 고객 중 한 분이 되어 주셔서 감사합니다.

어휘 valuation 평가, 가치(액), 판단 value 가치, 값, 유용성; 소중하게 생각하다

124 동사 어휘

해설 빈칸 뒤 목적어 talented sales agents 및 전치사구 from the rest와 적절히 어울려 쓰이는 동사를 선택하는 문제이다. 문맥상 '유능한 영업 대리인을 (나머지와) 신속히 판별하다'라는 내용이 되어야 자연스러우므로, 전치사 from과 함께 'A를 B와 구별하다, 판별하다'라는 표현을 완성하는 (A) distinguish가 정답이다.

번역 탕 씨는 유능한 영업 대리인을 신속히 판별할 수 있으므로 성공한 채용 담당자이다.

어휘 recruiter 채용 담당자 rest 나머지 persuade 설득하다 alter 바꾸다 assist 돕다

125 부사절 접속사

해설 빈칸 뒤에 오는 완전한 절(work stopped during the power failure)을 이끄는 접속사 자리이다. 따라서 '비록 ~일지라도'라는 의미의 부사절 접속사인 (A) although가 정답이 된다. (B) at은 전치사, (C) her는 소유격/목적격 인칭대명사, (D) never는 부사로 절을 이끌 수 없으므로, 빈칸에 들어갈 수 없다.

번역 페너 씨는 정전 기간 동안 작업이 중단되었지만 생산 목표치는 달성될 것이라고 우리에게 장담했다.

어휘 assure 장담하다, 보장하다   power failure 정전, 동력 고장
meet (의무를) 완수하다, 달성하다

126 부사 어휘

해설 빈칸 앞에 있는 동사 will be adjusted를 적절히 수식하는 부사를 선택하는 문제이다. 견적(quote)이 앞에서 언급된 주문 제작 울타리의 정확한 치수(dimensions)에 따라 조정된다는 내용이 되어야 자연스러우므로, 빈칸에는 '그에 맞춰, 그에 따라서'라는 의미의 부사가 들어가야 한다. 따라서 (B) accordingly가 정답이다. 참고로, (A) namely는 예를 나열할 때 쓰이는 부사로 뒤에 해당 항목들이 열거되어야 한다.

번역 고객님께서 세우고자 하시는 주문 제작 울타리의 정확한 치수를 주시면 그에 따라 견적이 조정됩니다.

어휘 dimension 치수   custom 주문 제작한, 맞춤의   quote 견적
adjust 조정하다   namely 즉   frequently 자주   supposedly
아마

127 동명사 _ 주어

해설 빈칸 뒤 명사 employees를 목적어로 취하면서 동사 is의 주어 역할을 하는 자리이므로, 동명사인 (C) empowering이 정답이다. 과거분사(형용사)인 (A) empowered는 명사 employees를 수식할 수 있지만 그렇게 될 경우 동사 is와 수가 일치하지 않게 되므로, 빈칸에 들어갈 수 없다.

번역 체스턴빌 은행의 부사장은 직원들에게 자율권을 부여하는 것이 회사의 성공에 필수적이라고 믿는다.

어휘 empower 권한[자율권]을 부여하다   vital 필수적인, 굉장히 중요한

128 명사 어휘

해설 빈칸은 동사 is posted의 주어 역할을 하는 명사 자리로, 전치사구 for the city council's Monday meeting의 수식을 받는다. 문맥상 회의(meeting) 전에 미리 웹사이트에 게시되어야(is posted) 할 대상을 나타내는 명사가 빈칸에 들어가야 하므로, '안건'이라는 의미의 (C) agenda가 정답이다.

번역 시 의회의 월요일 회의 안건은 그 전주 금요일 오후 3시까지 시 웹사이트에 게시된다.

어휘 municipal 시의   preceding 앞의   inventory 재고(품)

129 부사 자리 _ 형용사 수식

해설 빈칸은 「declared+목적어(the new facility)+목적격 보어(sound and ready to open)」의 구조에서 형용사 sound를 수식하는 부사 자리이므로, '구조적으로'라는 의미의 부사인 (D) structurally가 정답이다. (A) structured는 동사/과거분사, (B) structuring는 동명사/현재분사, (C) structural은 형용사로 모두 품사상 빈칸에 적합하지 않다.

번역 건축물 준공 검사 책임자는 신규 시설이 구조적으로 건실하며 개방될 준비가 되어 있다고 공표했다.

어휘 building inspector 건축물 준공 검사 책임자   declare 공표하다
facility 시설   sound 건실한, 건전한   structure 조직하다,
구조화하다

130 형용사 어휘

해설 빈칸 뒤 명사구 Brighton Award를 수식하는 형용사를 선택하는 문제로, 이 상의 특징을 적절히 묘사하는 형용사가 빈칸에 들어가야 한다. 따라서 '권위 있는, 명망 있는'이라는 의미로 상의 위상을 나타내는 (C) prestigious가 정답이다.

번역 우에르타스 박사는 식물 생물학에서의 획기적인 업적으로 권위 있는 브라이튼 상을 받았다.

어휘 groundbreaking 획기적인   overwhelmed 압도된
intentional 의도적인   deserving 받을 만한

PART 6

131-134 이메일

> 수신: 전 직원
> 발신: 조지 루이스
> 날짜: 7월 18일 수요일
> 제목: 중요한 고객
>
> 두 곳의 ¹³¹**지역** 신문 〈토론토 데이〉와 〈토론토 라이징〉의 음식 비평가들이 이번 주에 이곳에서 식사할 예정입니다. 완벽하게 업무를 수행할 수 있도록 특별히 노력합시다.
>
> 비평가들의 사진이 손님맞이 구역에 전시될 것입니다. 이 ¹³²**이미지들**을 활용하여 안내 담당 직원들은 비평가들을 알아보고 종업원들에게 말해 줄 책임이 있으며, 종업원들은 주방에 알려야 합니다. 서빙 직원들은 신속해질 수 있도록 노력해야 합니다. 또한 우리 식당의 일일 특선 요리들을 추천해야 합니다. ¹³³이는 우리가 제공하는 가장 독창적인 요리들입니다.
>
> 저는 우리 모두가 훌륭한 음식과 서비스로 이 비평가들에게 ¹³⁴**깊은 인상을 줄 것**이라고 확신합니다.
>
> 감사합니다.
>
> 조지 루이스
> 총지배인

131　형용사 자리 _ 명사 수식

해설　빈칸은 전치사 from의 목적어 역할을 하는 명사 newspapers의 앞 자리로, 문맥상 '지역 신문'이라는 의미를 완성하는 형용사가 들어가야 자연스럽다. 따라서 '지역의, 현지의'라는 의미의 형용사인 (A) local 이 정답이다. (B) locals은 명사로 newspapers와 복합명사를 이룰 수 없으므로 오답이고, (C) locally는 부사, (D) more locally는 비교급 부사로 모두 품사상 빈칸에 적합하지 않다.

어휘　locals 주민, 현지인

132　명사 어휘

해설　빈칸은 these가 한정 수식하는 명사 자리로, 현재분사 Using의 목적어 역할을 한다. 바로 앞 문장에서 비평가들의 사진(Photographs of the critics)이 손님맞이 구역에 전시된다고 했고, 뒤 문장에서는 안내 담당 직원들이 이를 통해 비평가를 알아봐야 한다고 했으므로, 빈칸에는 사진(photographs)과 유사한 의미의 명사가 들어가야 자연스럽다. 따라서 (D) images가 정답이다.

어휘　review 후기　issue 문제, 주제

133　문맥에 맞는 문장 고르기

번역　(A) 이는 우리가 제공하는 가장 독창적인 요리들입니다.
　　　(B) 우리는 벌써 광고를 냈습니다.
　　　(C) 근무 일정은 뒷문에 게시되어 있습니다.
　　　(D) 그들 중 한 명이 시간에 불만이 있었습니다.

해설　빈칸 앞 문장에서 서빙 직원들이 식당의 일일 특선 요리들을 추천해야 한다(They should also recommend our daily specials)고 했으므로, 빈칸에는 일일 특선 요리들을 부연 설명하는 내용이 들어가야 문맥상 자연스럽다. 따라서 (A)가 정답이다. 참고로, (A)의 지시대명사 These는 our daily specials를 가리킨다.

134　동사 어형 _ 시제

해설　빈칸은 that절의 주어 everyone의 동사 자리로, 명사구 these critics를 목적어로 취하고 있다. 첫 번째 단락에서 '음식 비평가들이 이번 주에 이곳에서 식사할 예정이다(Food critics ~ are expected to dine here this week)'라고 했으므로, 해당 문장은 '이 비평가들에게 깊은 인상을 줄 것이다'라는 미래와 관련된 내용이 되어야 자연스럽다. 따라서 미래 시제인 (B) will impress가 정답이다.

어휘　impress 깊은 인상을 주다

135-138　기사

쉐르빌, 지역 관광업을 간소화하다

5월 10일—쉐르빌 시는 멋진 건축 양식과 오래 전부터 주민들에게 인정받아 온 숨막히게 아름다운 교외 지역을 자랑한다. 최근에 도입된 열차 운행 서비스 덕분에 관광객들도 이제 이 도시를 ¹³⁵즐길 수 있다. 쉐르빌의 인기 상승에 힘입어 기존의 관광 관련 산업이 호황을 누리고 있다. ¹³⁶실제로, 식당과 호텔의 개업이 이어지고 있다.

관광객들과 업체들을 돕기 위해 쉐르빌 통상국은 시티카드를 처음 선보였다. 카드를 긁으면 지역 업체나 관광지에서 자동으로 ¹³⁷할인이 적용된다. 시 당국은 관광객들이 더 저렴한 가격으로 혜택을 보게 되어 시티카드에 만족할 것이라고 생각한다. ¹³⁸동시에, 이 카드는 소매 거래를 촉진할 것이며, 이는 업체들의 수익 증가로 이어질 것이다.

어휘　simplify 간소화하다　boast 자랑하다　architecture 건축(양식)　breathtaking 숨막히는, 굉장한　appreciate (진가를) 인정받다, 감상하다　popularity 인기　existing 기존의, 현재 사용되는　boom 호황을 맞다　debut (제품 등을) 새로 선보이다, 처음 연주하다　attraction 관광지, 명소　benefit from ~에서 혜택을 보다　retail traffic 소매 거래　profit 수익, 이익

135　동사 어휘

해설　「be able to + 동사원형」 구조를 완성하는 동사를 선택하는 문제이다. 빈칸을 포함한 절이 전치사구 Thanks to the recent introduction of a train service의 수식을 받고 있으며, 빈칸은 명사구 the city 를 목적어로 취한다. 따라서 빈칸에는 열차 운행 서비스 도입으로 관광객이 할 수 있게된 행위를 묘사하는 동사가 들어가야 자연스러우므로, '도시를 즐길 수 있다'라는 의미를 완성하는 (B) enjoy가 정답이다.

어휘　revisit 다시 방문하다　depart 떠나다　bypass 우회하다

136　문맥에 맞는 문장 고르기

번역　(A) 게다가, 그 건축가는 탑을 지을 것이다.
　　　(B) 시장이 환영사를 할 예정이다.
　　　(C) 기차 덕분에 지역민들은 여행이 더 수월하다.
　　　(D) 실제로, 식당과 호텔의 개업이 이어지고 있다.

해설　빈칸 앞 문장에서 기존의 관광 관련 산업이 호황을 누리고 있다(existing tourism-related businesses are booming)고 했으므로, 빈칸에는 이와 관련된 내용을 덧붙이는 문장이 들어가야 문맥상 자연스럽다. 따라서 (D)가 정답이다.

137　명사 자리 _ 동사의 목적어

해설　빈칸은 '적용하다'라는 의미의 동사인 applies의 목적어 역할을 하는 명사 자리이므로, '할인'이라는 의미의 명사인 (A) discounts가 정답이다. to부정사인 (C) to discount와 동명사인 (D) discounting 또한 동사의 목적어 역할은 할 수 있지만, '할인하는 것'이라는 의미로 행위를 나타내며 목적어를 취해야 하므로 빈칸에는 적절하지 않다.

138 접속부사

해설 빈칸 앞뒤 문장을 문맥상 연결하는 접속부사를 선택하는 문제이다. 빈칸 앞 문장에서는 카드 사용으로 관광객이 누리게 될 혜택(tourists, who will benefit from lower prices)을, 빈칸 뒤에서는 기업에 돌아갈 혜택(leading to increased profits for businesses)을 언급했으므로, 빈칸에는 유사한 내용을 이어 주는 접속부사가 들어가야 자연스럽다. 따라서 '동시에'라는 의미의 (C) At the same time이 정답이다.

139-142 회람

수신: 마코 전 매장 점장들
발신: 메리 반 블리엣, 최고기술책임자
날짜: 5월 22일
주제: 결제 시스템 업그레이드

다음 주에 세인트 토마스에 위치한 마코 매장의 모든 금전 등록기에 새로운 결제 처리 단말기가 설치됩니다. 결제 시스템 4.0은 푸에르토리코에 있는 당사 매장에서 몇 달 동안 ¹³⁹**운영되어 왔습니다.** 지금까지 고객¹⁴⁰**이나** 점장이 보고한 시스템상의 문제는 없습니다.

¹⁴¹결제 시스템 4.0은 다양한 이점을 제공합니다. 그것은 현재 결제 시스템보다 더 빠르고 더 많은 상거래 유형을 처리합니다. 또한 25달러 미만의 상거래에 대해서 ¹⁴²**추가로** 조회할 필요가 없도록 해줍니다.

설치와 관련된 문의가 있으면 언제든지 저에게 연락 주십시오.

어휘 processing 처리, 가공 terminal 단말기 install 설치하다 register 금전 등록기; 등록하다 a variety of 다양한 benefit 이점, 혜택 transaction 거래 eliminate 제거하다 verification 조회, 입증, 확인

139 동사 어형 _ 시제

해설 빈칸은 주어 Payment System 4.0의 동사 자리이므로, 문장에서 동사 역할을 할 수 있는 (B) will operate, (C) is operating, (D) has operated 중 하나를 선택해야 한다. 전치사구 for several months가 빈칸을 수식하고 있고, 바로 뒤 문장에 부사구 So far(지금까지)가 있으므로, 해당 문장은 '(몇 달 전부터 지금까지) 시스템을 운영해 왔다'라는 내용이 되어야 자연스럽다. 따라서 현재완료형 동사인 (D) has operated가 정답이다.

140 상관접속사

해설 빈칸 뒤 접속사 or와 짝을 이루어 명사 customers와 managers를 연결하는 상관접속사 자리이다. 따라서 'A나 B 둘 중 하나'라는 의미의 「either A or B」 구조를 완성하는 (C) either가 정답이다.

어휘 extra 여분의 total 총, 전체의

141 문맥에 맞는 문장 고르기

번역 (A) 결제 시스템 4.0은 다양한 이점을 제공합니다.
(B) 새로운 급여 소프트웨어가 곧 출시될 예정입니다.
(C) 6월에는 특별 할인 판매가 있습니다.
(D) 정확한 설치 날짜를 모두에게 이메일로 보내 드리겠습니다.

해설 빈칸 뒤에서 기존 결제 시스템보다 더 빨리 많은 상거래를 처리(It is faster and handles more transaction types)하고, 일정 금액 미만의 거래는 조회할 필요가 없게 해준다(eliminates the need for verification of transactions under $25.00)는 결제 시스템의 이점을 구체적으로 나열하고 있으므로, 빈칸에서 먼저 결제 시스템이 다양한 이점을 제공한다는 내용이 언급되어야 문맥상 자연스럽다. 따라서 (A)가 정답이다.

어휘 release (신상품, 영화 등을) 출시하다, 개봉하다

142 형용사 어휘

해설 빈칸 뒤 명사 verification을 적절히 수식하는 형용사를 선택하는 문제이다. 새로운 결제 시스템이 25달러 미만의 거래는 조회할 필요가 없도록 해준다는 내용으로, 빈칸에 '조회'의 특징을 나타내는 형용사가 들어가야 자연스럽다. 따라서 '추가의, 부가적인'이라는 의미의 형용사인 (B) additional이 정답이다.

어휘 available 이용 가능한 reserved 예약된 economical 경제적인

143-146 후기

앱 후기: 포워드 패스

¹⁴³**피트니스** 앱의 세계에서 아베들론 주식회사가 개발한 앱들은 혁신적이고 사용하기 쉬워 눈에 띕니다. 태블릿과 스마트폰¹⁴⁴**용으로** 최근 출시된 포워드 패스 앱도 예외가 아닙니다. 포워드 패스는 고정식 자전거와 로잉 머신(노젓기 운동 기구) 같은 가정용 운동 장비와 연동됩니다. 사용자들은 실제 경로 수십 개를 담은 비디오 영상을 선택할 수 있습니다. 그런 다음 해당 영상을 자신의 운동 속도에 ¹⁴⁵**맞게 해주는** 여러 가지 속도 옵션 중 하나를 선택할 수 있습니다. ¹⁴⁶그들은 심지어 날씨 상태와 계절도 지정할 수 있습니다. 실외 운동을 대체할 수 있는 것은 없지만, 포워드 패스는 현재 시중에 나와 있는 다른 어떤 앱보다 더 흡사하게 나왔습니다. 우리 시험 사용자들은 이 앱을 강력히 추천합니다.

어휘 stand out 눈에 띄다, 두드러지다 newly 최근 release 출시하다 exception 예외 stationary 고정된, 정지된 specify (구체적으로) 정하다, 명시하다 replace 대체하다 currently 현재

143 명사 어휘

해설 빈칸 뒤 명사 apps와 함께 복합명사를 이루는 명사를 고르는 문제로, 문맥에 맞는 단어를 선택해야 한다. 뒤에 오는 내용을 살펴보면, 아베들론 주식회사가 개발한 앱 중 하나인 포워드 패스가 가정용 운동 장비와 연동된다(Forward Path connects with home exercise equipment)고 했으므로, 빈칸에는 운동과 관련된 명사가 들어가야 자연스럽다. 따라서 '피트니스, 신체 단련'이라는 의미의 (B) fitness가 정답이다.

어휘 translation 번역 landscaping 조경 navigation 운행, 조종

144 전치사 어휘

해설 빈칸은 명사구 tablets and smartphones를 목적어로 취하는 전치사 자리로, 빈칸 이하의 전치사구가 명사구 The newly released Forward Path app을 수식한다. 따라서 두 명사구를 적절히 연결하는 전치사를 선택해야 한다. 문맥상 '태블릿과 스마트폰용으로 최근 출시된 포워드 패스 앱'이라는 내용이 되어야 자연스러우므로, '~를 위한, ~용의'라는 의미의 전치사인 (D) for가 정답이다.

145 to부정사 _ 형용사적 용법

해설 빈칸 앞에 완전한 절이 왔으며, 뒤에 명사구(the video)가 있으므로 빈칸에는 이 두 요소를 이어주는 한편 바로 앞 명사구(speed options)나 절을 수식할 수 있는 준동사가 들어가야 한다. 문맥상 '동영상을 자신의 운동 속도에 맞추게 해주는 여러 가지 속도 옵션'이라는 내용이 되어야 자연스러우므로, 형용사와 같은 역할을 하는 to부정사 (A) to time이 정답이다. (D) timed가 수동태의 과거분사라면 앞에 오는 명사를 수식해 줄 수 있으나 목적어(the video)를 취할 수는 없으므로, 빈칸에 들어갈 수 없다.

146 문맥에 맞는 문장 고르기

번역 (A) 그들은 심지어 날씨 상태와 계절도 지정할 수 있습니다.
(B) 다른 앱과 비교해 선택 사항이 다소 제한적입니다.
(C) 이 가격이라면 아주 인기가 많을 것입니다.
(D) 최소 1일 30분입니다.

해설 빈칸 앞에서 사용자들이 실제 경로 수십 개를 담은 비디오 영상을 선택하여 동영상을 자신의 운동 속도에 맞게 조절할 수 있다(Users can select video footage ~ their workouts)고 했으므로, 빈칸에도 이와 유사하게 사용자들이 선택할 수 있는 옵션과 관련된 내용이 들어가야 자연스럽다. 따라서 (A)가 정답이다. 지문에서 전체적으로 긍정적인 평가를 하고 있으며, 빈칸 뒤에서도 다른 어떤 앱보다(than any other app) 실외 운동과 흡사하다고 했으므로, (B)는 정답이 될 수 없다.

PART 7

147-148 공지

---

[147]지역 교통 알림 및 교통국 업데이트

[147]지역 교통국은 1월에 675번 간선도로에 있는 표지판 수리 및 교체 작업을 시작할 예정입니다. [148]새로운 표지판은 빛을 더 잘 반사해 더욱 읽기 쉽도록 고안되었습니다. 찾기도 더 쉬울 것입니다.

대부분의 작업은 교통량이 가장 적은 저녁에 시행되며 이때 고속도로 차선이 일부 폐쇄될 예정입니다. 주간 차량 통행에는 영향이 없을 것입니다. 작업은 6주에서 8주 정도 소요될 예정이며, 예정된 모든 작업은 날씨에 좌우됩니다.

어휘 authority 당국 regional 지역의 repair 수리하다; 수리 replace 교체하다 reflective 반사하는 entail 필요로 하다, 수반하다

147 주제 / 목적

번역 공지의 목적은?
(A) 교통량 증가 경고
(B) 작업 구간 안전 수칙 설명
(C) 개선 공사 설명
(D) 간선도로 신설 계획 발표

해설 공지의 제목인 '지역 교통 알림 및 교통국 업데이트(Area Traffic Alert and Transportation Authority Update)'와 첫 번째 단락의 '표지판 수리 및 교체 작업을 시작할 예정입니다(will begin repairing and replacing signs)'라는 문구를 통해 도로 개선 공사를 설명하기 위한 공지임을 알 수 있다. 따라서 (C)가 정답이다.

어휘 outline 개요를 서술하다

▶▶ Paraphrasing 지문의 repairing and replacing signs
→ 정답의 improvement

148 세부 사항

번역 새 표지판의 특징은?
(A) 훨씬 오래갈 것이다.
(B) 색상이 다양하다.
(C) 훨씬 크다.
(D) 가독성이 개선된다.

해설 첫 번째 단락에서 새로운 표지판은 빛을 더 잘 반사해 더욱 읽기 쉽게(more reflective and thus easier to read) 고안되었다고 했으므로, 가독성이 개선되었음을 알 수 있다. 따라서 (D)가 정답이다.

어휘 significantly 상당히 readability 가독성

▶▶ Paraphrasing 지문의 easier to read
→ 정답의 improved readability

149-150 양식

로린 인더스트리즈
환급 요청서

성명: 티모시 오스웰   **관리자 성명:** 로라 조
부서: 광고
ID: 8123976
직위: 프로젝트 매니저
항목별 경비:

날짜	명세	비용
1월 28일	회의장까지 교통비	3파운드
1월 28일	마지라 그룹의 야니크 러 미농과 점심	55파운드
1월 28일	사무실로 돌아오는 교통비	3파운드
	[150]총 환급액	61파운드

[149]항목별 영수증 없이는 직원에게 경비가 지급되지 않습니다. [150]청구 환급액은 격주로 지급되는 직원 급여에 가산될 것입니다. 100파운드가 넘는 금액은 해당 급여 지급 기간 중에는 처리되지 않습니다. 대신에 다음 분기말에 환급됩니다.

직원 서명: <u>티모시 오스웰</u>

관리자 서명: 로라 조	
요청서 접수일: 1월 30일	영수증을 첨부하셨나요? 예
경리부 환급 담당자 승인: 티아 제거팔크	

어휘 reimbursement 환급 supervisor 관리자, 상사
itemized 항목별로 나눈 expense 경비, 비용 description 명세,
(자세한) 설명 issue 지급하다, 발급하다 credit (추가되는) 금액
claim 청구하다, 신청하다 process 처리하다 quarter 분기
attach 첨부하다

149 세부 사항

번역 양식을 사용해 환급 가능한 것은?

(A) 100파운드 미만 금액만
(B) 교통비만
(C) 영수증과 함께 제출된 비용만
(D) 간부 직원의 경비만

해설 경비 내역 바로 아래 문장에서 항목별 영수증 없이는 직원에게 경비가 지급되지 않는다(Funds will not be issued to employees without itemized receipts)고 했으므로, 영수증과 함께 제출된 비용만 환급 가능하다는 것을 알 수 있다. 따라서 (C)가 정답이다.

150 추론 / 암시

번역 오스웰 씨에 관해 암시된 것은?

(A) 회사 신용카드를 사용했다.
(B) 매주 말에 급여를 받는다.
(C) 신규 고객과 거래했다.
(D) 다음 급여에 추가금을 받을 것이다.

해설 양식 하단을 보면 청구된 환급액은 격주로 지급되는 직원 급여에 가산(Credits ~ be added to the employee's regular biweekly paycheck)되지만, 100파운드가 넘는 금액은 해당 급여 지급 기간 중에는 처리되지 않는다(Amounts over £100 will not be processed during the current pay period)고 했다. 오스웰 씨의 총 환급액(Total reimbursement)은 61파운드이므로, 다음 급여와 함께 환급 신청한 비용을 받을 것임을 추론할 수 있다. 따라서 (D)가 정답이다.

151-153 이메일

수신: 전 직원
발신: 타카시 이무라
전송: 10월 7일 목요일 오전 9시 4분
제목: 엘리베이터 점검

151시 조례 시행청이 내일 오전 11시부터 엘리베이터 연례 점검을 실시합니다. 점검 목적은 우리 엘리베이터가 모든 안전 요건을 충족하는지 확인하기 위해서입니다. 우리 엘리베이터는 잘 관리되고 있어서 어떤 문제도 없을 것으로 예상합니다.

152개별 엘리베이터가 운행되지 않는 시간이 있을 것입니다. 하지만 그 시간이 언제든 간에 건물 내에서 적어도 한 대의 엘리베이터는 운행될 겁니다. 이번 검사는 공식적으로 오후 2시까지 계속될 예정입니다. 모든 엘리베이터가 다시 운행하게 되면 이메일로 알려 드리겠습

니다. 건물의 시설 웹사이트에도 메시지가 게시됩니다.

153점검 절차로 인한 불편에 대해 사과드리며 건물을 이용하는 직원과 고객에게 미치는 영향을 최소화하도록 하겠습니다. 양해 부탁드리며, 문의 사항이 있으시면 저에게 연락 주십시오.

타카시 이무라, 건물 관리인

어휘 inspection 점검 code 법규, 규정, 조례 enforcement 시행, 실시 annual 연례의 requirement 요건, 요구 사항 maintain (건물·기계 등을 보수해 가며) 유지하다, 관리하다 anticipate 예상하다 facility 시설 inconvenience 불편 minimize 최소화하다 impact 영향

151 세부 사항

번역 엘리베이터는 얼마나 자주 점검을 받는가?

(A) 한 달에 한 번
(B) 6개월마다
(C) 1년에 한 번
(D) 2년마다

해설 첫 번째 단락에서 엘리베이터 연례 점검을 실시한다(perform annual elevator inspections)고 했으므로, 1년에 한 번 점검을 받는다는 것을 알 수 있다. 따라서 (C)가 정답이다.

▸▸ Paraphrasing 지문의 annual → 정답의 Once a year

152 추론 / 암시

번역 직원과 고객에게 점검이 불편한 이유는?

(A) 최상층에 있는 사무실이 오전 11시 이후로 문을 닫을 것이다.
(B) 자주 이용하는 엘리베이터가 운행되지 않을 수도 있다.
(C) 월요일 오후 2시까지 엘리베이터가 운행되지 않는다.
(D) 이용자들을 위해 관계자들이 일부 엘리베이터를 운행해야 할 수도 있다.

해설 두 번째 단락에서 개별 엘리베이터가 운행되지 않는 시간(periods when individual elevators will be out of service)이 있을 예정이라고 했으므로, 이로 인해 직원과 고객이 불편함을 겪게 될 것임을 추론할 수 있다. (B)가 정답이다.

▸▸ Paraphrasing 지문의 will be out of service → 정답의 may not be working

153 문장 삽입

번역 [1], [2], [3], [4]로 표시된 곳 중에서 다음 문장이 들어가기에 가장 적합한 곳은?

"양해 부탁드리며, 문의 사항이 있으시면 저에게 연락 주십시오."

(A) [1]
(B) [2]
(C) [3]
(D) [4]

TEST 8

해설 주어진 문장에서 양해를 구한다(Thank you for your patience)고 했으므로, 이 문장 앞에 특정 문제에 대한 언급이 있어야 한다. [4] 앞에서 점검 절차로 인한 불편에 대해 사과(We apologize for any inconvenience caused by the inspection process)하며 직원과 고객에게 미치는 영향을 최소화하겠다(minimize the impact on staff and clients)고 덧붙였으므로, 이 뒤에 주어신 분장이 들어가야 글의 흐름이 자연스러워진다. 따라서 (D)가 정답이다.

154-155 온라인 채팅

> **케이티 밀레르:** (오전 10시 36분)
> 델 마르 씨, 제가 지금 **154다음 달 고객 감사 연회**를 위한 음식 준비 주문을 마무리하고 있어요. 하트포드 앤 메이슨 법률 사무소 고객들에게서는 답장을 못 받았는데요. 전화해서 확인해야 할까요?
>
> **알베르토 델 마르:** (오전 10시 38분)
> 아니요, 그럴 필요 없어요. **154, 155어제 하트포드 씨와 이야기했는데 자신들이 참석하지 못할 거라고 저한테 말했어요. 155그날 약속이 있어서 다른 주로 출장을 간다고 하네요.**
>
> **케이티 밀레르:** (오전 10시 39분)
> 그렇군요. 그분들은 연회에 참석하지 못하시니 선물 바구니를 사무실로 배달시킬까요?
>
> **알베르토 델 마르:** (오전 10시 41분)
> 네. 연회가 열리는 식당에서 사용할 수 있는 상품권과 나중에 그곳에서 저와 점심을 함께하자는 초대장도 넣어 주세요.
>
> **케이티 밀레르:** (오전 10시 42분)
> 알겠어요. 오늘 오후에 서명하실 수 있게 카드를 사무실로 가져다 드릴게요.
>
> **알베르토 델 마르:** (오전 10시 42분)
> 고마워요, 케이티.

어휘 finalize 마무리짓다 catering 음식 공급(업) appreciation 감사 banquet 연회 response 답장, 반응 confirm 확인하다 appointment 약속 attend 참석하다

154 사실 관계 확인

번역 하트포드 씨에 관해 명시된 것은?
(A) 다가오는 행사에 참석할 수 없다.
(B) 오후에 밀레르 씨에게 연락할 것이다.
(C) 회의를 준비하고 있다.
(D) 아직 출장 계획을 짜지 않았다.

해설 밀레르 씨가 오전 10시 36분 메시지에서 하트포드 앤 메이슨 법률 사무소 고객들이 다음 달 고객 감사 연회(next month's client-appreciation banquet) 참석 여부를 알려 주지 않았다고 하자, 이에 대해 델 마르 씨가 오전 10시 38분 메시지에서 하트포드 씨가 참석하지 못한다(Mr. Hartford ~ won't be able to make it)고 자신에게 말해 주었다고 했다. 따라서 (A)가 정답이다.

어휘 organize 준비하다, 조직하다

▸▸ Paraphrasing 지문의 next month's client-appreciation banquet → 정답의 an upcoming event
지문의 won't be able to make it → 정답의 is unable to attend

155 의도 파악

번역 오전 10시 39분에 밀레르 씨가 "그렇군요"라고 말한 의도는 무엇이겠는가?
(A) 고객에 관한 정보를 보고 있다.
(B) 델 마르 씨의 설명을 이해한다.
(C) 지금 선물 바구니 사진을 보고 있다.
(D) 델 마르 씨가 자신이 카드를 구매하기를 바란다는 사실을 알고 있다.

해설 델 마르 씨가 오전 10시 38분 메시지에서 하트포드 씨가 행사에 참석하지 못하는 이유가 그날 다른 주로 출장을 가기(traveling out of state for an appointment that day) 때문이라고 설명했고, 이에 대해 밀레르 씨가 '그렇군요(I see)'라고 응답했으므로, 델 마르 씨의 설명을 이해한다는 의도로 말한 것임을 알 수 있다. 따라서 (B)가 정답이다.

156-157 정보문

> 저는 제 생애 대부분을 콜로라도의 시골 숲에서 보냈고, 그곳에서 언제나 자연의 아름다움을 보며 영감을 얻었죠. **156저의 접시, 그릇, 도마는 숲속을 여기저기 돌아다니다가 발견한 쓰러진 나무에서 얻은 목재를 손수 깎아 만든 것입니다.**
>
> 제 목재 주방용품은 모두 단 하나뿐이며 자연의 곡선과 나뭇결을 살리도록 조각되었습니다. 이 독특한 소품들은 적절히 보관되고 다뤄지면 평생 사용 가능합니다. 습기에 장기간 노출되면 뒤틀리므로 절대 물속에 담근 채로 방치하면 안 됩니다. 때때로 미네랄 오일을 얇게 발라서 색이 바래는 것을 방지하는 것도 좋습니다. **157천연 목재 제품이 변질되는 것을 막는 최선의 요령들을 더 보시려면 www.hollyhollingsworth.com을 방문하십시오.** **156저의 제품을 구매해 주셔서 감사합니다!**
>
> – 홀리 홀링스워스

어휘 rural 시골의 inspiration 영감 carve 조각하다 forage 찾다 one of a kind 단 하나뿐인 것, 유일한 것 grain (종이나 나무 등의) 결 properly 적절히 soak 담그다, 젖다 prolonged 장기의 exposure 노출 warp 뒤틀리다, 휘다 prevent 방지하다 fade 색이 바래다 deterioration 변질, 악화 purchase 구매하다; 구매(품)

156 추론 / 암시

번역 정보문은 어디에 있겠는가?
(A) 제품 상자 안
(B) 미술관의 예술 작품 주변
(C) 자연 잡지 기사
(D) 신문 광고

해설 첫 번째 단락에서 자신의 접시, 그릇, 도마는 쓰러진 나무에서 얻은 목재를 손수 깎아 만들었다(My plates, bowls, and cutting boards are hand carved ~ from fallen trees)며 제품의 재료와 제작 방법을 설명했고, 두 번째 단락 후반부에서 제품을 구입해 주어 감사하다(Thank you for purchasing my products)는 인사말로 마무리했다. 따라서 제품 상자 안에 있는 설명문임을 추론할 수 있으므로, (A)가 정답이다.

157 세부 사항

번역 정보문에 따르면 독자들이 웹사이트에서 할 수 있는 일은?

(A) 판매하는 신상품 둘러보기
(B) 다양한 목재 유형 비교하기
(C) 제품 관리에 관한 상세한 설명 읽기
(D) 목각 기법 배우기

해설 두 번째 단락 후반부에서 천연 목재 제품의 변질을 막는 최선의 요령을 알아보려면(For more tips on how to best protect your natural wood product from deterioration) 웹사이트를 방문하라고 조언했으므로, (C)가 정답이다.

> ▸▸ Paraphrasing   지문의 For more tips on how to best protect your natural wood product → 정답의 detailed product-care instructions

158-160 양식

퍼넬리 호텔

고객님의 최근 행사를 위해 퍼넬리 호텔을 선택해 주셔서 감사합니다! 잠시 시간을 내셔서 이 설문 조사서를 작성해 주시기 바랍니다. 고객님의 긍정적인 경험을 동료, 친구들과 나누시길 바랍니다. ¹⁵⁸**고객님의 추천으로 예약을 받게 되면, 다음 행사 비용에서 5퍼센트를 할인해 드리겠습니다.**

고객 성명 및 이메일: 아이카 오타니, a.otani@bipmail.com
행사일: 4월 6일
¹⁶⁰⁽ᴮ⁾행사 장소: 오크우드 식당
다음 측면에 대해 저희 호텔에서 경험하신 것을 평가해 주세요.
(N/A = 해당 사항 없음)

	나쁨	보통	좋음	아주 좋음	N/A
음식의 질				X	
음식의 양			X		
직원의 친절도				X	
방 구성/분위기	X				
숙박 시설					¹⁶⁰X

의견/제안:

¹⁶⁰⁽ᴰ⁾**퍼넬리 행사 담당자가 이번 연례 행사를 준비하는 데 굉장한 도움을 주었습니다.** ¹⁶⁰⁽ᴬ⁾**음식이 맛있었고,** 손님들이 닭고기 구이를 극찬했어요! ¹⁵⁹**식당이 꽉 차면서 꽤 소란스러웠습니다.** 내년에도 다시 퍼넬리를 이용할 계획이지만, 그때는 꼭 다른 방을 요청할 겁니다.

어휘 associate 동료, 친구 referral 추천 rate 평가하다 aspect 측면, 양상 atmosphere 분위기 accommodation 숙박 (시설) coordinator 책임자, 담당자 rave 극찬하다 definitely 분명히

158 세부 사항

번역 오타니 씨는 어떻게 하면 할인을 받을 수 있는가?

(A) 4월 6일 이전에 행사를 예약해서
(B) 행사를 예약하는 사람을 추천해서
(C) 호텔 객실 한 구역을 예약해서
(D) 온라인 설문 조사를 작성해서

해설 첫 번째 단락에서 고객의 추천으로 예약을 받으면(If we receive a booking based on your referral) 다음 행사 비용에서 5퍼센트를 할인해 준다(give you a 5% discount on the cost of your next event)고 했으므로, (B)가 정답이다.

159 세부 사항

번역 오타니 씨가 겪은 문제는?

(A) 너무 소란스러웠다.
(B) 음식이 충분하지 않았다.
(C) 메뉴가 제한되어 있었다.
(D) 방이 작았다.

해설 오타니 씨가 작성한 의견/제안(Comments/Suggestions)란을 보면 식당이 꽉 차면서 꽤 소란스러웠다(The dining room got quite noisy as it filled up)고 했으므로, (A)가 정답이다.

> ▸▸ Paraphrasing   지문의 quite noisy → 정답의 too much noise

160 사실 관계 확인

번역 양식에서 명시되지 않은 것은?

(A) 손님들이 음식을 맛있게 먹었다.
(B) 행사가 오크우드 식당에서 열렸다.
(C) 오타니 씨의 손님들 중 많은 사람들이 하룻밤 투숙했다.
(D) 퍼넬리 호텔 직원들이 준비를 도왔다.

해설 의견/제안(Comments/Suggestions)란의 '음식이 맛있었어요(The food was delicious)'라는 평에서 (A)를, 행사 장소(Event location)가 '오크우드 식당(Oakwood Dining Room)'이라는 것에서 (B)를, 의견/제안(Comments/Suggestions)란의 '퍼넬리 행사 담당자가 이번 연례 행사를 준비하는 데 굉장한 도움을 주었습니다(The Pernely event coordinator provided excellent support in putting this annual event together)'에서 (D)를 확인할 수 있다. 그러나 오타니 씨의 손님들 중 많은 사람들이 하룻밤 투숙했는지는 언급되지 않았고, 숙박 시설 평가란에 해당 사항이 없다(N/A)고 했으므로, (C)가 정답이다.

> ▸▸ Paraphrasing   지문의 provided excellent support in putting this annual event together → 보기 (D)의 helped with planning

161-163 기사

케이프타운(10월 26일)—161현지에 기반을 두고 있는 로블링 비전이 케냐 나이로비에 본사를 둔 노비안토 테크놀로지와 합병할 예정이라고 어제 발표했다. 이 합병으로 로블링 비전은 연구 부서를 확장하여 최첨단 시력 기술을 전문으로 하는 팀을 포함할 수 있게 된다.

"당사가 내년에 새로운 안경 제품을 출시할 것이라는 점에는 의심의 여지가 없습니다." 로블링 비전 CEO 오바켕 반 디크가 말했다. "우리가 함께 노력한다면 할 수 있는 일에는 한계가 없을 것입니다."

162두 회사가 힘을 합치기 전에 요하네스버그에 있는 로블링 비전의 연구소는 훨씬 더 많은 인력을 수용할 수 있도록 확장될 것이다.

이곳 케이프타운에 본사를 두고 있는 로블링 비전은 전국적으로 센터를 보유하고 있다. 약 10년 전, 남아프리카공화국의 몇몇 유명인사들이 로블링 안경을 쓰기 시작한 이후, 그 인기가 상승했다. 이 회사는 안경과 콘택트렌즈를 제조하는 것으로 가장 유명하다. 이에 비해 잘 알려지지 않은 사실은 연구와 기술에 163전념하는 소규모 부서가 요하네스버그에 있다는 것이다.

어휘 merge with ~와 합치다 expand 확장하다 action 행동, 조치 cutting-edge 최첨단의 vision 시력, 시야 eyewear 안경류 solutions (특정 요구를 충족시키기 위한) 제품, 서비스 laboratory 연구소 accommodate 수용하다 manufacture 제조하다 division 부서 devoted to ~에 전념하는

161 주제 / 목적

번역 기사의 목적은?
(A) 새로운 유형의 안경에 대한 비평
(B) 시력 센터 개장 보도
(C) 두 회사의 합병 발표
(D) 최근의 패션 트렌드 설명

해설 첫 번째 단락에서 로블링 비전이 노비안토 테크놀로지와 합병 예정이라고 발표했다(Roebling Vision announced ~ it will be merging with Novianto Technology)고 하며 이후 관련 내용을 서술하고 있으므로, 두 회사의 합병을 알리기 위한 기사임을 알 수 있다. 따라서 (C)가 정답이다.

어휘 critique 비평하다

▶▶ Paraphrasing   지문의 be merging with
→ 정답의 the uniting of

162 세부 사항

번역 로블링 비전은 곧 무엇을 할 것인가?
(A) 연구소 수용 능력 늘리기
(B) 본사를 나이로비로 이전하기
(C) 생산 라인 중단하기
(D) 신임 CEO 채용하기

해설 세 번째 단락에서 로블링 비전의 연구소는 훨씬 더 많은 인력을 수용할 수 있도록 확장될 것(Roebling Vision's laboratories ~ will be expanded to be able to accommodate a much larger workforce)이라고 했으므로, (A)가 정답이다.

어휘 capacity 용량, 수용력 discontinue 중단하다, 단종시키다

▶▶ Paraphrasing   지문의 be expanded → 정답의 Increase
지문의 to accommodate a much larger workforce → 정답의 capacity

163 동의어 찾기

번역 네 번째 단락 8행의 "devoted to"와 의미상 가장 가까운 것은?
(A) ~에 감탄하는
(B) ~에 주력하는
(C) ~에 선택된
(D) ~로부터 지원받은

해설 "devoted to"를 포함한 부분은 '연구와 기술에 전념하는 소규모 부서(a small division devoted to research and technology)'라는 내용으로, 여기서 devoted to는 '~에 전념하는'이라는 뜻으로 쓰였다. 따라서 '~에 주력하는, ~에 중점을 둔'이라는 의미의 (B) focused on이 정답이다.

164-167 온라인 채팅

마거리트 오구스 (오전 9시 30분)
안녕하세요, 팀원 여러분. 우리 직원들을 위한 〈건강한 생활 방식〉 무료 시리즈는 어떻게 진행되고 있나요?

피터 젤리스 (오전 9시 31분)
2월 점심 회의 때 구내식당에서 이야기 나눈 대로 167(B)영양 섭취부터 시작하려고요.

태원 윤 (오전 9시 31분)
165우리 병원 소식지에 건강한 생활에 대한 칼럼을 쓰는 아담 리커트에게 말했어요.

피터 젤리스 (오전 9시 32분)
166그럼 3월 1일에 시리즈를 시작하는 것이 목표인가요, 태원?

마거리트 오구스 (오전 9시 33분)
아주 좋네요. 165그 사람이 숙면의 필요성에 관해 텔레비전에서 인터뷰하는 것을 본 기억이 나요. 그가 사람들 앞에서 실황으로 발표하는 데 능숙한가요?

피터 젤리스 (오전 9시 34분)
음, 지난달에 중요한 회의에서 그가 발표를 했어요.

태원 윤 (오전 9시 34분)
166네. 아담 리커트가 시리즈에서 처음 세 개의 세션을 맡겠다고 약속했어요.

마거리트 오구스 (오전 9시 35분)
잘됐군요. 방은 어때요?

피터 젤리스 (오전 9시 36분)
164시리즈 전체를 위해서 5월까지 병원 북쪽에 있는 아트리움을 예약해 뒀어요.

태원 윤 (오전 9시 37분)
167(A)시리즈 두 번째 주제도 벌써 정했습니다. 바로 신체 단련이에요.

마거리트 오구스 (오전 9시 38분)

훌륭해요. 이제 4월 세션에서 167(D)사회적 관계의 중요성에 대해 이야기할 시리즈의 세 번째 강연자를 선정해 봅시다.

어휘 nutrition 영양, 영양 섭취 marvelous 굉장한, 놀라운 deliver a presentation 발표하다 commit 약속하다

164 추론 / 암시

번역 강연자 시리즈에 관해 암시된 것은?

(A) 점심 식사가 포함될 것이다.
(B) 병원에서 열릴 것이다.
(C) 일반에게 개방될 것이다.
(D) 텔레비전에 방영될 것이다.

해설 젤리스 씨가 오전 9시 36분 메시지에서 시리즈 전체를 위해서 병원 북쪽에 있는 아트리움을 예약했다(The atrium on the north side of the hospital has been reserved)고 했으므로, 강연이 병원에서 열릴 것임을 추론할 수 있다. 따라서 (B)가 정답이다.

165 의도 파악

번역 오전 9시 33분에 오구스 씨가 "아주 좋네요"라고 쓴 의도는 무엇인가?

(A) 최신 소식지에 만족한다.
(B) 젤리스 씨가 채팅에 참여해서 기쁘다.
(C) 윤 씨가 선택한 강연자에 만족한다.
(D) 시리즈의 일부로 강연하게 되어 기쁘다.

해설 윤 씨가 오전 9시 31분 메시지에서 병원 소식지에 건강한 생활에 대한 칼럼을 쓰는 아담 리커트에게 말했다(I talked to Adam Rickert, who writes the column on healthy living for our hospital newsletter)고 했는데, 이에 대해 오구스 씨가 '아주 좋네요(Marvelous)'라고 응답한 후, 리커트 씨가 텔레비전에 나와 인터뷰하는 것을 본 기억이 있다(remember seeing his interview on television)고 했다. 따라서 윤 씨가 선택한 강연자인 리커트 씨에 대해 만족스럽다는 의도로 말한 것임을 추론할 수 있으므로, (C)가 정답이다.

166 세부 사항

번역 리커트 씨는 언제 강연할 예정인가?

(A) 2월
(B) 3월
(C) 4월
(D) 5월

해설 젤리스 씨가 오전 9시 32분 메시지에서 '3월 1일에 시리즈를 시작하는 것이 목표인가요(are we on target to start the series on March 1)'라며 윤 씨에게 질문을 했고, 이에 대해 윤 씨가 오전 9시 34분 메시지에서 '네(Yes)'라고 응답한 후, 아담 리커트가 시리즈에서 처음 세 개의 세션을 맡을 것(Adam Rickert ~ doing the first three session in the series)이라고 했으므로, 리커트 씨가 3월에 강연할 예정임을 알 수 있다. 따라서 (B)가 정답이다.

167 추론 / 암시

번역 채팅에 따르면 강연자 시리즈에서 논의되지 않을 것 같은 주제는?

(A) 신체 운동
(B) 잘 먹기
(C) 수면 습관
(D) 건강한 관계

해설 윤 씨의 오전 9시 37분 메시지에 언급된 신체 단련(the second topic in the series: physical fitness) 관련 강연에서 (A)가 논의될 것임을 알 수 있고, 젤리스 씨가 오전 9시 31분 메시지에서 '영양 섭취부터 시작하려 한다(we're starting with nutrition)'라고 한 것으로 보아 첫 강연에서 (B)가 논의될 것임을 추론할 수 있다. 그리고 오구스 씨의 오전 9시 38분 메시지에서 사회적 관계의 중요성에 대해 이야기할 시리즈의 세 번째 강연자(the third speaker of the series, who will discuss the importance of social relationship)를 선정하자고 했으므로, 해당 강연에서 (D)가 다뤄질 것임을 알 수 있다. 그러나 수면 습관과 관련된 내용은 언급되지 않았으므로, (C)가 정답이다.

168-171 보고서

롱아일랜드 지역 에너지국
주거 시설 검사서

대상 고객: 다라 헤닝거

건물 주소: 337 배럴 스트리트, 헴스테드, 뉴욕 11550

168검사 요청 사유: 고객이 가장 더운 몇 개월 동안 에너지 요금이 비정상적으로 많이 나오고 냉각 시스템이 비효율적이라고 신고했다.

방문일: 8월 26일

점검 요약: 건물 규모는 약 366제곱미터이며 건물 서쪽에 실외 에어컨 장치가 있다. 장치는 새 것으로 설치되었으며 이제 6년이 되었다.

169냉방 장치의 규모는 건물 규모에 비해 여유가 있다. 그런데 너무 작은 배기구를 통해 환기가 되고 있다. 현재의 배기구 크기를 확대하거나 인접한 벽에 추가 배기구를 만들면 이 문제를 바로잡을 수 있을 것이다.

171건물의 아치형 금속 지붕이 단열 처리가 잘 되어 있지 않다. 지붕의 단열 처리를 다시 할 것을 추천한다. 이것이 최우선 과제이다. 170더운 몇 달 동안에는 위층의 천장 선풍기 사용을 자제해야 한다. 지붕의 단열 처리가 잘 되어 있지 않아 여름에 천장을 통해 전달되는 열을 식히느라 선풍기가 과도한 양의 에너지를 사용하게 되어 방이 적절하게 냉각될 수 없다.

본 검사는 공인 에너지 검사관이 실시했다.

검사관: 케빈 앤더스

어휘 audit 검사, 평가 unusually 유난히, 평소와 달리 inefficient 비효율적인 inspection 점검 approximately 약 sufficient 넉넉한, 충분한 return air 환기 vent 배기구, 배출구 expand 확대하다 adjacent 인접한 insulate 단열[방음]하다 excessive 과도한 combat 제거하기 위해 노력하다, 싸우다 adequately 적절하게 certified 공인된

168 추론 / 암시

번역 헤닝거 씨가 검사 서비스를 요청한 이유는 무엇이겠는가?

(A) 주거 공간을 넓히고 싶다.
(B) 난방 설비의 수리가 필요하다.
(C) 부동산 매입에 관심이 있다.
(D) 여름철 에너지 비용을 줄이고 싶다.

해설 검사 요청 사유(Reason for audit request)를 보면 헤닝거 씨(The customer)가 가장 더운 몇 개월 동안 에너지 요금이 비정상적으로 많이 나오고 냉각 시스템이 비효율적이라고 신고했다(reported unusually high energy bills and an inefficient cooling system during the warmest months)고 했으므로, 여름철 에너지 비용을 줄이기 위해 검사 서비스를 요청했다고 추론할 수 있다. 따라서 (D)가 정답이다.

어휘 enlarge 확대하다, 확장하다

> ▶▶ **Paraphrasing** 지문의 **energy bills during the warmest months** → 정답의 **summer energy costs**

169 사실 관계 확인

번역 에어컨 장치에 관해 명시된 것은?

(A) 충분히 적당한 규모이다.
(B) 환기 시스템이 충분하다.
(C) 단종된 모델이다.
(D) 더운 공기를 만들어 내고 있다.

해설 점검 요약(Inspection summary)의 두 번째 단락에서 냉방 장치의 규모는 건물 규모에 비해 여유가 있다(The size of the cooling unit is more than sufficient for the building size)고 했으므로, (A)가 정답이다.

어휘 adequate (특정 목적이나 필요에) 충분한, 적절한

> ▶▶ **Paraphrasing** 지문의 **the cooling unit**
> → 질문의 **the air-conditioning unit**
> 지문의 **more than sufficient for the building size** → 정답의 **an adequate size**

170 세부 사항

번역 앤더스 씨가 천장 선풍기에 관해 조언하는 것은?

(A) 교체해야 한다.
(B) 다른 장소에 재설치해야 한다.
(C) 에어컨 장치 대신 써야 한다.
(D) 연중 일부 기간에는 꺼야 한다.

해설 점검 요약(Inspection summary)의 세 번째 단락을 보면, 앤더스 씨가 더운 몇 달 동안에는 위층의 천장 선풍기 사용을 자제해야 한다(The use of ceiling fans ~ should be avoided in the warm months)고 조언했으므로, (D)가 정답이다.

> ▶▶ **Paraphrasing** 지문의 **be avoided in the warm months**
> → 정답의 **be turned off for the part of the year**

171 문장 삽입

번역 [1], [2], [3], [4]로 표시된 곳 중에서 다음 문장이 들어가기에 가장 적합한 곳은?

"이것이 최우선 과제이다."

(A) [1]
(B) [2]
(C) [3]
(D) [4]

해설 주어진 문장에서 이것이 최우선 과제(This should be a top priority)라고 했으므로, 앞에서 먼저 우선적으로 처리되어야 할 작업 관련 내용이 언급되어야 한다. [3] 앞에서 건물의 아치형 금속 지붕이 단열 처리가 잘 되어 있지 않기(The building has a vaulted metal roof that is poorly insulated) 때문에 지붕의 단열 처리를 다시 할 것을 추천한다(Reinsulating the roof is recommended)고 했으므로, 이 뒤에 주어진 문장이 들어가야 글의 흐름이 자연스러워진다. 따라서 (C)가 정답이다. 참고로, '이것(This)'은 '지붕의 단열 처리를 다시 하는 것(Reinsulating the roof)'을 가리킨다.

172-175 회의 일정

5월 25일 회의 일정
오전 7:00-8:00　　　　 등록 (대강당, 1층)
오전 8:00-9:15　　 ¹⁷²**소프트웨어 솔루션** 전체 차량 및 제품 선적을 추적하고 운전자와 배차원 간의 소통을 원활하게 해주는 최고의 최신 소프트웨어 시스템에 대해 배우십시오. 강사: 니클라스 마슨
¹⁷⁵**오전 9:30-10:30**　　 ¹⁷²**항공 화물 유닛** ¹⁷³⁽ᴮ⁾국내 및 해외 운송, ¹⁷³⁽ᴬ⁾요금 및 수수료 산정, 귀중품 보호, ¹⁷³⁽ᶜ⁾발생 가능한 문제 해결 등의 영역에서 항공 화물 운용에 관한 새로운 통찰을 살펴보십시오. ¹⁷⁵**강사: 에진느 치오케**
¹⁷⁴**오전 10:45-11:45**　　 ¹⁷²**효율적인 운전자 교육** 법으로 규정되어 있습니다! 국가 교통 위원회에 따르면 고용주에게는 모든 운전자들이 ¹⁷⁴**정부 법률과 요건**을 숙지하도록 해야 할 책임이 있습니다. 최신 개정 법률에 대해 설명하고 효율적인 교육 프로그램을 기획하는 방법에 대한 정보도 다룹니다. 강사: 칭-리엔 우
오후 12:00-1:00　　　 ¹⁷²**보유 차량 관리** 차량, 정비사, 운전자, 판매 업체 및 연료 소비와 관련된 비용을 예상하고 관리하는 것을 포함하는 전체 보유 차량(승용차, 버스, 트럭, 운송 장비) 관리 분야의 최신 동향을 살펴보십시오. 강사: 니클라스 마슨
¹⁷⁵**오후 12시 세션을 제외한 모든 세션은 4층에 있는 제네바 회의실에서 열립니다.** 오후 12시 세션은 2층에 있는 하크니스 회의실에서 열립니다. 장비 설치 관련해서 도움이 필요한 발표자는 G14호에 있는 시설 담당 직원과 상의하십시오.

어휘 registration 등록 keep track of ~을 추적하다
fleet 전체 보유 차량[비행기, 선박] facilitate 원활하게 하다
dispatcher 배차원, 발송[발차] 담당자 instructor 강사 cargo
화물 troubleshooting 문제 해결[처리] be familiar with
~을 숙지하고 있다, ~에 익숙하다 requirement 요건 address
말하다 effective 효과적인 anticipate 예상하다, 기대하다
associated with ~와 연관된 fuel 연료 consumption 소비
facility 시설

172 추론 / 암시

번역 회의에 참석하는 사람은 누구이겠는가?

(A) 운송 회사 소유주
(B) 컴퓨터 소프트웨어 프로그래머
(C) 트럭 및 버스 운전사
(D) 경영학 교수

해설 회의의 세션별 주제를 살펴보면 운전자와 배차원간의 소통을 원활하게 해주는 소프트웨어 프로그램(Software Solutions), 항공 화물(Air Cargo Units) 운용, 운전자 교육(Driver Training), 보유 차량 관리(Maintaining Vehicle Fleets) 등 운송 회사 운영과 관련된 내용을 다룬다는 것을 알 수 있다. 따라서 (A)가 정답이다.

▸▸ **Paraphrasing**   지문의 **employers** → 정답의 **owners**

173 추론 / 암시

번역 오전 9시 30분 세션에서 다루어지지 않을 것 같은 주제는?

(A) 가격 책정
(B) 국제 운송
(C) 흔한 난관 해결하기
(D) 직원간 소통 개선하기

해설 요금 및 수수료 산정(calculating rates and charges)에서 (A)가, 국내 및 해외 운송(domestic and overseas transport)에서 (B)가, 발생 가능한 문제 해결(troubleshooting possible complications)에서 (C)가 논의될 것임을 추론할 수 있다. 그러나 직원간 소통 개선하기는 9시 30분 세션보다는 8시 세션에서 다루어질 만한 내용이므로, (D)가 정답이다.

▸▸ **Paraphrasing**   지문의 **calculating rates and charges**
→ 보기 **(A)**의 **Pricing**
지문의 **overseas transport**
→ 보기 **(B)**의 **International shipments**
지문의 **troubleshooting possible complications**
→ 보기 **(C)**의 **Solving common difficulties**

174 세부 사항

번역 법규 준수에 관한 세션은 언제 열리는가?

(A) 오전 8시
(B) 오전 9시 30분
(C) 오전 10시 45분
(D) 오후 12시

해설 효율적인 운전자 교육(Effective Driver Training) 세션에서 정부의 법률과 요건(government laws and requirements)에 대해 다룬다고 했다. 이 세션의 시작 시간을 보면 10시 45분이므로, (C)가 정답이다.

▸▸ **Paraphrasing**   지문의 **laws** → 질문의 **regulations**

175 세부 사항

번역 치오케 씨는 어디에서 세션을 진행할 것인가?

(A) 대강당
(B) 제네바 회의실
(C) 하크니스 회의실
(D) G14호

해설 일정표 하단을 보면, 오후 12시 세션을 제외한 모든 세션은 제네바 회의실에서 열린다(All sessions will be held in the Geneva Conference Room ~ except the 12 P.M. session)고 했으므로, 오전 9시 30분에 시작하는 치오케 씨의 세션은 제네바 회의실에서 진행될 예정임을 알 수 있다. 따라서 (B)가 정답이다.

176-180 매출 보고서 + 이메일

플래시드 문 커피

[179]**3월 매출 보고서—4월 4일 점장 코라 린 작성**

전체 제품의 점포 매출

제품	수익	비고
커피, 원두, 1파운드 봉지	14,000달러	전반적으로, 판매 수익이 더 높았음. [179]미스티 하이츠 블렌드 원두 봉지 제품이 가장 많이 판매되었으며, 3,000달러 남짓한 수입을 올림.
[176]커피, 조제 음료	18,200달러	[176]에스프레소 기계가 수리되는 동안 많은 음료가 제공되지 않음. 4월에는 판매량이 회복될 것임.
차, 조제 음료	5,500달러	이전 몇 개월과 판매량이 비슷함.
병 음료	2,200달러	이전 몇 개월과 판매량이 비슷함.
제과 제빵류	3,400달러	지난달 대비 7퍼센트 증가함.
소매(변질되지 않는 제품)	750달러	[177]판매 업체가 아직 주문품을 납품하지 않아 플래시드 문 커피 머그잔 재고가 여전히 없음.
3월 판촉		
단골 고객 프로그램	자료 없음	이번 달에는 단골 할인 카드가 고객에게 거의 배포되지 않음. [178]이 혜택을 홍보하는 데 있어서 직원들을 더 잘 교육해야 함.

어휘 revenue 수익, 이익 comparable 비슷한
nonperishable 보존할 수 있는, 변질되지 않는 out of stock
재고가 없는 fulfill an order 납품하다 distribute 배포하다

수신: coralin@placidmooncoffee.com

발신: tyrellharris@placidmooncoffee.com

179날짜: 4월 4일, 오후 6시 23분

제목: 회신: 3월 매출 보고서

3월 보고서를 신속히 제출해 주어 고맙습니다. **179**지난달 우리가 새로 선보인 원두 신제품이 많이 판매되어서 기쁩니다. 이 커피 블렌드의 매출을 4월까지 주의 깊게 살펴봅시다. 우리의 정규 제품군에 추가할 수 있을지도 모릅니다.

단골 고객 프로그램에 대한 제안이 마음에 듭니다. 덧붙여, 저는 금전 등록기 옆에 카드를 홍보하는 포스터를 붙이고 직원 휴게실에도 하나 붙일 것을 제안합니다. 이러한 시도가 효과가 있는지 월말에 알려 주십시오.

마지막으로, 좋은 소식이 있습니다. 유키히로 아사카와 씨가 12월부터 식당 본점에서 우리의 볼드 마코 종 커피를 제공했는데, 이제는 모든 지점에서 플래시드 문이 독점 공급업체가 되기를 바라고 있습니다. **180**당신이 얼마 전에 아사카와 씨에게 우리 커피를 소개했으니 이렇게 사업을 확장하게 된 것은 모두 당신 덕분입니다.

타이렐 해리스

플래시드 문 커피, 사장

어휘 promptly 신속하게 register 금전 등록기 effort 노력,
시도 impact 효과, 영향 flagship 본점, 주력 매장 exclusive
독점의 provider 공급 업체[자] expansion 확장

176 세부 사항

번역 예상보다 적게 판매된 제품은?

(A) 조제 커피 음료

(B) 조제 차 음료

(C) 병 음료

(D) 제과 제빵류

해설 매출 보고서의 커피, 조제 음료(Coffee, prepared drinks) 항목을 보면, 에스프레소 기계가 수리되는 동안 많은 음료가 제공되지 않았다(A number of drinks were not offered)고 하며 4월에는 판매량이 회복될 것(Sales should recover in April)이라고 했으므로, (A)가 정답이다.

177 세부 사항

번역 린 씨가 겪고 있는 문제는?

(A) 일부 디저트가 원하는 만큼 판매되지 않았다.

(B) 일부 머그잔이 배송되지 않았다.

(C) 일부 커피 원두 재고가 없다.

(D) 일부 포스터에 불명확한 정보가 있다.

해설 매출 보고서의 소매(Retail) 항목에서 판매 업체가 아직 주문품을 납품하지 않아(as our vendor has not yet fulfilled our order) 커피 머그잔 재고가 여전히 없다(mugs are still out of stock)는 문제점을 언급했으므로, (B)가 정답이다.

▸▸ Paraphrasing 지문의 has not yet fulfilled our order
→ 정답의 have not been delivered

178 세부 사항

번역 린 씨는 무엇을 추천하는가?

(A) 더 좋은 에스프레소 기계를 구입해야 한다.

(B) 단골 고객 프로그램을 중단해야 한다.

(C) 시간제 직원을 정규직으로 채용해야 한다.

(D) 직원들이 추가 교육을 받아야 한다.

해설 매출 보고서의 단골 고객 프로그램(Customer loyalty program) 항목에서 단골 고객 프로그램의 혜택을 홍보하는 데 있어서 직원들을 더 잘 교육시켜야 한다(We should better train staff in promoting this benefit)고 조언했으므로, (D)가 정답이다.

어휘 permanent 영구적인, 종신 고용의

▸▸ Paraphrasing 지문의 We should better train staff
→ 정답의 Employees should receive
additional training

179 연계

번역 미스티 하이츠 블렌드에 관해 암시된 것은?

(A) 3월에 처음 제공되었다.

(B) 플래시드 문 커피에서는 더 이상 판매하지 않을 것이다.

(C) 다른 커피 종류보다 비싸다.

(D) 다른 블렌드보다 향이 오래 간다.

해설 3월 매출 보고서(March Sales Report)의 커피, 원두, 1파운드 봉지(Coffee, whole bean, one-pound bags) 항목에서 미스티 하이츠 블렌드의 원두 봉지 제품이 가장 많이 판매되었다(Bags of whole-bean Misty Heights Blend were a top seller)고 했다. 관련 내용은 해리스 씨가 4월에 작성한 이메일에서도 확인할 수 있는데, 첫 번째 단락에서 지난달 새로 선보인 원두 신제품이 많이 판매되어(the strong sales of the new whole-bean product we introduced last month) 기쁘다고 했으므로, 미스티 하이츠 블렌드가 3월에 처음 선보인 제품임을 알 수 있다. 따라서 (A)가 정답이다.

▸▸ Paraphrasing 지문의 new → 정답의 for the first time

180 추론 / 암시

번역 린 씨에 관해 무엇이 사실이겠는가?

(A) 추가 업무를 맡기로 동의했다.

(B) 해리스 씨에게 새로운 에스프레소 메이커를 요청했다.

(C) 아사카와 씨에게 제품을 추천했다.

(D) 직원 휴게실을 개조했다.

해설 이메일의 마지막 단락을 보면 린 씨가 아사카와 씨에게 커피를 소개한(you introduced Mr. Asakawa to our coffee) 덕분에 플래시드 문의 사업이 확장되었다고 했으므로, 린 씨가 아사카와 씨에게 제품을 추천했음을 추론할 수 있다. 따라서 (C)가 정답이다.

181-185 기사 + 온라인 신청서

TV 제과 제빵 쇼 오디션

던모어, 펜실베이니아—차기 제과 제빵 스타가 될 자질을 갖추었다고 생각하시나요? 인기 제과 제빵 경연 쇼인 〈토니의 제과 제빵 달인〉이 이제 다섯 번째 시즌 오디션 일정을 잡았으니, 케이크 굽는 팬과 제과 제빵용 솔을 준비하세요!

181〈토니의 제과 제빵 달인〉은 5년 전에 처음 프로그램을 선보인 이래로 TV에서 공전의 182히트를 기록했습니다. 181이 쇼는 유명한 진행자인 제과 제빵사 아드리아나 토니의 이름을 땄습니다. TV 방송인으로 유명 인사가 되기 훨씬 전에, 그녀는 다국적 제과점 체인인 TKL 크리에이션즈를 설립했고, 이제는 181고전이 된 디저트 요리책 〈돌체 댄싱〉을 출간했습니다.

185아마추어 제과 제빵사, 즉 사업의 일환으로 제과 제빵을 한 경험이 없다면 〈토니의 제과 제빵 달인〉에 출연할 기회가 있습니다. 첫 번째 단계는 온라인 신청서 작성입니다. 쇼 제작자들은 약 50명의 유망한 지원자를 선정하여 대면 면접을 위한 초대장을 보낼 것입니다. 이 첫 번째 라운드를 통과한 지원자들은 TV 심사위원들 앞에서 이틀 동안 펼쳐지는 집중 제과 제빵 오디션에 참가하게 됩니다. 이 오디션에서 제과 제빵 달인 타이틀을 걸고 경쟁할 행운의 결선 진출자 16명이 선발될 것입니다!

당신이 구운 제품이 언제나 가족과 친구들을 감탄하게 합니까? 망설이지 말고 신청서를 제출해 빵을 구워 보세요!

어휘　competition 경연, 경쟁　premiere 처음 공개하다, 초연하다　celebrated 유명한　host (방송 등의) 진행자　celebrity 유명 인사　stand a chance ~할 가능성이 있다　application 신청(서)　promising 유망한　candidate 지원자, 후보　intensive 집중적인, 철두철미한　participant 참가자　finalist 결승전 진출자　compete for ~을 걸고 경쟁하다　hesitate 주저하다

---

http://www.tonisbakingace.com

홈	조리법	동영상	**오디션 신청**

성명: 데니스 파라
전화: 414-555-0112
이메일: dfarah@chemail.com

• 현재 직업:
1849년째 고등학교 화학 교사로 재직 중입니다.

• 언제부터 제과 제빵을 시작했으며 어떻게 배웠습니까?
5살 때부터 제 아버지와 함께 제과 제빵을 시작했습니다. 아버지는 가족과 친구를 위해 제과 제빵을 즐겨하셨고, 저는 아버지의 주방 보조가 되었습니다. 조리 기법을 연구하고, 제과 제빵 쇼를 시청하고, 또 저만의 조리법도 몇 가지 개발했던 일이 기억납니다.

• 특별한 품목이 있습니까?
파이입니다. 특히 새로운 파이 소를 시도해 보는 것을 좋아하기 때문입니다.

• 쇼에 출연하려는 이유는 무엇입니까?
저는 제과 제빵에 열정을 가지고 있습니다. 〈토니의 제과 제빵 달인〉이 처음 방영된 이래로 계속 시청해오고 있고, 그 쇼에서 봤던 최고의 조리법을 많이 시도해 보았기 때문에, 제 기량이 크게 향상되었습니다. 지난주 한 친구가 이 오디션에 대해 듣고는 신청서를 제출해 보라고 저를 설득했습니다.

• 제과 제빵 제품을 시장에 내놓거나 판매해 본 적이 있습니까?
185공식적인 제과 제빵 경험은 교내 스포츠 프로그램을 지원하기 위해 학교의 연례 크리스마스 세일 행사에 판매될 컵케이크를 기부한 것입니다.

183자기 소개 및 자신이 구운 제과 제빵류를 보여 주는 60초 분량의 영상을 업로드하십시오. 동영상을 업로드 하려면 동영상 탭으로 가십시오.

어휘　assistant 보조, 조수　experiment 시도, 실험　filling (음식의) 소[속]　passionate 열정적인　persuade 설득하다　formal 공식적인　amount to ~에 해당하다, ~에 이르다　donate 기부하다

181 사실 관계 확인

번역　〈토니의 제과 제빵 달인〉에 관해 기사에서 명시한 것은?

(A) 10대를 경연자로 받는다.
(B) 종종 외국 참가자도 선정한다.
(C) 우승자에게 상금을 수여한다.
(D) 유명한 저자가 진행한다.

해설　기사의 두 번째 단락에서 〈토니의 제과 제빵 달인(Toni's Baking Ace)〉의 유명한 진행자(its celebrated host)인 제과 제빵사 아드리아나 토니(Adrianna Toni)가 요리책을 출간한 적이 있다(published a dessert cookbook that has become a classic)고 했으므로, (D)가 정답이다.

182 동의어 찾기

번역　기사에서 두 번째 단락 2행의 "hit"와 의미상 가장 가까운 것은?

(A) 성공
(B) 영향
(C) 비용
(D) 격돌

해설　"hit"를 포함한 부분은 'TV에서 공전의 히트를 기록했다(has become a huge TV hit)'라는 의미로, 여기서 hit는 '히트, 성공'이라는 뜻으로 쓰였다. 따라서 '성공'이라는 의미의 (A) success가 정답이다.

183 사실 관계 확인

번역 온라인 신청서에 언급된 요건은?

(A) 계약서 서명
(B) 제과 제빵 속도 경연 통과
(C) 소개 영상 포함
(D) 지난 대회 참가

해설 온라인 신청서의 마지막 단락에서 자기 소개 및 자신이 구운 제과 제빵류를 보여 주는 영상을 업로드하라(Please upload ~ video introducing yourself and showing a baked creation of yours)고 요청했으므로, (C)가 정답이다.

> **Paraphrasing** 지문의 upload a video introducing ~
> → 정답의 Including an introductory video

184 세부 사항

번역 파라 씨가 자신의 신청서에 언급한 것은?

(A) 주방 보조가 있다.
(B) 교육자이다.
(C) 쇼를 본 적이 없다.
(D) 자신의 아버지가 곧 쇼에 출연할 것이다.

해설 파라 씨가 작성한 온라인 신청서를 보면 현재 직업(Current Occupation)을 묻는 항목에서 고등학교 화학 교사(a high school chemistry teacher)로 재직중이라고 답했으므로, (B)가 정답이다.

> **Paraphrasing** 지문의 a high school chemistry teacher
> → 정답의 an educator

185 연계

번역 파라 씨가 연례 행사에 대해 자세히 설명한 이유는 무엇이겠는가?

(A) 자신의 제과 제빵류가 얼마나 인기 있는지 보여 주려고
(B) 경연에 익숙하다는 것을 나타내려고
(C) 전문 제과 제빵사가 아니라는 것을 증명하려고
(D) 제한된 장비로 빵을 구울 수 있다는 것을 증명하려고

해설 온라인 신청서의 마지막 질문에 대해 파라 씨가 공식적인 제과 제빵 경험은 교내 연례 크리스마스 세일 행사에 판매할 컵케이크를 기부한 것(My formal baking experience amounts to donating cupcakes)이라면서 자세히 설명했다. 이렇게 설명한 이유는 기사를 통해 확인할 수 있는데, 세 번째 단락에서 사업의 일환으로 제과 제빵을 한 경험이 없어야(if you have never baked as part of a business) 토니의 제과 제빵 쇼에 출연할 기회가 있다는 조건을 제시했으므로, 파라 씨가 자신이 전문 제과 제빵사가 아니라는 것을 증명하기 위해 자세히 설명했음을 알 수 있다. 따라서 (C)가 정답이다.

어휘 evidence 증거

> **Paraphrasing** 지문의 amateur baker, baked as a part of a business → 정답의 not a professional baker

186-190 웹페이지 + 양식 + 이메일

http://www.lanarktheater.org/advertise

[186]래너크 극장에 광고하세요!

저희 극장의 프로그램 인쇄본에 광고를 내시면 수많은 저희 관람객들이 귀하의 업체를 보게 됩니다. 저희의 다가오는 공연 시즌이 막 발표되었는데, [187]1년 내내 공연을 펼칠 극단, 음악단, 무용단으로 구성된 멋진 진용을 갖추었습니다. 1년간, 혹은 연중 일부 기간 동안 저희 프로그램에 귀하의 업체를 실을 수 있으며, 광고 크기 역시 선택할 수 있습니다. 기본 광고 옵션은 다음과 같습니다.

종류	전면	절반 지면	[189]4분의 1 지면
1년 (12개월)	4,165달러	2,200달러	1,700달러
[189]반년 (6개월)	2,550달러	1,120달러	[189]780달러
1분기 (3개월)	1,330달러	760달러	440달러
1회 광고	440달러	300달러	150달러

[190]1년 광고주는 광고 계약 기간 중 래너크 극장에서 열리는 모든 공연 티켓을 15퍼센트 할인 받을 수 있는 특별 할인 카드를 받으실 수 있습니다!

시작하시려면 광고 신청서를 제출하십시오. 저희가 연락을 드려 귀하가 가장 적합한 광고 패키지를 선택하실 수 있도록 돕겠습니다. 신청서는 www.lanarktheater.org/advertise-request에 있습니다.

어휘 place an advertisement 광고를 하다 patron 고객, 손님 perform 공연하다 partial 부분적인, 일부의 good 유효한 duration 기간 suitable 적합한

래너크 극장
광고 신청서

성명: [188]루이스 샌더슨
이메일: l.sanderson@stanmorebistro.com
전화: 716-555-0145
업체: [188]스탠모어 식당

이전에 당사에 광고를 낸 적이 있습니까? 아니요.

어떤 경위로 이 광고 기회에 대해 알게 되었나요?
래너크 극장에서 공연을 자주 봅니다. 얼마 전에 친구의 업체가 극장 프로그램에 광고를 낸 것을 보았습니다. 그는 브레데일 의류의 소유주로, 귀사의 프로그램에 제 업체도 광고를 내라고 강력히 추천했습니다. [188]래너크 극장 관람객들이 제 식당에서 식사하는 것을 즐기게 될 거라고 확신합니다!

관심 있는 광고 종류는 무엇입니까?
1년 ____ [189]반년 _X_ 1분기 ____ 1회 ____ 모르겠음 ____

[189]최대 예산은 얼마입니까? 850달러

어휘 frequently 자주 bistro (소규모) 식당 budget 예산

수신: 마치에이 리치 〈m.ritchie@braedaleapparel.com〉
발신: 로사 초크펠 〈rosa.chokphel@lanarktheater.org〉
제목: 광고 갱신
날짜: 12월 13일

리치 씨께,

다가오는 시즌에 브레데일 의류 광고 패키지를 갱신해 주셔서 감사합니다. **190**1년간 4분의 1 지면 광고를 싣기로 다시 한 번 확정되셨습니다. 저희 래너크 극장은 귀사와 같은 지역 업체들의 도움 없이는 풍성하고 고무적인 예술 공연을 지역 사회에 제공하는 사명을 완수할 수 없을 것입니다!

최근에 추천을 해주신 것도 감사드립니다. 귀하의 추천 덕분에 루이스 샌더슨 씨가 저희 프로그램에 광고를 하게 되었습니다. 보내 주신 성원에 깊이 감사드립니다!

로사 초크펠
마케팅 직원, 래너크 극장

어휘 fulfill 완수하다, 충족하다 thought-provoking 생각하게 만드는, 고무적인 recent 최근의 referral 추천 appreciate 감사하다, 인정하다

186 주제 / 목적

번역 웹페이지의 목적은?
(A) 다가오는 공연 홍보하기
(B) 최근 공연 논평하기
(C) 광고 기회 알리기
(D) 공연자 구성 소개하기

해설 웹페이지의 제목 '래너크 극장에 광고하세요!(Advertise with Lanark Theater!)'와 첫 번째 단락의 '프로그램 인쇄본에 광고를 내시면 수많은 저희 관람객들이 귀하의 업체를 보게 됩니다(When you place an advertisement ~ your business will be seen by thousands of our patrons)'라는 문구를 통해 광고 기회를 알리는 웹페이지임을 알 수 있다. 따라서 (C)가 정답이다.

187 사실 관계 확인

번역 래너크 극장에 관해 언급된 것은?
(A) 다양한 예술 공연을 제공한다.
(B) 지역 신문에 광고한다.
(C) 최근에야 문을 열었다.
(D) 지역 그룹만 참여하는 공연을 선보인다.

해설 웹페이지의 첫 번째 단락에서 1년 내내 공연을 펼칠 극단, 음악단, 무용단으로 구성된 멋진 진용을 갖추었다(we have an exciting lineup of theater, music, and dance groups ~ throughout the year)고 했으므로, 다양한 예술 공연을 제공한다는 것을 알 수 있다. 따라서 (A)가 정답이다.

188 세부 사항

번역 샌더슨 씨는 어떤 업체를 소유하고 있는가?
(A) 광고회사
(B) 의류 매장
(C) 극장
(D) 식당

해설 광고 신청서(Advertisement Request Form)에 나온 업체명(Stanmore Bistro)과 래너크 극장 관람객들이 자신의 식당에서 식사하는 것을 즐기게 될 거라고 확신한다(Lanark Theater patrons would enjoy dining at my bistro)는 의견으로 미루어 보아, 샌더슨 씨가 식당을 소유하고 있음을 알 수 있다. 따라서 (D)가 정답이다.

▸▸ **Paraphrasing** 지문의 bistro → 정답의 restaurant

189 연계

번역 샌더슨 씨는 어떤 광고 옵션을 구매하겠는가?
(A) 전면 광고
(B) 절반 지면 광고
(C) 4분의 1 지면 광고
(D) 1회 광고

해설 샌더슨 씨는 광고 신청서(Advertisement Request Form)에서 반년(Half year)의 광고 기간을 선택했고 최대 예산(maximum budget)이 850달러임을 명시했다. 광고 옵션은 웹페이지에서 확인할 수 있는데, 반년에 해당하는 지면 크기 옵션 중 샌더슨 씨의 예산에 맞는 광고는 780달러인 4분의 1 지면(Quarter Page)이므로, 샌더스 씨가 이 광고를 구매할 것임을 추론할 수 있다. 따라서 (C)가 정답이다.

190 연계

번역 리치 씨에 관해 암시된 것은?
(A) 스탠모어 식당 공동 소유주이다.
(B) 할인 티켓을 받을 것이다.
(C) 자신의 광고 패키지를 업그레이드했다.
(D) 무용 공연보다 음악 공연을 선호한다.

해설 이메일의 첫 번째 단락에서 리치 씨가 1년 간 4분의 1 지면 광고를 싣기로 다시 한 번 확정되었다(You are once again confirmed for a quarter-page advertisement for the full year)고 했는데, 웹페이지를 보면 표 아래 단락에서 1년 광고주들은 광고 계약 기간 중 공연 티켓을 15퍼센트 할인 받을 수 있는 특별 할인 카드를 받는다(full-year advertisers receive a special discount card ~ 15% off tickets)고 했다. 따라서 리치 씨가 공연 할인 티켓을 받을 것임을 추론할 수 있으므로, (B)가 정답이다.

http://www.cheverlyartmuseum.com

| 홈 | 소개 | 전시회 | **여름 프로그램** | 연락처 |

세계적 수준의 미술 전시회를 감상한 후 ¹⁹¹**체벌리 미술관의 제10회 연례 여름 콘서트 시리즈** 기간에 프리 뮤직을 즐기십시오. 7월 14일부터 8월 4일까지 정문 근처의 아트리움 무대 또는 실외 광장에 있는 칠럼 무대에서 음악 공연이 열립니다. 콘서트는 오후 7시부터 9시까지 진행됩니다. 티켓 가격은 예매 시 10달러이고, 표가 남아 있는 경우 입구에서 15달러에 판매됩니다.

¹⁹⁵**7월 14일** 아트리움 무대
¹⁹⁵**현지 삼중주단인 킬럼루 사운즈가 활발한 아일랜드 전통 음악으로 시리즈를 시작합니다.**

7월 21일 아트리움 무대
유명한 재즈 피아니스트 릴리언 캐시가 5년 넘게 베스트셀러 음반인 〈키보드 스웨이〉에 수록된 혼이 담긴 곡들을 연주합니다.

7월 28일 칠럼 무대
¹⁹³**전국적으로 유명한 툴라 스톰퍼스가 미국 전통 민속 음악을 연주합니다.** 공연에는 ¹⁹³**리드 보컬 리아논 루이스**, 밴조 연주자 헥터 프리먼, 만돌린 연주자 린 트루먼, 바이올린 연주자 와이어트 데이븐포트가 출연합니다.

8월 4일 칠럼 무대
¹⁹²**헤네시 현악 사중주단이 자신들의 최근 음반 〈서머타임 클래식〉에서 선정된 곡을 연주합니다.**

어휘   exhibit 전시(회); 전시하다   free music 프리 뮤직, 저작권 사용료가 없는 음악   renowned 유명한   quartet 사중주단

수신: 리아논 루이스 〈rhianon.lewis@tgd.com〉
발신: 제임스 사보 〈j.sabo@cheverlyartmuseum.com〉
제목: 여름 콘서트 공연
날짜: 7월 17일

루이스 씨께:

저는 체벌리 미술관 프로그램 담당자입니다. 이번 시즌에 귀하께서 저희와 공연을 하시게 되어 정말 기쁩니다. 저희 콘서트는 언제나 호평을 받고 성황을 이룹니다.

¹⁹⁴**각 공연 1시간 전에 모든 장비가 제대로 작동하는지 확인하기 위해 무대 위에서 음향 점검을 실시합니다. 따라서 저희는 뮤지션들이 적어도 예정된 시작 시간 2시간 전에 도착하실 것을 권해 드립니다.** 또한 귀하 혹은 귀하의 밴드 멤버가 친구나 가족을 위한 티켓이 필요하시면, 저에게 알려 주세요. 기꺼이 준비해 드리겠습니다. ¹⁹³**티켓은 더 이상 구할 수 없지만, 예약 좌석이 몇 개 있어서 드릴 수 있습니다.**

만나 뵙기를 고대합니다!

제임스 사보
프로그램 담당자, 체벌리 미술관

어휘   well received 호평을 받는   well attended 관객이 많은   equipment 장비   properly 제대로

수신: 제임스 사보 〈j.sabo@cheverlyartmuseum.com〉
발신: 리아논 루이스 〈rhianon.lewis@tgd.com〉
제목: 회신: 여름 콘서트 공연
날짜: 7월 17일

안녕하세요, 제임스,

알려 주셔서 감사합니다. 저는 밴드와 함께 알링턴에서부터 운전해서 갈 예정이어서, 저희 모두 교통편이 마련되어 있습니다. 오후 5시 30분에 도착할 계획입니다.

별개의 문제로, 지금 장소 변경을 요청하기에 너무 늦은 건 아니었으면 합니다. ¹⁹⁵**제가 7월 14일 공연을 보러 왔었는데** 당시 공연했던 그룹이 연주하면서 뒤에 있는 스크린을 통해 동영상을 보여 주었습니다. 저희 그룹도 공연하는 동안 보여 드리고 싶은 이미지와 동영상이 있습니다. 무대 관리자와 이야기했는데 저희가 공연하기로 예정된 공간에서는 그런 설정이 가능하지 않을 것이라고 말했습니다. 이러한 요소들이 저희 쇼에서 필수적인 부분은 아니지만, 저희 관객들은 그것들이 매우 효과적이라고 생각해 왔습니다. 따라서 가능하다면 그런 요소들을 넣고 싶습니다.

감사합니다.

리아논

어휘   transportation 교통(편)   venue 장소   element 요소   powerful 강렬한, 매우 효과적인   incorporate 포함하다

---

191 사실 관계 확인

번역   콘서트 시리즈에 관해 웹페이지에 명시된 것은?
   (A) 해마다 열린다.
   (B) 클래식 음악에 집중한다.
   (C) 미술관 회원들에게만 공개된다.
   (D) 유명한 예술가들이 조직한다.

해설   웹페이지의 첫 번째 단락에서 '제10회 연례 여름 콘서트 시리즈 (tenth annual Summer Concert Series)'라고 했으므로, 콘서트 시리즈가 해마다 열린다는 것을 알 수 있다. 따라서 (A)가 정답이다.

▸▸ **Paraphrasing**   지문의 annual → 정답의 every year

---

192 세부 사항

번역   웹페이지에 따르면 최근 음반을 녹음한 공연자는?
   (A) 킬럼루 사운즈
   (B) 릴리언 캐시
   (C) 툴라 스톰퍼스
   (D) 헤네시 현악 사중주단

해설 웹페이지의 마지막 단락에서 헤네시 현악 사중주단이 자신들의 최근 음반에서 선정된 곡을 연주한다(The Hennessy String Quartet will play selections from their recent recording)고 했으므로, (D)가 정답이다.

어휘 act (음악) 공연자, 그룹

> ▸▸ Paraphrasing　지문의 their recent recording
> → 질문의 recently recorded music

193　연계

번역　툴라 스톰퍼스 콘서트에 관해 암시된 것은?

　(A) 이미 매진되었다.
　(B) 2시간 일찍 시작할 것이다.
　(C) 지역 초빙 음악가가 출연할 것이다.
　(D) 다른 날로 옮겼다.

해설　웹페이지에 나온 공연 프로그램 안내를 보면, 7월 28일에 전국적으로 유명한 툴라 스톰퍼스가 미국 전통 민속 음악을 연주(The nationally renowned Tulla Stompers play traditional American folk music)하는데, 여기에 리드 보컬(lead vocals)인 리아논 루이스(Rhianon Lewis)도 출연한다고 했다. 툴라 스톰퍼스의 공연에 대한 정보는 사보 씨가 루이스 씨에게 보낸 첫 번째 이메일에서도 확인할 수 있는데, 두 번째 단락 후반부에서 티켓은 더 이상 구할 수 없다(Tickets are no longer available)고 했으므로, 툴라 스톰퍼스 콘서트가 매진되었음을 추론할 수 있다. 따라서 (A)가 정답이다.

> ▸▸ Paraphrasing　지문의 Tickets are no longer available
> → 정답의 sold out

194　세부 사항

번역　첫 번째 이메일에 따르면 뮤지션들이 일찍 도착해야 하는 이유는?

　(A) 주차할 곳을 찾기 위해
　(B) 계약서에 서명하기 위해
　(C) 음향 장비를 점검하기 위해
　(D) 무대 관리자를 선정하기 위해

해설　두 번째 단락에서 각 공연 1시간 전에 무대 위에서 음향 점검을 실시하기(we run a sound check onstage an hour before each performance) 때문에 뮤지션들이 적어도 예정된 시작 시간 2시간 전에 도착할 것(musicians arrive by at least two hours before the scheduled start time)을 권한다고 했으므로, (C)가 정답이다.

> ▸▸ Paraphrasing　지문의 by at least two hours before the
> scheduled start time → 질문의 early
> 지문의 run a sound check
> → 정답의 test sound equipment

195　연계

번역　루이스 씨에 관해 명시된 것은?

　(A) 릴리언 캐시와 함께 곡을 녹음했다.
　(B) 체벌리 미술관에 교통편을 요청했다.
　(C) 이전에는 자신의 공연에 동영상을 사용한 적이 없다.
　(D) 킬럴루 사운즈 공연에 참석했다.

해설　루이스 씨가 사보 씨에게 쓴 두 번째 이메일의 두 번째 단락을 보면, 자신이 7월 14일 공연을 보러 왔었다(came to see the July 14 performance)고 했다. 7월 14일에 열린 공연과 관련된 정보는 웹페이지에서 확인할 수 있는데, 이날은 현지 삼중주단인 킬럴루 사운즈(Local trio Killaloe Sounds)가 공연한 날이므로, (D)가 정답이다.

196-200 목차 + 웹페이지 + 블로그 게시글

> 〈월간 재계 전망〉
>
> 3월 호 기사:
>
> **적임자**　　　　　　　　　　　　　　　11쪽
> 변화를 불러올 지원자를 찾아내라. 더그 테너가 4명의 관리자와 함께 그들의 196면접 접근 방식에 관해 이야기를 나누었다.
>
> **적합한 질문**　　　　　　　　　　　　27쪽
> 대형 국제 법인들은 신입 사원을 어떻게 물색할까? 릴리 짐블이 세계에서 가장 규모가 큰 인사부 세 곳을 방문해 196구인 공고와 구인 활동에 어떤 요소가 투입되는지 살펴본다.
>
> **그곳에 있다는 것**　　　　　　　　　38쪽
> 200지나 피멘텔이 가상 회의의 장점과 약점을 살펴본다. 원격 회의의 미래는 무엇이며, 이것이 과연 우리가 원하는 것일까? 200짧은 회의에는 유용하지만 더 긴 시간의 상호 작용에도 좋을까? 놀랍게도 일부 연구에 따르면 가상 회의가 직원 참여에는 거의 효과가 없다고 한다.
>
> **상용 회화집의 이점**　　　　　　　19744쪽
> 197멜리사 다이슨이 외국에서 영업할 때 현지인들과 소통하는 비결을 공유한다. 고객은 자신의 언어를 배우려고 노력하는 방문자들을 더 친절하게 대한다.
>
> **장기 체류**　　　　　　　　　　　　52쪽
> 199그렉 맥다니엘이 5주 동안 다섯 곳의 호텔에서 장기 체류 옵션을 경험했다. 그가 각 호텔의 장단점을 상세히 설명한다.

어휘　approach 접근(법)　recruiting 구인 (활동), 채용　virtual 가상의　distance meeting 원격 회의　interaction 상호 작용, 교류　engagement 참여　conduct 수행하다, 이행하다　warm 호의적으로 대하다　extended 길어진, 장기의　pros and cons 장단점

◀ ▶ http://www.farolgrandehotel.com/updates

파롤 그란데 호텔—업데이트

〈월간 재계 전망〉 잡지 3월 호에 저희 호텔에 대한 평가 글이 게재된 것을 최근 알게 되었습니다! 평가는 "비밀 작전"을 통해 이루어졌습니다. ^{198, 199}기자가 가상의 이름을 사용해 단골 고객으로 가장하고 저희 호텔에 5박을 머물렀습니다. 따라서 저희는 기사를 보고서야 그가 여기 왔었다는 것을 알았습니다! 저희 시설에 대한 철저한 분석글을 읽으시려면 http://www.bom.com/currentissues/march에 접속해 잡지를 보시기 바랍니다.

어휘 undercover 비밀리에 하는 fictional 지어낸, 허구의
analysis 분석

〈월간 재계 전망〉

편집자님께:

지나 피멘텔이 작성한 화상 회의 및 기타 가상 회의 기술의 현황에 관한 기사를 흥미롭게 읽었습니다. 화상 회의와 전화 회의가 직접 참석하는 회의에 대한 진정한 대안이 될 수 없다는 기자의 의견에는 공감하지만 미래에는 그것이 추세가 되지 않을까 합니다. ²⁰⁰하지만 최근의 기술 발전을 감안하더라도, 제 경험에 따르면 화상 회의는 상황 점검 같은 짧은 회의에 가장 효과적입니다. 협상에 관한 문제라면 대면 상호 작용만 한 것이 없습니다.

—엠레 오스만

어휘 take (1회분의) 기사, 원고 status (진행) 상황
sympathize with ~에 공감하다 sentiment 감정, 의견
alternative 대안; 대안이 되는 effective 효과적인 negotiation 협상

196 세부 사항

번역 잡지의 처음 두 기사는 어떤 점에서 비슷한가?

(A) 모두 직원 채용 업무에 대해 논의한다.
(B) 모두 기술의 새로운 활용에 초점을 맞춘다.
(C) 모두 신설 직책을 광고하는 법에 대해 논의한다.
(D) 모두 부정적인 면접 행위에 관해 비판한다.

해설 잡지 목차를 보면 첫 번째 기사에서는 면접 접근 방식(approach to interviewing)에 대해 다루고, 두 번째 기사에서는 기업의 구인 공고와 구인 활동(job postings and recruiting)에 대해 다룬다고 나와 있다. 따라서 두 기사 모두 직원 채용과 관련된 업무에 대해 논하고 있으므로, (A)가 정답이다.

197 세부 사항

번역 해외 여행객들에 대한 조언은 몇 쪽에 있는가?

(A) 11쪽
(B) 27쪽
(C) 38쪽
(D) 44쪽

해설 잡지 44쪽에 있는 기사인 '상용 회화집의 이점(Benefits of the Phrase Book)'에서 멜리사 다이슨이 외국에서 영업할 때 현지인들과 소통하는 비결(tips on communicating with locals when conducting business abroad)을 공유한다고 했으므로, (D)가 정답이다.

▸▸ Paraphrasing　　지문의 tips → 질문의 advice
　　　　　　　　　　　지문의 abroad → 질문의 international

198 세부 사항

번역 웹페이지에 따르면 기자가 한 일은?

(A) 3월에 호텔을 방문했다.
(B) 실제 신분을 숨겼다.
(C) 예약을 취소했다.
(D) 밤늦게 도착했다.

해설 웹페이지에서 기자가 가상의 이름을 사용하여(the reporter used a fictional name) 단골 고객으로 가장했다(posed as a regular guest)고 했으므로, 실제 자신의 신분을 숨겼다는 것을 알 수 있다. 따라서 (B)가 정답이다.

▸▸ Paraphrasing　　지문의 used a fictional name, posed as a regular guest → 정답의 hid his real identity

199 연계

번역 파롤 그란데 호텔에 묵은 사람은?

(A) 테너 씨
(B) 짐블 씨
(C) 다이슨 씨
(D) 맥다니엘 씨

해설 파롤 그란데 호텔의 웹페이지를 보면, 기자가 가상의 이름을 사용해 호텔에 투숙했다(the reporter used a fictional name ~ stayed with us)고 했다. 이 기자의 이름은 잡지의 목차에서 확인할 수 있는데, '장기 체류(Extended Stay)' 기사에서 그렉 맥다니엘이 다섯 곳의 호텔에서 장기 체류 옵션을 경험했다(Greg McDaniel went to five hotels ~ to experience their extended-stay options)고 했으므로, (D)가 정답이다.

200 연계

번역 피멘텔 씨와 오스만 씨가 가상 회의에 관해 동의하는 것은?

(A) 직원 참여가 늘어난다.
(B) 미래에는 차츰 사라질 것이다.
(C) 직접 참석하는 회의를 대체할 것이다.
(D) 신속한 정보 교환에는 효과적이다.

해설 잡지 목차를 보면, '그곳에 있다는 것(Being there)' 기사에서 피멘텔 씨가 가상 회의(virtual conferencing)가 짧은 회의에 유용하다(useful for brief meetings)는 의견을 밝혔음을 알 수 있다. 오스만 씨의 의견은 블로그 게시글에서 확인할 수 있는데, 자신의 경험에 따르면 화상 회의는 짧은 회의에 가장 효과적(videoconferences are most effective for short meetings)이라고 했다. 따라서 둘 다 가상회의가 신속한 정보 교환에는 효과적이라는 점에 동의한다는 것을 알 수 있으므로, (D)가 정답이다.

101 (B)	**102** (B)	**103** (C)	**104** (B)	**105** (D)
106 (C)	**107** (B)	**108** (A)	**109** (A)	**110** (A)
111 (C)	**112** (B)	**113** (C)	**114** (B)	**115** (C)
116 (A)	**117** (A)	**118** (B)	**119** (D)	**120** (D)
121 (A)	**122** (D)	**123** (D)	**124** (A)	**125** (C)
126 (A)	**127** (B)	**128** (C)	**129** (B)	**130** (D)
131 (C)	**132** (A)	**133** (D)	**134** (B)	**135** (B)
136 (A)	**137** (C)	**138** (A)	**139** (B)	**140** (D)
141 (C)	**142** (A)	**143** (C)	**144** (D)	**145** (A)
146 (D)	**147** (B)	**148** (D)	**149** (D)	**150** (B)
151 (A)	**152** (D)	**153** (C)	**154** (C)	**155** (D)
156 (B)	**157** (D)	**158** (A)	**159** (C)	**160** (B)
161 (C)	**162** (B)	**163** (D)	**164** (C)	**165** (C)
166 (C)	**167** (D)	**168** (A)	**169** (D)	**170** (A)
171 (B)	**172** (A)	**173** (D)	**174** (B)	**175** (C)
176 (B)	**177** (D)	**178** (D)	**179** (A)	**180** (B)
181 (D)	**182** (D)	**183** (D)	**184** (C)	**185** (A)
186 (D)	**187** (A)	**188** (C)	**189** (C)	**190** (B)
191 (C)	**192** (A)	**193** (B)	**194** (D)	**195** (C)
196 (B)	**197** (B)	**198** (D)	**199** (D)	**200** (C)

PART 5

101 인칭대명사의 격 _ 소유격

해설 빈칸은 전치사 by의 목적어 역할을 하는 명사구 expert chef를 한정 수식하는 자리이므로, 소유격 인칭대명사 (B) their가 정답이다. 참고로, Generita's Bistro 같이 특정 단체나 조직을 가리킬 때는 복수 대명사를 사용할 수 있다.

번역 제네리타즈 비스트로에 있는 모든 소스는 그들의 전문 요리사들에 의해 꼼꼼하게 가공 처리된다.

어휘 batch (음식 등) 한 번에 만드는 양   process 가공 처리하다   meticulously 꼼꼼하게   expert 전문가

102 부사 자리 _ 동사 수식

해설 Computerization of medical records가 주어, increases가 동사인 문장으로, 빈칸에는 동사를 수식하는 부사가 들어가야 한다. 따라서 '대단히, 크게'라는 의미의 부사인 (B) greatly가 정답이다. 원급인 (A) great과 최상급인 (D) greatest는 형용사, (C) greatness는 명사로 모두 품사상 빈칸에 적합하지 않다.

번역 의료 기록을 전산화하면 환자를 진단하고 치료하는 의사의 역량이 크게 향상된다.

어휘 computerization 전산화, 컴퓨터화   physician 의사   diagnose 진단하다   treat 치료하다   patient 환자

103 명사 어휘

해설 빈칸은 동사 use의 목적어 역할을 하며, 형용사 the freshest와 available의 수식을 받는다. 따라서 이들과 가장 잘 어울리는 명사를 선택해야 한다. 문맥상 '구할 수 있는 가장 신선한 재료들을 사용해 샐러드를 만든다'라는 내용이 되어야 자연스러우므로, '재료, 성분'이라는 의미의 (C) ingredients가 정답이 된다.

번역 로젤즈 파인 다이닝에서는 구할 수 있는 가장 신선한 재료들을 사용해 샐러드를 만듭니다.

어휘 application 지원(서), 응용 프로그램   subject 주제, 과목   factor 요인

104 전치사 어휘

해설 빈칸 뒤 명사구 the natural history conference를 목적어로 취하는 전치사 자리로, 빈칸을 포함한 전치사구가 동사구 will present his paper를 수식하고 있다. 따라서 빈칸에는 '논문을 발표하는 것이다'와 '자연사 학회'를 적절히 연결해주는 전치사가 들어가야 한다. 문맥상 '자연사 학회에서 논문을 발표할 것이다'라는 내용이 되어야 자연스러우므로, '~에(서)'라는 의미의 (B) at이 정답이다.

번역 벤귀귀 교수는 내일 있을 자연사 학회에서 논문을 발표할 예정이다.

어휘 natural history 자연사, 박물학   conference 대회, 학회

105 명사 어휘 _ 복합 명사

해설 빈칸 뒤 명사 date와 복합명사를 이루어 전치사 for의 목적어 역할을 하는 명사를 선택하는 문제이다. '새로 주문한 오븐의 배송일을 기다리고 있다'라는 내용이 되어야 자연스러우므로, 보기 중 불가산(단수)명사로 '배송'을 의미하는 (D) shipping이 정답이 된다. 참고로, shipment는 가산명사로 쓰일 경우 '수송품'을 뜻하며, 불가산명사로 쓰일 때만 date와 함께 '선적일'이라는 표현을 완성할 수 있다.

번역 요리사들은 2주 전에 주문한 새 컨벡션 오븐의 배송일을 여전히 기다리고 있다.

어휘 convection oven 대류식 오븐   shipper 운송업자

106 부사 어휘

해설 동사 works (with)를 적절히 수식하는 부사를 선택하는 문제이다. 내부 팀원들 및 다양한 지역의 영업 사원들과 협력한다는 내용이므로, 빈칸에는 협력 방식을 묘사하는 부사가 들어가야 자연스럽다. 따라서 '긴밀히'라는 의미의 (C) closely가 정답이다.

번역 강 씨는 내부 팀원들은 물론 다양한 지역의 영업 사원들과도 긴밀히 협력하고 있다.

어휘 regional 지역의   representative 사원   mildly 약간, 부드럽게   nearly 약, 거의   narrowly 간신히

107 명사절 접속사

해설 빈칸은 타동사로 쓰인 knows의 목적어 역할을 하는 자리이므로, 명사절을 이끌 수 있는 (B) when과 명사로 쓰일 수 있는 (C) need 중 하나를 선택해야 한다. 문맥상 '자신의 제품 종류를 언제 새롭게 바꿔

야 할지 알고 있다'라는 내용이 되어야 자연스러우므로, (B) when이 정답이다. 참고로, 명사절 접속사 when 뒤에는 완전한 절 또는 to부정사구가 올 수 있다.

번역 패션 디자이너 박혜자는 변화하는 취향에 부응해 자신의 제품 종류를 언제 새롭게 바꿔야 할지 알고 있다.

어휘 in response to ~에 부응해, 답하여 taste 취향

108 형용사 어휘 _ 과거분사

해설 빈칸은 '너무 …해서 ~하다'라는 의미의 「be+so+형용사+that ~」의 구문을 완성하는 형용사 자리이다. that절에 나오는 판단(정규 강좌 과목으로 만들기로 결정했다)의 근거가 되는 과거분사가 빈칸에 들어가야 자연스러우므로, 부사 well과 함께 '많은 사람들이 참석한, 참석자가 많은'이라는 표현을 완성하는 (A) attended가 정답이 된다.

번역 삼바 수업에 너무 많은 사람들이 참석해서 율라라 댄스 학원은 이 강좌를 정규 강좌 과목으로 만들기로 결정했다.

어휘 permanent 정규의, 상임의 educated 교육받은, 많이 배운 gathered 모아진, 주름이 잡힌 protected 보호된, 보호를 받는

109 전치사 어휘

해설 빈칸 뒤 명사구 the city's residential area를 목적어로 취하는 전치사 자리로, 빈칸을 포함한 전치사구가 부사 away와 함께 동사구 will be situated를 수식하고 있다. 문맥상 '주거 지역에서 멀리 떨어진 곳에 지어질 것이다'라는 내용이 되어야 자연스러우므로, '~에서 (부터)'라는 의미로 장소 간의 거리를 나타낼 때 쓰이는 (A) from이 정답이다.

번역 그 공장은 소음과 배기가스에 대한 불만을 줄이기 위해 시의 주거 지역에서 멀리 떨어진 곳에 지어질 것이다.

어휘 situate 위치시키다 residential 주거의 reduce 줄이다 emission 배기가스, 배출

110 형용사 자리 _ 명사 수식

해설 최상급 표현 the most와 함께 명사구 mailing option을 수식하는 형용사 자리이므로, '경제적인, 실속 있는'이라는 의미의 형용사인 (A) economical이 정답이다. (B) economy는 명사, (C) economize 및 (D) economized는 자동사로 품사상 빈칸에 적합하지 않다.

번역 쿠라모토 씨는 이용 가능한 가장 경제적인 발송 옵션을 선택했다.

어휘 economy 경제, 절약 economize 절약하다, 아끼다

111 동사 자리 _ 조동사 + 동사원형

해설 빈칸 앞에 조동사 can이 있고 뒤에 전치사 on이 있으므로, 빈칸에는 동사원형이 들어가야 한다. 따라서 '의존하다, 의지하다'라는 의미의 동사 (C) rely가 정답이다. (A) reliable은 형용사, (B) reliably는 부사, (D) relying은 동명사/현재분사로 품사상 빈칸에 들어갈 수 없다.

번역 정보 기술 전문가가 없는 기업들은 온라인 서비스 지원이 필요할 시 바이버 소프트웨어 어드바이저스에 의지하면 됩니다.

어휘 reliable 믿을 만한, 신뢰할 수 있는 reliably 신뢰할 수 있게, 확실히

112 관계대명사 _ 주격

해설 빈칸은 뒤에 오는 불완전한 절(is to review design portfolios)의 주어 자리이며, 빈칸 이하가 명사구 a new task를 부연 설명하고 있다. 따라서 빈칸에는 불완전한 절의 주어 역할을 하며 두 절을 이어 주는 접속사가 들어가야 하므로, 주격 관계대명사 (B) which가 정답이다. (A) although, (C) after, (D) because는 모두 완전한 절을 이끄는 부사절 접속사로 빈칸에 적합하지 않다.

번역 내년에 우리 팀은 새로운 과제를 맡게 되는데, 이 과제는 디자인 포트폴리오를 검토하는 것이다.

어휘 task 과제 review 검토하다

113 대명사

해설 빈칸은 to ensure의 목적어 역할을 하는 명사 readiness를 한정 수식하는 자리이며, 빈칸을 포함한 명사구가 to be eaten의 수식을 받고 있다. 문맥을 살펴보면 먹을 수 있게 준비되어야 하는 것은 고기(the meat)이므로, 고기를 가리키는 소유격 대명사 (C) its가 정답이다.

번역 고기를 먹을 수 있게 준비하려면 30분 동안 익히십시오.

어휘 readiness 준비가 되어 있음

114 형용사 _ 어휘

해설 동사구 will hire의 목적어인 interns를 적절히 수식하는 형용사를 선택하는 문제이다. '실험실 업무를 도울 인턴을 채용할 것이다'라는 내용이므로, '몇몇의, 여러'라는 의미로 불특정한 숫자를 나타내는 (B) several이 빈칸에 들어가야 자연스럽다. 참고로, (C) whole은 '(무언가의) 전부[전체]'라는 의미로 빈칸에 부적절하다.

번역 아목시트론의 연구팀은 실험실 업무를 도울 인턴 여러 명을 채용할 예정이다.

어휘 laboratory 실험실, 연구실 duty 업무 given 주어진 natural 자연스러운, 자연의

115 부사절 접속사

해설 빈칸에 적절한 접속사를 선택하는 문제이다. 문맥을 살펴보면, 빈칸이 이끄는 절은 '새 주스의 인기가 높은 것으로 나타났다'라는 내용으로, 주절에 나온 '생산량을 늘리기 위해 신속하게 움직여야 한다'라는 판단의 근거가 된다. 따라서 '~ 때문에, ~여서'라는 의미의 부사절 접속사인 (C) Since가 정답이다.

번역 새로운 아사이베리 혼합 주스가 아주 인기가 높은 것으로 나타났으므로, 우리는 생산량을 늘리기 위해 신속하게 움직여야 한다.

어휘 increase 늘리다 volume 양

116 명사 자리 _ 전치사의 목적어

해설 빈칸 앞에 단수 가산명사(engine)가 한정사(관사, 소유격 등) 없이 왔으므로, 빈칸에는 engine과 복합명사를 이루는 명사가 들어가야 한다. 문맥상 '엔진 제조 과정'이라는 내용이 되어야 자연스러우므로, '제조, 건축'이라는 의미의 불가산명사 (A) construction이 정답이 된다. 참고로, (D) construct는 '건설하다'라는 뜻의 동사 이외에도 '생각, 구조물'이라는 명사로 쓰일 수 있지만, 가산명사이므로 단수형으로 빈칸에 들어갈 수 없으며 의미상으로도 부적절하다.

번역 새로운 배기가스 기준 때문에 라이더 오토는 엔진 제조 과정을 수정해야 했다.

어휘 emission 배출, 배기가스   force ～하도록 강요하다   modify 수정하다   constructive 건설적인, 구조적인, 추정적인

117 동사 어휘

해설 빈칸은 명사구 business tasks를 목적어로 취하면서 전치사 for의 목적어 역할을 하는 동명사 자리로, 전치사구 with speed and precision의 수식을 받는다. 따라서 business tasks 및 with speed and precision과 적절히 어울려 쓰이는 동사를 선택해야 한다. 문맥상 '업무 과제를 신속하고 정확하게 수행하기 위한'이라는 내용이 되어야 자연스러우므로, '수행하기, 실행하기'라는 의미의 (A) executing이 정답이다.

번역 마키 카야노의 책은 업무 과제를 신속하고 정확하게 수행하기 위한 기법을 제공한다.

어휘 execute 수행하다   precision 정확(성)   equip 장비를 갖추다   involve 포함하다

118 부사 자리 _ 동사 수식

해설 빈칸 앞에 완전한 절이 있으므로, 빈칸에는 동사 will be installed를 수식하는 부사가 들어가야 한다. 따라서 '점진적으로, 서서히'라는 의미의 부사인 (B) gradually가 정답이다. 원급인 (A) gradual, 비교급인 (C) more gradual, 최상급인 (D) most gradual은 모두 형용사로, 품사상 빈칸에 적합하지 않다.

번역 비용을 통제하기 위해, 업데이트된 신용카드 판독기를 지점들에 점진적으로 설치할 예정이다.

어휘 install 설치하다   branch store 지점   gradually 점진적으로

119 전치사 어휘

해설 빈칸에 적절한 전치사를 선택하는 문제이다. 빈칸 앞에서 '매출을 예상한다'고 했고, 뒤에서 범위가 될 만한 특정 금액(£160,000 and £180,000)을 언급했으므로, 빈칸이 이끄는 전치사구는 '16만 파운드에서 18만 파운드 사이의'라는 내용이 되어야 자연스럽다. 따라서 접속사 and와 함께 'A와 B 사이의'라는 표현을 완성하는 (D) between이 정답이다. 참고로, (B) among은 '～ 중에, (셋 이상) 사이에'라는 의미로 뒤에 복수명사가 온다.

번역 이번 분기에 몬텔 베버리지사는 16만 파운드에서 18만 파운드 사이의 매출을 올릴 것으로 예상하고 있다.

어휘 expect 예상하다, 기대하다

120 대명사

해설 빈칸은 have reached의 주어 자리이므로, 보기에서 복수동사와 쓰일 수 있는 (A) any와 (D) few 중 하나를 선택해야 한다. 부사절에서 '아코욜라 산이 등반가들에게 무척 힘들기 때문에'라는 이유를 언급했으므로, 빈칸이 포함된 절은 이와 어울리는 결과에 관한 내용이 되어야 자연스럽다. 따라서 '소수(밖에 없는), 거의 없는 사람[것]'이라는 부정적 의미를 나타내는 (D) few가 정답이 된다. 참고로, (C) other는 단독으로 대명사 역할을 할 수 없다.

번역 아코욜라 산은 등반가들에게 무척 힘들기 때문에, 정상에 도달한 사람이 거의 없다.

어휘 challenging 힘든, 어려운   climber 등반가   peak 정상

121 전치사 자리 _ 어휘

해설 빈칸은 명사구 repair work를 목적어로 취하는 전치사 자리이며, 빈칸을 포함한 전치사구가 동사 will be closed를 수식하고 있다. 따라서 전치사로 끝나는 (A) because of와 (D) rather than 중 하나를 선택해야 하는데, 문맥상 '수리 공사 때문에 폐쇄될 예정이다'라는 내용이 되어야 자연스러우므로, (A) because of가 정답이 된다. 참고로, 부사절 접속사인 (B) so that과 (C) as if 뒤에는 완전한 절이 와야 한다.

번역 킹 스트리트 다리는 보수 공사로 인해 9월에 폐쇄될 예정이다.

어휘 repair 수리; 수리하다

122 부사 자리 _ 동명사 수식

해설 빈칸은 동명사 negotiating과 전치사 with 사이 자리이므로, 자동사로 쓰인 동명사 negotiating을 수식하는 부사가 들어가야 한다. 따라서 '효과적으로'라는 의미의 부사인 (D) effectively가 정답이다.

번역 타니구치 씨의 상사는 후루야마사와 효과적으로 협상한 것에 대해 그녀를 칭찬했다.

어휘 supervisor 상사   commend 칭찬하다   negotiate 협상하다   effectively 효과적으로

123 부사 자리 _ 관계부사의 생략

해설 빈칸 앞뒤에 완전한 절이 있으나 보기에 완전한 절을 이끌 수 있는 접속사가 없으므로, 빈칸과 they 사이에 관계부사가 생략이 되었다는 가정 하에 정답을 선택해야 한다. 본래 관계부사절은 명사를 수식하지만, 빈칸 바로 앞에 명사구(the conference room)가 있기 때문에 문장 구성상 빈칸에 대명사가 들어갈 수 없다. 따라서 의미상 명사를 포함하는 부사 (A) somewhere(=in/to some place)와 (D) anytime(=at any time) 중 하나를 선택해야 하는데, 문맥상 '필요할 때면 언제나 회의실을 예약할 수 있다'라는 내용이 되어야 자연스러우므로, (D) anytime이 정답이 된다. 복합관계대명사인 (B) whatever는 불완전한 절을 이끄는 접속사이므로 빈칸에 들어갈 수 없고, (C) everything은 대명사로 품사상 빈칸에 적합하지 않다.

번역 직원들은 필요할 때면 언제나 회의실을 예약할 수 있다.

어휘 reserve 예약하다

124 명사 어휘

해설 빈칸은 전치사 of의 목적어 역할을 하는 명사 자리이며, 전치사구 in English and Spanish의 수식을 받고 있다. 또한 '높은 수준의'를 의미하는 a high level of의 수식도 받고 있으므로, 언어를 구사하는 데 있어서 레벨 측정의 대상이 되는 명사가 빈칸에 들어가야 한다. 따라서 '유창함, 숙달'이라는 의미의 (A) proficiency가 정답이다.

번역 홍보 부장은 영어와 스페인어를 아주 유창한 수준으로 구사해야 한다.

어휘 public relations 홍보 advancement 발전, 승진 routine (통상적으로 하는) 습관, 일 strength 힘, 내구력

125 부사 어휘

해설 빈칸 뒤 동사 seeks를 적절히 수식하는 부사를 선택하는 문제이다. 혁신적인 방법을 모색하는 방식을 묘사하는 부사가 빈칸에 들어가야 자연스러우므로, '끊임없이, 지속적으로'라는 의미의 (C) continually가 정답이다.

번역 패터슨 프로덕츠는 변화하는 소비자의 요구를 충족하는 혁신적인 방법을 끊임없이 모색한다.

어휘 continually 끊임없이 meet 충족하다 demand 요구, 수요 dually 이중으로 favorably 호의적으로 generically 일반적으로

126 동사 어형

해설 접속사 so (that)가 이끄는 절의 동사를 선택하는 문제이다. so (that)가 '(~를 가능하게) 하기 위해'라는 의미로 쓰이며, 문맥상 '방해 없이 기술 보고서를 끝낼 수 있도록 내일 집에서 근무할 예정이다'라는 내용이 되어야 자연스러우므로, 가능을 나타내는 (A) can finish가 정답이다.

번역 볼란테 씨는 아무런 방해 없이 기술 보고서를 끝낼 수 있도록 내일 집에서 근무할 예정이다.

어휘 distraction 방해, 주의를 산만하게 하는 것

127 부사절 접속사

해설 빈칸은 뒤에 오는 완전한 절을 이끄는 접속사 자리이므로, 부사절 접속사인 (A) in order that과 (D) except that 중 하나를 선택해야 한다. 새 결제 코드를 넣어야 하는 것(new payment codes ~ inserted)은 모든 청구 절차가 동일하다는 것(All of the billing procedures ~ the same)의 예외 사항이므로, '~라는 것 이외에는'이라는 의미의 (D) except that이 정답이 된다.

번역 송장 문서에 새 결제 코드를 넣어야 한다는 점을 제외하면 모든 청구 절차는 동일하다.

어휘 procedure 절차 insert 넣다 invoice 송장, 청구서

128 형용사 어휘

해설 주어 The lightweight design of the new sedan을 적절히 설명하는 형용사를 선택하는 문제이다. 빈칸 뒤 부사절에서 '경량 설계

가 차를 미끄러지게 할 수 있기 때문에(because it can cause the vehicle to slide)'라는 특정 근거를 제시했으므로, 빈칸에는 이 근거에 따른 판단을 나타내는 형용사가 들어가야 자연스럽다. 따라서 '의문의 여지가 있는, 문제가 되는'이라는 의미의 (C) questionable이 정답이다.

번역 신형 세단의 경량 설계는 빙판길에서 차를 미끄러지게 할 수 있기 때문에 문제가 된다.

어휘 vehicle 차량 icy 얼음에 뒤덮인 mechanical 기계적인 multiple (명사 앞에서) 많은, 복합적인

129 명사 자리 _ 동사의 주어

해설 빈칸은 동사 was의 주어 역할을 하는 명사 자리이며, 정관사 the와 형용사 common의 수식을 받고 있다. 따라서 '예측, 추측'이라는 의미의 명사인 (B) assumption이 정답이다. 참고로, 동명사인 (C) assuming 또한 주어 역할을 할 수 있지만, assume은 타동사로서 목적어를 취해야 하며, 부사의 수식을 받으므로 빈칸에는 들어갈 수 없다.

번역 은행장이 은퇴했을 때 부행장이 인계하리라는 것이 일반적인 예측이었다.

어휘 retire 은퇴하다 take over 인계하다 assume 예측하다 assumable 가정할 수 있는

130 동사 어휘

해설 빈칸 뒤 목적어 fees for oversized items와 가장 잘 어울리는 동사를 선택해야 한다. 문맥상 '허용 중량 제한 범위 안의 특대 물품에 대해서는 수수료를 면제해 준다'라는 내용이 되어야 자연스러우므로, '(권리 등을) 포기하다', 즉 '(비용 등을) 면제해 주다'라는 의미의 (D) waives가 정답이다. 참고로, '협력하다'라는 의미의 (B) cooperates는 자동사로, 전치사 없이 바로 목적어를 취할 수 없다.

번역 웨스트 벵갈 항공은 허용 중량 범위 안에 있는 특대 물품에 대해서는 수수료를 면제해 준다.

어휘 oversized 특대의, 너무 큰 limitation 제한 transport 수송하다, 이동시키다

PART 6

131-134 이메일

수신: pmendoza@factmail.co
발신: recruiting@analystsassoc.org
날짜: 5월 2일
제목: ASA 가입

멘도자 씨께,

최근의 **131**대회 기간 동안 저희 단체에 관심을 보여 주셔서 감사합니다. 베버 정보 시스템 컨벤션 기간 중 ASA 부스에서 만나 뵙게 되어 반가웠습니다. 저와 나눈 대화를 기억하시리라 생각합니다만, 그때 우리

는 ASA의 월간 소식지에서 제공해 드리는 업계에 대한 통찰과 인맥 형성 기회를 통해 ASA 멤버십이 어떻게 귀하의 경력에 ¹³²**도움이 될 수 있는지** 논의했습니다. 정규 회비는 연 120달러에 불과하지만, 저희가 현재 신규 회원 할인을 제공하고 있습니다. ¹³³이번 달에는 정상 요금의 절반 금액에 가입하실 수 있습니다.

아직 가입 의사가 있으면 ¹³⁴**저에게** 우편 주소와 함께 답장을 보내 주시기 바랍니다. 그러면 신청 서류 일체를 전해 드리겠습니다.

애슐리 로렌, 회장
시스템 분석가 협회

어휘 recall 기억하다, 회상하다 opportunity 기회 insight 이해, 통찰(력) forward 전달하다 application 신청, 지원

131 명사 어휘

해설 바로 뒤 문장에서 베버 정보 시스템 컨벤션 기간(during the Weber Information Systems Convention)에 멘도자 씨를 만나서 반가웠다고 했으므로, 빈칸에 Convention을 가리키는 명사가 들어가야 흐름이 자연스러워진다. 따라서 Convention처럼 '대규모 회의'를 의미하는 (C) conference가 정답이다.

어휘 election 선거 broadcast 방송 performance 공연, 성과

132 동사 어형

해설 빈칸은 주어 ASA membership의 동사 자리로, 명사구 your career를 목적어로 취한다. 앞뒤 문맥을 살펴보면 멘도자 씨가 ASA 멤버쉽에 가입할 것을 권유하고 있으므로, 해당 부분은 'ASA 멤버십이 어떻게 귀하의 경력에 도움이 될 수 있는지 논의했습니다'라는 내용이 되어야 자연스럽다. 따라서 (A) can benefit이 정답이다.

어휘 benefit ~에게 이롭다, ~에게 도움이 되다

133 문맥에 맞는 문장 고르기

번역 (A) 렌터카 할인은 연회원권에 포함되어 있다.
(B) 저희 구인란은 꽤 포괄적입니다.
(C) 우리는 우리 유형으로는 최초의 단체입니다.
(D) 이번 달에는 정상 요금의 절반 금액에 가입하실 수 있습니다.

해설 빈칸 앞 문장에서 현재 신규 회원 할인 혜택을 제공한다(we are currently offering a new-member discount)고 했으므로, 빈칸에는 해당 할인 혜택을 구체적으로 설명하는 내용이 들어가야 문맥상 자연스럽다. 따라서 (D)가 정답이다.

어휘 annual 연간의, 연례의

134 대명사 어휘

해설 바로 뒤에 오는 문장을 보면, 로렌 씨가 '그러면(=멘도자 씨가 답장을 하면) 신청 서류 일체를 전해 드리겠습니다(I will then forward you an application packet)'라고 했으므로, 멘도자 씨의 답장을 받는 대상이 로렌 씨 본인이 되어야 문맥상 자연스럽다. 따라서 (B) me가 정답이다.

135-138 이메일

수신: 샘 하인즈
발신: 노스웨이즈 전문성 개발
날짜: 4월 20일
제목: 워크숍 4/28-4/30

워크숍 참가자들께,

디지털 스토리텔링 워크숍에서 여러분을 뵙기를 고대합니다. 첫날, 앨빈 대학 캠퍼스에 오시면 안내원들이 43지구와 토트먼 빌딩으로 여러분을 ¹³⁵**안내할** 것입니다. 우리는 9번 회의실에서 하루를 시작하게 될 겁니다. 아침마다 커피, 차, 간식, 과일이 ¹³⁶**제공될 예정입니다.** 점심은 블랙 호스 레스토랑의 샌드위치와 샐러드입니다. ¹³⁷드시지 못하는 음식이 있으면 알려 주십시오.

오후에는 컴퓨터 연구실에서 작업할 예정입니다. 프로젝트에 사용하고 싶은 이미지를 몇 개 모아서 정리할 것을 권해드립니다. 디지털 저장 장치에 미리 저장해 두면 ¹³⁸**유용할** 것입니다. 문의 사항이 있으시면 이 메일을 보내십시오.

지나 카푸스키

어휘 attendant 안내원, 수행원 assemble 모으다, 모아서 정리하다 storage 저장 beforehand 미리

135 동사 어휘

해설 빈칸은 주어 attendants의 동사 자리로, you를 목적어로 취하고 전치사구 to lot 43 and the Toteman Building의 수식을 받는다. 따라서 빈칸에는 안내원이 특정 장소에서 할 수 있는 행위를 나타내는 동사가 들어가야 자연스러우므로, '(사람을) 안내하다, (~에게) 길을 알려 주다'라는 의미의 (B) direct가 정답이다. 참고로, (A) offer와 (C) pass는 「동사 A to B」 형태로 쓰일 경우 B 자리에 사람 명사가 들어가며, (D) instruct는 「instruct A to+동사원형」 형태로 'A가 ~하도록 지시하다'라는 의미를 나타낸다.

어휘 instruct 지시하다

136 동사 어형_태_시제

해설 빈칸은 주어 Coffee, tea, snacks, and fruit의 동사 자리이므로, 보기에서 문장의 동사 역할을 할 수 있는 (A) will be provided, (B) were provided, (D) are providing 중 하나를 선택해야 한다. 주어 Coffee, tea snacks, and fruit은 제공되는 대상이며, 이들이 제공되는 워크숍은 미래에 진행될 예정이므로, 수동태 미래 동사인 (A) will be provided가 정답이 된다.

137 문맥에 맞는 문장 고르기

번역 (A) 이전에 디지털 파일로 작업을 수행한 경험이 있다고 가정합니다.
(B) 저작권이 있는 자료는 워크숍에 가져오지 마십시오.
(C) 드시지 못하는 음식이 있으면 알려 주십시오.
(D) 1회 주차 요금은 15달러입니다.

해설 빈칸 앞에서 아침과 점심에 제공되는 음식(Coffee, tea, snacks, and fruit ~ sandwiches and salads)에 대해 언급했으므로, 빈칸에도 음식과 관련된 내용이 들어가야 문맥상 자연스럽다. 따라서 (C)가 정답이다.

어휘 prior 사전의, ~보다 우선하는 copyrighted 저작권이 있는 dietary 음식물의, 식이의 restriction 제한

138 형용사 어휘

해설 가주어(It)와 진주어(to have them saved ~ beforehand) 구문에서 주어를 적절히 설명하는 형용사를 선택하는 문제이다. 앞 문장에서 이미지를 모아서 정리하라고(assemble some images) 제안했으므로, 빈칸을 포함한 문장은 그것들을 미리 저장해 두면 유용할 것이라는 내용이 되어야 문맥상 자연스럽다. 따라서 '유용한, 도움이 되는'이라는 의미의 (A) useful이 정답이다.

139-142 기사

변화하는 소비자에 부응하는 벤리 식품

샐러드에 들어 있는 토마토가 실제로 어디에서 왔는지 관심을 갖는 사람이 있을까? 소비자 단체가 수행한 연구에 따르면, ¹³⁹**분명** 점점 더 많은 사람들이 관심을 보이고 있다. 실제로, 이 연구에 따르면 신선 식품의 정확한 원산지를 밝히면 많은 소비자들이 평균 10퍼센트를 더 지불한다고 한다. ¹⁴⁰**대도시에서는 이 수치가 20퍼센트로 높아진다.** 보스턴에 있는 벤리 식품 같은 일부 식료품점은 이러한 추세에 편승하여 ¹⁴¹**더 영리한** 브랜딩 및 마케팅을 위해 이를 활용하고 있다. "우리가 제품에 대한 이야기를 해줄 수 있다면, 우리는 소비자의 마음 속에 ¹⁴²**가치**를 더한 것입니다." 벤리 식품 CEO 김민지 씨는 말한다.

어휘 responsive to ~에 부응하는, 응답하는 consumer 소비자 take advantage of ~을 이용하다, ~을 기회로 활용하다 implement 시행하다, 이행하다

---

139 부사 어휘

해설 빈칸 뒤 완전한 절을 수식하는 부사를 선택하는 문제이다. 해당 문장의 동사인 do는 앞 문장의 cares where the tomatoes in your salad actually came from을 대신하고 있는데, 앞 문장에서 토마토에 관심을 갖는 사람들이 있는지 미심쩍어하는 것과 달리, 여기에서는 근거를 내세우고(according to a study conducted by the Consumer Group) 있다. 따라서 '분명히 점점 더 많은 사람들이 관심을 보이고 있다'라는 내용이 되어야 문맥상 자연스러우므로, '분명히, 듣자 하니'라는 의미의 (B) Apparently가 정답이다.

어휘 formerly 과거에는 rarely 거의 ~하지 않는

140 문맥에 맞는 문장 고르기

번역 (A) 신선한 음식은 최장 이틀까지 냉장할 수 있다.
     (B) 많은 식료품점들이 영업 시간을 연장하고 있다.
     (C) 대부분의 연구는 소비자 잡지에 실린다.
     (D) 대도시에서는 이 수치가 20퍼센트로 높아진다.

해설 빈칸 앞 문장에서 일반적인 소비자들의 성향(many consumers would pay an average of 10 percent more)을 언급했고, 빈칸 뒤에서 보스턴에 있는 벤리 식품 같은 일부 식료품점은 이러한 추세에 편승했다(Some grocery stores, such as Venley Foods in Boston, have taken advantage of the trend)며 보스턴 시의 사례를 제시했다. 따라서 빈칸에는 대도시 소비자들의 성향과 관련된 내용이 들어가야 자연스러우므로, (D)가 정답이다.

어휘 refrigerate 냉장(보관)하다 extend 연장하다 publish 게재하다, 출간하다

141 형용사 자리 _ 명사 수식

해설 빈칸은 to implement의 목적어 역할을 하는 명사구 branding and marketing을 수식하는 형용사 자리이므로, '더 영리한'이라는 비교급 형용사인 (C) smarter가 정답이다. (A) smarts는 동사, (B) smartly는 부사, (D) smartness는 명사로 모두 품사상 빈칸에 적합하지 않다.

어휘 smart 영리한, 재치 있는; 쓰리다 smartly 영리하게, 호되게 smartness 세련됨, 쓰림

142 명사 어휘

해설 빈칸은 동사 have added의 목적어 역할을 하는 명사 자리로, 전치사구 in the minds of consumers의 수식을 받고 있다. 부사절에서 '우리가 제품에 대한 이야기를 해줄 수 있다면'이라는 조건을 나타냈으므로, 주절에는 이 조건이 충족되었을 때 나타나는 결과나 의의에 대한 내용이 나와야 자연스럽다. 따라서 '고객의 마음에 가치를 더한 것이다'라는 표현을 완성하는 (A) value가 정답이다. 참고로, (D) bonus는 가산명사로 한정사(관사, 소유격 등)나 복수형 어미 없이는 빈칸에 들어갈 수 없다.

어휘 value 가치 obstacle 장애(물) bonus 상여금, 뜻밖의 즐거움

143-146 기사

나일로브사, 최신 개발 프로젝트 발표

시애틀 (5월 1일)—기술 회사인 나일로브사의 연구원들이 환경적인 노출로 인한 부식을 감지할 수 있는 센서를 개발 중이다. 부식은 매년 항공기 산업에서 ¹⁴³**재정적** 손실을 야기하는 주요 원인이다. "이것은 민간 항공사의 주요 ¹⁴⁴**자산**이 될 것입니다." 나일로브사 CEO 멜 라보 씨는 말한다. "이 센서는 너무 많은 비용이 들지 않으면서 인건비와 정비 비용을 모두 절감해 줄 것입니다."

라보 씨에 따르면 센서는 부식된 물질을 제거함으로써 문제를 간단하게 해결할 수 있는 초기 단계에서 부식을 감지하는 방식으로 작동한다. ¹⁴⁵**이렇게 하면 비용이 많이 드는 구조 수리의 필요성이 줄어든다.** 대형 항공기 구조물에서 중요한 이음쇠 일부는 특히 부식에 취약할 수 있다. ¹⁴⁶**다행히도** 센서를 이용해 이러한 부분을 점검하고 문제가 될 가능성이 가장 높은 부분을 겨냥할 수 있다.

어휘 capable of ~할 수 있는 detect 감지하다 corrosion 부식 environmental 환경의 exposure 노출

---

contributor 원인, 기여자   aircraft 항공기   asset 자산   fleet
전체 보유 차량[비행기, 선박]   decrease 줄이다   labor 인력, 노동
maintenance 정비, 유지 관리   corroded 부식된   repair 수리
critical 중요한   susceptible to ~에 취약한, ~에 걸리기 쉬운
inspect 점검하다

143 형용사 자리 _ 명사 수식

해설   빈칸은 전치사 to의 목적어 역할을 하는 명사 losses 앞 자리로, 문
맥상 손실의 종류를 나타내는 형용사가 들어가야 자연스럽다. 따라서
'재정상의, 금융의'라는 의미의 형용사인 (C) financial이 정답이다.
과거분사인 (B) financed는 '출자된, 지원을 받은'이라는 의미로 문
맥상 어색하고, (D) finances는 복수명사로 쓰일 경우 '(특정 개인이
나 단체가 가진) 재정'을 뜻하며, losses와 복합명사를 이룰 수 없으
므로 빈칸에 적합하지 않다.

144 명사 어휘

해설   빈칸은 문장에서 보어 역할을 하며 지시대명사 This(=a sensor)
와 동격 관계를 이루는 명사 자리이다. 바로 뒤에 오는 문장에
서 센서(The sensor)가 인건비와 정비 비용을 모두 절감해 줄 것
(decrease both labor and maintenance costs)이라는 재정적
이점을 소개하고 있으므로, 해당 문장은 '이 센서가 민간 항공사의 주
요 자산이 될 것이다'라는 내용이 되어야 자연스럽다. 따라서 '자산(이
되는 물건)'이라는 의미의 (D) asset이 정답이다.

어휘   balance 균형   examination 시험, 조사   expectation 기대,
예상

145 문맥에 맞는 문장 고르기

번역   (A) 이렇게 하면 비용이 많이 드는 구조 수리의 필요성이 줄어든다.
(B) 그 부품들은 모두 고급 자재로 교체되었다.
(C) 프로젝트의 다음 단계는 손상된 영역에 대한 감식이 포함된다.
(D) 그것의 스타일과 매끈한 디자인으로 대중에게 인기를 끌었다.

해설   빈칸 앞 문장에서 '센서가 문제를 간단하게 해결할 수 있는 초기 단
계에서 부식을 감지하는 방식으로 작동한다(work by detecting
corrosion in its early stages ~ simply)'며 이점을 언급했고, 뒤
부분에서 대형 항공기의 취약점과 이 센서를 활용할 수 있는 방법을
설명했다. 따라서 빈칸에는 이러한 작동 방식이 주는 효과와 관련된
내용이 들어가야 자연스러우므로, (A)가 정답이다.

어휘   replace 교체하다   affected 손상된, 영향을 받은   sleek 매끈한

146 접속부사

해설   빈칸 앞뒤 문장을 의미상 연결하는 접속부사를 선택하는 문제이다. 빈
칸 앞 문장에서 대형 항공기(large aircraft) 이음새가 부식에 취약
하다는 점(some critical joints ~ susceptible to corrosion)
을, 뒤 문장에서 센서를 이용해 이 문제를 해결할 수 있는 방식(the
sensor ~ target the most likely areas of concern)을 언급했
다. 따라서 '다행히도'라는 의미의 접속부사가 빈칸에 들어가야 자연스
러우므로, (D) Fortunately가 정답이다.

어휘   meanwhile 한편으로는   similarly 비슷하게   otherwise
그렇지 않으면

PART 7

147-148 송장

송장 3987

샤우키 오피스 서비스, 두바이, 아랍에미리트

영어로 요청한 보고서

10월 18일

젠킨스 프레스
사서함 2291
두바이, 아랍에미리트

서비스

10월 12일에 접수된 전화 요청에 따라 10월 14일에 전구 교체 및
용지함 수리. 복사기 2대 잉크 교체. ¹⁴⁷기존 서비스 계약에 따라 복
사기 5대에 대한 연간 정기 점검을 실시.

인건비	330.00디르함
용지함	50.00디르함
전구	30.00디르함
복사기 잉크	220.00디르함
총계	630.00디르함

¹⁴⁸10월 31일까지 총액을 납부해 주셔야 합니다.
저희와 거래해 주셔서 감사합니다!

어휘   routine 정기적인, 통상의   maintenance 정비, 관리, 유지
보수   existing 기존의   contract 계약(서)

147 사실 관계 확인

번역   젠킨스 프레스에 관해 명시된 것은?

(A) 세계 여러 곳에 사무실이 있다.
(B) 복사기를 해마다 점검한다.
(C) 사무실 장비가 구식이다.
(D) 샤우키 오피스 서비스의 신규 고객이다.

해설   송장의 서비스(Service) 항목을 보면, 복사기 5대에 대한 연간 정기
점검을 실시했다(Performed routine yearly maintenance on
five copiers)고 했으므로, 젠틴스 프레스는 복사기를 해마다 점검한
다는 것을 알 수 있다. 따라서 (B)가 정답이다.

▸▸ Paraphrasing   지문의 **Performed routine yearly
maintenance**
→ 정답의 **get checked every year**

148 세부 사항

번역   지불 기한은 언제인가?

(A) 10월 12일
(B) 10월 14일
(C) 10월 18일
(D) 10월 31일

해설 송장 하단을 보면 총액을 10월 31일까지 납부해야 한다(Total amount must be received by 31 October)고 했으므로, (D)가 정답이다.

어휘 due 지급 기일이 된, 만기가 된

> ▸▸ **Paraphrasing** 지문의 **Total amount must be received by** → 질문의 **payment due**

149-151 광고

하버 뷰 아파트—포츠마도그, 웨일즈

149침실이 하나 있는 이 아파트는 휴가철 탈출구로 안성맞춤입니다! 조용한 곳에 위치하며 항구의 아름다운 전망이 보이는 테라스를 자랑합니다. 최근에 개조되어 가스레인지, 냉장고, 전자레인지, 커피포트를 갖춘 식당 겸 주방, 샤워실이 딸린 욕실, 대형 TV가 있는 거실이 있습니다. 그밖에 이 부동산의 생활 편의 시설 및 서비스에는 다음 사항이 포함됩니다:

- 식당 및 상점과 가까운 거리
- 해변까지 걸어서 5분
- 자동차로 20분 거리에 있는 공원과 유적지
- 난방 및 전기 포함
- 수건과 침대보 구비
- 150일일 청소 서비스 이용 가능 (추가 비용)
- 150무선 인터넷 접속 (추가 비용)

이 귀한 곳을 지금 예약하세요! 1513월 30일까지 계약하시면 임차료를 10퍼센트 절감할 수 있습니다. 계약하시려면 dbarrett@telarentals.co.uk로 딜런 배럿에게 연락하세요.

어휘 harbour 항구 boast 뽐내다, 자랑하다 amenity 편의 (시설) property 부동산, 건물 historic site 유적지 access 접속, 이용 gem 보석, 보석처럼 귀한 것

149 추론 / 암시

번역 광고에 관심을 가질 사람은 누구이겠는가?

(A) 출장 다니는 사람
(B) 포츠마도그 주민
(C) 부동산 투자자
(D) 단기 여행객

해설 첫 번째 단락의 '침실이 하나 있는 이 아파트는 휴가철 탈출구로 안성맞춤입니다!(This one-bedroom apartment is perfect for a holiday escape!)'라는 문구를 통해 휴가철에 숙소를 구하는 여행객을 위한 광고임을 추론할 수 있으므로, (D)가 정답이다.

150 사실 관계 확인

번역 임차료에 관해 명시된 것은?

(A) 유적지를 둘러보는 관광이 포함된다.
(B) 아파트의 모든 기능에 대한 비용을 충당하지는 않는다.
(C) 지역 식당에서 사용할 수 있는 상품권이 포함되어 있다.
(D) 최소 30퍼센트의 보증금을 미리 납부해야 한다.

해설 편의 사항(amenities) 항목을 보면, 일일 청소 서비스(Daily cleaning service)와 무선 인터넷(Wireless Internet)을 이용하려면 추가 비용(extra fee)을 지불해야 한다고 했다. 따라서 임차료로 충당되지 않는 비용이 있다는 것을 알 수 있으므로, (B)가 정답이다.

어휘 feature 특징, 기능 voucher 상품권, 쿠폰 deposit 보증금 in advance 미리

> ▸▸ **Paraphrasing** 지문의 **extra fee** → 정답의 **does not cover**

151 세부 사항

번역 배럿 씨에게 3월 30일까지 연락해야 하는 이유는?

(A) 임차료를 할인 받기 위해
(B) 아파트 개조 일정을 잡기 위해
(C) 남아 있는 마지막 부동산을 임차하기 위해
(D) 시즌 종료 전에 부동산을 팔기 위해

해설 마지막 단락에서 3월 30일까지 계약하면 임차료를 절감할 수 있고 (Signing a contract by March 30 will reduce the rental cost), 계약하려면 배럿 씨에게 연락하라(To sign a contract, contact Dylan Barrett)고 했으므로, (A)가 정답이다.

> ▸▸ **Paraphrasing** 지문의 **reduce the rental cost** → 정답의 **get a discount on rent**

152-153 문자 메시지

제이슨 솔터 (오후 1시 45분)
리즈, 15분 후에 회의가 시작해요. 어디예요?

리즈 오티즈 (오후 1시 47분)
기차가 잠시 선로에 멈췄어요. 뭔가 문제가 생긴 것 같아요. 153그래도 회의에 참석할 수 있으면 좋겠네요.

제이슨 솔터 (오후 1시 50분)
그렇군요. 당신 자리를 맡아 놓을게요.

리즈 오티즈 (오후 1시 59분)
방금 안내 방송이 나왔어요. 153앞에 고장 난 열차가 있대요. 시간이 좀 걸리겠어요.

제이슨 솔터 (오후 2시)
걱정 마세요. 152우리 부서에 대한 질문이 있으면 제가 처리할게요.

리즈 오티즈 (오후 2시 1분)
고마워요. 이따 전화할게요.

어휘 announcement 발표, 안내 (방송) disabled 고장 난, 장애가 생긴

174

152 추론 / 암시

번역 솔터 씨에 관해 암시된 것은?

(A) 회의를 주재하고 있다.
(B) 열차로 통근한다.
(C) 오티즈 씨에게 물어볼 질문이 많다.
(D) 오티즈 씨와 같은 부서에서 일한다.

해설 솔터 씨가 오후 2시 메시지에서 '우리 부서에 대한 질문이 있으면 제가 처리할게요(If there are any questions for our department, I'll handle them)'라고 했으므로, 솔터 씨와 오티즈 씨가 같은 부서에서 근무한다는 것을 추론할 수 있다. 따라서 (D)가 정답이다.

어휘 commute 통근하다

153 의도 파악

번역 오후 1시 59분에 오티즈 씨가 "시간이 좀 걸리겠어요"라고 쓴 의도는 무엇이겠는가?

(A) 회의가 늦게까지 계속되고 있다.
(B) 아직도 초안을 준비하고 있다.
(C) 회의에 참석하지 못할 것 같다.
(D) 아직 기차를 타지 않았다.

해설 오티즈 씨가 오후 1시 47분 메시지에서 그래도 회의에 참석할 수 있기를 바란다(I still hope to make the meeting)고 했지만, 1시 59분 메시지에서 앞에 고장 난 열차가 있다(There's a disabled train up ahead)고 한 후 시간이 좀 걸리겠다고 했으므로, 회의에 참석하지 못할 것 같다는 의도로 말한 것임을 추론할 수 있다. 따라서 (C)가 정답이다.

154-155 이메일

발신: tbogosian@sardhasconvention.com
수신: pradalaily@dmcv.com
날짜: 3월 22일
제목: 예약
첨부: ◎ 프라다 파티

프라다 씨께,

고객님의 8월 30일 행사 주최를 위해 사르다즈 연회장을 선택해 주셔서 감사합니다. ¹⁵⁴**아쉽게도, 웨스트 홀은 8월에 수리 예정이므로 고객님의 단체를 그 방에 모실 수 없게 되었습니다. 하지만 이스트 홀이 고객님의 일행에게 잘 맞을 것입니다.** 이 방은 바닥부터 천장까지 창문이 있어서 강의 전경이 한눈에 보입니다. 저희가 받은 15퍼센트의 예치금으로 예약은 유지됩니다.

¹⁵⁵**고객님께서 당사 웹사이트를 통해 요청서를 작성하셨을 때** 표시된 바와 같이 총 금액 1,600달러에는 애피타이저, 수프 또는 샐러드, 메인 코스 및 디저트가 포함된 풀코스 식사가 포함됩니다. 이 이메일에 첨부된 고객 제공 메뉴에는 애피타이저와 메인 코스 선택 사항이 있습니다.

토마스 보고시언
총지배인

어휘 accommodate 수용하다 comfortably 편안하게 feature (특별히) 포함하다 deposit 예치금, 보증금 attached 첨부된

154 주제 / 목적

번역 이메일의 목적 중 하나는 무엇인가?

(A) 예약 취소
(B) 실수 사과
(C) 방 변경 알림
(D) 추가 예치금 요구

해설 첫 번째 단락에서 프라다 씨가 예약했던 웨스트 홀이 수리 예정이므로 그 방에 프라다 씨 일행의 예약을 받을 수 없게 되었다(West Hall will be under renovation ~ be unable to accommodate your group in that room)고 하며 대신 다른 홀(East Hall)을 이용할 수 있다고 했으므로, 이메일의 목적 중 하나가 방 변경을 알리기 위함이라는 것을 알 수 있다. 따라서 (C)가 정답이다.

155 추론 / 암시

번역 프라다 씨에 관해 암시된 것은?

(A) 청구 금액을 전액 지불했다.
(B) 사르다즈에서 주기적으로 식사한다.
(C) 식품 업계에서 일한다.
(D) 온라인으로 예약했다.

해설 두 번째 단락의 '고객님께서 당사 웹사이트를 통해 요청서를 작성했을 때(when you completed your request through our Web site)'라는 문구를 통해 수신인인 프라다 씨가 온라인으로 홀을 예약했다는 것을 추론할 수 있다. 따라서 (D)가 정답이다.

▶▶ **Paraphrasing** 지문의 **through our Web site** → 정답의 **online**

156-157 회람

> **회람**
>
> 수신: 전 직원
> 발신: IT 관리자
> 제목: 운영 체제 업데이트
> 날짜: 5월 27일
>
> 멜버른과 빅토리아 사무실에 있는 모든 회사 컴퓨터의 운영 체제가 업데이트되어야 합니다. 이번 업데이트를 통해 컴퓨터는 7월 첫째 주에 도착할 새로운 버전의 회계 소프트웨어에 대한 채비를 갖추게 될 것입니다. ¹⁵⁶**기술자들이 6월 3일부터 새 운영 체제를 설치할 예정입니다. 6월 16일경 이 과정이 완료될 것으로 예상하며**, 회계 소프트웨어가 업로드되기 전에 해당 기간 동안 운영 체제상의 모든 버그를 해결할 수 있을 것입니다.

전체 과정을 완료하려면 시스템이 예상대로 작동하는지 저희가 확인할 수 있도록 여러분이 로그인을 해야 합니다. 따라서 ¹⁵⁷**이 기간 동안 휴가 계획이 있다면 자리를 비우게 될 날짜를 즉시 IT 지원팀에 알려 주십시오.** 그래야만 여러분의 일정에 맞춰 다른 날짜를 계획할 수 있습니다.

문의 사항이 있으시면, IT 지원팀 직원에게 내선 48번으로 문의하십시오.

> 어휘 accounting 회계 (업무) entire 전체의 verify 확인하다 as anticipated 예상대로 immediately 즉시 alternate 대안이 되는 accommodate 맞추다, 부응하다 extension 내선

156 세부 사항

번역 운영 체제 설치는 언제 완료될 예정인가?

(A) 6월 첫째 주
(B) 6월 중순
(C) 6월 말
(D) 7월 첫째 주

해설 첫 번째 단락에서 6월 3일부터 새 운영 체제를 설치하고(install the new operating system beginning on 3 June), 6월 16일경에 이 과정이 완료될 것으로 예상한다(expect the process to be completed around 16 June)고 했으므로, (B)가 정답이다.

> ▶▶ Paraphrasing 지문의 be completed → 질문의 be finished
> 지문의 around 16 June
> → 정답의 In the middle of June

157 세부 사항

번역 IT 지원팀에 연락하라는 요청을 받은 사람은?

(A) 회계 소프트웨어가 필요 없는 직원
(B) 이미 새로운 운영 체제를 사용하고 있는 회계사들
(C) 사무실 밖에서 일하는 직원
(D) 휴가를 내는 직원

해설 두 번째 단락에서 새 운영 체제 설치 기간 동안 휴가 계획이 있다면(if you plan to go on holiday) 즉시 IT 지원팀에 알려 달라(please inform IT Support immediately)고 요청했으므로, (D)가 정답이다.

> ▶▶ Paraphrasing 지문의 inform → 질문의 contact
> 지문의 go on holiday → 정답의 taking time off

158-160 편지

> **클라크-엘리스 건설**
> 머피 공업 단지 20번지
> 세인트 마이클 BB23028
> 1-246-555-0126
> *바베이도스 전역에 포괄적 서비스를 제공하는 업소 전문 도급업체*
>
> 6월 4일

아이다 구티에레스
달링 코브 호텔
망고 드라이브
포크스톤 BB24017

구티에레스 씨께,

지붕 공사를 위해 클라크-엘리스 건설에 연락 주셔서 감사합니다. 건물을 검사해 본 결과, 호텔의 주 지붕은 양호한 상태이며 이번에는 수리할 필요가 없음을 확인했습니다. ^{158, 160}**하지만 호텔의 현관 지붕이 적어도 20년은 된 것 같고, 수리가 불가능할 정도로 낡았습니다.** 그것은 교체되어야 합니다. ¹⁵⁸**클라크-엘리스 건설은 기존의 현관 지붕을 제거하고 새 지붕을 설치할 수 있습니다.** 교체 지붕은 호텔 주 지붕의 재질, 스타일 및 색상과 비슷할 것입니다. ¹⁵⁹**저희는 웨스트 인디즈 웨더푸르핑사에서 제조한 업소용 누수 방지벽, 단열재 및 지붕용 판자만 사용할 예정입니다.** 인건비와 자재비를 포함한 총 견적 원가는 3,260달러입니다. 현관 페인트칠 또는 현관 가림막 교체 등의 다른 개선 작업을 원하시면 추가 요금이 적용됩니다.

일정에 대한 논의나 작업에 대한 문의 사항이 있으시면 상기 번호로 전화 주십시오. 곧 연락 기다리겠습니다.

그레이슨 클라크
그레이슨 클라크, 공동 소유자, 클라크-엘리스 건설

> 어휘 industrial park 산업 단지, 공업 단지 contractor 계약 업체, 도급 업체 inn (작은) 호텔 inspect 점검하다 property 건물, 부동산 confirm 확인하다 porch 현관 beyond repair 수리할 수 없을 정도로 replace 교체하다 dispose of ~을 제거하다 existing 기존의 comparable to ~와 비슷한 leak 누수 barrier 장벽 insulation 단열 shingle 지붕용 판자 manufacture 제조하다 estimated cost 견적 원가 inclusive ~를 포함하는 screen 가림막, 가리개 improvement 개선

158 주제 / 목적

번역 클라크 씨가 편지를 쓴 이유는?

(A) 작업 제안서를 제공하려고
(B) 공사 연장을 요청하려고
(C) 점검 보고서를 요청하려고
(D) 수정된 비용 견적을 제출하려고

해설 첫 번째 단락에서 호텔 현관 지붕의 문제점(the roof of the inn's porch ~ is worn beyond repair)을 언급한 후, 기존의 현관 지붕을 제거하고 새 지붕을 설치할 수 있다(can remove and dispose of the existing porch roof and install a new one)고 했으므로, 작업 제안서를 제공하기 위한 편지임을 알 수 있다. 따라서 (A)가 정답이다.

어휘 extension 연장

159 사실 관계 확인

번역 웨스트 인디즈 웨더프루핑사에 관해 명시된 것은?

(A) 달링 코브 호텔에 현관을 새로 설치하고 있다.
(B) 페인트칠 서비스를 제공한다.
(C) 지붕 자재를 생산한다.
(D) 클라크-엘리스 건설이 소유하고 있다.

해설 첫 번째 단락 중반부에서 웨스트 인디즈 웨더프루핑사에서 제조한 업소용 누수 방지벽, 단열재 및 지붕용 판자(commercial-grade leak barriers, insulation, and shingles manufactured by West Indies Weatherproofing, Inc.)만 사용할 예정이라고 했으므로, 웨스트 인디즈 웨더프루핑사는 지붕 자재를 생산하는 업체임을 알 수 있다. 따라서 (C)가 정답이다.

> ▶ Paraphrasing 지문의 commercial-grade leak barriers, insulation, and shingles manufactured by
> → 정답의 produces roofing materials

160 문장 삽입

번역 [1], [2], [3], [4]로 표시된 곳 중에서 다음 문장이 들어가기에 가장 적합한 곳은?

"그것은 교체되어야 합니다."

(A) [1]
(B) [2]
(C) [3]
(D) [4]

해설 주어진 문장에서 '그것은 교체되어야 한다(It must be replaced)'고 했으므로, 앞에서 먼저 '그것(It)'에 해당하는 교체 대상이 언급되어야 한다. [2] 앞에서 호텔의 현관 지붕이 수리가 불가능할 정도로 낡았다(the roof of the inn's porch ~ is worn beyond repair)고 하며 이 지붕이 교체되어야 할 대상(It)임을 나타내고 있다. 따라서 이 뒤에 주어진 문장이 들어가야 자연스러우므로, (B)가 정답이다.

161-164 광고

직책: 보조 편집자	게시일: 3월 15일

설명

161북아메리카 원예를 중심으로 다루는 독립 출판사인 골드호스 프레스는 50년이 넘는 기간 동안 가정 원예사들을 위한 원예 관련 조언을 제공해 왔습니다. 당사는 현재 노스캐롤라이나 주 샬럿 시에서 규모를 확장하고 있는 팀에 합류할 보조 편집자를 찾고 있습니다. 162의료 보험과 치과 보험을 비롯해 훌륭한 복리후생을 제공합니다.

직무

편집자들을 도와 대중의 주목을 받을 만한 출판물 입수; 원고 개발, 외부 지원자와 공동 작업, 편집 주임 두 명과 긴밀히 협력.

요건/자격

• 관련 분야 학사 학위
• 최소 1년의 출판 업계 경력
• 163세부 사항에 주의를 기울이는 능력
• 팀원으로서의 원활한 업무 수행
• 원예 분야 경력 우대
• 즉시 입사 가능해야 함

164이력서와 급여 조건을 humanresources@goldhorsepress.com으로 보내 주십시오.

어휘 description 설명 independent 독립적인 expand 확대하다[되다] benefits (회사) 복리 후생, 수당 insurance 보험 acquisition 입수, 획득 title 출판물 manuscript 원고 bachelor's degree 학사 학위 related 관련된 industry 업계, 산업 availability 이용 가능함, 유용성 requirement 필요 조건, 요구

161 추론 / 암시

번역 골드호스 프레스는 어떤 책을 출판하겠는가?

(A) 〈제과 제빵 사업 확장하기〉
(B) 〈노스캐롤라이나 여행 가이드〉
(C) 〈여러해살이 꽃 심기〉
(D) 〈유능한 임원〉

해설 설명(Description) 부분에서 골드호스 프레스가 가정 원예사들을 위한 원예 관련 조언을 제공해 왔다(has provided gardening advice for home gardeners)고 했으므로, 〈여러해살이 꽃 심기(Planting Perennial Flowers)〉와 같은 원예 관련 책을 출판할 것으로 추론할 수 있다. 따라서 (C)가 정답이다.

어휘 perennial (오랫동안) 지속되는, 다년생의 efficient 효율적인

162 사실 관계 확인

번역 골드호스 프레스에 관해 명시된 것은?

(A) 편집보 2명을 채용하고 있다.
(B) 직원에게 보험을 제공한다.
(C) 업계 잡지를 출판한다.
(D) 최근 창립된 회사이다.

해설 설명(Description) 부분을 보면, 직원에게 의료 보험과 치과 보험을 비롯해 훌륭한 복리후생을 제공한다(We offer ~ medical and dental insurance)고 했으므로, (B)가 정답이다.

163 세부 사항

번역 광고하고 있는 직책에 필요한 요건은?

(A) 원예에 대한 열정
(B) 세세한 사항을 알아차리는 능력
(C) 관련 분야 석사 학위
(D) 감독 없이 일하는 능력

해설 요건/자격(Requirements/Qualifications) 부분에서 '세부 사항에 주의를 기울이는 능력(Ability to pay close attention to detail)'이 요구된다고 했으므로, (B)가 정답이다.

어휘 aptitude 소질, 재능, 능력 supervision 감독, 관리

> ▶ Paraphrasing 지문의 Ability to pay close attention to detail
> → 정답의 An aptitude for noticing details

164 세부 사항

번역 지원자들이 요청받은 일은?

(A) 구직 신청서 제출하기
(B) 추천인 목록 제출
(C) 근무 가능 여부 명시하기
(D) 희망 급여 명시하기

해설 마지막 문장에서 이력서와 급여 조건을 이메일로 보내 달라(E-mail résumé and salary requirements)고 요청했으므로, (D)가 정답이다.

어휘 reference 추천인, 추천서 indicate 표시하다, 명시하다

▶▶ Paraphrasing 지문의 **salary requirements**
→ 정답의 **desired pay**

165-168 온라인 채팅

데릭 마샬 [오전 8시 19분]
모두 안녕하세요. 리지우드사와의 합병에 관한 새 소식을 전하고, 혹시 여러분들이 그 동안 회의를 했는지 알고 싶었어요.

마이 청 [오전 8시 20분]
165우리의 데릭 부티크 매장들 중 어느 지점이 계속 운영될지 결정했나요?

데릭 마샬 [오전 8시 21분]
네, 165데릭 부티크는 의류 제품군 전체를 판매하는 35개 매장을 계속 운영할 겁니다. 166나머지 12개 매장은 재고품을 리지우드사 매장으로 옮길 거예요.

니키타 탐볼리 [오전 8시 22분]
이전 일정을 언제로 잡아야 하나요? 이번 달?

데릭 마샬 [오전 8시 23분]
아니요, 16712개 매장은 다음 달 말까지는 비우지 않아도 됩니다. 지금부터 5주 뒤로 일정을 잡아 주시겠어요?

앤서니 로시 [오전 8시 24분]
168이번 주 초에 점장들과 점심을 먹으면서 회의를 했습니다. 제가 막 채용한 두 사람을 포함해서요.

니키타 탐볼리 [오전 8시 25분]
그럼 되겠네요.

마이 청 [오전 8시 27분]
168저도 제가 관리하는 점장들과 회의하면서 매장 이전 계획을 검토할게요.

데릭 마샬 [오전 8시 28분]
다들 수고하셨어요.

앤서니 로시 [오전 8시 29분]
모든 과정이 언제 완료될까요?

데릭 마샬 [오전 8시 30분]
6개월 정도면 됩니다.

어휘 merger 합병 inventory 재고(품) vacate 비우다 transition 이전

165 추론 / 암시

번역 글을 입력한 사람들은 어디에서 일하겠는가?

(A) 마케팅 회사
(B) 의류 회사
(C) 부동산 중개업소
(D) 신문 출판사

해설 청 씨가 오전 8시 20분 메시지에서 '우리의 데릭 부티크 매장들(our Derek Boutique locations)'을 언급했고, 마샬 씨가 오전 8시 21분 메시지에서 데릭 부티크는 의류 제품군 전체를 판매하는 35개 매장을 계속 운영할 것(Derek Boutique ~ open with the full line of clothing)이라고 했다. 또한 대화 전반에서 의류 매장의 이전과 관련된 논의를 하고 있으므로, 대화 참가자 모두 의류 회사에서 근무하고 있음을 추론할 수 있다. 따라서 (B)가 정답이다.

166 세부 사항

번역 얼마나 많은 매장이 문을 닫을 것인가?

(A) 5
(B) 6
(C) 12
(D) 35

해설 마샬 씨가 오전 8시 21분 메시지에서 35개 매장은 계속 운영하지만(keep 35 stores open) 나머지 12개 매장은 재고품을 리지우드사 매장으로 옮길 예정(The other 12 will move their inventory to the Ridgewood, Inc., locations)이라고 했으므로, 12개 매장이 문을 닫을 것임을 알 수 있다. 따라서 (C)가 정답이다.

167 의도 파악

번역 오전 8시 25분에 탐볼리 씨가 "그럼 되겠네요"라고 쓴 의도는 무엇이 겠는가?

(A) 현재 재고가 두 배로 늘 것이다.
(B) 리지우드사는 2주 후 폐업할 것이다.
(C) 마샬 씨는 점장들과 회의할 것이다.
(D) 제안된 시간 안에 이전 일정을 잡을 수 있다.

해설 마샬 씨가 오전 8시 23분 메시지에서 12개 매장은 다음 달 말까지는 비우지 않아도 된다(the 12 locations don't need to be vacated until the end of next month)고 한 후 지금부터 5주 뒤로 일정을 잡아 달라(Could you schedule this for five weeks from now?)고 요청했다. 이에 대해 탐볼리 씨가 '그럼 되겠네요(That would work)'라고 응답했으므로, 마샬 씨의 요청대로 일정을 잡을 수 있다는 의도로 말한 것임을 추론할 수 있다. 따라서 (D)가 정답이다.

168 추론 / 암시

번역 청 씨와 로시 씨에 관해 암시된 것은?

(A) 다른 직원을 관리한다.
(B) 리지우드사에서 자주 쇼핑한다.
(C) 최근 점심을 먹으러 같이 갔다.
(D) 합병에 대해 우려한다.

해설 로시 씨는 오전 8시 24분 메시지에서 자신이 채용한 두 명을 포함해 점장들과 점심을 먹으면서 회의를 했다(I met over lunch with my managers ~ I just hired)고 했고, 청 씨는 오전 8시 27분 메시지에서 자신이 관리하는 점장들과 회의하겠다(I'll be meeting with the managers on my staff)고 했다. 따라서 둘 다 다른 직원을 관리하는 업무를 담당한다는 것을 추론할 수 있으므로, (A)가 정답이다.

어휘 supervise 감독하다, 관리하다 concern 우려 (사항)

169-171 기사

그늘에서 나와 각광받다

칼럼 엘우드 작성

169(C)나미비아 응용과학원의 농업 생명공학자인 에스더 누조마 박사는 생명공학의 실질적인 응용에 관한 다수의 책을 저술한 작가이다. 〈런던 데일리 레지스터〉의 도서 평론가인 페이지 키녹에 따르면, "누조마 박사는 매우 복잡한 과학적 소재를 쉬운 말로 옮기는 능력을 통해 일상생활에서 생명공학의 역할에 대한 대중의 인식을 높였다."

171그녀의 최근 작품인 〈그늘 뒤에서 빛나다〉는 늘 다루던 주제에서 벗어나 있다. 이 책의 초점은 생명공학을 실제 상황에 적용하는 것이 아니다. 170, 171오히려 이 책은 그녀의 아프리카 및 아시아 출신 동료 12명의 삶과 경력을 중점적으로 조명하고 있다. 169(A)3년 전 칠레에서 열린 회의에서 그 아이디어가 떠올랐다. 누조마 박사는 회상한다. "강연자의 이야기를 차례로 들으면서, 제 동료들 중 다수가 그간 잘 드러나지 않던 아프리카와 아시아 같은 지역 출신이라는 것을 깨달았습니다."

이 책은 꽤 흥미롭다. 누조마 박사는 동료들이 어떻게 그 직업에 이끌렸는지, 그리고 그들이 일에 쏟아 붓는 노력에 대한 이야기에 생명을 불어 넣는다.

그러나 이 책은 한 가지 측면에서 부족한 점이 있다. 바로 농업 생명공학 분야에서 일하는 사람들의 삶과 경력에 대한 통찰만을 제공한다는 것이다. 나라면 동물, 해양, 의학 생명공학을 전문으로 하는 사람들에 관한 이야기도 환영했을 것이다. 그럼에도 불구하고, 169(B)누조마 박사는 전문가와 비전문가 모두에게 호소하는 작품을 만드는 데 다시 성공했다.

어휘 agricultural 농업의 biotechnologist 생명공학자 institute 연구소 application 적용, 응용 critic 평론가 awareness 인식 translate 옮기다, 번역하다 departure 벗어남, 출발 peer 동료, 또래 친구 colleague 동료 region 지역 underrepresented 잘 드러나지 않은, 대표자가 불충분한 compelling 흥미로운, 주목하지 않을 수 없는 pour into ~에 쏟아 붓다 fall short 모자라다, 결핍되다 insight 통찰(력) specialize in ~을 전문으로 하다 expert 전문가 laypeople 비전문가

169 사실 관계 확인

번역 누조마 박사에 관해 명시되지 않은 것은?

(A) 칠레를 방문했다.
(B) 재능 있는 작가이다.
(C) 나미비아에 근거하고 있다.
(D) 〈런던 데일리 레지스터〉와 인터뷰했다.

해설 두 번째 단락의 '칠레에서 열린 회의에서 그 아이디어가 떠올랐다(The idea came to her ~ at a conference in Chile)'에서 (A)를, 마지막 단락의 '누조마 박사는 전문가와 비전문가 모두에게 호소하는 작품을 만드는 데 다시 성공했다(Dr. Nujoma has ~ succeeded in creating a work that speaks to experts and laypeople alike)'에서 (B)를, 첫 번째 단락의 '나미비아 응용과학원의 농업 생명공학자인 에스더 누조마 박사(Dr. Esther Nujoma, an agricultural biotechnologist with the Namibia Institute of Applied Sciences)'에서 (C)를 확인할 수 있다. 그러나 누조마 박사가 〈런던 데일리 레지스터〉와 인터뷰를 했다는 내용은 언급되지 않았으므로, (D)가 정답이다.

170 세부 사항

번역 엘우드 씨가 〈그림자 뒤에서 빛나다〉에 관해 언급한 것은?

(A) 아프리카와 아시아 출신 과학자들에 초점을 맞추고 있다.
(B) 3년 전에 출판되었다.
(C) 누조마 박사가 자신의 직업을 선택한 이유를 상세히 설명한다.
(D) 생명공학의 다양한 분야를 설명한다.

해설 두 번째 단락에서 누조마 박사의 책(The book = *Shining Behind Shadow*)이 그녀의 아프리카 및 아시아 출신 동료의 삶과 경력을 중점적으로 조명한다(highlights the lives and careers ~ of her peers from Africa and Asia)고 했으므로, (A)가 정답이다.

> ▶▶ Paraphrasing 지문의 highlights her peers
> → 정답의 focuses on scientists

171 문장 삽입

번역 [1], [2], [3], [4]로 표시된 곳 중에서 다음 문장이 들어가기에 가장 적합한 곳은?

"이 책의 초점은 생명공학을 실제 상황에 적용하는 것이 아니다."

(A) [1]
(B) [2]
(C) [3]
(D) [4]

해설 주어진 문장에서 '이 책의 초점은 생명공학을 실제 상황에 적용하는 것이 아니다(Its focus is not on applying biotechnology in real-life situations)'라고 했으므로, 앞에서 먼저 '그것의(Its)'에 해당하는 구체적인 대상이 언급되어야 하고, 뒤에서는 초점을 맞춘 내용이 무엇인지 밝혀야 한다. [2] 앞에서 누조마 박사의 최근 저서인 〈그늘 뒤에서 빛나다〉(Her latest book, *Shining Behind Shadows*), 즉 '그것의(Its)'의 구체적인 대상을 제시했고, [2] 뒤에서 실제 초점을 맞춘 내용(Rather, the book highlights the lives and careers of twelve of her peers)을 언급하고 있으므로, 이 사이에 주어진 문장이 들어가야 글의 흐름이 자연스러워진다. 따라서 (B)가 정답이다.

172-175 공지

킹스턴-가넷 섬 여객선 서비스

일반 정보

¹⁷²5월 15일부터 킹스턴-가넷 섬 여객선 서비스가 여름철 8주 동안 운항을 재개합니다. 매일 오전 7시부터 오후 8시까지 30분마다 여객선이 운항됩니다. 가넷 섬으로 가는 마지막 여객선은 오후 7시 30분에 출발합니다. 가넷 섬에서 오는 마지막 여객선은 오후 8시에 떠납니다.

여객선에는 자전거를 실을 수 있습니다. ¹⁷³**자전거 이용자들은 출발 30분 전에 도착해서 자전거 특별 통로에서 기다렸다가 자전거를 먼저 실어야 합니다.** 여객선마다 자전거 50대를 고정시킬 수 있는 거치대 5개가 있습니다.

¹⁷⁴**가넷 섬에는 엔진이 달린 차량이 허용되지 않습니다.** 야간 주차는 킹스턴에 있는 여객선 주 터미널 주차장에서 가능합니다. 요금은 4시간까지는 시간당 5달러이고, 4시간부터 24시간까지는 균일 요금인 25달러입니다.

당사 웹사이트 www.kgferryservice.com을 방문해 여객선 사진, 가넷 섬 지도, 섬 내 지역 명소 목록, ¹⁷⁵**혼잡 시간대 요금 할증** 및 단체 할인 정보를 확인하십시오.

어휘 resume 재개하다 depart 출발하다 permit 허용하다 prior to ~ 이전에 motorized 엔진이 달린 flat fee 균일 요금 attraction (관광) 명소

---

172 사실 관계 확인

번역 여객선 서비스에 관해 명시된 것은?

(A) 특정 계절에만 이용할 수 있다.
(B) 최근 배를 개조했다.
(C) 섬에 도착하는 데 1시간이 소요된다.
(D) 주말에는 더 자주 운항한다.

해설 첫 번째 단락에서 여객선 서비스가 여름철 동안 운항을 재개한다(Passenger Ferry Service will resume service ~ during the summer season)고 했으므로, 특정 계절에만 이용할 수 있음을 알 수 있다. 따라서 (A)가 정답이다.

▸▸ Paraphrasing 지문의 resume service during the summer season → 정답의 available only seasonally

173 사실 관계 확인

번역 여객선에 타는 자전거 이용자들에 관해 사실인 것은?

(A) 마지막으로 승선한다.
(B) 특별 티켓을 구매해야 한다.
(C) 오후 7시 30분에는 여행할 수 없다.
(D) 터미널에 일찍 도착해야 한다.

해설 두 번째 단락에서 자전거 이용자들은 출발 30분 전에 도착해야 한다(Bicyclists should arrive 30 minutes prior to departure)고 했으므로, (D)가 정답이다.

▸▸ Paraphrasing 지문의 30 minutes prior to departure → 정답의 early

174 세부 사항

번역 가넷 섬에서 허용되지 않는 것은?

(A) 자전거 대여
(B) 자동차 운전
(C) 야영
(D) 사진 촬영

해설 세 번째 단락에서 가넷 섬에는 엔진이 달린 차량이 허용되지 않는다(No motorized vehicles are permitted on Garnet Island)고 했으므로, 자동차 운전이 허용되지 않는 것을 알 수 있다. 따라서 (B)가 정답이다.

▸▸ Paraphrasing 지문의 permitted → 질문의 allowed
지문의 motorized vehicles → 정답의 cars

175 사실 관계 확인

번역 페리 티켓에 관해 명시된 것은?

(A) 킹스턴에 있는 가게에서 구입할 수 있다.
(B) 어린이용은 저렴하다.
(C) 여행 시간에 따라 가격이 달라진다.
(D) 배에서 구입하면 더 비싸다.

해설 마지막 단락에서 혼잡 시간대 요금 할증(peak-hour fare increases)에 관한 정보를 웹사이트에서 확인할 수 있다고 했으므로, 여행 시간에 따라 가격이 달라진다는 것을 알 수 있다. 따라서 (C)가 정답이다.

176-180 영수증 + 이메일

그린 스트라이프 프레스에서 구매해 주셔서 감사합니다.

¹⁷⁷**주문 번호**: GSP20896

고객 정보: 슈박스 마운틴
제이슨 호 〈jasonho@shoeboxmountain.com〉
주문일: 12월 14일 (선납: 온라인 주문)
¹⁷⁷**배송 예정**: 12월 18-20일

수량	품번	품목	가격
1	CAL201	무료 야생 동물 달력	0.00달러
7	ARB132	회계 장부 (각 19.99달러)	139.93달러
		소계:	139.93달러
		할인:	0.00달러
		세금 6%:	8.40달러
		¹⁷⁶**운송 및 취급**:	0.00달러
		총계:	148.33달러

¹⁷⁶**기업 고객에게는 운송 및 취급비가 부과되지 않습니다.** 주문 관련 문의 사항이 있으시면 customerservice@greenstripepress.com으로 연락하십시오.

어휘 complimentary 무료의 charge 요금 corporate 회사의, 기업의 account 계정, 고객

어휘   deliver 배송하다   accounting record book 회계장부   refund 환불하다   incur (비용을) 발생시키다   proceed 진행하다   on a different note 그건 그렇고, 화제를 바꾸어서   stunning 멋진

176   세부 사항

번역   호 씨가 배송비를 부과받지 않은 이유는?

(A) 판촉을 이용했다.
(B) 회사용으로 구매했다.
(C) 물건을 직접 가서 가져왔다.
(D) 이전 주문에서 배송비를 초과 지불했다.

해설   영수증의 마지막 단락에서 기업 고객에게는 운송 및 취급비가 부과되지 않는다(There is no charge for shipping and handling for corporate accounts)고 했으므로, 그가 회사용으로 구매했기 때문에 배송비가 청구되지 않았음을 알 수 있다. 따라서 (B)가 정답이다.

어휘   overpay 초과 지불하다

▸▸ Paraphrasing   지문의 for corporate accounts
→ 정답의 for his company

177   연계

번역   호 씨의 주문품에 관해 사실인 것은?

(A) 운송 중에 파손되었다.
(B) 깨지기 쉬운 물건이 포함되었다.
(C) 수표로 지불되었다.
(D) 제때에 배송되었다.

해설   이메일 첫 번째 단락에서 오늘 배송된 가장 최근의 주문(my most recent order(#GSP20896))에 대해 글을 쓴다고 했는데, 이메일 발신 날짜가 12월 18일이므로, 이날 호 씨의 주문품이 배송되었다는 것을 알 수 있다. 해당 주문품에 관한 정보는 영수증을 통해 확인할 수

있는데, 상단에 배송 예정(Expected Delivery)일이 12월 18일-20 일이라고 적혀 있으므로, 호 씨의 주문이 제때에 배송되었다는 것을 알 수 있다. 따라서 (D)가 정답이다.

어휘   transit 운송, 수송   fragile 깨지기 쉬운

178   세부 사항

번역   이메일에 따르면 실수로 호 씨에게 배송된 것은?

(A) 주문하지 않은 성에 관한 책
(B) 지난해 달력
(C) 잘못된 환불 수표
(D) 여분의 회계 장부

해설   호 씨가 보낸 이메일의 첫 번째 단락을 보면, 자신은 회계 장부 6권을 주문했지만(I ordered six accounting record books), 그린 스트라이프 프레스에서 7권을 보냈다(You sent us seven copies)고 했으므로, 회계 장부 1권이 실수로 배송되었음을 알 수 있다. 따라서 (D)가 정답이다.

179   주제 / 목적

번역   호 씨가 이메일을 쓴 이유 중 하나는?

(A) 물품 칭찬
(B) 가격에 대한 불만 제기
(C) 사진첩 주문
(D) 그래픽 디자이너 추천

해설   이메일의 두 번째 단락에서 지난해에 보냈던 〈고대의 성〉 달력보다 이번에 보내준 달력 사진이 훨씬 더 멋지다(The photos are even more stunning than those ~ last year)고 했으므로, 이메일을 보낸 이유 중 하나가 새 달력을 칭찬하기 위해서임을 알 수 있다. 따라서 (A)가 정답이다.

180   동의어 찾기

번역   이메일에서 두 번째 단락 4행의 "our way"와 의미상 가장 가까운 것은?

(A) 우리 스타일로
(B) 우리 주소로
(C) 우리 비용으로
(D) 우리를 위하여

해설   "our way"를 포함한 문장은 '저희 쪽으로 2부 더 보내 주시겠습니까?(Would you mind sending two more our way?)'라는 의미로, 여기서 our way는 '우리의 구역, 지역'이라는 뜻으로 썼다. 따라서 '우리 주소로'라는 의미의 (B) to our address가 정답이다.

181-185   연락처 양식 + 이메일

저는 영화 촬영지 섭외자로 근무하고 있습니다. 이번에는 의뢰인의 단편 영화를 위한 장소를 찾고 있습니다. ¹⁸¹**영화의 배경은 1930년대 초반이며, 힐그레이브에 그 시대의 흥미로운 건축물이 있다고 알고 있습니다.**

다음 달에 제가 힐그레이브에 가면 방문해야 할 장소들을 제안해 주시겠습니까? ¹⁸³**특히 저는 줄무늬 차양 및 테두리를 두른 진열창 같이 독특한 디테일을 갖춘 고풍스러운 상점이 있는 빈 건물을 찾고 있습니다.** 전기를 쉽게 사용할 수 있으면 이상적이겠지만 ¹⁸²**크게 중요하지는 않습니다.** 필요시 사용할 수 있는 발전기를 제 의뢰인이 갖고 있습니다. 제 의뢰인의 미적 요구 사항들이 가장 중요한 고려 사항입니다. 도와주시면 감사하겠습니다.

어휘 architecture 건축 (양식), (집합적) 건축물 specifically 특히, 구체적으로 말하면 vacant 비어 있는 old-fashioned 오래된, 고풍스러운 storefront 상점 (앞), 점두 distinctive 독특한 awning 차양, 천막 generator 발전기 aesthetic 미적인, 심미적인 requirement 요구 사항, 요건 assistance 도움

수신: roger@witmondtlocations.com
발신: brandi_schaertl@hilgravehistoricalcommission.org
날짜: 9월 28일
제목: 요청하신 정보
첨부: 📎 힐그레이브 유적지

위트몬트 씨께,

힐그레이브 역사 위원회에 연락해 주셔서 감사합니다. 첨부한 소책자에는 힐그레이브에서 역사적으로 흥미로운 주요 지역의 목록이 담겨 있습니다. 일부 건물이 귀하의 요구 사항에 모두 부합하지 않을 수도 있지만, 고려할 가치는 있을 것 같습니다.

첨부된 목록에는 없는 건물 하나는 ¹⁸³**메인 스트리트 188번지에 있는 오래된 레코드 가게입니다.** 지난 10여 년 동안 영업을 하지 않았지만, ¹⁸³**귀하의 기준에 맞는 것 같습니다.** ¹⁸⁴**소유주인 루크 닐런드 씨는 현재 그 건물을 창고로 사용하고 있습니다.** ¹⁸⁴**기꺼이 그와 연락이 닿도록 해 드리겠습니다.** 그에게 공간 사용을 허락받기가 어려울 것 같지는 않습니다. 힐그레이브가 한때는 붐비는 마을이었지만, 요즘은 운영 중인 사업체들 수가 줄어들었습니다. ¹⁸⁵**단편 영화로 이 지역에 관심이 쏠린다면 많은 마을 주민들이 고맙게 생각할 것입니다.**

브랜디 쉐틀

어휘 criteria 기준 storage 저장, 보관 permission 허락 bustling 붐비는 appreciate 고마워하다, 환영하다 attention 주의, 주목, 관심

181 세부 사항

번역 위트몬트 씨가 힐그레이브에서 촬영 장소를 물색하는 이유는?

(A) 경치 좋은 산 전망으로 유명하다.
(B) 그의 사무실에서 가까운 거리이다.
(C) 그곳의 상업 지구가 다른 영화에 나왔다.
(D) 건물들이 특정 시대를 나타낸다.

해설 연락처 양식의 첫 번째 단락에서 의뢰인의 영화 배경이 1930년대 초반인데, 힐그레이브에 그 시대의 흥미로운 건축물이 있다고 알고 있다(The film will be set in the early 1930s, ~ Hilgrave has some interesting architecture from that era)고 했으므로, (D)가 정답이다.

어휘 scenic 경치 좋은 represent 나타내다, 보여 주다

▸▸ Paraphrasing 지문의 some architecture
→ 정답의 Its building
지문의 that era
→ 정답의 a particular time period

182 동의어 찾기

번역 연락처 양식에서 두 번째 단락 4행의 "critical"과 의미상 가장 가까운 것은?

(A) 판결의
(B) 필수적인
(C) 지속 가능한
(D) 이용할 수 있는

해설 "critical"을 포함한 부분은 '전기를 쉽게 사용할 수 있으면 이상적이겠지만 크게 중요하지는 않다(While having easy access to electricity would be ideal, it is not critical)'는 의미로, 여기서 critical은 '결정적인, 굉장히 중요한'이라는 뜻으로 쓰였다. 따라서 '필수적인'이라는 의미의 (B) essential이 정답이다.

183 연계

번역 메인 스트리트 188번지에 관해 암시된 것은?

(A) 한때는 주거지로 사용되었다.
(B) 관광객들이 자주 방문한다.
(C) 여러 층으로 되어 있다.
(D) 장식이 있는 디자인이 특징이다.

해설 쉐틀 씨가 보낸 이메일의 두 번째 단락을 보면, 메인 스트리트 188번지에 있는 오래된 레코드 가게(the old record store at 188 Main Street)가 위드몬트 씨가 제시한 기준에 맞는 것 같다(it seems to meet your criteria)고 했다. 위드몬트 씨가 제시한 기준은 연락처 양식에서 확인할 수 있는데, 두 번째 단락에서 줄무늬 차양과 테두리를 두른 진열창 같이 독특한 디테일을 갖춘 고풍스러운 상점이 있는 빈 건물(a vacant building with an old-fashioned storefront that has distinctive details like ~ framed display windows)이라고 했으므로, 메인 스트리트 188번지는 장식이 있는 디자인이 특징이라는 점을 알 수 있다. 따라서 (D)가 정답이다.

184 세부 사항

번역 쉐틀 씨는 무엇을 하겠다고 제안하는가?

(A) 곧 개봉할 영화 광고하기
(B) 건물 청소 준비하기
(C) 위트몬트 씨와 건물 주인 연결해 주기
(D) 위트몬트 씨가 마을에서 필요한 허가 얻도록 돕기

해설 이메일의 두 번째 단락에서 건물 주인인 루크 닐런드 씨(The owner, Luke Nylund)와 연락이 닿도록 해 주겠다(I would be happy to put you in touch with him)고 제안했으므로, (C)가 정답이다.

어휘 forthcoming 곧 있을 acquire 얻다, 호기득하다

> ▶ Paraphrasing 지문의 **would be happy to** → 질문의 **offer to**
> 지문의 **put you in touch with him**
> → 정답의 **Connect Mr. Witmondt with a building's owner**

185 추론 / 암시

번역 쉐틀 씨는 힐그레이브에 필요한 것이 무엇이라고 시사하는가?

(A) 더 많은 관심
(B) 추가 주차 구역
(C) 창고 시설
(D) 상공인 인명록

해설 쉐틀 씨가 보낸 이메일의 두 번째 단락을 보면, 단편 영화로 이 지역에 관심이 쏠린다면 많은 마을 주민들이 고맙게 생각할 것(Many of the town's residents would appreciate the attention)이라고 했다. 따라서 그가 힐그레이브 지역에 대한 관심이 필요하다고 생각하고 있음을 추론할 수 있으므로, (A)가 정답이다.

어휘 publicity (매스컴의) 관심, 홍보

> ▶ Paraphrasing 지문의 **the attention** → 정답의 **More publicity**

186-190 이메일 + 이메일 + 웹페이지

수신: 코넬리아 페인 〈cpayne@roughwing.co.uk〉
발신: 프라야 메타 〈pmehta@airsky.in〉
제목: 강연
날짜: 1월 18일
첨부: 📎 원고

코넬리아에게,

186늦게 알려 주게 되어 미안하지만, 제가 강연에 합류할 수 없게 되었어요. 뭄바이에 있는 대학교에서 맡은 새로운 직책 때문에 캠퍼스에 남아 있어야 해서요.

당신이 혼자서 강연을 할 만반의 준비가 되어 있다는 것을 알지만, 제가 일전에 발표를 위해 준비했던 원고 한 부를 첨부합니다. 원고를 검토한 후, 제가 추가할 수 있는 것이 있다면 알려 주세요.

처음으로 바하마 프리포트로 여행을 가는 것과 당신을 다시 만나게 되는 것을 무척 고대했었어요. **189시립 대학교에서 당신과 함께 일했던 시절이 정말 그리워요.**

강연 잘 하길 바랄게요.

프라야

어휘 deliver a lecture 강연하다

수신: 에즈라 헐톤 〈ehalton@ansonhouse.org〉
발신: 코넬리아 페인 〈cpayne@roughwing.co.uk〉
제목: 정보
날짜: 1월 20일

헐톤 씨께,

앤슨 하우스에서 강연하기에 3월 19일이 괜찮다는 점을 확인해 드리게 되어 기쁩니다. 전화로 말씀드렸듯이, 저 혼자 강연할 예정입니다.

187, 188제 출판사인 알파감마 프레스에서 프라야 메타 박사와 제가 공동 집필한 최신작 30부를 귀하의 기관으로 발송할 예정입니다. 책이 발송되면 귀하의 기관과 저는 알파감마에서 보낸 확인 메일을 받을 겁니다. 책은 적어도 강연 일주일 전에 도착할 예정입니다.

곧 만나 뵙기를 바랍니다.

코넬리아 페인

어휘 publisher 출판사 coauthor 공동 집필하다; 공동 집필자 institution 기관

---

http://www.theansonhouse.bs

| 방문 | 전시회 | 강연자 시리즈 | 연락처 |

앤슨 하우스
프리포트, 바하마

강연자 시리즈

각 강연의 티켓은 35달러이며 3회 시리즈는 할인가인 90달러에 구매하실 수 있습니다. 무료 다과가 제공됩니다. **190예약이 필수는 아니지만 하시는 것이 좋습니다.**

3월 7일, 오후 7시 – 8시 30분, 자넬 피어스 씨
프리포트에서 평생 거주한 역사학자 자넬 피어스 씨와 함께 앤슨 하우스의 이면을 살펴보세요. 피어스 씨가 앤슨 하우스에 원래 살던 거주자들의 일상을 설명합니다.

3월 12일, 오후 7시 – 8시 30분, 그레고리 리 씨
저희 원예 장인이 고대 정원 복원의 어려움에 대해 이야기합니다. 그는 찰스턴, 사우스캐롤라이나, 그리고 프랑스 파리에 있는 정원에서 근무해왔습니다.

3월 19일, 오후 7시 – 8시 30분, 코넬리아 페인 박사
188페인 박사가 프라야 메타 박사와 공저하여 최근에 발간한 저서, 〈19세기 대서양 건너편 세상〉에 관해 이야기합니다. **189페인 박사는 약 25년 동안 영국 스토크온트렌트의 시립 대학교에 재직하며 가르쳐 왔습니다.**

어휘 purchase 구매하다; 구매(품) reduced rate 할인가 complimentary 무료인 refreshments 다과 recommend 권장하다 restore 복원하다 historic 오래된, 역사적인

번역 메타 박사가 페인 박사에게 이메일을 보낸 이유는?

(A) 휴가 계획을 취소하려고
(B) 강연 원고를 요청하려고
(C) 회의를 확정하려고
(D) 사과하려고

해설 메타 박사가 페인 박사에게 쓴 이메일의 첫 번째 단락을 보면, 늦게 알려 미안하지만 자신이 강연에 합류할 수 없게 되었다(I am sorry for the late notice, but I will not be able to join you for the lecture)고 했으므로, 사과를 전하는 이메일임을 알 수 있다. 따라서 (D)가 정답이다.

번역 두 번째 이메일에 따르면 페인 박사가 한 일은?

(A) 배송 준비하기
(B) 힐튼 씨에게 선물하기
(C) 프레젠테이션 수정하기
(D) 주소 변경 알리기

해설 페인 박사가 보낸 이메일의 두 번째 단락을 보면, 알파감마 프레스가 자신의 최신작 30부를 힐튼 씨의 기관으로 보낼 것(My publisher, Alphagamma Press, will be sending 30 copies of my most recent work ~ to your institution)이라고 했으므로, 자신의 저서가 배송되도록 준비했다는 것을 알 수 있다. 따라서 (A)가 정답이다.

번역 알파감마 출판사에 관해 명시된 것은?

(A) 본사가 바하마에 있다.
(B) 앤슨 하우스에 정기적으로 자료를 배송한다.
(C) 〈19세기 태평양 건너편 세상〉을 발간했다.
(D) 페인 박사의 여행과 숙박 비용을 지불하고 있다.

해설 페인 박사가 보낸 이메일의 두 번째 단락을 보면, 알파감마 출판사에서 자신과 메타 박사가 공동 집필한 최신작을 배송할 예정(My publisher, Alphagamma Press, will be sending my most recent work, coauthored with Dr. Pragya Mehta)이라고 했으므로, 이 출판사에서 해당 저서가 출간되었음을 알 수 있다. 페인 박사가 출간한 책에 관한 정보는 웹페이지에서도 확인할 수 있는데, 강연자 시리즈 마지막 일정을 보면 페인 박사가 메타 박사와 공저하여 최근에 발간한 저서(her most recently published book ~ coauthored with Dr. Pragya Metha)가 〈19세기 대서양 건너편 세상〉(The Transatlantic World of the Nineteenth Century)이라고 했으므로, (C)가 정답이다.

번역 메타 박사와 페인 박사는 어디에서 동료였겠는가?

(A) 뭄바이
(B) 프리포트
(C) 스토크온트렌트
(D) 찰스턴

해설 첫 번째 이메일의 세 번째 단락에서 메타 박사가 시립 대학교에서 페인 박사와 함께 일했던 시절이 정말 그립다(I certainly miss working with you at the City University)고 했다. 그들이 함께 일했던 시립 대학교에 대한 정보는 웹페이지를 통해 확인할 수 있는데, 강연자 시리즈 마지막 일정에서 페인 박사가 영국 스토크온트렌트의 시립 대학교에 재직하며 가르쳐왔다(Dr. Payne has taught at the City University of Stroke-on-Trent in England)고 했다. 따라서 그들이 스토크온트렌트에서 함께 근무했음을 추론할 수 있으므로, (C)가 정답이다.

번역 강연자 시리즈에 관해 웹 페이지에 명시된 것은?

(A) 할인이 불가능하다.
(B) 예약은 선택 사항이다.
(C) 오전에 행사가 열린다.
(D) 다과가 포함되지 않는다.

해설 웹페이지의 첫 번째 단락에서 예약이 필수는 아니지만 하는 것이 좋다(Reservations are not required but are recommended)고 했으므로, 예약이 선택 사항임을 알 수 있다. 따라서 (B)가 정답이다.

▸▸ Paraphrasing   지문의 **not required but are recommended**
→ 정답의 **optional**

CRYN 그룹: 귀사를 위해 최고의 사원을 찾아 드립니다.

게시:	11월 25일
직책명과 코드:	• 운영 이사, TL0015
	• 마케팅 이사, TL0023
	• 품질 관리 이사, TL0027
	• 194상품군 관리 이사, TL0045
지원 방법:	게시 번호 2098을 제목란에 적어서 mdoro@ cryngroup.ca.com으로 이력서를 보내 주세요.

회사:

192저희 의뢰 업체는 내년에 라틴 아메리카에서 영업을 시작할 계획으로 그곳에서 진취적인 성장을 계획하고 있습니다. 이 업체는 북아메리카에서 소비자 건강 제품을 판매하는 것으로 이름이 널리 알려져 있으며 최근에는 유럽과 아시아에서도 유명해지기 시작한 건실한 회사입니다.

자격 요건:

191지원자는 경영학 정규 학위와 최소 한 곳의 해외 환경에서 관리자로 일한 증빙 기록이 있어야 합니다. 191온라인 영업 및 마케팅 경력 우대합니다.

어휘 operation 운영, 영업 quality control 품질 관리 aggressive 진취적인, 의욕적인, 공격적인 well-established 탄탄한, 안정된 formal 공식적인, 정규의

수신: 스벤 아비드슨 〈sarvidson@barkent.de.com〉
발신: 마리아 도로 〈mdoro@cryngroup.ca.com〉
제목: 게시 번호 2098
날짜: 12월 10일

아비드슨 씨께:

이력서를 제출해 주셔서 감사합니다. 귀하가 저희 의뢰 업체에게 적절한 선택일지 판단하기 위해 가능한 한 빨리 예비 통화 일정을 잡고 싶습니다. ¹⁹²특히 저희 의뢰 업체의 해외 신규 시설에서 근무할 준비가 되셨는지 논의하고 싶습니다.

¹⁹³다음 주 월요일이나 화요일 동부 표준시 오전 10시에서 오후 2시 사이에 30분 정도 통화하실 수 있는지 알려 주세요. 가능한 한 빨리 이메일로 답장 주시기 바랍니다.

마리아 도로
CRYN 그룹

어휘 submit 제출하다 preliminary 예비의 determine 판단하다, 결정하다 particularly 특히 facility 시설 at one's earliest convenience 되도록 일찍, 형편 닿는 대로

즉시 보도용

자세한 정보는 416-555-0103으로 줄리 드라이든에게 연락하세요

타예르슨사, 신임 이사 지명

토론토, 4월 5일—타예르슨사가 오늘부터 한 달 뒤에 개업하는 새로운 해외 지점에 계속 직원을 충원하고 있다. 이번에 행운의 지원자는 스벤 아비드슨 씨이다. "¹⁹⁴상품군 관리는 비교적 새로운 영역으로, 제가 이사로서 즐겁게 개척하고 발전시킬 영역이라고 확신합니다." 아비드슨 씨는 말했다. "¹⁹⁵주요 온라인 영양제 판매사로서 타예르슨은 더욱 활기차고 수익성 있는 회사가 되어 더 나은 삶을 향한 길을 인도할 준비가 되어 있습니다."

아비드슨 씨는 경력을 쌓으면서 몇 가지 핵심적인 관리직을 맡아 왔으며 가장 최근에는 독일에 있는 바켄트 제약회사에서 근무했다. 그는 또한 MSZ 컨설팅 그룹의 공동 출자자로서 캐나다와 중국에 있는 일류 소비재 회사들을 이끄는 데 있어 필요한 마케팅 관련 조언을 제공했다.

어휘 outpost 지점, 출장소, 전초 기지 candidate 지원자, 후보 relatively 비교적 explore 개척하다, 탐험하다 nutritional supplement 영양제 be poised to + 동사원형 ~할 만반의 태세를 갖추다, ~할 것을 각오하다 vibrant 활기찬 profitable 수익성이 좋은 partner 공동 경영자, 공동 출자자

---

191 세부 사항

번역 광고에 따르면 지원자에게 요구되는 조건이 아닌 것은?

(A) 경영학 학위
(B) 과거 관리직 근무 경력
(C) 해외 근무 경험
(D) 온라인 영업 및 마케팅 경험

해설 자격 요건(Qualifications) 부분을 보면 지원자는 경영학 정규 학위와 최소 한 곳의 해외 환경에서 관리자로 일한 증빙 기록(a formal business degree and a proven management record in at least one international setting)이 있어야 한다고 했으므로, (A), (B), (C)가 필수적인 자격 요건임을 알 수 있다. 그러나 온라인 영업 및 마케팅 경력은 우대(Experience with online sales and marketing preferred)한다고 했으므로, 이는 필수 조건이 아니라는 것을 알 수 있다. 따라서 (D)가 정답이다.

▸▸ Paraphrasing
지문의 preferred → 질문의 not required
지문의 a formal business degree
→ 보기 (A)의 A degree in business
지문의 a proven management record
→ 보기 (B)의 Previous employment in a managerial position
지문의 in one international setting
→ 보기 (C)의 overseas

192 연계

번역 아비드슨 씨가 지원한 직책이 있는 장소는 어디겠는가?

(A) 라틴 아메리카
(B) 북아메리카
(C) 유럽
(D) 아시아

해설 도로 씨가 보낸 이메일의 첫 번째 단락에서 아비드슨 씨가 의뢰 업체의 해외 신규 시설에서 근무할 준비가 되었는지(whether you would be prepared to work at our client's new facility overseas) 논의하고 싶다고 했으므로, 아비드슨 씨가 해외 신규 시설에 있는 직책에 지원했음을 알 수 있다. 해당 시설이 있는 장소는 광고에서 확인할 수 있는데, 회사(Company) 설명 부분에서 내년에 라틴 아메리카에서 영업을 시작할 계획(Latin America, where it plans to start operations next year)이라고 했으므로, (A)가 정답이다.

193 세부 사항

번역 도로 씨가 아비드슨 씨에게 답장으로 제공해 줄 것을 요청한 것은?

(A) 리더십 역량에 대한 정보
(B) 면접 가능 여부
(C) 현재 이력서
(D) 추천인 두 사람의 이름

해설 도로 씨가 보낸 이메일의 두 번째 단락을 보면, 아비드슨 씨에게 다음 주 월요일이나 화요일 중 30분 정도 전화 통화가 가능한지 알려 달라(Let me know if you are available for a 30-minute phone call)고 했으므로, 전화 면접 가능 여부를 통보해 달라고 요청했음을 알 수 있다. 따라서 (B)가 정답이다.

▸▸ Paraphrasing
지문의 if you are available
→ 정답의 His availability

194 연계

번역 아비드슨 씨는 지원하면서 어떤 직책 코드를 언급했겠는가?

(A) TL0015
(B) TL0023
(C) TL0027
(D) TL0045

해설 보도 자료의 첫 번째 단락에서 아비드슨 씨가 상품군 관리는 비교적 새로운 영역(Category Management is a relatively new area)으로 자신이 이사로서 즐겁게 개척하고 발전시킬 영역이라고 확신한다(I'm sure I'll enjoy exploring and developing as director)고 했으므로, 그가 상품군 관리 이사직을 맡았다는 것을 알 수 있다. 직책 코드는 광고에서 확인할 수 있는데, 상단을 보면 상품군 관리 이사직(Director of Category Management)의 코드가 TL0045라고 나와 있다. 따라서 (D)가 정답이다.

195 세부 사항

번역 보도 자료에 따르면 타예르슨사가 판매하는 것은?

(A) 의료 기구
(B) 회계 소프트웨어
(C) 영양제
(D) 운동 기구

해설 보도 자료의 첫 번째 단락에서 타예르슨이 주요 온라인 영양제 판매사(As a major online marketer of nutritional supplements)라고 했으므로, (C)가 정답이다.

196-200 소책자 + 이메일 + 일정표

FGJ's
FGJ의 비즈니스 전문가 시리즈
잠재 고객 데이터 구매
45분 웨비나
5월 11일, 오후 2시 30분

사업상 결정을 하려면 조직의 모든 부서는 정보가 필요합니다. **196특히 마케팅 전문가들은 좋은 결과를 얻기 위해 잠재 고객에 대한 정확한 데이터를 필요로 합니다.** 이번 웨비나에서 **198파일 원 마켓 데이터의 최고 재무책임자인 브리아나 카레라 씨가 196불완전한 데이터 수집의 위험을** 피하는 방법을 설명하고, 다음 데이터 배치가 원하는 결과로 이어지려면 장래의 데이터 제공자에게 무엇을 요구해야 하는지에 관한 조언을 제공합니다.

어휘 prospect (경제) 잠재 고객 webinar 웨비나(웹과 세미나의 합성어) organisation 조직, 단체 pitfall (숨어 있는) 위험 acquire 수집하다, 얻다 prospective 장래의, 가능성 있는 batch 배치, (일괄 처리되는) 한 묶음

수신: 산드라 레스퀴르
발신: 지노 스텔레티
날짜: 5월 12일
제목: 제목: FGJ의 웨비나

산드라에게,

제가 어제 참석한 데이터 수집 관련 웨비나에 대한 보고서를 달라고 요청했었잖아요. **197솔직히, 진행자가 확실히 아는 것은 많았지만 제가 이미 알고 있는 것만 말했습니다.** 저는 그녀가 여러 종류의 데이터베이스 간의 차이점을 보여 주었으면 했지만, 그 주제는 전혀 언급하지 않았어요. 이러한 웨비나 전부가 유용한지 잘 모르겠습니다. **198결국 이런저런 특정 회사에서 제품을 구매하도록 언제나 유도하는 것 같아요. 이번 경우에는 파일 원이었습니다.** 그래도 새로운 일정이 막 나왔고, 곧 또 다른 웨비나가 있는데, **199제가 원하는 데이터 저장 및 분류 방법에 관한 정보를 제공해 주었으면 좋겠네요. 저는 이미 신청했습니다.** 제가 배운 내용을 당신에게 계속 알려 줄게요.

지노

어휘 facilitator 진행자 knowledgeable 박식한 steer 유도하다, 조종하다 sign up for ~을 신청하다

FGJ's

200다가오는 45분간의 웨비나, FGJ의 비즈니스 전문가 시리즈

시장 조사의 기초	6월 1일, 오전 9시 30분	에드 퀴노네스	12.00유로
매출 촉진 비결	6월 12일, 오전 9시 30분	카메론 스톤	16.00유로
시장 자동화란 무엇인가?	7월 5일, 오전 11시	에드 퀴노네스	12.00유로
199적합한 데이터 베이스 선택하기	**1997월 17일,** 오후 2시	셀리나 투치	12.00유로

비즈니스 전문가 시리즈는 뚜엣 응우옌 씨가 준비합니다. 문의 사항은 tnguyen@fgj.org로 그녀에게 보내십시오. 추후 시청 용도로 웨비나를 녹화하지 않으므로, 웨비나 내용을 보시려면 참석하셔야 합니다.

어휘 expert 전문가 accelerate 촉진하다 attendance 참석

---

196 추론 / 암시

번역 소책자에 따르면, 잠재 고객 데이터 구매 웨비나에서 가장 많은 도움을 받을 것 같은 사람은?

(A) 재무 분석가
(B) 마케팅 관리자
(C) 소비자 서비스 담당 직원
(D) 정보기술 전문가

해설 소책자에서 마케팅 전문가들은 잠재 고객에 대한 정확한 데이터를 필요로 한다(Marketing professionals ~ rely on accurate data about potential customers)며 이번 웨비나에서 불완전한 데이터 수집의 위험을 피하는 방법(how to avoid the pitfalls of acquiring incomplete data)을 알려 주고 장래의 데이터 제공자에게 무엇을 요구해야 하는지(what to ask your prospective data provider)에 관해 조언을 제공한다고 했으므로, 마케팅 관리자 가장 많은 도움을 받을 것으로 추론할 수 있다. 따라서 (B)가 정답이다.

197 세부 사항

번역 웨비나에 대한 스텔레티 씨의 불만은?

(A) 형식이 마음에 들지 않았다.
(B) 새로운 내용을 아무것도 배우지 않았다.
(C) 전부를 듣는 데 어려움이 있었다.
(D) 주제가 너무 복잡했다.

해설 스텔레티 씨가 보낸 이메일을 보면, 웨비나 진행자(the facilitator)가 자신이 이미 알고 있는 것만 말했다(did not tell me anything I didn't already know)고 했으므로, 새로운 내용을 배우지 못한 것이 불만임을 알 수 있다. 따라서 (B)가 정답이다.

> ▸▸ Paraphrasing   지문의 **did not tell me anything I didn't already know**
> → 정답의 **did not learn anything new**

198 연계

번역 스텔레티 씨가 카레라 씨에 관해 암시한 것은?

(A) 최근 새로운 회사에 취직했다.
(B) 데이터베이스 관리 경험이 있다.
(C) 웨비나를 신청하라고 요청했다.
(D) 자신의 회사 서비스를 판매하려고 했다.

해설 스텔레티 씨가 보낸 이메일의 중반부를 보면, 웨비나가 이런저런 특정 회사의 제품을 구매하도록 유도(steering us to purchase from one particular company or another)하는 것 같다며 이번 경우에는 파일 원이었다(in this case, it was Pile One)고 했다. 소책자를 보면, 웨비나 진행자인 카레라 씨가 파일 원 마켓 데이터의 최고재무책임자(chief financial officer of Pile One Market Data)라고 나와 있으므로, 카레라 씨가 자신의 회사 서비스를 판매하려 했음을 추론할 수 있다. 따라서 (D)가 정답이다.

> ▸▸ Paraphrasing   지문의 **steering us to purchase**
> → 정답의 **tried to sell**

199 연계

번역 스텔레티 씨는 언제 다른 웨비나에 참석하겠는가?

(A) 6월 1일
(B) 6월 12일
(C) 7월 5일
(D) 7월 17일

해설 스텔리티 씨는 이메일에서 데이터 저장 및 분류 방법(how to store and sort data)에 관한 정보를 제공해 줄 것으로 기대되는 웨비나에 이미 신청했다(I have already signed up for it)고 했다. 일정표를 보면, 스텔리티 씨가 희망하는 주제를 다룰 것으로 추정되는 '적합한 데이터베이스 선택하기(Choosing the Right Database)'라는 제목의 웨비나가 7월 17일에 있을 예정이므로, (D)가 정답이다.

200 세부 사항

번역 일정표에 따르면 모든 웨비나의 공통점은?

(A) 비용이 동일하다.
(B) 오전에 열린다.
(C) 진행 시간이 동일하다.
(D) 나중에 재생할 수 있도록 녹화된다.

해설 일정표 상단을 보면 '다가오는 45분간의 웨비나(Upcoming 45-Minute Webinars)'라고 했으므로, 모든 웨비나가 45분간 진행된다는 것을 알 수 있다. 따라서 (C)가 정답이다.

101 (B)	**102** (D)	**103** (C)	**104** (A)	**105** (A)
106 (D)	**107** (B)	**108** (B)	**109** (C)	**110** (A)
111 (D)	**112** (A)	**113** (D)	**114** (A)	**115** (D)
116 (D)	**117** (B)	**118** (B)	**119** (A)	**120** (C)
121 (D)	**122** (C)	**123** (C)	**124** (A)	**125** (B)
126 (C)	**127** (B)	**128** (D)	**129** (C)	**130** (D)
131 (B)	**132** (C)	**133** (A)	**134** (A)	**135** (D)
136 (A)	**137** (B)	**138** (C)	**139** (B)	**140** (C)
141 (A)	**142** (D)	**143** (D)	**144** (A)	**145** (C)
146 (A)	**147** (C)	**148** (A)	**149** (A)	**150** (C)
151 (B)	**152** (A)	**153** (C)	**154** (D)	**155** (C)
156 (B)	**157** (B)	**158** (A)	**159** (C)	**160** (D)
161 (D)	**162** (C)	**163** (C)	**164** (A)	**165** (D)
166 (C)	**167** (B)	**168** (B)	**169** (B)	**170** (A)
171 (C)	**172** (B)	**173** (B)	**174** (C)	**175** (A)
176 (D)	**177** (A)	**178** (C)	**179** (B)	**180** (A)
181 (B)	**182** (C)	**183** (B)	**184** (A)	**185** (B)
186 (B)	**187** (A)	**188** (C)	**189** (B)	**190** (C)
191 (C)	**192** (D)	**193** (C)	**194** (B)	**195** (A)
196 (A)	**197** (C)	**198** (D)	**199** (B)	**200** (C)

PART 5

101 인칭대명사의 격 _ 주격

해설 빈칸은 if절의 동사인 need의 주어 역할을 하는 자리이므로, 주격 인칭대명사인 (B) you와 소유대명사인 (D) yours 중 하나를 선택해야 한다. 주절인 명령문의 동사원형 contact 앞에 주어 you가 생략되어 있고, 연락하는(contact) 주체와 대체 부품을 필요로 하는(need) 주체가 동일인이어야 문맥상 자연스러우므로, 주격 인칭대명사인 (B) you가 정답이다.

번역 대체 부품이 필요하시면 소매점이 아닌 제품 유통업체에 연락하세요.

어휘 distributor 유통업자, 배급사 retail store 소매점 replacement 교체 part 부품

102 전치사 어휘

해설 빈칸은 기간을 나타내는 명사구 the last three years를 목적어로 취하는 전치사 자리이며, 빈칸을 포함한 전치사구가 현재완료형 동사구 have remained steady를 수식하고 있다. 따라서 빈칸에는 '변동이 없었다'와 '지난 3년'을 적절히 연결해 주는 전치사가 들어가야 하므로, '~ 동안'이라는 의미로 현재완료와 자주 쓰이는 (D) for가 정답이다.

번역 AGU 그룹의 보험료는 지난 3년간 변동이 없었다.

어휘 insurance rate 보험료 steady 꾸준한, 안정된

103 형용사 자리 _ 명사 수식 _ 비교급

해설 빈칸은 a variety of(다양한)의 명사 variety를 수식하는 형용사 자리이므로, 형용사의 원급인 (A) wide, 최상급인 (B) widest, 비교급인 (C) wider 중 하나를 선택해야 한다. 뒤에 비교급과 쓰이는 than이 있으므로, 비교급인 (C) wider가 정답이 된다.

번역 세이지 비스트로의 메뉴에는 알매이너 파빌리온의 메뉴보다 더욱 다양한 해산물이 있다.

어휘 feature (특별히·중점적으로) 포함하다, 특징으로 삼다

104 부사 어휘

해설 「동사(enables)+목적어(our technicians)+목적격 보어 (to resolve ~)」의 구조에서 목적격 보어인 to resolve most computer problems를 적절히 수식하는 부사를 선택하는 문제이다. 문맥상 '잦은 교육을 통해 문제를 신속히 해결할 수 있게 된다'라는 내용이 되어야 자연스러우므로, '신속히, 즉시'라는 의미의 (A) swiftly가 정답이다.

번역 잦은 교육을 통해 우리 기술자들은 대부분의 컴퓨터 관련 문제를 신속히 해결할 수 있게 된다.

어휘 frequent 잦은, 빈번한 enable A to + 동사원형 A가 ~할 수 있게 하다 avoidably 피할 수 있게 doubtfully 미심쩍게, 불확실하게 rigidly 엄격히, 완고하게

105 명사 자리 _ 전치사의 목적어

해설 빈칸 앞 trade(무역)와 복합명사를 이루어 전치사 as a result of의 목적어 역할을 하는 명사 자리이므로, '협정'이라는 의미의 명사인 (A) agreement가 정답이다.

번역 대부분의 제조 부문은 무역 협정의 결과로 더 높은 수익을 기록했다.

어휘 manufacturing 제조 profit 수익 trade 무역

106 부사절 접속사

해설 빈칸 뒤 완전한 절(it thickens)을 이끄는 접속사 자리이다. 빈칸이 이끄는 절이 동명사 구문 letting the sauce simmer를 수식하므로, 빈칸에는 부사절 접속사가 들어가야 한다. 따라서 (A) whereas와 (D) until 중 하나를 선택해야 하는데, 문맥상 '소스(it=the sauce)가 걸쭉해질 때까지 끓도록 두다'라는 내용이 되어야 자연스러우므로, (D) until이 정답이 된다. 부사인 (B) likewise와 (C) instead는 절을 이끌 수 없으므로 빈칸에 들어갈 수 없다.

번역 요리 설명에 따르면 불을 줄이고 소스를 걸쭉해질 때까지 끓도록 뒤야 한다.

어휘 call for ~를 필요로 하다 reduce 줄이다 simmer 끓다 thicken 걸쭉해지다

107 부사 자리

해설 빈칸은 형용사 short를 수식하는 부사 자리로, 문맥상 '놀랄 만큼 짧은 시간'이라는 내용이 되어야 자연스럽다. 따라서 '놀랍게도, 의외로'라는 의미의 부사인 (B) surprisingly가 정답이 된다.

번역　컬링포드 다리는 보수하는 데 놀랄 만큼 짧은 시간이 걸렸다.

어휘　repair 수리하다, 고치다

108 부사 어휘

해설　수동태 동사구 is held를 적절히 수식하는 부사를 선택하는 문제이다. be동사 뒤에서 과거분사를 수식할 수 있는 (B) always와 (C) much 중 하나를 선택해야 하는데, 문맥상 '항상 시외 지역에서 개최된다'라는 내용이 되어야 자연스러우므로, (B) always가 정답이 된다.

번역　회사 하계 야유회는 항상 시외 지역에 있는 워렌 카운티 레이크사이드 파크에서 개최된다.

109 명사 어휘

해설　빈칸 앞 명사 assistant와 복합명사를 이루어 to fill의 목적어 역할을 하는 명사 자리이므로, to fill 및 assistant와 가장 잘 어울리는 명사를 선택해야 한다. 문맥상 '비서관 자리를 채우다'라는 내용이 되어야 자연스러우므로, '자리, 직책'이라는 의미의 (C) position이 정답이다.

번역　나바로 씨는 가능한 한 빨리 행정 비서관 자리를 채우고 싶어 한다.

어휘　fill a position 자리를 채우다 administrative 행정적인 employment 고용, 일

110 형용사 어휘

해설　빈칸은 주어 The item (that ~ catalog)을 설명하는 형용사 자리로, 전치사구 until 16 October의 수식을 받는다. 따라서 박 씨가 주문한 제품이 특정일까지 어떤 상태인지 적절히 묘사하는 형용사가 빈칸에 들어가야 하므로, '이용할 수 없는, 획득할 수 없는'이라는 의미의 (A) unavailable이 정답이다.

번역　박 씨가 우리 카탈로그에서 주문한 제품은 10월 16일까지 구할 수 없다.

어휘　occupied 사용 중인, 분주한 uneventful 특별한 일이 없는 delivered 배송된

111 재귀대명사

해설　빈칸은 전치사 by의 목적어 역할을 하는 자리이므로, 소유대명사인 (A) theirs, 목적격 인칭대명사인 (C) them, 재귀대명사인 (D) themselves 중 하나를 선택해야 한다. 빈칸 뒤에 '우유와 곁들이면 훨씬 더 맛있다'라는 내용이 왔으므로, 빈칸을 포함한 부분은 '그 자체로 맛있는'이라는 내용이 되어야 자연스럽다. 따라서 주어인 Kespi Brand cookies와 동일한 대상을 나타내는 재귀대명사 (D) themselves가 정답이다. 참고로 by oneself는 '스스로, 그 자체로'라는 의미로 자주 쓰이는 표현이니 암기해 두는 것이 좋다.

번역　케스피 브랜드 쿠키는 그 자체로도 맛있지만 우유와 곁들이면 훨씬 더 맛있다.

어휘　be paired with ~와 병행되다, ~와 짝이 이루어지다

112 동사 어휘

해설　빈칸은 주어 The North India Electricians Association의 동사 자리로, 명사구 various online courses를 목적어로 취한다. 따라서 '협회' 및 '다양한 강좌'와 가장 잘 어울리는 동사를 선택해야 한다. 협회가 강좌를 가지고 할 수 있는 행위를 생각해 보면, '제공하다'라는 의미의 (A) offers가 빈칸에 들어가야 가장 자연스럽다. 참고로, (B) takes도 courses와 자주 쓰이는 동사지만, 협회가 강좌를 이수하는 주체는 아니므로 문맥상 빈칸에 적절하지 않다.

번역　북인도 전기 기사 협회는 자격 취득, 안전 및 기술 관련 내용을 다루는 다양한 온라인 강좌를 제공한다.

어휘　electrician 전기 기사, 기술자 association 협회 licensure 자격 취득, 면허 교부

113 형용사 자리 _ 주격 보어

해설　빈칸은 that절의 주어인 our downtown store를 설명하는 주격 보어 자리이므로, 명사인 (A) conveniences와 (C) convenience, 형용사인 (D) convenient 중 하나를 선택해야 한다. 문장 구조상 '교외 매장보다 도심에 있는 매장이 더 편리하다'라는 내용이 되어야 하므로, more와 함께 비교급 표현을 완성하는 형용사 (D) convenient가 정답이 된다.

번역　최근 조사는 도심에 있는 매장이 교외의 매장보다 지역 쇼핑객들에게 더 편리하다는 사실을 보여 준다.

어휘　survey 조사 suburban 교외의

114 전치사 어휘

해설　빈칸은 명사구 women ages 18-34를 목적어로 취하는 전치사 자리이며, 빈칸을 포함한 전치사구가 명사구 the most popular television show를 수식하고 있다. 따라서 빈칸에는 '가장 인기 있는 TV 프로그램'과 '18-34세 여성들'을 적절히 연결해 주는 전치사가 들어가야 한다. 문맥상 '18-34세 여성들 사이에서 가장 인기 있는 TV 프로그램'이라는 내용이 되어야 자연스러우므로, '~ 사이에, ~ 중에'라는 의미의 (A) among이 정답이다.

번역　〈위빙 파이어〉는 18-34세 여성들에게 가장 인기 있는 텔레비전 프로그램이다.

115 부사절 접속사

해설　빈칸 뒤에 완전한 절과 콤마가 왔으므로, 빈칸에는 접속사가 들어가야 한다. 빈칸이 이끄는 절이 먼저 일어날 일(원형 제품을 완성하다)에 대한 내용이고, 주절이 그 다음에 일어날 일(나머지 팀원들은 그 제품을 평가하라는 요청을 받을 것이다)에 대한 내용이므로, '~한 후에'라는 의미의 (D) After가 정답이 된다. 참고로, (B) Whether는 부사절을 이끌 경우 or not과 함께 쓰인다.

번역　디자이너가 원형 제품을 완성하고 나면, 나머지 팀원들은 그 제품을 평가하라는 요청을 받을 것이다.

어휘　complete 완료하다 prototype 원형 critique 비평하다, 분석하다

116 부사 어휘

해설 빈칸 앞에 있는 delete them(=routine e-mails)을 적절히 수식하는 부사를 선택하는 문제이다. 문맥상 '일상적인 이메일을 보관하기보다는 삭제하라'라는 내용이 되어야 자연스러우므로, '대신에'라는 의미로 상반되는 내용을 나타내는 (D) instead가 정답이다.

번역 일상적인 이메일은 보관하지 말고 삭제하십시오.

어휘 archive 파일을 보관하다 especially 특히 likewise 또한, 마찬가지로

117 동사 어형 _ 시제

해설 빈칸은 관계사절의 주어 he의 동사 자리이므로, 보기에서 (B) apologized, (C) apologize, (D) will be apologizing 중 하나를 선택해야 한다. 빈칸이 포함된 「전치사(during)+목적격 관계대명사(which)」가 이끄는 절이 yesterday를 수식하고 있으므로, '어제'와 시제가 일치하는 과거형 (B) apologized가 정답이 된다.

번역 칸 씨는 어제 전화를 걸어 와서 의류 주문 배송이 지연된 점에 대해 사과했다.

어휘 delay 지연 shipment 배송, 수송

118 명사 어휘

해설 빈칸은 전치사 on의 목적어 역할을 하는 명사 자리로, 전치사구 for the new perfume bottle의 수식을 받고있다. 새로운 향수병에 관해 결정(decided)할 수 있는 것을 생각해보면, '스타일, 모양'이라는 의미의 (B) style이 빈칸에 들어가야 가장 자연스럽다.

번역 마케팅 팀은 수개월의 연구 끝에 마침내 새 향수병 스타일을 결정했다.

어휘 research 연구

119 to부정사 _ 부사적 용법

해설 등위접속사 or가 특정 목적을 나타내는 전치사구 For more information about product warranties와 빈칸 이하를 연결하여 주절을 수식하고 있으므로, 빈칸에도 특정 목적을 나타내는 내용이 들어가야 문맥상 자연스럽다. 따라서 '새 제품을 등록하기 위해'라는 목적을 표현하며 부사의 역할을 할 수 있는 to부정사 (A) to register가 정답이다. (B) registered는 동사/과거분사(형용사), (C) registers는 동사, (D) registration은 명사로 품사상 빈칸에 들어갈 수 없다.

번역 제품 품질 보증서에 관한 더 자세한 정보가 필요하거나 새 제품을 등록하려면 고객 서비스에 연락하십시오.

어휘 warranty 품질 보증(서) appliance 기기

120 등위접속사

해설 빈칸 앞뒤 절을 자연스럽게 연결하는 접속사를 선택하는 문제이다. 문맥을 살펴보면, 빈칸 앞의 절이 '중요한 파일을 백업해 달라(please back up any important files)'는 요청의 이유(내일 소프트웨어 업그레이드가 있을 예정이다)를 나타내고 있다. 따라서 '그래서, 그러므로'라는 의미의 등위접속사인 (C) so가 빈칸에 들어가야 자연스럽다. 참고로, (A) rather는 부사이므로 절을 이끌 수 없다.

번역 내일 소프트웨어 업그레이드가 있을 예정이니 서버에 저장한 중요 파일을 백업해 주십시오.

121 부사절 접속사 _ 복합관계대명사

해설 빈칸은 뒤에 오는 절(it was)을 이끄는 접속사 자리이므로, 보기에서 접속사 역할을 할 수 있는 복합관계대명사 (A) whoever와 (D) whatever 중 하나를 선택해야 한다. 문맥을 살펴보면, 빈칸이 이끄는 절의 주어인 it이 each job을 대신하고 있다. 따라서 '무엇이든지'라는 의미의 (D) whatever가 정답이 된다. 참고로, (A) whoever는 사람을 대신할 때 쓰인다.

번역 차투르베티 대사는 자신의 회고록에 그의 부모님이 어떤 일이든 잘 해내라고 가르쳤다는 이야기를 썼다.

어휘 ambassador 대사, 사절 memoir 회고록

122 부사 자리 _ 동사 수식

해설 빈칸은 미래 시제 동사 will rise 사이에서 동사원형 rise를 수식하는 부사 자리이므로, '꾸준히'라는 의미의 부사인 (C) steadily가 정답이다. 형용사의 원급인 (A) steady와 비교급인 (D) steadier, 동명사/현재분사인 (B) steadying은 모두 품사상 빈칸에 적합하지 않다.

번역 나트륨 컴포스트를 토양에 뿌리면 뜰에서 거두는 수확량이 꾸준히 늘어날 것이다.

어휘 yield 수확량 soil 토양

123 명사 자리 _ 어휘

해설 빈칸은 product와 복합명사를 이루어 동사 handles의 목적어 역할을 하는 명사 자리이므로, 보기에서 (B) distributor와 (C) distribution 중 하나를 선택해야 한다. 접속사 and가 빈칸을 포함한 복합명사와 customer service를 연결하고 있으므로, 문맥상 '제품 유통 및 고객 서비스를 처리한다'라는 내용이 되어야 자연스럽다. 따라서 '유통, 배포'라는 의미의 (C) distribution이 정답이 된다.

번역 도쿄 사업부는 회사에서 제품 유통 및 고객 서비스를 처리한다.

어휘 division 사업부, 분과 distributor 배급[유통] 업자[회사]

124 명사 어휘

해설 빈칸은 전치사 for의 목적어 역할을 하는 명사 자리로, 빈칸 뒤 전치사구 between the marketing and accounting departments의 수식을 받는다. 또한 빈칸을 포함한 전치사구(for ~)가 형용사 responsible을 수식하므로, 빈칸에는 두 개의 부서 사이에서 담당할 일을 구체적으로 나타내는 명사가 들어가야 자연스럽다. 따라서 '업무 조율, 조정'이라는 의미의 (A) coordination이 정답이다.

번역 우리의 신임 보좌관은 마케팅 부서와 회계 부서 간 업무 조율을 담당할 예정이다.

어휘 executive assistant 보좌관, 비서 accounting 회계 attention 주의, 관심, 배려 appreciation 감사, 감상, 인정 consideration 고려 (사항), 배려

125 관계대명사 _ 소유격

해설 빈칸 뒤에 오는 절(primary role will be expanding ~ region)을 이끄는 관계대명사를 선택하는 문제이다. 가산명사인 primary role 앞에 한정사(관사, 소유격 등)가 없고, a sales representative와 primary role이 '영업 담당자의 주요 임무'라는 소유 관계를 나타내므로, 소유격 관계대명사인 (B) whose가 정답이다.

번역 헴린 코퍼레이션은 서북쪽 지역 사업 확장이 주요 업무가 될 영업 담당자를 찾고 있다.

어휘 sales representative 영업 담당자 primary 주된 expand 확장하다

126 형용사 어휘

해설 to eliminate의 목적어 역할을 하는 명사 inventory를 적절히 수식하는 형용사를 선택하는 문제이다. 문맥을 살펴보면, 주절에서 언급된 가격 인하(has cut prices)는 '겨울용 겉옷 재고품 없애기(To eliminate ------- inventory of winter outwerwear)'라는 특정 목적을 달성하고자 취한 조치임을 알 수 있다. 따라서 제거 대상이 될 만한 재고품의 특성을 나타내는 형용사가 빈칸에 들어가야 자연스러우므로, '초과한'이라는 의미의 (C) excess가 정답이다.

번역 애슐리 패션은 겨울용 겉옷의 남아도는 재고품을 없애기 위해 코트, 모자, 스카프 가격을 모두 인하했다.

어휘 eliminate 없애다 inventory 재고 (목록)

127 명사 자리 _ 전치사의 목적어

해설 빈칸은 전치사 for의 목적어 역할을 하는 명사 자리로, 최상급 형용사인 the most current and detailed와 전치사구 of investment options의 수식을 받는다. 따라서 '설명'이라는 의미의 명사인 (B) explanation이 정답이다. (C) to explain도 명사와 같은 역할을 할 수 있지만, 전치사의 목적어 자리에 들어갈 수 없으므로 정답이 될 수 없다.

번역 투자 옵션에 관한 최신 상세 설명을 보시려면 라베세 파이낸셜 웹사이트를 살펴보세요.

어휘 current 현재의 detailed 상세한 investment 투자

128 동사 어휘

해설 주어 The last paragraph와 to부정사구 to have been added to the contract를 연결할 수 있는 동사를 선택해야 한다. 또한 문맥상 '마지막 단락은 계약서에 추가된 것 같다'라는 내용이 되어야 자연스러우므로, 연결 동사로서 to부정사와 함께 '~인 것 같다'라는 표현을 완성하는 (D) appeared가 정답이다. 참고로, The last paragraph는 (A) arranged(마련하다, 정리하다), (B) permitted(허락하다), (C) transferred(이동하다, 이체하다)의 주체가 될 수 없으므로, (A), (B), (C) 모두 빈칸에 부적절하다.

번역 마지막 단락은 뒤늦게 계약서에 추가된 것으로 보인다.

어휘 contract 계약서 afterthought 나중에 (생각나서) 덧붙인 것

129 동사 어형 _ 시제

해설 빈칸은 주절의 주어 work on the lobby floor의 동사 자리이므로, 문장에서 동사 역할을 할 수 있는 (A) has commenced, (C) will commence, (D) commenced 중 하나를 선택해야 한다. 조건 부사절 접속사인 Unless가 이끄는 절의 현재형 동사 arrives가 미래를 대신하므로, 주절에도 미래를 나타내는 동사가 들어가야 한다. 따라서 미래 시제인 (C) will commence가 정답이다.

번역 타일이 일찍 도착하지 않는다면 로비 바닥 작업은 휴일 이후에 시작될 것이다.

어휘 shipment 배송 commence 시작되다

130 형용사 어휘

해설 빈칸은 주격 관계대명사 that이 대신하는 명사구 a synthetic blend를 설명하는 형용사 자리로, 빈칸 뒤 전치사구 to staining의 수식을 받는다. 따라서 빈칸에는 합성 혼합 소재와 얼룩의 관계를 적절히 묘사하는 형용사가 들어가야 자연스러우므로, 전치사 to와 함께 '~에 취약한, ~에 피해를 입기 쉬운'이라는 표현을 완성하는 (D) vulnerable이 정답이다. (A) exposed와 (C) limited 또한 전치사 to와 어울려 쓰이지만 각각 '~에 노출된', '~에 국한된'이라는 의미로 문맥상 적절하지 않다.

번역 니슨 프로 의류는 얼룩에 취약한 합성 혼합 소재로 만들어졌다.

어휘 garment 의복, 옷 synthetic 합성의 blend 혼합 stain 얼룩지다, 더러워지다 automatic 자동의, 반사적인

PART 6

131-134 회람

수신: 전 직원
제목: 서버 보수 알림
날짜: 3월 11일

IT 부서가 필수 서버 점검 및 업데이트를 ¹³¹**실시할** 예정임을 알려 드립니다. ¹³²<u>이 절차는 내일 저녁에 시작됩니다.</u> 3월 12일 수요일 저녁 7시부터 3월 13일 목요일 오전 9시까지 건물 내 인터넷 서비스가 중단될 예정입니다. 아울러 원격 접속도 불가능합니다. 이에 따라 회사 외부에서 서버에 로그인할 수 없습니다. 정기 점검 기간 ¹³³**중에는** 이메일, 일정표, 연락처를 이용할 수 없습니다. 직원 여러분께서는 이에 따라 계획을 세우셔야 합니다. 불편을 끼쳐 드려 ¹³⁴**죄송합니다.**

어휘 maintenance 정비, 유지 보수 reminder 상기시키는 것 mandatory 의무적인 in addition 게다가, 덧붙여 remote 원격의 regularly scheduled 정기의 have access to ~에 접근할 수 있다, ~를 이용할 수 있다 accordingly 그에 맞춰 inconvenience 불편

131 동사 어휘

해설 빈칸은 to부정사의 동사원형 자리로, 명사구 mandatory server maintenance and updates를 목적어로 취한다. 빈칸 앞 the IT department가 의미상 주어가 되며, 빈칸을 포함한 to부정사구가 명사 time을 수식하고 있으므로, 문맥상 'IT 부서가 필수 서버 점검 및 업데이트를 실시할 시기'라는 내용이 되어야 자연스럽다. 따라서 '수행하다, 실시하다'라는 의미의 (B) perform이 정답이다.

어휘 suggest 제안하다 revise 변경하다

132 문맥에 맞는 문장 고르기

번역 (A) 업데이트는 전 직원에게 이메일로 발송될 예정입니다.
(B) 참가를 원하시면 회신해 주십시오.
(C) 이 절차는 내일 저녁에 시작됩니다.
(D) 시작시간이 적힌 메모가 회람될 예정입니다.

해설 빈칸 앞 문장에서 필수 서버 점검 및 업데이트를 실시할 예정(to perform mandatory server maintenance and updates)이라고 했고, 빈칸 뒤 문장에서 이로 인해 건물 내 인터넷 서비스가 중단될 예정(There will be no Internet service in the building)이라고 했으므로, 빈칸에도 서버 점검 및 업데이트 실시 계획과 관련된 내용이 들어가야 문맥상 자연스럽다. 따라서 (C)가 정답이다. 참고로, (C)의 '절차(The process)'는 '서버 점검 및 업데이트 실시(to perform mandatory server maintenance and updates)'를 가리킨다.

어휘 participate 참가하다 process 절차 과정 distribute 돌리다, 유통시키다 indicate 나타내다, 보여 주다

133 전치사 자리

해설 빈칸 뒤 명사구 this regularly scheduled maintenance를 목적어로 취하는 전치사 자리이므로, '~ 동안'이라는 의미의 전치사인 (A) During이 정답이다. (B) Now는 명사/부사, (C) When은 접속사, (D) Finally는 부사로 명사를 목적어로 취할 수 없으므로, 빈칸에 적합하지 않다.

134 동사 자리

해설 빈칸은 주어 We의 동사 자리이므로, '유감으로 여기다, 후회하다'라는 의미의 동사인 (A) regret이 정답이다. (B) regretting은 동명사/현재분사, (C) regrettable(유감스러운)은 형용사, (D) regrettably(유감스럽게도)는 부사로, 모두 문장에서 동사 역할을 할 수 없다.

135-138 편지

4월 22일

안나 스쿨
로데잔트 334
3011 AV 로테르담
네덜란드

스쿨 씨께,

네덜란드, 벨기에, 룩셈부르크에서 거두신 놀랄 만한 135성과를 축하드립니다. 스쿨 씨 담당 지역은 지난 7분기 동안 정시 배송 실적이 향상되었습니다. 136이러한 업적은 인정받아 마땅합니다.

스쿨 씨께 유럽 지사의 지사장직을 제안하게 되어 기쁩니다. 해당 직책은 독일 함부르크에 137기반을 두고 있습니다. 전근으로 인해 어려운 점이 있을 것입니다. 138하지만 시간을 충분히 두고 이 기회에 대해 생각해 보셨으면 합니다. 조속한 시일 내에 연락 주시면 우려하실만한 사항에 대해 이야기 나눌 수 있을 겁니다.

유노시티 운송의 가족이 되어 주셔서 감사합니다.

시아 수, 사업 부장
유노시티 운송 주식회사

어휘 remarkable 놀랄 만한, 주목할 만한 improve 향상되다 on-time 정시의, 제때의 quarter 분기 promotion 진급 relocate 이전하다, 전근하다 consider 고려하다 opportunity 기회 at one's earliest convenience 되도록 일찍, 형편 닿는 대로

135 명사 어휘

해설 빈칸은 Congratulations on의 목적어 역할을 하는 명사 자리로, 형용사 remarkable의 수식을 받고 있다. 바로 뒤에 오는 문장에서 정시 배송 실적이 향상되었다(has improved its on-time delivery performance)는 성과를 밝히고 있으므로, 이와 관련된 축하 대상을 나타내는 명사가 빈칸에 들어가야 한다. 따라서 '(노력의) 성과'라는 의미의 (D) efforts가 정답이다.

136 문맥에 맞는 문장 고르기

번역 (A) 이러한 업적은 인정받아 마땅합니다.
(B) 비서관을 만나 보십시오.
(C) 약 1주일 전에 배송됐습니다.
(D) 저는 다음 달에 벨기에에 갈 겁니다.

해설 빈칸 앞 문장에서 스쿨 씨가 이룬 성과(Your region has improved its on-time delivery performance)에 대해 언급했으므로, 빈칸에는 그 성과를 치하하는 내용이 들어가야 문맥상 자연스럽다. 따라서 (A)가 정답이다. 참고로, (A)의 Such work는 앞 문장 전체를 가리킨다.

어휘 deserve ~할 자격이 있다, ~해야 마땅하다 recognition 인정

137 동사 어형 _ 태 _ 시제

해설 빈칸은 주어 The position의 동사 자리이므로, 문장에서 동사 역할을 할 수 있는 (A) was based, (B) is based, (D) bases 중 하나를 선택해야 한다. 주어인 The position이 동사 base(~에 근거지를 두다)의 대상이 되므로 수동태가 쓰여야 하며, 앞 문장에서 제안된 승진(a promotion)으로 맡게 될 직책이므로 현재 시제가 쓰여야 자연스럽다. 따라서 (B) is based가 정답이 된다.

138 접속부사

해설 빈칸 앞뒤 문장을 의미상 연결하는 접속부사를 선택하는 문제이다. 빈칸 앞 문장에서 전근으로 인해 어려운 점이 있을 것(relocating may be difficult for you)을 안다고 했지만, 빈칸 뒤에서 시간을 충분히 두고 기회에 대해 생각해 볼 것(you will take time to consider this opportunity)을 제안하고 있으므로, 빈칸에는 대조적인 내용을 연결하는 접속부사가 들어가야 자연스럽다. 따라서 '하지만'이라는 의미의 (C) However가 정답이다.

139-142 이메일

수신: 우 인베스트먼트 서비스 직원 여러분
발신: 에일린 쉔, 사무장
제목: 제이콥 우
날짜: 8월 15일

전 직원 여러분께,

많은 분들이 알고 계시듯이, 오랫동안 자리를 지켜 주셨던 제이콥 우 회장님께서 10월 1일자로 ¹³⁹**퇴임하실 예정입니다.** 우 회장님은 20년 전 국제적 역량을 갖춘 홍콩 기반의 서비스 업체 설립을 계획했습니다. ¹⁴⁰그리고 분명 자신의 목표를 이루었습니다. 우 인베스트먼트 서비스는 현재 17개국에 고객을 두고 있으며 이 중 95퍼센트가 저희와 장기적으로 투자를 하고 있습니다.

우 회장님의 뒤는 아들인 토마스 우 씨가 ¹⁴¹이을 것입니다. 토마스 우 씨는 지난 4년간 우 인베스트먼트 서비스의 부사장을 역임했습니다.

우 회장님의 ¹⁴²**성공적인** 경력을 기리기 위해 9월 28일 회식이 있을 예정입니다.

해당일에 가까워지면 행사에 관한 추가 정보를 보내 드리겠습니다. 감사합니다.

에일린

어휘 investment 투자 be aware 알고 있다 long-standing 오랫동안 Chief Executive Officer 최고경영자 set out 착수하다, 계획하다 scope 능력, 여지 currently 현재 for the long term 장기간 동안 gathering 모임 further 추가의

139 동사 어형_시제

해설 빈칸은 주어 Jacob Wu, our long-standing Chief Executive Officer의 동사 자리로, 전치사구 on 1 October의 수식을 받는다. 회람을 작성한 날짜(8월 15일)로 미루어 보아 우 회장이 작성일 기준으로 미래에 퇴임할 예정임을 알 수 있으므로, 미래진행형 동사인 (B) will be retiring이 정답이 된다.

140 문맥에 맞는 문장 고르기

번역 (A) 곧 공식 초청장을 받으실 것입니다.
(B) 행사는 직원실에서 개최 예정입니다.
(C) 그리고 분명 자신의 목표를 이루었습니다.
(D) 그곳에서 뛰어난 학업 성적으로 졸업했습니다.

해설 빈칸 앞 문장에서 우 회장의 기업 설립(set out to create a Hong Kong-based services firm with an international scope)을 언급했고, 빈칸 뒤 문장에서 기업의 현재 성과(Wu Investment Services ~ for the long term)에 대해 구체적으로 설명하고 있다. 따라서 빈칸에도 우 회장이 기업 설립 후 이룬 성과와 관련된 내용이 들어가야 자연스러우므로, (C)가 정답이다.

어휘 formal 공식적인 take place 열리다 with distinction 뛰어난 성적으로

141 동사 어휘

해설 빈칸 앞에서 우 회장이 퇴임할 예정이라고 했으므로, 해당 문장은 '우 회장의 뒤는 아들인 토마스 우 씨가 이을 것이다'라는 내용이 되어야 자연스럽다. 따라서 '(자리·지위가) 승계되다'라는 의미의 (A) succeeded가 정답이다.

어휘 achieve 달성하다, 성취하다 accomplish 완수하다, 성취하다 resolve 해결하다, 결심하다

142 형용사 어휘

해설 빈칸은 명사 career를 수식하는 형용사 자리이며, 빈칸을 포함한 명사구가 to celebrate의 목적어 역할을 하고 있다. 따라서 기릴만한 경력이나 업적의 특성을 묘사하는 형용사가 빈칸에 들어가야 자연스러우므로, '성공적인, 유명한'이라는 의미의 (D) distinguished가 정답이다.

어휘 promising 전도유망한, 장래성이 있는 technical 기술적인 foremost 맨 앞의, 주요한

143-146 회람

발신: 마들렌 데브리스, 사업 부장
수신: 전 직원
날짜: 6월 1일
제목: 출장 규정

¹⁴³**비용** 절감을 위해 중역들은 회사의 출장 규정을 변경하는 쪽에 투표를 했습니다. 변경된 규정은 6월 15일 자로 ¹⁴⁴**도입될** 예정입니다. 이후로 국내 출장을 가는 직원 여러분은 늦어도 출발일 3주 전까지 출장 요청서를 회계과에 제출해야 합니다. ¹⁴⁵해외 출장 요청서는 최소 한 달 전에 보내야 합니다.

본 규정에 관한 ¹⁴⁶**모든** 예외 사항은 건별로 결정되며 반드시 상사의 승인을 먼저 받아야 합니다.

어휘 reduce 줄이다 vote 투표하다 policy 정책, 규정 revise 변경하다, 수정하다 from that point forward 그 후로는 be required to ~해야 한다 submit 제출하다 accounting 회계 no later than 늦어도 ~까지는 departure 출발 exception 예외 case-by-case 사례별로 처리하는, 건별의 approve 승인하다 individual 각각의

143 명사 자리 _ 동사의 목적어

해설 빈칸은 동사 reduce의 목적어 역할을 하는 명사 자리이므로, 보기에서 (C) spender와 (D) spending 중 하나를 선택해야 한다. 빈칸 앞에 한정사(관사, 소유격 등)가 없으므로, '지출, 비용'이라는 의미의 불가산명사인 (D) spending이 정답이 된다. (C) spender는 '돈을 쓰는 사람, 낭비하는 사람'이라는 의미의 가산명사이므로 빈칸에 들어갈 수 없다.

144 동사 어휘

해설 앞 문장에서 회사의 출장 규정을 변경하는 쪽에 투표했다(have voted to change the company's travel policy)고 했으므로, 해당 문장은 '변경된 규정은 6월 15일 자로 도입 예정이다'라는 내용이 되어야 문맥상 자연스럽다. 따라서 '도입된, 제정된'이라는 의미의 (A) instituted가 정답이다.

어휘 examine 조사[검토]하다, 검사하다   overturn 뒤집다

145 문맥에 맞는 문장 고르기

번역 (A) 회계과는 다음 주 보수 공사로 휴무입니다.
(B) 출장은 고객과의 관계 유지에 중요한 요소입니다.
(C) 중역들은 주요 회사 정책을 주기적으로 검토 및 수정합니다.
(D) 해외 출장 요청서는 최소 한 달 전에 보내야 합니다.

해설 빈칸 앞 문장에서 국내 출장을 가는 직원(employees traveling within the country)의 출장 요청서와 관련된 절차(will be required to submit travel requests to ~ departure)를 언급했으므로, 빈칸에도 이와 관련된 내용이 들어가야 문맥상 자연스럽다. 따라서 해외 출장 요청서 관련 절차를 안내한 (D)가 정답이다.

어휘 renovation 개조, 보수   maintain 유지하다   relationship 관계   periodically 주기적으로   in advance 미리

146 형용사 어휘

해설 빈칸 뒤에 있는 명사 exceptions를 적절히 수식하는 형용사를 선택하는 문제이다. ------- exceptions는 will be decided on a case-by-case basis의 주어로, 전치사구 to this policy의 수식을 받는다. 문맥상 '본 규정에 관한 모든 예외 사항은 건별로 결정될 것이다'라는 내용이 되어야 자연스러우므로, '(특정 범주 내에 있는) 누구나, 무엇이나'라는 의미의 (A) Any가 정답이다.

어휘 additional 추가의   previous 이전의, 사전의

PART 7

147-148 영수증

시오반스 토론토, 온타리오

4월 14일	오전 9시 23분	내부에서 식사
주문: 55234		종업원: 안토니오 K.

[147,148]미디엄 커피 1	[148]2.25달러	
설탕 X		
우유 X		
[147]라지 커피 1	2.75달러	
설탕 3		
우유 X		
[147]크로아상 2	4.00달러	
소계	9.00달러	
통합소비세 13퍼센트	1.17달러	
총계	**10.17달러**	

****

[148]오늘의 서비스에 대해 평가하고 무료 미디엄 커피 한 잔을 받으세요! www.siobhans.ca/survey에서 온라인 설문조사에 응답하시면 됩니다.
페이스트리를 정가로 구매하시면 무료 미디엄 커피 한 잔을 받으실 수 있는 코드를 드립니다.

어휘 fill out a survey 설문에 응하다   regular-priced 정가의   HST 통합소비세(= Harmonized Sales Tax)

147 추론 / 암시

번역 어떤 종류의 사업체에서 영수증을 제공했겠는가?
(A) 음식 공급 업체
(B) 청과 시장
(C) 카페
(D) 온라인 소매업체

해설 주문한 제품 목록의 '커피(Coffee)'와 '크로아상(Croissants)'을 통해 카페에서 제공한 영수증임을 추론할 수 있다. 따라서 (C)가 정답이다.

148 세부 사항

번역 설문 참여자는 얼마의 금액을 절약할 수 있는가?
(A) 2.25달러
(B) 2.75달러
(C) 4.00달러
(D) 9.00달러

해설 영수증 하단에서 '오늘의 서비스에 대해 평가하고 무료 미디엄 커피 한 잔을 받으세요!(Tell us how we did today and get a free medium coffee!)'라고 했으므로, 설문에 참여하면 미디엄 커피 한 잔 가격인 2.25 달러를 절약할 수 있음을 알 수 있다. 따라서 (A)가 정답이다.

어휘 participant 참가자

▸▸ Paraphrasing   지문의 get a free medium coffee
→ 질문의 save money

149-150 광고

어휘   tip 조언   trick 요령, 비결   award-winning 상을 받은   take pride in ~를 자랑하다   scrumptious 아주 맛있는   article 기사   aspect 측면   expert 전문가   landscape 조경   horticulturalist 원예사   botanist 식물학자   practical 실용적인   do-it-yourself 스스로 하는, 손수 하는   recommendation 추천   step-by-step 단계적인   spectacular 극적인   subscribe 구독하다   cover price 정가

149 추론 / 암시

번역   광고는 누구를 대상으로 한 것이겠는가?

(A) 초보 정원사
(B) 조경 디자이너
(C) 꽃집 주인
(D) 잡지 출판인

해설   네 번째 문장에서 독자 대부분이 잡지 주문 전에는 씨앗 한 톨 심어 본 적이 없다고 말했지만(Most of our readers say ~ before ordering our magazine) 이제 아름다운 꽃과 맛있는 채소 재배에 자부심을 느낀다(now they take pride in ~ vegetables)고 했으므로, 초보 정원사를 대상으로 한 잡지 광고임을 추론할 수 있다. 따라서 (A)가 정답이다.

어휘   publisher 출판인

150 세부 사항

번역   광고에 따르면 잡지에 실리는 것은?

(A) 제품 광고
(B) 독자들이 보낸 원예 관련 조언
(C) 원예 전문가들이 작성한 기사
(D) 식물 삽화

해설   광고 중반부를 보면, 기사는 전문 조경 디자이너, 원예사 및 식물학자가 작성한다(Out articles ~ are written by expert landscape designers, horticulturalists, and botanists)고 했으므로, (C)가 정답이다.

어휘   feature 특별히 포함하다   professional 전문가   botanical 식물의

▸▸ **Paraphrasing**   지문의 expert landscape designers, horticulturalists, and botanists → 정답의 gardening professionals

151-152 이메일

어휘   request 요청   place 두다, 배치하다   edge 가장자리   ream 연 (종이의 단위를 나타내는 단어)   exceed 초과하다, 넘다   recycle 재활용하다   true-to-size 실제 크기의   attention ~ 앞, 귀하   approve 승인하다

151 추론 / 암시

번역   아라밀라 씨는 누구이겠는가?

(A) 비서
(B) 그래픽 디자이너
(C) 회계사
(D) 매장 관리자

해설   첫 번째 단락에서 요청에 따라 라벨에 넣을 문구를 보낸다(Per your request, below is the text for the labels)며 디자인 관련 요구 사항(The design should include the tree graphic)을 덧붙였고, 두 번째 단락에서 실제 크기, 실제 색상의 라벨 견본을 만들어 달라(Please create a true-to-size and true-to-color sample version)고 부탁했다. 따라서 이메일의 수신인인 페드로 아라밀라 씨가 문구를 받아 라벨을 디자인하는 그래픽 디자이너임을 추론할 수 있으므로, (B)가 정답이다.

어휘   administrative 행정의   accountant 회계사

152 사실 관계 확인

번역 견본에 대해 명시된 것은?

(A) 그림을 포함한다.
(B) 최종본보다 크다.
(C) 녹색 잉크로 인쇄된다.
(D) 켄싱턴 씨의 승인이 필요하다.

해설 첫 번째 단락에서 라벨 디자인에 나무 그래픽이 들어가야 한다(The design should include the tree graphic)고 했으므로, 라벨 샘플에도 그림이 포함된다는 것을 알 수 있다. 따라서 (A)가 정답이다.

어휘 approval 승인

▸▸ Paraphrasing   지문의 the tree graphic → 정답의 an image

153-154 온라인 채팅

> **아티 제퍼스 [오후 5시 40분]**
> 선정, ¹⁵⁴회의실 전등이 비정상적으로 깜빡거리는데요. 관리실 직통 전화로 연락했지만 응답이 없군요. ¹⁵³관리팀 직원 누군가가 아직 있나요?
>
> **선정 박 [오후 5시 41분]**
> 저런! ¹⁵⁴20분 후에 거기서 라크스퍼 임원들과 회의가 있는데요. 패티 그랜트 씨에게 메시지를 보내 보세요. 관리 팀장인데, 보통 늦게까지 일해요.
>
> **아티 제퍼스 [오후 5시 45분]**
> 좋은 소식이에요! 패티 씨에게 응답이 왔어요. 직원이 그 문제를 처리하려고 오는 중입니다.

어휘 overhead 머리 위의 blink 깜빡이다 oddly 이상하게 maintenance 유지 보수 hotline 직통 전화 respond 응답하다 address a problem 문제를 처리하다

153 주제 / 목적

번역 제퍼스 씨가 박 씨에게 메시지를 보낸 이유는?

(A) 회의 일정을 잡기 위해
(B) 늦게까지 일할 수 있는지 알아보기 위해
(C) 직원이 있는지 물어보기 위해
(D) 다가오는 행사를 연기하기 위해

해설 제퍼스 씨가 오후 5시 40분 메시지에서 '관리팀 직원 누군가가 아직 있나요?(Is anyone from maintenance still in for the day?)'라고 했으므로, 직원이 있는지 문의하기 위해 메시지를 보냈다는 것을 알 수 있다. 따라서 (C)가 정답이다.

어휘 availability 이용 가능성 postpone 연기하다 upcoming 다가오는

▸▸ Paraphrasing   지문의 anyone from maintenance still in → 정답의 staff availability

154 의도 파악

번역 오후 5시 41분에 박 씨가 "저런!"이라고 쓸 때, 그 의도는 무엇인가?

(A) 회의실을 준비하지 않았다.
(B) 그랜트 씨의 전화번호를 찾을 수 없다.
(C) 임원 회의에 참석할 수 없다.
(D) 보수 문제를 우려하고 있다.

해설 제퍼스 씨가 오전 5시 40분 메시지에서 회의실 전등이 비정상적으로 깜빡거린다(the overhead lights in the conference room are blinking oddly)는 문제점을 언급했고, 이에 대해 박 씨가 '저런(Oh no)'이라고 응답한 후 20분 후 회의실에서 임원들과 회의가 있다(We have a meeting there in 20 minutes with the ~ executives)는 일정을 언급했다. 따라서 박 씨가 곧 있을 회의 때문에 회의실 보수 문제가 우려된다는 의도로 말한 것임을 추론할 수 있으므로, (D)가 정답이다.

어휘 attend 참석하다 be concerned about ~에 대해 우려하다

155-157 양식

> **빌 갈라도스 수트**
>
> **상품 세부 사항**
>
> | | |
> |---|---|
> | 구매자: | 리차드 소여 |
> | 의복: | #PC36 (남색 / 모) |
> | 가격: | 89.99달러   세금: 5.40달러 |
> | ¹⁵⁷수선: | 무료 (비고란 참조) |
> | ¹⁵⁵판매자: | 래리 웨이 |
> | 배정자: | 플로리안 가트너 |
>
> **수선**
>
> | 상의 | | 하의 | |
> |---|---|---|---|
> | 옷깃: | | 허리: | |
> | ¹⁵⁶소매: 짧게 수선 | | 길이: | |
> | 어깨: | | 허벅지: | |
> | 기장: | | 무릎: | |
> | 허리: | | 밑단: | |
>
> **비고**
> ¹⁵⁷최초 측정 시 사무원의 착오가 있었음.

어휘 garment 의복, 옷 alteration 고침, 변경 charge 요금 assign 할당하다, 배정하다 clerical 사무직의, 사무원의 initial 처음의 measurement 측정

155 추론 / 암시

번역 웨이 씨는 누구이겠는가?

(A) 재단사
(B) 디자이너
(C) 판매원
(D) 업체 소유주

해설 상품 세부 사항(Item details) 부분을 보면, 판매자가 래리 웨이(Sold By: Larry Wei)라고 적혀 있으므로, 그가 판매원임을 추론할 수 있다. 따라서 (C)가 정답이다.

어휘 tailor 재단사

156 세부 사항

번역 소여 씨에게 정확히 맞지 않는 부분은 어디인가?

(A) 다리
(B) 팔
(C) 목 둘레
(D) 허리 둘레

해설 수선(Alterations) 부분의 '소매: 짧게 수선(Sleeves: shorten)'이라는 문구를 통해 소매가 소여 씨에게 길다는 것, 즉 팔 부분이 정확히 맞지 않다는 것을 확인할 수 있다. 따라서 (B)가 정답이다.

어휘 correctly 정확하게

157 세부 사항

번역 무료 수선이 제공되는 이유는?

(A) 쿠폰 교환을 했다.
(B) 제품을 온라인으로 구매했다.
(C) 결함 있는 제품이 판매됐다.
(D) 직원이 실수를 했다.

해설 상품 세부 사항(Item details) 부분에서 수선비(Alteration)가 무료(no charge)라고 하며 비고란(remarks)을 확인하라고 했는데, 비고란을 보면 최초 측정 시 사무원의 착오가 있었다(clerical error during initial measurement)고 했다. 따라서 직원의 실수로 인해 무료 수선이 제공된다는 것을 알 수 있으므로, (D)가 정답이다.

어휘 redeem 현금이나 상품으로 바꾸다 purchase 구매하다 defect 결함

▸▸ Paraphrasing 지문의 no charge → 질문의 free
지문의 clerical error
→ 정답의 A staff member made a mistake.

158-160 고객 후기

9월 23일 금요일 오후 12시 34분, 게시자 패드마 프래던

158금이 간 액정 문제로 도움을 받으려고 리바스 대로와 23번 가에 있는 비비스 테크 수리점에 휴대전화기를 가져갔습니다. 화요일 오후에 전화기를 떨어뜨렸고 159수요일 아침이 되어 수리 가격을 알려 주는 견적서를 이메일로 받았습니다. 견적을 수락하기 위해 전화를 했고 신용카드 번호를 알려 주었습니다. 159그 다음날 퇴근길에 새것 같은 휴대전화기를 찾을 수 있었습니다. 책임감 있는 전문가를 찾는다면 비비스 테크 수리점이 적합할 것입니다.

휴대전화기를 찾으려고 매장에 있을 때 다른 손님이 들어왔습니다. 그 손님도 망가진 전화기를 찾으러 온 것이었는데, 물에 심각하게 파손되어 기기를 수리할 수 없다고 기술자가 알려주었고, 그래서 그 손님은 돈을 낼 필요가 없었습니다. 고객이 기술자에게 무료 진단을 받을 수 있고 기기 수리가 160어려울 경우 돈을 지불할 필요가 없다는 점이 인상적이었습니다.

어휘 cracked 금이 간 quote 견적(서) fix 고치다, 수리하다 accept 수락하다 responsible 책임감 있는 damaged 손상된 severe 심한 diagnostic 진단; 진단의

158 추론 / 암시

번역 비비스 테크 수리점에 대해 암시된 것은?

(A) 매장이 여러 곳 있다.
(B) 최근에 설립됐다.
(C) 휴대전화만 수리한다.
(D) 신용카드로만 결제할 수 있다.

해설 첫 번째 단락에서 휴대전화를 리바스 대로와 23번 가에 있는 비비스 테크 수리점(the Vivi's Tech Fix location on Rivas Boulevard and 23rd Street)에 가져갔다고 했으므로, location이라는 단어로 미루어 보아 비비스 테크 수리점 매장이 두 군데 이상 있다는 것을 추론할 수 있다. 따라서 (A)가 정답이다.

어휘 multiple 다수의 payment 지불

▸▸ Paraphrasing 지문의 the Vivi's Tech Fix location on Rivas Boulevard and 23rd Street
→ 정답의 multiple stores

159 세부 사항

번역 프래던 씨는 언제 휴대전화기를 찾았는가?

(A) 화요일
(B) 수요일
(C) 목요일
(D) 금요일

해설 첫 번째 단락에서 수요일 아침에 견적서를 받았고(by Wednesday morning I had received a quote), 그 다음날 휴대전화기를 찾을 수 있었다(I was able to pick up the mobile the next day)고 했으므로, 목요일에 휴대전화기를 찾았음을 알 수 있다. 따라서 (C)가 정답이다.

160 동의어 찾기

번역 두 번째 단락 5행의 "beyond"와 의미상 가장 가까운 것은?

(A) ~보다 우수한
(B) ~하는 데 비용이 많이 드는
(C) ~가 즉시 필요해서
(D) ~의 범위 밖에 있는

해설 "beyond"를 포함한 부문은 '기기 수리가 어려울 경우(if a device is beyond repair)'라는 의미로, 여기서 beyond는 '~을 넘어서는, ~할 수 없는'이라는 뜻으로 쓰였다. 따라서 '~의 범위 밖에 있는'이라는 의미의 (D) outside the reach of가 정답이다.

어휘 superior 우수한 costly 비용이 많이 드는 immediate 즉각적인

161-163 회람

즉시 열람 요망

수신: 전 직원
발신: 정보 기술 서비스
날짜: 7월 28일

¹⁶¹어젯밤 메인 웹메일 서버 정지로 인해 회사 전체의 이메일 및 웹 서비스가 영향을 받았습니다. 밤새 호스트 서버 webmail.raass.net에 오류가 발생해 메일 서비스가 중단된 것입니다. ¹⁶¹그 결과 이메일을 여는 데 시간이 훨씬 오래 걸립니다. 많은 경우에 있어 계정이 전혀 응답하지 않을 수 있습니다.

현재 서비스는 완전히 복구되지 않았습니다. ¹⁶³문제의 원인을 파악하고 있으며 해결을 위해 작업 중입니다. 안타깝게도 그게 언제가 될지는 잘 모르겠습니다. ¹⁶²자동 음성 메시지를 통해 추가 통지를 계속 보내 드릴 예정이니 전화에 신경 써 주십시오. 불편을 드려 죄송합니다.

어휘 outage 정전 affect 영향을 주다 interrupt 방해하다
account 계정 restore 복구하다 investigate 조사하다 keep
~ posted ~에게 계속 알려 주다 automated 자동화된 ignore
무시하다 apologize 사과하다 inconvenience 불편

161 세부 사항

번역 메모에서 설명하고 있는 것은?

(A) 비밀번호 변경하는 방법
(B) 새 이메일 계정 신청하는 방법
(C) 직원들이 매우 많은 음성 메시지를 받은 이유
(D) 직원들이 이메일 사용에 어려움을 겪은 이유

해설 첫 번째 단락에서 메인 웹메일 서버 정지(an outage of the main webmail server)로 인해 이메일을 여는 데 시간이 훨씬 오래 걸리고(it takes much longer to open e-mail) 많은 경우 계정이 전혀 응답하지 않을 수 있을 것(In many cases, accounts may not respond at all)이라며 직원들이 이메일 사용에 어려움을 겪은 이유를 설명하고 있다. 따라서 (D)가 정답이다.

어휘 apply for ~에 지원하다, 신청하다 access 접속하다, 이용하다

▸▸ Paraphrasing 지문의 to open e-mail
→ 정답의 accessing e-mails

162 세부 사항

번역 직원들은 무엇을 하라고 요청받았는가?

(A) 안내 데스크에 연락하기
(B) 게시판에 메시지 올리기
(C) 사용자 정보 업데이트하기
(D) 추후 공지 기다리기

해설 마지막 단락에서 자동 음성 메시지를 통해 추가 통지를 계속 보내 줄 예정이니 전화에 신경 써 달라(We will keep you posted with further notices ~ do not ignore your phone)고 요청했으므로, (D)가 정답이다.

어휘 board 게시판 announcement 공지, 안내

▸▸ Paraphrasing 지문의 further notices
→ 정답의 further announcements

163 문장 삽입

번역 [1], [2], [3], [4]로 표시된 곳 중에서 다음 문장이 들어가기에 가장 적합한 곳은?

"안타깝게도 그게 언제가 될지는 잘 모르겠습니다."

(A) [1]
(B) [2]
(C) [3]
(D) [4]

해설 주어진 문장에서 '안타깝게도(Unfortunately)'라는 표현을 사용하여 부정적인 결과를 예측하고 있으므로, 앞에서 먼저 특정 결과를 얻고자 하는 시도나 노력과 관련된 내용이 언급되어야 한다. [3] 앞에서 문제의 원인을 파악하고 있으며 해결을 위해 작업 중(We are investigating the cause of the problem and working to resolve it)이라고 했으므로, (C)가 정답이다. 참고로, 주어진 문장의 that은 문제 해결(resolve it)을 가리킨다.

164-167 이메일

수신: jgonzalez@centralavemarketing.com
발신: pamison@dantonpubliclibrary.org
제목: 도서관 업데이트
날짜: 5월 10일
첨부: 📎 자원봉사 기회

곤잘레즈 씨께,

¹⁶⁴지난해 댄튼 공립 도서관에 다시 한 번 기부해 주셔서 감사합니다. 귀하와 다른 분들의 기부 덕분에 도서관 이용자들이 사용할 신규 컴퓨터 20대를 구매할 수 있었습니다. 또한 어린이실에 소장할 신규 비소설 도서를 구매했습니다.

¹⁶⁶이번에는 추가 기금을 통해 완료하고자 하는 다른 프로젝트에 대해 말씀드리고 싶습니다. ¹⁶⁶, ¹⁶⁷오래되고 낡은 책들을 전자 파일로 변환해 후추 사용할 수 있도록 내용을 보존하는 프로젝트입니다. ¹⁶⁷이러한 시도는 비용이 많이 듭니다. 헌신적인 후원자들의 재정적 지원과 직원들의 추가 근무 시간이 모두 필요합니다. ¹⁶⁴, ¹⁶⁷이 새로운 목표에 적은 금액이라도 힘을 보태 주실 수 있다면 매우 감사하겠습니다.

추가로 금전적인 기부를 하실 수 없다면 저희가 올해로 예정해 둔 소규모 개조 프로젝트를 완료할 수 있도록 도와주십시오. 해당 프로젝트들의 목록을 첨부하였습니다. 귀하의 관심을 끄는 프로젝트를 찾으셨으면 합니다. ¹⁶⁵귀하와 같이 열정적이고 열심히 노력하는 지역 사회 일원과 함께 힘을 합해 도서관의 밝은 미래를 만들 수 있기를 고대합니다.

피터 아미슨, 지역 사회 지원 담당자

댄튼 공립 도서관

164 세부 사항

번역   아미슨 씨가 곤잘레즈 씨에게 이메일을 보낸 이유는?

(A) 도서관을 도운 이력이 있기 때문에
(B) 새 프로젝트를 감독하고 있기 때문에
(C) 댄튼에 대한 책을 썼기 때문에
(D) 도서관 컴퓨터를 자주 사용하기 때문에

해설   첫 번째 단락에서 '지난해 댄튼 공립 도서관에 다시 한 번 기부해 주셔
서 감사합니다(Thank you for your generosity in donating to
the Danton Public Library once again last year)'라고 인사
말을 한 후, 다음 단락에서 다른 프로젝트를 도와 달라고(If you are
able to contribute even a small amount ~ appreciated) 부
탁하고 있다. 따라서 곤잘레즈 씨가 예전에 도서관을 도운 적이 있어
서 아미슨 씨가 그에게 이메일을 보냈다는 것을 알 수 있으므로, (A)
가 정답이다.

어휘   oversee 감독하다   frequent 빈번한

165 추론 / 암시

번역   곤잘레즈 씨에 대해 사실인 것은?

(A) 은퇴한 사서이다.
(B) 도서관 일자리에 지원했다.
(C) 북 스캐너를 갖고 있다.
(D) 댄튼 주민이다.

해설   마지막 단락에서 댄튼 공립 도서관에 기부했던 곤잘레즈 씨를 '귀하와
같이 열정적이고 열심히 노력하는 지역 사회 일원(enthusiastic and
engaged community members like yourself)'이라고 칭했으
므로, 그가 댄튼 주민이라는 것을 추론할 수 있다. 따라서 (D)가 정답
이다.

어휘   retired 퇴직한, 은퇴한   resident 거주자, 주민

▶▶ Paraphrasing   지문의 community members
→ 정답의 a resident of Danton

166 세부 사항

번역   댄튼 공립 도서관은 현재 어떤 프로젝트를 완료하려고 하는가?

(A) 신규 도서 구매하기
(B) 낡은 컴퓨터 교체하기
(C) 책을 전자 형식으로 옮기기
(D) 비소설 부문 재구성하기

해설   두 번째 단락에서 추가 기금을 통해(with additional funds) 오래
되고 낡은 책들을 전자 파일로 변환하여 추후 사용할 수 있도록 내용

을 보존하는 프로젝트(converting many of our old, worn-out
books into electronic files ~ for future use)를 완료하고자 한
다고 했으므로, (C)가 정답이다.

어휘   current 현재의   replace 교체하다   transfer 옮기다

▶▶ Paraphrasing   지문의 converting many of our old,
worn-out books into electronic files
→ 정답의 Transferring books to electronic
format

167 문장 삽입

번역   [1], [2], [3], [4]로 표시된 곳 중에서 다음 문장이 들어가기에 가장
적합한 곳은?

"헌신적인 후원자들의 재정적 지원과 직원들의 추가 근무 시간이 모두 필
요합니다."

(A) [1]
(B) [2]
(C) [3]
(D) [4]

해설   주어진 문장에서 헌신적인 후원자들의 재정적 지원과 직원들의 추
가 근무 시간이 모두 필요하다(It will require both financial
resources from dedicated patrons and additional staff
hours)고 했으므로, 앞에서 먼저 '그것(It)'이 가리키는 대상이 언급되
어야 하고, 이는 재정적인 지원과 추가 근무 시간 모두를 필요로 하는
것이어야 한다. [2] 앞에서 새로운 프로젝트(converting many of
our old, worn-out books into electronic files)를 언급한 후,
이러한 시도는 비용이 많이 든다(This is a costly endeavor)고 했
으므로, 이 다음에 주어진 문장이 들어가야 자연스럽다. 따라서 (B)
가 정답이다. 지문의 a costly endeavor를 주어진 문장에서 both
financial resources from dedicated patron and additional
staff hours라고 구체적으로 표현했다.

어휘   financial 재정의   dedicated 헌신적인

168-171 온라인 채팅

마리아 재신토 [오전 10시 24분]
안녕하세요, 여러분. 아이카 오쿠라 씨, 채팅에 합류하신 것을 환영합
니다.

아이카 오쿠라 [오전 10시 24분]
안녕하세요! 168, 169올해 저희 서점이 작가 회의를 공동 후원할 수 있어
기뻐요. 저희에게는 멋지고 새로운 기회입니다.

마리아 재신토 [오전 10시 25분]
저희도 마찬가지입니다. 회의를 이틀로 늘렸는데 추가 후원이 큰 도움
이 됐습니다. 회의가 커지면 세션이 더 많아지고 호텔 준비도 추가로 해
야하니까요.

아서 루포 [오전 10시 26분]
호텔 이야기가 나와서 말인데요... 작년에 로타운 호텔이 아주 좋았는데
이번엔 필요한 날짜에 예약이 다 찼어요. 하지만 170페어마운트 앳 클라
크는 10월 17일과 18일에 이용할 수 있습니다. 회의 공간이 더 크고 뷔
페 선택권도 더 많으니 더 나을 것 같아요.

마리아 재신토 [오전 10시 28분]
좋습니다. 가격 세부 정보를 보내 주시겠어요?

아서 루포 [오전 10시 29분]
회의 참석자들에게는 특별 객실 요금을 제공할 수도 있답니다. 세부 정보를 받는 대로 모두에게 이메일로 보내겠습니다.

마리아 재신토 [오전 10시 30분]
좋아요. 기조연설자는 어떻게 되어가죠?

아이카 오쿠라 [오전 10시 31분]
¹⁷¹**델로라 레테 씨가 잠정적으로 승낙했습니다.**

아서 루포 [오전 10시 32분]
아, ¹⁷¹**최근 그분의 추리물이 정말 좋았어요!** 그렇게 빨리 베스트셀러가 된 이유를 알 것 같아요.

아이카 오쿠라 [오전 10시 33분]
네, 훌륭하시죠. 연설도 훌륭하다고 들었어요. 런던에서 10월에 다른 일정이 있는데 두 행사 모두 참여할 수 있는지 확인하고 싶어 하십니다. 이번 주말까지 확정해 주실 겁니다.

마리아 재신토 [오전 10시 34분]
좋아요. 다 되어가는 것 같군요. 금요일에 다시 확인할게요.

어휘 **expand** 확대시키다, 늘리다 **sponsorship** 후원 **arrangement** 준비, 마련 **availability** 이용 가능성 **attendee** 참석자 **keynote speaker** 기조연설자 **tentatively** 잠정적으로 **engagement** 약속[일정]

---

168 사실 관계 확인

번역 오쿠라 씨에 대해 사실인 것은?
(A) 소설을 출간한다.
(B) 사업체를 소유하고 있다.
(C) 이전에 레테 씨를 만난 적이 있다.
(D) 회의 준비를 도왔다.

해설 오쿠라 씨가 오전 10시 24분 메시지에서 자신의 서점이 작가 회의를 공동 후원할 수 있다(my bookstore is able to cosponsor the writers' conference)고 했으므로, 오쿠라 씨가 사업체(서점)를 소유하고 있음을 알 수 있다. 따라서 (B)가 정답이다.

어휘 **publish** 출판하다 **previously** 이전에

▸▸ **Paraphrasing** 지문의 my bookstore
→ 정답의 owns a business

169 사실 관계 확인

번역 회의에 대해 명시된 것은?
(A) 런던에서 개최될 것이다.
(B) 후원사가 한 곳이 넘는다.
(C) 최초로 개최되는 것이다.
(D) 금요일까지 할인 요금을 제공한다.

해설 오쿠라 씨가 오전 10시 24분 메시지에서 자신의 서점이 작가 회의를 공동 후원할 수 있다(my bookstore is able to cosponsor the writers' conference)고 했으므로, 오쿠라 씨의 서점 이외에도 후원사가 더 있음을 알 수 있다. 따라서 (B)가 정답이다.

---

170 의도 파악

번역 오전 10시 28분에 재신토 씨가 "좋습니다"라고 쓸 때, 그 의도는 무엇인가?
(A) 제안된 회의 장소가 마음에 든다.
(B) 호텔 가격에 합리적이라고 생각한다.
(C) 루포 씨가 뷔페에 함께 가기를 원한다.
(D) 로타운 호텔을 선호한다.

해설 루포 씨가 오전 10시 26분 메시지에서 페어마운트 앳 클라크(The Fairmount at Clark)를 올해의 회의 장소로 제안한 이유(they have a larger meeting space and more options for the buffet)를 언급했고, 이에 대해 재신토 씨가 '좋습니다(That sounds good)'라고 응답했으므로, 루포 씨가 제안한 회의 장소가 마음에 든다는 의도로 말한 것임을 알 수 있다. 따라서 (A)가 정답이다.

어휘 **reasonable** 합리적인

171 추론 / 암시

번역 레테 씨는 누구이겠는가?
(A) 행사 기획자
(B) 여행사 직원
(C) 작가
(D) 서점 주인

해설 오쿠라 씨가 오전 10시 31분 메시지에서 기조연설자(keynote speaker)로 레테 씨(Delora Lette has tentatively agreed)를 언급했고, 루포 씨가 오전 10시 32분 메시지에서 레테 씨의 최근 추리물이 정말 좋았다(I loved her latest mystery)고 한 후 그렇게 빨리 베스트셀러가 된 이유를 알 것 같다(I can see why it became a best seller so quickly)고 했다. 따라서 레테 씨가 작가임을 추론할 수 있으므로, (C)가 정답이다.

172-175 사보 기사

사원 소식

¹⁷²**앨리샤 포털스카 씨께 축하의 말씀을 전합니다. 1월 1일로 신임 마케팅 부서장직을 맡으실 것입니다.** 지난주 소식에서 전한 루이스 라슨 부서장님의 연말 퇴임 소식에 이은 것입니다.

포털스카 씨는 4년 전 수습 마케팅 사원으로 입사하여 최근 마케팅 책임자로 승진했습니다. ¹⁷³**마케팅 부서에 대한 포털스카 씨의 헌신과** ¹⁷⁴**탁월한 기여에 대해 감사드리고 싶습니다.** 포털스카 씨의 업적은 저희 매출액에 지대한 영향을 주었습니다. ^{173, 174}**올해 매출 목표를 초과한 것은 어느 정도 포털스카 씨의 부단한 노력 덕분입니다.** 축하드립니다, 포털스카 씨! 당신의 선례가 저희 모두에게 영감이 됩니다.

어휘 **extend one's congratulations to** ~에게 축하를 전하다 **vice president** 부(서)장, 부사장 **retirement** 은퇴, 퇴직 **trainee** 수습 (직원) **recently** 최근 **be promoted** 승진하다 **dedication** 헌신 **outstanding** 뛰어난 **contribution** 공헌 **have an impact on** ~에 영향을 미치다 **sales figures** 매출액 **tireless** 지칠 줄 모르는 **inspiration** 영감, 자극을 주는 것

172 주제 / 목적

번역 기사를 쓴 목적은?

(A) 직원들에게 매출액에 대해 알리기 위해
(B) 직원의 승진을 통지하기 위해
(C) 올해 마케팅 전략의 개요를 설명하기 위해
(D) 직원이 상을 받았음을 알리기 위해

해설 첫 번째 단락에서 신임 마케팅 부서장직(new Vice President of Marketing)을 맡을 포털스카 씨에게 축하를 전한다(We would like to extend our congratulations to Alicia Portalska)고 했으므로, 직원의 승진을 알리기 위한 사보 기사임을 알 수 있다. 따라서 (B)가 정답이다.

어휘 give notice of ~를 통지하다 outline 개요를 서술하다 strategy 전략 receive an award 수상하다

173 사실 관계 확인

번역 기사에서 포털스키 씨에 대해 명시한 것은?

(A) 인기가 많다.
(B) 열심히 일한다.
(C) 혁신적이다.
(D) 경험이 부족하다.

해설 두 번째 단락에서 마케팅 부서에 대한 포털스카 씨의 헌신과 기여(her dedication and outstanding contribution to the marketing department)에 대해 감사하다고 하며, 그녀의 부단한 노력 덕분에(thanks to her tireless efforts) 매출 목표를 초과했다(we have exceeded our sales targets)고 했다. 따라서 포털스카 씨가 열심히 일한다는 것을 알 수 있으므로, (B)가 정답이다.

어휘 innovative 혁신적인 lack ~이 없다

> ▸▸ Paraphrasing 지문의 her tireless efforts
> → 정답의 She works hard.

174 동의어 찾기

번역 두 번째 단락 5행의 "outstanding"과 의미상 가장 가까운 것은?

(A) 임박한
(B) 완전한
(C) 놀랄 만한
(D) 예상치 못한

해설 "outstanding"을 포함한 부분은 '마케팅 부서에 대한 탁월한 기여(outstanding contribution to the marketing department)'라는 의미로, 여기서 outstanding은 '탁월한, 두드러진'이라는 뜻으로 쓰였다. 따라서 '놀랄 만한, 두드러진'이라는 의미의 (C) remarkable이 정답이다.

175 사실 관계 확인

번역 올해 최종 매출액에 대해 명시된 것은?

(A) 예상보다 좋았다.
(B) 작년 매출액과 같았다.
(C) 최근 직원 회의에서 논의되었다.
(D) 금요일 기념식에서 발표되었다.

해설 두 번째 단락에서 올해 매출 목표를 초과했다(we have exceeded our sales targets this year)고 했으므로, 예상보다 실적이 좋았다는 것을 알 수 있다. 따라서 (A)가 정답이다.

어휘 anticipate 예상하다, 기대하다 ceremony 의식, 식

> ▸▸ Paraphrasing 지문의 have exceeded our sales targets
> → 정답의 were better than anticipated

176-180 이메일 + 문자 메시지

수신: 아스트리드 마틴 〈amartin@elpost.com〉
발신: 쿼일 에어라인 〈reservations@quailairlines.com〉
제목: 항공편 확정
날짜: 3월 15일

마틴 씨께,

오늘 구매하신 항공권 정보는 아래와 같습니다.

여행객	편명	좌석	확정 번호
아스트리드 마틴	QA566	18D	EV4363592

여행 일자	출발	도착
4월 10일	벨기에 브뤼셀, 오전 10시 35분	캐나다 토론토, 오후 1시

탑승 시간: 오전 9시 35분 ~ 오전 10시 05분
177수하물 예약: 수하물 가방 1개, 기내용 가방 1개

여행 당일 쿼일 에어라인 카운터로 오셔서 탑승권을 수령하시고 수하물을 부치십시오. **176, 177쿼일 트래블 카드 회원 자격으로 수하물 1개, 기내용 가방 1개를 무료로 가져가실 수 있습니다.** 수하물 요금에 대한 설명은 아래의 표를 참조하십시오.

	1개	2개	3개	4개
수하물 가방	0.00달러	30.00달러	60.00달러	90.00달러
기내용 가방	0.00달러	–	–	–

179항공편이 세 시간 이상 지연될 경우, 쿼일 트래블 카드를 이용해 쿼일 프리퍼드 클럽룸에 입장하실 수 있습니다. 179클럽룸에서는 휴식을 취하거나 고속 무선 인터넷 서비스를 이용하고 스낵바에서 무료 음식과 다과를 즐기실 수 있습니다.

어휘 confirmation 확정 departing 출발 reservation 예약 carry-on 기내 휴대용 가방 proceed to ~로 나아가다 boarding pass 탑승권 free of cost 무료로 in the event of ~할 경우에는 complimentary 무료로 제공하는 refreshment 다과

수신: 아스트리드 마틴
발신: 쿼일 에어라인 항공편 QA566
179날짜: 4월 10일 오전 6시

178, 179본 문자 메시지는 180악천후로 인해 금일 캐나다 토론토행 QA566편이 4시간 지연됨을 알려 드리기 위한 것입니다. 탑승은 오후 1시 35분에 시작됩니다.

불편을 끼쳐 드려 죄송합니다.

176   사실 관계 확인

번역   마틴 씨에 대해 사실인 것은?

(A) 캐나다 출신이다.
(B) 단체로 비행기에 탑승한다.
(C) 출장을 가는 길이다.
(D) 쿼일 트래블 카드 회원이다.

해설   이메일의 수하물 예약(Baggage Reservation) 부분에서 쿼일 트래블 카드 회원 자격으로(As a Quail Travel Card member) 수하물 1개, 기내용 가방 1개를 무료로 가져갈 수 있다(you are allowed one checked bag and one carry-on bag free of cost)고 했으므로, 수신인인 마틴 씨가 쿼일 트래블 카드 회원임을 알 수 있다. 따라서 (D)가 정답이다.

어휘   business trip 출장

177   세부 사항

번역   마틴 씨는 가방에 대해 얼마를 지불해야 하는가?

(A) 0.00달러
(B) 30.00달러
(C) 60.00달러
(D) 90.00달러

해설   이메일의 수하물 예약(Baggage Reservation) 부분을 보면, 마틴 씨가 수하물 가방 1개와 기내용 가방 1개(1 checked bag, 1 carry-on bag)를 예약한 것을 알 수 있는데, 바로 아래 단락의 두 번째 문장에서 쿼일 트래블 카드 회원 자격으로 수하물 1개, 기내용 가방 1개를 무료로 가져갈 수 있다(As a Quail Travel Card member, ~ free of cost)고 했다. 따라서 마틴 씨는 비용을 지불하지 않아도 되므로, (A)가 정답이다.

178   주제 / 목적

번역   마틴 씨에게 문자 메시지가 전송된 이유는?

(A) 탑승권 구매를 확정하기 위해
(B) 가격 인상을 알리기 위해
(C) 시간 변경을 알리기 위해
(D) 출발 게이트를 알려 주기 위해

해설   문자 메시지에서 악천후로 인해(due to poor weather conditions) 항공편이 4시간 지연됨을 알린다(to inform you that your flight ~ has been delayed 4 hours)고 했으므로, 출발 시간 변경을 알리기 위한 문자 메시지임을 알 수 있다. 따라서 (C)가 정답이다.

> ▶▶ Paraphrasing   지문의 has been delayed 4 hours
> → 정답의 a time change

179   연계

번역   마틴 씨는 4월 10일에 무엇을 받을 수 있는가?

(A) 무료 여행용 가방
(B) 무료 간식
(C) 무료 좌석 업그레이드
(D) 무료 항공편 재배정

해설   문자 메시지에서 마틴 씨의 금일(today=Date: 10 April) 항공편이 4시간 지연된다(your flight ~ has been delayed 4 hours)고 했다. 지연에 따른 항공사 정책은 이메일에서 확인할 수 있는데, 이메일의 표 아래 단락에서 항공편이 세 시간 이상 지연될 경우(In the event of an airline delay of more than three (3) hours), 클럽룸의 스낵바에서 무료 음식과 다과를 즐길 수 있다(you may ~ enjoy complimentary food and refreshments at our snack bar)고 했으므로, 마틴 씨가 무료 간식을 받을 수 있음을 알 수 있다. 따라서 (B)가 정답이다.

어휘   reassignment 재배정, 재할당

> ▶▶ Paraphrasing   지문의 complimentary food and refreshments → 정답의 A free snack

180   동의어 찾기

번역   문자 메시지에서 첫 번째 단락 3행의 "poor"와 의미상 가장 가까운 것은?

(A) 나쁜
(B) 약한
(C) 적은
(D) 두꺼운

해설   "poor"를 포함한 부분은 '악천후로 인해(due to poor weather conditions)'라는 의미로, 여기서 poor는 '(날씨가) 좋지 못한'이라는 뜻으로 쓰였다. 따라서 '나쁜, 안 좋은'이라는 의미의 (A) bad가 정답이다.

181-185   이메일 + 이메일

수신: custserv@xanthusflowers.co.uk
발신: mnair@nortraxpetrol.co.uk
날짜: 7월 27일
제목: 주문 번호 9871

담당자께:

181, 182(B)저는 7월 24일에 저희 회사 노트랙스 석유를 대표해 백장미와 분홍 백합 세 다발을 180파운드에 온라인으로 주문하였습니다. 181, 182(D)꽃은 그 다음날 저녁 회사 연회에 사용하기 위해 오전 10시까지 배송되기로 예정되어 있었습니다.

182(D)안타깝게도 꽃은 정오까지 도착하지 않았습니다. 182(B)게다가 꽃다발은 분홍색과 흰색 카네이션으로 구성되어 있었습니다. 182(A)무엇보다도 꽃은 대부분 시들었거나 꽃잎이 떨어지고 있어서 계획대로 연회장을 꾸미는 데 사용할 수 없었어요. 183저희 노트랙스 석유가 지난 5년간 신뢰하고 의지한 산투스 플라워가 기대를 저버렸다는 데 놀랐고 실망했습니다.

꽃은 일회성 행사용이었기 때문에 교체 주문은 사실상 해당 사항이 아닙니다. ¹⁸⁴**따라서 환불을 받고 싶습니다.**

이 문제를 처리해 주시면 감사하겠습니다.

민디 네어
기업 행사 담당자
노트랙스 석유

어휘 place an order 주문하다   on behalf of ~를 대표하여
be meant to be ~할 예정이다, ~하기로 되어 있다   banquet
연회   consist of ~로 구성되다   wilted 시든   shed 떨어뜨리다
petal 꽃잎   as planned 계획대로   let down 기대를 저버리게
하다   replacement 교체, 대체   attention 주의, 처리

수신: mnair@nortraxpetrol.co.uk
발신: custserv@xanthusflowers.co.uk
날짜: 7월 28일
제목: 주문 번호 9871

네어 씨께,

귀하의 주문 건과 관련하여 최근 겪으신 문제에 대해 진심으로 사과의 말씀을 드립니다. ¹⁸⁵저희는 최근 더 큰 시설로 이전하였고 적응 과정에서 몇 가지 어려움을 겪었습니다. 모든 주문에 대해 정시 배송 및 고품질 꽃을 제공하는 것이 저희 업체의 목표입니다. 이번 주문이 저희의 높은 기준에 맞지 않았던 점에 대해 유감스럽게 생각합니다.

¹⁸⁴180파운드짜리 환불 수표가 귀하의 업체로 발급되었습니다. 저희 측 실수이므로 다음 주문 시 무료 배송과 함께 20퍼센트 할인 혜택을 제공해 드리고자 합니다.

저희 업체를 애용해 주셔서 감사합니다. 빠른 시일 내에 다시 모실 수 있기를 바랍니다.

빌 맥케이브
고객 서비스 관리자

어휘 sincerely 진심으로   apologize 사과하다   recently 최근
transition 이행, 변화; 이동하다, 변화하다   facility 시설   adjust
적응하다   on-time 정시의, 늦지 않는   live up to (기대에) 부응하다
standard 기준   issue 발행하다   free delivery 무료 배송
loyal customer 충성 고객, 단골 고객

---

181 세부 사항

번역 노트랙스 석유가 준비한 연회는 언제 개최되었는가?

(A) 7월 24일
(B) 7월 25일
(C) 7월 27일
(D) 7월 28일

해설 첫 번째 이메일의 첫 번째 단락에서 7월 24일에 온라인으로 꽃을 주문했고(On 24 July, I placed an online order for ~ roses and pink lilies), 그 다음날 저녁 회사 연회에 쓰기 위해(the following day for a company banquet that evening) 오전 10시까지 꽃이 배송되어야 했다고 했으므로, 회사 연회가 7월 25일이었음을 알 수 있다. 따라서 (B)가 정답이다.

어휘 organize 조직하다, 마련하다

182 사실 관계 확인

번역 네어 씨가 언급한 꽃에 대해 맞지 않는 것은?

(A) 용인하기 어려운 상태였다.
(B) 종류가 잘못되었다.
(C) 너무 비쌌다.
(D) 늦게 배송되었다.

해설 첫 번째 이메일 두 번째 단락의 '꽃은 대부분 시들었거나 꽃잎이 떨어지고 있었다(many of flowers were either wilted or were shedding petals)'에서 (A)를, 첫 번째 단락의 '백장미와 분홍 백합을 주문했다(I placed an online order ~ arrangements of white roses and pink lilies)' 및 두 번째 단락의 '꽃다발은 분홍색과 흰색 카네이션으로 구성되어 있었다(the bouquets consisted of pink and white carnations)'에서 (B)를, 첫 번째 단락의 '오전 10시까지 배송되기로 되어 있었다(The flowers were meant to be delivered by 10 A.M.)' 및 두 번째 단락의 '꽃은 정오까지 오지 않았다(the flowers did not arrive until noon)'에서 (D)를 확인할 수 있다. 그러나 가격 관련 내용은 언급되지 않았으므로, (C)가 정답이다.

어휘 unacceptable 받아들일 수 없는

▸▸ Paraphrasing   지문의 were either wilted or were shedding
petals → 보기 (A)의 Their condition was
unacceptable
지문의 did not arrive until noon
→ 보기 (D)의 were delivered late

183 추론 / 암시

번역 네어 씨에 대해 암시된 것은?

(A) 이벤트 기획 업체에서 일한다.
(B) 매월 꽃을 배송받고 싶어 한다.
(C) 필요한 것보다 더 많은 꽃다발을 주문했다.
(D) 이전에 산투스 플라워와 거래한 적이 있다.

해설 첫 번째 이메일 두 번째 단락에서 노트랙스 석유가 지난 5년간 산투스 플라워를 신뢰하고 의지해 왔다(Xanthus Flowers, a company we at Nortrax Petroleum ~ over the last five years)고 했으므로, 네어 씨가 산투스 플라워와 이전에도 거래한 적이 있다는 것을 추론할 수 있다. 따라서 (D)가 정답이다.

어휘 flower arrangement 꽃꽂이   do business with ~와
거래하다

184 연계

번역 네어 씨가 기대하지 않는데 맥케이브 씨가 제공하는 것은 무엇인가?

(A) 추후 주문 건 할인
(B) 향후 모든 구매 건 무료 배송
(C) 전체 주문 가격 환불
(D) 불만족스러웠던 꽃을 대신할 새 꽃

해설 두 번째 이메일의 두 번째 단락에서 맥케이브 씨가 180파운드짜리 환불 수표(A refund cheque in the amount of £180) 및 다음 주문 시 무료 배송과 함께 20퍼센트 할인(a 20% discount plus free delivery on your next order) 혜택을 제공하겠다고 했다. 네어 씨의 요구 사항은 첫 번째 이메일에서 확인할 수 있는데, 세 번째 단락에서 환불을 받고 싶다(would like to receive a refund)고만 했으므로, 맥케이브 씨가 제공한 것 중 네어 씨가 기대하지 않았던 것은 (A)이다.

어휘 entire 전체의 unsatisfactory 만족스럽지 않은

▸▸ **Paraphrasing** 지문의 **a 20% discount ~ on your next order**
→ 정답의 **A discount on a future order**

185 사실 관계 확인

번역 산투스 플라워에 대해 언급된 것은?
(A) 신속한 서비스로 잘 알려져 있다.
(B) 새 사무실에서 영업 중이다.
(C) 최근 배송 차량을 구입했다.
(D) 꽃 종류를 늘릴 계획이다.

해설 두 번째 이메일의 첫 번째 단락에서 최근 더 큰 시설로 이전했다(We have recently transitioned to a larger facility)고 했으므로, 새 사무실에서 영업 중임을 알 수 있다. 따라서 (B)가 정답이다.

어휘 expand 확장하다 selection 선택된 물건들

▸▸ **Paraphrasing** 지문의 **recently transitioned to a larger facility**
→ 정답의 **operating from a new location**

186-190 웹페이지 + 주문 양식 + 이메일

http://www.singhsupplies.com

| 홈 | **소개** | 제품 | 주문 | 연락처 |

싱 서플라이즈 LLC

싱 서플라이즈 LLC는 여러분에게 운송·포장용 자재를 공급해 드리는 일류 업체입니다. ¹⁸⁶설립자인 차타르 싱은 30여년 전 사업을 시작하고 "적은 비용으로 최고의 효과를"이라는 좌우명을 만들었습니다.

¹⁸⁶그의 자녀와 손주들인 저희가 그분의 약속을 어떻게 실현하고 있을까요? 저희는 모든 재료를 대량 구매하고 절감된 금액을 소비자에게 돌려드립니다. ¹⁸⁷여러분은 운송용품 업계 최저 가격 및 최상의 품질은 물론 가장 세심한 고객 서비스까지 누리실 수 있습니다.

✓ 주문은 모두 24시간 이내에 처리됩니다.
✓ 전화, 팩스, 이메일, 또는 문자 메시지를 통해 주문이 가능합니다.
✓ 고객 서비스 담당자가 상시 대기하고 있습니다.
✓ 북동 지역에 5개의 배송 센터가 있어 비용을 최소화하고 배송 시간을 줄일 수 있습니다.

저희의 고객 만족 보증 제도는 다음과 같습니다: 전적으로 만족하지 못하셨다면 구매 이후 10일 이내에 주문 건에 대해 전액 환불을 받으실 수 있습니다. ¹⁹⁰10일 경과 후에는 주문 금액을 1년 동안 유효한 크레딧으로 돌려 드립니다. 반품 배송비는 고객 부담이라는 점을 유의하십시오.

어휘 shipping 운송 packaging 포장 founder 설립자, 창립자 coin 만들다 pledge 약속 in bulk 대량으로 pass along 다음으로 전달하다 savings 절약된 금액 attentive 배려하는, 주의를 기울이는 fill an order 주문을 충족시키다 minimize 최소화하다 guarantee 확약, 보장 completely 완전히 full refund 전액 환불 credit 크레딧 (현금처럼 쓸 수 있는 포인트), (추가되는) 금액 valid 유효한 responsibility 책임, 부담

싱 서플라이즈 LLC

날짜: 7월 10일   **이름:** 몬트조이 앤티크, 배송 부서 귀하
배송 주소: 102 댄버리 스트리트, 밸리빌, 뉴햄프셔 03038

제품 번호	설명	수량	단가	총액
MB 01267	판지 상자 (대)	80	1.75	140.00
MB 01257	판지 상자 (중)	200	1.50	300.00
¹⁸⁹MB 01268	¹⁸⁹보강 상자	50	15.78	789.00
TR 01345	테이프 롤	30	2.90	87.00
BW 01456	버블 랩 롤	10	5.60	56.00

거래해 주셔서 감사합니다!

소계: 1372.00
배송료: 140.12
총계: 1512.12

어휘 antique 골동품 attn. (= for the attention of) ~앞, 귀하 quantity 수량 unit price 단가 reinforced 보강된 crate (나무·철제) 상자 subtotal 소계 delivery charge 배송료

수신: 김정희 〈jhk@montjoyantiques.com〉
발신: 프란신 마요 〈fmayo@montjoyantiques.com〉
¹⁹⁰날짜: 8월 12일
제목: 주문 관련 문제

안녕하세요, 정희,

배송 부서와 막 확인을 마쳤습니다. ^{188, 190}싱 서플라이즈에서 7월 10일 주문 건을 평소처럼 신속하게 배송해 주어 만족스럽네요. ¹⁸⁹하지만 해당 제품을 창고로 옮기고 보니 실수로 견고한 상자를 너무 많이 주문한 것 같아요. 이 상품은 잘 쓰지 않기 때문에 이렇게 많은 수량을 다 쓰려면 몇 년이 걸릴 겁니다. 아울러 상자가 커서 복원 부서에 여러 개를 쌓아 두어야 했는데, 이곳은 이미 공간이 부족한 곳입니다. ^{189, 190}애친트 싱 씨께 오늘 연락해서 절반을 돌려보내도 되는지 알아봐 줄 수 있나요? 싱 씨의 지시 사항을 저에게도 알려 주면 그에 따라 진행하겠습니다.

고마워요!

프랜

어휘 promptly 신속하게 as usual 평상시대로 now that ~이므로 warehouse 창고 inadvertently 부주의로, 무심코 sturdy 견고한 crate 상자 rarely 좀처럼 ~ 않는, 드물게 stack 쌓다, 포개다 restoration 복원, 복구 at a premium 구하기 힘든[품귀 상태인], 할증이 붙어서

186 사실 관계 확인

번역 싱 서플라이즈에 대해 명시된 것은?

(A) 비교적 신생 업체이다.
(B) 가족이 경영한다.
(C) 제품을 전 세계로 배송한다.
(D) 판매하는 제품을 제조한다.

해설 웹페이지의 첫 번째 단락에서 설립자인 차타르 싱이 "적은 비용으로 최고의 효과를"이라는 좌우명을 만들었다(Our founder, Chatar Singh, ~ coined the company's motto, "Expect the best for less")고 한 후, 그 다음 단락에서 '그의 자녀와 손주들인 저희가 그의 약속을 어떻게 실현하고 있을까요?(How do we, his children and grandchildren, make his pledge a reality today?)'라고 했으므로, 가족이 대를 이어 싱 서플라이즈를 경영한다는 것을 알 수 있다. 따라서 (B)가 정답이다.

어휘 relatively 비교적, 상대적으로 manufacture 제조하다

> ▸▸ Paraphrasing　지문의 **his children and grandchildren**
> → 정답의 **members of a family**

187 세부 사항

번역 웹페이지에서는 업체의 어떤 측면을 강조하는가?

(A) 세심한 고객 서비스
(B) 다양한 제품
(C) 타 업체와의 제휴
(D) 편리한 위치에 있는 소매점

해설 웹페이지의 두 번째 단락에서 싱 서플라이즈 고객은 운송용품 업계 최저 가격 및 최상의 품질은 물론 가장 세심한 고객 서비스까지 누릴 수 있다(You will receive ~ the most attentive customer service)고 했으므로, (A)가 정답이다.

어휘 aspect 양상, 측면 emphasize 강조하다 conveniently 편리하게 retail location 소매점

188 세부 사항

번역 이메일에서 마요 씨가 싱 서플라이즈에 대해 칭찬한 것은?

(A) 연락이 쉽다.
(B) 제품을 안전하게 포장한다.
(C) 주문 건을 신속하게 배송한다.
(D) 제품 견본을 보낸다.

해설 이메일의 첫 번째 단락에서 마요 씨는 싱 서플라이즈에서 평소처럼 신속하게 배송하여 만족스럽다(I am pleased that ~ was delivered promptly by Singh Supplies as usual)고 했으므로, (C)가 정답이다.

어휘 praise 칭찬하다 securely 안전하게

> ▸▸ Paraphrasing　지문의 **was delivered promptly ~ as usual**
> → 정답의 **delivers ~ quickly**

189 연계

번역 마요 씨가 반품하고 싶어 하는 제품은?

(A) MB 01257
(B) MB 01268
(C) TR 01345
(D) BW 01456

해설 이메일의 첫 번째 단락에서 실수로 견고한 상자를 너무 많이 주문한 것 같다(we inadvertently ordered far too many of the sturdy crates)며 두 번째 단락에서는 절반을 돌려보내도 되는지 알아봐 달라(find out if we can send half of them back)고 요청했다. 주문서를 보면 보강 상자(reinforced crate)의 제품 번호가 MB 01268이라고 나와 있으므로, (B)가 정답이다.

> ▸▸ Paraphrasing　지문의 **send ~ back** → 질문의 **return**
> 주문서의 **reinforced crate**
> → 이메일의 **sturdy crates**

190 연계

번역 싱 씨는 김 씨의 요청에 어떻게 응답하겠는가?

(A) 마요 씨에게 추가 제품을 보낸다.
(B) 김 씨에게 실수에 대해 사과한다.
(C) 몬트조이 앤티크에 크레딧을 발행한다.
(D) 몬트조이 앤티크에 전액 환불을 해 준다.

해설 8월 12일에 마요 씨는 김 씨에게 이메일을 보내 7월 10일 주문 건(our July 10 order)의 절반을 돌려보내도 되는지 싱 씨에게 알아봐 달라(find out if we can send half of them back)고 요청했다. 웹페이지의 마지막 단락을 보면, 싱 서플라이즈 LLC에서 구매한 지 10일이 경과된 제품을 반품할 시 해당 주문금액을 크레딧으로 돌려준다(After 10 days you may return an order for a credit)고 했으므로, 거의 한 달이 경과한 몬트조이 앤티크의 주문에 대해 싱 씨가 해당 금액을 크레딧으로 돌려줄 것임을 추론할 수 있다. 따라서 (C)가 정답이다.

191-195 기사 + 이메일 + 개요

톨리, 지역 농장들에 찬사 보내

맨체스터 (6월 2일)—[191]지역 원예학 전문가인 카산드라 톨리가 금요일 저녁 맨체스터에 있는 버튼 오디토리엄에서 강연을 할 예정입니다. [193, 195]윈드햄 카운티 인근의 그린 리지 농장 소유주인 톨리 씨는 지역 농가 지원 및 홍보의 중요성에 대해 논할 것입니다.

소규모 영농인의 열렬한 지지자인 동시에 본인 역시 소규모 영농인으로서, 리 씨는 지난 수년간 많은 곳을 다니며 "지역에서 나는 음식을 먹자"라는 메시지를 전했습니다.

"식재료를 지역에서 조달하고자 노력한다면 지역 경제를 유지하고 도울 뿐 아니라 시장에서 다양성을 꾀할 수 있습니다." 톨리 씨는 말합니다. "이는 소비자에게 이익입니다."

"[192]모두 주말에 시간을 내어 지역 농산물 시장을 둘러봐야 합니다."라고 그녀는 덧붙입니다. "그곳은 여름철에 식료품을 사기에 가장 좋은 장소입니다."

금요일 저녁 강의는 7시에 시작합니다. 무료로 제공되는 강의지만 좌석이 한정되어 있으니 일찍 도착하시기 바랍니다. 주 전역에 있는 여름철 농산물 시장의 전체 목록을 보시려면 www.vermontfarmersmarkets.org를 방문하십시오.

수신: 쿡 투데이 집필진
발신: 잭 에르난데스 편집장
제목: 카산드라 톨리 강연
날짜: 6월 8일

집필진 여러분,

금요일에 카산드라 톨리 씨가 강연을 합니다. 가실 수 있는 분은 알려주십시오. 그분이 지역 재배자 관련 기사에 좋은 소재를 제공할 것을 확신합니다. 193작년 그린 리지 농장에서 톨리 씨의 이야기를 들을 기회가 있었습니다. 멋지면서도 재미있는 분이셨습니다.

잭

〈쿡 투데이 잡지〉 8월 호 특집 기사 개요

특집 기사 제목	주제	저자
지역 산물	195지역 생산자 및 재료 탐색하고 소개하기	195이라 뉴튼
194일 년 내내 나는 약초	194실내 식용 약초 텃밭 가꾸기	마카라 영
맛있는 비건 요리	현대적이고 영양 풍부한 유기농 비건 조리법	케이언 데이비스
멋진 8월	8월 행사 일정표	재은 박

191 주제 / 목적

번역 기사를 쓴 목적은?

(A) 지역 업체를 광고하기 위해
(B) 지역 경제에 관해 논의하기 위해
(C) 다가오는 행사를 홍보하기 위해
(D) 새로운 시장에 대해 소개하기 위해

해설 기사의 첫 번째 단락에서 지역 원예학 전문가인 카산드라 톨리가 금요일 저녁에 강연을 할 예정(Local horticulture expert ~ deliver a lecture Friday night)이라고 하며 관련 내용을 서술하고 있으므로, 다가오는 행사를 홍보하기 위한 기사임을 알 수 있다. 따라서 (C)가 정답이다.

어휘 advertise 광고하다 promote 홍보하다 upcoming 다가오는 profile 개요를 알려주다

192 세부 사항

번역 톨리 씨가 사람들에게 하라고 권하는 것은?

(A) 그녀의 웹사이트 방문하기
(B) 그녀의 저서 읽기
(C) 자신만의 농작물 기르기
(D) 농산물 시장에서 쇼핑하기

해설 기사의 네 번째 단락에 나온 톨리 씨의 인터뷰 내용을 보면, 모두 주말에 시간을 내어 지역 농산물 시장을 둘러봐야 한다(Everyone should spend their weekends browsing the regional farmers' markets)고 권하고 있으므로, (D)가 정답이다.

어휘 produce 농작물

▸▸ Paraphrasing 지문의 browsing the regional farmers' markets → 정답의 Shop at farmers' markets

193 연계

번역 에르난데스 씨에 대해 명시된 것은?

(A) 톨리 씨의 친구이다.
(B) 톨리 씨의 강연을 준비했다.
(C) 톨리 씨의 업체를 방문한 적이 있다.
(D) 톨리 씨의 강연 입장권을 판매하고 있다.

해설 에르난데스 씨가 보낸 이메일을 보면, 자신이 작년에 그린 리지 농장에서 톨리 씨의 이야기를 들을 기회가 있었다(had a chance to hear her speak last year at Green Ridge Farm)고 했다. 그린 리지 농장과 톨리 씨의 관계는 기사에서 확인할 수 있는데, 기사의 첫 번째 단락에서 '인근 윈드햄 카운티의 그린 리지 농장 소유주인 톨리 씨(The owner of Green Ridge Farm ~ Ms. Tolley)'라고 했으므로, 에르난데스 씨가 톨리 씨의 업체를 방문한 적이 있음을 알 수 있다. 따라서 (C)가 정답이다.

▸▸ Paraphrasing 지문의 The owner of Green Ridge Farm ~ Ms. Tolley → 정답의 Ms. Tolley's business

194 세부 사항

번역 독자들이 집안에 텃밭을 가꾸는 데 도움이 되는 특집 기사는 어떤 것인가?

(A) 지역 산물
(B) 일년 내내 나는 약초
(C) 맛있는 비건 요리
(D) 멋진 8월

해설 개요에 나온 특집 기사 목록 중 실내 식용 약초 텃밭 가꾸기(Growing and maintaining an indoor kitchen herb garden)를 주제로 다룬 기사인 '일년 내내 나는 약초(Herbs All Year)'가 집안에서 텃밭을 가꾸는 독자에게 도움이 될 것임을 알 수 있다. 따라서 (B)가 정답이다.

▸▸ Paraphrasing   지문의 Growing ~ an indoor kitchen herb garden
→ 질문의 grow a garden inside their home

195 연계

번역 톨리 씨의 강연에 누가 참석했겠는가?

(A) 뉴튼 씨
(B) 영 씨
(C) 데이비스 씨
(D) 박 씨

해설 기사의 첫 번째 단락에서 톨리 씨가 지역 농가 지원 및 홍보의 중요성(the importance of supporting and promoting local farmers)이라는 주제로 강연을 한다고 했다. 이 강연의 참가자는 개요를 통해 짐작할 수 있는데, 톨리 씨의 강연 주제와 유사한 '지역 생산자 및 재료 탐색하고 소개하기(Sourcing and showcasing local producers and ingredients)' 기사를 작성한 사람이 뉴튼 씨이므로, (A)가 정답이다.

어휘 attend 참석하다

196-200 엽서 + 양식 + 이메일

---

¹⁹⁶마데라 호텔 회원 보상제도

** 4월 특별 혜택 **

¹⁹⁷4월 1일과 8월 31일 사이에 저희 호텔의 어느 지점에서든 3박 이상 투숙하는 예약을 4월 30일까지 완료하시고, 다음 중 한 가지 혜택을 받으세요.

¹⁹⁷(1) 구매 1달러당 20포인트 + 500 보너스 포인트

¹⁹⁹(2) 마데라 호텔 식당 전점에서 사용 가능한 50달러짜리 식당 상품권

(3) 투숙 기간 중 스파 서비스 40퍼센트 할인

(4) 투숙 기간 동안 예약한 렌터카 할인

브라이언 카렐리
815 어빙 스트리트,
뉴욕, NY 10005

¹⁹⁶자주 찾아주시는 고객 여러분께 감사드리며, 마데라 호텔을 계속 이용해 주셔서 고맙습니다.

어휘 frequent customer 단골 고객

---

http://www.maderahotels/customersupport/form.com

마데라 호텔 회원 보상제 고객 지원:
본 양식에 가능한 한 자세한 정보를 기입하여 주시면 지원이 더욱 용이합니다.

¹⁹⁸금일 날짜: 7월 14일

호텔명: 더 그랜드 마데라   예약번호: XWQ43R2

위치: (택1) ☐ 덴버 ☑ 로스앤젤레스 ☐ 뉴욕 ☐ 워싱턴 DC

호텔 투숙 시작일: 5월 12일

이름: 브라이언 카렐리

회원 번호: B11932013

이메일: bcarelli@pointinvesting.com

전화번호: 555-0101

의견/문의 사항:

¹⁹⁷저는 최근 로스앤젤레스 그랜드 마데라 호텔에 5월 투숙 예약을 하고 4월 특별 혜택을 받았습니다. 온라인 예약 시 보너스 포인트 제공을 요청했는데, ¹⁹⁸6월 회원 보상제 내역을 받았을 때 포인트가 제 계정에 적용되지 않은 것을 알게 되었습니다. 아직 보너스 포인트를 받을 수 있는지 알려 주세요. 감사합니다.

어휘 complete a form 양식을 기입하다 property 건물 take advantage of ~를 이용하다, ~의 혜택을 받다 request 요청하다 offer 제공 statement 내역서 apply 적용하다 account 계정, 계좌

수신: 브라이언 카렐리 〈bcarelli@pointinvesting.com〉
발신: 올리버 벨트란 〈obeltran@maderahotels.com〉
날짜: 7월 16일
제목: 귀하의 문의 – B11932013

카렐리 씨께,

마데라 호텔 회원 보상 프로그램의 소중한 회원이 되어 주셔서 감사합니다. 업체 회의 및 개인적인 여행을 위해 저희 마데라 호텔을 이용해 주시는 데 대해 감사 말씀을 드립니다. 회원님의 요청 사항을 살펴보았는데, 회원님께서 말씀하신 내용이 맞는 것 같습니다. ¹⁹⁹저희가 회원님의 투숙 기간에 해당하는 보너스 포인트를 회원님의 계정에 지급하지 않고, 회사 주소로 식당 상품권을 보내 드렸습니다. 이 착오에 대해 사과드리며, 즉시 회원님의 계정에 포인트를 지급하겠습니다. ²⁰⁰아울러 저희 실수에 대한 보상의 의미로 포인트를 두 배로 제공해 드리겠습니다.

올리버 벨트란
고객 지원 수석 관리자
마데라 호텔

어휘 valued 귀중한, 소중한 conference 회의 apologize 사과하다 compensate for ~를 벌충하다, 보상하다

196 추론 / 암시

번역 카렐리 씨는 왜 엽서를 받았겠는가?

(A) 마데라 호텔 객실을 자주 예약한다.
(B) 5월에 차량을 대여했다.
(C) 뉴욕에 있는 마데라 호텔을 마지막으로 방문했다.
(D) 호텔 식당에서 식사하는 것을 좋아한다.

해설 엽서 마지막 단락의 '자주 찾아주시는 고객 여러분께 감사드리며, 마데라 호텔을 계속 이용해 주셔서 고맙습니다(We appreciate our frequent customers and thank you for continuing to choose Madera Hotels)'라는 문구를 통해 카렐리 씨가 마데라 호텔을 자주 예약하기 때문에 엽서를 받았음을 추론할 수 있다. 따라서 (A)가 정답이다.

어휘 frequently 자주

197 연계

번역 카렐리 씨의 호텔 투숙에 관해 사실인 것은?

(A) 회의를 위해 투숙했다.
(B) 스파 방문이 포함되어 있었다.
(C) 최소 3박 이상 투숙했다.
(D) 선물로 비용을 지불했다.

해설 카렐리 씨가 작성한 양식의 의견/문의 사항(Comments/ Concerns) 부분을 보면, 최근 4월 특별 혜택을 받았고(I recently took advantage of your April Specials), 보너스 포인트 제공을 요청했다(I requested the bonus points offer)고 했다. 이와 관련된 내용은 엽서를 통해서도 확인할 수 있는데, 카렐리 씨가 요청한 보너스 포인트(bonus points)는 4월 특별 혜택 중 (1)번에 해당한다. 따라서 호텔에 3박 이상 투숙하는 예약(Make a reservation ~ for a three-night or longer stay)을 하여 혜택 적용 조건을 충족했음을 추론할 수 있으므로, (C)가 정답이다.

어휘 in advance 미리

▸▸ **Paraphrasing** 지문의 **a three-night or longer stay**
→ 정답의 **at least three nights long**

198 세부 사항

번역 양식에 따르면 카렐리 씨는 언제 자신의 계정 관련 문제를 알렸는가?

(A) 4월 1일
(B) 5월 12일
(C) 6월 30일
(D) 7월 14일

해설 카렐리 씨가 작성한 양식의 의견/문의 사항(Comments/ Concerns) 부분을 보면, 6월 회원 보상제 내역을 받았을 때(when I received my June Member Rewards statement) 포인트가 자신의 계정에 적용되지 않은 것을 알게 되었다(I noticed that the points had not been applied to my account)며 관련 문제를 처음 언급했으므로, 그 양식을 작성한 날짜인 7월 14일에 해당 문제를 제기했다는 것을 알 수 있다. 따라서 (D)가 정답이다.

199 연계

번역 카렐리 씨가 잘못 받은 4월 특전 보상은 어떤 것인가?

(A) (1)
(B) (2)
(C) (3)
(D) (4)

해설 이메일의 중반부에서 벨트란 씨는 포인트를 지급하지 않고 카렐리 씨 회사 주소로 식당 상품권을 보냈다(we sent the restaurant gift card to your business address)며 착오(mistake)에 대해 사과했다. 카렐리 씨가 잘못 받은 식당 상품권은 엽서에 나온 (2)번 특전 '마데라 호텔 식당 전점에서 사용 가능한 50달러짜리 식당 상품권($50 restaurant gift card for use at any Madera Hotel restaurants)'에 해당하므로, (B)가 정답이다.

어휘 mistakenly 잘못하여, 실수로

200 세부 사항

번역 벨트란 씨가 하겠다고 제안한 것은?

(A) 회원 자격 업그레이드하기
(B) 예약 변경하기
(C) 보너스 포인트 추가 지급하기
(D) 업체 회의 일정 잡기

해설 벨트란 씨가 보낸 이메일의 후반부를 보면, 자신들의 실수에 대한 보상의 의미로 포인트를 두 배로 제공하겠다(to compensate for our mistake, I will double the offer)고 했으므로, (C)가 정답이다.

어휘 additional 추가의

▸▸ **Paraphrasing** 지문의 **double the offer**
→ 정답의 **Give additional bonus points**